KT-176-382

KA 0061859 4

The Archaeology of Late Celtic Britain and Ireland *c.* 400–1200 AD

The Archaeology of Late Celtic Britain and Ireland *c.* 400–1200 AD

Lloyd Laing

Methuen & Co Ltd
11 New Fetter Lane London

First published 1975 by Methuen & Co Ltd
11 New Fetter Lane London EC4P 4EE

Printed in Great Britain by Butler & Tanner Ltd
Frome and London

ISBN hardbound 0 416 65970 5
ISBN paperback 0 416 82360 2

Distributed in the USA by
HARPER & ROW PUBLISHERS INC.
BARNES & NOBLE IMPORT DIVISION

to Jen

Contents

Acknowledgements ix
List of plates xi
Notes on the plates xv
List of text figures xxi
Preface xxv

Part 1 The regional field archaeology of Late Celtic Britain and Ireland

1 The culture of the Early Christian Celts 3
2 Southern Scotland 20
3 Northern Scotland 46
4 Wales and the Isle of Man 89
5 South-west England 120
6 Ireland 145
7 The Norse in Scotland 177
8 The Norse outside Scotland 208
9 Celtic survival 232

Part 2 The material culture of the Early Christian Celts

10 Technology and trade 245
11 Subsistence equipment 260

12 Personal adornment 297

13 Art and craftsmanship 339

14 The Church 374

Appendix A Celtic manuscript art 389

Appendix B The chronology of some historical personages mentioned in the book 395

Abbreviations of journals 397
Select bibliography 399
Notes 421
Index 440

Acknowledgements

The author and publishers would like to thank the following for permission to use figures based on figures in the publications cited:

Aberdeen University Press for figures on pp. 23–31 of S. H. Cruden, 'Excavations at Birsay, Orkney', in E. Small (ed.), *Fourth Viking Congress* (Figures 60 and 62); The Clarendon Press, Oxford, for Figure 2, page 13, from E. T. Leeds, *Early Anglo-Saxon Art and Archaeology* (Figure 137); Her Majesty's Stationery Office for Figures 61 and 58 from J. R. C. Hamilton, *Excavations at Jarlshof* (Figures 59 and 65); *Medieval Archaeology* for Figure 43 from A. C. Thomas, 'Dark Age imported pottery in Western Britain' (Figure 88); Routledge and Kegan Paul for Figure 27 from I. Foster and G. Daniel, *Prehistoric and Early Wales* (Figure 90); the Royal Irish Academy for Figure 42 from H. O'N. Hencken, 'Balinderry crannog 1' (Figure 52) and Figures 62 (No. 1302) and 70 from 'Lagore crannog, and Irish royal residence of the 7th to 10th centuries AD' (Figure 75), for Figure 15 from S. P. O'Riordain, 'Excavation of a large fort at Garranes' (Figure 74), for Figure 9 from M. J. O'Kelly, 'Excavation of two ring forts at Garryduff' (Figure 104), all in the *Proceedings of the Royal Irish Academy*; Thames and Hudson for Figures 12, 18, 15, 16 and 29 from I. Henderson, *The Picts* (Figures 13, 14, 15, 16 and 17); the Society of Antiquaries of Scotland for Figure 4, page 287, and Figure 6a, page 298, from the volume for 1955–6 (Figures 2 and 27), and Figure 2, page 138, from the volume for 1959–60 (Figure 26), all in the *Proceedings of the Society of Antiquaries of Scotland*; the *Ulster Journal of Archaeology* for Figure 10, page 35, from E. M. Jope, 'Iron Age brooches in Ireland' (Figure 131); the University of Wales Press for Figures 28, 40 and 27 from L. Alcock, *Dinas Powys* (Figures 81, 84 and 86).

List of plates

1A Dinorben Hillfort, Denbighshire (photo: National Museum of Wales)
1B Dinas Powys, Glamorganshire (photo: L. Alcock)
2A Dinas Emrys, Caernarvonshire. Hillfort. 'The Pool' during excavation (photo: H. Savory, National Museum of Wales)
2B Mote of Mark, Kirkcudbright: vitrified rampart during excavation (photo: author)
3A Tynron Doon, Dumfriesshire. Hillfort (photo: author)
3B Broch of Gurness, Aikerness, Orkney. Post-broch settlement (photo: author)
4A Cadbury Congresbury, Somerset. Post-Roman hall during excavation (photo: P. Rahtz)
4B South Cadbury, Somerset. Hillfort (photo: L. Alcock)
5A Staigue Fort, Co. Kerry (photo: Irish Tourist Board)
5B Tara, Co. Meath, from the air (photo: Irish Tourist Board)
6A Raths, near Cork, from the air (photo: Aerofilms Ltd)
6B Dun, Strathtay, Perthshire (photo: author)
7A Tintagel, Cornwall, from the air (photo: Aerofilms Ltd)
7B Inishmurray, Co. Sligo. Monastic site (photo: Commissioners of Public Works, Eire)
8A Skellig Michael, Co. Kerry. Monastic cells (photo: R. A. Markus)
8B Eileach-an-Naoimh, Argyll. Monastic site (photo: Department of Environment)
9A Cashel, Co. Tipperary, from the air (photo: Irish Tourist Board)
9B St Kevin's Church, Glendalough, Co. Wicklow (photo: Irish Tourist Board)
10A Temple Macdara Church, Co. Galway (photo: Commissioners of Public Works, Ireland)

10B Papil, West Burra, Shetland (photo: author)
11A Spooyt Vane Keeill, Michael, Isle of Man (photo: Manx Museum)
11B The Braaid, Marown, Isle of Man (photo: Manx Museum)
12A The Moylough Belt Shrine (photo: Irish Tourist Board)
12B The Westness Brooch (photo: National Museum of Antiquities of Scotland)
13A St Ninian's Isle hanging bowl (photo: NMAS)
13B St Ninian's Isle silver bowl (photo: NMAS)
14A St Ninian's Isle strap end with Pictish inscription (photo: NMAS)
14B St Ninian's Isle, silver mount (photo: NMAS)
15A Part of Viking silver hoard, Skaill, Orkney (photo: NMAS)
15B Balladoole, Isle of Man, horse gear from boat burial (photo: Manx Museum)
16A Fragmentary bronze mount, probably Pictish, Stromness, Orkney (photo: NMAS)
16B Pictish wooden box, Birsay, Orkney (photo: NMAS)
17A Pictish cross slab, Papil, West Burra, Shetland (photo: NMAS)
17B 'The Drosten Stone', St Vigeans, Angus (photo: Department of Environment)
18A Pictish cross slab, Meigle No. 2, Perthshire (photo: Department of Environment)
18B Pictish cross slab, St Vigeans No. 7, Angus (photo: Department of Environment)
19A Pictish cross slab, Invergowrie, Angus (photo: NMAS)
19B Pictish cross slab, Meigle No. 3, Angus (photo: Department of Environment)
20A Iona. St Martin's Cross (photo: Department of Environment)
20B Iona. St John's Cross (photo: Department of Environment)
21A Kildalton, Islay. High cross (photo: Department of Environment)
21B Cross shaft, Govan, Lanarkshire (photo: Department of Environment
21C Kirkinner, Wigtown. Cross slab (photo: Department of Environment)
22A Sueno's Stone, Morayshire (photo: Department of Environment)
22B Cross slab, Riskbuie, Kiloran, Colonsay (photo: NMAS)
23A Head of Irneit's cross slab, Maughold, Isle of Man (photo: Manx Museum)
23B 'Crux Guriat' Stone, Maughold, Isle of Man (photo: Manx Museum)
24A Calf of Man Crucifixion slab (photo: Manx Museum)

24B Thorwald's cross slab, Andreas, Isle of Man (photo: Manx Museum)
25A Gaut's Cross, Michael, Isle of Man (photo: Manx Museum)
25B Briamail's Cross, Llandyfaelog-Fach, Breconshire (photo:
26 Margam, Glamorgan, wheel-headed cross (photo: National Museum of Wales)
26A Margam, Glamorgan, wheel-headed cross (photo: National Museum of Wales)
27A Enniaun's Cross, Margam, Glamorgan (photo: National Museum of Wales)
27B Cross shaft fragment, Bardsey, Caernarvonshire (photo: National Museum of Wales)
28A North Cross, Ahenny, Co. Tipperary (photo: Irish Tourist Board)
28B Bealin Cross, Co. Westmeath (photo: Commissioners of Works, Ireland)
29A Moone Cross, Co. Kildare (photo: Irish Tourist Board)
29B North Cross, Castledermot, Co. Kildare (photo: Commissioners of Works, Ireland)
30A Cross of Patrick and Columba, Kells, Co. Meath (photo: Commissioners of Works, Ireland)
30B East (unfinished) Cross and round tower, Kells, Co. Meath (photo: Irish Tourist Board)
31 Cross of Muiredach, Monasterboice, Co. Louth (photo: Irish Tourist Board)
32A Cross, Dysert O' Dea, Co. Clare (photo: Commissioners of Works, Ireland)
32B Round tower, Ardmore, Co. Waterford (photo: Irish Tourist Board)

Acknowledgements

The author and publishers would like to thank the following people and institutions for allowing them to reproduce copyright material: Plates 5A, 5B, 9A, 9B, 12A, 28A, 29A, 30B, 31, 32B, Bord Failte Eireann; 1A, 2A, 25B, 26, 27A, 27B, The National Museum of Wales, Cardiff, and Dr H. N. Savory; 11A, 11B, 15B, 23A, 23B, 24A, 24B, 25A, The Manx Museum, Douglas, Isle of Man; 6A, 7A, Aerofilms Ltd; 12B, 13A, 13B, 14A, 14B, 15A, 16A, 16B, 17A, 19A, 22B, The National Museum of Antiquities of Scotland, Edinburgh; 7B, 10A, 28B, 29B, 30A, 32A, The Commissioners of Public Works, in Ireland; 8B, 17B, 18A, 18B, 19B, 20A, 20B, 21A, 21B, 22A, 22B, 22C, 22A, Department of the Environment; 4A, Cadbury Congresbury Excavation Committee, and P. Rahtz; 8A, Dr R. A. Markus; 15B, Professor D. M. Wilson; 1B, 4B, L. Alcock. Mr and Mrs Peter Fowler are to be thanked for permission to base Figure 135 on one of their original drawings.

Notes on the plates

1A Dinorben Hillfort, Caernarvonshire. This fort, now largely quarried away, was occupied as early as Iron Age 'A', and after a long period of Iron Age settlement was reoccupied in the late Roman period when a round farmstead was built, and in the sub-Roman period, when a timber hall was constructed.

1B Dinas Powys, Glamorganshire. The most important of the Welsh reoccupied hillforts, this site appears to have been inhabited after a break in the Roman period from the fifth to the seventh century, and has produced imported pottery and glass as well as metalwork.

2A Dinas Emrys, Caernarvonshire. This site, important in Welsh folklore for its associations with Ambrosius Aurelianus, was refortified in the post-Roman period. The photograph shows a cistern built probably to water animals and a platform partly built over it over the peaty fill, during excavation.

2B The Mote of Mark, Kirkcudbright. This is one of the major Scottish Dark Age forts, occupied mainly in the sixth century. The vitrified rampart.

3A Tynron Doon hillfort, Dumfriesshire. This fort was occupied in the Iron Age but seems to have had both medieval and Early Christian occupation as well, evidence for the latter taking the form of a midden on the hill slope.

3B Broch of Gurness, Aikerness, Orkney. An Iron Age broch tower round which grew up an extensive settlement of stone huts in the post-Broch period. A penannular brooch and other finds show it was occupied in the fifth to sixth centuries; Viking houses and a burial are also known from the site.

4A Cadbury Congresbury, Somerset.

4B View of the Early Christian timber hall, South Cadbury, Somerset, during excavation.

5A Staigue Fort, Co. Kerry. A good example of the Irish type of stone-walled 'cashel' of the Iron Age and Early Christian period. The series of stairs giving access to the wall head should be noted.

5B The Hill of Tara, Co. Meath, from the air. In the centre can be seen the conjoined ringforts, the Teach Cormaic and the Torradh, within the larger enclosure of the Rath Na Riogh. The cluster of trees just above centre partly overlies the Rath of the Synods, which can be seen to the immediate left. Behind it is visible the Tech Midchuarta, while in front of it can be seen the chambered Neolithic tomb known as the Mound of the Hostages.

6A Raths, near Cork, from the air.

6B A typical dun, Strathtay, Perthshire. Strathtay is noted for its concentration of stone-walled forts of dun type, occupied in the Iron Age and later.

7A Tintagel, Cornwall, from the air. The later castle can be seen in the centre of the photograph; the cells of the Celtic monastery can be seen as clusters of grass-covered foundations in the bottom right hand sector of the picture.

7B Inishmurray, Co. Sligo. A classic example of an Early Christian monastery. The beehive cell to the left of the centre of the picture should be noted, as should the *leacht* just below the centre. The cashel wall can also be seen.

8A Skellig Michael, Co. Kerry. This famous example of a monastery is situated on a remote rock stack in the Skelligs. The photograph shows two adjoining beehive cells.

8B Eileach-an-Naoimh, Garvellochs, Argyll. A good Scottish example of an eremitic monastery. The photo shows a ruined beehive cell.

9A Cashel, Co. Tipperary, from the air. On the rock can be seen the medieval church, to the immediate left of which is Cormac's Chapel, a remarkable Romanesque building with earlier features. To the right is the earliest surviving building, a round tower. In the distance is a medieval abbey.

9B St Kevin's Church, Glendalough, Co. Wicklow. A stone-built church, probably eleventh-century.

10A Temple Macdara Church, St Macdara's Island, Co. Galway.

The notable features are the stone antae, skeuomorphic of wood.

10B Papil, West Burra, Shetland. West bank of vallum of small monastery visible under modern church enclosure wall. The site has produced several fine Early Christian sculptured stones.

11A Spooyt Vane Keeill, Michael, Isle of Man. Typical example of Manx chapel site of the Early Christian period.

11B The Braaid, Marown, Isle of Man. Enigmatic site, originally interpreted as a megalithic monument, now reinterpreted as a roundhouse of the Iron Age with two associated Viking longhouses.

12A Moylough Belt Shrine, detail. The buckle is skeuomorphic, and does not open. The belt shrine, made to contain a fragmentary leather belt, is a classic encyclopedia of techniques and motifs available to the Irish metalworker of the seventh century.

12B The Westness Brooch. Found in a Viking grave on Rousay, Orkney, this is a good example of an ornate penannular brooch of the early eighth century.

13A The St Ninian's Isle treasure – hanging bowl. Probably Northumbrian, this is one of only two known silver hanging bowls; the other is now lost.

13B St Ninian's Isle – bowl with animal ornament, in silver.

14A St Ninian's Isle – silver strap end with Pictish inscription in 'Irish' lettering.

15A Part of a Viking silver hoard, from Skaill, Orkney. Found in 1858, the largest Norse hoard from Scotland. It is coin dated to the late tenth century.

15B Items of horsegear from a Viking boat burial at Balladoole, Isle of Man. The fittings are probably of 'Celtic' manufacture.

16A Fragmentary bronze mount, from Stromness, Orkney. The animal design recalls that on the Birka Pail, and is probably Pictish of the eighth century.

16B Pictish wooden box, Birsay, Orkney. Made of alder, it was probably the toolbox of a leather-worker. Probably eighth century.

17A Pictish cross-slab, Papil, West Burra, Shetland. The meaning of the bird-headed figures with the human head between their beaks is unknown.

17B The 'Drosten' Stone, St Vigeans, Angus. The only Class II Pictish stone with an inscription in 'Irish' lettering. It relates to someone called 'Drosten'.

18A Meigle No. 2, Pictish cross-slab, Perthshire. One of the largest Pictish slabs, decorated in the 'Boss Style'.

The reverse shows Daniel and a cavalcade of hunters.

18B Pictish cross-slab, St Vigeans No. 7, Angus. Another of the very large (originally at least 7 feet high) stones, it is Notable for the fine work. The subject matter includes the hermit saints Paul and Anthony.

19A Pictish slab, Invergowrie, Angus. The design shows three clerics in a style reminiscent of the Irish, and two typically Pictish beasts. They should be compared with the St Ninian's Isle treasures. The front has a cross only.

19B Pictish slab, Meigle No. 3, Angus. A lively rendering of a rider. The sword chape should be noted.

20A St Martin's Cross, Iona. One of the finest of the Iona school high crosses. The present stumpy appearance of the arms is due to there once having been missing fragments tenoned into them.

20B Iona, St John's Cross. Originally probably the finest of the Iona high crosses, it is very fragmentary, but has recently been restored and re-erected. This shows the restored design.

21A Kildalton, Islay. The finest of the Scottish high crosses outside Iona.

21B Cross shaft, Govan, Lanarkshire. One of the late Viking-influenced stones of the Govan school. The figure above the interlace should be noted, as it shows Pictish influence.

21C Kirkinner, Wigtownshire, cross-slab. A good example of the 'Whithorn' school of sculpture, with characteristic disc head and stumpy shaft. The interlace shows Viking influence.

22A Sueno's Stone, Morayshire. A late monument with elaborate figural work, showing the continuation of Pictish sculpture after the absorption of Pictland by Scotland.

22B Cross-slab, Riskbuie, Kiloran, Colonsay. Probably seventh-century. This type of face cross is rare, and occurs mainly in Ireland. The prototype is east Mediterranean.

23A Head of Irneit's cross-slab, Maughold, Isle of Man. It commemorates a bishop (Irneit) of the late seventh century. Below the marigold are Chi-Rhos with inscriptions.

23B 'Crux Guriat' Stone Maughold, Isle of Man. It stands about 7 feet high, and dates from the early ninth century. Guriat is probably Gwriad, a Welsh prince who went to Man about 825.

24A Calf of Man crucifixion slab, Isle of Man. This remarkable altar frontal dates from the eighth century, and its iconography shows east Mediterranean links.

24B Thorwald's Cross, Andreas, Isle of Man. This tenth-century Norse slab shows scenes from Ragnärok, Odin being eaten by the Fenris wolf.

25A Gaut's Cross, Michael, Isle of Man. The most famous of the Norse Manx stones, it shows the type of ring-chain devised by Gaut, who is commemorated in a runic inscription. Tenth-century.

25B Briamail's Cross, Llandyfaelog-Fach, Breconshire. Late tenth-century cross, with Viking influence, notably in the 'Jellinge Beast'. The use of a figure is unusual.

26 Margam, Glamorgan, wheel-headed cross. Probably the finest of the Welsh sculptures, it is characteristic of Glamorganshire. Late tenth- to eleventh-century.

27A Enniaun's Cross, Margam, Glamorgan. Late ninth- to tenth-century. Notable for the good style of its workmanship.

27B Cross shaft fragment, Seven Sisters, Merioneth. The figure is in the Early Christian attitude of prayer, and is reminiscent of Roman sarcophagi and Merovingian 'Daniel' buckles. Ninth- to tenth-century.

28A North Cross, Ahenny, Co. Tipperary. One of the two Ahenny crosses which typify the group.

28B Bealin Cross, Co. Westmeath.

29A Moone Cross, Co. Kildare. The stiff carving is the result of the use of hard stone.

29B North Cross, Castledermot, Co. Kildare.

30A Cross of Patrick and Columba, Kells, Co. Meath One of the finest Kells group crosses.

30B Unfinished East Cross, Kells. This illustrates the way in which the design was blocked out prior to detailed carving.

31 Cross of Muiredach, Monasterboice, Co. Louth. Probably the finest of the Irish high crosses.

32A Dysert O'Dea Cross, Co. Clare. A late cross of 'Crucifixion' type.

32B Ardmore Round Tower, Co. Waterford.

List of text figures

1 Map of the Irish settlements and other migrations in western Britain 8
2 Plan of the phases of Traprain Law, WEst Lothian 22
3 Plan of Dalmahoy, Midlothian 26
4 Anglian cross shaft, Aberlady, Midlothian 29
5 Plan of the Mote of Mark, Kirkcudbright 32
6 Plan of Trusty's Hill, Anwoth, Kirkcudbright 34
7 Anglian whetstone, Collin, Dumfriesshire 40
8 Map of southern Scotland in the Early Christian period 41
9 Map of the diocesan divisions of southern Scotland 42
10 Early Christian memorial stones, south-west Scotland 43
11 Map of the distribution of *pit-* names in Scotland 52
12 Class I Pictish symbol stones (1) Sandside, Caithness (2) Huntly, Inverness 54
13 Map of the distribution of Class I Pictish symbol stones 54
14 Class I Pictish symbols 55
15 The 'declining' Pictish symbols 57
16 Map of the distribution of Class II Pictish cross-slabs 60
17 Fantastic animals on Class II Pictish stones 62
18 Plan of souterrain at Carlungie, Angus 70
19 Brechin round tower, Angus 71
20 Doorway of Brechin round tower, Angus 72
21 Map of the distribution of Irish placenames in Scotland 73
22 Plan of (a) Dunadd, Argyll (b) Dundurn, Perthshire 74
23 Objects from Dunadd, Argyll 75
24 Plan of Period II of the dun at Kildonan, Argyll 77
25 Broch of Gurness, Aikerness, Orkney. Plan of broch and post-broch structures 80
26 Plan of wheelhouse, a' Cheardach Mhor, South Uist 85

27 Plan of Dun Cuier, Barra 86
28 Welsh enclosed hut groups 91
29 Map of the distribution of Irish placenames and ogham inscriptions in Wales and south-west 94
30 The ogham alphabet 95
31 The tombstone of Vortepor, Carmarthenshire 102
32 Map of key sites in early Wales 103
33 Plan of Dinas Emrys, Caernarvonshire 107
34 Plan of Garn Boduan, Caernarvonshire 108
35 Plan of Dinas Powys, Glamorgan 109
36 Plan of the hall at Dinas Powys, Glamorgan 110
37 Map of key sites in south-west England 124
38 Comparative plans of reoccupied sites of the Early Christian period 126
39 Plan of Cadbury Congresbury, Somerset 127
40 Plan of South Cadbury Castle, Somerset 128
41 Plan of Chun Castle, Cornwall 130
42 Plan of halls at Castle Dore, Cornwall 131
43 Plan of Early Christian period huts at Gwithian, Cornwall 134
44 Plan of Mawgan Porth, Cornwall 136
45 The Cardinham Cross, Cornwall 140
46 Plan of living cells in the monastery, Tintagel, Cornwall 141
47 Plan of Cahercommaun, Co. Clare 148
48 Plans of Irish hillforts 152
49 Plan of Leacanabuaile Fort, Co. Kerry 153
50 Plans of raths: (a) Lissue; (b) White Fort, in Ulster 158
51 Plan of 'The Spectacles', Lough Gur, Co. Limerick 159
52 Plan of Ballinderry 1 crannog, Co. Westmeath 162
53 Map of key secular sites in Ireland 163
54 Map of key ecclesiastical sites in Ireland 165
55 Types of Irish cross-slabs 167
56 Plan of Skellig Michael, Co. Kerry 172
57 Plan and elevation of Gallarus oratory, Co. Kerry 172
58 Map of the Norse settlements in Scotland 182
59 Plan of Norse settlement at Jarlshof, Shetland, in the tenth century 188
60 General plan of the Brough of Birsay, Orkney 192
61 Plan of Norse houses, Birsay, Orkney 193
62 Plan of ecclesiastical remains at Birsay, Orkney 195
63 Plan of Norse settlement at Freswick Links, Caithness 198
64 Oblong brooches, probably Irish, from a Viking burial in Oronsay 200
65 Viking bone pins, Jarlshof, Shetland 202
66 Plan of Viking burial with underlying long-cist burials, Balladoole, Isle of Man 209

67 Plan and section of Viking burial mound, Ballateare, Isle of Man 210
68 Hiberno-Norse coins, Dublin mint 230
69 Map of Viking period finds in Ireland 231
70 Bone 'trial pieces' Lagore, Co. Meath 249
71 Stone 'trial pieces', Kingarth, Bute 249
72 Crucibles, Types 1–5 250
73 Crucibles, Types 8 and 9 251
74 Millefiori rod and holder, Garranes, Co. Cork 256
75 Glass stud mould and glass bracelet, Lagore, Co. Meath 257
76 Wheel-turned wooden vessels, Ireland 261
77 Stave-built wooden vessels, Ireland 262
78 Wooden scoops and shovels, Ireland 263
79 (a) Wooden mallet, Lagore, Co. Meath; (b) Wooden pack-saddle, Ballinderry 1, Co. Westmeath 264
80 Miscellaneous wooden objects, Ireland 265
81 Vessel glass, Dinas Powys, Glamorgan 266
82 Examples of A Ware 269
83 Distribution map of A Ware 270
84 Examples of B Ware 271
85 Distribution map of B Ware 271
86 Examples of D Ware 272
87 Distribution map of D Ware 273
88 Examples of E Ware 274
89 Distribution map of E Ware 275
90 Very Coarse Pottery, Pant-y-Saer, Anglesey 276
91 Very Coarse Pottery, Votadinian, Traprain Law, West Lothian 277
92 Souterrain ware, Ulster 278
93 Grass-marked pottery, Cornwall 280
94 Bar lug pottery, Gwithian, Cornwall 280
95 Wheelhouse pottery, Jarlshof, Shetland 283
96 Wheelhouse pottery, Hebrides 284
97 Types of spindle whorls 285
98 Irish weapon types 286
99 Iron knife types 288
100 Iron axehead types 289
101 Iron blade tools 290
102 Iron horse gear 291
103 Miscellaneous iron tools 292
104 Reconstruction of the Garryduff padlock, Co. Cork 293
105 Miscellaneous ironwork 295
106 Iron objects of Irish types 296
107 Leather shoes, Ireland 299
108 Types of bone combs 300
109 Penannular brooches, Types 1–8 305

110 Penannular brooches, Types 9–17 307
111 Penannular brooches, Types 18–23 309
112 Penannular brooches, Types 24–5 311
113 Penannular brooches, Types 26–9 312
114 The Kilmainham Brooch, Dublin 313
115 The Hunterston Brooch, Ayrshire 315
116 The Tara Brooch 316
117 The Mull Brooch 317
118 Ring brooches, unprovenanced, Ireland 318
119 Kyte brooch, Co. Kilkenny 318
120 Types of heads of ringed pins 319
121 Ringed pin types 320
122 The development of the hand-pin 322
123 Stick pins, Types 1–14 325
124 Stick pins, Types 15–29 328
125 Stick pins, Types 30–40 330
126 The development of the latchet brooch 332
127 Buckles, Lagore, Co. Meath 333
128 Tanged studs, Lagore, Co. Meath 334
129 Finger rings, Ireland 335
130 Types of beads 336
131 Roman metal openwork 345
132 Animal art in Europe, I – backward-looking animals 347
133 Animal art in Europe, II – shoulder spirals 348
134 Styles I and II, typical ornamental details 350
135 Three roundels showing widespread occurrence of interlace 351
136 'Grammar' of Dark Age art 352
137 Triskele motifs from hanging bowl escutcheons 353
138 Lough Erne shrine 360
139 The Monymusk reliquary 361
140 Hanging lamp, Ballinderry 1 crannog 364
141 The shrine of St Patrick's bell 369
142 Hoddom crozier shrine, Dumfriesshire 370
143 Celtic bells' (a) Armagh (b) Birnie, Nairn 372
144 Plan of vallum, Iona 378
145 Plan of 'catstane' cemetery, Kirkliston, Midlothian 379
146 Plan of the Hill of Knockea, Co. Limerick 380
147 Reconstruction of St Ninian's Isle corner post shrine 381
148 The 'Altoir Beag' *leacht*, Innishmurray, Co. Sligo 382
149 Plan of Church Island, Co. Kerry 383
150 Plan of Ardwall Isle, Kirkcudbright 384
151 Butterfly gable finials, Ireland 385

Preface

With the increasing number of admissions to archaeology degree courses in British universities, and the growing number of adult education classes in various aspects of the subject, there is an ever increasing need for general textbooks which provide a background framework on which the student can build up a more detailed knowledge. Any archaeologist would be hesitant to write such introductory textbooks, knowing that the speed with which knowledge advances will mean that any book will be at best slightly out of date by the time it is published. Moreover, increasing specialization means that no individual can be master of a fairly wide field of study, as was perhaps possible forty years ago.

This book is an attempt in part to rectify the problem. It is concerned primarily with surviving material culture. That is not to say that the non-archaeological material is totally neglected: where possible the archaeological evidence is matched with evidence from documentary and toponymic sources.

Certain topics have been dealt with somewhat cursorily. The Church has received inadequate treatment since it has recently been the subject of illuminating discussion by Professor Charles Thomas in the Hunter-Marshall Lectures – *The Early Christian Archaeology of North Britain* (1971). Historical matter has been confined to essential background, but readers are referred to a useful survey which puts the archaeological and documentary sources in perspective – Professor Leslie Alcock's *Arthur's Britain* (1971). The relationship between Celt and Saxon in the period up to *c.* 650 is dealt with in the same book, and is minimized here for that reason. Manuscript art is confined to an appendix, since manuscripts, except as sources for comparison with other categories of artistic product, are perhaps more suitably dealt with by the art historian than by the archaeologist. The importance of Ireland has also perhaps been minimized, since the Early Christian archaeology of the region is generally better known and has been dealt with in a number of works, most notably *Early Christian Ireland* (1958) by Maire and Liam de Paor.

In the absence of the existence of type series of common objects, I have devised my own lists. These are not intended as in any way definitive or exhaustive; I have no doubt omitted much that should have been included. Where I have differed from currently accepted opinion, or diverged from currently accepted classification, I have done so only after great deliberation. The limitations imposed by the nature of the book have prevented me from justifying my divergence fully in every case, but I hope elsewhere to set out in full the evidence on which the divergence has been based.

In a work of this kind, which is largely derivative of the work of numerous scholars, every statement, site and find should be fully documented. Such a process, however, would have resulted in the text becoming unreadable and the book as a whole becoming inconveniently long. Text references have therefore been confined to most statements of opinion where I am not the originator, and to sites and finds which are not documented in the select bibliography. Where a site or find is discussed at any length in the text without a bibliographical reference, the reader can assume that the discussion is based on information given in the excavation report for that site, which will be listed in the bibliography. To simplify finding the relevant report, the bibliography has been arranged in chapters.

The book is divided into two parts, the first consisting of a series of regional surveys of the field archaeology, the second comprising a discussion of the material culture to be found in all the areas under review in the period. In the first part of the book I have extended the discussion to include the subject of the Viking raids and subsequent settlements. The Viking impact on Celtic Britain was a major one, and an understanding of it is essential to appreciate the cultural changes that took place as a result.

Some justification for the use of the term 'late Celtic' in the title is perhaps necessary. I have called the book simply *The Archaeology of Late Celtic Britain and Ireland* because I believe there is some justification in reviving the term, once used to denote the last phase of the La Tène Iron Age, as a new usage to denote the period covered by this book, since there are now other terms in current archaeological nomenclature to take the place of its former usage. The alternatives – 'Early Christian', 'Dark Age', 'Post-Roman Iron Age', 'Arthurian' or 'early Medieval' seem to be emotive, restrictive or vague. For the purposes of this book 'medieval' is taken to mean after 1200 and before 1600.

The book was written as an extension of lectures given to first-year undergraduates at Liverpool University and the text was completed in 1971–2. While some revisions take into consideration material published subsequently, most sections were not revised after March 1972. The work would no doubt have been improved had I been able to incorporate the results of recent unpublished research, but some workers were reluctant to permit me to make use of the results of their research prior to definitive publication.

Few can be as aware of the deficiencies of the work as I am. The specialists who have devoted much time to the elucidation of particular problems will no doubt find much to criticize in the sections of which they have detailed knowledge. This book, however, is not for the collectors and critics of what Childe so aptly termed 'postage-stamp archaeology'; it is for students for whom the minutiae can come later. For this reason I have resisted the temptation to make in these pages a personal statement about what seem to me the most important aspects of the archaeology of the period.

Finally, it gives me great pleasure to record my thanks to those who have been so helpful while this book was being written. Acknowledgement for the illustrations is given elsewhere, and my debt to many who provided illustrations is not merely confined to my thanks for permission to use them but for help in their selection. Professor T. G. E. Powell has read the text and offered me advice on a number of points, while some chapters have been read to their great advantage by Dr Peter Harbison, Dr Maire de Paor, Dr H. N. Savory, Mr R. B. K. Stevenson and Professor Charles Thomas. Mr Aidan Macdonald, my colleague and friend on so many Early Christian field surveys in Scotland, has freely allowed me to make use of some of the results of his research on the Early Christian archaeology of Scotland, and a number of my students, most notably Mr Tony Holden, Mr Stuart Wrathmell and Mr Peter Fasham have allowed me to draw upon their particular research. Mr David Longley has redrawn some of my diagrams. If I single out the staff of the National Museum of Antiquities in Scotland and Dumfries Burgh Museum for special thanks among the many museums that have allowed me to make use of their resources, it is because I have spent more time there than elsewhere. As always, thanks to the above is due for any merits the book may have, the faults are all my own.

Liverpool, October 1973

Part 1 The regional field archaeology of late Celtic Britain and Ireland

1 The culture of the Early Christian Celts

The concept of the 'Dark Ages'

The terms 'Dark Ages', 'Migration Period', 'early medieval period' and 'early feudal age' have all been applied at some time as convenient blankets to cover what was regarded as a barbarian interval between the civilization of the Roman Empire and the emergence of feudal Christian civilization. The fifth to twelfth centuries were regarded as a period of chaos dominated by barbarian folk migrations, which gradually terminated in the establishment of small kingdoms, the importance of which lay mainly in their later development into medieval states. In tracing the emergence of medieval civilization, historians looked to the foundation of the Carolingian Empre in AD 800, casting only an uneasy glance at the Merovingian world of Pepin and before that, the Age of the Great Migrations.

To some extent it is the school of historical thought that grew up in the shadow of Gibbon that has led to the artificial isolation of the Migration Period, and the growth of the opposing concepts of 'Roman' and 'barbarian'. Recent work by ancient historians, especially A. H. M. Jones,[1] has shown that the late Roman Empire, particularly of the fourth century, was another world from the Rome of Augustus; it was essentially *Romania*, Christian Rome, an empire with a moving frontier in which Roman and barbarian elements were profoundly mixed, and in which a barbarian could rise to a position of supreme authority. One should not forget that the great Roman general, Stilicho, whose campaigns were so successful in prolonging the myth of Rome, was by birth a Vandal.

From the archaeological evidence the Roman Empire in Europe can be interpreted as the provider of a few centuries of cultural influence, the heritage of which was more material than political or social. The archaeologist, working within a far broader chronological framework than the historian, views the Migration Period as the last, and perhaps the most extensive, phase of European folk movement – part of a pattern which repeats itself sometimes on a modest, sometimes on a grand scale from the Mesolithic onwards. In this light, the peoples of the Migration Period are simply the direct descendants of the higher barbarian cultures of later prehistoric Europe, which continued to develop outside the Roman *limes*, sometimes acquiring the trappings of Roman materialism by trade or cultural contact. Within the Empire, despite the more heavily Romanized upper social stratum, peasant society maintained the traditional ways of life.

The Celts

'Celt' is a linguistic term which has acquired a cultural meaning only at a secondary stage. The Celtic languages developed from the parent language of Indo-European as did the Teutonic, Romance and Balto-Slavonic languages, as well as the classical languages of Greek and Latin and a number of ancient languages such as Hittite and Tocharian.[2] Complex linguistic evidence points to the region west of the Urals and north of the Black Sea as the original area of Indo-European speech. Late Neolithic settlers known as the Corded-Ware-Battle-Axe-Single-Grave People moved into northern Europe in the third millennium BC, and it is possible that they introduced an Indo-European language which was spread when they fused with a group of people, possibly of central European origin, known as the Beaker folk. The resultant amalgam of peoples spread through Atlantic Europe, including Britain.

If this is not the case, it is difficult to guess when Indo-European could have entered subsequently, since the Bronze Age in western Europe is notable for internal development and cultural continuity. There was no major folk movement or upheaval that could have resulted in the introduction of the language until the late Bronze Age,[3] by which time, however, it is inferred that a primitive form of Celtic was already being spoken.

Three main dialects of Celtic are known: *Gaulish*, the language of the European Celts, now known only from a few inscriptions; the *Goidelic* languages, comprising Irish, Scots Gaelic and Manx, and the *Brythonic* languages which include Welsh, Cornish and Breton. In general terms the Brythonic languages are later than the Goidelic – Brythonic probably developed in the early Iron Age, though O'Rahilly suggested in 1946 that it developed on the Continent and was introduced from there either fully or partly formed.[4]

Languages tend to become simpler with time, and the languages spoken in the seventh century were very different from those spoken by the Iron Age

Celts. In the sixth century AD Primitive Cornish and Primitive Breton emerged from a common Brythonic language that had been undergoing considerable change in the Roman period.[5] This period also saw the development in north-west Britain of Cumbric – a language related to Welsh. The introduction of Scots Gaelic to Scotland was the result of the Irish settlement of Dalriada and the subsequent expansion of Irish-speaking people in Scotland in the Early Christian period. By a similar process the Isle of Man, Brythonic-speaking in the beginning of the period, changed its language to Goidelic as a result of Irish settlement.

Celtic origins[6]

The Urnfield people were the largest group of people in late Bronze Age Europe and flourished between *c.* 1200 BC until the emergence of a fully Celtic culture in Transalpine Europe *c.* 600 BC. The commencement of the Urnfield period is marked by an expansion of population and the wide adoption of the rite of cremation, together with new technological skills, especially in bronze working. The Urnfield people penetrated northern Italy and the Iberian peninsula. Placenames incorporating the Celtic element *-briga* are known from Spain and Portugal and may be the outcome of an Urnfield incursion by way of Languedoc and Catalonia.

The spread of iron working, and the impact of Oriental styles on the Urnfield peoples led to the development of the Hallstatt iron-using culture that began in the late eighth century BC. The Hallstatt culture, named after a famous cemetery excavated in Upper Austria in the nineteenth century, held a frontier against intrusive groups variously designated Thracian and Scythian, who brought with them the rudiments of a Eurasiatic 'animal style' art.

The development and spread of the Hallstatt culture followed by that of La Tène is a subject of considerable complexity.[7] The Hallstatt culture (*c.* 700–500 BC) represents partly a continuity from the late Urnfield culture and partly a response to new influences from Anatolia and the eastern Mediterranean. Improved metal technology, and the adoption of larger horses for riding, facilitated expansion. It is the late Hallstatt culture of the sixth century BC centred mainly in south-west Germany, Switzerland, Burgundy and the Middle Rhineland that may with some confidence be equated with the Celts as first mentioned by Greek geographers at the end of that century and shortly afterwards by Herodotus.

The archaeology of the Hallstatt culture in the sixth century BC is dominated by trade with the classical world. Classical merchandise was traded north from Greek colonies, especially from Massilia (Marseilles), up the Rhone and Saône to within the western Hallstatt province. Although some Etruscan products reached the Hallstatt province as early as the opening of the sixth century BC they probably passed through Massilia. At the end of that century, and during the fifth century, Etruscan bronze vessels flooded north mainly by Alpine passes. A distinctive type of beaked wine jug was found in the princess's grave at Vix together with other Greek works indicating a date *c.* 500 BC. By about 450 BC many of the Hallstatt strongholds had been abandoned, and Greek and Etruscan products have been found in princely tombs in new areas, in particular around the Middle Rhine and in Champagne.

This succeeding La Tène culture, named after the find-spot of a large votive deposit on Lake Neuchâtel, marks the great age of Celtic supremacy in Europe. To it belongs the first great art style developed north of the Alps and manifested mainly in fine bronze drinking vessels, personal ornaments, weapons and helmets. Celtic artists produced their own abstractions based on Greek and Oriental motifs – acanthus leaves, running scrolls, peltas. By the third century BC the Celtic world was at its greatest extent. Celtic tribes had already invaded Italy and had sacked Rome in 390 BC. They raided far to the south, and by 368 BC had served as mercenaries in Sicily. Other movements to the Middle Danube and Balkans culminated in the sack of Delphi in 279 BC.

The Celts in Britain

As a whole the fragmentary story of Iron Age Britain tells of native continuity from the late Bronze Age (eighth century BC) with the gradual appearance of small groups of settlers from the Continent introducing Hallstatt and La Tène derived elements.[8] It is now no longer valid to speak of large-scale immigrations of continental Celts (a supposed initial wave of Iron Age 'A' incomers of Hallstatt stock, followed by 'B' invaders from the Marne). Only the Belgic culture of Iron Age 'C', the final pre-Roman phase in southern Britain, introduced a unitary intrusive continental culture. Incoming craftsmen of Hallstatt and La Tène tradition can be inferred, but they were numerically small and are associated with cultures developed locally rather than with large intrusive assemblages. The Belgic settlers are represented archaeologically by coins (which indicate six separate immigrations) and began to settle in south-west England in the late second century BC.[9]

The Belgae reached their peak in the period between the time of Caesar and the Claudian invasion, when on the basis of coin evidence it is possible to recognize numerous tribal groups and dynasties, and to trace the expansion of Belgic influence until it affected much of lowland Britain. In this period they engaged in a vigorous trade with the Romanized world, and developed a particularly fine insular art at a time when Celtic art was almost dead on the Continent.

Roman and barbarian – characteristics

The respective legacies of the Roman and barbarian worlds must be stressed since they are of crucial importance in understanding Migration Period and early medieval Europe. Much of the character of the early Middle Ages is the result of the uneasy relationship between the two. Essentially Roman civilization represents a tradition that remained unbroken from the emergence of early civilizations in the Near East, through the cultures of the east Mediterranean and Greece. Later, the tradition was kept alive partly through the deliberate classicism of the Carolingian Empire and its ultimate inheritor, the Romanesque culture of western Europe, and partly through the hybrid Eastern-Roman culture of Byzantium. It has passed directly into modern thinking by way of the Italian Renaissance and eighteenth- and nineteenth-century neo-classicism. The essence of this tradition is order and the classification of all experience within rigorous, if artificial, schemes. It is realist, and its art accordingly is naturalistic. To the barbarian, the twentieth-century concept of order would be as irrelevant as the classical concern with realism and naturalism. Barbarian art may revert to naturalism, but only as a springboard from which pattern can be developed. For the classical artist, symmetry was essential; for the barbarian it was only an occasional device and where it did occur was frequently due to classical influence. Barbarian society was tribal, familiar and flamboyant; humanity was viewed from a personal standpoint, and consisted of the acquaintances of the individual. Accordingly society was fragmented, and the abstract concept of the state was irrelevant.

The society with which this book is concerned was fundamentally a higher barbarian culture, the inheritor of one of the most significant cultures of prehistoric Europe. Although in most respects it was barbarian, it was by no means wholly so. In spite of what has frequently been written, it did not remain unchanged from the Pre-Roman Iron Age through the period of Roman occupation in Britain to emerge little altered in the fifth century. During these centuries many of the characteristics of Iron Age society were modified, and some died out completely. In the process much was acquired materially from the Roman world, and something of the Roman concept of territorial administration passed into Celtic thinking. However, it remains a point of debate to what extent Romano-British ideas would have outlived the fifth century had it not been for Christianity, or how far the Celtic world of the fifth century would have reverted to its Iron Age condition. This religion, though embodying a 'Mystery' element probably quite in keeping with the Celtic view of the universe, nevertheless was Roman in its trappings, its organization and its demand for logical thought.

In Britain, it is important to remember that there were grades of Romanization, and that not all regions were equally Romanized. In the west and north Roman occupation, where it existed at all, was largely military and its cultural influence was proportionately less than in the south and east. Moreover, Britannia was a frontier province, and did not enjoy the same level of cultural attainment as the long-Romanized provinces in the heart of the Empire. Furthermore the differences between the 'Celtic west' and the rest of Britain were accentuated by the fact that the densest Anglo-Saxon settlement was in the areas where Roman influence had been strongest.

Early Christian Celtic cultural interplay

While in many ways Celtic society of the Migration Period differed little from the other major barbarian groups that were its contemporaries, it was settled

Figure 1 Irish settlements in western Britain (After Thomas)

in character. There were no large-scale folk movements from Britain comparable with those of the Franks, Visigoths or Huns, and indeed the chief Celtic migrations of the post-Roman period were of the Irish and the minor migration from south-west England to Brittany.

The Irish settlements were felt most strongly in western Scotland and Wales, though there is evidence for extensive additional settlement in south-west England. The first mention of the Scotti or Irish in mainland Britain is in the writings of Ammianus Marcellinus, who in speaking of the events of

AD 360 refers to 'Scottorum Pictorum gentium ferarum excursus'.[10] It would seem that early in that year the Scots of Ireland joined forces with the Picts to ravage the northern frontier of Roman Britain, breaking the terms imposed on them earlier in the century. The events of the 360s, however, were not the first signs of contact between Ireland and the Romanized world. For the first two centuries AD there was a limited amount of peaceful trading between Ireland and Britain, and Tacitus, writing around the turn of the first century, recorded that 'the interior regions (of Ireland) are little known, but through trade and the merchants there is better knowledge of its harbours and approaches'.[11] The Irish exports seem to have been mainly wolfhounds, hides and cattle, and imports certainly included Roman pottery and metalwork which have been found on a number of sites including Lagore and the Rath of the Synods at Tara. Irish literature reflects widespread looting as well as trade. Niall of the Nine Hostages made seven expeditions to Britain. Traditionally his mother was a British captive, and slave-raiding appears to have been one of Niall's chief objectives.[12] The Roman material in Ireland dating from the fourth and fifth centuries reflects the same situation of uneasiness. Early fifth-century hoards of looted silver are recorded from Coleraine, and makers' stamps on pieces from Balline indicate their manufacture in Britain.[13]

Roman military policy in western Britain around the turn of the third century was probably dictated by Irish raids; forts such as Chester were refurbished and new forts constructed at Caer Gybi on Holyhead and at Cardiff. If these defences delayed the Irish settlements in Wales, it was not for long. The raids had probably been motivated by a thirst for booty and adventure: the settlements had other causes. The political situation in Ireland in the fourth century was one of constant internal feuds, probably partly the outcome of an increase in population – the result of improved farming methods and iron technology. Entire tribes seem to have been displaced as a result of civil strife, while Irish laws of primogeniture had always resulted in the disinheritance of younger sons. The legendary expulsion of one tribe, the Desi, accounts for an extensive Irish settlement in Pembroke, and similar factors may have resulted in the settlement of the Lleyn peninsula of Caernarvonshire. Cornwall may have been in part colonized from the Irish settlements of south Wales; a separate movement led to the foundation of the kingdom of Dalriada in Argyll while others resulted in settlements in south-west Scotland and the Isle of Man.[14] The documentary evidence for the settlements, which seem to be concentrated in the later fourth and early fifth centuries, is confusing; much of the evidence comes from placenames and memorial stones with Irish ogham inscriptions (Fig. 1). The archaeological evidence is virtually non-existent though this may partly be accounted for by the difficulty of recognizing distinctively 'Irish' objects of the fourth and fifth centuries.

The settlements of the British in Brittany were of a different character from those of the Irish in Britain.[15] Traditionally, the migration was led by a prince from Gwent in south Wales, and the leaders are described as eastern Welsh chieftains, although in fact the majority of the emigrants probably came from Cornwall. The migration was an organized operation, and appears to have met with little resistance. Some of the chiefs held both their estates in Wales and new territory in Brittany, which was partly opened up by the clearance of forest. The outcome was the establishment of Breton in Brittany. The settlement is difficult to date more precisely than to some time between the fifth and seventh centuries.

Modern nationalism has tended to define Scotland, Ireland, Wales, Man and south-west England as political and cultural units, and for convenience there is a tendency to study each of these regions separately. Such divisions would have been meaningless in the Early Christian period, the main distinction being between the Goidelic Celtic speakers of Ireland and the areas they colonized, and the Brythonic Celtic speakers of 'British'. The Celts themselves probably had no concept of Celtic nationality; territorial awareness was mainly confined to their individual kingdoms, with a more nebulous feeling of identity with linguistically related areas. Thus the people of Wales felt some kinship with the Gwyr y Gogledd ('Men of the North') who occupied Cumbria. The Picts represent a separate grouping.

Within this framework a pattern of internal and external cultural contacts and transmissions is apparent, a pattern best viewed against the geographical setting, and which was probably instrumental in the preservation of the overall character of Celtic society. All the Celtic-speaking areas of Early Christian times fall within the 'Highland Zone' defined by Sir Cyril Fox in 1932.[16] This region was characterized by cultural continuity and conservation. Influences from northern Europe were felt in north-east Scotland as a result of traffic across the North Sea, and contacts with the Mediterranean were felt round the Atlantic coast and the Irish Sea. Accordingly it is not surprising to find that Christianity came to western Britain by the same route as Mediterranean imports such as pottery, while slightly later Ireland was visited by clerics from Visigothic Spain.

It has been suggested by Alcock that Fox's division into Highland and Lowland Zones should be modified by the recognition of a third – the Irish Sea province.[17] The coastal areas of the south-western part of this 'province', together with most of Ireland, are relatively flat, and in terms of the economy they could support are in many ways similar to parts of the Lowland Zone. This concept of the 'Celtic Pond' as it has been termed was recognized as long ago as 1902 by Mackinder, who saw further divisions within it: (1) the north-western parts of Ireland and Scotland, (2) the Irish Sea with Man in its centre and (3) southern Ireland, most of Wales, south-west England and Brittany.[18] Some degree of unity can be seen within each.

Cultural continuity

On the Continent, Celtic civilization had become largely submerged by Roman, and, following the barbarian migrations, did not recover in the post-Roman period. Gaulish appears to have continued as a spoken language in the Roman period, but was obsolete by the late fourth century. Something of the Celtic tribal structure was preserved, however, in the territorial administration, and the population, in spite of its Roman veneer, must have been in essence Gaulish in its institutions and beliefs.

In Britain cultural continuity from the Iron Age into the Early Christian period is most readily apparent on a peasant level. It is most clearly demonstrated in Scotland, where the four culture provinces of the Iron Age remain valid divisions for the Early Christian period. In the Atlantic province brochs were replaced by wheelhouses and stone huts which were frequently erected among the crumbling ruins of the brochs themselves. The wheelhouse culture shows close affinities to that of the late broch period, while certain types of objects, such as fluted-rim pottery, show a remarkable conservatism from the earliest Iron Age of Shetland through to the period of Norse settlements. A similar degree of continuity can be traced in the Western Isles, while in the western Highlands Early Christian occupation of the characteristic 'duns' of the Iron Age can be attested at sites like Kildonan Bay, Argyll. In south-west Scotland crannogs appear to have been built in the Early Christian period along similar lines to those of their Iron Age predecessors, while there is also some evidence for the reoccupation of hillforts such as Trusty's Hill, Anwoth (Kirkcudbright). In southern Scotland too another Iron Age type, the scooped settlement, appears to have continued into the Middle Ages. What little native pottery of the post-Roman period is known from southern Scotland appears likewise to be Iron Age in character.

A type of fort which utilizes natural outcrops for defensive purposes is distinctive of the Early Christian period in the areas occupied by Picts and Scots. These 'nuclear forts', best exemplified by the Scottic citadel of Dunadd, have their counterparts outside Scotland. The fort of Dinas Emrys, Caernarvonshire, bears more than a superficial similarity to Dunadd in its profile and location, while the Mote of Mark, Kirkcudbrightshire, for instance, though lying outside the main area of nuclear forts shares many of their characteristics. Apart from Dinas Emrys there are a series of other reoccupied hillforts in Wales and the south-west, of which Dinas Powys (Glamorgan), Coygan Camp (Glamorgan), South Cadbury (Somerset) and Castle Dore (Cornwall) are good examples. In Ireland there is as yet little evidence for the reoccupation of hillforts, but of the few that have been excavated, one at least, Downpatrick, Co. Down, was occupied in the Early Christian period. The basic Irish settlement type, the rath or ringfort, appears to have been in use throughout the first millennium AD, and there is some evidence for the occupation if not the construction of raths until the eighteenth and nineteenth centuries. As in Scotland, crannogs were a feature of Early Christian settlement patterns, the royal site of Lagore being just such a lake dwelling. Earth-houses or souterrains are another type of Iron Age structure in use in the Christian era, in Ireland at least.

The economy of the Early Christian Celts

Most of the information available about the economy of the Early Christian Celts comes from Ireland, since more sites of the period have been excavated there than in Britain.

A recent survey has shown that the distribution of raths and cashels (stone-built ringforts) is restricted to areas of modern cultivated land in the lowlands, and to valleys which extend into the uplands.[19] It has been demonstrated that if a family's dietetic needs and the apparent yield per acre is estimated as slightly less in the Early Christian period than in the Middle Ages, then a farmer would require between 40 and 80 acres to supply the needs of his farm. It has been similarly shown that in County Down, if raths are plotted in relation to potential cultivable land, there is adequate land for 60-acre farms associated with each settlement. Some potentially cultivable land does not, however, appear to have been utilized by rath farmers – these gaps in distribution may be explained by other forms of settlement which have left no trace in the area, and it has been suggested that they might have taken the form of clustered undefended settlements appearing as *buaile* (*bally* placenames) and occupied by farmers of inferior status to rath owners.

The economy was predominantly pastoral, and literary sources show that wealth and tribute were measured in numbers of animals, of which the most important were cattle.[20] The bones from excavations, where these have been preserved, substantiate this. Only on one rath site, Boho, Co. Fermanagh, are there less than 70 per cent of cattle bones, and at Cahercommaun, Co. Clare, the percentage was as great as 97. Second in importance to cattle and also well suited to partially cleared woodland were pigs. The bones from excavated sites suggest a slender breed. The dearth of sheep bones from sites may perhaps partly be the result of the animals being kept for wool rather than for meat, and certainly sheep shears are common finds on Early Christian sites in Ireland. Sheep were not kept in large numbers in the wetter lowlands, being more suited to the hilly regions. Horses may occasionally have been eaten, as the evidence from the Ballinderry crannogs suggests, but were more usually used for riding or draught. There was a relatively high proportion of horse bones at Garranes (9 per cent) but this was possibly because the site is traditionally the seat of the Eóganacht chieftains, who would have required mounts. Evidence for the keeping of poultry is slight, domestic fowl being represented on only a few rath sites. The chicken was probably introduced from the Roman world.

The direct evidence for cultivation is meagre, but the picture is filled out by literary references.[21] Two types of plough are known from antiquity; the light two-ox plough without a coulter, wheels or mould board, usually known as an 'ard', used in cross-ploughing and widely present in prehistoric Europe; and the heavy coultered plough, often with wheel and mould board. The latter was suited to heavier soils, and though known from Europe as early as the fifth century BC does not appear to have been introduced to Britain until the arrival of the Belgae in the second century BC. Thereafter it was common in Britain. A few early coulters and ploughshares are known from Ireland indicating the use of a fairly heavy plough as well as a type of 'ard'. Relatively few sites have produced coulters or shares, which are known only from the major crannogs, the Early Christian occupation at Dundrum, and four raths. The plough according to literary sources was pulled by a team of two, four or six oxen. Sickles and reaping hooks were used for cutting the crops, as well as for fodder and thatch. Two spades have survived, and there is some evidence for their use, as cut turves and peat of the period are known. Evidence of pollen, charcoal and soils from beneath rath banks indicate some clearance of woodland in the neighbourhood prior to rath construction. Five grain crops are known from both literary and archaeological sources: 'red' and 'white' wheat, oats, barley and rye. Flax seeds were found at Lissue, and the plant is mentioned in literature along with various vegetables including kale, onions, leeks, garlic and dye-plants. The scythe does not appear to have reached Ireland until the Middle Ages – reaping was invariably done with a sickle, the ears being cut at the top of the stalk. For threshing, a stick was used rather than a true flail. Corn was sown directly on the furrow and harrowing is mentioned in the *Crith Gabhlach* (a collection of Irish law codes), though the date of its introduction is unknown.

The fields at 'The Spectacles', Lough Gur, and at Cush are examples of the rare instances where field layouts can be traced. Most have been destroyed by later cultivation. It is possible that the fields and huts at Caherguillamore and Two Mile Stone were contemporaneous. Those at Two Mile Stone are large and irregular, bounded by short lines of walling, and would have been used for pasture. On the slopes below the settlement were terraces which were possibly used for cultivation. The Irish Laws imply that although most fields were fenced and were family property, there was also a certain amount of common land with elaborate rules for its use.

Corn-drying kilns are known from a number of sites such as Letterkeen, Ballymacash and Garranes, and possibly also Uisneach and Nendrum. At Cush grain may have been stored in granaries supported by four posts, while grain storage pits of 'Little Woodbury' type are known. Rotary querns, often decorated in the Early Christian period with lines and rings in relief, are found on

Irish sites. There is evidence in literature for large mills but the only archaeological remains are from Ballinderry 1 which produced a sandstone millstone 28 inches in diameter and $11\frac{1}{2}$ inches thick. Although fragmentary, it weighed 350 lb and must have been used in a water-driven mill due to its weight.

As far as can be deduced, specialization in either crop cultivation or animal husbandry to the exclusion of the other was very rare. The majority of Early Christian sites for which there is adequate evidence show that both types of farming were practised, with emphasis on pastoralism. A few sites have produced evidence for cultivation alone.

The diet was supplemented by red deer and to a lesser extent wild pig, though it is not always possible to distinguish the bones of wild pig from the domesticated variety. Fowling and fishing were rare. Only Carraig Aille and Leacanabuaile have produced bird bones, and fish bones and line sinkers are uncommon. To some extent this might be due to the low survival level of such small bones in acid soil.

There is evidence of industrial activity on a great number of sites. Iron working, and the production of iron tools, was a home industry. The less frequent working of bronze was widespread, and not confined to the richest or most important sites. Lead too was worked. Spinning and weaving were usual in the home, and the working of bone, shale, jet, lignite and horn occurred.

Although most sites occupied in the period give the impression of being self-sufficient, some internal trade, especially in metal ores, existed. Jet, shale, glass and a number of small luxury objects were traded, and pottery was imported from as far afield as the Mediterranean. The homogeneity of material culture in much of the Irish Sea area implies frequent interchange. Literary sources attest the existence of roads and bridges, and transport was provided by wheeled vehicles and boats (p. 258).

In Celtic society the craftsman was mobile. Travelling smiths repaired tools and also set up temporary forges for the production of new utensils and articles of personal adornment. This fact alone must have contributed to the homogeneity of material culture within the Irish Sea area, and the rapid transmission of new styles and ideas.

The evidence from Britain indicates that the economy was generally similar to that in Ireland. Although exceptionally rich, the site of Mote of Mark, Kirkcudbright, shows that the Britons of Rheged lived on a similar cultural level to the occupants of Garranes, Co. Cork. At Mote of Mark iron, bronze and possibly lead were worked, while jet or lignite was imported from Yorkshire to make bracelets and spindle whorls. Bones show that cattle predominated in the economy, followed by pig; deer antlers imply that these were hunted. Only one fragmentary rotary quern was recovered, perhaps suggesting that bread was of minor importance in the diet. Of the more homely crafts, there was some evidence for spinning, bone and flint working, and possibly the working of antler. Glass, pottery and scrap bronze were imported, while iron ores and the stone used for tools were local. The pattern is repeated at Dinas Powys in Glamorgan, where the middens yielded a preponderance of cattle and pig bones with sheep and, in contrast to Irish sites, a few fowl. Horse bones were absent, and the diet here was supplemented to some extent by fish and limpets. There is no evidence that the early Welsh were nomadic or partly nomadic, as was once suggested; the basis of the economy was settled farming.[22] In Cornwall evidence for cultivation methods comes from Gwithian, where an arable field cultivated by a fixed mould-board plough was excavated. Sickles similar to those used in Ireland occurred on this site (pp. 133–5).

Political and social structure

On a higher social level cultural continuity is less apparent. The kingdoms of Early Christian Britain traced their origins to Roman administration, and the kings and chiefs of the fifth century, at least, were cast in a Romano-British mould. For all their barbarian dependence on the loyalty of their immediate followers, Vortigern and Cunedda were essentially Romano-Britons, trying to keep alive Romano-British standards of law and order in a disordered world. Such leaders lived in timber halls like those at South Cadbury or Dinas Powys.

Nevertheless as the memory of Rome grew fainter the world of the British chiefs became more obviously heroic, and further removed from that of provincial Roman administration.[23] Poetry of the period shows that a chief of the sixth century lived with his followers and shared with them the feasting, music and poetry of the court. His position was maintained by the personal loyalty of his followers and the qualities which they most admired in him were courage and generosity, in return for which they would die for him. The bands were generally small, and their leaders held their positions through the hereditary right of their aristocracy. Among the Early Christian Celts the kingship of the tribe was open to every male member of the royal lineage whose great-grandfather had been king. In this respect, though usually patrilineal (the exception being the probably matrilineal Pictish kingdom), the inheritance did not depend on primogeniture, and among the special legal privileges of a king in the Welsh laws of Hywel Dda was the right to nominate his successor. In the absence of organized administration, government depended on complex economic and hereditary law codes, which seem to owe little to Roman legal procedures and are based on a more archaic native structure which was periodically adapted to changing conditions. Fundamental to the law codes and to Celtic society was the maintenance of family ties and the adherence to the clan, which had a corporate unity in law equal to that of the individual in modern society. Within the tribe were two main classes, the nobility and the free peoples, below which there was a further class of slaves. Although the basic social and political structure varied slightly from region to region and at various periods, the heroic character of Celtic society was universal, and was little affected by the spread of Christianity.

Celt and Saxon[24]

The relationship between Celt and Saxon is important in a consideration of the transmission of cultural traits in the Celtic world. The differences have perhaps been exaggerated, and, except in Northumbria, the independence of the two groups overstressed. Anglo-Saxons and Celts were culturally on a similar level, with comparable basic equipment. Both were societies of farmers, without coinage, urban administration or political unity until these were developed by the Saxons in the seventh and later centuries. Both were heroic societies in which political unity depended on individual loyalties and family connections, and both were divided by civil warfare between rival factions. Both built round huts and larger rectangular halls, and though the Anglo-Saxons appear to have formed a settlement pattern based on the *gawondorf* (the nucleated hamlet) rather than the *einzelhof* (the isolated farmstead), the differences in settlement type may be more apparent than real, due to the accident of archaeological survival. For both Celt and Saxon, internal trade was sporadic and conducted on a relatively small scale: in the case of Anglo-Saxon England, within a ten-mile radius, if deductions can be made about the nature of trade from the travels of the products of Anglo-Saxon potters.[25] One reason why pagan Saxon England seems in such contrast to the Celtic west lies in the nature of the archaeological evidence. For Anglo-Saxon England there are extensive and rich cemeteries, furnished with grave goods, which provide the framework for archaeological study. The Celtic areas, Christian from an early date, lack furnished burials – there is no pagan Celtic burial known from the post-Roman period – and accordingly Celtic archaeology has probably been deprived of a wealth of evidence. The finds from pagan Saxon settlements are notably impoverished, though they include native pottery, which Celtic sites do not, and the everyday objects such as bone combs, spindle whorls, knives and other ironwork are virtually identical in both areas. Both regions drew upon a common tradition of material culture widespread in Migration Period Europe, the ultimate origins of which are often to be found within the Roman Empire. Celt and Saxon alike drew on common artistic traditions from Migration Period Europe, and between the two there was an artistic interplay.

The traditional view of Celto-Saxon relations stems from Bede. It must be remembered that Bede was writing some centuries after the Anglo-Saxon settlements, and was trying to rationalize the evidence available to him about the settlements in the light of the subsequent formation of the kingdoms of the Heptarchy. He was also writing from a theological standpoint, and differences of doctrine between the Anglo-Saxon and Celtic Church represented to him fundamental differences between Celt and Saxon. Such differences were more religious and political than cultural. The story of waves of Anglo-Saxon invaders in the mid-fifth century can no longer be sustained. The Anglo-Saxon settlements were a gradual process that began probably in the third century and continued increasingly until the mid-fifth, when the already existing Germanic population was augmented by a phase of uncontrolled settlement. The pagan Saxon population, however, was relatively small, and the Britons would probably have numerically outweighed the incomers. Archaeology in no way suggests that the British were extensively massacred by the incomers, nor that they migrated westwards, and it must be assumed that to some extent they coexisted with the Anglo-Saxon who initially occupied parts of the countryside never densely populated by the Romano-Britons. A gradual cultural fusion seems likely, and the finds of British types of penannular brooches, hanging bowl escutcheons and other small objects in Anglo-Saxon contexts may be manifestations of it.

The cultural achievement of the Early Christian Celts

The Early Christian Celts contributed nothing of any consequence to the development of technology, and few items of their equipment could not be found elsewhere in Europe. They are not notable for their political or social institutions, nor were they outstanding traders. The Celtic contribution to European civilization is one which is only partly reflected in archaeology. In great part it stems from their religion, and has its archaeological reflection in their art. While the 'Celtic Church' did not exist as a unity throughout the Celtic areas it is possible to recognize a Celtic Christian ethos which in many ways embodies the less militant qualities of Christianity.[26]

From the Celtic Church stems much of the surviving literature of the Celts, although it also embodies a wealth of heroic material, notable among which is the work of the Welsh poets Taliesin and Aneurin.[27] Celtic poetry is distinguished by its compression, brevity and cumulative quality; it builds up to an emotional climax, except in the case of some short poems which are distinguished by simplicity and unity of thought. Apart from saints' *Lives* and historical material, Celtic prose includes a body of traditional stories. The finest collection, though set down in medieval form, was that gathered together in the last century by Lady Charlotte Guest as the *Mabinogion*; beneath the overlay of medieval romance and Christianity, it is possible to read stories with origins in the Iron Age, such as the legend of Lludd and Llefelys.

The sources of Celtic art are complex, and as far as can be ascertained little of La Tène insular art survives in the manuscripts, metalwork and sculpture of the post-Roman era. It was an amalgam of Roman, European barbarian and native elements which managed, during the seventh and eighth centuries at least, to maintain a careful balance between classical order and barbarian chaos. Careful discipline produced an intricate beauty which was frequently only just preserved from over-ornateness by the mastery of the artists. It can be seen at its best in metalwork, notably the Ardagh Chalice, but it is apparent in some manuscripts such as Durrow or Lindisfarne.

The nature of the evidence[28]

The evidence for the culture of the Early Christian Celts is both archaeological and historical. Early medieval historical writing is far removed from what is today regarded as history. The nearest documents to a historical narrative are *annals*: catalogues of events listed chronologically, some of which represent compilations from earlier sources, others of which are based on genuine historical knowledge. Most of these were set down in monasteries. Among the most important of this period are the *Annals of the Four Masters, The Annals of Tigernach* and the *Annales Cambriae*, the first two being Irish compilations, the last Welsh. Related in form are *genealogies*, which are king-lists compiled to provide an ancestry for a ruling dynasty. The earlier part of such dynasties is usually entirely mythical, the later entries more reliable. Notable among existing genealogies are those incorporated in the Welsh MS *Harley 3857*. Historical information can sometimes be provided by *inscriptions*; most of these are simple memorials on tombstones, though a few monuments, such as the Pillar of Eliseg, near Llangollen, provide more information. *Narrative histories* are very rare; the *De excidio* of Gildas, set down in the sixth century, belongs to this category, but is an unreliable diatribe. To this category also belongs the *Historia Brittonum*, a work now regarded as a compilation by many hands, including that of Nennius. The remaining documentary sources were never intended as historical writings, and consist of *Lives* of saints, *homilies* and other religious tracts, *poetry*, notably historical narrative poems like the *Gododdin*, and *law codes*. All these sources are of varying degrees of unreliability, and the first task of the historian is to try to determine what can be regarded as historical facts and how these facts can be fitted to a chronological framework.

The archaeological evidence is equally scant and difficult to interpret. Much of the evidence comes from a few sites, the majority of which are in Ireland. In Britain only one site in Wales (Dinas Powys) and two in Scotland (Dunadd and Mote of Mark) have produced a considerable range of finds; the important site of Gwithian in Cornwall is as yet unpublished, so a comparable site for the south-west is so far lacking. Furthermore, the field has been neglected in Britain in comparison with other fields of archaeological study, and there are correspondingly few recent excavations. Where work on the period has been done, it has been concentrated on ecclesiastical archaeology and art history. In Scotland almost no work had been done on possible Pictish settlement sites until 1970, and even at the time of writing many of the major Early Christian period sites such as Dundurn, Perthshire, have not been sampled by excavation. Because it is seldom possible to use documentary evidence for establishing a chronology for sites, dating is dependent on the internal evidence. Even in the case of sites which do produce a range of finds, dating is difficult. The most important datable material is imported pottery, but it has not been possible to arrive at a close date for individual wares on the Continent, nor, by extension, for their currency in Britain. As far as can be established, most classes of material culture remained very little altered throughout the Early Christian period; the exceptions are brooches and other forms of dress fasteners, which to some extent can be arranged in a chronological sequence. Except in a few rare cases, however, the date brackets that it is possible to assign to particular types are seldom narrower than a century. Apart from Pictish settlements, there are other major gaps in archaeological knowledge. Little is known from archaeology about settlements in Britain from the seventh to the eleventh centuries. In no region outside Ireland is it possible to attempt a regional survey of settlement patterns in the period, and population estimates, ecology and land utilization can only be guessed.

2 Southern Scotland

Three groups of people can be recognized in the Early Christian period in the area of modern southern Scotland. Of these the British represent the native Celtic stock and their ancestors can be traced to the anonymous peoples of the Iron Age. The other two groups were intrusive, and comprise the Angles and the Irish. Although not strictly relevant to the subject of this book, the Angles of Northumbria must be considered because of their important impact on the north Britons. At the height of their power the Northumbrians occupied all south-east Scotland and made some inroads into the south-west. Although there is little archaeological evidence for the settlement, place-names suggest that there were groups of Irish in Galloway in the period. South-east Scotland is considered separately from the south-west, as the archaeology and history of the region is governed by its distinctive Iron Age background and by its early assimilation into Northumbria; the south-west possessed a more diverse Iron Age background and this to some extent resulted in regional variation in the post-Roman period and in the growth of two distinct kingdoms.

The pre-Roman Iron Age[1]

As elsewhere in Britain, there is no sharp division between the late Bronze Age and early Iron Age in Scotland. In the late Bronze Age it is possible to recognize the appearance of hillforts with timber-laced defences and 'palisaded settlements' (a type of site on which a palisade encloses one or more huts). Such settlements should be seen as an indigenous development which was a response to changing social conditions, increased stability of economy, and population growth during the first millennium BC.

During the fifth to fourth centuries BC new hillfort types appeared for the first time in southern Scotland, with univallate defences, usually of stone or earth, sometimes with some timber lacing. Their appearance was due to the spread of Hallstatt-influenced culture in Britain as a whole. In a few cases, such as Hownam Rings, Roxburgh, univallate hillforts were constructed on top of pre-existing palisaded sites.[2]

In the early to mid-first century BC there was a general movement of La Tène peoples into Scotland from England. These peoples, designated 'Iron Age B' in England, may have been driven north from eastern England by the pressure of Belgic colonists who were, by the mid-first century BC, dominating much of south-east England. The colonists introduced a new type of fort with multivallate defences, which rapidly became a characteristic monument of the southern Scottish Lowlands.[3]

As early as the end of the third century BC a flourishing school of ornamental metalworking was established in southern Scotland, the products of which, both native and intrusive, have been used to classify the later stages of the southern Scottish Iron Age.[4] The last group of ornamental metalwork prior to the arrival of the Romans was introduced in the first century AD by Belgic refugees from England, possibly displaced by the expansion of the Catuvellauni under Tasciovanus in the early part of the first century.

Hillforts were the predominant type of settlement in southern Scotland in the Iron Age, but other settlement types are recognizable. First, there are a few brochs and duns, outliers of their own province to the north of the Forth–Clyde line. Secondly, there are crannogs and souterrains. The first widespread appearance of crannogs, or lake dwellings, in southern Scotland is probably contemporary with the earliest hillforts, though it is possible that some examples, as in Ireland, may be as early as the Bronze Age. The majority of excavated examples belong to the period of Roman military occupation. While they tend to be of western distribution (they spread as far as the Biggar Gap), their northerly limit is less restricted, stretching into the Highlands. Most of the few souterrains in southern Scotland appear to have been occupied as late as the Roman military advance. With the exception of one at Yardhouses, Carnwath, Lanarkshire, the six remaining known examples are all in the south-east. They are an extension from the souterrain province of Angus. Thirdly, there are several classes of homesteads and enclosed hut groups, most of which appear to belong to the Roman Iron Age.

The basic settlement pattern established in Lowland Scotland and northern England during the first millennium BC continued into the Roman period and beyond. The reoccupation of some Iron Age hillforts in the post-Roman period is indicative of continuing settlement in the same areas, and it is likely that the economy of the region in the post-Roman period was similar to that of the pre-Roman and Roman Iron Age. Crannogs continued to be constructed in the post-Roman period, and where new forts were built in the Dark Ages, the sites chosen were in areas where Iron Age settlement appears to have been fairly dense. The fort of Dalmahoy, Midlothian, for example, is adjacent to the Pre-Roman Iron Age fort of Kaimes Law, while the Mote of Mark, Kirkcudbright, is near what is probably an Iron Age fort with medieval occupation at Castlehill Point.

The Roman Iron Age[5]

The principal source of information about the tribes of southern Scotland in the early centuries AD is the *Geography of Ptolemy*. To a lesser extent the sixth-century compilation known as the *Ravenna Cosmography* is also used since it draws on second-century sources. Ptolemy lived during the time of Hadrian and Marcus Aurelius, but he obviously used information collected

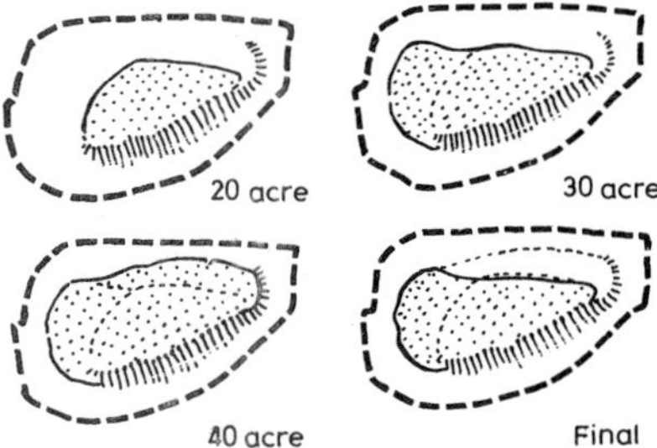

Figure 2 Phases of Traprain Law (After Feachem)

about the time of Agricola. Although erroneous on matters concerning latitude and longitude, a tribal map can be worked out from his writings and this can in part be amplified and substantiated by other classical sources.

In Lowland Scotland four tribes can be distinguished. The *Votadini* occupied the east coast from the Tyne to the Forth and to the west of them, centred on Roxburgh, were the *Selgovae*. In Wigtown, and extending into Kirkcudbright, were the *Novantae*, while the *Damnonii* were concentrated in the Clyde valley and Ayrshire and probably extended into Dunbarton.

Against this tribal background the character of the hillforts falls into clearer perspective. The largest forts (both univallate and multivallate) were the equivalent of oppida or tribal capitals. The largest in north Britain are Traprain Law, East Lothian, and Eildon Hill North, Roxburghshire.

Traprain Law[6] was the oppidum of the Votadini (Fig. 2). It possibly began as an open Bronze Age settlement, replaced by a small 10-acre enclosure. This putative enclosure was subsequently enlarged first to about 20, then 30 and finally 40 acres, before reduction in the late Roman period. The lack of stratified finds hinders the precise dating of the earlier phases, but the 40-acre fort appears to have been occupied in the first and second centuries. Occupation ceased at some point in the fifth century.

Eildon Hill North[7] was the capital of the Selgovae. The primary enclosure was about 2 acres in extent, but was subsequently extended to 9 and finally 40 acres. Within the defences some 300 house floors have been recognized, and up to 200 more have probably been destroyed. No excavations have taken place.

Apart from the two oppida, the Votadini and Selgovae occupied other large forts. In both Votadinian and Selgovian territory the evidence points to the continued reduction in the size of the minor forts, suggesting increased political stability and gradual cohesion of various small groups of people.

In the territory of the Damnonii the largest fort is Walls Hill, Renfrewshire, occupying 18½ acres. The next largest is Carmen, Dunbarton (5½ acres) followed by Duncarnock, Renfrewshire (4½ acres). Further south, in the territory of the Novantae, the most important fort was that of Birrenswark (17 acres) in Dumfriesshire, later used for manœuvres by the Roman army from Birrens.

The Roman military advance into Scotland was carried out by Agricola. It was probably his successor who had a series of camps built to block the mouths of the Highland glens in a line through Perthshire.[8] These forts seem to have been abandoned in AD 86–7, and by AD 100 all the forts north of the Tyne–Solway were likewise deserted.[9]

Early in the second century a series of forts, fortlets and watchtowers were constructed on the Stanegate. These were replaced by Hadrian's Wall which was begun in 122 and itself superseded *c.* 142 by the Antonine Wall stretching from the Forth to the Clyde. This was defended until *c.* 158.[10] During the following period of abandonment, inscriptions attest the reoccupation of Hadrian's Wall. Current thinking favours the view that the Antonine Wall remained unoccupied from *c.* 158 until the 180s when, as a result of a barbarian invasion which broke Hadrian's Wall, it was reoccupied and held until the end of the century.[11] Around 207 the Antonine Wall and part of Hadrian's Wall were destroyed, and in 208 Septimius Severus came to Britain with his sons, focusing his attention on the Maeatae. He established a legionary fortress at Carpow[12] on the Tay, and built a series of large camps stretching into Moray. After his death in York in 211, his son Caracalla concentrated on the defence of Hadrian's Wall which henceforth controlled the natives beyond the frontier.

The Roman military advance did very little to alter the general way of life or the economy in north Britain.[13] The appearance of the rotary quern, whether introduced by the Romans or as early as the second century BC, did no more than improve milling. The Belgic plough has only been found in Roman contexts in the north. There is some evidence, however, that although the Roman military obtained their supplies by sea from the south, they actively encouraged native farming. The site at Tamshiel Rig, Roxburgh, is a stone-built version of a southern British type of farm, with 30 acres of adjoining fields.

The appearance of enclosed hut groups in Northumberland, Durham and the adjoining parts of the Scottish Lowlands is probably due to this official encouragement of farming.[14] These huts, like the Welsh hut groups, show features such as stone walling not present before the Roman advance. The wool industry was indubitably an incentive to farming; for example it is quite possible that some of the famed British woollen cloaks mentioned in Diocletian's *De Maximis Pretiis* edict came from the north. The presence of a Roman votive clay model of a bale of wool from a Skye broch points to such a trade.

Native centres of resistance, such as major hillforts, were rapidly rendered inoffensive, and only a few sites, such as Traprain and Dalry, remained in occupation. Traprain from the outset seems to have held a special status. Occupation continued through the Roman period, possibly because the chiefs of the Votadini may have had special privileges. Beyond the frontier Roman pottery and gewgaws spread among the natives.[15] Roman pottery occurs in crannogs in Galloway, in caves on the Solway, souterrains in Angus, hillforts in Ayrshire and brochs in Orkney. Although diffusion of Roman objects was wide, their significance is generally minimal, particularly when compared with the wealth of Roman material beyond the German *limes*, where it had but little effect on the way of life of the Germanic tribes.

The beginnings of the post-Roman kingdoms

The 'Conspiratio Barbarica' of 367 was the most extensive of the disruptions of the northern frontier in the fourth century. It had been preceded by a serious disturbance *c.* 343, the details of which are lost. It certainly seems that the Picts or proto-Picts had ravaged the territory north of Hadrian's Wall, and around this time a number of forts in north Britain, notably High Rochester, Risingham and Bewcastle, were badly damaged. The emperor Constans thought the matter sufficiently serious to call for a visit to Britain, and apparently employed the *areani* of the hinterland of the Wall to assist in this reorganization. The precise status of the *areani* or *arcani* is difficult to determine. They seem to have been federates deployed on the frontiers to keep check on native activities; the term *areani* means 'men of the open spaces', or 'men of the sheepfolds', the term *arcani* meaning 'intelligence agents'. If these people were strictly speaking *areani*, then it is likely that they were the occupants of the enclosed hut groups of the Borders.[16]

In 360 a further uprising of the Picts, this time aided and abetted by the Scots of northern Ireland, presumably in contravention of the terms agreed upon with Constans, seems to have been a prelude to the events of 367, when there were successful attacks on Britain by Picts, Scots, Attacotti and Saxons. It is the first instance of a consortium of barbarians in the north. Previous raids had been the outcome not of an alliance, but of individual tribal initiative, and the Attacotti were new, as far as is known, to the list of raiders. Their homeland is disputed; they either came from Ireland or the Western Isles, and St Jerome attested their barbarism on one occasion in Gaul, when he noted that they were cannibals.

The Wall was overrun, and the Count of the Saxon Shore killed, while the Duke of Britain was captured or besieged. The *areani* failed to give advance warning and gave information to the enemy, and the situation was further aggravated by widespread desertion in the Roman army.

Under Count Theodosius the defences were reorganized. The Wall was refortified and a chain of lookouts was built along the Yorkshire coast. Corbridge, which had been one of the main supply forts for the Wall and which had been destroyed in *c.* 350, was repaired. The final abandonment of Hadrian's Wall took place some time after 385 as coin evidence and the *Notitia Dignitatum* suggest.[17] Although some years were to elapse between the raid of 367 and the abandonment of the Wall, it seems that during this time the area behind the Wall was hostile, for few finds postdating 367 have been found there. Most of the *vici* or civil settlements outside the Wall forts seem to have been abandoned in the late fourth century, civilians probably moving inside the forts, though Chesterholm seems to have been occupied as a *vicus* into the fourth and possibly the fifth century.[18]

Following the restoration of Count Theodosius, Roman protectorates were set up in what was to become Strathclyde (the former territory of the Damnonii) and that part of the Votadinian lands subsequently known as *Manau.* This would certainly seem to be corroborated by the story of Cunedda. This Votadinian leader migrated to Wales in the fifth century (p. 100) and the names of the early rulers of Manau and Strathclyde are Roman. However, the adoption of Roman names may merely signify the adoption of Christianity and have no political significance. The policy would have been in accordance with Roman tradition, and the absence of federate tribes would be more surprising than their presence – the migration of Cunedda would be largely inexplicable unless part of the Votadinian lands were held by Votadini federates.

The names of the early Votadinian kings are preserved in the genealogies of Hywel Dda, and the predecessors of Cunedda are given as Tacitus, Paternus and Aeternus. Of these, Tacitus may have been a Roman decurion sent north to rule the Votadinian confederacy as *praefectus gentium*. It could have been a hereditary command, paralleled by that of the Syagrii of Gaul.

Traprain, after exceptional prosperity in the mid-second to mid-third centuries AD, continued to flourish, importing and using Roman goods throughout the third and fourth centuries.[19] Stone-built enclosed settlements belong to this period, for instance Kaimes Law, Midlothian, and the classic site of Hownam Rings.

South-east Scotland in the fifth to seventh centuries

The genealogies provide little information about the dynasties of the fifth and sixth centuries in the south-east, and cut short many of the surviving lines in the early sixth century. In spite of his title 'Gwledig' ('great'), Cunedda does not seem to have been king of all the territory formerly occupied by the Votadini and known in the Early Christian period as Gododdin. In fact he seems to have ruled over only Manau. From this it can be inferred that of Gododdin in the late fourth century, only Manau was a Roman confederacy. Typiaun, who according to the story of the Migration of Cunedda was left

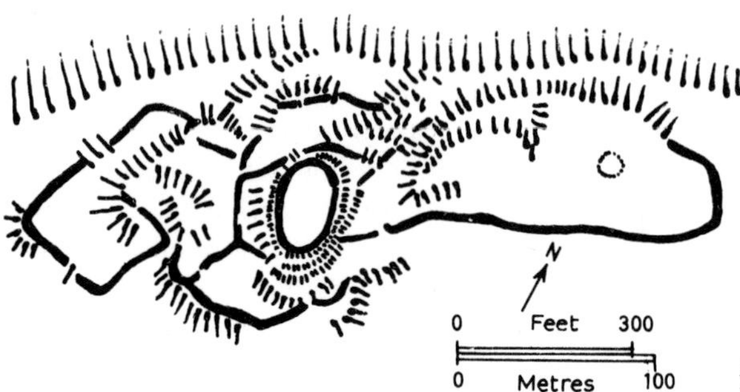

Figure 3 Plan of Dalmahoy, Midlothian (After Stevenson)

behind to rule over Manau, does not appear in the genealogies and the subsequent events in his kingdom are not chronicled. An important Early Christian memorial stone from Yarrow, Selkirk, records the names of Nudus and Dumnogensus, who appear to have been princes. Their father is called Liberalis, but none of them appear in the genealogies.[20]

The relationship between the southern Picts and the British of Gododdin seems to have been ambivalent. That Pictland extended for a time south of the Forth is suggested by Class 1 symbol stones from Edinburgh and Borthwick, and it is not improbable that the nuclear fort at Dalmahoy, Midlothian (Fig. 3), represents the southern boundaries of the Pictish realm. At a later date a strong connection between Pictland and Northumbria can be seen in the art of both areas.

Enclosed hut groups of circular stone dwellings similar to those in Northumberland, Durham, Roxburgh and Selkirk in the Roman Iron Age are found in the south-east of Scotland. Most belong to the second to fourth centuries, but there is evidence that some continued into the post-Roman period. The only sites which can be securely placed in this period are Crock Cleugh (Roxburgh), Whiteside Rig and Shaw Craig, Peeblesshire, and Hownam Law.

A few further putatively post-Roman forts may be noted from eastern Scotland. At Peniel Heugh, Roxburgh, there is a single oval enclosure partitioned by a cross-wall, inside an earlier fort, and at Woden Law, Roxburgh, within the inner rampart of the Iron Age fort a similar wall is associated with stone huts. A citadel at Chatto Craig, Roxburgh, has a passageway about 21 feet long formed by two stone walls, and similar passage entrances occur in stone-walled enclosures at Stobshiel and Harelaw, East Lothian.

With the exception of the timber halls at Doon Hill (p. 28), the house plans in south-east Scotland are normally circular. In the latest levels at Traprain several groups of interconnected subrectangular rooms, about 15 feet by 30 feet, were encountered, each group probably representing a single house. The date of these structures must remain in doubt, but it is possible that they are products of Romanized native activity and belong to the fourth century rather than later.

The sixth century in south-east Scotland was dominated by the rise of Bernicia and the Anglian advance.[21] Documentary evidence for it is sparse. The only reference to an early clash comes from the unreliable pages of Nennius, who relates that Ida founded the kingdom of Bernicia in 547 and fought a British warrior (otherwise unknown) called Dutigirn. The next mention of the Anglian expansion comes in the 580s when the kingdoms of West Rheged and Strathclyde were involved. One reference in the Welsh *Triads* hints at fairly peaceful annexation when it states that 'all the Llaegrians became one people with the Saxons, whose only excepted in the Commot of Caroban in Deira and Bernicia'. The *Gododdin* of Aneurin describes the enemy of Gododdin as the men of Bryneich and Deywr, as well as the Saxons, and there may have been an Anglian alliance with the tribes of Bryneich, whose name they adopted.

Towards the end of the sixth century the expansion of Bernicia increased. An alliance was formed with Urien of Rheged, whose kingdom approximates to Dumfries and Galloway, but he was murdered by his rivals. Another attempted coalition at the turn of the century resulted in the expedition to Catterick, chronicled in the *Gododdin* poem, which ended in disaster. An entry in the *Annals of Ulster* for 637 refers to the 'Obsessio Etin'. This must refer to Edinburgh, and marks the Anglian annexation of the Lothians.

Archaeological evidence for the Anglian advance is similarly sparse. Only two cemeteries (Yeavering and Howick) of pagan Saxon date are recorded north of the Tyne. Two fifth-century brooches from Corbridge suggest the presence of foederati at the eastern end of Hadrian's Wall, while three burials at Barrasford, Great Tosson and Capheaton (the last with hanging bowl escutcheons) would indicate a primary area of Anglian settlement around Bamburgh, Yeavering and along the river valleys and coast. This would substantiate the literary tradition that the original focus of Bernicia was Bamburgh. At present under excavation, Bamburgh has produced a pagan grave. From this area there was a southern expansion to link with other Saxon groups further south, notably those centred on York.

From northern England a northwards expansion, at least into the Lowlands south of the Lammermuirs, brought the Angles into Scotland. The absence of graves may be explained by the comparative lateness of the movement, for pagan graves are unlikely to have had a long duration. The solitary pagan grave from Scotland, that at Dalmeny, Midlothian, contained a necklace of beads of a type associated with the latest pagan Saxon cemeteries in southern England, suggesting a mid-seventh-century date.[22]

There are a few other finds of the period. A gold object shaped like a truncated pyramid and decorated with filigree and garnet inlay is known from Dalmeny, and must date from the seventh century. Its shape is similar to the sword-harness mounts from Sutton Hoo, while the filigree is reminiscent of the products of Kentish and East Anglian workshops. The only other finds are a bun-shaped loom weight from Yetholm, Roxburghshire, and a ring with an Anglian runic inscription of slightly later date.[23] Excluding sculpture, Anglian objects of any period are very rare in eastern Scotland. A seventh-century sword pommel from Culbin Sands, Moray,[24] the Burghead drinking-horn mount in late Saxon 'Trewhiddle Style',[25] a pin from Perthshire and a couple of strap ends complete the list.[26]

The two major Bernician settlements to have been excavated are the palace complex at Yeavering and the hall at Doon Hill near Dunbar, East Lothian. A site similar to Doon Hill at Hogbridge in Peeblesshire and what would appear to be another palace complex have been noted by aerial photography.

The excavations at *Yeavering* and *Doon Hill* are particularly important for shedding light on British–Anglian relations in the sixth and seventh centuries. The first hall at Doon Hill[27] measured 75 feet in length and was built of posts set in single sockets except for the gables which were of 'open book' formation and composed of sleeper beams into which the posts were set. The walls had buttress posts and internally the hall was divided by two rows of three posts. This hall was laid out on exactly the same proportional basis as the earliest at Yeavering, and the excavator, Hope-Taylor, has suggested that this relationship was due to British influence on the earliest halls at Yeavering, these being a regional development of a native type under royal patronage. However, it is also possible that Hall 'A' at Doon Hill was the result of Anglian influence on a British lord. Hall 'A' was probably destroyed *c.* 640 during the reign of Oswald, and replaced by Hall 'B' which was similar to the seventh-century halls at Yeavering. This has prompted Hope-Taylor to suggest that both seventh-century halls stem from a British prototype. Certainly the evidence argues in favour of a two-way traffic between the British and the Angles in the sixth and seventh centuries, which is perhaps not surprising since early Northumbria was almost as British as it was Anglian.

The most important group of archaeological remains of the Anglian period are the sculptures.[28] One of the earliest is a magnificent panel from Jedburgh, Roxburghshire, decorated with inhabited vinescroll: birds and animals pecking and biting at fruit. The panel was probably done by the same hand as the Ruthwell Cross and may have been intended for a chancel screen. It should be dated to the seventh century. Probably of the early eighth century are the fragments of a cross from Aberlady, East Lothian, which was close in spirit to the other major Northumbrian cross at Bewcastle. One face bears an angel, with interlaced serpentine animals above, while the back carries a panel of interlocking heads and legs of four birds, with a formal key pattern. The sides carry formal vinescroll (Fig. 4). The other sculptures from south-east Scotland are less notable and are in general fairly late. There is a good collection at Abercorn on the Forth, the site of a monastery.

Fig. 4 Aberlady, Midlothian. Anglian cross shaft

South-west Scotland in the fifth to seventh centuries

Historically the picture in the south-west is of British kingdoms emerging in the fifth century from the early Iron Age tribal structure which prevailed in the Roman period. Strathclyde was the descendant of the former tribal area of the Damnonii, while the nucleus of historical Rheged was probably the tribal area of the Selgovae and Novantae.

From archaeological evidence the south-west appears to have supported a particularly thriving fourth-century population. There are three fourth-century coins from the area and a massive gold brooch that has sometimes been suggested as having belonged to Constantius Chlorus. It was dropped at the beginning of the fourth century on a Roman road at Erickstanebrae, Dumfriesshire. The Roman fort at Birrens appears to have had sub-Roman occupation, while at Blacketlees,[29] near Annan, excavation revealed an enclosure which had probably contained a sub-Roman hut, though the structure itself was not located. The enclosure was rectangular with one curved side through which ran a causeway. It was defended by a ditch 7 feet deep which produced a red deer antler knife-handle which could date from the fourth century. A few other enclosures, such as the circular site at Kirkbryde, seem to have had sub-Roman rectilinear additions.

The transitional character of the period is evident from the Iron Age fort at Camps Hill, Trohoughton,[30] where within the ramparts a pagan cemetery with carelessly oriented graves was gradually replaced by a Christian burial ground with well-oriented graves set close together. This may imply a sub-Roman Christian community in Dumfriesshire, just as the early cemetery at Whithorn implies a pre-Ninianic Christian sector in Galloway. At Whithorn the early cemetery was of standard long-cist type, though with the inhumations were other, presumably pagan, cremation burials.

By themselves these pieces of evidence amount to little, but they provide some explanation for the emergence of the British kingdoms. It seems probable that the kingdoms of the Solway–Clyde were established as part of deliberate Roman policy, a situation existing similar to that in the territory of the Votadini. The Strathclyde dynasty traced its origins back to Ceretic, who is identifiable with Coroticus.[31] In about 450 Patrick wrote to the soldiers of Coroticus condemning them and their master for trafficking in Christian slaves. The genealogy gives Ceretic's grandfather and great-grandfather as Cinhil and Cluim. These have been seen as British versions of 'Quintillus' and 'Clemens', implying a Roman origin for the dynasty of Strathclyde in the fourth century.

The two major kingdoms of south-west Scotland were Rheged and Strathclyde. *Rheged*[32] flourished mainly in the later sixth century. Urien of Rheged fought with Rhydderch Hael against the Angles of Bernicia about AD 580. References at this time to the activities of Urien indicate the extent of his kingdom. It seems to have included Carlisle and, as the placename Dunragit (the 'fort of Rheged') suggests, part of Wigtownshire. Taliesin's poems support the assumption that Urien's influence reached the Eden Vale, Westmorland and Ayrshire. Tradition says Urien was killed through jealousy of another of the Coel line, and evidence points to the disappearance of Rheged at the time of the advance of Æthelfrith of Bernicia (592–604) and the subsequent Anglian advance (604–16). Of crucial importance is the Battle of Degsastan in 603, when Aidan of Dalriada was defeated by Æthelfrith. Bede asserts that the latter ravaged the Britons more than any other. Later, Edwin of Northumbria is stated by Bede to have influence in Man, implying his control of the Solway area. By 638 at the latest Rheged was finally absorbed by Northumbria when Oswiu married the great-granddaughter of Urien.

Strathclyde[33] does not appear by name until after the Anglian penetration of south-west Scotland. It is mentioned first in the *Annals of Ulster* in an entry for AD 872, and shortly afterwards in the *Anglo-Saxon Chronicle*. Prior to this the kingdom appears to have been known from its principal seat *Alclud* (Dumbarton Rock), and Adamnan refers to it when he describes Rhydderch Hael, the powerful sixth-century king, as the monarch who 'in petra

Cloithe regnavit'. Similarly Irish annals refer to the kings as the 'reges Alocluaithe'.

The documentary evidence for early Strathclyde comes not from native sources but from Irish and Welsh literary traditions. Of these, the *Annals of Tigernach* and the *Annals of Ulster* are the primary Irish sources, and the *Annales Cambriae*, the Welsh *Triads* (groups of three poems on related subjects) and genealogies are the sources from Wales.

The Welsh sources for the most part owe their preservation to the interest shown in the Britons of the Solway–Clyde by Owain ap Hywel Dda of Dyfed in the tenth century. Under his direction a copy of the Strathclyde genealogy was redacted, and a copy of this, the *Harley 3857*, has survived. This is simply a king-list. With cross-references from annalistic and other sources, however, it is possible to establish a relative chronology. The same source records the genealogies of some of the other dynasties in southern Scotland – significantly, these seem to end in the first half of the seventh century, while the dynasty of the rulers of Strathclyde continues to *c.* 920.

The picture that the genealogies provide for the Strathclyde Britons is of a network of small sub-kingdoms, of which many traced their ancestry back to Coel Hen (sometimes called Goutepauc). No fewer than eight lines, including that of Urien of Rheged, stemmed from him.

The areas occupied by the kingdoms of Strathclyde are not easily defined. One, which may have been known as *Aeron*, appears to be closely connected with Coel Hen himself. It was centred on the Ayr valley and is known chiefly from placename evidence, notably the occurrence of the placename Coylton. A fleet of Aeron is mentioned in the *Gododdin* poem. *Alclud* had its own dynasty, and the Upper Clyde was ruled over by Morcant. Two other kingdoms lay in the south-west, and a third which adjoined Rheged was ruled by a vassal of Urien. *Danuting* was probably in Cumbria since a *regio Danuting* was presented at Ripon in 675. The whereabouts of the others are not known.

The dynasty centred on Dumbarton, or Alclud, was not descended from Coel Hen. Rhydderch Hael, the best known of its kings, claimed descent from Ceretic, and the dynasty had connections with the east of Scotland, Rhydderch's wife coming from the Lothians. Rhydderch was the last king of note in Strathclyde – after his rule the kingdom appears to have been eclipsed by the rising sun of Bernicia, and to have fallen to the second line descended from Dumngual Hen. It is likely that Ecgfrith was the first Northumbrian king to dominate the Strathclyde Britons, the annexation having taken place at an unknown date prior to his death at Nechtan's Mere in 685.

Settlements in Rheged

In the Early Christian period, south-west Scotland was an area of continuing Iron Age traditions. In Dumfries and Galloway Iron Age hillforts appear to have been reoccupied, while some nuclear-defended sites may be local manifestations of the nuclear fort tradition found elsewhere in post-Roman Britain. Perhaps the most outstanding factor that emerges from a study of the archaeological evidence is the wealth of the considerable population of Dumfries and Galloway. The coastal plain of Ayrshire seems only slightly less rich and contrasts with Lanarkshire, which is under-endowed except for its few sculptured stones of Anglian date (tenth century or later).

Hillforts dominate the landscape of the Clyde valley. Numerous hilltops in the Upperward of Lanarkshire were occupied in the Iron Age. Few, however, appear to have had post-Roman additions, though some sites have 'satellite' forts which may be later than the original construction. A fort at Culter incorporates a smaller enclosure which may be a similar phenomenon to that at Garn Boduan, Caernarvonshire. Only one Upperward hillfort excavation has been published (this was at Cairngryffe near Lanark, prior to quarrying) and it is possible that some of the Upperward forts were reoccupied in the Early Christian period along with some of the other earthworks in the county that are of uncertain date.

In Dumfries and Galloway there are three main forts from the post-Roman period: Trusty's Hill, Tynron Doon and the Mote of Mark.

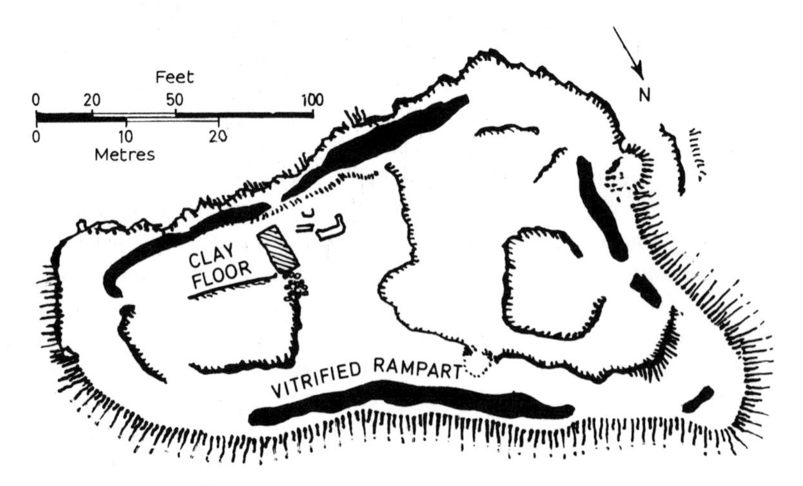

Figure 5 The Mote of Mark

Trusty's Hill, Kirkcudbright (Fig. 6) is a small knoll near Gatehouse-of-Fleet, fortified on the southern and north-eastern sides. Two phases have been recognized, the first consisting of a rampart wall on the hilltop with a substantial bank and ditch cutting off the north-eastern approach, together with a guard hut. This is a 'double promontory' fort of the common Iron Age type, probably constructed and occupied during the first two centuries AD, the date being suggested by a rotary quern. The second phase consisted of a series of outlying ramparts and the extension of the original fort entrance with out-turned banks. The technique of construction used in these, with an outer revetment and rubble make-up behind, is characteristic of both secular and ecclesiastical valla in the Early Christian period. The excavators thought that there had been timber lean-to shacks built against the ramparts at that period, since pieces of vitrifaction were found on the site. Since excavation failed to produce evidence of timber lacing, it was deduced that the firing of these lean-to buildings, after the Pictish sack of the site in the sixth century, had produced the vitrifaction. Evidence for this takes the form of Pictish symbols – a double disc and Z-rod – incised on the rock near the guard hut. It is one of the most convincing pieces of evidence that there were occasional bands of Pictish raiders in south-west Scotland in the sixth century.

Tynron Doon (Plate 3A)[34] is a well-preserved multivallate hillfort in Dumfriesshire, associated in local legend with the 'heidless horseman' who is supposed to have ridden down from it as an omen of death, a story which possibly has some origin in a Celtic head cult. The fort was modified with the addition of a courtyard on the north-eastern side, which was later converted to a motte. Excavation of a midden on the steep slope on the south side produced evidence of Early Christian occupation. The midden finds included a piece of a blue-ribbed glass bead, two bone pins, a curved piece of bone, possibly a toggle, decorated with ring-and-dot, an iron knife, a vitreous playing piece, miscellaneous iron including a link from a chain, fragments of iron bloomery waste and pieces of vitrifaction. A sherd of pottery (from the midden) was possibly Early Christian, but in view of the later medieval occupation could be thirteenth- or fourteenth-century. In 1927 a fragment of a gold filigree bracteate was found on the site. This is of seventh-century date, and is probably Anglo-Saxon.

It is possible, but no more than speculation, that from Tynron Doon come fragments of copper decorated with vinescroll and other motifs of late Antique inspiration, and coated with gold foil, now in the National Museum, Edinburgh. These have been identified as belonging to a series of central European embossed copper ornamental plates with gold foil known as *pressblech*, which are most commonly found on Merovingian helmets of the type known as *spangenhelmen*.[35] They span the period from the fifth to the mid-seventh centuries. The Dumfriesshire fragments are not from a *spangenhelme* but from some other form of helmet, and probably belong to the seventh century. How they reached the area is uncertain, but they appear to have been scrap metal and may have been loot from the troubles in Northumbria in 633. Such objects as the helmet were favoured as diplomatic gifts in the seventh century.

The Mote of Mark[36] in Kirkcudbright (Fig. 5; Plate 2B) is the most important site in the south-west, and the 'Mark' has been identified with the Mark of medieval romance who supposedly had his seat at Castle Dore in Cornwall. The Mote of Mark is at the mouth of the Urr estuary, at Rockcliffe, and is a denuded rocky outcrop. It was excavated in 1913 by Dr A. O. Curle, and in 1973 by the author.

The 1973 excavations showed the site to have been occupied in the period *c.* 475–625 AD, reduced occupation continuing probably through much of the

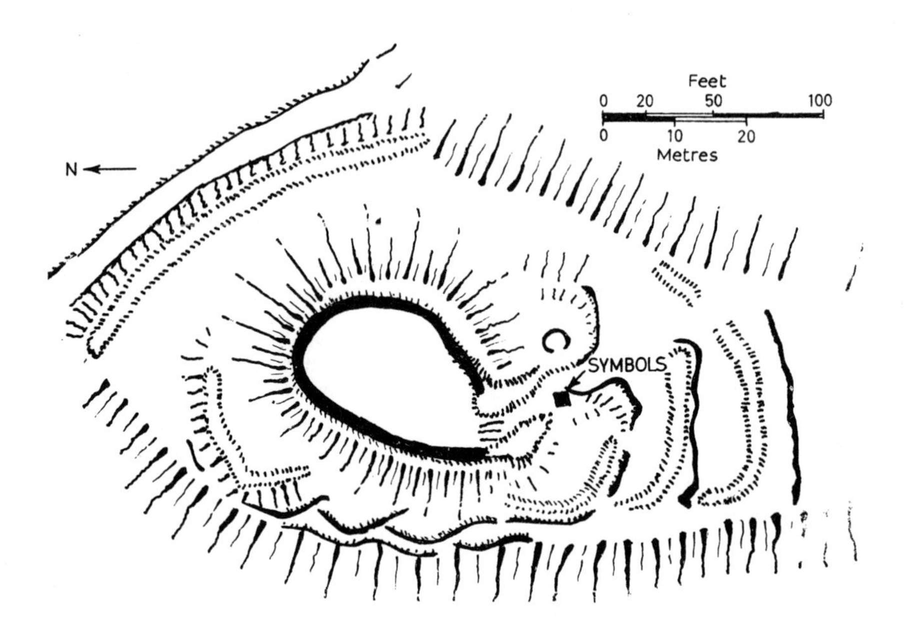

Figure 6 Trusty's Hill, Anwoth, Kirkcudbright

seventh century. In the first period of occupation (Ia) there appears to have been open settlement on the hilltop. Due to the depth at which the structural remains of this period lay, they were not excavated extensively, but a hearth and a post-hole of a hut belonging to this phase were investigated, and an iron-smelting hearth found in 1913 may also belong to this period.

Period Ia appears to have been of short duration. Period Ib is marked by the construction round the hill of a rampart composed of a bank of stones and earth, timber-laced at the front and measuring originally about 10 feet wide and probably attaining a similar height. This rampart was broken by an entrance on the south side with a timber gateway, and by a postern on the north. At about the same time a stone wall was built round the central hollow on the site, in which the main area of occupation was concentrated. Period Ib marks a phase of considerable activity on the site, and can probably be assigned to the sixth century, extending until the early seventh. During this period ornamental metal working took place in bronze and less certainly in gold and silver, and there was also iron working. Shale or lignite, imported probably from Ayrshire, was worked into bracelets, beads and spindle whorls, and fragments of partly worked shale were recovered. Considerable quantities of white trailed glass, mainly from cone beakers, pouch bottles and similar vessels, were imported from the Rhineland, presumably as raw material for glass-making. Glass beads, both of the usual plain blue type and also of an Irish type with green and white cables, were found, and glass inlays may have been produced as is suggested by a find made in 1913. Bone and antler were both worked on the site.

The remains relating to ornamental metal working include numerous fragments of clay moulds, fragments of triangular, bag-shaped and 'dog's dish' crucibles (one with the imprint of tongs upon it), tuyères, slags, scrap bronze (some possibly from Anglo-Saxon bucket mounts) and ores. A stone ingot mould was found, as well as two bronze ingots. The moulds were for a variety of objects, of which the brooches and pins are the most common. One nearly complete mould for a Class G penannular brooch was found in 1973, and others for the same type of brooch were found in 1913. Pin moulds include some for thistle-headed, nail-headed and ball-headed types. A bone pin was associated with some moulds, and another found in 1913 was found with the mould it had been used to form. Stud moulds were common, and a strip of four studs, still with their 'flash', was found. Of the decorated moulds the most interesting were for round and square mounts, probably for caskets. Among these was a mould for a round mount decorated with interlace, closely paralleled by a mount from Caenby, Lincs. The context of this mould showed that it could not be later than the early seventh century. A similar mould fragment for another round mount was found in 1913. Another mould fragment has concave-sided triangle ornament, while moulds from the 1913 excavations include two fragments of Class H brooches, decorated with double-strand interlace on their terminals. A piece of silver and a small spiral ornament of gold ribbon may belong to penannular brooches.

In period Ib the gateway may have been additionally defended on the interior by a stone barbican, which may have fallen into disuse before the end of period Ib and used as a forage – subsequently a midden grew up around it. A small circular hut, about 9 feet in diameter, constructed with an irregular footing of pebbles and with a gravel floor, can be assigned to this period. Adjacent to it was a cobbled yard. Another similar hut was excavated in 1913.

The ironwork and stonework of period Ib is very varied. The iron-working remains include a 'furnace bottom' and the iron objects include tweezers and a large rock-splitting wedge. Considerable numbers of worked flints appear to have been gathered from a nearby Mesolithic site and re-used, possibly as strike-a-lights and small tools. Over fifty sherds of imported E Ware were recovered in 1973, representing at least ten vessels, and more were found in 1913, as well as one sherd of D Ware (p. 272).

Period Ic is marked by the firing of the original rampart, which caused the granite to vitrify into a stone mass. The impression of an upright timber was preserved in it at one point (Plate 2B). Following the firing of the rampart, the entrance was hurriedly blocked, a bank of stones and midden material being heaped up over the fallen timbers.

At the beginning of period II the rampart was deliberately demolished. A cobbled surface was laid down over the partly demolished rampart, the internal subsidiary walling and the period Ib structures. A rectangular clay platform, overlying the main metal-working area and sealing the deposit, may belong to either a late stage in period Ib or to period II.

In the time of Urien of Rheged the fort was probably a princely stronghold subsequently taken by the Angles. Two Anglian runic inscriptions have been recovered from the site. The first, on a polished bone, reads 'Athili . . .' and is presumably a personal name. The second has not yet been deciphered, and is on a piece of sandstone. A few finds associated with the period II occupation can be provisionally identified as Anglian in character. They include a rock crystal bead and a single-sided bone comb with ring-and-dot decoration. The period II evidence suggests that the Anglian annexation of Rheged may not have been as peaceful as is sometimes suggested.

Castle Haven, Kirkcudbright, was apparently occupied in the Early Christian period. It is a stone fort, built like a dun, measuring 60 feet by 35 feet internally, and with intramural galleries. The plan is subrectangular, and except on the west, where it is defended by a rock face, the fort has an outer courtyard. Whether this is an Iron Age dun, reoccupied in the Early Christian period, or purely an Early Christian structure cannot be ascertained. The finds, apart from a blue glass bead with white trail and a penannular brooch, are unspectacular and no pottery was found. A spiral finger ring may be Iron Age but could equally well be later.

Belonging to this period, but still unexcavated, are a series of 'courtyard forts', notably Suie Hill, Almorness, Dunguile, Stroanfreggan and Balliehill Island.

Settlements in Strathclyde

In Ayrshire in the Early Christian period a series of crannogs, notably Buston, Lochlee and possibly Lochspouts, are recognizable. One of the main problems in assessing the crannogs of south-west Scotland is the fact that only one, Milton Loch, Kirkcudbright, has been excavated this century in accordance with scientific methods. Milton Loch dated from the second century AD and had no occupation in the Early Christian period. Although at least a few of the crannogs excavated last century were the subject of very detailed and apparently accurate reports, it is not possible to correlate structural phases with periods. A number of sites, including the important example at Hyndford, Lanark, were reoccupied in the Middle Ages. *Lochspouts*[37] appears to have been occupied at some fairly late date in the Early Christian period. At *Lochlee* primary occupation in the Roman Iron Age is attested by Roman fibulae, a dress fastener and a Roman melon bead. The site was reoccupied in the Early Christian period, and produced a fine ringed pin with decorated head, probably of ninth-century date. A number of other finds, such as a wooden trough and possibly some of the ironwork, belong to the period. A flesh hook from Lochlee may be medieval, and a knife blade with brass mount is of the seventeenth century.

Buston Crannog[38] is notable as the type site for Class E Ware, the distinctive form being the 'Buston Beaker'. The site has also produced related pottery, probably of Frankish origin, notably the top of a tubular spouted pitcher and a pot with corrugated shoulder. Of more diagnostic date is a contemporaneous forgery of a seventh-century Anglo-Saxon gold 'thrymsa' or tremissis, of a type found in the Crondall hoard. The remainder of the finds are of indeterminate date but would not conflict with a seventh-century *floruit* for the crannog.

The crannog was a raft made up of layers of branches, kept in place by rings of piles linked both radially and concentrically. On this platform the house was built, but it had been too badly damaged for a detailed plan to be established. It appeared, however, to have been oval, about 50 feet in diameter with a hearth in the centre some 10 feet across. The walling was of stone and timber. Round the house was a platform and immediately opposite the door was a midden. Access to the crannog was by boat, and a dugout canoe, with a separate stern board and pegged strakes, was found beside it.

The finds from Buston include two fine composite bone combs with ring-and-dot decoration, horn points and a knife handle, five iron knives, an iron axehead, iron punch, awl, spearhead and arrows, two gold spiral finger rings, two bronze pins – one with a blue glass bead inset in its head – an annular brooch, a cylindrical bead with trailed red and yellow glass decoration, a jet slider, flints, spindle whorls, polishers and whetstones, and four curious iron objects, two with spiral heads and one with a spring which is probably from a barrel padlock, the fourth being fishtailed and possibly being used as compasses.

It is possible that in Ayrshire hillforts were reoccupied in the Early Christian period. The royal castle of *Dundonald* stands within an earthwork which follows the contours of the hill as do the defences of nuclear forts.

In Renfrewshire, on comparison with the Lothian forts, it seems likely that forts with stone revetments or terraced ramparts between the 500- and 600-feet contours were reoccupied in the Early Christian period. Into this category falls *Duncarnock*, with its terraced rampart which has yielded a stray find of a sherd of 'Damnonian' pot – a type of coarse ware akin to Votadinian ware.

Marshall Moor and Castle Hill also belong to this category. The excavated fort at *Walls Hill* has a built-up terrace with a stepped foundation surmounted by a stone revetted rampart. This type of defence also occurs at the Meikle Reive, and probably also at Chatto Craig. Some of the square homestead enclosures common in Renfrewshire may belong to this period, but without excavation this cannot be proved.

Dumbarton Rock,[39] Dunbarton, is a volcanic plug of basalt. It is similar in character to the rocks frequently chosen for nuclear forts, but apart from those of the medieval castle the summit is devoid of defences. The site was very badly disturbed as a result of the building in the Middle Ages, and no Early Christian objects have been found there. Bede described it as 'civitas Brettonum munitissima' – 'a well-fortified city of the Britons' – and there can be no doubt that it was extensively occupied in the period.

Two timber halls are known from south-west Scotland:

Kirkconnel, Dumfries, measured about 18 feet by 55 feet, and was constructed with single posts of whole and split trunks. On the north side was a putative entrance screened by a light partition. The main timbers were buttressed lightly with drystone walling, between which the walls were probably of turf, planking or wattle. There was no internal division or aisling. The west end was angular, possibly of the 'open book' formation found at Doon Hill, though the outlying post might be interpreted as a buttress. Occupation in the sixth or seventh centuries was substantiated by a glass eye bead, a sherd of very coarse pottery and an iron knife. It is not impossible that the hall belongs to the period of Anglian penetration, which is known to have started in Dumfriesshire around 600, for the plan bears close resemblance to late Anglo-Saxon buildings at, for example, Thetford, or even to pagan Saxon halls such as Linford, Essex.

Castlehill, Dalry, Ayrshire, was excavated in the nineteenth century and is less definitive. A large mound, possibly a motte, was found to cover a timber building 46 feet long by 20 feet wide built of single posts with wickerwork between. Some of the timbers were well preserved. There was a hearth at one end. No datable finds were discovered, and a Beaker found nearby does not seem to be contemporary. It has been suggested that Dalry is a Neolithic 'mortuary house' but no similar Neolithic structures exist for comparison. It is more explicable as the ancestor to a Norman motte.

The Angles in south-west Scotland

According to the unreliable twelfth-century *Life of Kentigern* by Jocelyn of Furness, there were pagan Angles 'worshipping Woden' in the neighbourhood of Hoddom to whom Kentigern preached shortly after the battle of Ardderydd in 573. The placename Pennersaughs (near Hoddom) is British, meaning 'head of the Saxons', and probably dates from this period.

By the end of the seventh century Dumfriesshire as well as Strathclyde was dominated by Northumbria. An Anglian bishopric was set up at Whithorn in 720 and lasted until at least 803. In 752 (not 750 as in the *Baedae Continuatio*) Kyle in Ayrshire was annexed by Eadberht of Northumbria, prior to which it was probably part of Strathclyde. How long Kyle remained under Northumbrian domination is unknown. Present evidence suggests that a Northumbrian wedge separated the Strathclyde British from the Cumbrians until about 875. At this date Bishop Eardulf of Lindisfarne and Abbot Eadred fled to Whithorn, in the Northumbrian area, with the relics of St Cuthbert and the Lindisfarne gospels. This domination was probably ended by the Scandinavian raids. Apart from the finds from the Mote of Mark, the archaeological evidence for the Northumbrian period in south-west Scotland is almost exclusively ecclesiastical. The secular finds, with the exception of the Talnotrie hoard, consist entirely of Northumbrian copper coins of the reigns of Æthelred I (789–96), Eanred (806–40) and Æthelred II (841–4 and 844–9), most of which were found at Luce Sands.[40] There are also a number of strap ends from Luce Sands, Wigtown, and Stevenston Sands, Ayrshire, some of which may have served as book tags.[41] Together with one from the Talnotrie hoard and another from Coldingham Priory, Berwickshire, they date to the ninth century. The Talnotrie hoard, buried *c.* 910, is almost certainly hack-silver, possibly looted by the Vikings (strap ends of the Talnotrie type are well known from Whitby for example).[42] The Luce and Stevenston strap ends are bronze and that from Talnotrie is of silver decorated with animal ornament and niello inlay. The strap ends are all in Trewhiddle Style, a style named after the Trewhiddle hoard buried in Cornwall *c.* 875. About seventy such strap ends are known from Britain and Scandinavia.[43]

The Talnotrie hoard also contained the globular head of a pin with scroll-work in filigree, a lead weight with an interlaced brass top, a plain gold finger ring, two pins of silver with round plate heads, once joined by a chain, several metal scraps, a piece of glass, three claystone spindle whorls, a perforated piece of jet, an agate and some waxy substance. With these objects were twelve coins: six Northumbrian coins including a copper styca of Wulfhere of York (854–910) and one of Osberht (845–67), four silver pennies of Burgred of Mercia (853–74), a Carolingian denier and an Arab dirhem of one of the Abbasid caliphs of Baghdad. The hoard was found in 1912 by a shepherd's wife, who saw the objects falling out of her peats as she was putting them on the fire. Some were already melted before being recognized. They were found near some hut circles and a rectangular building. All the objects were compatible with late Saxon metal-working traditions.

The fragmentary whetstone with facing human head from Collin, Dumfries-shire, may be ascribed to the period of Anglian domination.[44] Stylistically it is similar to the whetstone from the seventh-century Lincolnshire cemetery at Hough-on-the-Hill, and the other more famous and earlier ceremonial whetstone from Sutton Hoo. The Hough and Collin stones are probably contemporary (Fig. 7).

There is a very important series of Anglian sculptured stones from Dumfriesshire, including a number of works of the 'classic' period of Northumbrian sculpture from the end of the seventh to the eighth century.[45] The most famous is the Ruthwell Cross, Dumfriesshire, with another group from Hoddom.[46] The Dumfries school of sculpture appears to have been in contact with the latest developments in Northumbria and beyond, and some motifs appear to be directly inspired by continental models. The richness of the school may be in part due to a thriving Anglian Christian community centred

Figure 7 Whetstone from Collin, Dumfriesshire

on Hoddom, where a church was built of re-used Roman stones from Birrens *c.* 700 with plain split-slab footings – a similar technique to that used at Jarrow. The Ruthwell Cross should probably be assigned to the beginning of the eighth century, and two of the Hoddom crosses may belong to the second half of the same century, while a third cross shaft and a cross head date probably from the ninth century. Five of the crosses carved in St Ninian's cave in Wigtownshire are also putative Anglian works of the eighth century. The Hoddom stones show a connection with the Hexham tradition in their prolific use of rosettes, while the early cross head has an *Agnus Dei* for which the closest parallel is on a silver medallion set on a fifth-century ivory book cover in Milan. Another Hoddom cross head had a seated figure and bust of Christ, which is paralleled in western Yorkshire and Breedon, Leicestershire, the latter in Mercian territory. This does not imply a direct link, only that common models were shared by Mercia and Dumfries at this period. A few other stones from Hoddom are more local in character.

Of the later Anglian sculptures the cross shafts from Closeburn and Thornhill (Nith Bridge) are the finest, and date from the end of the ninth or early tenth century. The Thornhill Cross is probably the earlier of the two and shows affinities with less developed Hoddom work and also work done in western Yorkshire. Viking influence is apparent in the slightly later tenth-century cross from Glencairn, which is still within the mainstream of the Dumfries Anglian tradition, while the final phase before the Normans is represented on stones from Penpont, Closeburn and Kirkconnel, and links up with the traditions of other regions in the south-west, notably the 'Whithorn' school and the 'Govan' school (p. 205).

The Irish in south-west Scotland

It has been suggested on the basis of placename evidence that there was a settlement of Irish in Galloway.[47] The placename element which is most relevant as evidence for this settlement is *slew-*, from the Gaelic *sliabh*, meaning a hill. It has a fairly dense distribution in the Rinns of Galloway, but not elsewhere in the south of Scotland. It seems to be pre-Norse, and in Galloway denotes 'moor'. The same element may be seen as an outlier at Slamannan, near Linlithgow, West Lothian. Also valid as placename evidence are certain forms of the word *carraig*, meaning a rock, which are also found in Galloway.[48]

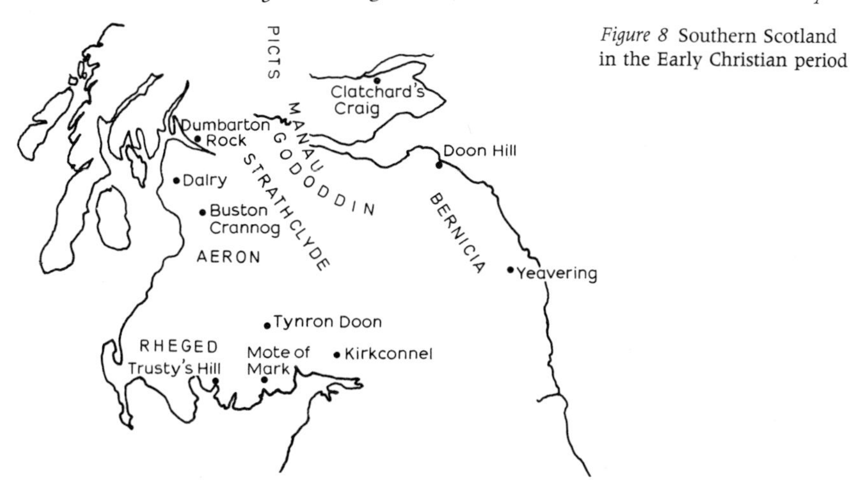

Figure 8 Southern Scotland in the Early Christian period

A limited amount of archaeological evidence has been put forward. The most notable is a decorated bronze ring brooch from Luce Sands, which, with two other small ring brooches, has been cited as Irish and as datable to the fifth or sixth century.[49] This identification cannot now be held valid, as the Irish provenance for the main Luce brooch was based on the fact that the terminals were decorated with a type of concave-sided triangle and hatching believed unparalleled in Scotland. A pin from Orkney has a head decorated with this motif, and the general type of brooch (Type H2/3, see p. 307) is not specifically Irish. Some pins from the Luce Sands area that came from a private collection and are now in Kelvingrove Museum, Glasgow, have also been advanced as Irish. However all are late types and not necessarily Irish.[50]

If there is no archaeological evidence of a secular nature for Irish contacts with Galloway, there is now no reason to doubt the evidence for ecclesiastical contacts. The site at Ardwall Island, Kirkcudbright, has its closest parallels at Church Island, Co. Kerry (p. 383), and finds from there included a fragment of a gable finial of Irish type. In the same context there are links between the Whithorn area and Ireland.

It need not be supposed that Galloway was an Irish kingdom, but it was certainly not Pictish and the Anglian expansion from Northumbria did not affect the extreme west of Galloway until the end of the seventh century. Neither was it, except possibly in the sixth century, a part of the British kingdom of Rheged, so a mixed Irish–British population in this area in the fifth century is to be expected. Later Irish objects and placenames in Scotland belong to the period of mixed Irish–Norse movements at the time of the Viking raids and settlement.

Christianity in southern Scotland (Fig. 9)

Early Christianity in southern Scotland must be viewed within the framework of the British kingdoms and their Iron Age tribal predecessors, and all the evidence points to a diocesan structure among the north Britons, as elsewhere

Figure 9 Diocesan divisions of southern Scotland (After Thomas)

in Britain and Ireland. Thomas has suggested that there was a diocese already in existence by the fifth century at Carlisle with an offshoot in western Galloway that served Rheged.[51] By the sixth century three other dioceses can be recognized, one centred on the Tweed valley serving the area of Bryneich (Bernicia), a second centring on the Forth and serving Gododdin, and a third at Strathclyde.

The archaeological evidence for these early dioceses is primarily memorial stones of the fifth and sixth centuries. It has already been suggested that there were existing Christian communities centring on Whithorn and Carlisle in the late Roman period, and that Ninian went from Carlisle to serve as bishop in the Whithorn community. Whithorn itself, in addition to the evidence afforded by the very early cemetery, has produced a memorial stone to Latinus which belongs on epigraphic evidence to the late fifth century, and there are three other very early stones from Kirkmadrine in the Rinns of Galloway. One may be slightly earlier than the Latinus stone, and commemorates two priests, Viventius and Mavorius. The second, which has two

Figure 10 Early Christian memorial stones. (1) 'St Peter's' stone, Whithorn; (2) 'Latinus' stone, Whithorn; (3) 'Viventius' stone, Kirkmadrine.

names one of which is Florentius, is probably contemporary with the Latinus stone. The third, with an inscription reading 'Initium et Finis . . .', belongs to the early sixth century. The Kirkmadrine stones are probably not *in situ* and may have come from a now lost cemetery at Curgie a few miles away, where a stone is recorded as having an inscription commemorating Ventidius, a subdeacon of the church. A further stone from Whithorn has the inscription LOCI PETRI APUSTULI, and dates from the seventh century. The stone implies continental, probably north Gaulish, connections, and hints that by that date Whithorn had acquired some important relic (Fig. 10).[52]

There is a traditional connection between the Isle of Man and the Whithorn area, and it is possible that the diocese of Whithorn extended its influence to Man. There are two early memorial stones on the island, one inscribed to Ambicatus, from Knock-y-Doonee, Andreas, which also has an ogham inscription, and another from Santon inscribed to Avitus (or Avitos). The Andreas stone is late fifth century in date, the Santon stone a century later.[53]

The Tweed basin has produced no stones as early as those from Whithorn and Kirkmadrine though it is possible that Cunedda and his followers were Christians which would explain the later traditions which regarded them as saints. Christianity, however, need not have reached any but the ruling sector of the community, and the date of the earliest memorial stones indicates its extension from the extreme south-west to the rest of Lowland Scotland. There are a number of inscribed stones of the sixth century and later from Greater Tweed-dale. One from Manorwater, Peeblesshire, belongs to the late sixth century and the Yarrow stone with its inscription to Nudus and Dumnogenus, the sons of Liberalis, has already been mentioned (p. 26). A further stone, now lost, is recorded from Peebles, while a sixth-century stone from Over Kirkhope depicts what has been variously interpreted as an *orans* (praying) figure or a Celtic godling.[54]

The Gododdin area, with the exception of the Catstane from the cemetery at Kirkliston, near Edinburgh, has no early memorial stones. There is, however, a concentration of long-cist cemeteries (such as that at Parkburn, Midlothian) on both sides of the Forth, and it is not unlikely that sixth-century Christianity affected both the 'British' and the 'Pictish' sides of the estuary. This situation seems even more likely in view of the possibility that the Pictish boundary came as far south as Dalmahoy at some stage.[55]

The origins of Christianity in Strathclyde are far from clear – there are no memorial stones and the earliest Christian remains are the chapel and cemetery at St Ninian's Point on Bute, which appear to have a sub-Roman origin. Documentary sources, however, particularly some relating to Kentigern, point to Christianity in the area by the sixth century, possibly as a result of the extension of the activities of the Whithorn diocese.

The main ecclesiastical sites in Rheged were Whithorn and Hoddom. Nothing remains of the latter, and at Whithorn the only visible remains are those of the medieval priory. A small oratory, however, has been found in excavation and appears to be of Irish type, perhaps dating from as early as the seventh century. It was constructed of stones set in clay, plastered within and without with white mortar. The white mortar has given rise to the speculation that this was the 'Candida Casa' of Ninian, but 'Candida' means 'pure' or 'holy' rather than 'white' and the original name of Whithorn was probably unrelated.[56] In any case, the oratory cannot be as early as Ninian himself as his chapel would have been of timber. Nearby are two related sites, on St Ninian's Isle and at Physgyll (St Ninian's cave). The existing chapel on St Ninian's Isle is twelfth-century but the vallum probably predates it. The only other early ecclesiastical site in the area is that on Ardwall Isle (p. 383). At Chapel Finnian on Luce Bay excavation revealed the plan of a tenth- or eleventh-century chapel with lateral *antae* within an earlier enclosure. A well was associated with the site. Further north, nothing remains of the putative monastic site at Govan on the Clyde, or of the original site of St Kentigern's church at Glasgow. A site at Cambuslang and possibly one at Paisley have left no traces.

In the Central Tweed basin the site of *Mailros*, Old Melrose, was a monastery of Irish type founded from Lindisfarne after 635 and situated in a loop in the Tweed. The vallum can still be traced. Further north, at St Abb's Head in Berwickshire, a vallum indicates another early monastic site – this has sometimes been taken to be the 'Urbs Coludi' of Bede which could also have been at Coldingham. Coldingham has produced some late Anglian sculpture, have revealed two rectangular buildings, one with drystone walling, 'Trewhiddle Style' strap end.[57]

On the Forth the key site is Abercorn,[58] the 'Aebbercurnig' of Bede, raised to a temporary see in 681 and likely to have been founded about 638. Excavations at Abercorn, which has a few important pieces of Anglian sculpture, have revealed two rectangular buildings, one with drystone walling, the other with sleeper beams and possibly median post-holes. These lay within the oval vallum, which can still be partly traced. Dating was provided by E Ware.

Old Melrose and Abercorn as well as Coldingham were Anglian foundations, but it is very likely that they both had earlier, British, predecessors.

Apart from ecclesiastical sites and sculptured stones, there are a few ecclesiastical objects from southern Scotland. The finest is a fragmentary crozier shrine from Hoddom of cast bronze, which should be assigned to the tenth century.[59] It has affinities with the contemporary Anglian work and also shows some Viking influence. It is probably a native product of south-west Scotland.

A fragmentary object from Monybuie has been identified as a bell shrine.[60] It is in a fragile condition, and is made of two sheets of cast bronze, folded over and riveted, with bronze-covered cord along the bottom and up the sides. It is more likely to be a bell than a bell shrine, and its date remains in dispute.

Finally, there is a rectangular bronze flask from Barr of Spottes, which measures $2\frac{1}{2}$ by $2\frac{1}{8}$ inches and is $\frac{1}{4}$ inch thick.[61] It is without precise parallel, but seems to be a type of pilgrim's flask. There are worn traces of interlace of a type which would indicate a tenth-century date. Some doubt has been cast on its authenticity but it is probably genuine. A sixteenth- or seventeenth-century date has also been suggested for it.

3 Northern Scotland

Since the documentary and archaeological evidence for the Picts is so inadequate, they have become one of the romantic mysteries of Early Christian Britain. Because they are known historically and can be seen to have possessed a monumental art, it is frequently assumed that they should exist in the archaeological record as a distinct culture, with their own settlement, pottery and metalwork types. If documentation existed for prehistoric Britain, one suspects that many of the cultural labels would have to be reconsidered when the political boundaries were found to cut across the cultural.

If this is borne in mind and distinctively Pictish material culture is not sought, at least some of the problems of studying Pictish archaeology become less formidable. The material culture of non-Germanic Britain and Ireland is remarkably uniform. The Picts probably shared this culture, as indeed excavation of such sites as Clatchard's Craig, Fife, and the distribution of fifth- and sixth-century brooches in Pictland seem to verify. The Picts, however, should not be regarded as a culturally homogenous group, for historical Pictland embraced areas where the Picts were merely the dominant element in a native society of different cultural background. This is true of the Northern and Western Isles – the 'Atlantic province', where a separate cultural tradition derived from earlier Iron Age broch and wheelhouse communities can be recognized in the historical period. From the seventh century onwards, when regional developments in traditions of metal working are distinguishable in Ireland, Pictland produced a distinctive tradition of ornamental metalwork that embraced not only the more splendid objects represented in the St Ninian's Isle hoard, but also simpler bronze penannular brooches, pins and 'swivel rings'. Except where they are demonstrably imports, objects found in historical Pictland of the fifth to eighth centuries should be ascribed to the Picts. The range of such products is sufficient to demonstrate with certainty that there is no 'lost culture' of the Picts, and no objects incised with Pictish symbols as the 'trademark' are waiting to be unearthed.

The sparse documentation does not indicate that the Picts were more barbarous or less literate than their well-recorded neighbours. Indeed it is possible that the Picts also kept detailed records.[1] Original documents dating from before AD 850 are relatively rare in England and Ireland and what does survive is mainly the result of medieval transcription. Although Anglo-Saxon and Old Irish were understood in the twelfth century, Pictish had ceased to exist as an official language in favour of Latin after the accession of Kenneth mac Alpin, and would probably have been beyond the comprehension of medieval copyists. It can only be assumed that any Pictish documents set down in Latin were lost or destroyed in the Edwardian campaigns, the Scottish Reformation or possibly the Viking raids.

The prehistory of the Picts

Around 700 BC in north-east Scotland various phenomena were introduced from north Germany, of which the most important were timber-laced forts, with vertical and horizontal beams which were used to build up a framework for a stone rampart. The forts and associated material are distributed over the whole of eastern Scotland north of the Forth–Clyde valley, and there are some outlying finds even from Orkney and the Inner Hebrides.[2] The population of the region, however, remained basically derived from that of the local late Bronze Age. At a later stage there were further intrusive elements in the region from southern Scotland and possibly northern England, but in general terms cultural continuity can be observed in north-east Scotland until the first century AD. During this long period from the seventh century BC ferrous metallurgy was gradually introduced to the region, but ironwork was always relatively rare and it is difficult to determine at what point iron objects were produced locally rather than imported.

North-east Scotland became the main area occupied by the historical Picts, and its prehistory is important in providing a clue to Pictish origins. The historical Picts were only partly Celtic, and what little is known about their language shows that they probably retained some elements in their speech from a pre-Celtic past (p. 51). The timber-laced fort builders should be regarded as the ancestors of the Picts.

The Northern and Western Isles of Scotland along with the north-west mainland belong to a separate tradition from that of the timber-laced forts. The problem relating to this Atlantic province are complex, and still under considerable debate.[3]

In the Hebrides a mixed native population partly made up of people from western France and from eastern England developed a type of small stone fort built with a double wall bonded together with transverse slabs, a technique known as 'hollow walling'. These forts were probably being built around the middle of the first millennium BC.[4] In Shetland similar types of stone forts appear at a slightly later date.

Around 75 BC further developments in stone-fort building took place in the Hebrides, possibly the outcome of the arrival of Belgic refugees from England. This development involved the building of the fort wall to a much greater height, producing a tower of a type known as a broch.[5] From the Hebrides brochs spread to the north mainland and the Northern Isles, where the most extreme variants were built. Here, in response to the less rugged terrain, the walls were built with a solid base. Although they vary in design, brochs conform to a basic plan. At ground level a drystone wall was built enclosing a central court some 25–35 feet in diameter. This wall was about 12 feet thick, and was pierced by a passage with door checks. Two intramural chambers opened from the entrance passage, one serving as a guard chamber, giving access to an internal staircase. The inner wall face had a ledge about 6 feet from the floor which supported a timber range. Brochs usually had a central well, and at a very late stage in their history had fixed stone furnishings such as water tanks in the floor.

The economy of the broch people was primarily agricultural, though it was to some extent supplemented by fishing, whaling and piracy. The brochs were the Iron Age equivalent of the castles of the Middle Ages. It was a troubled age, and evidence of the violence of the times comes from the Broch of Gurness, Orkney, where the bones of two hands, deliberately severed at the wrist, were found in a midden.

Brochs continued in use until about the second century AD when they were replaced by smaller, stone-built huts of different types. The historical Picts extended into the territory previously occupied by the broch builders, and the broch peoples can be regarded as ancestral to one element in the Pictish population.

The history of north-east Scotland

Classical sources indicate that the area bounded by the Moray Firth, the Great Glen and the Forth–Clyde divide was occupied in the early centuries AD by four tribes: the *Caledonii*, the *Vacomagi*, the *Taezali* and the *Venicones*.[6] The most important of these were the Caledonii, whose territory ran from Perthshire to the Beauly Firth. They have given their name to Shiehallion, the sacred mountain of the Caledonians, and to Dunkeld, which means 'fort of the Caledonians'. The Vacomagi seem to have centred on Strathmore, the area from the Tay to the Dee. The Taezali were based on the river Don in Aberdeenshire, and the Venicones occupied Fife.

By the beginning of the third century AD these four tribes were apparently grouped into confederacies, for Cassius Dio, in recording the events in Scotland in the time of Severus, mentions only the Caledonii and the Maeatae north of the Forth–Clyde. Dio asserts that the Maeatae lived close to the Antonine Wall with the Caledonians beyond them. The Maeatae were presumably an amalgam of the Vacomagi and Venicones, but the status of the Taezali is in doubt. In the later fourth century this division was still in existence according to Ammianus, who asserts that the Picts were comprised of the Dicalydones (who must be the Caledonians) and the Verturiones (who were probably the Maeatae). There can be little doubt that these tribes constitute the Proto-Picts, and since there is no evidence to the contrary they can be identified with the mixed prehistoric stock of north-east Scotland.

Archaeologically, little is known about the Proto-Picts in the first two or three centuries AD, except that they were responsible for a school of metalwork known as the 'Caledonian'.[7] Characteristic of this metalwork is a series of massive bronze armlets produced in the period between AD 50 and 150. The starting point is represented by a snake armlet from Culbin, Moray, and by the Deskford carnyx (the mouthpiece of a boar's head trumpet) from Banff. While essentially local products, the Caledonian is linked to the 'Brigantian' metalwork of Yorkshire[8] and to a northern Irish school.

The name 'Pict' appears in the classical writers for the first time towards the end of the third century. It has often been taken to mean 'painted' and to allude to the Pictish custom of tattooing. The native name in the Early Christian period was *Cruithni*. By the fourth century the Picts were a historical entity, and are recorded as taking part in the great raid of AD 367 (p. 24). The division of Proto-Picts into Maeatae and Caledonii may have continued into historic times, for Bede speaks of the northern and southern Picts, though possibly only for convenience. An early legend tells how the first king of the Picts, called Cruithne, had seven sons who gave their names to the seven regions of Pictland. This origin legend is obviously an attempt to explain regional names by mythology, but omits to provide the names of the districts. For the later history of the Picts,[9] four regions are important: *Athflotla* or Athol, *Circinn*, which consisted mainly of Strathmore, *Forthriu* or Fortrenn (the upper Earn and Forth) and *Fib*, or Fife. All these are southern, those in the north being less prominent.

Pictish history begins with Bridei mac Maelcon, the first king to be mentioned in a source independent of the *Pictish Chronicle*. His father Maelcon may have been Maelgwn of north Wales, who traditionally came from southern Scotland. Bridei won a victory over Gabran of Dalriada some time in the second half of the sixth century, and fifteen years' peace between Picts and Scots followed. Bridei is prominent in Scottish tradition as 'King Brude', who was converted by Columba, according to the conventional account by the saint's biographer, Adamnan. The full extent of Bridei's kingdom is unknown, but it probably included Orkney, the sub-king of which was at Bridei's court at the time of Columba.

Around 574 Aidan mac Gabran, one of the most important figures in early Scottic history, became king of Dalriada. He campaigned in Orkney (which conceivably was in opposition to its Pictish overlords at this time) and later encroached on Manau, which was probably in Pictish hands. In 584 Bridei died, leaving the way open for Aidan mac Gabran to annex a sizable area of Pictland. Whether he availed himself of this opportunity is debated, since he may have been more concerned with the Anglian advance. Certainly, acting both for the Dalriadic Scots and the Strathclyde Britons he attacked Æthelfrith of Northumbria at the battle of Degsastan in 603, and his army was almost totally destroyed.

Documentary evidence for Pictish history in the first half of the seventh century is scanty and virtually confined to king-lists. The Picts probably suffered at the hands of the Dalriadic Scots under Domnall Brecc, although he was much preoccupied with the Britons and probably did not campaign extensively in Pictland.

At some point after 650 the Anglians annexed part of Pictland, possibly the whole region south of the Mounth. They were not driven back until their defeat at the battle of Nechtan's Mere (probably Dunnichen in Angus) in 685, despite the Pictish revolt *c.* 672, led possibly from outside the occupied territory. More cordial relations with Northumbria were brought about by Nechtan mac Derelei, who succeeded in 706. After skirmishes early in his reign, he invited guidance from the Northumbrian Church on the method of calculating the date of Easter. Nechtan's reign ended with three others contesting his throne. The ultimate victor was Oengus mac Fergus, one of the most important figures in the early history of Scotland. On his accession he campaigned vigorously in Dalriada. By 741, after ten years' fighting there and probably also in Ireland, he subjugated the Irish in Scotland who had already been weakened by internal Dalriadic disputes.

Not content with Dalriada, Oengus did not wait to consolidate his position but turned his attention to the stronger kingdom of Strathclyde. At this time there was ostensible peace with Northumbria, though an unsuccessful attempt was made in 740 on the part of Eadberht of Northumbria to move into Pictland while Oengus was preoccupied elsewhere. Oengus seems to have been prepared to ally himself with anyone willing to take up the offensive against Strathclyde, including Cuthred of Wessex. In one campaign in Strathclyde Oengus's brother was killed and the combined forces of Oengus and Eadberht were crushed there in 756.

Oengus died in 761. Dalriada did not long remain under Pictish domination, for Aed Finn, son of Eochaid, won back its independence, probably before 778. Picto-Scottish relations in the following years are difficult to unravel; it seems that at some times Dalriada was free of the Picts, at others under their domination. While the confusion of the documentary sources at this period is understandable, the total absence of records for the rise of Kenneth mac Alpin, the Scottic king who annexed the throne of Pictland, is surprising. One explanation for this is the concern of chroniclers with the Scandinavian raids. Warfare between Picts and Scots was probably endemic and not deemed worthy of comment. It can only be assumed that Kenneth annexed Pictland rapidly, presumably through a military campaign. The success of this move must be attributed to a Dalriadic policy which involved not only the subjection but also the colonization of Pictland by the Scots, to relieve population pressures. The date of this event is uncertain, though 849 or 850 is likely. From this date onwards subsequent kings ruled the Scots as well as the Picts, who ceased to exist as an independent power.

The Pictish language[10]

The archaeological background of the Picts may explain why their language shows a mixture of elements. Not a single sentence of Pictish has survived in a document, and the sources for the language are a few brief inscriptions in Pictish ogham, a couple in Latin letters, placenames and a number of personal names and other references in late classical and early medieval writings. From these sources it has been possible to show that Pictish was Brythonic rather than Goidelic.

The Celtic element in Pictish was an earlier form than Old Welsh, and has certain affinities to Gaulish. Pictish, however, was not a pure Celtic language and contains a much earlier substratum belonging to a pre-Celtic and probably non-Indo-European language. This element was probably the language of the Bronze Age natives of north-east Scotland who were the ancestors of the Picts. The relatively few Brythonic placenames in the north and west can be explained partly by the heavy overlay of Irish and Norse populations and partly by their being outside the primary settlement area of the Picts.

The Picts probably acquired the ogham alphabet as a result of contact with the Irish of Dalriada, possibly as late as the eighth century, though one of the two inscriptions from Dalriada was probably set up following the sack of Dunadd by the Picts. The twenty to thirty surviving ogham inscriptions that are legible record personal names. The remarkable Newton stone has an inscription in an unknown alphabet.[11] The suggestion that this is a nineteenth-century forgery must be discounted from the evidence of the inscription technique. Among the notable placenames are those which incorporate the element *pit-* (Fig. 11). These do not occur south of the Forth–Clyde, and their distribution coincides remarkably with that of the Class I symbols. An almost identical distribution is shared by placenames of Brythonic derivation north of the Antonine Wall. These names include *carden, lanerc, pert, pevr* and *aber* elements.

One of the surviving inscriptions in Latin (using Irish minuscule) is on the Drosten stone, now in St Vigeans, Angus. It is inscribed in a panel on the side of the Class II stone and reads

drosten/ipeuoret/ettfor/cus

Drosten, Uoret and Forcus are personal names. Ipe is probably Pictish.

Figure 11 Distribution of pit-names in Scotland (After Wainwright)

Another inscription appears in the St Ninian's Isle hoard,[12] and reads in majuscules

IN NOMINE D(EI) S(UMMI)
RESADF(or K)ILISPU(or B)SSCIO

Resad and Spusscio are personal names and the 'fili' is probably a Latinized version of the 'maqq' which appears on some Pictish ogham stones, meaning 'son of'.

Pictish art (Figs 12–17)

The main category of archaeological evidence for the Picts consists of the important and unique series of sculptured stones. They have been divided into three main classes according to their style of execution.[13]

Class I: simple undressed stones decorated with incised symbols.
Class II: dressed slabs of varying dimensions with sculpture in relief. This consists of a cross on one side decorated with interlace and frequently subsidiary motifs. On the other face Pictish symbols are found in relief, frequently combined with other iconographic detail.
Class III: sculptures related in style and technique to Class II but lacking Pictish symbols.

In addition to the monuments, the Picts are responsible for some examples of ornamental metalwork, some of the earliest of which bear symbols, and for a series of engravings on cave walls.

The meaning and origin of the symbols on Class I and II Pictish stones has long mystified archaeologists and art historians. The symbols fall basically into two groups:

(1) Animals, executed in a distinctive style and with great economy of line. These consist of the horse, boar, bull, stag, wolf, fish, eagle, goose and some representations which seem to be a horse's head, a seal or otter, the head of a hunting dog and an animal called the 'Pictish beast' or 'swimming elephant'. There is also a snake and a beast called the 'Pictish S-dragon'. With the exception of the 'swimming elephant' and 'S-dragon' all these animals could be found in Pictland at the time they were carved.
(2) Abstract symbols, known by various descriptive terms such as 'notched rectangle', 'Z-rod', 'V-rod', 'triple disc', 'crescent and V-rod' or 'mirror and comb case'.

These symbols appear repeatedly with little variation in the form of their depiction in various combinations on Class I stones.

Class I stones

Certain points may be noted about the Class I stones that shed some light on their origin and purpose:

None of the surviving Class I stones is likely to date from before the fifth century, since with one exception none have been found in Dalriada.

If they had been used as tattoos or inscribed on some perishable material such as wood, leather or cloth for some centuries before they were inscribed on stone, the symbols might be expected to be artistically degenerate, which is not the case. Degeneration, however, can be detected during their period of

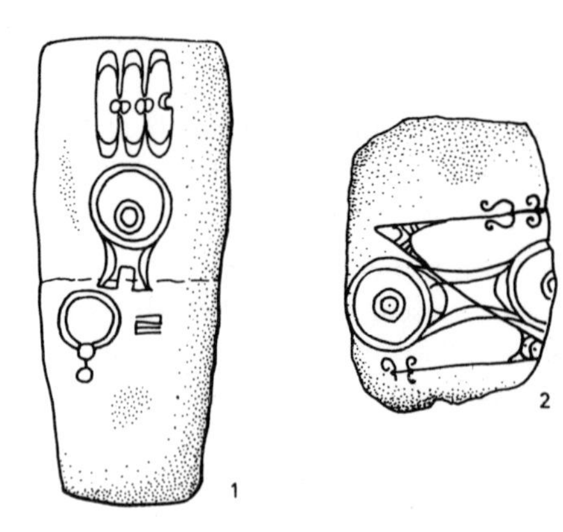

Figure 12 Class I Pictish symbol stones. (1) Sandside, Reay, Caithness; (2) Huntly

Figure 13 The distribution of Class I Pictish symbol stones

use on Class I and II stones. Also to be expected would be regional variation, which does not occur in the early stones.

The animals show close affinities with beasts which appear in Hiberno-Saxon manuscript art, notably the *Book of Durrow*, the *Book of Echternach* and the *Corpus Christi 197*. They are, however, better executed than their Northumbrian counterparts, which could imply either that they predated and

Figure 14 Class I Pictish symbols (After Henderson)

influenced the Northumbrian, or that both Picts and Northumbrians were relying on a common source.[14] Some Class I stones have inscriptions in Pictish ogham carved on them. The style of the ogham indicates that they are not earlier than the eighth century, though it is possible that the ogham inscriptions were later additions to early stones.[15]

Crucial to the dating of Pictish symbols is the hoard of silverwork from *Norrie's Law*, Fife.[16] This consisted of two silver plaques, three hand-pins, some coins and hacksilver, which included the distorted fragment of the bowl of a silver spoon of late Roman work that would not have been out of place in a hoard such as that of the fifth century from Traprain Law. The latest coin is Byzantine, dating from 582 and unlike most of the others it seems genuinely associated with the hoard. Typologically the hand-pins are in keeping with a late sixth-century date and like the silver plaques bear Pictish symbols. The silver plaques from the hoard have been seen as Pictish versions of Roman *phalerae*, and a counter argument to the late sixth-century date has been advanced on the basis that these objects and the Roman hacksilver is unlikely to have been circulating in Pictland three centuries after the Roman withdrawal. Roman silver, however, was used in the Early Christian period for making other objects and it is possible that a source was available – possibly a hoard that had been unearthed. An extreme argument has been improbably suggested that the hoard may date as late as *c.* 700, on account of the superficial similarity between a dog's head symbol on the plaques and an animal in the Lindisfarne gospels.

The suggestion that Class I stones are memorial stones copied from Roman tombstones is possible but unprovable.[17] There is only one recorded association of a Pictish stone and a burial, from Birsay, Orkney, and the relation of these is not certain. Class I stones are found widely scattered, in contrast to Class II which seem to be associated with ecclesiastical sites. The fact that Pictish symbols are associated with Christian cross-slabs (Class II monuments) indicates that they were not distasteful to the Christian Picts. This merely indicates that they were not of pagan religious significance. From the above, Class I symbols can be dated from between the fifth and the eighth centuries, and appear to be secular and probably developed in the post-Roman period.

Thomas has suggested that the Class I stones are memorial stones to the dead, and that the symbols of animals are clan badges while the others are descriptive and denote rank.[18] He has pointed out that they appear in various combinations: sometimes a single animal, sometimes a pair of symbols (usually an animal and an object), sometimes in a triple or quadruple combination. In the case of comb and mirror symbols, which have been seen to be indicative of a female, they occur together with an animal.

He has suggested that the animals are derived from a long tradition of Eurasiatic animal art, transmitted to Scotland in the early Iron Age by English intermediaries, while the object symbols represent items familiar in the society of the ancestral Caledonians; he has pointed out various Iron Age counterparts for the objects figured. He has postulated that the symbols should therefore be seen as originating in the Iron Age, and should be connected with the hierarchy of Iron Age society, originally appearing as tattoos.[19]

This very attractive theory is difficult to substantiate. One of the most serious obstacles is the absence of objects decorated in the animal style along its postulated route of transmission. It is true that there are instances of animal representations in Scottish Iron Age art – notably on some rare sherds of Hebridean pottery, but an animal art as such is absent in Pictland. Where such animals occur, they are neither very close to Eurasiatic animals nor to the later Pictish beasts. Secondly, while it cannot be denied that a few object symbols do appear to be identical to Iron Age objects, a number (such as the mirror and comb symbols) have equally good Early Christian period counterparts. Viewed in isolation, the 'Iron Age' object symbols must be admitted to be too stereotyped to be representations of conclusively Iron Age objects.

It is easier to see the tradition as part of the general amalgam of artistic

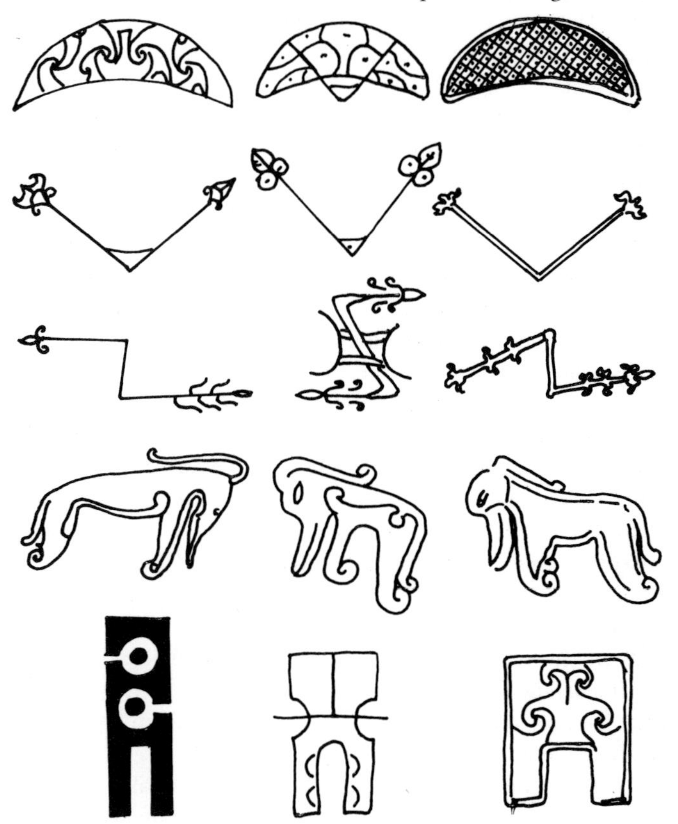

Figure 15 The 'declining' Pictish symbols (After Henderson)

traditions reaching Britain in the post-Roman period. Elements of the Eurasiatic animal style occur in a variety of contexts in Migration Period Europe, and motifs can be detected in Anglo-Saxon metalwork, including some pieces from Sutton Hoo. A stag with a shoulder spiral in Eurasiatic tradition appears on the Lullingstone hanging bowl, and would not be out of place in Pictland, while certain motifs such as beaked bird's heads occur at varying periods in different parts of Britain and Europe. Other elements in the Pictish bestiary, for instance the S-dragon, may have come from late Roman traditions, though this particular motif is widespread in various guises in Migration Period art and is not confined to Romano-British dragonesque fibulae.

An alternative explanation for Class I symbols has recently been advanced by Henderson, who has suggested that the symbols were the invention of one man to be used as marks of ownership.[20] She regards the symbol stones as marking the boundaries of territorial divisions. Following this explanation the Class II stones could indicate the bounds of church lands. Henderson has suggested that the custom of erecting stones probably began in the north, round the Moray and Dornoch Firth, where the most carefully executed and stylistically early occur. From there, they probably spread down into Aberdeenshire, where there is a concentration in the Don–Uire valley and in Strathspey. Thence they spread outward through Pictland.[21] She has suggested a seventh-century date for their invention, though the evidence of the Norrie's Law hoard points to a sixth-century date.

It has been suggested that during the period in which the symbols were in use a decline in the standard of representation can be detected and the principle of the 'declining symbol' has been used to provide a chronology for the stones.[22] While it is likely that there is a 'correct' form for the symbols, and that some are a degenerate version, this chronology cannot be accepted without reservation. The Brandsbutt stone, for example, which has been dated by the style of the ogham inscription to the eighth century, has symbols which are typologically early. It is not always possible to determine the 'true' form of the symbol. The 'notched rectangle' of the Newton stone could for instance be either very early or very late, depending on the interpretation. It is true to say, however, that the symbols on Class II stones are more degenerate than many of those in Class I. It is feasible that this was not a universal process and that typologically early and developed symbols were carved contemporaneously. One practical argument for Class II stones being more developed lies in the difficulties of carving the symbols in relief, since they are essentially linear and designed for painting or incising. It is possible that the degenerate symbols on Class I stones date mostly from the period when modified symbols were being used on Class II stones.

Pictish symbols of the type found on Class I stones occur also on early Pictish silverwork including the find at Norrie's Law (p. 55) and a series of ten chains. The chains are all constructed by the same technique and each has a terminal ring with expanded flanges.[23] These necklets are akin to the torcs of the Iron Age, and two of them, from Parkhill, Aberdeenshire, and Whitecleuch, Lanarkshire, have early Pictish symbols on their terminal rings. They are usually dated to the seventh or early eighth century though a date in the late sixth or early seventh century would be as valid. A few of the chains have simpler ring terminals. They are widespread, with seven coming from the Lowlands, notably from Traprain Law, Haddington, Whitlaw, Greenlaw, Hordwheel and Walston as well as Whitecleuch. They could be explained in terms of loot taken from Picts, but may also have been brought into the area by raiders, which would be more explicable in the sixth century than later. Raiders too are probably responsible for the appearance of Pictish symbols in the Lowlands. That from Anwoth, Kirkcudbright, for instance, is near the fort of Trusty's Hill (p. 32) which was possibly taken by Pictish raiders.[24]

The Gaulcross Hoard, Banff,[25] is one of the most important finds of early Pictish silverwork. It was found before 1840 in the ring cairn of a Bronze Age stone circle. One of the greatest losses to Pictish studies was that of the pins and brooches, before their publication, which would presumably have provided dating for the hoard. As it survives today, the Gaulcross hoard consists of a silver chain, bracelet and hand-pin, and what may be the silver mounts of knife handles. The hand-pin is decorated with triple hairspring spirals like dodo heads, and stylistically is sixth century in date. A two-pronged wooden tool and die were probably used in the manufacture of the chains, which suggests that already by the sixth century the Picts were skilled silversmiths, a fact to be borne in mind when considering the silverwork of the St Ninian's Isle treasure (p. 65) or the Cadboll brooches (p. 315).

A few other objects bear Pictish symbols. These include a scratching on a piece of bone from the Broch of Burrian in Orkney and symbols carved on a number of round sandstone discs. The Burrian bone cannot be used for dating evidence, since the excavations in the nineteenth century failed to record its exact associations. The broch also produced a Celtic bell, suggesting a post-broch occupation well into the Early Christian period. A bronze crescent-shaped object, now lost, from Monifeith, Angus, reputedly came from a broch-like structure, possibly a dun, and had declined Pictish symbols inscribed on it.

Class II stones (Fig. 16; Plates 17–19)[26]

Class II stones are usually dated to the later eighth to the tenth centuries. It has already been noted that Class II stones differ from Class I in that they have a cross in relief. This cross is not free-standing as in the case of early Northumbrian examples, but is added to the slab to form what is termed a cross slab. These slabs have interlaced crosses apparently derived from contemporary manuscripts. It is tempting to see Northumbrian prototypes, but it is possible that Pictish gospel books could have provided models. There are fourteen different types of cross, of which the most common are those with round armpits and those with double square armpits. The round armpit is a feature of both Northumbrian and Irish sculpture, while the double square can be seen in Northumbrian manuscripts such as the *Book of Durrow,* or the Lindisfarne gospels. The type with a quadrilobate nimbus instead of the more usual circular form seems to be purely Pictish, and occurs on an early group, of which the most famous example is that in Aberlemno churchyard. Some later Manx stones show the same feature presumably derived from Pictland. Class II stones show a variety of interlace designs, some of which are the products of local schools. Some of the more ornate interlace appears on the earliest Class II stones.

The close similarity between Pictish and Northumbrian art might suggest

Figure 16 The distribution of Class II Pictish cross slabs (After Henderson)

that the Class II stones and manuscripts are contemporaneous, and it is not unreasonable to suppose that there was a period of Northumbrian influence in Pictland, following the Pictish affiliation to the Northumbrian Church in AD 710. It could have been a two-way current, and Pictish-style figures of the type represented on the Inchbrayock stone can be seen on the Northumbrian whalebone box known as the Franks casket.

An early group of works are distinguishable, including the stones from

Aberlemno churchyard, Rossie Priory and certain examples from the collections at Meigle and St Vigeans.[27] All these, and related stones, display fairly low relief sculpture. Significantly, this group is of southern Pictish provenance, but a number of probably early stones come from the north, including one from Birsay and the earliest of the group, which comes from Papil.

Around AD 800 a further development in Class II sculpture can be seen, represented by the remarkable stone from Hilton of Cadboll in Easter Ross. Standing almost 8 feet high, it is covered with a mass of detail, with a hunting scene under three Pictish symbols at the top. The nearest antecedent is the Glamis stone, which is a foot higher but less accomplished.

In the ninth century the *Boss Style* of Pictish sculpture developed.[28] The Nigg Cross, Aberlemno No. 3, and the St Andrew's shrine belong to the first or 'Early Boss Style'. The latter, a corner-block shrine (p. 381) dates from about 825, and may belong to the time when relics of St Andrew were brought to Scotland by Oengus, who ruled from 820 to 834. The decoration of this shrine is probably inspired by Mercian work via the Kells school, and the style can also be paralleled by a series of other works, including the ninth-century crosses at Iona. Aberlemno No. 3 (sometimes called the Roadside Cross) echoes the hunting scene of the Hilton of Cadboll stone.

A feature of all the above stones is the use of round bosses, decorated with interlace, as part of the design. The use of bosses in Scotland, as elsewhere in Early Christian sculpture, is no doubt derived from metalwork and can be traced in earlier manuscripts. The Boss Style degenerated during the ninth century, when after such elaboration there was a trend to simplification. Typical of this phase from the north is the sculpture from Rosemarkie. In the south, continuity can be traced from the Aberlemno Roadside Cross to Meigle No. 2 (Plate 18A) which stands 8 feet high and which is distinguished by the absence of Pictish symbols for the first time.

The Late Boss Style in the north, with its large, almost extravagant symbols, may be seen as a display of northern Pictish independence. In the south the stones of this late period do not always carry bosses,[29] being more subdued. Bosses do appear on the Dunfallandy stone in Perthshire and on a stone from Fowlis Wester. The same extravagant style, but without the bosses, can be detected on the Drosten stone (St Vigeans No. 1) (Plate 17B).

Class III[30]

Class III monuments belong to the period after the merging of Dalriada with the kingdom of Pictland under Kenneth mac Alpin in the ninth century. Though an upsurge of Irish influence, spreading from Dalriada with the accession of a Dalriadic king, might be expected, little is apparent, and the free-standing high crosses of Irish type encountered in the west, most notably at Iona and Kildalton on Islay, are not found in eastern Scotland.

With the disappearance of the Pictish kingdom traces of traditional Pictish art continued in the area. The distribution of crosses having a cross-ring decorated with meanders or step patterns (Class II) seems to be confined to the old territory, although Pictish influence extended further and figures which are related to the older tradition of Pictish figurative work appear in Strathclyde, notably in the collection at Govan (p. 205). From there the figures and the cross-slab type spread to the Isle of Man about the middle of the tenth century.

A few major works of this late period occur in Scotland. The first is the free-standing cross at *Duplin*, near Perth, where Anglian elements are apparent,

Figure 17 Fantastic animals on Class II stones. (1)–(2) Rossie, Perthshire; (3) Gask, Perthshire; (4) Woodwray, Perthshire; (5) Meigle; (6) Gask (After Henderson)

though the figure composition is in the Pictish tradition with perhaps hints of Irish influence. *Sueno's stone*, at Forres, stands 20 feet high, and is skilfully executed with a mass of tightly packed figures, though uninspired interlace suggests a late date (Plate 22A). To this late period should probably be assigned a series of stones with evangelistic scenes, notably St Vigeans No. 11, and the fine stone from *Aldbar* now in Brechin Cathedral and probably datable to the last quarter of the ninth century.

The iconography of Class II and III stones (Fig. 17)[31]

The very unusual secular iconography of the Class II and III stones seems to have been derived in part from an embroidery tradition. Such tapestries are known to have existed elsewhere in the Early Christian period and would explain why many scenes seem to have been taken from a secular narrative tradition. With certain exceptions, including the unique battle scene on the back of the Aberlemno churchyard stone, the scenes seem to be put together at random from different sources to fill the vacant spaces on the stone. Secular themes are rare in Early Christian period art in Britain, appearing in the late Manx stones and a group of northern English stones which may have been influenced in part by Pictish tradition as well as by Scandinavian art.

The hunting scene on the *Hilton of Cadboll* stone, and the *St Andrew's shrine*, may belong to a particular Pictish tradition. Another tradition in the secular iconography centres around depictions of monsters, of which eight types are represented and which are clearly not derived from ornamental lacertines. These may be derived from a *Physiologus* or from another illustrated book current in the Early Christian period – *Marvels of the East* – a copy of which seems to have been available in Northumbria. Near Eastern elements are also present, though the precise source cannot be determined. A *World Chronicle* source, such as that used by the carver of the Franks casket, may have contributed, but if so the scenes should be less haphazard and more narrative in character.

Henderson has suggested that the secular iconography owes something to Celtic tradition, and has cited the Gundestrup cauldron and the Gallehus Horns from Scandinavia as a parallel for the imagery.[32] This theory is too tenuous, and similarities are more likely to stem from the pre-Roman tradition that secular iconography in Early Christian Europe draws upon.

The Christian iconography is less varied. Henderson has argued convincingly that the David iconography, which is so important on the St Andrew's shrine, the Hilton of Cadboll stone and the Nigg stone, is derived from Mercian sculpture.[33] She has pointed to its relationship with the school typified by the *Book of Kells*, and detectable in the Aberlemno Roadside Cross. She sees the appearance of mourning angels on either side of the cross as due to Carolingian influence by way of models such as the Metz ivories. This tradition must have been transmitted by way of the Kells school.

Other Christian themes that appear on the Pictish stones are two of the Old Testament types of salvation (types and anti-types were integral to Early Christian iconography and were current in Northumbria), the two being Daniel and Jonah, both popular with the Picts, doubtless because they involved the depiction of animals.

Samson also figures in the iconography, along with the illustrations relating to Saints Paul and Antony, two hermit saints who had a wide appeal for not only Pictish but also Northumbrian and Irish clerics.

Early Pictish metalwork

Except for a few examples from the Northern Isles, Pictland has produced no penannular brooches which can be ascribed with certainty to the fifth or sixth centuries, and it is possible that the penannular brooch, along with other metal-working traditions, arrived in Pictland some time in the sixth century.

The date of the beginning of Pictish metalwork depends on two hoards, *Norrie's Law* (Fife) and *Tummel Bridge* (Perthshire).[34] Both these hoards contained penannular brooches of silver with undecorated, expanded flattened terminals, of Type H (p. 308). It has been suggested that the Norrie's Law hoard cannot be earlier than the end of the sixth century, and may even be as late as 700 (p. 56). The dating of the Tummel Bridge find is less clearcut.

As well as three penannular brooches, the Tummel Bridge hoard contained fragments of a hanging bowl with openwork escutcheons decorated with four peltas. The traditional date for openwork escutcheons is the fifth century since they are similar to Roman openwork. They need not all, however, be as early, and the recent discovery of a mould for casting openwork hanging bowl escutcheons at Craig Phadrig, Inverness,[35] suggests that some at least were being made in the sixth century. The mould was associated with sherds of E Ware, which was not being imported to Britain prior to *c.* 525–50 AD. Craig Phadrig was undoubtedly occupied by the Picts (p. 68).

The Type H brooches from the two hoards have been dated to the fifth century by Fowler, who sees the type as a native Scottish development out of her Type Aa brooches, current in the Roman period, though it is possible that they had a different origin, and are later (p. 308).[36] In the light of this the Tummel Bridge find can be regarded as having been deposited perhaps in the late sixth century, perhaps even in the seventh.

From Castle Tioram, Moidart, comes a fragment of a hanging bowl with an openwork pelta pattern escutcheon which is also probably Pictish.[37] The excavations of the Pictish site at Clatchard's Craig, Fife, produced a small bronze mount which is related to a class of enamelled hanging bowl escutcheon.[38] Measuring three-quarters of an inch across, this disc has a triple pelta enamelled decoration, and is datable to the sixth or seventh century. The motif is very similar to that on the escutcheon of a hanging bowl from Winchester, and the disc could have been soldered to a small bowl. In addition to that from Craig Phadrig, other moulds have been found in Pictland, notably a series from Clatchard's Craig, which may date from the period.

As a whole the evidence indicates that at a date not far removed from 600, metal working was already established in Pictland. Between the late sixth and the eighth century a number of objects are recognizable in Pictland which are almost certainly of local workmanship. Pictish symbols on three hand-pins from Norrie's Law show them to be undoubtedly Pictish work, and apart from the more ornate examples from Gaulcross and Norrie's Law, there is a series of about ten, which includes one from Culbin Sands with a minute head a few millimetres across.

The *Monymusk Reliquary*,[39] the most famous object of Early Christian date from Scotland, should be assigned to the end of the seventh century (p. 361). The reliquary combines three features shared by the later St Ninian's Isle metalwork; the technique and manner of the animal ornament on the bowls from the hoard, the type of bronze-gilt and enamelled appliqué work found on one of the bowls and the open concentric curvilinear pattern. The hinges of the Monymusk Reliquary recall some hanging bowl escutcheons, while the open-mouthed animals are reminiscent of some later Pictish animals on the Dunbeath Brooch. The details of decoration on the Monymusk Reliquary are closely comparable with the ornament in the Lindisfarne gospels, and this fact alone might suggest some Northumbrian influence before the early eighth century in Pictland. The *Birka Pail* (p. 363) and a bronze object from *Vinjum*, Sogn og Fjordane, Norway, are probably Pictish and certainly in a related tradition.[40] Other objects of Pictish metalwork include a bronze wheel-shaped object from Moan, Mainland, Orkney,[41] decorated with roundels similar to those on the terminals of Croy hoard penannular brooches. It may have been the head of a ring brooch of annular type. It was found with an assortment of Early Christian period beads, a cruciform mounting which once had a central inlay, another piece of bronze and some fragments of slag and pottery. The group came from a stone cist.

From the Class H brooches represented in the Norrie's Law hoard stem a series of elaborate Pictish brooches (discussed on p. 313). Simpler types of penannular brooches were also being produced in the Pictish area in the seventh and eighth centuries (Nos 17 and 18, p. 308), and the numerous mould fragments from Birsay show that a variety of Pictish penannulars were being made on the site, probably in the early eighth century.[42]

A small bronze mount from Stromness and a bronze mount found nearby at Monker Green may both be Pictish.[43] The Monker Green mount is decorated with interlaced biting animals, and bears some affinities to objects like the Birka Pail and also to the St Ninian's Isle treasure (Plate 16A).

The St Ninian's Isle treasure (Plates 13–14)[44]

The hoard of silverwork found in the 1958 excavations at St Ninian's Isle, just off the Shetland mainland near Spiggie, must rank as the most important discovery of 'Celtic' metalwork hitherto made. The hoard was found in a larchwood box, buried under a broken sandstone slab inscribed with a cross, near the chancel arch of a twelfth-century church. Iron Age occupation also occurred on the site, and seven post-stones of a corner-post shrine were recovered, decorated with Pictish symbols.

The hoard consisted of seven silver bowls (one almost hemispherical, the others with omphaloid bases), a hanging bowl, two sword chapes, three pepperpot-shaped objects, a sword pommel, a spoon and a single-pronged claw-shaped implement, possibly for eating shellfish, and twelve penannular brooches along with the jawbone of a porpoise. There is good reason to suppose that not all the objects are of the same date – some, such as the inscribed sword chape, show signs of considerable wear. In all probability, however, the hoard was buried in the late eighth or early ninth century, almost certainly in the face of the Norse invasion threat. It is unlikely to be Norse loot, since the site was ecclesiastical and in regular use, and there is an absence of hacksilver and objects of non-Scottish origin. It follows therefore that it belonged to a Pictish chief, since Shetland at this time would have been under Pictish domination. Moreover, the inscription and other factors to be considered below indicate that Pictland provides the most likely provenance for all the objects, except perhaps the hanging bowl.

A case has been made in support of the treasure being ecclesiastical and not secular.[45] The 'pepperpots' and sword pommel have been interpreted as part of a *flabellum* or processional standard, the chapes as strap ends, which, along with the brooches, would have been part of the trappings of a cleric's vestments. The spoon has been explained as eucharistic, the six bowls as chalices, the hemispherical bowl as an aquamanile, the hanging bowl as a votive chalice and the pronged implement as a eucharistic knife. While this is an interesting and possible explanation, a stronger case has been advanced for the treasure's secular character.

The bowls are decorated with punched dots; in four cases this is in the form of interlace or rectilinear patterns, in two there is a frieze of animals. The smallest bowl has an internal mount with red enamel on the centre of the base. The hemispherical bowl has complex geometric decoration, consisting of curves of incised lines bordered with punched dots. The hanging bowl has three ribs in the form of boars. In the centre of the base there is a chip-carved roundel with animal ornament, with a circular disc in the same position on the exterior. The sword chapes are decorated with animal ornament and blue glass studs, while the 'pepperpots', which may be buttons or belt fasteners, are decorated in a similar style. The spoon is ornamented with a dog's head at the base of the handle, appearing to lick from the bowl. Both spoon and pronged implement have a loop for suspension, possibly at the waist. The twelve penannular brooches are with one exception gilt on their faces. They belong to two main classes, those with lobed terminals and those with plate terminals, and all are decorated with carved interlace, with occasional animal motifs.

The bowls are the most useful for ornamental comparison. Those with animals can be compared with some of the late Pictish stones of Class II which also show hints of Northumbrian influence, such as vinescroll ornament, the closest parallels for the animals being on the stones from Aberlemno and Meigle. The single animals on the best-preserved of the two bowls can be matched on stones from Glamis, Meigle and Lasswade.

Pictish influence, however, is not the only inspiration behind the St Ninian's Isle bowls. There are certain similarities of treatment between the scrolled hindquarters of the animals on the bowls and animals on the early eighth-century Tara Brooch. Further parallels can be seen in Northumbrian manuscripts, most notably the Lindisfarne gospels. There are many points of similarity of treatment – animals on both have spiral hindquarters, reversed legs and looped necks. Certain features on the St Ninian's Isle bowls postdate the Lindisfarne gospels, such as the foliation on the tips of the tails and tongues. This is mainly a feature of late eighth-century Anglo-Saxon art and can be seen for example on the Witham Pins from Lincolnshire.

The three 'pepperpots' have decoration which is most closely paralleled in the *Book of Kells*, though a more remote comparison can be seen in one of the panels of the Nigg stone. The *Book of Kells* is usually thought of as Irish, but the script is more in accordance with Northumbrian palaeography. Kells was a foundation of Scottish monks fleeing from Iona in the face of Viking advance *c.* 800, and it is likely that the *Book of Kells* was taken with them, in a finished or more probably unfinished form. It is possible that Iona monks were using a Northumbrian script, though it is conceivable that the book was executed by a Northumbrian monk.

The hanging bowl is anomalous in the hoard. The closest parallels for its decoration come from Northumbria, and it is closely comparable with the lost bowl from the Witham, Lincolnshire. The animals on the border of the internal mount are related to Style II Anglo-Saxon work, of the type that appears on objects from Sutton Hoo or in the *Book of Durrow*. Other details of the bowl suggest Irish influence, but the cumulative impression is of Anglo-Saxon work, done very probably in Northumbria in the late seventh or eighth century. It is thus the oldest object in the hoard.

Pommel and chape are difficult to attribute, showing late eighth-century Anglo-Saxon elements as well as Celtic. This ancestry may in some way be connected with the general influence of Merovingian manuscript models in the period.

The brooches from the hoard are discussed on p. 309f.

The hoard is important since it proved that a distinctive Pictish school of metal working had developed in the eighth century AD that was previously only suspected. In addition, the hoard has extended the known metalwork to include classes of objects other than brooches and has shown artistic influences that were at work in Pictland. It is clear that the contact with Northumbria postulated as beginning after the affiliation between the Northumbrian and Pictish Church at the beginning of the eighth century had an effect on art forms other than sculpture. Although the character of the hoard is Pictish, the Northumbrian and other Anglo-Saxon influences should not be minimized, nor should the Irish influence be ignored, though it is less important than might have been suspected.

The Birsay box (Plate 16B)[46]

A further example of Pictish craftsmanship can be seen in a wooden box found at Birsay, Orkney, in the nineteenth century. Measuring 11½ by 5 by 3 inches, it is cut from a block of alder, with a sliding lid, originally held down with metal bands which were later replaced by leather thongs. The faces and lid were decorated with chip-carved running S-scrolls and C-curves. It was probably the work of a leatherworker, and the eight handles found in it were of leather-working tools. Although prehistoric examples of wooden tool boxes are known, there is only one other probably Early Christian period example, from Dromiskin, Co. Louth, though there is a series of Scandinavian examples. The Birsay box can tentatively be dated to the eighth century.

Settlement sites

Until recent excavations little information was available about settlement sites in Pictland. The Picts lived on a variety of different sites, depending on the region, the chief settlement type in mainland Scotland being the *reoccupied hillfort*.

Craig Phadrig is a rocky outcrop on the Beauly Firth, near Inverness. At some point in the fourth century BC a timber-laced rampart was constructed on the hill, to which a second rampart defence was added. The fort was accidentally fired, producing vitrifaction. After the initial occupation the fort was deserted until the Early Christian period. Local tradition associates it with Bridei mac Maelcon; this is probably a fairly recent invention, although the mould and E Ware from the site corroborates reoccupation at about the time of his reign. The pottery and escutcheon mould belonged to an occupation level with several hearths, though only one hut site was recognizable, indicated by a clay floor. Associated finds consisted of bone, a spindle whorl, whetstones and a palette. A radiocarbon date for this occupation of around AD 370 was obtained, but this was probably too early.

Cullykhan, Banff, is another example of a timber-laced fort with later reoccupation (see p. 47). Much of the Pictish occupation material was destroyed by medieval castle builders. A complex of post-holes, however, was encountered during excavation from which it has been possible tentatively to reconstruct a rectangular house with porch, associated with a charred wooden object which has provided a radiocarbon date of *c.* AD 370.

Burghead, Morayshire, is remarkable in that one of the two forts there was timber-laced and constructed possibly as late as the time of the historical Picts. The upper fort was constructed possibly in the fourth century AD and has produced late Roman coins among other finds. The lower fort was probably not much later, and both appear to have been occupied until the arrival of the Norse. Finds include stones with Pictish bull symbols on them – the symbol is known accordingly as the 'Burghead Bull'. About twenty-five to thirty have been noted from the site. Of somewhat later date in the Early Christian period is a slab shrine, and there is also a record of 'numerous bronze spears given away to any English tourist who happened to be passing'. In the ninth century the fort was fired, and left unoccupied until the twelfth or thirteenth century. Radiocarbon dating for the rampart of the upper fort dates construction to the fourth century, though a slightly later date is possible. The fort is very extensive, and was probably one of the most important in Pictland.

Clatchard's Craig, Fife, was a multivallate Iron Age fort about 550 feet by 300 feet and was reoccupied in the Pictish period, when the area was reduced to 300 feet by 200 feet and a rampart was constructed utilizing Roman masonry. Within the fort was a timber hall of beam-slot construction, and the associated finds of the Pictish phase included penannular brooches, moulds and glass eye beads, bone combs and other bone objects generally in keeping with assemblages from elsewhere, such as the Mote of Mark or Dunadd. Pottery included E Ware.

Similar material points to a post-broch occupation at *Hurly Hawkin*, Angus.

A series of *nuclear forts* should also probably be associated with the Picts,[47] since although also found outside the area, they are more abundant in Pictland than elsewhere. They share a preference for rocky sites where natural outcrops can be incorporated into the defensive scheme. This scheme consists of a central enclosure or 'citadel' and a series of outworks forming subsidiary enclosures. One of the most characteristic is *Dundurn*, Perthshire. Here the citadel occupied the top of a rock outcrop, measuring 70 feet in internal diameter and defended by a stone wall linking the natural rock outcrops. Beyond are a series of walls which link further outcrops. Dundurn is probably the *Duinduirn* mentioned in the *Annals of Ulster* as having been besieged in 683. Dundurn commands upper Strathearn, and may have been the main fort of the Picts of Fortrenn (Fig. 22).

Moncrieffe Hill near Perth is another good example of a nuclear fort. Here the first defences consisted of a stone wall following the edge of the hill, converting it into a contour fort. This phase probably belongs to the early Iron Age, and at a later stage an oval citadel was built, about 160 feet by 120 feet. This was probably contemporary with the building of an 'outer courtyard'. Moncrieffe is probably the *Monad Croib* mentioned as the scene of a battle in 729.

Further south, *Dumyat* in Stirlingshire is another example, with a citadel defended by outer defences following fairly regular courses. The name may mean 'the fort of the Maeatae'.

Ringforts or *duns* may also be associated with the Picts. These forts, which are characterized by a very thick stone wall with a single entrance enclosing usually a comparatively small area, are in all probability descended from the mainstream of Iron Age stone-walled forts in Scotland, but they seem to have been occupied or reoccupied not only in the Early Christian period but even later. They are particularly common in Strathtay, Perthshire, the heart of Pictland (Plate 6B).

In some cases ringforts are found inside earlier forts. This is the case at *Turin Hill*, Angus, where a ringfort was constructed within a contour fort. Here the wall is about 12 feet thick, and encloses an area about 80 feet in diameter. It partly overlies an earlier enclosure, which may be a timber-laced fort of Abernethy type, which in turn is situated within a more orthodox

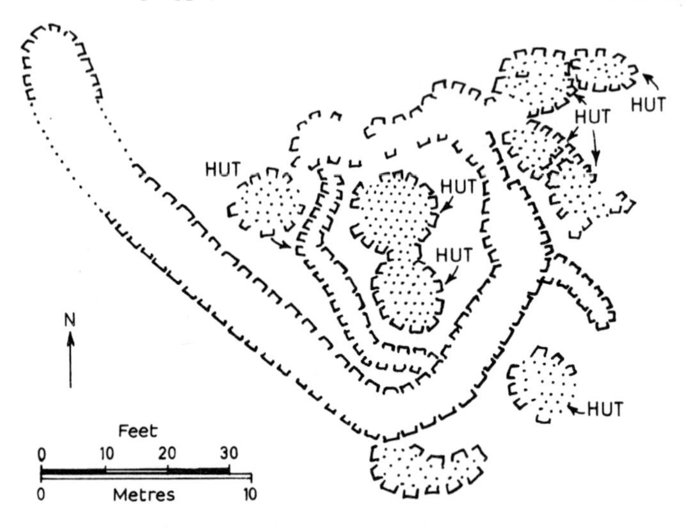

Figure 18 Carlungie, Angus, souterrain (After Wainwright)

multivallate Iron Age fort. A similar but less complex and striking feature can be seen at *Dunearn*, Fife.

A group of souterrains in southern Pictland should probably be associated with the Proto-Picts.[48] Evidence points to their being used in the first two centuries AD by agriculturalists who lived in above-ground huts. Such huts have been recognized on two sites in Angus – *Carlungie* (Fig. 18) and *Ardestie*. All the evidence, however, points to the southern Pictland souterrains falling out of use in the third century AD. Where evidence is available it seems that some at least were deliberately dismantled and filled in by souterrain folk who continued to live on the same site. Evidence for post-souterrain occupation comes from Ardestie and Carlungie, and as this occupation appears to have continued at least until the fifth century the post-souterrain people may be equated with the historical Picts.

Pictish ecclesiastical architecture

Restenneth Priory, Angus, is a twelfth-century priory which incorporates an earlier tower.[49] The tower displays a number of features in accordance with

Anglo-Saxon work, notably a round-headed south doorway outlined by plain square pilaster-strip work and hood moulding. The upper part of the tower is probably medieval work, but the lower part has been dated to the eighth century and may have been the porticus of a church built by masons from Monkwearmouth around 710 on the order of Nechtan mac Derelei of the Picts. The upper part may have been added around 1100 by Alexander I.

Abernethy, Perthshire, has a round tower of Irish type, one of the two remaining examples in Scotland. It dates to the eleventh century and a Pictish Class I stone now stands nearby.

Brechin, Angus (Figs 19–20), incorporates the second round tower in Scotland into the later cathedral. A few feet from the ground its round-headed doorway is decorated with figure sculpture. It is crowned with a Crucifixion and the jambs have flanking figures of hooded clerics. At the base are a pair of fantastic beasts. The style of the sculpture would suggest a date around 1000, and Irish influence is detectable.

St Regulus' Tower, St Andrews, Fife,[50] is similar to Restenneth in that the remains comprise a very tall square tower together with a slightly wider chancel to the east. Additions were made to it in the twelfth century, but they have not survived. It has windows and other features characteristic of Anglo-Saxon work, and probably dates from the eleventh century.

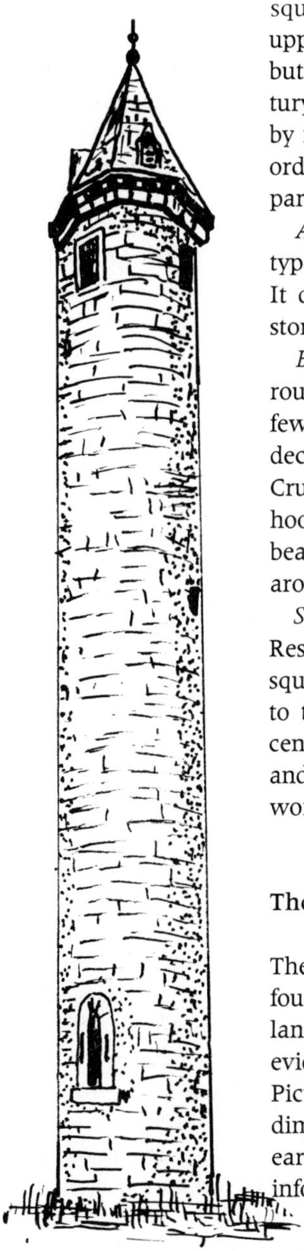

Figure 19 Brechin round tower

The Scots of Dalriada

The kingdom of Dalriada centred on Argyll and was founded by fifth-century colonists of Scotti from Ireland for whom there is very little archaeological evidence. The kingdom was eventually united with Pictland *c.* 849. The initial period of colonization is dimly reflected in later documentary tradition. The earliest source for it is the *Duan Albanach*, which informs us that

> The three sons of Erc, son of Eochaidh, the valiant
> Three who obtained the blessing of Patrick,

Took Alban, exalted their courage,
Loarn, Fergus and Angus.[51]

A later account, preserved in the twelfth-century *Chronicle of the Scots*, tells us that Fergus was 'the first of the race of Conaire to take the kingdom of Alban from the mountain of Druimalban to the Irish Sea and the Isles of the Gael'.[52] His death is given in the *Annals of Tigernach* as taking place around 501. Conaire is identified as Conaire mac Moga Lama, one of the kings of Munster.

The Scottish king-lists trace first the kings of Dalriada, then the kings of the Picts and Scots together down to Malcolm III (d. 1095). They give Fergus

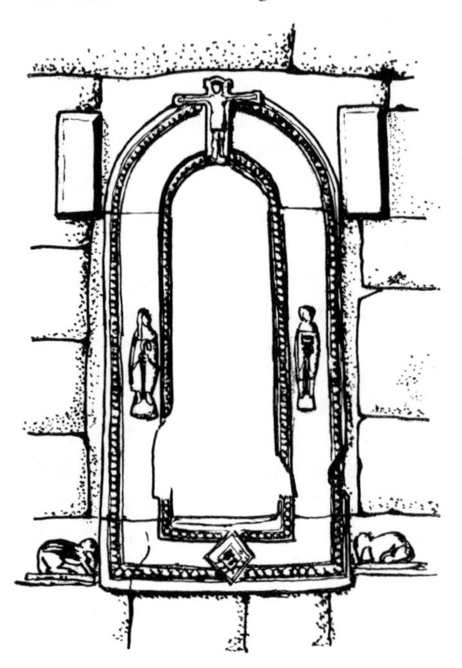

Figure 20 Brechin round tower – doorway

mac Erc as a common ancestor. The first part of the list comes from the *Chronicle of Dalriada*.[53] Other evidence that the Irish were well informed of events in Dalriada is contained in the chronicle kept from the seventh century within Dalriada itself, probably at Iona, which may have provided a source for Irish annalistic entries. Indeed its existence is only known from other sources.

A survey drawn up in the seventh or eighth century gives a general muster of sea and land in Dalriada, and a sketch history.[54] According to this source the sons of Erc came in a fleet of 150 men, led by Fergus, Loarn and Angus. The family of Loarn (the Cinel Loarne) occupied northern Argyll (i.e. Lorne), and were traditionally based on Dunollie, a fort with a medieval castle which stands above Oban. The family of Angus occupied Islay, while Gabran, the descendant of Fergus, had Kintyre and Knapdale, and occupied as his stronghold Dunadd in the Crinan Moss. There is no doubt that the sons of Erc came from that part of Antrim known as Dalriada; traditionally their homeland stronghold is Dunseverick. The Irish were known as the 'Scots' – the term

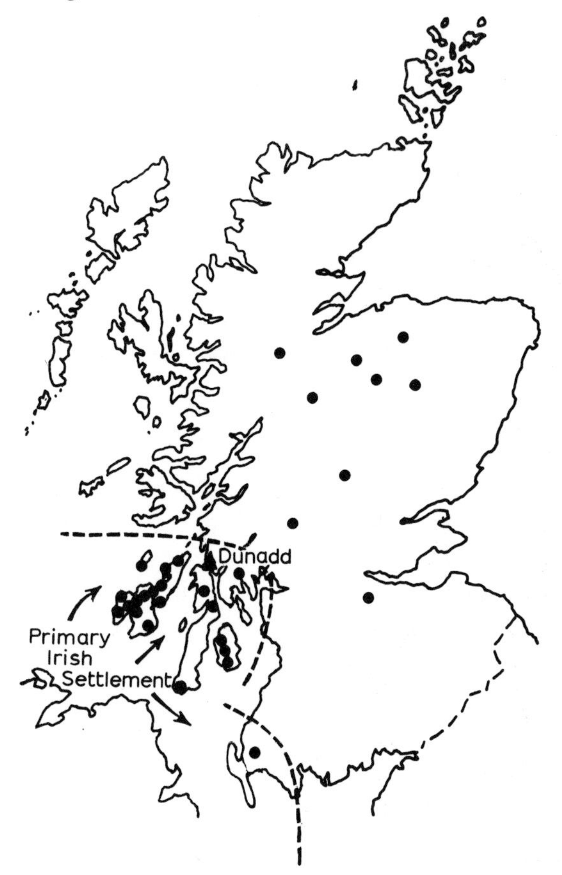

Figure 21 Distribution of Irish placenames in Scotland (After Nicholaisen)

'Scotti' may be derived from a verb meaning 'to plunder' but is Goidelic rather than Brythonic and was probably the name used by the expeditionaries themselves. The name of Argyll appears to be derived from *air-gailne*, 'eastern vassals', a reference to their Antrim origins.

The initial movement probably took place in the last quarter of the fifth century, if the information given in the chronicle is reliable. According to this, Loarn ruled for ten years and was followed by Fergus who reigned for twenty-seven years. The early history of Dalriada is one of rivalry between the families of Loarn and Gabran. It is likely that the area settled was sparsely populated, and there was little initial friction between the natives and the Irish colonists.

The most important effect of the Irish settlement of Dalriada was the introduction of Goidelic to Scotland, Scots Gaelic being the result. The language spoken in Ireland and Dalriada was what is known as 'common Gaelic'. While initially confined to Dalriada, Gaelic had at least entered Pictland before

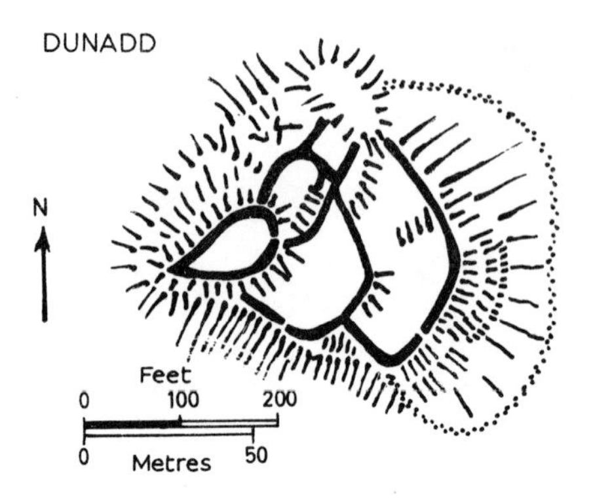

Figure 22 Dunadd and Dundurn plans

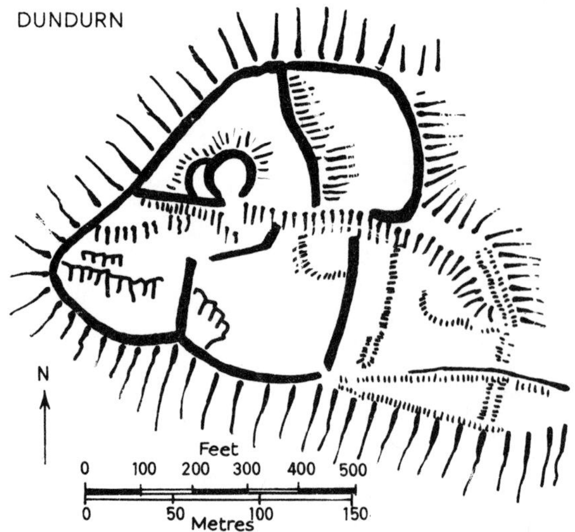

its union with Dalriada in the ninth century, as a result of ecclesiastical activity, probably from Iona. The main expansion of Gaelic, however, was a late phenomenon, not directly connected with the Dalriadic expansion, but the result of hybrid Irish-Norse movements in the tenth century. By the eleventh century Gaelic was in use throughout Scotland except for a narrow belt along the English border and in the Norse-speaking areas of the Hebrides and Northern Isles. The divergence of Scots Gaelic from the Irish probably began in the tenth century.

The Picts acquired the ogham alphabet from the Irish of Dalriada in the sixth or seventh century, and ogham inscriptions, all of which are unintelligible, appear on some Class I Pictish symbol stones. There are, however, only two ogham-inscribed memorial stones from Dalriada, one from near Dunadd, the other from the island of Gigha.[55]

Placenames belonging to the Dalriadic phase are known:[56] the name *sliabh* meaning a 'hill' is almost entirely confined to Dalriada but with a scatter in Pictland. It is related to the placename element *slew* which has been used as evidence for Irish settlement in the Rinns of Galloway (Fig. 21).

The most important site of the period in Dalriada is the nuclear fort of *Dunadd* (Fig. 22), a rocky outcrop in the Crinan Moss, now drained but once a serious barrier to would-be attackers. The first reliable reference to the occupation of the site was in 683, when an Irish annalistic entry refers to a siege of Dunadd or *Duinatt* by Fearchar Fadha, at a time when another nuclear fort, Dundurn, was also besieged. The *Annals of Tigernach* also refer

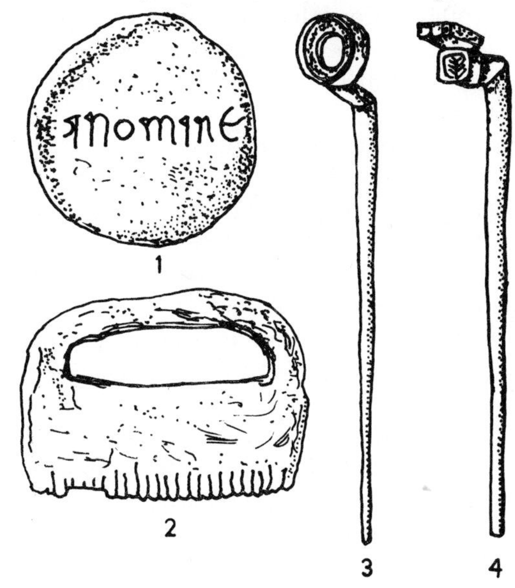

Figure 23 Objects from Dunadd. (1) Stone disc; (2) Iron saw; (3) Projecting headed pin; (4) Hand-pin. All actual size except (2), which is ½

to a further siege and capture of the site by Oengus mac Fergus, king of the Picts, in 736. Historically, then, occupation is known in the seventh and eighth centuries, and the archaeological finds from the site attest an earlier occupation.

The excavation at Dunadd at the start of this century left little undisturbed for subsequent excavation in 1929. The defences are stone built with traces of stone buildings within, one of which, at least, seems from the report to have been rectilinear. Within the fort is a carving of a boar and an incised footprint, which is similar to other 'inauguration' footprints, paralleled at the Iron Age site of Clickhimin, Shetland. The boar is stylistically related to Class I Pictish symbol stones, and is of sixth- or more probably seventh-century date.

The finds start with a Neolithic carved stone ball, presumably imported to the site, a fragment of a food vessel (Bronze Age), some sherds of Roman pottery, and finally a series of objects of Early Christian date. Among the distinctively Irish objects are slot-headed iron implements, a long-handled iron saw and an iron comb (p. 296). A hand-pin of sixth-century date could be Irish or indigenous, while an unfinished incised carving on a piece of stone depicts a type of penannular brooch common in seventh-century Ireland. The pottery consists mainly of E Ware, together with the sub-Roman classes D and F. The absence of A and B Wares, and the presence of certain bronzes and moulds for bronzes (notably penannular brooches), indicates that the site was occupied from the end of the fifth or beginning of the sixth century (Fig. 23).

Among the finds are a carved stone with late interlace and an enamelled bronze disc with skein ornament. A stone is inscribed (I) NOMINE in a script akin to Irish minuscule of the seventh century, which attests the presence of literate Christians in the fort. As on most sites occupied in the period the finds consist of nondescript 'Irish Sea province' metalwork, both iron and bronze, and copious evidence for metal working.

Few other sites in Dalriada have produced evidence for occupation during the Early Christian period. Of particular note, however, is a crannog in *Loch Glashan*, Argyll, excavated in 1960.[57] The crannog was built up of brushwood laid on the mud in the loch on the landward side, and layers of logs, sometimes revetted with stones, laid on top of the brushwood on the other side. Piles were sunk into the lake round the perimeter and there was a scatter of stones on the surface. Two structural phases were recognized, the first associated with a rectangular structure, about 25 feet by 15 feet, defined by substantial parallel oak timbers, the tops of some of which were flattened, possibly to serve as a floor. The north-east end was paved with stone slabs, and may have had a hearth. The rectangular building was replaced by a circular hut, about 12 feet in diameter, and may have been preceded by an earlier structure, which could not be properly examined as it was below water level.

The finds included a large number of wooden objects, such as a trough, four trough-like bowls, a paddle, a scoop, pegs and pins. There was also a considerable amount of scrap leather, including fragments of sheaths, shoes and a jerkin. Metal finds included an iron bearded axe and a penannular bronze brooch, perhaps originally silvered and set with amber or brown glass. Numerous querns were recovered, and the pottery was E Ware. The site compares very closely with Irish crannogs, such as Ballinderry 2, and on the evidence of the brooch and E Ware can be dated between the sixth and ninth centuries.

Raths – a type of settlement found in Ireland – do not occur in Dalriada. Instead, there are 'duns', at least some of which were occupied in the Early Christian period. One good example at *Kildonan Bay*, Kintyre, has been excavated (Fig. 24). It had a stone-built wall 14 feet thick at its widest point and enclosing a roughly triangular area some 63 feet by 42 feet across. First a wall of half the thickness of the final defence was constructed, with outer facing revetments and an inner rubble core. Various intramural features were then built, notably a cell and staircase, and finally the gaps between these features were filled up and the inner wall faced, somewhat roughly. Inside, the floor level was made up on the bedrock to provide an even surface; in places the deposit was 4 or 5 feet deep. The fort was entered by a narrow

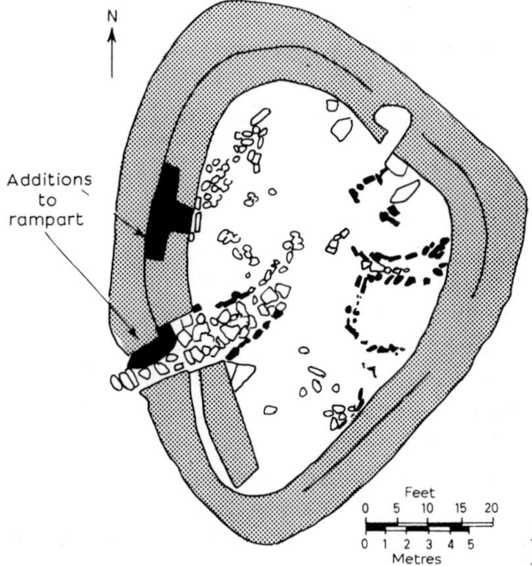

Figure 24 Dun at Kildonan, Argyll. Period II Plan

passage, ending with a trip step, at the end of which was a guard chamber furnished with a hearth. This entrance arrangement seems to have been a secondary modification of a simple passage with door checks and barhole, the original width being reduced by additional masonry. Within the fort were small, roughly circular huts, and areas of rough paving. The site was re-occupied in the fourteenth century. The period of main occupation of the dun at Kildonan is difficult to calculate: evidence would point to the Early Christian occupation lying within the seventh to eighth centuries, and a brooch which may belong to either one of the first two phases should probably be assigned to the seventh century rather than later. Another find of half a red and yellow enamelled disc also points to a date probably not later than the seventh century. Pottery from the Early Christian period occupation was coarse, reddish-brown, and showed simple, rounded, upright rims. Other finds included a spearhead, knives, two beads, moulds, a crucible and the usual range of whetstones, stone discs, whorls, iron nails, bronze fragments and querns. In all, the assemblage had much in common with the material from Dunadd. A sherd of samian ware led the excavator, Fairhurst, to postulate that the fort was occupied or built before the Early Christian period, but samian ware occurs frequently on post-Roman sites and is not significant.

Near the Kildonan dun at *Ugadale Point* is a small stack fort. It utilized the natural defences of a rock stack. On the flat crest an irregular univallate rampart enclosed a roughly rectangular area about 63 feet by 37 feet, and an inner revetment held back the rampart for part of its course at least. The only excavated structure within the fort was post-medieval, but finds from the site included beads, a bronze needle, jet armlet fragments and crucible fragments. These finds, particularly the beads, indicate occupation in the seventh to eighth centuries, and other Argyll stack forts of similar type are equally likely to have Early Christian occupation.

In Bute, the fort of *Little Dunagoil* was occupied in the period and has produced E Ware.

Monasteries

Although later than the Irish colonization, the Irish-founded monasteries of Dalriada are of importance in understanding the archaeology of the area as a whole. The greatest, *Iona*,[58] was founded in 567 by Columba, who had probably crossed over to this remote island to serve a community of already Christian Irish. There was another foundation at *Lismore*, on the Firth of Lorne, which was founded traditionally by St Moluag, whose death is recorded in the Irish annals for 592. Two other early Irish monastic foundations were probably in Pictish territory, that at Eigg, in the Inner Hebrides, and Applecross in Wester Ross, the latter founded by St Maelrubha from Bangor *c.* 673, and maintaining connections with its parent monastery until the ninth century.

The status of *Kingarth*, Bute, is difficult to assess.[59] Traditionally, it was founded by St Blane in the sixth century. Blane (Blaan) is called a bishop in Irish martyrologies, and another bishop of Kingarth is mentioned in the same source. The Irish *Annals* give obits of bishops of Kingarth for the years *c.* 659 and 688, while the obits entered under the years 737, 776 and 790 are for abbots. It might be inferred from this that until the early eighth century Kingarth was the seat of a diocese, and thereafter became a full monastery, possibly as a result of the transference of a community from elsewhere. Whatever the truth of the matter, the site at Kingarth is of some complexity, and although many of the structural phases visibly postdate the Viking raids, the stone-built vallum (or more strictly cashel wall), some small cells and some fragmentary grave-slabs probably belong to the eighth century. As at Iona, the vallum is not a simple, single period structure but has subsidiary enclosure walls. A small ringfort associated with the site may be a rath of Irish type, but could be an earlier, Iron Age fort, as is the case of Dun Bhuirg, Iona.[60]

Iona was undoubtedly the most important of the Irish monastic foundations, partly because of the personal standing of Columba and his successors. Iona's role in the conversion of the northern Picts cannot seriously be doubted, even if the literal truth of Bede's assertion that Iona had the leadership over the monasteries of the Picts is not accepted. Little is known about the early monastery contained within the vallum (discussed p. 377), though it may be inferred that the buildings were of timber. However, the early monastery was situated in all likelihood round the rock outcrop known as Torr Abb, where a hut, complete with stone bed, has been excavated. However, on Dun Bhuirg a hut excavated to the north-east of the fort had been constructed in a similar fashion, with a roof of bundles of heather resting on poles bedded in the walls. The pottery from this hut was related to broch and wheelhouse wares, implying that it was pre-Columban.[61] In view of this, the attribution of the hut on Torr Abb to the time of Columba must remain speculative. Round Torr Abb, however, were traces of structures possibly connected with the first monastery. Near the rebuilt medieval abbot's house an area of metal working was dated to the seventh century from a sherd of A Ware stratified above it. Also belonging to the early phase of the monastery was grass-marked pottery, possibly of Irish origin, some early inscribed grave-slabs, which can be paralleled at Clonmacnois, and a small bronze human head of the seventh or eighth century.[62]

Iona has also produced free-standing high crosses, including St Martin's and St John's Crosses (Plates 20–2). These are probably of the ninth century, and while Irish in character may have been influenced by the inspiration of 'Boss Style' Pictish sculpture. The precise relationship between the Iona school of sculpture and the Irish high crosses has been in dispute; Stevenson has advanced a case for the Iona crosses having influenced the Irish, rather than vice versa.[63] Iona was to remain an important centre in the later development of the west Highland school of sculpture, and another high cross on the island, MacLean's Cross, dates from the fifteenth century. Related to the Iona school, the exceptionally fine ninth-century cross at Kildalton, Islay, is an outlier (Plate 21).

Orkney and Shetland

There can be little reason to doubt that Pictish influence extended to the Northern Isles as both the documentary sources and the distribution of Pictish stones of Class I and II in the Northern Isles suggest. It is likely, however, that the political control of the Picts in the Northern Isles did little to affect the native population, who enjoyed a continuity of tradition from the Iron Age.

Brochs continued in use only until around the second century AD and thereafter ceased to be occupied as such, though the sites in many cases have produced evidence of occupation continuing until the period of Norse settlement in the early ninth century. The cause was probably a period of peace, brought about by the preoccupation of the main enemies of the broch people, the mainlanders, with the force of military Rome. For a time at least the old brochs seem to have been kept in good repair; at the Broch of Gurness, Aikerness, on the Orkney mainland, a bastion was built round the broch

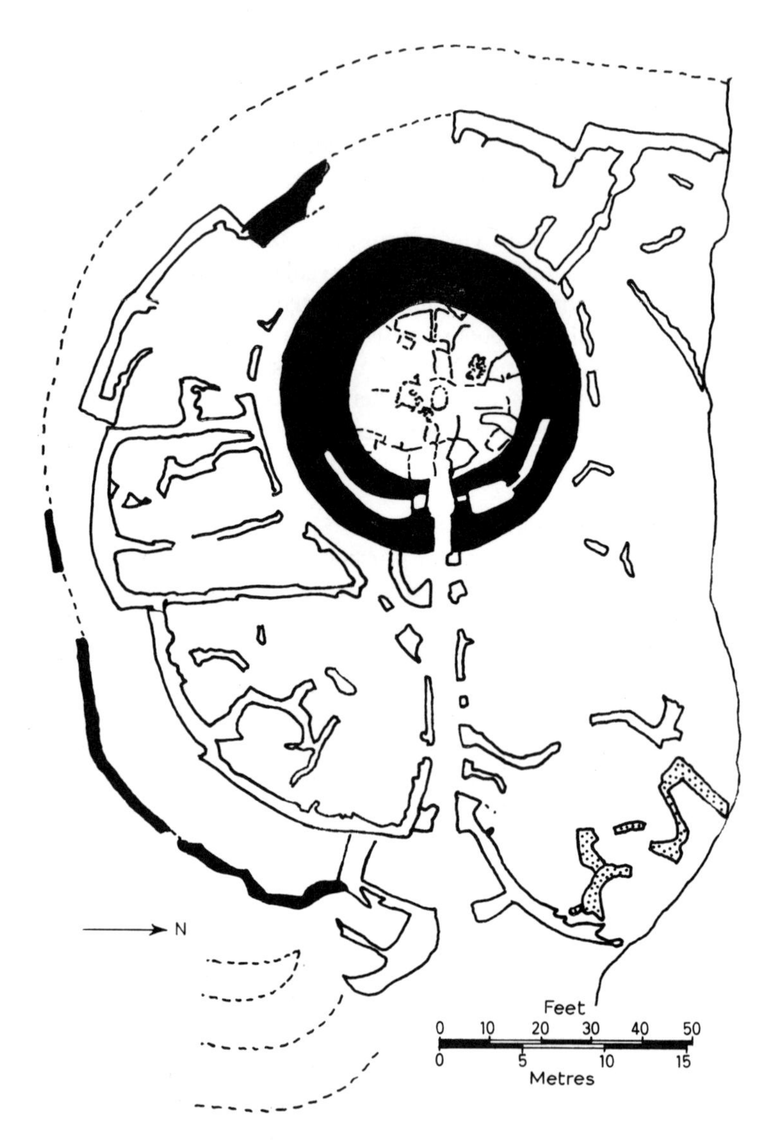

Figure 25 Aikerness, Broch of Gurness. Heavy lines indicate broch period structures

platform, while at Midhowe on Rousay there were secondary additions to the stone rampart (Fig. 25). Inside the brochs themselves the open court was divided up into more manageable units with the aid of sandstone partitions. This happened both in the Isles, as at Midhowe or Gurness, and on the north mainland, as at Carn Liath, Caithness. Gradually as the brochs fell into decay the stone was used to construct complexes of stone huts which clustered round the base of the ruined broch and gradually began to encroach upon it, exemplified by Midhowe, Gurness and Lingro in Orkney or Carn Liath.

In Shetland there was a more marked transition. At Jarlshof part of the courtyard wall of the broch was taken down to build a roundhouse with some broch-like features, notably an internal timber range. At a secondary stage radial stone piers were inserted, turning the house into something more akin to the roundhouses of the earlier Bronze and Iron Ages of the Northern Isles. This house-building phase was followed, probably around the third century, by the appearance of wheelhouse builders, themselves the descendants of the broch builders, who constructed a wheelhouse which remained the basic settlement unit on the site until the arrival of the Vikings in the ninth century. At Clickhimin, following the decay of the broch, a wheelhouse was built within the ruin. Wheelhouse occupation of a similar nature is associated with a number of other brochs, including Mousa and Clumland.

Wheelhouses spread from Shetland to the Hebrides and did not exist in Orkney. The typical wheelhouse consisted of a circular drystone building with radial piers like the spokes of a wheel dividing up the interior into compartments, roofed with corbelled slabs about 9 or 10 feet above floor level. On average wheelhouses were about 30 to 40 feet in diameter. In the centre or 'hub' of the wheel was an open hearth.

Hamilton has seen the wheelhouses of Shetland as being derived from the older stone hut or 'courtyard house' tradition of the Shetland Bronze and Iron Ages, and has suggested that the compartments with radial piers are simply an elaboration of earlier side cubicles.[64] Certainly the evidence from Jarlshof suggests that the development of the wheelhouse was a Shetland phenomenon, and at Jarlshof the emergence of the true wheelhouse can be seen from a transitional phase in which aisled wheelhouses were constructed, with a gap between the radial piers and the outer wall, tied with stone lintels. An alternative explanation is that the radial piers developed out of the supports of the internal timber ranges.[65] The development from the transitional stage of the 'aisled wheelhouse' to the wheelhouse proper may have resulted from the inadequacy of the aisled construction for supporting the roof, and at Jarlshof one pier was blocked up in an aisled wheelhouse for just this reason.

The adoption of the wheelhouse suggests that there was also a change in family structure in Shetland (and judging by the character of post-broch structures also in Orkney and Caithness), with a reversion to the small unit rather than the larger group involved in stone fort building and occupation.

Frequently wheelhouses were constructed in isolation, away from broch sites, as is almost invariably the case in the Hebrides. In Shetland occupation continued within the older brochs, despite the crumbling masonry which must have posed a serious threat to the occupants.

A date for the beginning of the wheelhouse phase and the end of the brochs is available, since many of the sites in the Northern Isles have produced Roman imports.[66] A fragment of glass of the late first or early second century came from the early wheelhouse occupation at Clickhimin, while at Dun Mhor Vaul in the Hebrides Roman glass and samian pottery indicate a date in the second century for the end of the broch. At Lingro in Orkney the post-broch settlement produced two coins of Antoninus Pius (138–61 AD) and a bone parallelopiped die which was associated with a coin of Crispina (180–3 AD). Presumably these date from the end of the broch period. Roman pottery has been found in secondary levels at Midhowe and Aikerness (Orkney) and Keiss (Caithness), all suggesting that the wheelhouse phase began in the second or third century.

Wheelhouse culture generally is remarkably conservative. At Clickhimin, fluted rims and double rims continue the tradition of broch and pre-broch pottery. The wheelhouse period pottery at Jarlshof represents a new tradition, but it too is ultimately derived from that of the brochs. There were a few innovations: notched slate sticks were used to separate the ear from the corn stalk in harvesting. They also modified the field system at Jarlshof, the result of improved farming techniques.

Metal working continued, and from Jarlshof have come the remains of mould gates and moulds, as well as iron lumps and a ring-headed bronze pin of the type familiar in broch horizons. At Jarlshof and Clickhimin were found a curious series of painted stone pebbles, similar to those from secondary occupation levels at Keiss and Burrian. Their function is unknown, but may have been connected with a cult.

At some point in time the wheelhouse people of Jarlshof became Christian – a rough slab with a cross incised on it was recovered from wheelhouse levels. At Jarlshof the final phase before the arrival of the Norse involved the occupation of a couple of huts and an associated earthhouse. This building, the Passage House, consisted of a long sloping passage over 25 feet in length leading to three chambers, with walls built of upright slabs supporting horizontal facing stones. It was probably first used as a habitation, and subsequently as a byre.

At Clickhimin the final phase of occupation was equally impoverished, and there was a tendency to dig huts or storage pits into the earlier middens. During the earlier period the strait which separated the island from the mainland had silted up, and a causeway was constructed, over 80 feet long, possibly in order to drive cattle to the islet. The most remarkable feature of this final phase is a stone in the threshold of the gateway, which bears the mark of two 'footprints' with a circular depression at either end, between the toes and between the heels. Such footprints are known from elsewhere in

Scotland – Dunadd, for example – and are traditionally associated with the inauguration of kings. There is an example in Orkney, now at St Mary's Church on South Ronaldsay.

The story so clearly told by the occupation of Clickhimin and Jarlshof in the post-broch period is not so clear in Orkney and the mainland, for most of the sites were excavated in the nineteenth century and so far there has been no recent excavation published to give a properly documented sequence. (Plate 3B) It is clear, however, that although wheelhouses, themselves were not built (though there are related structures), the general cultural tradition was the same as that in Shetland, and the pottery of the wheelhouse period at Jarlshof tallies favourably with the post-broch pottery from Orcadian sites.

Recently a new class of habitation site has been recognized as belonging to this period in Orkney and the Hebrides. This is the figure-of-eight house, one of which has been excavated at Buckquoy, Birsay (Orkney).[67] The Buckquoy house was probably Pictish, and produced bone pins, iron knife blades, pottery, a painted pebble and an ogham-inscribed spindle whorl. Beneath it was an earlier celled structure of more usual post-broch Orcadian type. Figure-of-eight houses are well represented in the Hebrides at the Udal, North Uist (p. 86).

Documentary evidence suggests that a rebellion of Orkney necessitated the presence of the subregulus of Orkney in Bridei mac Maelcon's Pictish court at the time of Columba's visit. The 582 campaign led by Bridei mac Bile was probably also to put down insurrection. There was certainly a strong tradition, evidenced by Nennius, Bede and Gildas, that Orkney came under Pictish rule, and even earlier, at the turn of the fourth century, Claudian referred to the Picts in Shetland.[68]

There are nine Pictish symbol stones from Orkney, of which more than half have come from recorded contexts, mostly brochs, one being used as a partition slab in a post-broch hut. Shetland has produced more Pictish oghams than any other Scottish county, while the Northern Isles together have produced more than half the recorded total from Scotland. It has already been noted that these Pictish oghams mainly date from the eighth century, and the script was adopted from the Dalriadic Scots (p. 51). It is perhaps not fanciful to suppose that their abundance in the Northern Isles is the outcome not only of a strong Pictish element in the population, but also of an Irish element. The name Nechton (Nehton) appears on a stone from Lunnasting, while the Scottic element is suggested by the use of the formula *meqq* and also the use of *crossc* (a version of the Irish name for 'cross') on the Bressay stone. This Irish element was probably supplied by Irish clerics – the Papae who have given their names to many places in the Northern Isles, such as Papil.

An account set down around 1200 by a Norse writer states that the Orkneys were first inhabited by the Picts (Peti) and Irish-Scottish priests (Papae) and that the Picts were little more than pygmies who did wonders in the morning and evening, building towns, and at midday completely lost their strength and hid themselves in underground houses. It also reports that the Orkneys were called Pictland (*terra Petorum*) and that the Papae were so called on account of their white robes. The reference here to underground houses is particularly significant, bearing in mind the Passage House of the final pre-Norse phase at Jarlshof.

Some Scandinavian placenames in the Northern Isles incorporate elements that imply the presence of Picts, such as Pettadale (valley of the Picts), Petester (homeland of a Pict), or Pettafell (mountain of the Picts), while the Pentland Firth itself means 'firth land of the Picts'. While no obviously Pictish names survive in the Northern Isles, there is a stratum of Celtic names, with Goidelic elements, presumably introduced by the Irish, together with a few others which are not Irish such as *maen, penn, tref* and *pitt*, but which cannot with any certainty be ascribed to the Picts.

The Hebrides

It is difficult to determine to what extent the Hebrides were Pictish. Skye was almost certainly dominated by the Picts for a while, but the archaeological evidence for the period has produced almost no material which can be ascribed definitely to any historically known peoples. The migrants from England in the Iron Age who developed the broch in the Hebrides may also have introduced the aisled farmhouse, which is a stone version of the 'Little Woodbury' type of house of southern England, the shortage of wood in the islands necessitating stone building. Two examples have been excavated, Clettraval (Uist) and Allasdale (Tigh Talamhanta) on Barra. These two sites were probably cattle farms, since the absence of querns and their situation on open moorland suggests that they were not, like Little Woodbury, agricultural. Allasdale was occupied probably in the first or second century AD, to judge from a copy of a Roman fantail brooch of 'Aesica' type found there. Clettraval, which may have been occupied slightly earlier, has pottery showing strong Wessex influence (it gives its name to the Clettraval Style).

The aisled farmhouses of the Hebrides are comparable with the round-houses of Jarlshof and the 'aisled wheelhouses' there. The wheelhouse was probably introduced to the Hebrides from Shetland (p. 81). Hebridean wheel-houses are frequently termed 'earth houses' in excavation reports, as they were usually partly dug down into the surrounding sand.

As in the Northern Isles, the wheelhouses of the Hebrides had a long continuity. At *a' Cheardach Mhor* (Fig. 26) five phases of occupation were recognized, the first with degenerate Clettraval ware probably of the second century AD, though bone pins of 'Roman' type might suggest a slightly later date. The finds from phases I–III were closely comparable to those from Dun Cuier, Barra, where the main occupation was probably of the fifth to sixth century. Phase IV takes the sequence well into the Early Christian period, when a squatter hut was built within the wheelhouse with robbed slabs, associated with a ringed pin, another bone pin, and a sherd of what is probably Class B amphora. This, together with other finds, implies a sixth-century

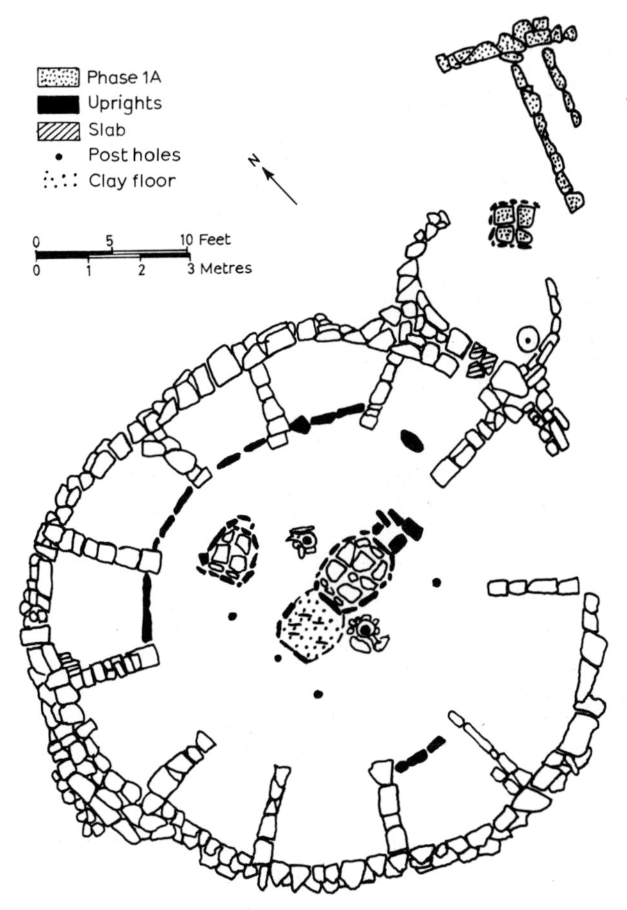

Figure 26 a' Cheardach Mhor, South Uist (After Young)

date for this phase of occupation. The structure shows close similarities to the Passage House at Jarlshof. A final phase, V, was represented by a scatter of finds, including a spindle whorl, a composite bone comb and an iron knife, all of Early Christian type.

Another wheelhouse at Garry Iochdrach, North Uist, produced a fourth-century Roman coin, though the precise context is not certain, while samian ware was found at Bac Mhic Connain, Vallay. Both *Bac Mhic Connain* and *Foshigarry*, though producing evidence of occupation at least as early as the third century AD, have also produced later material. From the former comes a unique knife handle with an inscription in Pictish ogham, while from the latter comes a fine bone composite comb with ring-and-dot decoration as well as some bone pins which appear to be copies of Early Christian bronze types.

A further category of settlement is represented in the Hebrides only at *Coileagean an Udail* (The Udal) on North Uist.[69] This comprises the figure-of-eight houses encountered also in Orkney. The Udal houses consisted of a small

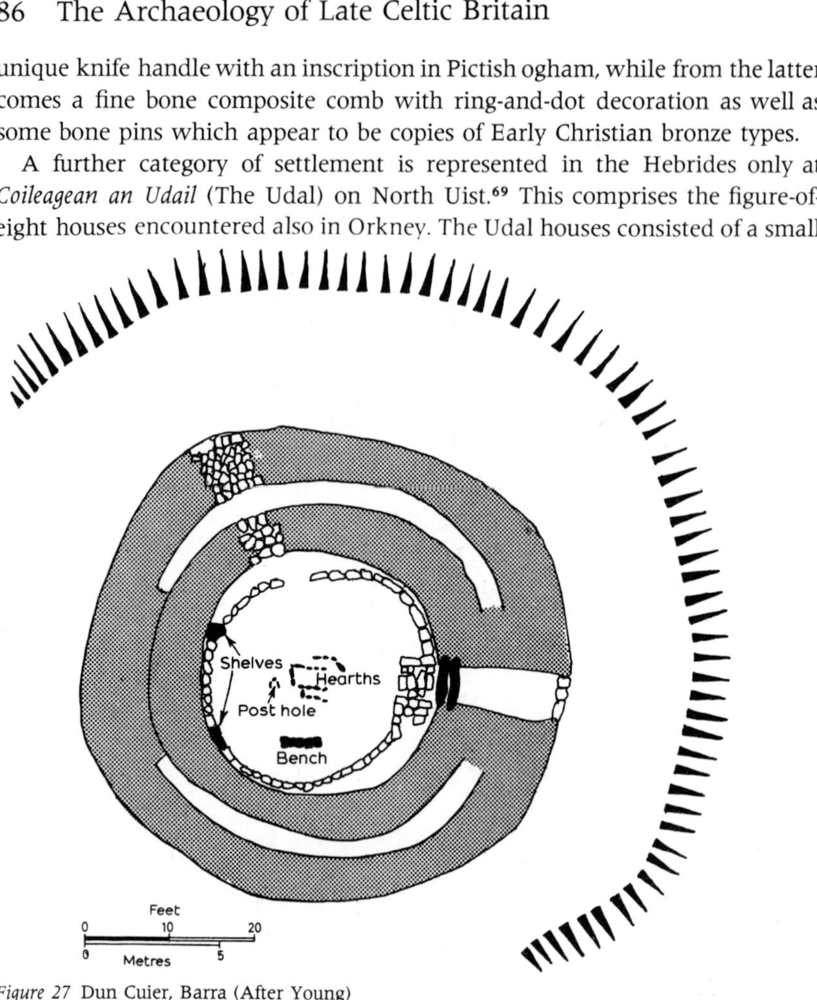

Figure 27 Dun Cuier, Barra (After Young)

circular cell leading from a larger ovoid chamber, with one or more turret-like rooms lying along little corridors off the main building. The main room contained slab-lined and floored hearths flanked by low revetments for sleeping platforms. Uprights in the revetting took the roof. Associated with the houses were outbuildings. The finds included elaborate bone combs, gaming pieces, crucibles, clay-moulds, bronze pins, decorated bone pins, iron knives, a fish spear, pottery, including two possible sherds of imported Mediterranean red painted ware, and worked whalebone. These houses postdate a wheelhouse-building phase, which seems to have ended with a squatter occupation some time between the second and fifth centuries. The phase represented by the figure-of-eight houses spans the period from *c.* 400 AD until the coming of the Norse.

Dun Cuier, Barra (Fig. 27), is a galleried dun, utilizing the natural rock surface, consisting of three separate walls, an outer, an inner and a main wall, approached by a paved entrance passage. The majority of the finds were indeterminate, but included, in addition to a decorated bone comb, baggy, undecorated pottery which has been suggested was the result of Irish influence from Dalriada (see p. 283).[70] There are a number of similar galleried duns in the Hebrides, which in so far as they can be dated, fall within the Early Christian period.

There are a number of factors which argue against the influence from Dalriada in the Western Isles. The most important is that the pottery from Dun Cuier, while superficially similar to the crude shapes of Irish souterrain ware, cannot be closely paralleled in Ireland and lacks the characteristic 'grass marking'. If the tradition were intrusive from Dalriada it would be expected to occur there too – in fact similar pottery is almost totally absent. The Hebridean pottery of this Dun Cuier phase (it is represented on a number of other sites, including a' Cheardach Mhor) probably represents a coarse tradition parallel to that of the Passage House phase at Jarlshof, and is simply a degenerate version of the long-established local tradition.

There is very little evidence in favour of Irish influence in the Hebrides, and the post-broch Hebridean sequence should be seen in terms of a native culture upon which some new elements were imposed – first wheelhouse architecture, then certain types of bone equipment, most notably pins and combs. It is possible that wheelhouses gradually went out of use in the Early Christian period in favour of less substantial stone buildings, sometimes using wheelhouse sites, and open settlement on the machair and sand dunes. A considerable quantity of material, including Early Christian objects such as bronze pins, is known from casual finds on sand-dune sites in the Hebrides. The duns may represent a revival of the old traditions of fortification in much the same way that forts appear to have been reoccupied or in a few instances constructed for the first time in other parts of Scotland.

The Church in northern Scotland

The question of the date of the conversion of the Picts to Christianity is debatable, dependent as it is on the interpretation of the career of Ninian. Bede asserted that the southern Picts had been converted to Christianity by Ninian prior to the time of Columba. Because it is not generally held that Ninian was engaged in active missionary work outside south-west Scotland, this statement of Bede's has sometimes been doubted.[71] Recently, however, Thomas has pointed out that long-cist cemeteries, a feature of fifth- and sixth-century Christianity in Scotland, occur in considerable numbers on both sides of the Forth, the traditional British–Pictish boundary, and has suggested that the population in this region may have been to some extent a British–Pictish mixture, and the Picts of this region may have been converted at an early date to Ninianic Christianity by the British.[72] Whatever the truth of this, the conversion of the northern Picts seems to have followed the activities of Columba. By the end of the seventh century, Pictland appears to have been Christian. The date of the conversion of the Northern Isles has similarly been disputed, but probably follows the visit of Cormac, the follower of Columba, to the Northern Isles around 575, and the appearance in the Isles of the Papae, or Irish clerics.[73] The conversion of the Western Isles also probably followed activity by the Dalriadic Church. The Pictish Church was essentially monastic, but very little is known of its organization; it appears to have conformed to the organization of the Columban Church. The late seventh century was dominated in Pictish ecclesiastical affairs by the Easter controversy; around 710 it terminated with a reform of the Pictish Church by Nechtan mac Derelei, who took the Roman side in the controversy and brought Pictland in line with Northumbria. Thereafter the history of the Pictish Church is confused until its disappearance in the ninth century.[74]

Archaeologically, apart from the few stone structures already mentioned (p. 71) very little is known about the church in Pictland outside the Isles. The important monastic foundation at *Applecross*, Wester Ross, (p. 78) was founded probably in the seventh century, and traces of the oval vallum remain.[75] Surviving remains on a number of chapel sites or sites of possible minor monasteries indicate, however, that the ecclesiastical structures were similar in Pictland to those found elsewhere in the Celtic west.

More information is available about some of the known sites in the Northern and Western Isles.[76] At *Papil*, West Burra (Shetland), the modern churchyard wall is built on top of a roughly rectilinear vallum, and the present ruined church, built in 1815, is situated on top of an earlier chapel (Plate 10B). The site has produced a famous Pictish cross slab (the Papil stone), a second cross slab and the remains of one single and one double corner-post shrine. Although probably converted through Irish activity, the Northern Isles show in the eighth century signs of Northumbrian influence, such composite shrines being one manifestation of it. In Orkney, traces of the vallum of the important monastery on the *Brough of Birsay* along with associated burials were found on excavation predating the later Norse graveyard, while at *Deerness* in Orkney, at *Birrier*, Yell, and *Northmavine*, Kame of Isbister, there are good examples of small eremitic monasteries on isolated stacks, once joined to the mainland by land-bridges. Of the chapel sites two good examples are those on *St Ninian's Isle*, Shetland, and at *Markwick*, Orkney, the latter possibly of Norse date.

In addition to the Dalriadic sites the site of *Eileach an Naoimh* in the Garvellochs has a small monastery with graveyard, chapel and beehive cells reminiscent of those at Skellig Michael (Plate 8A). The remains of circular cells are also present at *Annait*, on Skye, a small monastic foundation on a promontory, while a further eremitic monastery within a stone-built cashel wall of roughly circular shape is situated at *Sgor Nam Ban-Naomha*, on Canna.

4 Wales and the Isle of Man

Apart from rich epigraphic material of the fifth to seventh centuries, a few settlements and a series of later sculptured stones, Wales has very few archaeological remains until the period of Norman penetration. The documentary evidence is more rewarding though confused.

The pre-Roman and Roman Iron Age

While there is a certain amount of early pottery comparable to 'Iron Age A' wares in England, except for some from sites in the Welsh Marches and some very late pottery from the south, Wales was virtually aceramic in the Iron Age. Even in the Marches, where the forts are far less impoverished than in the rest of Wales, pottery is very frequently of the 'VCP' (Very Coarse Pot) type which is probably ultimately derived from the Bronze Age and is unclassifiable and undatable. In the absence of diagnostic finds, types of field monuments have been used as a basis for the study of the Welsh Iron Age, but the limitations of this line of approach are obvious.

Throughout the Iron Age, hillforts are the dominant settlement type in Wales and their origins can be traced back to the late Bronze Age. Between the eighth and the fourth centuries BC a series of forts was built with timber-framed ramparts or double palisades enclosing complexes of square buildings. The overall pattern was of continuity from the Bronze Age through the Iron Age with new elements appearing from outside and the development of regional variations. It is noteworthy that some of the excavated Marches forts such as Midsummer Hill and Croft Ambrey show evidence of repeated rebuilding, the gateways having as many as fifteen reconstructions, a pattern reflected in the distribution and rebuilding of huts within the defences.[1] Such a pattern points to a continuous occupation of the forts from generation to generation.

Irish contacts with Wales are recognizable in the Iron Age; the Tal-y-Llyn hoard of ornamental metalwork shows that Welsh ornamental styles were partly related to those in Ireland, the transmission of ideas perhaps being connected with the Dublin–Holyhead trade route.[2] Similarly the small plateau and hilltop enclosures of south-west Wales and the associated concentric earthworks can be paralleled in the coastal areas of Connaught and Munster.[3] Stone ramparts with internal terracing and sometimes *chevaux de frise* are found in the same area with parallels in west Wales and Caernarvonshire.[4] Among the tribes of the later Iron Age was the Gangani which was located in the Lleyn peninsula, Caernarvonshire. It was a north-west Irish tribe, and its extension into Lleyn was a foretaste of the Irish settlements in the same area in the Early Christian period.

The Romans in Wales[5]

The initial cause of the Roman campaigns in Wales was unrest among the Silures and Ordovices in the south. The early campaigns were directed against the Silures, but in AD 61 attention was turned to Anglesey, where an unfinished campaign was completed by Agricola, who used Chester as a base to set up a string of forts and connecting roads in north Wales, his key fort being Caernarvon. Agricola's predecessor, Frontinus, had completed the conquest of south Wales where another series of forts, of which the most important was Caerleon, maintained control. Around AD 75, the Roman town of Caerwent was founded.

Except in the south, Roman control and influence was essentially military. Elsewhere civil Roman settlements did not exist, apart from the *canabae* that grew up round forts such as Caernarvon, though there is some evidence for industrial sites at Prestatyn and possibly Tremadoc. In the south, however, were the towns of Caerwent and Carmarthen and villas are known from Ely near Cardiff, Llantwit Major, and the vale of Glamorgan.

Roman material appears as trade objects on a variety of native sites in Wales. These sites fall into two main categories, hut groups and hillforts, and seem to span the entire period of Roman occupation.

Native settlements in Wales (Fig. 28) fall into six regional groups.[6] In the *south-west* such sites as Cwmbrwyn and Trelissey were occupied during the second and third centuries, and Roman pottery occurs on fortified sites such as Bosherton where the earthwork is pre-Roman. In the *south-east* there is enough first- and second-century pottery from native defended sites to indicate that the zone became civil at a later date. In *west and central Wales* native occupation of the Roman period is lacking, though there are many Iron Age hillforts. In the *north Marches* there is a single native type of farm, near the Breiddin, with a D-shaped banked and ditched enclosure. It had at least one round wooden hut, and evidence of Roman period iron working. Two styli suggest that the inhabitants were literate. The evidence from the *north-east* comes from the hillfort at Dinorben, where soon after the mid-third century a round house, 65 feet in diameter, was built in the abandoned fort. Most of the evidence, however, comes from the *north-west*, where there is a long tradition of stone-built hut groups. These enclosures fall into three main categories: (1) oval with thick walls, (2) oval with thin walls, (3) polygonal. In the last, an enclosing wall was set out in straight lines and angles, enclosing both round and rectangular huts. The entrance usually led through one of the

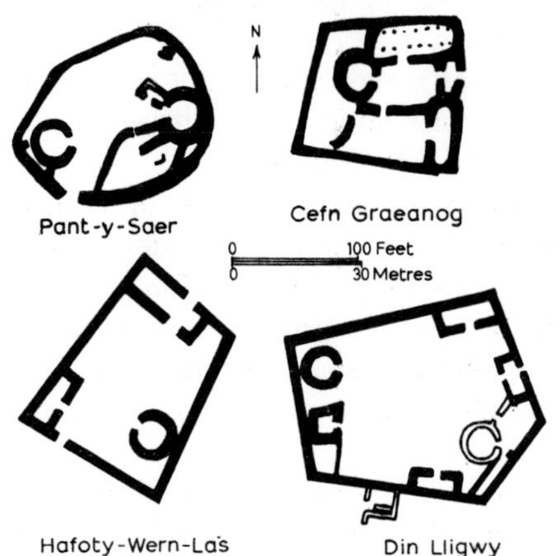

Figure 28 Welsh enclosed hut groups

rectangular buildings, which may have been a porter's lodge. The best examples are those from Hafoty-wern-Las, Din Lligwy and Graeanog.

The hut groups represent the homes of single families, though they may also have accommodated labourers who perhaps lived in the isolated huts sometimes found nearby. The main homestead stood in a block of farmland, usually about 15 acres, divided into terraced fields of various sizes. Most of them are on high ground, and have produced evidence of metal working. Generally, on excavation they indicate a low level of prosperity.

With the exception of Pant-y-Saer in Anglesey, there is no evidence for post-Roman occupation. A number of possible explanations have been forwarded; they could have been the result of deliberate Roman resettlement of a depopulated area, or settlement of an underpopulated area; or they could have been a natural evolution under Roman influence, of native Iron Age traditions. Certainly the rectilinear planning of the polygonal hut groups indicates Roman influence as it does in Cornwall and northern England. Most of the settlements were founded at a comparatively late date – some time in the early third century. It is possible that the rectilinear hut groups, if not the others too, represent an attempt by the Romans to settle mercenaries in the area as a defence against the third-century Irish raids.

Hillforts, too, show occupation in the Roman period, though there is no evidence for deliberate refortification. At Dinorben, the third- and fourth-century occupation sprawls over the defences. At Braich-y-Dinas, Penmaenmawr,[7] occupation continued throughout the Roman period, though most of the Roman finds came from between the ramparts. Din Silwy and Carn Fadrun hillforts also had probable occupation in the Roman period, and Tre'er Ceiri, in Lleyn, has produced much Roman material of the second to late third centuries.[8] Not all hillforts were occupied in the Roman period, but none the less there is enough evidence to indicate that the Romans tolerated native occupation of forts, presumably because the inhabitants were seen as convenient allies in the face of outside threats.

In south Wales this story is echoed to some extent at Coygan Camp where in the late third century a rectangular stone building and three smaller structures where built within the ruined Iron Age defences.

The Isle of Man, like Wales, was virtually aceramic for most of the Iron Age. In addition there are insufficient excavated sites to provide a framework for adequate study. There was no Roman occupation of the island which accordingly enjoyed a cultural continuity from the Iron Age to the Early Christian period. Hillforts in Man are relatively rare,[9] the two classic sites being *South Barrule* and *Cronk Sumark*, which dominate the southern and northern plains of the island.

The remaining Iron Age sites in Man fall into two general categories, promontory forts and a type of monument usually called after their excavator 'Bersu hut sites'. Of the promontory forts the most important is *Close ny Chollagh*, Scarlett.[10] Three 'Bersu hut sites' were excavated by Gerhard Bersu,[11] two at *Ballacaggan* and a third a mile away at *Ballanorris*. All three were in the flood plain of a river, and prior to excavation were recognizable as ring ditches. The three roundhouses were exceptionally large – from 70 to 90 feet in diameter, and their roofs were supported on seven concentric rings of posts, of which the third ring acted as a partition dividing the inner from the outer room. The economy of the inhabitants was essentially pastoral. Ox, sheep, pig and pony were represented in that order of frequency in the food bones. Rotary querns imply agriculture to some degree.

Only one settlement of the Early Christian period is known in Man – at Ronaldsway.[12] A full report is not available, but published finds suggest an occupation in the seventh or eighth century.

Irish raids and settlements

Around the turn of the third century Roman military policy in Wales was very probably directed against the Irish raids. Rebuilding at Chester took place on the west walls of the fort, and the Wroxeter forum seems to have been destroyed in a major raid. In the late third century the new fort at Lancaster was built, modelled on the Saxon Shore forts and in the time of Constantius Chlorus the forts at Caer Gybi on Holyhead and at Cardiff were constructed, probably as defences against the Irish.[13] Irish raids are reflected also in the pattern of late third-century coin hoards in Wales; these are mostly coastal in distribution, and while many end with coins of the Tetrici (AD 268–73), there is reason to suppose that they were not buried till the end of the century.[14] Almost half the coin hoards of Carausius and Allectus (AD 287–96) found in Britain have come from Wales. It is probable, however, that Allectus withdrew the garrisons of the Welsh forts as indicated by the absence of his coins from Caernarvon, Forden Gaer and Brecon Gaer.

An expulsion legend provides a key to the understanding of one of the main Irish settlements in Wales. The story of the 'Expulsion of the Desi' states that

> Eochaid, son of Artchorp, went over the sea with his descendants into the territory of Demed (Dyfed) and it is there that his sons and grandsons died. And from them is the race of Crimthann over there, of which is Teudor son of Regin, son of Catgocaun, son of Cathen, son of Cloten, son of Nougoy, son of Arthur, son of Petr, son of Cincar, son of Guortepir, son of Aircol, son of Triphun, son of Aed Brosc, son of Corath, son of Eochaid Allmuir, son of Artchorp.[15]

The same story tells of the slaying of Conn mac Cormaic and the partial blinding of Cormaic of Tara by Eochaid's brother. This event is also recorded in the *Annals of the Four Masters* for the year 265. Accordingly it was for long believed that the Expulsion of the Desi took place in about 270.[16] This is, however, probably too early.[17] Guortepir mac Aircol may be the Vortipor who was hated by Gildas in the sixth century, and if it is assumed that he ruled *c.* 530, which is in accordance with the date of Gildas, and that a generation might be about thirty years, the arrival of the Desi in Wales could be as late as 380.

It is quite possible that the Desi were invited over by the Romans as federates, for the Romans were still in control in south Wales at the end of the fourth century: the coin sequence at Cardiff continued until the time of Gratian (367–83) and at Caerleon to the time of Arcadius (395–408). At Caerwent coins and late Gallo-Roman metalwork indicate that town life still continued until 400.[18] Pertinent to this is the memorial stone from Castell Dwyran, Carmarthenshire (see p. 101).

The 'Expulsion of the Desi' is perhaps the most valuable documentary source for the Irish settlements in Wales, but it is not the only one. A ninth-century Irish document, *Cormac's Glossary*, makes interesting reference to the Irish settlements in western Britain.[19] It is a late attempt to explain, either by fact or fiction, the derivation of certain archaic words but it nevertheless draws on old tradition. The relevant text is quoted here:

> For at that time great was the power of the Gaels over the Britons. They had divided Alba among them into estates, and each of them knew his friends' abode. And the Gaels used to dwell to the east of the sea not less than in Scotia. And their dwellings and royal forts were built there. . . . Thus every tribe divided on that side for its property on its east was equal to that on the west, and they long continued in power, even after the coming of Patrick.[20]

The *Vitae* of Welsh saints (and less frequently Irish) refer to the Irish–Welsh contacts. One *Life of St Carannog* refers to Irish invasions, and another version refers to fighting between Irish and Welsh in Ceredigion.[21] In other saints'

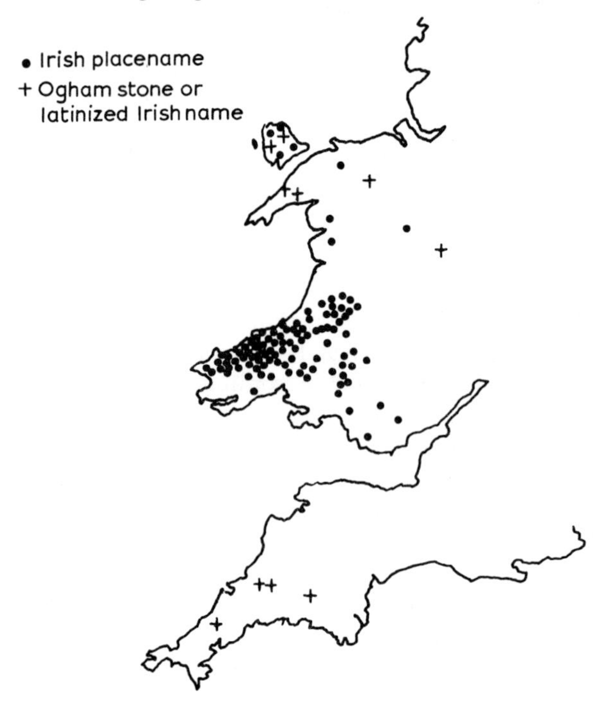

Figure 29 Irish placenames and ogham inscriptions in Wales and the south-west (After Richards *et al.*)

Lives there are references to the rulers of the Irish dynasty in Dyfed, namely Tryffin and Aergol. While these references are all late they point to a traditional sixth-century dynasty.[22] Ptolemy as early as the second century suggested an Irish connection when he called Lleyn the 'Promontory of the Gargani' (p. 90).[23]

The most important category of archaeological evidence for the Irish settlements in Wales is that of the memorial stones with ogham inscriptions of which fifty have been noted in Wales.[24] These stones are often inscribed with explicitly Christian formulae in Latin or in Irish ogham, or sometimes bilingually. Ogham was chiefly developed in southern Ireland, probably in the fourth century as a result of contact with Roman Christian civilization and the Roman alphabet. The ogham alphabet consisted of twenty letters, with additional symbols, which were arranged in sets of five along a guide line, usually the edge of the stone (Fig. 30). Ogham does not lend itself to complicated inscriptions, and was probably evolved either from a finger language or from a method of counting livestock on a tally stick. Initially it

Figure 30 The ogham alphabet

was probably put to secular and pagan recording. Because of the large number of ogham inscriptions in Wales it has been somewhat improbably suggested that it was developed by the Irish there and taken back to Ireland. Normally the Welsh ogham stones are cut along one or both angles of the face, reading from bottom to top and sometimes continuing across the top. Very occasionally the inscription reads up on the left and down on the right. Since many are bilingual, and the letters used in the Latin inscriptions are Roman capitals or mixed capitals and half uncials, the stones are datable to the fifth and sixth centuries, most of them antedating 550.

The ogham inscriptions follow very simple formulae. Usually they give the name of the deceased, in the genitive, with some introductory word meaning 'the stone' or 'the memorial' understood. In this category falls the stone from Brynkir, Caernarvonshire, with its inscription ICORIGAS – 'The stone of Icorix'. An extension of this formula gives the name of the father of the deceased, usually employing the word *Maqi*, meaning 'son of' with the second name in the genitive. Thus the inscription usually follows the pattern of the example from Nevern, Pembroke, with its inscription reading MAGLICUNAS MAQI CLUTARI, meaning '(the stone) of Maglicu, son of Clutarius'. Occasionally instead of *Maqi* are the words *Avi* (grandson or descendant), or *Inigenia* (daughter). A stone from Llangeler, Carmarthen, attempts to render the Latin formula HIC IACET in ogham. Most of the personal names recorded are Irish, but there are also a few Roman ones.

It must be remembered that ogham stones do not represent primary evidence for the Irish settlements in Wales, but rather the subsequent continuity of the Irish communities. The initial settlements were of pagan Irish. It seems probable that at a later phase Christianity was introduced to the already settled Irish in mainland Britain, with the ogham stones as its manifestation.

In this light the relatively sparse distribution of ogham stones in north Wales becomes more readily understood. By the time ogham memorials were in vogue among the Irish colonists, the Irish population in Lleyn had been largely assimilated. Also, and equally relevant, Lleyn was especially connected with northern Ireland, not the areas where ogham was widespread.

In north Wales by the fifth and sixth centuries the British dynasty of the descendants of Cunedda was well established, and it seems likely from the distribution of ogham stones that the boundary between the British-speaking tribes and the Goidelic-speaking Irish of south-west Wales lay along a line from the Dee to the Teifi. This indeed is implied by the Harleian genealogies. If the relative absence of ogham stones in north Wales reflects the domination of the sons of Cunedda, it might be asked why any ogham inscriptions are found there at all, especially in view of the statement by Nennius that Cunedda's sons held all the territory between the Dee and the Teifi and expelled all the Irish. The words 'expulsi sunt' in this text are probably used to mean not 'driven out' but 'relegated to an inferior position', and it is equally likely that there were for a long period enclaves of Irish in north Wales, until their subjection was completed in Caernarvonshire and Anglesey by Cadwallon in the seventh century. A reference in the *Life of St Carannog* suggests that Ceredig had to contend with an Irish influx fairly late in his life.[25]

Ogham stones are certainly the memorials of members of the ruling class. In a few cases continuity of their names can be traced in local placenames. An Anglesey stone, from Llanfaelog, has the name of Cunogusos, which is preserved in the neighbouring placename Pencaernisiog, a corruption of Conysiog.[26] Earlier forms of this are Comissok or Conussok. The *-iog* suffix is territorial and implies that Cunogusos was a ruler in the district.

Placename evidence itself provides useful corroboration of other sources of information.[27] The name given to western Caernarvonshire – Lleyn – incorporates the same element as the name Leinster. The district of Gwynedd seems to derive its name from *Feni*, the name of a group of people who appear to belong to the Connachta whose expansion was at the root of much displacement in Ireland in and around the fourth and fifth centuries AD. Single names such as Dinllaen and Llyn in Caernarvonshire, or Mallaen in Carmarthen, have a root probably derived from the proper name *Laigain*. Names which describe natural features such as river names, brook names or hill names are usually the oldest strata in placenames. Into this category fall names with the Irish suffix *-ach*, which usually appear as river names, or those incorporating the element *-cnwc* (a hillock), which stems from the Irish *-cnoc*. Another word of Irish derivation is *loch*, usually in the form *lloch* or *llwch*, the latter, however, being unreliable for plotting Irish settlement since it can also be a variant of a Welsh word for stagnant water. The distribution of *-cnwc* names is mainly in Pembrokeshire and Cardiganshire south of the Ystwyth, extending over to the upper reaches of the Teifi and Tywi and down into Carmarthen, with some outliers. This distribution corresponds well with the ancient boundaries of the kingdom of Dyfed as it was in the Early Christian period though certain areas had debatable frontiers.[28]

It is difficult to determine how early these Irish placenames are. Certainly they do not all date back to the fourth, fifth or sixth centuries, but their distribution must at least reflect fairly accurately where words borrowed from the Irish remained current. Irish was certainly being spoken in south-east Wales until the end of the sixth, and probably into the seventh century.

In addition there are church dedications to St David. While dedications are unreliable for tracing the activities of the saints concerned, dedications to St David are noticeably absent from north Wales, generally coinciding with the area of Irish settlement. Many elements in the *Life* of St David are Irish in origin, and it is quite possible that David settled in Pembroke to minister to an already Christian Irish community, as Ninian went to Whithorn or Columba went to Iona.

While not in itself evidence of Irish settlement, the linear earthwork known as the Clawdd Mawr corroborates the putative boundary of Dyfed in the Early Christian period.[29] This earthwork, similar in some respects to Offa's Dyke, or Wat's Dyke, consists of a single rampart and ditch running along high ground separating the Teifi and Tywi river valleys. It was probably constructed by the Irish-derived inhabitants of Dyfed as a defence in the eighth century, at a time when there was an expansion of Welsh-speaking peoples in the vale of Tywi.

There is very little archaeological evidence apart from the memorial stones for Irish settlement in Wales, or indeed anywhere else. This is not really surprising, since in the present state of archaeological knowledge specifically Irish objects of the fourth and fifth centuries, the period of primary Irish colonization, cannot be distinguished. The period from the fourth to the later sixth centuries was an era in which a great variety of traditions was available to craftsmen on either side of the Irish Sea, and a similar culture was shared by both British and Irish. Only in the sixth century can regional traditions be seen to emerge. Furthermore, at no point in time can a distinctively Irish cultural assemblage be recognized, as most types of objects were also common to the areas occupied by the Irish or the British.

There are objects of the seventh century and later of Irish provenance from the areas known to have been settled at an earlier date by the Irish, but their value as evidence is limited. They are too few in number to be statistically significant, and it is hardly necessary to argue the presence of Irish in a given area to account for a stray brooch or pin. Apart from Dunadd, Argyll, which has produced a range of material comparable with the assemblages from Irish sites, the only places to have produced groups of objects with Irish parallels are Lesser Garth Cave (Glamorgan) and Gwithian (Cornwall), though in neither case can the finds be regarded as conclusive evidence for an Irish culture.

The supposition that, once established on British soil, the Irish settlers proceeded to make and use the type of objects current in their homeland, and kept up their connections with Ireland generation after generation, is at best unlikely. In many cases the Irish were exiles who were unlikely to have maintained contacts with their homeland, more probably adopting the native culture of the area in which they settled, or evolving a culture of their own.

An important group of Irish finds in Wales comes from *Lesser Garth Cave*, Glamorgan.[30] The cave had prehistoric and Roman as well as Early Christian period occupation, of which the most distinctive find was a ring brooch of Irish type, with a pseudo-penannular head decorated with two scrolls. Although precise parallels for the type are difficult to find, examples date mainly from the eighth and ninth centuries in Ireland, a few being earlier, such as one from Lagore which is dated tentatively to the mid-seventh century. The Lesser Garth example is probably eighth century. Another object of Irish origin from Lesser Garth is an iron slotted-headed object of the type discussed on p. 296. Such objects appear to be exclusively Irish and cannot be closely dated, occurring down to the Viking period. In Britain they occur on two other sites with Irish associations, Dunadd and Gwithian.

Three other caves in Wales have produced Early Christian finds with Irish affinities. The best known is Minchin Hole, the other two being Bacon Hole and Culver Hole,[31] all in Gower. In the past the brooch from Bacon Hole has been described as Irish, but there is no reason for this identification since the type is also as common in Britain. Similarly a penannular brooch from Kenfig Burrows, Glamorgan, has frequently been described as Irish.[32] The type belongs to Class H1 (p. 308), of which the only recorded example comes from Lagore.

There is a pin with a double spiral head from Castlemartin Burrows, Pembroke, and a further double spiral-headed pin from Caerwent.[33] While some double spiral pins are now known to be Anglo-Saxon, the Welsh finds are almost certainly Irish. A ringed pin has been published from the site of Gateholm, Pembroke (p. 111), and has been unconvincingly suggested to be Irish.[34] Finally, a lead pattern for a penannular brooch from Dinas Powys, Glamorgan, belongs stylistically to the Irish series, though it has no precise counterpart. It dates from the sixth century and, along with the slight evidence for millefiori working on the same site, can perhaps suggest the presence of an itinerant Irish smith in south Wales.[35]

A series of circular earthworks or ringforts akin to Irish raths exist in Dyfed (roughly modern Pembroke) which are, however, clearly not the work of Irish settlers. One, Walesland Rath,[36] was recently excavated and shown to be Iron Age. Two others, Cwmbrwyn[37] and Trelissey,[38] enclose Roman buildings. They should probably be viewed within the general tradition of small forts in western and northern Britain, a class embracing duns in Scotland and rounds in Cornwall. There are a great many such earthworks in south-west Wales, and few have been investigated. Until more have been excavated the possibility that the Desi on reaching Wales took up an already existing tradition of ringfort building remains hypothesis.

Much of the evidence for the Irish settlements in the Isle of Man has been obliterated by centuries of Norse cultural overlay.[39] It would appear, however, that the first recognized dynasty of kings in Man had Brythonic names such as Tudwal (Tutuvallus), and dates from the fifth century. Manx, however, is a Goidelic language and from placenames and personal names it seems that Man changed its language from Brythonic (i.e. British) as a result of the Irish settlements there in the fifth century and possibly later. A few examples from the series of memorial stones have Brythonic names such as Andreas, in Latin and ogham, apparently of the fifth century. But by this time it is quite clear that Irish was being established in Man, and indeed the presence of ogham itself attests it. Man was not thickly populated at the time of the Irish settlements, could readily absorb immigrants, and was ideally situated in the 'Celtic Mediterranean'. A connection between Man and south-west Scotland, where there also appears to have been some Irish settlement, is suggested by the Brythonic tradition of early rulers associated with both, and on Man there are a number of dedications to Ninian (Trinian in the Manx form).

Early historical Wales

Except for a number of sculptured cross slabs and other stones which can confidently be ascribed to the period there is almost no other surviving material from the seventh to twelfth centuries in Wales. The absence of ornamental metalwork later than the sixth or seventh century must lead to the conclusion that it was not being produced. Of the settlement sites likewise nothing is known, though it is probable that there was continuation from the post-Roman pattern. If the *Laws* of Hywel Dda, formalized though they are, can be thought to reflect a realistic situation in Wales it would not be unreasonable to suspect the existence of open settlements similar to the Anglo-Saxon, at least in the less mountainous regions and the areas most susceptible to Anglo-Saxon influence. Earlier, in the time of Merfyn Vrych and his son Rhodri Mawr, there were connections between Gwynedd and the Continent, notably the court of Charles the Bald. In such a context some tangible evidence for the cultural revival that literary evidence attests, at least in ninth-century Gwynedd, might be expected. The contrary would seem to be the case, to judge from the degenerate style of Welsh sculpture.

'Maxen Wledig was emperor of Rome, and he was a comlier man, and a better and wiser than any emperor that had been before him.'[40] Thus begins the *Dream of Maxen Wledig*, a medieval Welsh romance which preserves a dim but favourable folk memory of the usurper Magnus Maximus. It is with Maximus that any study of early Welsh history should begin, for before he was killed at Trieste in 388 he had done 'some great and memorable thing' for Wales. What this was can only be inferred indirectly from other sources. The inference that can be drawn from the Pillar of Eliseg[41] is that no less an important figure than Vortigern married Maximus's daughter, and the frequent occurrence of Maximus in the genealogies, even though suspect, suggests that he was responsible for the organization that lay behind the formation of the early kingdoms of Wales. It is quite probable, in the light of current thinking, that he invited Cunedda to settle in Wales as a buffer against the Irish – the dating of the Cunedda episode (p. 93) seems to fit such a hypothesis.

Whether or not Maxen Wledig was personally responsible for the policy, it is quite clear that late Roman provincial organization left an ineradicable mark on Wales. The Roman policy of encouraging native allies to organize themselves in defence of depredations from without almost certainly underlay the formation of the early kingdoms, which, significantly, traced their origins back to late Roman founders.

In this context the story of Cunedda assumes a special prominence.[42] According to Nennius – who, to judge by his spelling of the name 'Cunedag', used a version of the story which dates back at least to the seventh century – Cunedda left that part of Gododdin (formerly the territory of the Votadini) known as Manau in the south-east of Scotland and migrated to Wales. He took with him all his sons except the eldest. In Wales, Cunedda held out against the Irish, and at his death the kingdom was divided between his sons, who founded independent kingdoms and probably expanded the territory ruled over by their father. Nennius relates that this event took place 146 years before the time of Maelgwn, who is known to be a contemporary of Gildas. This would place the event before AD 400.[43] Attempts have been made to compute the date through the genealogies, but these tend to be unreliable. Both Cunedda's father and grandfather had Roman names – Uetern (Aeternus) and Patern Pesrut (Paternus).

While the similarity between two spearheads and a bronze brooch from Kenfig in south Wales and finds from Traprain can be discounted as evidence for Cunedda's migration, the similarity between either the rectangular stone-built structures at Gateholm[44] and the final phase at Traprain,[45] or between the enclosed hut groups of the Votadini and those in north Wales, cannot be dismissed so easily. The only stone-built Welsh huts, however, which can with confidence be ascribed to a date after AD 400 are those from Pant-y-Saer[46] and Garn Boduan,[47] and there are comparably few of post-Roman date in the Votadinian areas. The similarity of the hut groups in both areas is probably due to a uniform Roman policy, though the polygonal hut groups do compare very closely with a class found in Northumbria. It is possible that Cunedda's followers, being in the habit of living in such dwellings, and finding them already present in Wales, continued to construct them.

All this evidence, slight though it is, is compatible with an early date for Cunedda's migration, and indeed such a migration is only explicable in terms of the federate policy in operation in late Roman Britain. The extent of the territory ruled over by the eight sons of Cunedda can probably be seen from the concentration of memorial stones with ogham inscriptions south of the river Teifi, with none to the north of it, suggesting that this was the boundary of the British expansion. Beyond lay terrain in which Irish would have been as familiar a language as Welsh. Certainly the memorial stones postdate the time of expansion of Cunedda's sons, but the significance remains. The evidence can be reinforced by the Clawdd Mawr,[48] a linear earthwork in north Carmarthenshire which probably demarcates the eastern boundary of Dyfed, constructed in the face of possible eastern expansion by the British dynasts. This can also be substantiated by a tenth-century genealogy appended to a version of Nennius, which lists Cunedda's sons and says, 'This is their boundary, from the Dee to the Teifi, and they held many districts in the western parts of Britain.'

While not all the Welsh kingdoms traced their dynastic origins back to the sons of Cunedda, all plotted them to the Roman period, and there seems to have been a ninth-century attempt to clarify the genealogies and provide a convenient retrospective explanation for their origins.

In Dyfed, the area settled by the Irish, there is some evidence for Romanizing elements, which has led Alcock to postulate that the Irish settlements of Dyfed were invited by Magnus Maximus, acting in the same way that Vortigern had when he had invited Hengist and Horsa to settle.[49]

The custom of inviting outside barbarians to settle and act as federates against other external threats seems to have been a widespread phenomenon, and certainly there is some echo of Roman military organization in the dynastic structure of Dyfed. The memorial stone from Castell Dwyran (Fig. 31)[50] has a bilingual inscription, of which the Latin reads:

MEMORIA VOTEPORICIS PROTICTORIS.

Protector is a technical title, applied to certain categories of officer-cadet in the late Roman army.[51] Vortepor could not have been a *protector* of this type himself, but it is not impossible that he was using a title that had become hereditary, which an ancestor of his had acquired. Vortepor is known from historical sources, namely Gildas, who around 530 refers to 'Vorteporius usurper in Dyfed'. His genealogy is informative if garbled. The earliest line is given as 'Maxen guletic map Protec map Protector', suggesting that Magnus Maximus was regarded as the starting point. Vortepor's ancestor may have been a bodyguard-hostage at the court of Maximus, following the custom of holding the son of a federate leader as a hostage. To further underline the Roman military connotations in the dynasty, both Irish and Welsh versions give the name of Vortepor's father as Agricola and his grandfather as Triphum, which is clearly a blundered version of *tribunus*, the commander of a military unit.

Gildas mentions four other kings in Britain: Constantine, Aurelius Caninius, Cuneglasus and Maglocunun. Of these Constantine seems to have ruled in Dumnonia, or, less probably, in the old territory of the Damnonii, that is, Strathclyde. Aurelius Caninius probably ruled over south-west Wales or the Lower Severn. Cuneglasus, who is known from Nennius as Cinglas, is given

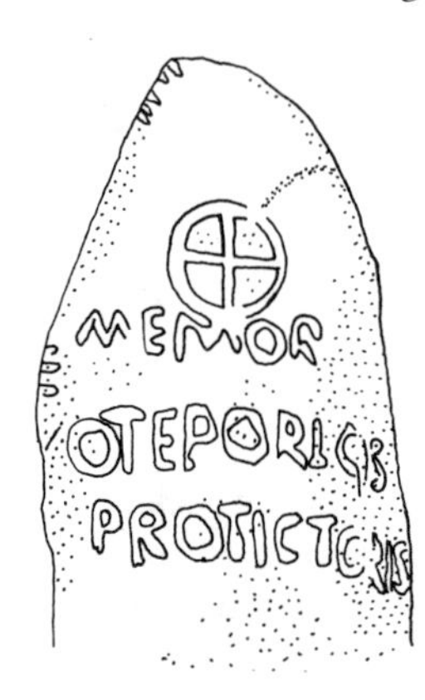

Figure 31 The tombstone of Vortepor

the same grandfather as Maglocunun. The latter is without doubt Maelgwn of Gwynedd, who is described by Gildas as the 'dragon of the isles'.

Maelgwn was the king of Gwynedd, and after an early youth devoted to the Church he became in the mid-sixth century a ruthless, heroic chieftain, who was to be honoured by medieval Welsh poets – he figures in the story of *Taliesin* and the *Dream of Rhonabwy*.

Dyfed and Gwynedd, thus, are two kingdoms for which the genealogies are fairly certain, the one being Irish, possibly fostered by Magnus Maximus, the other being one of the kingdoms founded by Cunedda.

The other Welsh kingdoms have less certain origins.[52] *Brycheiniog* in south-central Wales (modern Brecknock) had a dynasty which lasted until the tenth century, and seems to have had mixed Irish–Welsh origins. The dynasty of *Builth* on the Wye claimed descent from Vortigern, but this seems unlikely though it was never disputed by the early Welsh chroniclers. Vortigern was also claimed as the founder of the kingdom of *Gwerthyrion* (the name itself is derived from an archaic form of the name Vortigern), while the *south-eastern Welsh kingdoms* claimed to be derived from the old tribal territory of the Silures, with their dynasty traced back to Caractacus. *Powys* on the Welsh March was focused on the old territory of the Cornovii. Its dynastic origins, however, are confused.

It is therefore clear that Wales in the sixth century consisted of a number of small kingdoms, ruled by dynasties rooted in Roman tradition. During this period the British (Brythonic) language was going through the final stages of its development into Primitive Welsh, and borrowing from Latin. This process had begun in the third century, and continued till the sixth century and beyond, though in later centuries the borrowings were of a 'learned' nature. Latin probably remained the upper-class language throughout the

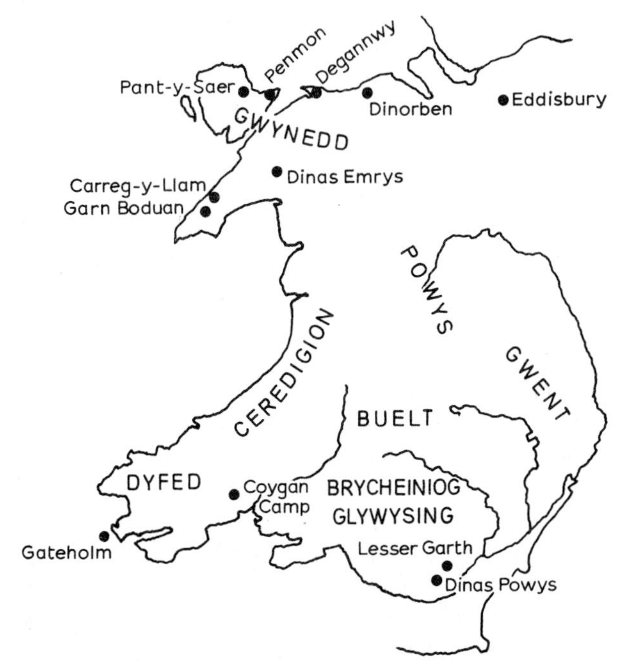

Figure 32 Early Wales – key sites

sixth century with the British-Latin pronunciation that had developed in the fifth century, and this continued to be the language of the Church. There can be little doubt that the Welsh chiefs of the sixth century maintained some veneer of Romano-British culture. In sixth-century Dyfed, Irish was certainly being spoken.

The developments of the seventh century[53] brought about the severance of Wales from Cumbria – the land of the *Gwyr y Gogledd* or Men of the North – and the ensuing development of their dialects. Up to this point there had been considerable traffic northwards from Wales through Lancashire, presumably by way of the Roman road from Chester to Ribchester, though some of Lancashire must have been uninhabited and largely impassable due to the Chat Moss. The kingdom of Elmet in the south of the Yorkshire Pennines seems also to have been linked with Wales until the conquest of the area by Edwin of Northumbria in the period around 617. A memorial stone from Llanaelhaern, Caernarvonshire, commemorating an ALIORTVS ELMETIACO, shows that at least one native of Elmet was living in north Wales in the late fifth to early sixth centuries. Æthelfrith of Northumbria had expanded south-west to win a decisive victory at Chester *c.* 615. The Anglo-Saxon settlement of Lancashire, Cumberland and Westmorland seems to have been a fairly slow process, but with this penetration in the later seventh century the final severance of Wales from Cumbria took place.

The seventh century was also a period of considerable activity on the eastern frontier of Wales. In the early part of the century the kingdom of Gwynedd seems to have been of considerable importance, and was ruled over by Cadfan, whose memorial stone has been found at Llangadwaladr in Anglesey with the proud inscription:

> CATAMANUS REX SAPIENTIS(S)I/MUS OPINATIS(S)IM/US OMNIUM REG/UM
>
> 'Catamanus, wisest and most renowned of all kings lies here'

The language echoes the phraseology of the Byzantine court. His son was Cadwallon, who allied with Penda of Mercia and waged war on Edwin of Northumbria, defeating and killing him at Hatfield Chase in 632. After the death of Cadwallon the alliance with Penda was continued by Cadafael, who after a brief and ignominious rule was followed by Cadwaladr, who was regarded by Welsh tradition as a great deliverer.

Penda had extended the influence of Mercia during his lifetime along the Upper Severn, and by the mid-seventh century had reached the area round Wroxeter. It seems likely that the 'short dykes' of the central Welsh March, where the Mercian frontier was most exposed and penetration by the Welsh to the Mercian capital at Tamworth most likely, belong to this period. About this time too Penda's activity extended into Cheshire, and is attested by place-names. The area round the Hereford plain and the southern Shropshire highlands became a political unit known as *Magonsaetan*, and was ruled over by a Northumbrian client family who had aided Penda. The function of *Magonsaetan* seems to have been to act as a buffer between Mercia and Powys.

The frontier was peaceful until the early eighth century, when in 705 and 709 there were Welsh raids on Mercia. The outcome was the Mercian construction of the linear earthwork known as *Wat's Dyke*,[54] which extended from the southern extremity of the Dee estuary at Basingwerk to the Morda between Oswestry and Maesbury in Shropshire. It was built by Æthelbald (716–57), and was intended not simply as a boundary line but as a declaration of Mercian conquest. Between the building of Wat's Dyke and Offa's Dyke lay a period of considerable unrest on the frontier. On the evidence supplied by the Pillar of Eliseg at Valle Crucis near Llangollen, northern Powys suffered repeated Mercian attacks in the later seventh century. This period of Mercian offensive was to culminate with *Offa's Dyke*,[55] built between 784 and 796 and which extended from Prestatyn in Flintshire to Sedbury

Cliff on the Severn estuary. It served as a boundary, not a military frontier.

In the next phase of Welsh history the number of kingdoms was reduced and united by a series of marriage alliances. Towards the end of the eighth century dynastic changes in Gwynedd led to the accession of Merfyn Vrych, a descendant of Maelgwn Gwynedd. His court seems to have been in direct contact with that of Charles the Bald at Liège, and there is some reason to suppose that it was a port of call for Irish travellers on their way there. Merfyn married the sister of Concenn of Powys, and his reign marks the opening of Wales again to external stimuli after a long period of isolation.

Rhodri Mawr, Merfyn's son, continued his father's policy. By marrying the sister of the king of Cardigan he expanded the kingdom of Gwynedd until it embraced a large part of Wales. Rhodri probably continued to liaison with the court of Charles the Bald, and under him there was something of a cultural revival. The oral traditions both of the northern British and of the Welsh were probably set down in writing at his court. His military campaigns were on two fronts. He successfully kept the Vikings at bay, killing the Danish leader Horm off Anglesey in 876, while his control of Powys also meant having to combat the serious threat from Mercia and Wessex along the frontier. In 822, according to the *Annals of Wales*, Deganwy had been attacked by the Saxons, who at that time had also dominated Powys. In 828 Mercia was conquered by Wessex, which was then in direct conflict on the borders with the Welsh, and by the middle of the century Burgred of Mercia is described as reducing Wales with the help of Æthelwulf. Exaggerated though the extent of the Anglo-Saxon conquest of Wales may be in the documentary sources, there can be no doubt that Rhodri was faced with an explosive situation. The conflict with the Anglo-Saxons on the Marches occupied much of his attention during his reign, and he and his son Gwriad both died at the hands of the Saxons while fighting in 878.

It seems probable that Rhodri had some ambition to unite the Celtic peoples of Britain, and it may be that in anticipation of the union of the north Britons and Welsh he compiled the transcripts of north British traditions. By the time of his death, marriage alliances had united all Wales except Dyfed and the south-east under the control of Gwynedd.

Following the death of Rhodri, his kingdom was divided between his sons. In the ensuing period a sharp division grew up between those who were violently opposed to union with England (the supporters of this cause being mainly in the north), and those who favoured it (mainly the south, which had allied with the Saxons against Rhodri). The matter was to be settled by Hywel Dda, the grandson of Rhodri, who brought unity by annexing south-west Wales, and pacified resistance in Dyfed by marrying the ruler's daughter. From 942 he was virtually sole ruler of Wales, and pursued a strong pro-English policy, allying with Æthelstan. A landgrant of Æthelstan signed at Luton in 931 describes Hywel as a 'subregulus', and it seems probable that he was a client king. His pro-Saxon policy is well illustrated by the fact that coins were struck in his name at Chester in the last years of his reign.[56] Although sometimes regarded as evidence for a coinage struck by him, only one coin has survived, which implies a very limited output probably struck by the Anglo-Saxons as a diplomatic gift to him. After Hywel's death in 949 or 950, Wales was increasingly pro-Anglian. The anti-English feelings of the north were to linger on, and flared up throughout the Middle Ages. In the south the process of Normanization was rapid, with little resistance to the English.

Welsh settlement sites

Most of the archaeological evidence for Early Christian Wales comes from a series of excavations carried out since the mid-1950s on hillforts that appear to have been reoccupied in the late and post-Roman period. The phenomenon of reoccupied hillforts is widespread in late Celtic Britain (pp. 126–33).[57] The few forts known to have been reoccupied in the Roman period used to seem anomalous: the picture has now radically changed.

In Wales there are some thirteen sites that were reoccupied in the late or post-Roman period, some of which have produced only a few sherds of pottery as evidence. Coygan Camp, for instance, yielded only a small number of sherds of A and B imported Wares, although it was earlier extensively reoccupied in the late Roman period. None of the three main Welsh Marches hillforts, Eddisbury (Cheshire), Old Oswestry (Shropshire), and the Breiddin (Montgomeryshire) were refortified; the post-Roman evidence from Eddisbury[58] and Old Oswestry[59] consists of huts built within the ditches of the Iron Age fort.

Dinas Emrys, Caernarvonshire (Fig. 33; Plate 2A), has more impressive evidence for reoccupation. This site closely resembles a nuclear fort in character and was identified from the ninth century with Ambrosius Aurelianus (Emrys is a Welsh form of the name). Traditionally this was the site where Vortigern attempted to build his tower, which repeatedly collapsed, and which required the blood of a fatherless young man to be sprinkled on it before work could continue. Legend also associated it with Merlin, and with the battle of the Red and White Dragons described in the story of Lludd and Llefelys in the *Mabinogion*. The identification of this site with the legends certainly took place as early as the twelfth century. It attracted the attention of antiquaries at a relatively early date, and extensive excavations by Breese at the beginning of this century uncovered the base of a tower which was believed to be Vortigern's but which was in fact a Norman Welsh castle. Breese also found evidence of the Iron Age occupation and badly disturbed the area of post-Roman occupation without recognizing it. Excavations between 1954 and 1956 clarified the sequence. The first phase consisted of a small settlement with a timber structure, probably a hut or granary, on a wooden platform. This was defended by a flimsy palisade. The date of initial occupation is not known, though evidence points to the immediately post-Roman period. The sub-Roman and post-Roman occupation are distinguishable phases. In the first a native type of stone-walled homestead was occupied, with circular huts and outbuildings. Iron and possibly also bronze was worked and cultivation terraces and huts on the slope of the hill may be contemporary. At about this time two ramparts were built to utilize the naturally defensive character of the hill. This settlement was occupied in the fifth century; as well as late Roman pottery, sherds of imported wares were found, including a Chi-Rho stamped base sherd from a lamp, and sherds of A and B Wares. Other finds from this settlement included late Roman glass and a triangular crucible. About the time of the construction of the defences, a cistern was built to water sheep and cattle sheltered within the ramparts. Later in the

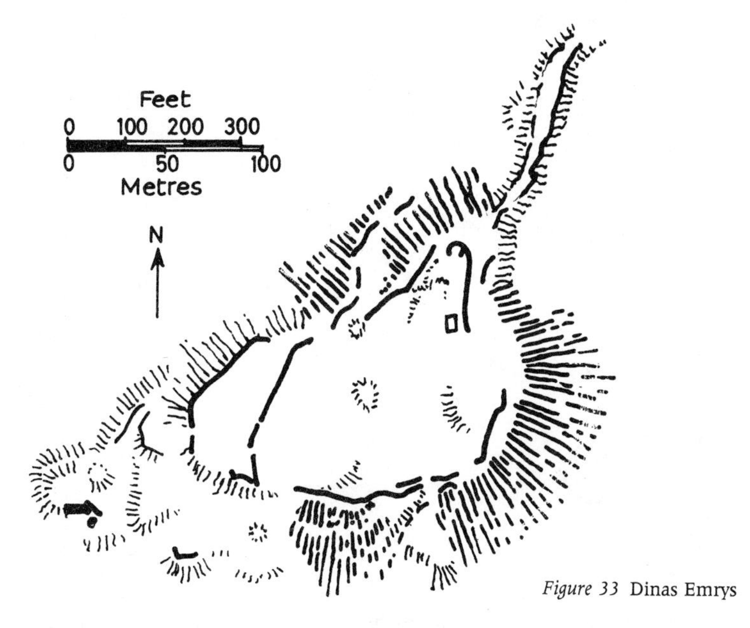

Figure 33 Dinas Emrys

Early Christian period, possibly not much earlier than the tower, a platform was built to give access to the cistern. Belonging to this, or a slightly later phase, may be the putative timber structure beneath the tower, excavated by Breese, with the now lost metalwork finds, which included a gold-plated bronze strip, similar to one from Lesser Garth Cave, and a series of twelve bronze studs with gold plating which were possibly similar to one from Dinas Powys.

Degannwy Castle is another Caernarvonshire site with traditional associations with Maelgwn. Standing opposite Conway, the chief surviving remains are of a castle built by Henry III, destroyed in 1263 by Llewelyn ap Gruffydd. The earliest occupation on the hill probably belongs to the Roman period. The inner face of a stone rampart which may belong to the original defences has been excavated. Some of the pottery from the site belongs to the first or early second century, implying occupation of the site at least as early as this.

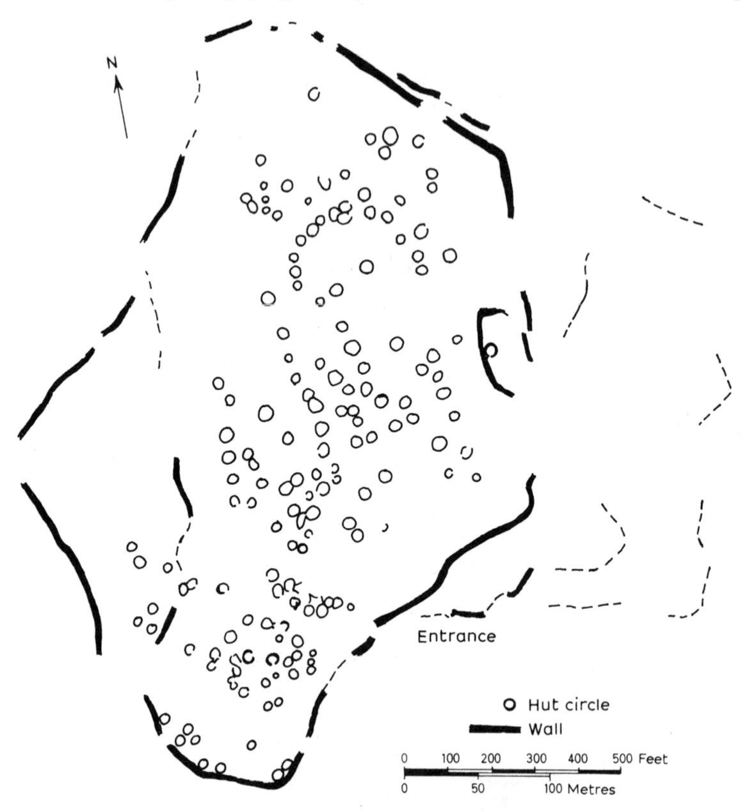

Figure 34 Garn Boduan, Caernarvonshire

The site was certainly occupied in the late Roman period, for there is a good pottery and coin sequence, the coins extending from Gallienus (260–8) to Valens (364–78) – possibly the site was reoccupied to act as a buffer against Irish raids. A dozen sherds of Class B imported amphorae demonstrate post-Roman occupation. Later building on the site, together with the selective nature of excavation so far, has meant, however, that structural remains of the period are still lacking.

Garn Boduan (Fig. 34) is a third Caernarvonshire site. This stone-built fort similar to Tre'er Ceiri was occupied during the Roman period. The post-Roman occupation of the site consisted of a much smaller fort, built within the earlier circuit. The small fort is generally better built than the Iron Age one. Both sides of the rampart walls are well faced. Originally this wall was probably less than 10 feet high, access to the top being by steps set into the wall. Originally it had two entrances, both merely gaps in the circuit, but

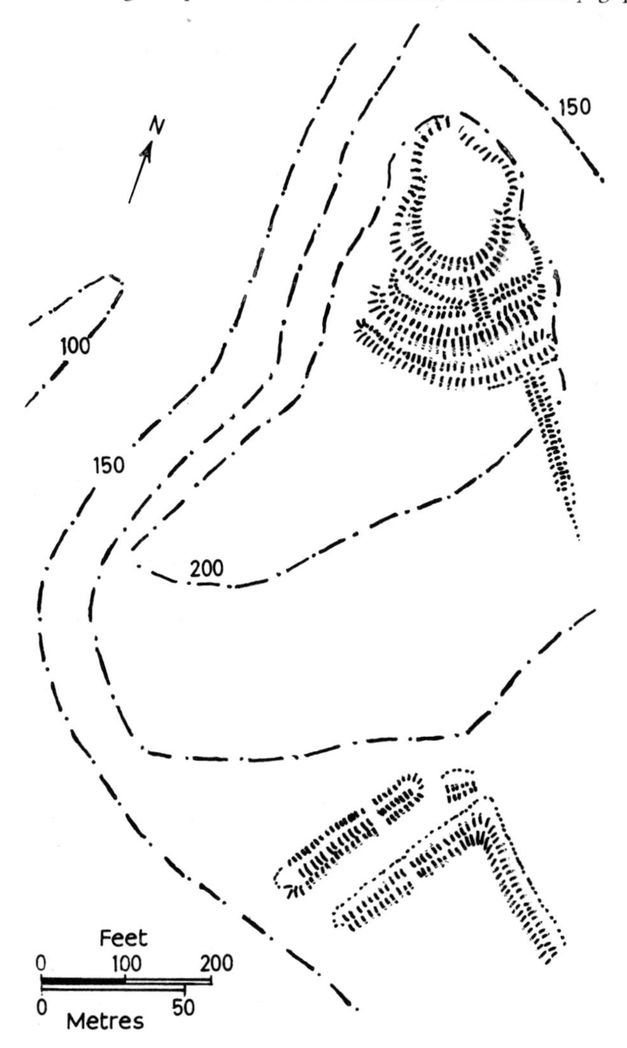

Figure 35 Plan of Dinas Powys (After Alcock)

later one was elaborated. Inside were two huts, circular in plan and similar to those in the Iron Age fort. Finds were few – some beads, a worn stray sherd of a second-century mortarium, and some sherds of Very Coarse Pot.

Dinas Powys, Glamorgan (Fig. 35; Plate 1B) is undoubtedly the most impressive site occupied in Early Christian Wales. The hilltop was first occupied in the early Iron Age, the earliest finds being of Iron Age 'A' pottery, flint flakes and animal bones without associated structures. Somewhat later a hill-slope fort was begun but not completed. Only one rampart was constructed and was later incorporated into the post-Roman earthworks. In the fifth and sixth centuries AD the northern end of the hill was defended by insubstantial earthworks. Within this area, about 150 feet across, it seems that two buildings were constructed, their plans having been reconstructed from drainage gulleys. These consisted of a hall with bowed-out sides, some 40 feet long, and a smaller building, which appears to have been preceded by an unfinished

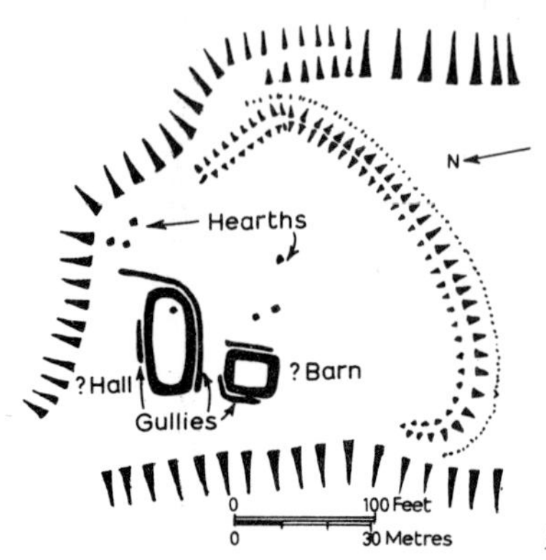

Figure 36 Dinas Powys – Hall (After Alcock)

timber structure. Evidence for this takes the form of five post-holes, which have been identified as the remains of a building measuring approximately 17 by 20 feet, with a central post, probably for a roof support. The hall which replaced it could have been made of stone and measured 50 feet by 20 feet. The barn was about 30 feet by 20 feet in dimension. The two were set at angles to one another, forming a courtyard in which were a number of hearths used for a variety of activities, including metal working. There was no dating evidence for the buildings themselves but this was inferred from the associated finds outside, mainly from middens. These produced pottery and glass and, among other scrap metal, a fragment from an Anglo-Saxon bucket. Bronze working seems to have been quite extensive: presumably the site was the stronghold of a local chieftain. The final phase of occupation on the site was connected with the construction of a substantial earthwork of ringwork type in the late eleventh century, possibly constructed in the face of the Norman conquest of Glamorgan.

Dinorben, Denbighshire (Plate 1A), has produced problematic structural evidence in the form of post-holes which the excavator interpreted as an aisled hall, at least 55 feet long by 25 feet wide. The post-holes were seen to be in six lines, roughly aligned. Dating evidence is entirely dependent on sequence – the post-hole structure is certainly later than a large round hut on the site, which was dated to the late Roman period.

Caer Mynydd, Caernarvon, is an example of a hut group built in the period of Roman military occupation in Wales, but which may have been occupied into the fifth century. Finds include a fourth-century rotary quern and a quantity of late Roman pottery, including some sherds which have been identified as possibly Class A imported ware.

Pant-y-Saer, Anglesey, undoubtedly had some post-Roman occupation. The site consisted of two circular stone huts at opposite ends of a hilltop enclosure. Cultivation was carried out on a terrace on the slope of the hill, and excavated bone indicates that the inhabitants domesticated cattle, sheep, pigs and horses. Hearths were absent, suggesting that cooking was done outside. The smaller hut had a stone bench by the door, and a rubbish pit. At the back was a raised semicircular bench, presumably a sleeping place, at the end of which was a stone mortar set in the floor, and a saddle quern. Apart from pottery, finds included whetstones, hammerstones, flint scrapers and stone pot lids. At a later date two further huts were built against the wall of the first. These were rectangular, and a silvered brooch of Class H was recovered from the floor of one. There is no reason to suppose that the first constructional phase is later than the Roman period.

A cave at *Longbury Bank,* Pembroke, has produced sherds of imported A and B Wares, but the finds come from outside the cave, and need not imply actual occupation in the Early Christian period.

Gateholm Island, Pembroke. The site was once attached to the mainland, and rectangular huts have been noticed both on the mainland and the island itself. The complex consists of about 130 huts, mostly arranged in rows end-on, around small courtyards. Occupation began in the third century, as evinced by a coin of Carausius and by Roman pottery, and certainly continued into the Early Christian period, for the finds included a ringed pin. The houses were built of turf with stone facings, the roof being carried on a ridge-pole between the posts. The site has been interpreted variously as a native Roman settlement with later occupation, and as an early monastic complex like Tintagel. The latter seems unlikely, since it would appear that some at least of the huts were built in the Roman period.

For a short period at least after the withdrawal of the Roman forces the sites of *Caerwent* and *Caerleon* remained in occupation. The evidence from Caerwent comprises a double spiral-headed pin and a series of unprovenanced Byzantine coins of the sixth to ninth centuries, the authenticity of which has been questioned. The pin is of a type for which a sixth- to seventh-century date seems likely. Other evidence for continuing occupation at Caerwent takes the form of squatter occupation above the latest Roman levels and the building of a basilican structure, sometimes suggested as a church, on top of the debris of the fallen peristyle of the Roman baths. Evidence for continuity at Caerleon consists of A Ware and squatter occupation in the vicus.

There are few remaining Early Christian period finds from Wales (apart from inscribed stones); a purple and yellow glass bead from Gors-y-mur, Anglesey, and a bead which is probably Early Christian in date from a hut group at Porth Dafarch, Anglesey. To this sparse list can be added a few penannular brooches from Castell Collen (Radnorshire), Llangenedd (Glamorgan) and Trevor Rocks, Llangollen (Montgomery).[60] A double-headed whetstone, possibly of the ninth century and showing similarities to two from Scotland, was found near Colwyn Bay, Caernarvonshire.

Christianity in early Wales[61]

Compared to Ireland, Scotland, Man or south-west England, church sites in Wales with some visible remains which may predate the twelfth century are sparse. To some extent the absence of field monuments is offset by the abundance of memorial stones and later ecclesiastical sculpture, and it is upon this body of evidence, along perhaps with the dubious information provided by placenames and dedications, that the picture of Christianity in early Wales must be constructed.

There is no reason to doubt, however, that the general character of Welsh ecclesiastical sites must have been similar to that encountered in Ireland and Scotland, and recent excavations at Burry Holms, Glamorgan, have provided Wales with an equivalent of Church Island or Ardwall, in which the sequence of timber oratory to stone chapel can be traced. Apart from Burry Holms, however, the evidence is difficult to assess, and comes mainly from the north. The best-known site is the small monastery on *Ynys Seiriol* (Puffin Island), Anglesey.[62] Here the remains consist of a ruined cashel wall, now about a foot high, enclosing a rough oval of about three-quarters of an acre round the church. The existing ruined church tower has been ascribed to the twelfth century, but excavation has shown that it was preceded by an earlier stone chapel about 5 feet square, possibly dating from the tenth century. In turn this was preceded by an earlier, putative oratory. Grouped round the north-west sector of the wall are the remains of three or four rectangular cells, and to the north and east are further enclosures, with three small fields lying beyond the cashel to the west. Cashel and cells may be pre-Viking.

Penmon[63] is situated on the Anglesey mainland opposite Ynys Seiriol. A holy well and cell may predate 1200 – the cell is of rough stone construction, circular internally, built against a rock face. Nearby is a rectangular structure which may represent the nave and chancel of an early chapel. The site is traditionally associated with the sixth-century saint, Seiriol, but almost all the visible remains belong to the period of the medieval monastery on the site.

Llangybi, Caernarvon,[64] has a spring and pool dedicated to St Gybi in a building which has 'Megalithic' masonry. Though rectangular in plan it shows signs of rising to a beehive vault. The structure adjoins an eighteenth-century farmhouse, and has been suggested to be the product of eighteenth-century 'archaism', but the structure is probably medieval and may predate 1200.

St Beuno's Chapel, Clynnog Fawr, Caernarvon,[65] is more determinate. Beneath a later chapel are the remains of an earlier church, 18 feet by 9 feet 9 inches, built of rough clay-bonded stones and oriented along the same axis. The proportions are roughly 2 : 1 and a date in the tenth century is not impossible for it.

Bardsey[66] has a monastic complex too disturbed by later burials to repay excavation, while that on *St Tudwal's Isle*[67] has on excavation proved to have no surviving remains datable with any certainty to before the twelfth century.

Of the great monasteries of Wales almost nothing survives. Camden recorded ruins at *Bangor-Is-Coed*[68] in the sixteenth century. At *Bangor Fawr*,[69] the modern Bangor (Caernarvonshire), some remains were uncovered during building operations for the university, but the excavation was partial and not sufficiently extensive to determine the precise nature of the site. A rough rubble-built structure was uncovered, rectangular in plan, with clay bonding and surrounded by burials, which is likely to be pre-Norman but need not date from the time of the monastery of St Deiniol in the sixth, seventh or eighth century. The burials, however, were in cists (cf. p. 380), and the site seems to have been scarped on a terraced platform on the hillside. Other structures were also noted. More recent excavations on the site found only modern walling.

Slight evidence from *Caer Gybi*, Holyhead (Anglesey)[70] suggests that the custom of constructing early ecclesiastical sites within pre-existing Roman forts was as usual in Celtic as in Saxon areas.

The major south Welsh monasteries such as that of Illtud at Llantwit Major, Glamorgan, or at St David's, Pembroke, have produced nothing except a few sculptured stones from the latter.

Burry Holms,[71] Glamorgan, excavated by Mr D. B. Hague, confirms that the character of Welsh early ecclesiastical sites was in keeping with those in the other areas of Celtic-speaking Britain. Beneath a twelfth-century church on the site were four corner post-holes of a timber church on a slightly different alignment, which had been standing when the stone church was built, the posts being pulled out for its construction. This timber chapel was probably the work of Caradog (d. 1124), and therefore should be assigned to the end of the eleventh century or beginning of the twelfth. The timber chapel measured 11 feet by 10 feet, and the south-east post-hole was cut into an earlier disturbed grave. It would seem that the site was occupied until the Viking period, plundered by the Vikings and then reoccupied after a period of abandonment. Excavation of the cashel wall showed a sequence which would fit in with the rest of the evidence from the site. The first phase consisted of a vallum of turf with a revetment of small stones, which after a short abandonment had a palisade erected on top, presumably at the time of the erection of the timber chapel. The final phase was the replacement of this by a stone cashel wall consisting of a double line of large orthostats enclosing an egg-shaped area, almost certainly contemporary with the twelfth-century stone church. Other buildings on the site were of later medieval and post-medieval date, belonging to a Benedictine foundation.

Llandegai,[72] near Bangor, Caernarvonshire, is a prehistoric site with a later structure, of sleeper-beam construction, measuring 12 by 14 feet. It was associated with medieval graves, and may have been a timber oratory.

At present no detailed fieldwork has been done in Wales on potential Early Christian chapel sites, except that by the Royal Commission. It seems likely, however, that a number remain to be recognized. For instance, the circular or oval graveyard in Wales may preserve the line of an earlier vallum in some cases. The churchyard at Llangybi, near St Gybi's well, for example, shows traces of a circular vallum within the graveyard and has also produced a stone of the Early Christian period.

There is growing evidence to suppose there was some Christianity in Wales, particularly in the south, by the fourth century AD. That Eastern cults were reaching Wales as early as the second century is clearly shown at the Roman fort at Segontium, where a gold gnostic charm and a later mithraeum are recorded.[73] There is some evidence for the existence of a Christian community on the border at Wroxeter; a fourth-century lead tablet from Bath seems to be a letter from a cleric at Wroxeter writing about Arian. Recently, a Latinized memorial stone with an Old Irish inscription CUNORIX MACUS MAQUI-COLINE was ploughed up on the site, and should be ascribed to the sixth century.[74] Excavations on the forum site in 1860 and again in 1923–7 produced evidence of a post-Roman cemetery, and certainly the town continued in occupation, on an impoverished scale, into the fifth century. The nearby church of St Andrew shows masonry belonging to the earliest phase of Anglo-Saxon church architecture, and continuity of Christianity from the Roman period is not impossible.[75]

Early Christian remains have been found on a number of Roman sites in Wales. The villa at Llantwit Major had skeletons buried on the remains of a mosaic pavement, and other graves were cut through the walls of rooms. In view of the proximity of the early foundation of St Iltud these are almost certainly Early Christian in date.[76] The Roman baths at Tremadoc, Caernarvonshire, produced a number of post-Roman bones. At Caerhun a church was built within the Roman fort and the coin sequence from the site implied occupation at least until the end of the fourth century. The church at Llanbeblig, at Caernarvon, overlies Roman cremation burials belonging to the fort of Segontium, again implying continuity of site. At Caerwent a building interpreted as a church was excavated above Roman baths (p. 111), and nearby were post-Roman burials.

A lead coffin from Anglesey has an inscription in reverse and symbols of possibly Christian significance; the type of coffin belongs to a series of late Roman products, many of which are Christian, and the Anglesey example is probably fifth-century.

Memorial stones[77]

Nash-Williams in his monumental study of the Early Christian monuments of Wales recognized a Group I which consisted of stones with simple memorial formulae in debased Latin or ogham script, on rough pillars or slabs of stone. These date from the fifth and sixth centuries, and are the main archaeological evidence for the first phase of Christianity in Wales. A few stones probably represent the continuation of late Roman memorial tradition and can be classed along with late Roman gravestones – they have inscriptions set in parallel lines on the stones, horizontally, in Roman capitals. These are found in north-west Wales, two important examples coming from Aberdaron, Caernarvonshire. These are exceptional, however, and the majority of the memorial stones reflect another tradition, new in Wales and belonging to the spread of memorial stones during the fifth and sixth centuries from the Mediterranean through Gaul and western Europe. The formulae employed on the stones betray their origins, most being of the type found in Gaul (in certain cases, Africa), while a stone of the late sixth century from Llantrisant, Anglesey, may actually commemorate a Gaulish immigrant. Another, from Penmachno, Caernarvonshire, bears an inscription indicating that it was set up 'in the time of the consul Justinus'. Justinus's name appears in a restricted area round Lyons, and the inscription both provides a date for the stone (of 540) and sound evidence for direct contact with the Lyons area.

The distribution of two types of inscription – those with HIC IACIT and those with FILIUS is important. The HIC IACIT (here lies) inscription seems to originate in Gaul, and is found there in the provinces of Gallia Belgica and Germania as well as round Vienne – elsewhere in Gaul the common formula is HIC REQUIESCET. The HIC IACIT inscriptions have a distinct concentration in north-west Wales, and their distribution implies that the north-west was the area most strongly influenced by the new Gaulish Christianity.

The inscriptions with FILIUS, normally in the form A FILIUS B (A son of B) belong to a different phenomenon. This is a direct translation of the ogham A MAQQI B, and is very rare in Gaul, there being one example at Vienne and another commemorating a member of the royal house of Burgundy. It was frowned on as it seemed to disobey Matthew 23 : 9, 'Call no man your father upon the earth', and it has been suggested that filiation is connected with the Pelagian heresy. This seems unlikely, and is more probably the natural outcome of Celtic (and particularly Irish) tribal structure. The distribution of stones with FILIUS is concentrated in south-west Wales, and is the outcome there of the Irish settlements. Irish influence too must be seen behind inscriptions in vertical lines (again following ogham, which could not readily be inscribed horizontally), the use of the genitive '(the stone) of X' being understood, and bilingual ogham-Latin stones.

The dating for the Group I memorial stones as a whole is difficult, but the broad span can be confirmed by the close dating of comparable Gaulish monuments. Of the Gaulish series, 4 are fourth century, 54 are fifth, 131 are sixth, and 20 date from the seventh. Within the series Nash-Williams tried to provide a detailed chronology based on the gradual transition from Roman to half uncial lettering. While in the main this transition is valid, and can be paralleled in Gaul, the character of the epigraphy of any one stone cannot be used to provide a firm date for it, since there are too few firmly dated inscriptions from Wales to provide an absolute chronology. Furthermore it is highly probable that the transition did not proceed everywhere in Wales at the same rate, and archaism in lettering was probably fairly widespread, uniformity being concomitant with an official school of inscription carving.

Nash-Williams's scheme for Welsh monuments recognized a Group II – stones with plain incised crosses. Nash-Williams assigned a chronological span to them from the seventh to ninth centuries. These stones belong to a general class designated by Thomas as 'primary cross-marked stones'.[78] They represent typologically the earliest and simplest form of grave marker, and have a relationship with the uninscribed monoliths of prehistory. In Wales they are found concentrated in the north, and Thomas has suggested that they are connected with the spread of Irish Christianity in north Britain. Certainly they are found in areas of Irish settlement, but significantly they do not seem to be concentrated in the areas which have produced the most ogham inscriptions. The reason for this, it has been suggested, is that ogham inscriptions are most densely concentrated in the areas settled from southern and eastern Ireland, while primary cross stones emanate from the northern Irish colonization ventures. Behind the stone memorials in all probability lie wooden ancestors. The dating, in spite of efforts to establish some kind of fixed sequence, must remain fluid. The cross was in vogue on the Continent prior to the seventh century, and some at least probably date from the sixth century – a cross on the 'Catamanus' stone (dated by Nash-Williams to *c.* 625) can be paralleled with one on a Gaulish memorial stone of 503. At the other end of the scale such cross slabs were probably being erected in Scotland well into the Middle Ages, and there is no reason to suppose that they did not recur intermittently in Wales as well. Certainly the relationship of crosses to Group I inscriptions and to half uncial script would suggest that many were current in the seventh century or later.

Some Group I stones have been found in association with long-cist burials, notably the stones from Pentrefoelas (Denbigh), and Ffestiniog (Merioneth). In other instances two or more stones have been found together, when an Early Christian period site can be inferred. Stray stones are misleading, since often they are not on their original sites. In most of north Wales, where the evidence is clearest, the distribution of sites with two or more Group I stones coincides notably with the distribution of enclosed hut groups, though in Anglesey the memorial stones have been found in the inland forest areas, away from the coastal settlements.

Diocesan organization and the early Welsh Church

From the evidence it seems increasingly clear that there may have been some continuity of Christian worship in Wales from the Roman period. The contribution of Romano-British Christianity must not be over-emphasized, however. The distribution of memorial stones and of potentially early ecclesiastical sites admittedly coincides remarkably with the pattern of native settlement in the Romano-British period, but it need not imply that Christianity too was continuous. The explanation should probably be sought in a continuation of the basic settlement pattern in the post-Roman period, the same areas being inhabited in the sixth as in the second or third century.

Much of the incentive behind the blossoming of Welsh Christianity in the sixth and seventh centuries must be sought in the reintroduction of Christian beliefs and practices from the Continent, particularly from Gaul. That this was concomitant with the seaborne trade from the Continent, as witnessed by imported pottery, cannot be doubted, and is illustrated by the sherd of a lamp from Dinas Emrys with a stamped Chi-Rho between alpha and omega. In the context of this intercourse between Britain and Gaul, the presence of the British cleric Faustus at Lérins, and the account of Patrick travelling with sailors from Ireland to Gaul, should be borne in mind.

This Christianity was to be reinforced, particularly in the areas of Irish settlement, by a further contact with Irish Christianity, itself in great part fostered by the same continental contacts. This activity must be viewed as secondary to the settlements brought about by missionaries coming over to preach to Irish Christian communities.

The early Welsh Church, like the early Church in the other Celtic-speaking areas of Britain, appears to have been diocesan, or more accurately administered by *paruchiae* under bishops. In southern Scotland this can be demonstrated with greater certainty, but the same sort of organization in the immediate post-Roman period seems equally valid for Ireland, Wales and probably the south-west. There is no archaeology of the Patrician church in Ireland in the fifth century, but the documentary evidence for the sixth century points to administration through the *paruchia*, which represented the *plebs* or 'tribe'. In Ireland the system of tribal bishops seems to have been gradually submerged in the seventh century with the rise in importance of the monastery. In Wales the situation was probably similar, though in the seventh-century *Life* of St Samson of Dol the bishop is represented as the main authority in south

Wales. Apart from the *Lives*, reinforcement for this picture of ecclesiastical organization comes from Gildas. The system of tribal bishoprics was the adaptation of the urban structure of the Roman diocesan religion to the needs of a tribal society where towns which could act as bishops' seats were totally absent.

The historical picture is confirmed to some extent by the evidence of memorial stones, for some of these reflect a degree of settled civil existence which might at first seem surprising for post-Roman Wales. The two Aberdaron stones commemorate Veracius and Senacus who are described as *presbyter*, while stones from Bodafon, Caernarvonshire, and Llantrisant, Anglesey, commemorate *sacerdotes*. Other terms, notably *magistratus* and *medicus*, imply advanced secular as well as ecclesiastical organization.

Against this background the picture of the wandering Celtic saint travelling by the western seaways and preaching to wild unconverted sheep farmers in Snowdonia, so often suggested, has very little place. This picturesque form of evangelization probably had little part in the early days of the Church in Britain, and 'missionary' saints usually began by preaching to the converted before extending their influence.

The introduction of monasticism in the sixth century from the Continent almost certainly had considerable impact on the Welsh Church, and as in Ireland the *paruchia* probably took on a monastic meaning. The Welsh *Vitae*, notably that of St Samson, taken with the other evidence, point to the growth of monasticism being a fairly prolonged process, though many of the great Welsh monasteries appear to have been founded during the sixth century. Once established, the Celtic monasteries of Wales were as longlasting as their Irish counterparts. The monasteries of Bardsey (Enlli) and Ynys Seiriol along with another community at Beddgelert survived into the twelfth century and the similar communities at Bangor, Penmon and Clynnog Fawr seem to have survived the Viking period. The monastic zeal of the twelfth-century Norman-English does not seem to have greatly affected Wales, though towards the end of the twelfth century Llewelyn Fawr was influenced by the Cistercians. It was not the Cistercian movement, however, which finally swamped the Celtic eremitic monastic organization. The old Celtic monasteries of Beddgelert, Bardsey, Ynys Seiriol and possibly St Tudwal's Island were refounded as Augustinian houses, probably before the English conquest of north Wales. A similar situation could be seen in the south and east, where new monastic foundations of the Middle Ages were more abundant.

Church dedications[79]

The interpretation afforded by church dedications has in the past been stretched beyond the limits of reasonable inference. Bowen attempted to define the spheres of activity of the early saints in Wales through the distribution of dedications to them, on the assumption that a dedication indicated that the church had been founded by the saint himself or his followers. He has argued that, on the basis of the *Vitae*, the traditional picture of the area of activity of particular saints coincides with the distribution pattern of dedications to them.

In this connection certain points should be noted. No Welsh dedication is attested before the Norman period, and so at best the distribution is that of medieval dedications. Secondly in the fifth and sixth centuries, the period with which Bowen was concerned, church dedications appear to have been mainly to Peter and Paul, followed by other major biblical saints and later by ascetics, notably St Martin of Tours. By far the greatest number of dedications to local saints can be shown to be the result of later medieval revival of the cults, especially in the twelfth century, when there seems to have been a revival of interest in *Vitae* – the *Vita* of St Kentigern written in the twelfth century by Jocelyn of Furness almost certainly led to a spate of dedications to Kentigern in Strathclyde. Similarly, offshoots of older foundations frequently adopted the dedication of the parent church in the Middle Ages. The subject could be elaborated, but lies outside the scope of archaeology. It should be said in conclusion, however, that some distribution patterns do seem to be significant in the light of what is known of the saints concerned. The dedications to St Bueno and St Tysilo have distinct and separate distributions in north Wales, which must be a reflection of local traditions.

5 South-west England

The Celtic south-west had a fluctuating boundary, due to gradual encroachment on its eastern limit by Anglo-Saxons. Cornwall and Devon, never very Romanized, preserved native cultural traditions into the Early Christian period and later, and were not absorbed into the mainstream of English cultural developments until the ninth century. By the late fifth century, Anglo-Saxon settlement extended as far as the Upper Thames, with some penetration into the valley of the Warwick Avon. By 550 the Saxon front lay along a curved line approximately from Southampton to Warwick, and by the early seventh century approximately from Weston-super-Mare to Bournemouth. Access by land to south-west England was limited by the marshland of the Somerset Levels to routes across Salisbury Plain and the Dorset Downs. The north–south flow of the rivers was equally impeding to transit from east to west. Surrounded on three sides by water, the south-west peninsula was thus more vulnerable to contacts from continental Europe and Ireland than from the rest of the British mainland. The archaeology of the region reflects both local cultural developments and frequent seaborne influences from France and Iberia. Despite its metal resources, the south-west was more culturally impoverished than the rest of southern England.

The pre-Roman and Roman Iron Age

From the seventh century BC onwards new ideas began to affect the native Bronze Age peoples of south-west England, and gradually with the introduction of iron metallurgy Iron Age cultures can be discerned.[1] Throughout the period it is possible to trace repeated contacts with the Continent, particularly with Brittany, a pattern which was to continue into the post-Roman period when it seems there was a reversal of the flow of influences with the migration of a group of British to Brittany. The distribution of hillforts with widely spaced ramparts in the later Iron Age of south-west England and south Wales also in some measure represents a foretaste of the contacts that were to exist in the Early Christian period between the two regions.[2]

In general terms it is possible to recognize, in the pattern of the post-Roman settlement, that of the Iron Age – a continuity emphasized by the reoccupation of such Iron Age sites as Castle Dore and Chun Castle in Cornwall or South Cadbury and Cadbury Congresbury in Somerset. Although some phenomena are fairly widespread throughout south-west England in the early Iron Age, regionalism is apparent. Geographical factors are probably in part responsible for the concentration of hillforts in Somerset and Dorset; further west other types of settlement seem to have been more favoured. Similarly, geographical factors are probably responsible for the lake villages such as Glastonbury and Meare in Somerset, and for the distribution of cliff castles round the Devon, Cornwall and Scilly coasts.

A trading site at Mount Batten, Devon,[3] shows that at a very early date in the Iron Age trading contacts were established with Normandy or Brittany; by the second century BC it is possible to recognize a complex of apparently related phenomena which reflect contacts with Armorica – pottery styles and settlement types including *fogous* or souterrains (underground passageways).[4] Also appearing for the first time were *courtyard houses* – stone-built huts within an enclosure wall which also enclosed subordinate byres and sheds and which are best exemplified at Chysauster. Such hut groups occur elsewhere in Britain especially in north Wales and Northumberland, where they seem to be of slightly later date. A third category of settlement which made its appearance around this time is the *cliff-castle*, a type of small fort erected on a promontory, classic examples of which are Trevelgue and Gunnard's Head. It has been suggested that the appearance in this period of *rounds* – small ringforts – was in some way related to the activities of the Veneti, an Armorican tribe who are recorded by Caesar as operating a fleet between Brittany and Britain.[5]

Continuing contact with Brittany is indicated by the spread from Cornwall during the first century BC of Glastonbury Ware, a type of richly decorated pottery of Breton inspiration produced by craftsmen versed in Breton traditions. It appears as an intrusive element in the lake village of Glastonbury to which it owes its name.[6]

The destruction of the fleet of the Veneti by Caesar in 56 BC drastically curtailed contacts between the extreme south-west of England and the Continent in the later first century BC. From then on Dumnonia lay outside the distribution of many of the categories of later Iron Age antiquities in southern England, and underwent a period of cultural impoverishment and isolation.[7]

The last phase of continental influence in the Iron Age is associated with the emergence of the Durotrigian culture, named after the tribe of the Durotriges in Dorset. This culture was made up of a mixture of elements derived from Brittany and also from the Belgae, who were being pushed into Dorset by mounting pressures from further east at about the time of Caesar.[8] These two elements combined with others already present in Dorset, and the resulting amalgam was an important and powerful force in southern Wessex into the Roman period – the Durotriges were responsible for the final Iron Age fort of Maiden Castle. Native Durotrigian farmsteads, such as Tollard Royal, Rotherley or Woodcuts, show clearly how native Iron Age culture lingered on into the Roman period.[9]

The sack of Maiden Castle by Vespasian in AD 43 or 44 was part of a general campaign to overthrow the power of the hillforts in Wessex. From about AD 65–70 the Second Legion was based on Gloucester, and a number of subsidiary forts were in operation in the first century, one being temporarily established within the captured hillfort at Hod Hill, Dorset.[10]

After the initial impact of Roman military activity, the south-west (east of Dumnonia) seems to have settled down to enjoy the benefits of Roman civil life. Dorset remained comparatively unchanged by the Roman conquest, except for the town of Dorchester, but Somerset supported a number of Roman villas, and was the centre for various industrial activities.[11]

There is little to suggest that Dumnonia represented an area of strong resistance. In the main the policy seems to have been one of *laissez-faire*. Some early military penetration can be inferred from the fort at Nanstallon and other Roman sites in the coastal region.[12] Although the geographer Ptolemy lists three *poleis* (communities) they were probably native settlements. The only villa known is at Magor, Illogan, which might represent the home of a Dumnonian retiring after a career in Roman service.[13]

Settlement in Dumnonia in the Roman period was agricultural and impoverished, with only minimal Roman influence. The settlements are of three types: 'rounds', which are evenly distributed throughout the region; open settlements, which are a feature of the uplands; and courtyard houses which are peculiar to the granite highlands in the area of Land's End. The rounds have a comparable density and distribution to Irish raths and some are rectilinear, reflecting Roman influence. There is some evidence that attendant on the economy of the round was an extension of agriculture, more ground being opened up as the result of innovations acquired from the more Romanized areas to the east. In this connection the curved iron sickle and ploughshare, as well as the use of a mould board on the plough, may have gained currency in the Roman period. There is post-Roman evidence and iron sickles are likely to have been introduced much earlier.

Generally speaking it is apparent that although the Roman impact was felt in the south-west soon after the Claudian invasion, in Dumnonia at least it had little effect on the way of life of the people, and an overall continuity can be observed in the economy and settlement pattern from the Iron Age to the post-Roman period. Perhaps the most lasting effect of the Roman occupation was the introduction of land-divisions. The *civitas* seems to have been divided into *pagi* which may be the ancestors of the six 'hundreds' of tenth-century Anglo-Saxon Cornwall.[14]

The six Roman towns of the south-west continued in occupation in the sub-Roman period. Imported pottery as well as Byzantine coins (of Anastasius and Justinian) have been found at Ilchester,[15] while at Gloucester sherds of imported pottery (one probably B iii amphora) and a complex of post-holes imply continuity.[16] The evidence, though flimsy, points also to the survival of the Roman town defences into the fifth century. At Cirencester[17] there are suggestions that the forum was kept clean and the streets surfaced in the fifth century, while the destruction of one house in Insula XI occurred some time after the fourth century. There are further suggestions of late occupation in the form of timber buildings on top of the late fourth-century street metallings, and finds include buckles of a type which Mrs Hawkes considers fifth century, as well as Byzantine coins and some fairly crude calcite gritted pottery. Evidence for a more orthodox type of post-Roman pottery has come from the excavations at Abbeygate Street, Bath, which produced a ceramic sequence extending from the late fourth into at least the fifth century.[18] Similar pottery has been noted from the latest phases at Witcombe villa. The evidence from Gloucester, Cirencester and Bath implies a surviving sub-Roman community in the fifth century, and it would be reasonable for this to have remained in existence until taken by the Saxons following the battle of Deorham in 577.

At Poundbury,[19] Dorchester, outside the town walls and above the late Roman cemetery, three rectilinear post-hole and beam-slot structures have been interpreted as three rooms round an open yard – a British imitation of a Roman arrangement, for which parallel might be cited in the sub-Roman buildings at Wroxeter.[20] Exeter[21] has produced no archaeological evidence for continuity but it certainly existed in the 630s when it was besieged by Penda of Mercia, and there was a monastery there at the time of the Saxon attack in 690. There is also documentary evidence for a British quarter in the Anglo-Saxon city until 928.[22]

Outside the towns, villas were occupied to the end of the fourth and a few continued into the fifth century. Important evidence comes from Witcombe, Gloucester,[23] where squatter occupation in the fifth century re-used old materials and erected a timber structure requiring post-holes within the walls of the villa. Finds associated with this phase were two penannular brooches, a bronze dog and a double-sided bone comb with ring-and-dot decoration. Although not yet fully published the pottery was described as 'native' in type. A similar situation is recorded from a number of other villas and there is some ground for assuming that the buildings were abandoned by their more Romanized owners and taken over by native elements. A local revival of native cults is suggested in Somerset by the reconstruction of the temple at Pagan's Hill.[24] This situation is echoed on the opposite side of the Bristol Channel at Lydney,[25] and at Yatton,[26] Somerset.

Dumnonia, never very Romanized, probably enjoyed continuity of traditions. There is some evidence for the adoption in the post-Roman period of Roman ceramic styles, the forms imitating those of coarse wares. The fabrics of this local pottery follow the traditional Iron Age wares, both wheel-turned and hand-made.[27] It is known as 'Gwithian Style' and is well represented at Gwithian itself, and Trebarveth-in-Lizard (p. 279). The village of

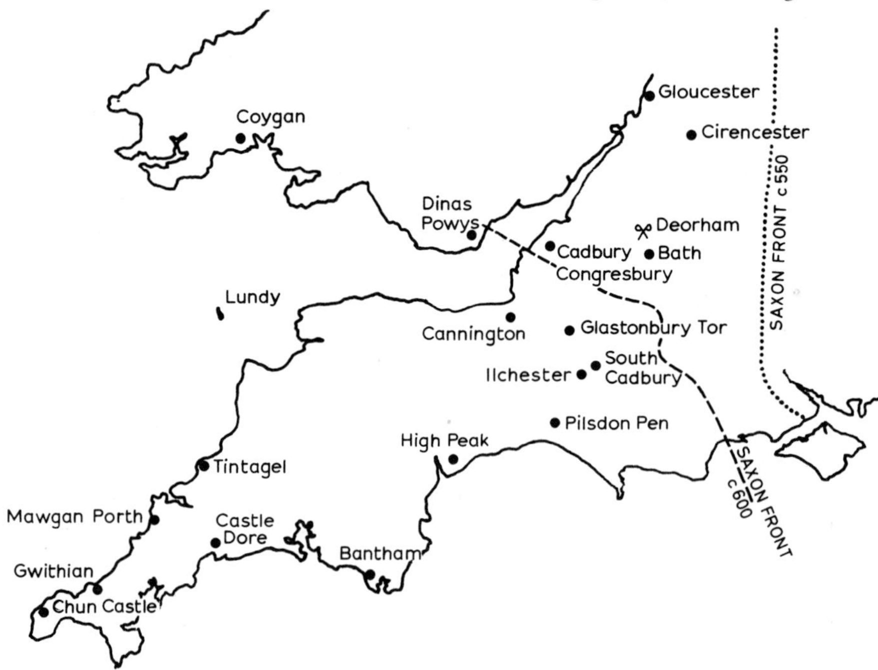

Figure 37 Key sites in south-west England

courtyard houses at Porthmeor[28] on the Land's End peninsula has produced 'Gwithian Style' pottery associated with pottery of Class Ai, indicating an occupation from the late fourth into the fifth century. Elsewhere the evidence for such continuity is lacking, and some courtyard settlements such as Chysauster were already abandoned in the Roman Period.

The Irish in the south-west

The evidence for Irish settlement in the south-west is confused. There seem to have been several distinct movements of people, not all of which are well attested. The main Irish settlement was in north Cornwall and Devon, and it seems likely that this represents a secondary migration from the Irish-occupied areas in south Wales, particularly Carmarthen. The evidence for this settlement is primarily ogham stones, which suggest that the migration took place at some point in the fifth century.

Ogham-inscribed stones in the south-west appear almost exclusively in north-east Cornwall and south-west Devon.[29] Among the few outliers are a late fifth- to early sixth-century bilingual stone from St Clement, near Truro, and others from Lewannick, Worthydale, St Endellion and St Kew. A group of stones with Latin inscriptions but Goidelic names are found in the same area, with only one outlier from Gulval near Penzance, dated to the mid- to late sixth century.[30] The name SAGRANUS was added in the late seventh century to an already standing memorial stone at Fardel, Ivybridge, indicating the continuity of Irish traditions. A few Cornish stones have the same personal names as the Welsh.

The movement from Wales is attested by the reference in *Cormac's Glossary* where a gloss on the name 'Dind Tradui' refers to an extension of the Irish settlement in Dumnonia. It seems probable that this was twofold – an ecclesiastical movement concomitant with a secular. An extension of this area of settlement can be seen as far afield as Glastonbury where the Irish were connected with the monastery in the seventh century.

In favour of the theory of an Irish settlement from Ulster is the large group of dedications to Irish saints,[31] such as St Ia (St Ives) and St Gwinear (Gwithian) in Cornwall and Scilly. These saints are associated with each other in tradition and in later *Vitae*, and one, St Breaca, is reported in a fragmentary *Vita* as having come from north-east Leinster, which borders on south-east Ulster.

At Gwithian a number of objects of suggested Irish origin[32] include small iron tanged knives (which were also made in Britain, however), long-handled saws and oval-headed pins. A variety of other objects as yet unpublished were reported by their excavator as being fairly closely paralleled in northern Ireland on sites such as Ballintoy, Co. Antrim. The worked bone from Gwithian also has affinities with finds from major northern Irish sites of the period.

Medieval dedications to the 'Children of Brychan' (the Brychan who gave his name to Brycheiniog) are similar to those found in Ireland[33] and have a distribution in Wales and Cornwall very similar to that of ogham stones. A memorial stone with an ogham inscription was found on the site of the Roman town of Calleva at Silchester.[34] The inscription is on a Roman column and reads EBICATO(S MAQ) I MUCO, and dates from the late sixth or seventh century. Further testimony of Irish penetration far inland in western Britain is the Latinized inscription ploughed up at Wroxeter which reads CUNORIX MAQUICOLINE, and dates from the sixth century.[35]

British settlements (Fig. 38)

There is a growing amount of evidence for the reoccupation of hillforts in the south-west, similar to the pattern in Wales and Scotland.[36] A few sites have long been known in this connection, Castle Dore in Cornwall for instance, but only since recent excavation of the interior of two Somerset forts, South Cadbury and Cadbury Congresbury, has attention been focused on what can now be seen as a widespread phenomenon. Some forts appear to have been reoccupied in the late Roman period, others in the fifth century.

In Gloucestershire a series of sites was reoccupied in the late Roman period,

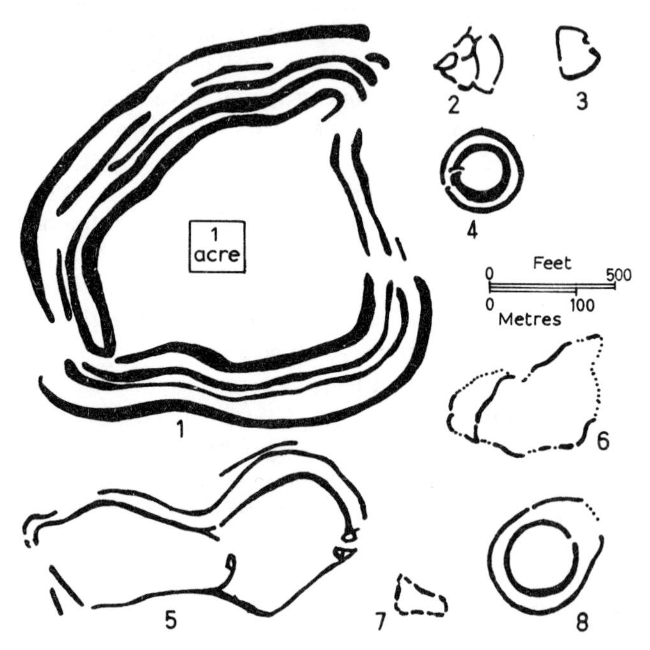

Figure 38 Comparative plans of reoccupied sites of the Early Christian period. (1) South Cadbury; (2) Dunadd; (3) Dinas Powys; (4) Chun Castle; (5) Cadbury Congresbury; (6) Dinas Emrys; (7) Mote of Mark; (8) Castle Dore

though how many were in occupation in the fifth century is uncertain. The reoccupied fort at *Crickley* has produced evidence for sixth-century metal working.

In Devon the fort at *High Peak* seems to be entirely the work of the post-Roman period. The fort appeared to have some Neolithic pre-fort occupation, followed by a long period of abandonment until the defences were constructed. These were dated by Class B amphorae to the fifth century.

Four recent excavations in Somerset have shed light on the reoccupation:

Cannington had occupation possibly contemporary with a sub-Roman cemetery which extended from the fourth to the eighth centuries, a type which is now known from a series in Somerset. The fort is dated by sherds of late Roman pottery and the cemetery by a possible sherd of B Ware and radiocarbon.

Glastonbury Tor has evidence for occupation on the hilltop in the form of an open site, probably a small look-out post. The site has produced late Roman pottery, not associated with any structures, followed by a very indeterminate complex of post-Roman structures. Dating is provided by fourteen sherds of

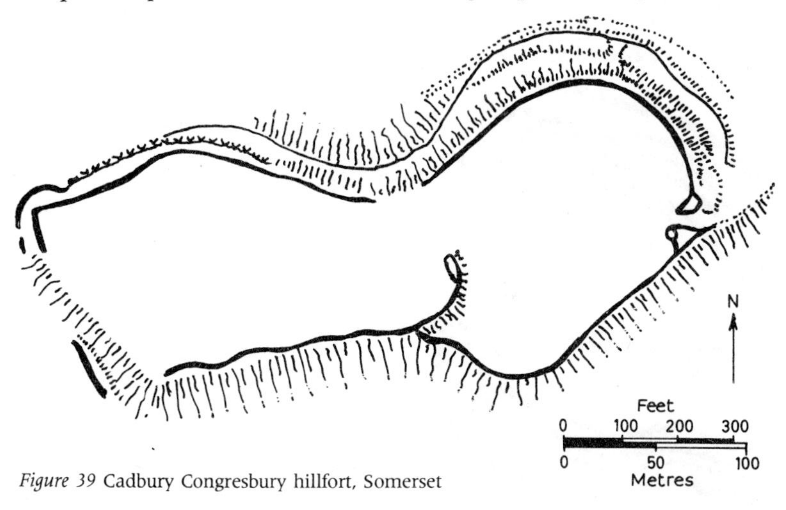

Figure 39 Cadbury Congresbury hillfort, Somerset

B Ware. Structural remains suggest possibly as many as five post-hole and beam-slot timber buildings. Metal working was represented by a hearth, metal-working refuse, and a particularly fine bronze head with iron core, which may have come from the top of a crozier of Ekerö type.

Cadbury Congresbury (Fig. 39; Plate 4A) is still being excavated at the time of writing, and would appear to have extensive post-Roman defences. A section across the defences suggested that the sequence was:

(1) Primary settlement in the pre-Roman Iron Age, in circular huts.
(2) The construction of a rock-cut ditch which supplied building materials for an associated flat-topped platform with a timber or turf façade. This phase may tentatively be assigned to the fifth century.
(3) The gradual decay of the existing defences, during which time the first imported pottery appeared on the site (before 500) after which occupation continued for a while in spite of the ruined defences. There is some evidence that the fifth-century bank may have been refurbished with D-shaped annexes or bastions.

Of the internal buildings, structure I is of rectangular, bipartite plan with a central ridge, a screen and rock-cut upper end. It measured about 24 feet by 9 feet and generally resembled a later longhouse. Pottery evidence suggests a date of *c.* 500 for its occupation. Another substantial structure (No. 7) is indicated by huge post-pits. A third structure was circular, about 36 feet in diameter, with a rock-cut post-trench broken by a gap on the south-east, in the centre of which was a post-hole. Set back from this were three large post-holes in alignment, with two post-holes roughly in the centre and one in the west sector. A number of other structures are probably, but not certainly, of post-Roman date.

Among the finds at Cadbury Congresbury were more sherds of imported pottery than have been found anywhere else, with the exception of Tintagel.

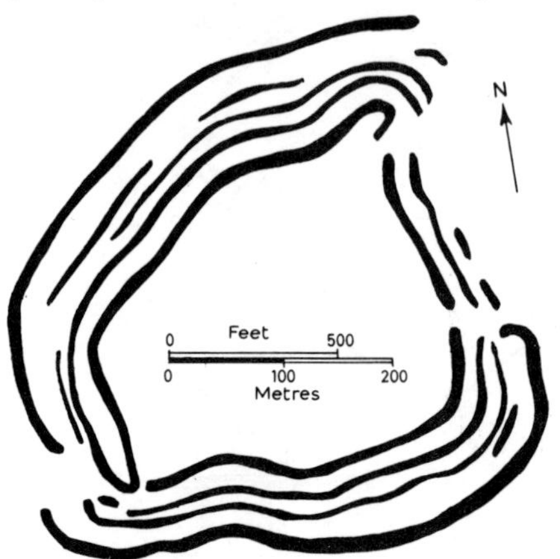

Figure 40 South Cadbury Castle hillfort, Somerset

The wares represented were Class A and B, together with a hitherto unrecognized class of quartzite gritted buff ware with rouletting on the shoulder, which may be Gaulish. There is a considerable quantity of glass, mostly Roman, though some probably Rhenish. Roman glass, all fragmentary, was probably the raw material for glass working or enamel-making. Other finds included an iron ploughshare, knives, an iron mount in the shape of an ox-head, a door stud, glass beads and slag from metal working, some associated with furnaces. Samian pottery is present in post-Roman levels just as it is for instance at Dinas Powys, Lagore, Ballycatteen and Kiondroghad. Evidence from Jarrow suggests that it was there used for grog in a seventh-century *opus signinum* floor, and it may have been used in post-Roman Britain for a variety of purposes such as colouring.

South Cadbury (Fig. 40; Plate 4B), though producing less pottery than Cadbury Congresbury, has more impressive evidence of reoccupation. At South Cadbury the occupation came to an end when Vespasian sacked the fort and dismantled the fortifications. The fort remained unused until the late third or fourth century, when a Romano-British temple was erected. This, to judge by coins from the site, was in use till the end of the fourth century, and may have been visited by pilgrims in the following century. In the fifth century the fortifications were completely refurbished with a wall or rampart of drystone construction incorporating Roman masonry. The rampart was a fairly low bank of rubble with stones piled up at the rear to form a revetment. In some sectors there were also signs of an outer revetment. The rampart was tied together with a framework of vertical, longitudinal and transverse beams, possibly to support some kind of fighting platform.

The rampart was probably broken by two entrances, at the south-west and north-east corners, where there had also been breaks in the Iron Age rampart. The archaeological evidence suggests that the south-west gate had two pairs of doors, 5 feet wide, hanging from uprights and closing against the sill beams. The uprights of the entrance framework were set in a square and were fairly substantial, implying that there was a lookout and fighting platform rising above the level of the rampart walk at this point, over the entrance. This type of single-tower entrance represents a type found usually in small forts in the Roman Empire. The type continued as late as the third century at Richborough. Single-tower gateways are known from the Continent in Carolingian times. Like the Roman ones, these have three pairs of main uprights rather than the two represented at South Cadbury. At either side of the entrance passage the rampart had been shored up with planking and a roadway taken through it.

A *terminus post quem* for the defences is provided by a Roman coin of 393–402 found in the make-up of the rampart. The roadway through the gateway was repaired, and below the upper surface a silver ring or buckle with chip-carved animal ornament was found dating from the later sixth century. This implies that the road was repaired possibly at the time of the Anglo-Saxon advance and capture of Gloucester, Cirencester and Bath in 577. A date in the early sixth or late fifth century for the first construction of the gate would be indicated.

Within the fort, one large timber building was excavated belonging to this period. Measuring 63 feet by 34 feet, it was divided by a screen about a third of the way from the east end. There is evidence for a northern row of posts, and slighter evidence for a southern, implying that it was aisled. Some 12 feet away from this hall was a smaller structure, the evidence for which was a pair of beam slots 13 feet long and 6 feet apart. Comparison with other sites suggests that this was a kitchen.

Finds from South Cadbury include imported pottery of Classes A, B iv, B i, and D suggesting reoccupation around 470. The most notable feature of the reoccupation is that the entire fort of some 18 acres was refortified, implying not merely a small group of refugees, but a large-scale operation involving considerable organization and manpower. The final phase of the site was the brief reoccupation and refortification from 1010 to 1017, when Æthelred II occupied it as a *burh*.

The reoccupation so clearly demonstrated in Somerset is repeated in Dorset and Cornwall. In Dorset, at *Pilsdon Pen*, two post-Roman buildings lie within an Iron Age fort, one circular and one rectilinear. In Cornwall there are two important sites: *Chun Castle* and *Castle Dore*.

Chun Castle (Fig. 41) is an Iron Age fort on open moorland, consisting of two concentric stone walls. The inner, enclosing an area almost 180 feet in diameter, is 12 feet wide, and stood 15 feet high in the seventeenth century. The outer wall is less substantial. The Iron Age entrances consisted of two straight passageways, but were altered, probably at the time of the reoccupation, to give a narrow twisting approach for better defence. The interior of

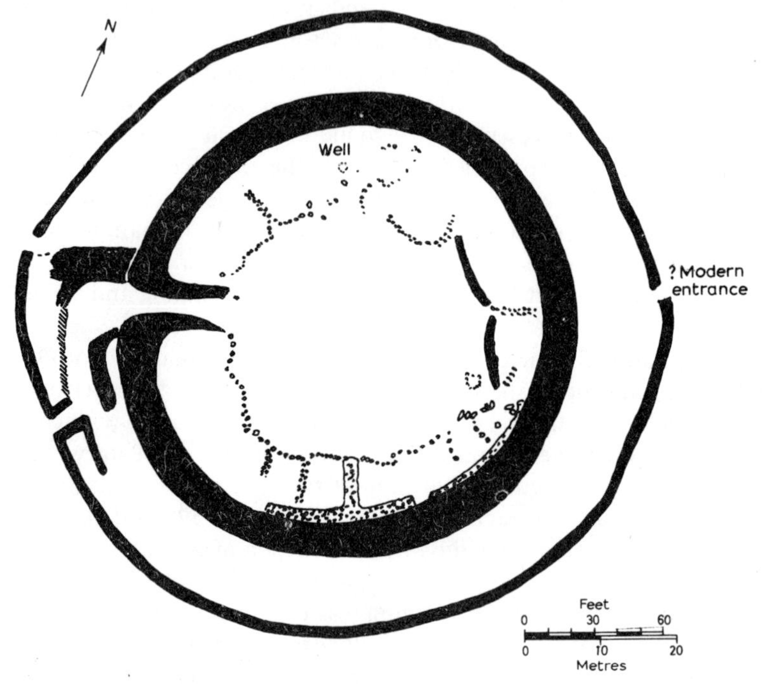

Figure 41 Plan of Chun Castle, Cornwall

the fort was divided into compartments in which houses were erected. This phase of occupation is dated to the sixth century by finds which include a grass-marked pot and sherds of Class B ware, as well as a lump of tin ore and a smelting furnace.

Castle Dore (Fig. 42). This consists of a double rampart and ditch, which opened out at the entrance into a roughly triangular 'green'. In the period of secondary occupation the defences seem to have been repaired and a porter's lodge, 24 feet by 18 feet, was built inside the inner entrance. Within the fort the excavator Radford uncovered a complex of post-holes from which he reconstructed two halls, one measuring 90 feet by 40 feet, with a projection on the north side which he interpreted as a porch. Adjoining it he reconstructed a smaller, less substantial building about 24 feet square, and interpreted it as a kitchen. He was able to distinguish a second and later hall, measuring 65 feet by 35 feet, and other buildings, including a doubtful granary and an uncertain paved building. The occupation was dated by a sherd of an uncertain class of pottery ('sub-Roman' in Thomas's 1959 scheme). The lack of datable finds was the result of extensive ploughing which removed the upper level. The post-hole alignments were very irregular, and their interpretation therefore only a personal view.

The discussion could be extended to a number of other hillforts, for instance

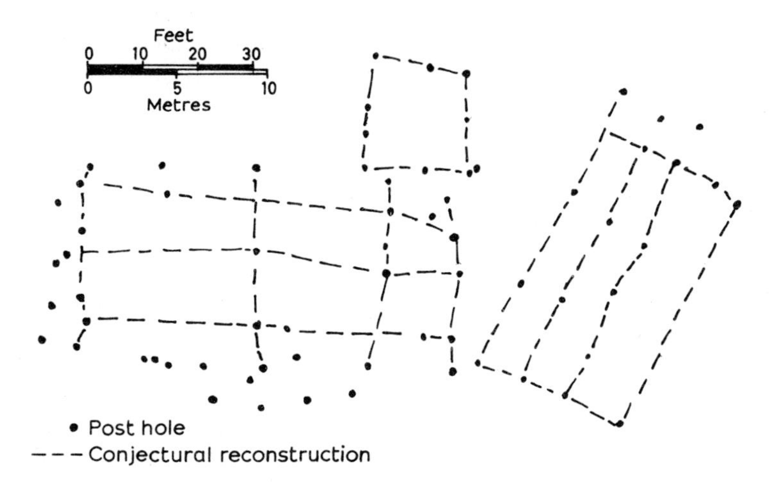

Figure 42 Castle Dore, Cornwall – Plan of halls (After Radford)

Cissbury, Sussex, which had a late Roman or post-Roman rampart, and Oldbury Camp, Wiltshire, which has occupation into the fifth century. The total distribution of sites which have produced either late Roman or post-Roman occupation or for which there is historical evidence is impressive. In Somerset alone there are sixty-two forts, of which twelve are likely to have been reoccupied. It has been estimated that an average of 20 per cent of the known English hillforts may have had some reoccupation.

The initial motive behind the growing tendency in the late fourth century to reoccupy hillforts was very frequently religious (and in this sense it is re-use rather than reoccupation), Romano-Celtic temples being established within the earlier defences. This revival of Romano-Celtic religion is well demonstrated at Lydney Park, Gloucestershire, where the site was reoccupied and guest buildings and a temple built, to continue flourishing into the fifth century. Possibly the religious revival was connected in some way with a general 'British revival' in the third and fourth centuries when native elements reasserted themselves. Some hillforts seem to have been used as cemeteries, either within or outside the defences, for instance at King's Weston near Bristol, Brean Down, Henley Wood, near Cadbury Congresbury, Cannington and Worlebury. In two cases, Henley Wood and Brean Down, all three features, temple, hillfort and cemetery, were closely associated.[37]

The religious use of hillforts precludes the theory that reoccupation was the result of some local warleader mustering a trusty band to hold out against the invading Saxons and refortifying the ancestral fort. The fact that so many were being reoccupied in the fourth century rules out the Saxon menace as the sole impetus. In many forts the reoccupation cannot be closely dated. Even at South Cadbury, for instance, the dating evidence for the initial post-Roman fortification is no closer than 'after 410 and before 550'.[38] Refortification in Wales and Scotland as well as England must certainly be explained by the general uncertainty of the times rather than by any particular menace.

House plans from Cadbury Congresbury, South Cadbury, Castle Dore and possibly Pilsdon Pen, together with information from Dinorben, Doon Hill, Dalry, Kirkconnel and Dinas Powys, provide evidence for the tradition of rectangular timber building, most notably of halls, in the early post-Roman period.

The basic building tradition in Iron Age Britain was the round *einzelhof*, and until recent years there were few examples of Iron Age rectilinear plans known in this country, the notable examples being at West Harling, Norfolk, and the rectilinear temple at Heathrow, London, both associated with roundhouses.[39] Recent excavations, most notably at Danebury, Hampshire,[40] and in the Welsh Marches,[41] suggest, however, that rectilinear plans may have been fairly widespread in southern England in the immediately pre-Roman period. Nevertheless, there is little as yet to support the idea that rectilinear plans were usual in the north or west, since when they occur in Welsh or northern English hut groups or the south-western rounds, for example, they appear to be the result of direct Roman influence. On the Continent the rectilinear plan was long established in the Iron Age, and even earlier examples are known.

It is highly unlikely that the rectilinear plan in post-Roman Britain represents a survival from the Iron Age; there are no aisled or large rectilinear buildings known from the British pre-Roman Iron Age, and no suggestion that they continued during the centuries of Roman domination.[42] The Romano-British aisled house is unlikely to have played any part in the origins of the rectangular hall of the post-Roman period since those closest in plan to the post-Roman structures are also the earliest and therefore the most chronologically remote.

Similarly there is no strong case in favour of the suggestion that the hall at South Cadbury is a devolved Roman basilica. In Somerset it is true that there were Roman models fairly readily available, but in some of the other areas there were no such sources of inspiration.

The conclusion which is most tenable is that the plan was introduced in the post-Roman period from outside, from one or more of the four possible sources: Anglo-Saxon England; the Mediterranean; northern Europe; Ireland.

The possibility of its being derived from Anglo-Saxon England can be ruled out since the evidence from South Cadbury points to the plan being established before there was any likelihood of Saxon building traditions affecting the region. If this is true for South Cadbury, it is even more likely for some of the more remote sites such as Castle Dore, Dinas Powys or Kirkconnel. It is possible that the plan came from the Mediterranean along with imported pottery and certain aspects of Christianity, but it should be borne in mind that the halls represent a way of life essentially barbarian, a far reach from Mediterranean stone-building traditions. Ireland remains a likely source since there is evidence that rectilinear timber building of a comparably skilled nature was long established there. Documentary evidence, allowing for borrowings at a later date and for literary effect, likewise indicates an Irish tradition of large timber buildings – the *Tech Midchuarta* at Tara is shown in a plan in the *Yellow Book of Lecan*. The law code known as the *Crith Gabhlach*, formalized in the ninth century but incorporating earlier material, also points to the existence of aisled halls in Early Christian Ireland.[43]

Most of the known halls are in areas where the Irish raided or settled. Although there is no evidence for early Irish settlement in Somerset, the Silchester ogham stone shows that one Irishman at least reached as far inland as Hampshire. The case for an Irish inspiration for the Somerset halls is admittedly not strong, but the present state of knowledge is too insubstantial for the case for the only remaining possible source, northern Europe, to be proved or disproved.

In Dumnonia reoccupied hillforts do not constitute all the evidence for settlement in the fifth and sixth centuries. In Devon an extensive midden has been investigated at *Bantham*, near Thurlestone. It lies at the end of a promontory with a sheltered harbour, where there are good internal lines of communication, as the promontory lies at the end of a ridgeway which links up with others. The finds from the site include sherds of B ii and B iii Wares as well as Class E, together with two double-sided bone combs, a spindle whorl decorated with incised dots and two iron javelin heads. It has been suggested that it was a trading post at which imported pottery first arrived. This theory was more probable when it was published in the 1950s than today, since very little imported pottery from other sites had then been recognized. Another similar site lies a few miles away to the west, at Mothecombe, on the mouth of the Erne.

Gwithian, Cornwall (Fig. 43), lies on the east side of St Ives bay. Excavations, carried out since 1948, have shown that occupation extended from the Mesolithic to early modern times. Four main sites at Gwithian, known as I, IV, Y and XX, have produced evidence for fifth- to sixth-century occupation.

The main site, I, is situated on a long low sand dune about a mile north of the present day Gwithian. Before the early Middle Ages the dune was attached to dry land to the east, and protruded into the estuary of the Red and Connar rivers. Three phases of occupation were recognized: Layers A, B and C, which were represented by a sequence of structures and dark bands separated by layers of clean yellow sand.

Layer C represented occupation from the fifth to the early seventh centuries, and produced traces of huts, almost entirely destroyed by stone robbing, along with 'Gwithian Style' pottery, a few sherds of grass-marked ware and sherds of imported A and B Wares. There were a few pieces of slag which indicated some metal working.

Layer B had an occupation extending from the seventh century to around

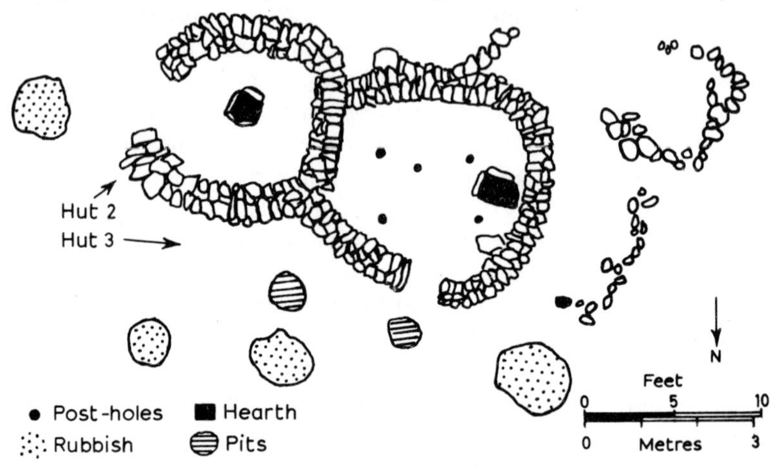

Figure 43 Gwithian, Cornwall – Plan of Early Christian period huts (After Thomas)

800 or 850 AD. There were three, possibly four, huts represented, of which Hut II was roughly circular, measuring 13 feet by 11 feet externally. Its entrance was on the east side, and the walls were composed of drystone without bonding material and made up of slabs of slate and blocks of quartz. In the centre was a large hearth, shaped into a pentagon by matching halves of rotary quern and other quern fragments. The absence of internal post-holes indicated that the roof rose directly from the wall head. Hut III was slightly larger and of the same general type, but postdated Hut II. The hearth was square, lined with granite and slate slabs. Four post-holes represented the roof supports. Hut IV was fragmentary, and measured about 6 feet in diameter. Both Huts III and IV were surrounded by collapsed turf, which had been used as an outer revetment for the walls, and both were extensively robbed during the next phase and used as middens.

There was abundant evidence for iron working in Layer B. Iron objects included tanged knives, long-handled saws, pins with oval heads, and square-section nails. There were also small quantities of lead and some bronze, including an awl and a piece of sheet metal. A pair of tweezers was found in the open space to the north of Huts II and III, of the sort encountered in Anglo-Saxon graves, notably at Abingdon. Stone implements including strikers, leather tanners and a 'limpet detacher' were abundant in both phases. A further range of finds came from a midden used in both phases. The pottery from Layer B consisted mainly of grass-marked ware, with some imported A and B Wares and a percentage of E Ware. E Ware also occurred in Layer C in similar quantities. Towards the end of the occupation represented by Layer B, bar lug pottery appeared. The occupation represented in Layer A was dated to the tenth and eleventh centuries and comprised a long dwelling of a type similar to those at Mawgan Porth.

A notable feature of phase B at Gwithian was an arable field (Site XX) contemporary with it.[44] This measured 90 feet by between 120 and 300 feet long. The northern long side was demarcated by a wide shallow boundary ditch, and on the southern side was a lynchet above the mud flats of the estuary. The field was some distance inland from the houses, due to the nature of the terrain. At the base of the plough soil in one cutting, stripes of sands separated horizontally and vertically by bands of dark soil were interpreted as the turned furrow slices produced by a fixed mould-board plough. Dating for the field was provided by three sherds of B i amphora, some Gwithian Style pottery and a considerable quantity of early grass-marked ware, which possibly reached the field in manure. Sickles and other indications of agriculture occurred at all levels on the site.

A village of approximately the same date as Gwithian Layer A has been excavated at *Mawgan Porth*, not far from St Mawgan-in-Pyder, Cornwall. This is the classic site for *bar lug* pottery, and a general date has been provided for it by a coin of Æthelred II immured there around AD 1000. It does not provide an absolute date for any one phase of the settlement, which lies somewhere between 850 and 1050 or a little later. The presence of this coin implies that the inhabitants of the settlement were not totally isolated from Anglo-Saxon influence. Other Anglo-Saxon coins have been found in Cornwall, and the Trewhiddle hoard of coins and ornamental silverwork suggests growing Anglo-Saxon cultural influence from the early ninth century onwards. Although the bar lug pottery derives some of its characteristics from northern Europe, the tradition represented at Mawgan Porth is essentially that of the native Cornish descendants of the occupants of Gwithian Layer B.

The site comprises a village and its associated cemetery. The hamlet was partly scarped into the slope of the hill, the cemetery and, one must assume, its attendant chapel (though this has not been found) dominating it from a great height. Two main clusters of buildings have been investigated, a third is known and a fourth may have existed.

The houses were rectilinear, built by stripping the hillside of its turf (later used for roofing) and red clay, and then partly quarrying the house platforms into the hill, so that they were level. On the uphill side of the site some of the rock was left upstanding to provide the base for walls, on average 2½ feet thick, built of quartz and roughly hewn blocks of quarried stone. They were built with facing stones and a rubble core, without mortar, though clay was used as pointing material. Slab-lined recesses were made into the walls, 3 or 4 feet from the ground, and slab-lined box beds and other furnishings were constructed, the slabs being set in quarried slots and kept in place with clay packing and stones. The roofs were supported by timber uprights, and after the floor had been levelled with surface shillet, earth was spread over it.

One main complex excavated proved to be a courtyard house comprising four main rooms round an open space, with doors opening off it. The main west room measured 33 feet by 14–15 feet with a long narrow annexe and a further small room opening off that. The whole complex covered an area about 70 feet by 54 feet. The main room was of 'longhouse' type, with both byre and living quarters under the same roof. The byre sector had a drain

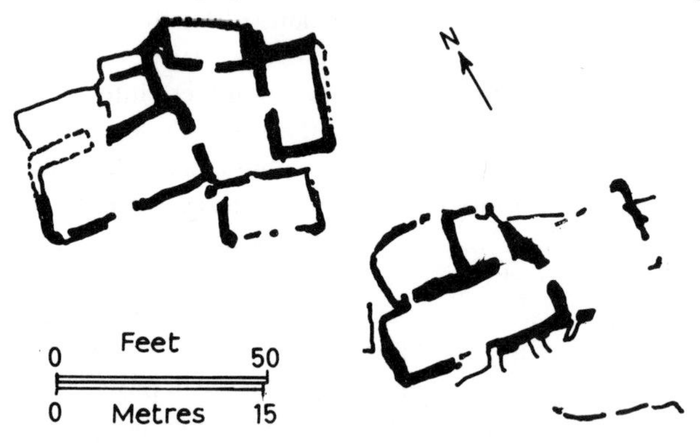

Figure 44 Mawgan Porth, Cornwall – Plan (After Bruce-Mitford)

in the south-west corner, and what was interpreted as a pile of decomposed fodder. A centrally placed pole doubled as a gable post and rubbing post. The byre was partitioned from the living room. This was furnished with box beds, rather more than 5 feet by 3 feet 6 inches, set in the wall angles. Along the south wall ran another slab-demarcated area, 10 feet by initially 18 inches wide but later widened to just over 2 feet, which may have been used as a 'keeping place' or less probably beds for children. Very near it was a hearth pit, which was associated with four small sharply defined holes which may have taken an iron pot support. This hearth was later replaced with another, central to the room. Other features included a countersunk polygonal basin, which may have held a tub, other slab-lined features and two large boulders which probably served as seats. The back room was used for storage – its only domestic feature was a cupboard, though its annexe may have been a sleeping room. The courtyard had a roofed recess which conceivably could have been a dog kennel. The north room was well built and had traces of internal rough-cast, and to the east of the door, in the south wall, a recess was built, possibly to catch the light from a window. The south room was contemporary with the original plan, the east a later development.

In the later complex the general pattern was the same, the courtyard in this instance being furnished with a slab-covered drain. Several phases of rebuilding were recognizable in both complexes. They should probably be seen as a parent steading with the dwellings of members of the extended family, and in this respect the pattern echoes Viking Jarlshof. Associated with the buildings were a terraced garden strip and wattle pen.

The finds from Mawgan Porth show that the inhabitants were essentially pastoralists, shell gatherers and fishermen. A notable feature is the virtual absence of metal, their implements being made of stone and bone. The most abundant finds were hammerstones, pounders, polishers, bone points and bodkins. A fragment of a bone comb and facings from two bone knife handles were decorated with ring-and-dot motifs. They ate mussels and snails, keeping the mussels unopened in slab tanks. They kept oxen, sheep and goats, as well as horses, dogs and cats, and possibly fighting cocks. The only evidence for agriculture was a granite quern built into one of the walls.

The cemetery consisted of slate cist burials, which were oriented east–west, with a very large proportion of child burials, which seem to have been grouped together to the west of the main burial area.

Early Christianity in the south-west[45]

As in the other areas of western Britain, there may have been some Christians in Cornwall in the late Roman period, presumably as the result of external contact coming by way of the river estuaries, as evidence from around the Hayle estuary might suggest. Further east, the six sub-Roman cemeteries known from Somerset imply a fairly strong surviving Christian community from the late and sub-Roman period. It is possible that Christianity was established early in the post-Roman period at Wareham, Dorset, as suggested by a group of post-Roman memorial stones.

In the fifth century, west Cornwall was one of the first areas of western Britain to receive a fresh wave of Christianity from the Continent. Along the coastal belt from the Camel estuary to the Devon border a group of early monastic sites can be recognized: St Kew (Landocco), Padstow (Lanwethiog), probably Cranstock and Perran, as well as the earliest excavated in mainland Britain, Tintagel.

It can be assumed that the early Church in Cornwall as elsewhere in Celtic Britain was initially based on a diocesan organization. In spite of its early monastic foundations it probably remained diocesan until at least the seventh century, at a time when the Irish Church was becoming increasingly monastic in emphasis. Bede refers to British bishops meeting St Augustine somewhere in the west, while a later legend refers to a bishop Gwethinoc, who, if he existed, probably lived in the sixth century. Later still, in the ninth century, a bishop Kenstec of Dinnurrin wrote a letter to Coelnoth, archbishop of Canterbury, and the names of several of his successors are known. It can only be speculated where the seat of the early bishops may have been – by the tenth century they were possibly based on the monasteries of St German and St Petroc.

No early timber oratories survive from Cornwall. The earliest archaeological remains are inscribed memorial stones – some with Latin inscriptions and some with inscriptions also in ogham, which are the result of the Irish settlements in Cornwall and the ensuing period of renewed Christian activity by the Irish. There are nine certain inscriptions of the fifth to sixth centuries in Cornwall, with a further five more dubious and fragmentary examples. Six stones carry ogham inscriptions. Many of these may have been originally associated with isolated graves – the *Cunaide* stone was erected over a burial in an abandoned round in the fifth century at Carnsew, Hayle.

A group of four stones from Beacon Hill cemetery on the island of *Lundy* appear to be in their original setting if not the original positions. The cemetery itself is a polygonal enclosure with a twelfth- or thirteenth-century church within. It does not appear, on present findings, to be the latest of a series on the site; as can be found on other sites in the Celtic west. The four stones, which range in date from the fifth to the seventh centuries, are, however, associated with a series of cist graves, of which the focus seems to have been a type of *cella memoria*, comprising a small enclosure, 7 feet 6 inches from east to west and about 17 feet from north to south, formed of upright slabs. Within this enclosure were three graves, covered by a low cairn of granite stones.

In Cornwall the presence of the placename element *lan* is possibly an indicator of a pre-eleventh-century cemetery.[46] The sequence in Cornwall, as elsewhere, was undoubtedly from undeveloped to developed cemetery, and as in Scotland many pre-Norman cemetery sites seem to have continued into the later medieval period with the addition of a medieval parish church. It has been estimated that there were approximately 700 chapels in Cornwall, of which many may be pre-Norman in origin. On a few classic sites the pre-Norman appearance has been preserved, the oval 'lan' at *Merther-Uny* in Wendron being one outstanding example.

Cornwall is notable for its variety of specialized chapel sites, which include *well chapels, landing-place chapels* and *lighthouse chapels*.[47] Well chapels were established where traditionally water first sprang from the ground for a saint. They are usually dedicated to the particular saint, the earliest surviving example in Cornwall being that of St Constantine at St Merryn, which may date from the ninth or eighth century. Landing-place chapels are sited where traditionally a patron saint landed from Ireland or Wales – Chapel Jane at Zennor is a good early example. Those lighthouse chapels associated with a beacon light tend to be late in the period.

Hermitage chapels form another category of specialized chapel sites. The most noteworthy is that excavated on *St Helens* in the Scilly Isles. The complex comprised a round hut, an oratory, a chapel and three rectangular huts enclosed by a precinct wall. The earliest structure was the round hut, which measured just under 12 feet in diameter, with walls 3 feet thick. The roof may have been of beehive form. The associated oratory, which was of more primitive 'megalithic' appearance, measured 15 feet by 8 feet with an altar containing a relic cavity. The chapel had three phases of construction, of which the first seems to have been built round a founder's grave, which would have been under the altar. Finds associated with these buildings were indeterminate, all medieval, but the oratory and cell could have dated to the seventh or eighth century and the first phase of the chapel certainly predated the twelfth century, though it is not certain by how much. The later phases of the chapel were twelfth century. The other buildings were medieval, the site having remained in use probably until the sixteenth century.

Some masonry chapels of the pre-Norman period have survived, at least in a fragmentary state. The double-square plan was favoured in Cornwall in contrast to the 3 : 2 ratio for the walls in most of Ireland. The double-square plan was probably due to Roman influence.

Later sculptured stones

Apart from the Latin-lettered stones and the ogham stones of the fifth and sixth centuries, there is in Cornwall an important group of later stones: a series starting in the seventh century with Irish-type half uncial inscriptions; a series of sculptured free-standing crosses; and a few hog-backed grave covers.

There are at least 500 free-standing crosses or fragments in Cornwall, but a great number of them date from the Middle Ages. They span the period from the ninth to the fifteenth centuries, and were erected for a variety of purposes.[48] The most important class which dates from the Early Christian period (but which overlaps into the Middle Ages) is that of *churchyard crosses*, set within churchyards, often on the right-hand side of the entrance. A few of these can be assigned to the ninth and tenth centuries, and some show strong Anglo-Saxon influence; it is possible that some were inspired by an important series of crosses associated with the monastery of St Petroc at Bodmin. A second group comprise *churchway crosses* which were set up to mark the route to a church and were used as stations where funerary processions could rest and say prayers. These all tend to be of the eleventh century or later. Two remaining classes are *sanctuary crosses*, used to indicate the extent of Church land, or the Church glebe, and *ornamental crosses*.

The most important of the pre-Conquest crosses are a series with wheel heads and decoration in late Hiberno-Saxon style. The general style seems to have been a product of Anglo-Scandinavian traditions in northern England, which spread to affect Welsh sculpture (p. 224). The Cornish series seems to be an offshoot from that of south Wales, and shares a number of decorative features in common with the Welsh – in addition the distribution is concentrated along the north Cornish coast and in the neighbourhood of the peninsula roads.

The decorative schemes used on the Cornish crosses are basically those of the vinescroll and interlace, ring-chain of Viking origin being particularly favoured, though key-and-fret patterns, step patterns, and triquetras are also common, as are alternately inverted T's. The so-called 'Jellinge Beast' and

Figure 45 The Cardinham Cross

'Ringerike scroll' were obviously borrowed directly from Viking sculpture. A number of the Cornish crosses have inscriptions in devolved Hiberno-Saxon lettering.

The finest of the Cornish crosses is that at *Cardinham* near Bodmin (Fig. 45). This cross has on one face a very degenerate vinescroll, more reminiscent of a running spiral than true vinescroll, with an interlaced head, while the sides carry step patterns, ring-chain and ring-twist interlace. The ring-chain is of the type first encountered on Gaut's cross on Man (p. 215), and dates from the tenth century.

Two crosses, from *Sancreed* and *Lanherne*, along with a third, from *Waterpit Down*, illustrate between them the range of motifs commonly employed on tenth-century crosses in Cornwall. The Sancreed Cross bears a Crucifixion on its head, probably one of the earliest of a long series of such representations on Cornish crosses.

As in Wales and the west Highlands, the traditions of the pre-Norman crosses continued into the later Middle Ages, and in the thirteenth century there seems even to have been a deliberate revival of the Hiberno-Saxon style

– the best example of this type is at Quethiock, which combines debased vine-scroll with Gothic detail.

Of the other categories of sculptured monument of the Early Christian period mention may be made of three hog-back stones, exotic in Cornwall but presumably ultimately derived from the Danelaw or elsewhere in northern England where they were popular. In style the Cornish examples are distinctive, and obviously products of a local school. They date from the tenth to eleventh centuries. Finally, there are a series of altar stones, of which the altar frontal known from its inscription as the 'Levvit stone' (tenth century) and the altar mensa from Treslothan (probably eleventh century) are the most notable.

Tintagel (Fig. 46; Plate 7A)

One of the most famous sites of Early Christian Cornwall is the monastery at Tintagel. The site is an exposed promontory, associated with Arthurian

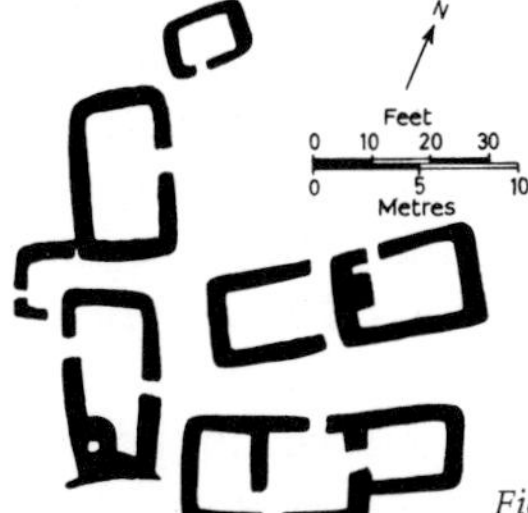

Figure 46 Tintagel – Plan of living cells

legend and crowned with the ruins of a medieval castle. The monastic remains were found almost by chance during consolidation. The remains comprise groups of small rectangular cells of stone and clay walling, butted onto one another. They probably had thatched roofs. The most important group of cells adjoins a Norman chapel, which presumably had a pre-Norman predecessor. Within the associated graveyard are the bare foundations of a *leacht* about 5 feet square.

Among the other buildings are further groups of cells on a shelf on the headland and a building identified as a scriptorium, furnished with benches. A small structure with a burned paved floor may have served as a vapour bath. A corn-drying kiln on the cliff edge indicates that originally there had been associated fields, presumably some distance away.

Four building periods were distinguished, taking the occupation down to the ninth century. At its greatest extent it seems to have housed about thirty monks.

The Anglo-Saxon advance

The problem of the Anglo-Saxon penetration of Wessex is one which has taxed scholars for fifty years, and the solution to it is not yet certain. What is fairly clear, however, is that in the period prior to 450 there was a gradual expansion of Saxon settlement up the Thames valley, concentrated on Roman towns such as Dorchester. At sites such as Abingdon, Berkshire, where there is ample evidence for early settlement, it seems likely this grew up round small Roman communities.[49] This Thames valley spread may be connected with the formation of a boundary between the area to the north of the Thames and that to the south of it, for cremation cemeteries are found north of the Thames, while inhumations are to the south. Along the Thames itself some cemeteries of mixed character occur. Whatever the explanation, this pattern is reinforced after 450 – the years that have recently been designated the period of uncontrolled settlement, when the style of pottery characterized by arched 'eyebrow' decoration known as *stehende bogen* gave way to elaborately decorated urns with bosses known as *buckelurnen*.[50] The spread of early *buckelurnen*, coupled with the distribution of equal-armed and other types of fifth-century brooches, shows the westward expansion of the Saxons, and it is generally held that the initial settlement of the Thames valley was augmented by a further spread from the north-east down the Iknield Way into Wessex from Middle Anglia. The map of *buckelurnen* shows that penetration extended as far as Warwickshire, and a small accessory vessel with faceted carination from the cemetery at Fairford implies that they reached the borders of Gloucestershire around 450 if not before. Until the end of the fifth century, however, there was no penetration of Somerset, Dorset or Hampshire.

In the traditions of early post-Roman history in England is the battle of *Mons Badonicus*. According to one interpretation of Gildas, the Saxon advance was halted following a great massacre of the invaders at a place called Mons Badonicus (Mount Badon), which he dates to the year of his birth, forty-four years before the time at which he was writing. This cannot be precisely dated, but it must lie between 490 and 516, probably around 500. Gildas asserts that since the battle there had been no further Saxon advance, which would mean a general halt during the first half of the sixth century. Archaeology confirms this assertion, and indeed might even imply that there was a slight reverse migration as the areas not very strongly held were relinquished.[51]

The settlement was not however in any way as extensive as Gildas might imply, and can only be argued for certain areas where the inhumation cemeteries show a break in the pottery sequence. In the areas of cremation burial, the pottery sequence continues unbroken up to the seventh century.

In Hampshire and the Isle of Wight in contrast to the rest of the south-west there is evidence for some fresh Anglo-Saxon settlement in the early sixth century. The cemetery at Worthy Park,[52] taken with the evidence provided by three urns from Fareham, implies Anglo-Saxon advance into Hampshire, the pots covering an unbroken sequence from a little before 500. Perhaps this is connected in some way with the traditional landing of Cerdic and his followers.[53] Further north, in the valley of the Warwick Avon, the story echoes that in Hampshire. There is little evidence for Saxon penetration prior to about 500, but, once established, the Saxon settlements flourished, as exemplified by cemeteries at Baginton, Stratford and Bidford-on-Avon.[54]

It would seem that the sequence on the upper Thames valley is disrupted around the early sixth century, for although the early types of *buckelurnen* (Classes I–IV) are encountered here, Class V, though widespread elsewhere, does not occur in the Upper Thames or its tributaries.[55]

From the mid-sixth century onwards there was a rapid expansion of the Anglo-Saxon advance. The expansion of Wessex under Ceawlin between 556 and his death in 593 brought the kingdom of Wessex into prominence. Apart from annexing Kent and probably the Surrey Saxons, Ceawlin consolidated the Saxon position on the Upper Thames, capturing Gloucester, Cirencester and Bath in 577. The same year had seen the defeat of three British kings at the battle of Deorham in Gloucestershire, and presumably the collapse of British supremacy in this area. Were the three chiefs, perhaps, the leaders of the still surviving three towns? Archaeologically, the campaigns of Ceawlin are difficult to follow, though it has been argued that the distribution of late panel style pottery with pendent triangles may reflect the arena of his activities.[56]

The remarkable linear earthwork known as Wansdyke, once believed to be a British defence against the Saxons, was probably a west Saxon boundary put up shortly after the treaty with Penda in 628.[57] By this date Wessex had already taken shape. The west Saxons occupied the northern and eastern perimeter of the Somerset Levels, while the British continued to hold the islands in the marshy lowlands. This would appear to be the situation until some time during the first half of the seventh century, for until then South Cadbury, Cadbury Congresbury and Glastonbury appear to have been in British hands, though Glastonbury was the site of an Irish monastic foundation established by clerics who had probably travelled inland from Cornwall. West Dorset was still British, though there is evidence, notably from the Saxon cemetery at Hardown Hill, that the population was already somewhat mixed.

A scatter of Anglo-Saxon finds have been recorded from the lowlying areas of Somerset – these include a button brooch from South Cadbury, two disc brooches and a square-headed brooch from Ilchester which mark the fringe area, while there are skeletons and an Anglo-Saxon sword from Queen Camel and a possible Anglo-Saxon cemetery at Long Sutton.[58]

The year 614 probably saw the Saxon advance into Devon, for in that year, according to the *Anglo-Saxon Chronicle*, Cynegils and Cwichelm fought at

Beandun and killed 2,045 Britons. The site overlooks the estuary of the Axe, so the operation may have been partly naval. In 658 the Saxons won the battle of *Peonnan*, sometimes identified as Penselwood on the Somerset–Wiltshire border, but more probably Pinhoe, just outside Exeter. The Saxon advance into Devon was furthered in 661 at the battle of Ponsbury, which gave command of north Dartmoor, and in a further battle in 682 effective control of Devon was gained. The British were pushed north-eastwards, and a flourishing British community must have existed as late as the eighth century at Cannington, to judge by the 350 or more graves in the cemetery there.

The Saxon inroad into Cornwall did not take place until 838, when a Viking fleet appeared off Cornwall and the Cornishmen joined forces with the raiders. Such a situation could not be tolerated by Eadgar, who defeated a combined Cornish-Danish force at Hingston Down. This military victory was followed up by Æthelstan, Eadgar's son, who infiltrated Cornwall by making grants of land to Saxons and the Saxon Church, setting up a diocese there. In 926 he received the submission of the king of Cornwall, Huwal, and nominally at least Cornwall was English from this time onwards. The effect of the Anglo-Saxons on Cornish life, however, was probably negligible, though it no doubt opened up a limited amount of trade. An Anglo-Saxon mint was opened at Launceston, and a small hoard of nine Anglo-Saxon pennies ranging from Æthelstan to Eadgar (925–75) was found near St Austell.[59] The manumissions in the Bodmin gospels show that from the early tenth century the slave-owning class in Cornwall was increasingly Anglo-Saxon, though there are some Celtic names and even some Anglo-Saxon slaves. By the late eleventh century, the English were predominant in Cornwall.

6 Ireland

Cultural continuity is a dominant factor in the study of later prehistoric and early historic Ireland. Yet the limitations of the available evidence are such that this continuity is perhaps more apparent than real, and while certain settlement and artefact types may have been of long duration, other facets of Irish society may have been less conservative.

The Iron Age

The Irish Iron Age is very imperfectly understood, due to the general scarcity of diagnostic types of sites or finds that can be used to establish a framework for the period. There is virtually no pottery, few graves and few classes of site which can be ascribed to the period. The same types of settlement appear to have been occupied from the late Bronze Age until the Early Christian period; often only excavation can show them to have been occupied in the Iron Age, and many of those that are recognized are culturally impoverished and produce few finds.

It is becoming apparent, however, that there is no sharp cultural break in Ireland between the late Bronze and early Iron Ages. During the seventh to third centuries BC it is possible to recognize a period when both Bronze Age and hybrid Bronze Age/Hallstatt cultures were systadial in Ireland,[1] and to this period probably belong a series of palisaded settlements such as that recently excavated at Navan,[2] and possibly also a few univallate hillforts. By 200 BC alongside Hallstatt-derived elements it is possible to distinguish elements of La Tène derivation. In 1958 a picture of the 'dual La Tène colonization' of Ireland was advanced which has won widespread acceptance.[3] The basis of this classification is the recognition of two distinct groups of objects, the first seen to be derived directly from the Continent, the other, rather later, derived indirectly through British intermediaries. Careful study of the two groups raises certain doubts. The list of continental 'imports' consists mainly of exotic objects not matched by a comparable list of the smaller, everyday objects which are essential if extensive cultural transmission is to be postulated. These exotic objects are evidence only for trade contacts between Ireland and the Continent in the late third or early second century BC, with possibly a few settlers in the west.

An examination of the Irish La Tène Style metalwork stresses more strongly the case against extensive continental influence. It has recently been cogently argued that the great majority of Irish objects decorated in a La Tène Style are without parallel outside Ireland. They include fibulae, which are the most informative, for if there was contact other than trade or casual transmission the incidence of more fibulae of direct continental origin might be expected than is in fact the case. This is not to deny any artistic contact with the Continent – certain patterns in use in both areas imply some type of direct link between Ireland and eastern Gaul and the Rhineland.

If the idea of extensive settlement in Ireland from the Continent can be dismissed, so probably can the case for extensive settlement from Britain. The theory that influences reached Ireland from Yorkshire by way of south-west Scotland must be rejected, as it rests largely on the similarity between the unique Torrs pony cap and certain pieces of Irish metalwork; the pony cap itself may be an import to Kirkcudbrightshire from much further afield.[4] In general, north Wales possibly played a greater part in the field of British–Irish contacts, and there are stylistic affinities between some of the metalwork from the Tal-y-Llyn hoard and the Lisnacroghera scabbards, while the Llyn Cerrig Bach find included an Irish trumpet of Lough-na-Shade type.[5]

The evidence, then, points to the gradual development in Ireland of an insular culture or cultures with elements introduced from outside either through trade or possibly through the sporadic settlement of small groups of people. In this connection it is worth mentioning the finds from the rath of Feerwore, Co. Galway,[6] which in fact constitute the only assemblage of this type. Here, if nowhere else, the finds imply a settlement of people from outside Ireland, almost certainly continental Europe. Taken on its own, however, it is hardly sufficient for general conclusions to be drawn.

From the first century AD onwards in Ireland further new elements, of Roman derivation, can be recognized. At Rathtinaun, Lough Gara, Co. Sligo, one phase of occupation of a crannog ended in desertion, probably because of a rise in the water level.[7] Radiocarbon dating and the character of the finds suggest that the site was reoccupied in the second century AD. The finds do not include any material of characteristically 'La Tène' type, but do include a range of objects of the sort usually encountered on sites of the Early Christian period. This has caused some speculation in Ireland, and it has been suggested that many accepted 'Early Christian period' sites should be dated much earlier, and are strictly speaking Iron Age.[8] This trend in 'backdating' sites has arisen possibly out of a dearth of sites in Ireland that can be ascribed with any certainty to the first five centuries of the Christian era. If it is accepted that certain types of objects were coming to Ireland during this period and continuing for much of the first millennium this hiatus is removed.

The source of the 'Roman' elements in the material culture of Early Christian Ireland has long been debated. Although the Romans did not reach Ireland, many everyday objects on Irish Early Christian period sites are of Roman derivation. The argument that these types were introduced in the very late Roman or post-Roman period at the time of the Irish raids on Britain and the ensuing settlement is not convincing, since there is very inadequate evidence that they were in regular use in the areas of western Britain actually affected by Irish raids and settlements.

The list of 'Roman' finds from Lagore Crannog, Co. Meath,[9] is typical of a pattern repeated on other sites. On present evidence Lagore was first occupied around 600, though it is possible that occupation may have begun in the sixth century. First, there is a series of tools derived from the Roman – axes, adzes, draw knives, forks, socketed pronged tools and certain features of swords. The toilet articles are Roman in inspiration, as are many of the pin types and possibly the bronze bowls. A number of objects – barrel padlocks and keys, rings with sliding knots, twisted-iron bucket handles with a flat grip in the middle, and some bead types, are of Roman origin, but found fairly widely in post-Roman Europe as well. Apart from these there are a number of objects which are also found in La Tène contexts, such as iron knives and shears, bill hooks, and certain types of spear. Other types of spear are of purely Roman derivation.

Many of these 'Roman' elements probably do belong to the period of coming and going between Britain and Ireland in the sub-Roman and post-Roman period, for example dress fasteners of various types, bronze bowls and possibly, but by no means certainly, weapons. The other objects belong to the native economic milieu, and are the adjuncts not so much of fashion but of the way of life that was already gradually emerging in the last two centuries BC but which did not develop fully until the early centuries AD (p. 7). It was in this period, not later, that many of the everyday objects probably made their first appearance in Ireland.

Cahercommaun and chronology (Fig. 47)

The dating of certain Early Christian sites in Ireland is of critical importance. Recently Raftery has put forward the suggestion that Cahercommaun, a stone fort in Co. Clare, which is regarded as a 'classic' site occupied in the Early Christian period, is in fact Roman Iron Age, and in so doing has cast doubt on the dating of a number of other major sites.[10] His case for backdating

Cahercommaun is based on the 'Roman' character of many of the finds, and the fact that the most closely datable find, a silver brooch of *c.* AD 800, came from a souterrain which might be secondary to the fort itself. However, none of the finds can be conclusively proved to be Iron Age and, furthermore, there

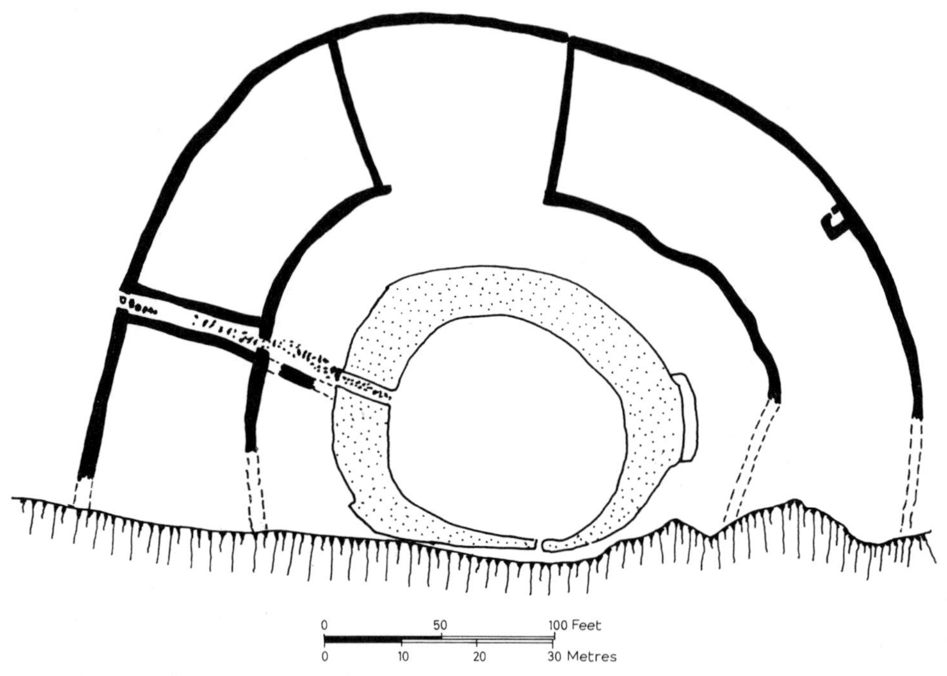

Figure 47 Cahercommaun, Co. Clare – Plan

are many finds which could not predate the fifth century AD. These include a fragment of a penannular brooch of Type E, a type that evolved out of Type D brooches which in turn developed in the fourth century (p. 000). An enamelled ring for a type of ringed pin uses red and yellow enamel in L-shaped cloisons, and belongs to a class of ornamented pin which is a cross between a true ringed pin and a penannular brooch. Typologically such an object is compatible with an eighth-century date, and while a case might be made for a slightly earlier date it could not conceivably be earlier than the seventh century, as the prototypes were not in existence. The tanged bronze studs of the type found at Cahercommaun are only known from Early Christian sites, and their affinities are Germanic – they were securely dated at Dinas Powys, Glamorgan. Even more characteristic are the shears, which have semicircular recesses at the top of the blades. The type occurs very rarely in Scandinavia in tenth-century burials, and in England, with the exception of a Middle Saxon example from Maxey, Northants, is apparently thirteenth century or later. As a type it apparently evolved in Early Christian Ireland, and there are no known earlier examples. Various pin types, the spindle whorls, the combs, the knives, the barrel padlocks, the bell and glass bracelet fragments from Cahercommaun all have their counterparts on other Early Christian period sites. Reviewing the whole assemblage from Cahercommaun, there is nothing that cannot be paralleled from other Early Christian sites, and the majority of the finds can be paralleled from them alone. It may be argued from this that the sites used for comparative purposes have also been wrongly dated, as indeed Raftery has suggested. However, several of the comparable sites have totally independent dating of the Early Christian period provided by imported pottery, and are not confined to Ireland but include Dinas Powys in Wales and Dunadd in Scotland.

The revised dating for the site at Cahercommaun has become fairly widely accepted, and on this basis other sites such as Lagore, the two Ballinderry crannogs, Garranes, Ballycatteen and Carraig Aille have likewise been redated, although in some of these cases the evidence for an Iron Age date is even weaker – Carraig Aille and 'The Spectacles' have produced conclusive evidence of occupation in the Viking period.[11] It is not enough, however, to date an Irish site simply because some finds from it can be compared with those from major Early Christian period sites, and extreme caution should be used for dating sites which have not produced diagnostic objects, more particularly imported pottery, glass, penannular brooches or pins of known Early Christian type. Furthermore, it is possible that a few may have had an earlier occupation in the Christian period as well as a later. On the basis of diagnostic material, the *floruit* of some of the major Irish Early Christian period sites would seem to be:

Garranes	*c.* 500
Garryduff 1	*c.* 650
Ballycatteen	*c.* 600
Ballinderry 2	*c.* 500–700
Lagore	*c.* 600 or possibly slightly earlier–1000
Cahercommaun	*c.* 600–800
Carraig Aille I	*c.* 650–950
Carraig Aille II	*c.* 700–1000 or later
Ballinderry 1	*c.* 975–1100

Contacts with the Roman world

The list of the Roman material from Ireland compiled by S. P. O'Riordain in the 1940s can now be extended and it is increasingly apparent that it cannot simply be confined to the period of the Irish raids.[12] The earliest material, which must predate the Roman occupation of Britain, consists of sherds of

Arretine ware, a type of red-gloss pottery that was ousted by south Gaulish samian in the Claudian period. Arretine has been found at Ballinderry and Tara,[13] while samian and other Romano-British pottery comes from Lagore. These are presumably later residuals, brought to the sites from elsewhere, but Roman material has been found in Iron Age contexts. At Freestone Hill, Co. Kilkenny, the finds of undoubted Roman origin include a coin of 337–40 AD. A coin was also found along with Roman pottery at the Rath of the Synods at Tara, and Roman coins were present at Newgrange. The site on Lambay Island, Dublin, produced a series of graves with Roman and Romano-British objects.[14] The imports include an iron mirror and four bronze brooches. A fifth brooch is a native copy in which the pin and catch plate are cast as one.

The series of Irish brooches shows very clearly the extent of influence from Roman Britain. The *Navan* series of brooches appears to have been developed in Ireland in the first century AD and the features of divided bow, openwork pattern and bulbous snout-like foot are derived partly from the Roman divided-bow brooches and openwork mounts (Fig. 131).[15] The evidence is supported by some of the metalwork from the Somerset (Galway) find, which included thin bronze discs with cut openwork, which may be derived from Roman enamelled disc brooches, or, less certainly, late pre-Roman Iron Age enamelled roundels.[16]

The evidence, then, is that Roman objects were brought into Ireland from the first century AD and assimilated by the Irish who developed their own variants of at least some. Of necessity the evidence takes the form of metalwork and pottery, but it may be assumed that less concrete influences were also felt. The ogham alphabet must have been formed as a result of contact with Roman literacy, and there are strong classical elements in the body of Early Irish literature, though much of this may be due to the classical education of the monks who set down lore in the Early Christian period.

Early Irish history

Irish history may be said to begin with the arrival of St Patrick in Ireland. Belonging to the period before this, however, is a considerable body of myth and quasi-history, set down by the monks in later centuries. Much of this quasi-history is enigmatic, but it quite certainly incorporates a genuine core of history and is therefore worthy of study by the historian. In the period of the legends the beginning of the struggle between Leinster and central Ireland can be seen: in the fourth century Cormac mac Airt, who ruled at Tara, exacted a tribute from Leinster. Munster figures little in proto-history.

With the fifth century came the rise of Niall of the Nine Hostages, Niall Noigiallach. He and his sons began by conquering Meath, and he ruled from Tara. The events of his reign are largely legendary. He is credited with raiding in the Western Isles, and seems to have gained virtual control over Ireland

and under him and his sons Ireland became split in two. Northern Ireland was ruled over by his family, known as the northern and southern Ui Neill, while southern Ireland was dominated by the ruling family of Munster. It is from this time that the development of Tara as the seat of the north and Cashel of the south can be recognized, with the emergence of the High Kingship of Tara. Of the two branches of the Ui Neill, the eldest sons became the southern Ui Neill and were based on Tara, while the younger sons comprised the northern Ui Neill which remained unified until the eighth century.

Northern Ireland was the most prominent area in the period preceding the Viking raids. The main source for its history is the *Annals of Ulster*. The history of southern Ireland is less well documented, and probably was fairly peaceful until the time of the Vikings and the rise of Brian Boru. There were some disputes between Munster and Leinster, but Munster tended to be oriented towards the Continent and was culturally more progressive. For the history of the south, the *Annals of Innisfallen* is one of the most useful sources.

Settlements

To make a distinction between sites occupied in the post-Patrician and pre-Patrician eras is false, for it is clear that though there are chronological differences the economy and settlement pattern of Ireland remained basically the same for the whole of the first millennium.

A small group of 'Pagan' *ceremonial sites* have been recognized. It is now apparent that a number of sites frequently referred to in Irish legends particularly as places of inauguration, which were well known in the Early Christian period, have origins in the early Iron Age. Three important sites at which excavations have taken place are *Temair* (Tara; Plate 5B), Co. Meath, *Emain Macha* (Navan Fort), Co. Armagh, and *Dun Ailinne* (Knockaulin), Co. Kildare. Peculiar to these ceremonial sites is the sprawling nature of the univallate enclosure, with internal subsidiary structures. Although not built on high hills, they command a wide view of the surrounding countryside. The ramparts are frequently outside the ditch.

Hillforts of a type found in Britain (timber-laced or with earth univallate or multivallate defences) are far less common in Ireland than the smaller ringforts or raths. Some of them are undoubtedly related to their British counterparts, but their investigation is as yet in its infancy. A recent study[17] has recognized about forty examples and has classified them into three categories.

Class I. *Univallate forts with or without a ditch.* There are some twenty of these which include the ritual sites as well as a variety of other monuments ranging from small forts of about an acre, such as Dun Beag, Co. Down, to the very large such as Dun Ailinne (34 acres). The distribution of the univallate forts is almost exclusively eastern. The forts at Freestone Hill and Downpatrick have been excavated. Finds from Freestone Hill seem to imply that it was a product of the fourth century AD but many univallate forts may be much earlier. At Downpatrick the earth rampart was strengthened by internal timber lacing.[18]

Class II. *Multivallate forts with widely spaced ramparts* which are situated either (a) on hilltops or (b) on clifftops. These forts represent a distinctive group, predominantly western in distribution. A feature of four of the forts is the

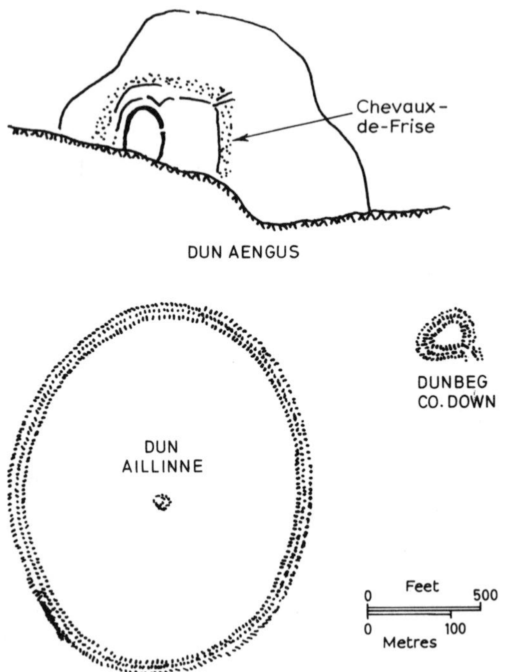

Figure 48 Irish hillforts (After Evans)

use of *chevaux de frise*, a type of fortification employing stones set with jagged points upwards in an area to prevent a ready assult on the defences. *Chevaux de frise* appear to have started as timber staking in Hallstatt C Europe, and were possibly spread by the arrival of horsemen from east Europe around 700 BC. From central Europe they spread to Spain and to Britain.[19]

The Class II monuments also show certain affinities with a small group of forts with widely spaced ramparts in Scotland, such as Arbory Law or the two Caterhuns, though the relationship is not certain. The forts in Classes I and II seem to have a distribution pattern that is almost mutually exclusive.

Class III. *Inland promontory forts.* These forts are very few in number, and may be univallate or multivallate. In some instances, such as Lurigethan, Co.

Antrim, the nature of the promontory is such that defences are only required on one side, where there are three closely set ramparts. Some forts have as many as four or six ramparts. In a few cases, as for example Caherconree, Co. Kerry, the rampart is of stone. As in Britain, a few of the Irish hillforts may have been reoccupied in the Early Christian period. The most convincing evidence for this comes from Downpatrick, which was occupied intermittently until the thirteenth century.

A group of *stone-walled forts*, which are typologically related to the ringforts discussed below, have entrance passages checked for doors, and staircases up to wall walks. They are very like outsize examples of Scottish 'duns' and are

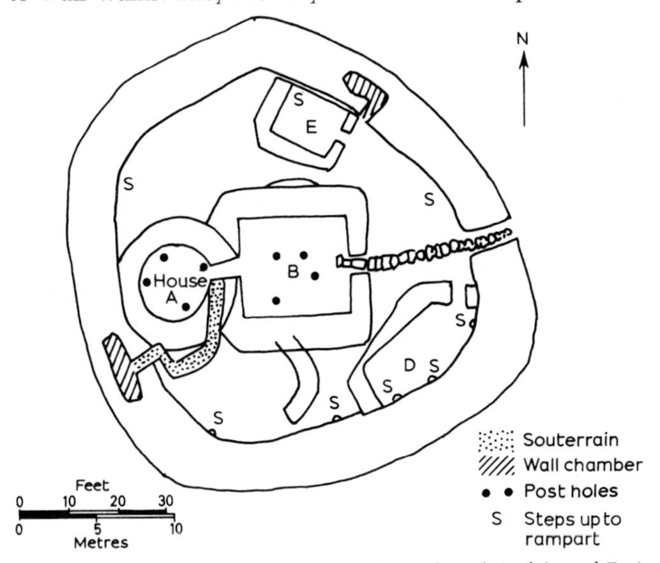

Figure 49 Leacanabuaile fort, Co. Kerry – Plan (After O'Riordain and Foy)

possibly related to the stone forts of the Scottish Atlantic province. Some, such as the *Grianan of Aileach*, Co. Derry, or *Staigue Fort* (Plate 5A), Co. Kerry, have been postulated as Early Christian mainly on the basis of tradition, since excavation has never been carried out. An argument in favour of a late date for Staigue and the Grianan is that the similar fort of Leacanabuaile, Co. Kerry (Fig. 49) was shown to be probably Early Christian. Leacanabuaile, however, is more closely related to Scottish duns, which have been argued as belonging to a very long tradition from the second century BC into the Early Christian period. Since for instance the Grianan shows close affinities to the Iron Age site at Clickhimin in Shetland, as well as Early Christian period characteristics, it would seem that the large stone forts also belong to a long-lived tradition. It is fairly certain that some of the Irish forts continued in occupation well into the Early Christian period. The Grianan almost certainly attained its maximum importance in the fifth century. *The Martyrology of Oengus the*

Culdee, written about AD 800, implies that Rathcrogan, Dun Ailinne and Navan were destroyed at some time before that date. The destruction of the Grianan of Aileach is recorded by the *Annals of the Four Masters* under the year 1101.[20]

Apart from the inland promontory forts, there are about 200 forts situated on rocky promontories on headlands mainly in the south and south-west of Ireland. Their main feature is their use of ramparts across one side of the headland only as in the case of the inland forts. In contrast to those inland, the forts are generally small, and represent a special group. They cannot be readily dated – the site at Ballygalley Head, Co. Antrim,[21] appears to have been used in Neolithic times, while others seem to be medieval or later. Where evidence is available the only provable date for occupation has been in the Early Christian period. It seems probable, however, that many are Early Iron Age like their British counterparts.

The dating of *Cahercommaun* has been discussed above (p. 148). The fort consisted of three limestone walls without ditches, the two outer enclosures being used as cattle kraals, a few huts in the outer enclosure probably belonging to herdsmen. The entrance to the fort was a straight path with paving stones which led through the three lines of walls (Fig. 47). Only the inner wall was defensive, and within it were a dozen small irregularly built structures, including a guard house, a sentry post, a chief's dwelling with two souterrains, one leading out under the fort wall to the ravine, the other the servants' quarters, and a further dwelling. There was some evidence for two phases of occupation but without a substantial break. The economy of the fort was primarily pastoral, with some limited cultivation, supplemented by the hunting of red deer. Iron working was carried out extensively to the exclusion of bronze working.

By far the largest class of monument in first millennium Ireland is the ringfort (Fig. 50; Plate 6A). There are at least 30,000, possibly 40,000, and of these only about 100 have been excavated. In almost every example examined certain features have been identified to distinguish it from the others. The forts are known by a variety of names; *rath*, *caiseal* (cashel) and *dun*, of which the term *caiseal* should be reserved for stone-built forts. In Ireland the term *dun* is usually reserved for large, substantially built forts, which often have stone or stone-faced ramparts, such as Dun Aenghus and Dun Beag.

Certain ringforts may date to the Neolithic/early Bronze Age – Carrigillihy, Co. Cork, has been assigned to the early Bronze Age.[22] O'Riordain excavated a group of conjoined ringforts at Cush, Co. Limerick,[23] and believed them to be late Bronze Age, though currently most are regarded as early Iron Age with some possible Early Christian occupation. The primary occupation of the Rath of Feerwore, Co. Galway, was certainly Iron Age, though here too there is some evidence of an Early Christian period occupation.[24] The early ringforts, however, remain problematical, and the large majority seem to date from the Early Christian period.

The essential feature of the rath or cashel is the central enclosed area, which is usually circular and ranges between 80 and 200 feet in diameter, the most typical being about 100 feet across.[25] This area is enclosed normally with a single rampart, less frequently by two or more concentric banks, with quarry ditch or ditches. Normally the ditches are absent from the stone-walled cashels, but at Lissachigel there was a partial ditch to provide drainage. To some extent the nature of the terrain seems to have dictated whether the construction was in earth or stone, but both raths and cashels can occur in the same area. Raths and cashels are not entirely a homogeneous group, and variations in the types are encountered, some being more akin to hillforts or promontory forts; for example Cahercommaun is sometimes described as a cashel.

It is becoming increasingly clear that the rath or cashel belongs to a different tradition from the forts, for they seem to have been simply nuclear farmsteads. They represent the parallel tradition to that of the single roundhouse found throughout Iron Age Britain, and can be seen as a native Irish development in response to the economic environment, suggesting an Irish equivalent of Little Woodbury. A wide variety of features, such as working hollows or pits (as at Garranes), entrance features (as at Ballycatteen) and storage pits (as at Kiltera)[26] belong to the basic tradition of the 'Little Woodbury economy'. The initial stimulus for the appearance of the rath may have come from outside Ireland, but the wide dissemination of this type of settlement was due to native developments under the stimulus of new techniques and economies – settled agriculture and an expanding rural economy facilitated by the use of iron. In this context the Bronze Age precursors of the raths must be seen as one of the native settlements in Ireland which proved to be more suited than the many other types to the new economy, since the enclosing rampart or wall enabled the stock to be kept together, an increasing necessity with the presumed increase in the size of herds.

There is a growing body of evidence that some at least of the raths were preceded by earlier settlements on the same sites. At Lisnagade 2 the first occupation phase consisted of an irregular and shallow V-shaped ditch with inner bank, which later became infilled and the area increased by the construction of a new, much larger bank and ditch outside.[27] At Langford Lodge the sequence was similar, primary occupation consisting of a house with drainage gulley enclosed by a larger ditch, being followed by a secondary phase with a larger ditch enclosing the first.[28] At Sallagh (Co. Antrim)[29] and the two Castle Skreen (Co. Down) sites there was evidence of open settlement preceding the raths.[30] On three further sites, Dressogagh, Glenloughan and Croft Road, Holywood, there was occupation material from below the bank of the raths.[31] At Lismahon,[32] the initial occupation seems to have consisted of a palisade structure with post-holes set in a post-trench, which was subsequently revetted with timber and earth before being finally encapsulated in a castle mound around 1200. The evidence from these sites, and a number of others, points to both the pre-rath and the rath phase belonging to the Early Christian period, and as yet there is little evidence for an Iron Age open settlement preceding a rath, though at Feerwore there is some evidence for settlement prior to the construction of the bank, and at Grange, Co. Limerick,[33] a house was enclosed within a ringfort. The evidence from Feerwore and Grange might represent a transitional stage when the normal open settlement type became enclosed in an earthwork rather than a simple ditch, and it is possible that influences may have come from contemporary hillforts. The evidence from Downpatrick, for example, points to the late Bronze Age undefended site being subsequently defended, in the Iron Age, with ramparts.

The majority of the excavated raths and cashels appear to have been occupied between the fifth and the thirteenth centuries. The site at Lissue, Co. Antrim, is dated by a decorated slab assigned to the late tenth century. At Sallagh, Co. Antrim,[34] the dating is mainly dependent on a pin of a type usually assigned to the Viking period but which on evidence from elsewhere seems to have also been in use as late as the thirteenth century. A hanging bowl escutcheon suggests a date for Castle Skreen 1,[35] while on Ulster sites 'souterrain ware' has been taken as a chronological signpost. Only a few sites have produced a variety of well-dated finds; Garranes, Ballycatteen, Garryduff and Carraig Aille perhaps being the most notable.

Beal Boru, Co. Clare, demonstrates that the building of raths continued as late as the Viking period, and lends support to the rural tradition in Ireland that raths are Danes' forts. Beal Boru was built in the eleventh century, and had a bank with an internal stone revetment and external palisade. Dating is provided by two Hiberno-Norse coins and other coins including a trial piece and a series of bronze pins. The fort was of native construction and was occupied for a considerable period before its abandonment, possibly following the destruction recorded in the *Annals of the Four Masters* in the year 1116. In the thirteenth century the bank was encased in a larger defence, which may have been an unfinished motte.

The evidence for continuing occupation into the medieval period is fairly substantial, particularly for Ulster, where raths were still occupied or re-used as castle sites in the Anglo-Norman period.[36] In Ulster, sites such as Glenkeen and Drumee have produced occupation material datable to the twelfth to sixteenth centuries. A few sites such as Thady's Fort and Garrynamona, Co. Clare, produced finds of seventeenth-century date. The Ordnance maps of the nineteenth century show occupied raths, though these may well be simply cottages built within existing rather than newly built examples. It seems reasonable to deduce that while raths may have been refurbished as late as the seventeenth century, construction did not continue later than the Middle Ages.

A considerable variety of structures have been found inside raths, ranging from dwellings to general farm buildings and stores. Only rarely as at Garryduff 2 were they used solely as farmyards. Timber, stone, clay, turf, wattle and daub were employed in the construction and in the case of cashels the stone huts were often butted on to the cashel wall to economize on building materials. At *Leacanabuaile* (Fig. 49) corbelling was used, as in ecclesiastical buildings in Ireland, though its use was not distinctive of the post-Roman period, being found also in Neolithic chambered tombs.

It is notable that the excavated structures bear little similarity to the impressive buildings that are suggested by literary evidence to have existed in Early Christian Ireland. Documentary sources describe large timber halls with thatched roofs, as well as smaller round buildings of wattle with domed wicker roofs and subsidiary complexes of pigsties, calf and sheep houses. The law tract known as *Crith Gabhlach* gives a formalized specification for the buildings and equipment appropriate to the various ranks of farmer. Since only one measurement is given for each building (presumably the length of the ridge-pole or the diameter if the house was round), the information is of little use. Archaeological evidence indicates one main dwelling with a few subsidiary barns, which were sometimes butted on to the inner revetment of the bank.

The buildings that have been excavated within raths were on average about 15 feet in diameter, or 14 feet square. In addition there are farm buildings less than 20 feet square. In many cases the roofs were probably very low – there are literary accounts of animals eating the roofing material. It is also possible that some two-storeyed buildings existed, similar to the reconstruction suggested for the White Fort, Drumaroad (Co. Down).[37] Circular and rectilinear buildings appear to occur with equal frequency.

Exceptional to the general traditions of raths is the much debated site at *Lissue*, Co. Antrim. Here excavation revealed several concentric rings of post-holes which were interpreted as the supports for a roof covering the entire area of the rath. This indicates an unusually large roofed area, some 100 feet in diameter, though the living quarters would have been only the central area, some 30 feet in diameter. It has also been suggested that Lissue had an earlier free-standing building which was destroyed by the roofing of the rath. Such a design would apparently have its parallel in the rath at Doon, Draperstown (Co. Tyrone).[38] Here excavation produced remains of a large free-standing house within the rampart. Suggestions of a ritual function for Lissue have been forwarded that would make it akin to Navan Fort or Dun Ailinne.

Since generalizations about the buildings within raths are almost impossible, consideration should be given to the features of the most important sites.

Garryduff. At Garryduff 1 two flimsy houses of timber were excavated.

House 1 was identified by an area of post-holes of different periods occupying a trapezoidal area about 10 feet wide by 20 feet long. Within this area was a hearth almost 5 feet in diameter, associated with small post-holes which presumably held pot hangers. The second house was more clearly defined, with more determinate post-holes marking out a rectangular area 21 feet by 10 feet. It had three very large central posts, adjoining one another, presumably taking some kind of ridge-pole. The floor of the southern part of the house was paved, and the hearth was also in this sector. It has been deduced that the house had a low thatched roof supported by three main posts and

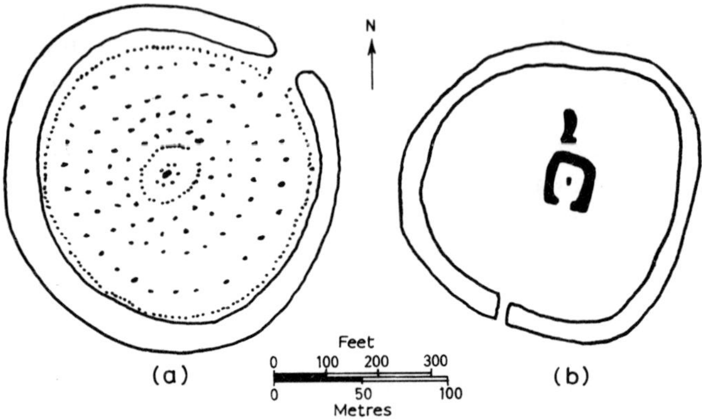

Figure 50 Raths – (a) Lissue; (b) White Fort, Drumaroad

the four corner posts. Three southern posts may have formed a portico. Elsewhere in the fort were other hearths, paved areas and a pit. The entrance passage was gravelled, and it had a timber gateway.

Garryduff 2 had no habitation and may have just been a farmyard. It had an unusual gateway with a palisade set into the walling.

Lough Gur – Carraig Aille. The two forts at Lough Gur known as Carraig Aille I and Carraig Aille II are particularly informative. Carraig Aille I was occupied possibly from about 650 to 950, while Carraig Aille II was occupied from *c.* 700 to *c.* 1000 AD. At Carraig Aille I the houses were stone-built and associated with areas of paving, but the walling was badly preserved. Most of the structures seem to have butted on to the rampart and were not more than 5 to 10 feet long. There was abundant evidence for hearths, and some suggestion of occupation of rough hollows in the rock above which flimsy shelters had been erected. Nearby was a group of rectilinear stone-walled structures which produced no dating evidence but were interpreted as animal shelters contemporary with the rath. At Carraig Aille II the earliest phase of occupation was associated with huts, stone-built with curvilinear plans. In the second phase the structures appear to have been rectilinear, and the best preserved measured about 20 feet internally with walls about 2½ feet thick. The original width of the building could not be determined, but was probably about 15 feet. There was paving inside the house and some outside. A less substantial annexe, 4 feet by 5 feet internally, was butted on to the gable wall. Evidence points to continuing occupation after the abandonment of the fort, as some of the adjoining house sites were butted on to the fort wall and one was built over it. In character these rough rectilinear structures with yard walls were similar to those inside the fort. At both Carraig Aille I and II the fort walls were provided with substantial gateways and steps in the ramparts.

The Spectacles. A number of 'open' sites have produced other evidence for Early Christian house types. The best known is 'The Spectacles' at Lough Gur,

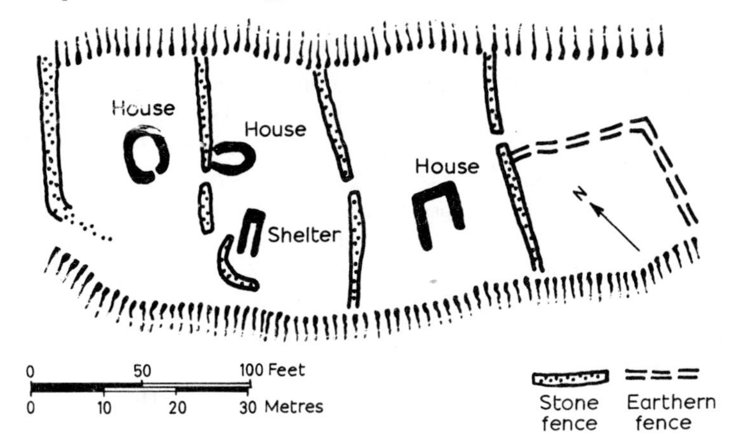

Figure 51 'The Spectacles', Lough Gur – Plan (After O'Riordain)

Co. Limerick. The settlement, on the shore of the lough, consisted of several huts with associated yard walls. Two round stone buildings and a third rectilinear structure were interpreted as houses. A further stone-built construction had only three sides and is regarded as a cattle shelter. One of the round huts, 15 feet in diameter, had internal post-holes for the roof and two hearths near the wall. The hut was approached by a paved pathway to a stepped entrance and porch. The rectangular house, 14 feet by 12 feet, had an open gable end across which ran a line of post-holes. The stone yard walls were identified as field boundaries. Steps led down to the lough from the site (Fig. 51).

St Gobnet's house, Ballyvourney, was a round stone-built hut with two faces and a rubble core to the 5-feet-thick walls. It was 20 feet in diameter and the roof, presumably thatched, was supported by a substantial timber post. The door had a hanging and a meeting post. There was a well nearby. The occupants of the house had engaged in iron smelting and there was an abundance of metal-working refuse from the site. Most of the finds were of an indeterminate nature, so the building could not be dated more precisely than the first millennium AD. The stone house had been preceded by a rectangular timber house or houses, associated with an earlier phase of iron working, with an elaborate scheme of drainage ditches. Details of the house plan, however, could not be ascertained due to clearance of the site for construction of the stone houses. The site was traditionally associated with the sixth- to seventh-century saint, Gobney, and there were traces of seventh-century activity nearby – a stone standing near the building, known as St Gobnet's stone, was datable to this time, and it is not impossible that the house belongs to this period or slightly later.

Inishkea North, Co. Mayo. A number of coastal sand-dune sites of the period are known in Ireland, of which one group is located on the island of Inishkea North. Here House A, Site 3, was a large timber-framed hut, about 24 feet long, with wattle and daub wall filling and a thatch or shingle roof which seems to have been used as a workshop for making purple dye and working chlorite. It was dated to the late seventh century by a brooch. A handle of a bronze mirror from the site was Iron Age in character (reminiscent of the Balmacellan mirror), but could have been Early Christian. A stone-lined pit (called a 'cellar' in the excavation report), measuring about 5 feet across, may have held a barrel or similar vessel. On a nearby site stone huts with wooden subsidiary structures imply that both timber and stone were in use around the same period.

Beginish, Co. Kerry, was the settlement associated with the ecclesiastical site on Church Island nearby. At Beginish there was a complex of eight houses, of which one was better preserved than the others. This had two rooms, the main one being circular and partly subterranean. It was approached by a sloping passageway with retaining walls, which led into a lintelled passage through the wall. The walls of the main room were slightly corbelled, but it did not originally have a corbelled roof – there were six holes in the masonry near the wallhead which had held the ends of radial roof timbers. The roof must have been thatched. The second room was rectangular, and was butted on to the first. The partly subterranean nature of the first room may have been to provide adequate headroom while still projecting as little as possible above ground level to counteract winds. Although some of the finds are possibly as early as the early ninth century, a runic inscription from the house implies that it was not built before 1050, and is quite possibly later, the excavator suggesting 1100–1200. In the medieval period there were further flimsy structures on the site. A number of houses at Beginish belong to the phase that preceded House 1, probably dating in some cases to the late ninth century. Associated with the settlement was a complex of fields and cairns.

Crannogs, in spite of their external appearance, are no more than the lacustrine or marshland equivalent of raths. Like raths, they had a lengthy existence in Ireland and many, including the important Iron Age example at Lisnacroghera, were destroyed by peat cutting as late as the nineteenth century. A few may be Neolithic in origin, such as Island MacHugh, Co. Tyrone, while others date to the Bronze Age such as the first phase of occupation at Ballinderry 2 or the destroyed site at Ballykinler, Co. Down.

A crannog is an artificial platform, built sometimes in water, sometimes on boggy land, composed of layers of brushwood, on top of which a timber dwelling was normally constructed. Crannogs are found in a variety of apparently unrelated European contexts. The majority of Irish examples date from the Early Christian period, those in Scotland from the Roman Iron Age. In both Scotland and Ireland occupation appears to have been long continued on the sites, with instances of new crannogs being built in the sixteenth and seventeenth centuries. Although weapons have been found on some crannog sites, there is no reason to suggest that they were primarily defensive. It would have been possible to transport stock to them.

The precise number of crannogs in Ireland is not known. In the nineteenth century Wood-Martin conservatively estimated the number at 220, but there are probably twice as many. They are concentrated in the counties of Cavan and Fermanagh and in Ulster generally, though some counties have relatively few (Co. Down has only thirty). This is probably due to the distribution of marsh and shallow lakes, which are abundant in the north. The word *crannog* comes from the Irish *crann* meaning a tree, a derivation stemming either from the amount of wood used in them, or from their more recent tree coverings. Crannogs are notable for the wood-working skill displayed in both their construction and the objects found in them, and familiarity with tenon and mortice jointing is attested as early as the Bronze Age.[39] The wet conditions in crannogs allow much organic material to be preserved.

Four crannogs in Ireland were carefully excavated and produced abundant finds. These are the two crannogs at Ballinderry, the Lough Faughan crannog and the royal site at Lagore.

Ballinderry 2 (Co. Offaly) began as a late Bronze Age settlement of wicker huts and a larger structure. The site was swamped by a rise in lake level and not reoccupied until the Early Christian period when the crannog was built as an extension of a natural island. Its outline, as with most crannogs, was defined by a circle of substantial posts, within which were a number of lesser circles, used to consolidate the marshy edge of the island. In the southern and south-western part of the site an area of flooring was recognizable, but the actual house or houses could not be reconstructed from the available evidence. Occupation of the crannog extended from the sixth to the eighth centuries.

Ballinderry 1 (Co. Offaly) was situated on the same lake as Ballinderry 2 and was built in a swampy shallow in the tenth century, when a large round wooden building was constructed occupying almost the whole area of the island. The floor of this house was roughly horseshoe-shaped, measuring 56 feet in diameter at its greatest extent, and appears to have been originally circular. Around 1000 a second house was built over the first, and this was replaced in the Middle Ages by a third. The site was occupied intermittently into the nineteenth century. Prior to excavation it appeared as a hillock 4 feet 6 inches high, 100 feet long and 60 feet wide. As at Ballinderry 2 the platform was surrounded by a palisade of piles inside which was a partial palisade of planks. An entrance through the pile palisade was later abandoned, for the plank palisade continued across it. A raft in the centre of the island had held a hearth and the main support of the building (Fig. 52).

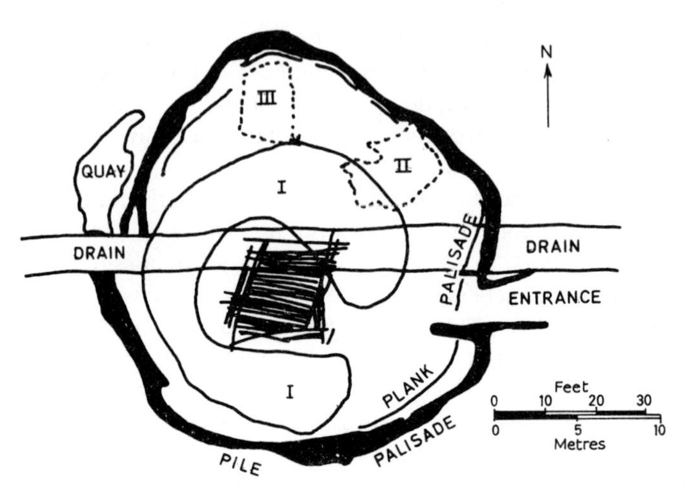

Figure 52 Ballinderry 1 crannog (After Hencken)

Lough Faughan, Co. Down, is now a reed swamp, but was once in open water. The crannog was about 115 feet in diameter, and consisted of layers of brushwood and peat, 14 feet thick, on the natural marsh deposits of peat. There were some vertical stakes and local areas of staging, but the structural evidence for the crannog was less substantial than at Ballinderry. The upper surface of the crannog was covered by woven wicker matting, but there was no evidence for a house, though several hearths were found. It seems to have been occupied in the period between the seventh and the tenth centuries with an additional later occupation.

Lagore, Co. Meath, is exceptional in that it was a royal residence, and without doubt is the richest Early Christian period site so far excavated. Its occupation started in *c*. 600, and the destruction of the site is recorded in 934. On a foundation of animal bones the artificial island was built up to a height of almost 10 feet. The platform was secured by bow-shaped timbers and a dugout boat incorporated into the bottoming. On this was laid brushwood, some of it woven into matting. The island was built up with layers of brushwood and peat with occasional timbers, with a circle of heavy piles around the perimeter. Hazel nuts suggested an autumn construction. Pieces sliced off the backs of skulls attested a massacre during the construction, presumably of the workmen. There were three circles of palisades made of piles, posts and planks, which represent three periods of occupation. The last two were refortifications and large numbers of piles outside the crannog may have served as *chevaux de frise*. No information about the structures that stood on the island was available due to extensive disturbance – when the site was first recognized in 1839 some 150 cartloads of bones had already been removed and transported to Scotland to make fertilizer.

There are a wide variety of sites classed as *souterrains*,[40] the simplest of

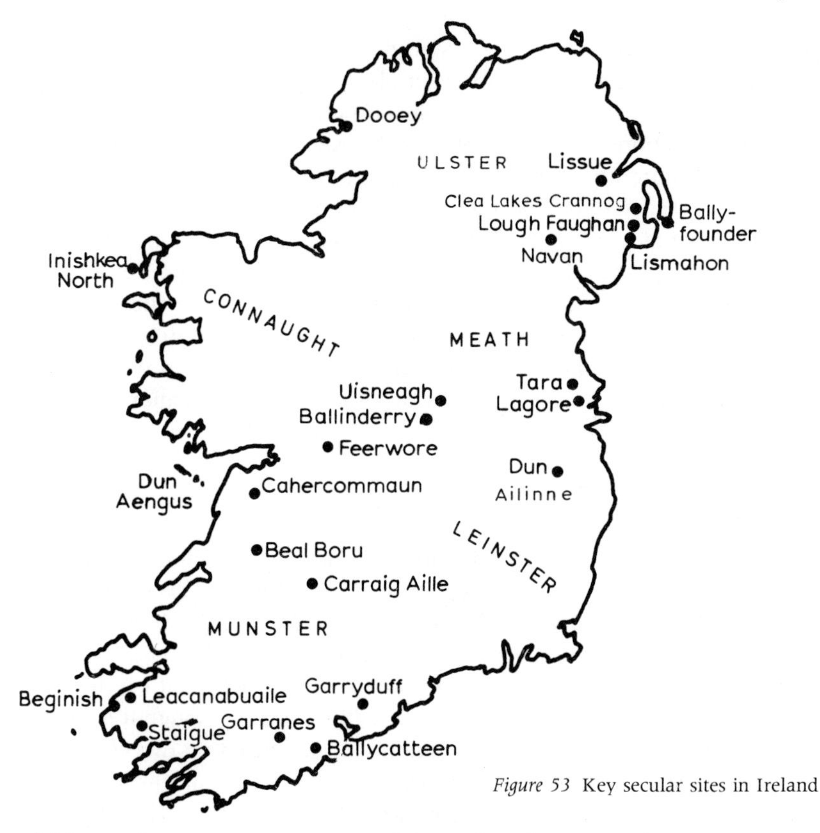

Figure 53 Key secular sites in Ireland

which are long narrow passages. More often, however, they consist of short low stretches of passage linking small chambers. Some elaborate examples have lintelled chambers, corbelled beehive rooms, right-angled bends, blind tunnels, concealed passages and various types of 'traps'. The many thousands of examples in Ireland do not fall as readily into distinct regional groups as the Scottish souterrains. On the whole the Irish souterrains are more complex than either the Scottish or the Cornish equivalents, the *fogous*.

The function and origin of Irish souterrains remains obscure (p. 36). Where dating evidence is available, it is of the Early Christian period. There are no known Bronze Age souterrains in Ireland to correspond with Jarlshof in Shetland and relatively few are likely to be early Iron Age, so they should be regarded as the contemporaries of raths, cashels and crannogs in the first millennium AD with possibly some slightly earlier precursors. This contrasts with the Scottish souterrains which are generally datable to the Roman Iron Age, and with the Cornish which are pre-Roman Iron Age. The suggestion that souterrains spread from Brittany to Cornwall and thence to Ireland and Scotland is unproven, and there is little in common between the various groups.

The majority of Irish souterrains seem to have been associated with above-ground structures. They occur for example in association with raths and cashels, and where above-ground remains are now lacking it is possible that the surface indications have been ploughed away. The presence of steps and the very low headroom of many Irish souterrains precludes their universal use as byres or sheepfolds, and the presence of drains and chimneys as well as hearths in some show that a few at least were occupied. A number have features suggesting that they were used for storing dairy produce – one in Belfast had remains of stave-built milk coolers in hollows in the floor, and the nature of 'souterrain ware' would have been well suited to storing dairy produce.[41] Some, particularly the elaborate coastal examples in western and eastern Ireland, may have been places of refuge, possibly in many cases at the time of the Viking raids.[42]

The introduction of Christianity to Ireland

The figure traditionally associated with the introduction of Christianity to Ireland, St Patrick, is surrounded by controversy.[43] With the exception of his own writings, the *Confession* and the *Letter to the Soldiers of Coroticus*, a body of writings set down from the seventh century is the only source.

Archaeological and historical sources do not shed much light on the early development of the Church in Ireland in the fifth century, though it is certain that by the sixth century the Irish Church was organized on diocesan lines, each bishop having authority over his own *paruchia*, which at this period can be translated as 'diocese' but which was based on the tribe. This structure therefore was related to that current in Britain, with variations stemming from the native structure of Irish society.[44]

The wealth of memorial stones available from Wales and Cornwall does not exist in fifth- or early sixth-century Ireland. A series of ogham inscriptions give early formulae of the type 'of A the son of B', the genitive being used for all three words.[45] Ogham stones were frequently regarded by the Early Christian Irish as pagan in character, and probably had a pagan use from the late fourth to the fifth centuries, with increasing Christian usage in the later fifth and sixth. The range of bilingual inscriptions in Latin and ogham that are to be found in Britain are absent from Ireland. The extent of influence of the continental Church at this early period can only be postulated, though there is ample evidence for it later, and certainly the trade which brought it to western Britain, as evidenced by imported pottery, also affected Ireland.

Figure 54 Key ecclesiastical sites in Ireland

Early cross-slabs (Fig. 55)

Apart from the buildings, the most important monuments of early Irish Christianity are the memorial stones and the free-standing crosses.

Inscribed memorial stones may possibly be descended from prehistoric menhirs. The earliest are simply monoliths with ogham inscriptions, which need not be Christian, but by the sixth century they often have inscribed crosses also. A related class has pillars with crosses but no inscriptions.

Grave markers consist of a series of much smaller uninscribed stones, many of which were buried with the dead or laid flat on the surface of the ground to mark graves. They are frequently the wrong shape and size for setting upright.

Recumbent cross-slabs are flat stone slabs with a cross in light relief, and were probably designed to lie flat on a grave. They are possibly an Irish type in origin, and may be derived from grave markers, though Gaulish influence has been suggested. They are mainly seventh-century and later.

Cross slabs are upright slabs similar in purpose to modern tombstones and can be very elaborate, with ornamental detail and inscriptions.

Free-standing crosses seem to be stone translations of wooden prototypes, and have the cross shaped out of stone. They developed into high crosses.

The earliest categories of cross-marked stones, with simple crosses, are known as primary cross-slabs and primary grave markers, and are unlikely to be earlier than the end of the sixth century. Uncommon in Ireland, they are likely to have been rustic versions of more elaborate pieces. Openwork metal book covers of the sort well represented in later Ireland, for example by the Athlone Crucifixion Plaque, may have been one source of inspiration for them.[46] Another inspiration might have been the Chi-Rho or cross symbols found on imported A Ware or lamps such as the example from Dinas Emrys in Wales.[47] A primary cross-slab from Kildreenagh, Co. Kerry, has a double outline cross with a stylized alpha and omega below the side arms which can be paralleled fairly closely by a similar cross with a hook forming the Rho, from a seventh-century manuscript, the *Codex Usserianus Primus* in Trinity College, Dublin. This similarity may be fortuitous, but the possibility of manuscript influence in the widespread adoption of the cross motif at the end of the sixth century cannot be disregarded. The distribution of primary cross-slabs is concentrated in the north and west of Ireland with that of the ogham stones mainly to the south.[48]

Recumbent cross-slabs are numerous in Ireland; about 800 or 900 have been recorded, scattered over the entire area with a concentration in Co. Offaly and a rich collection from Clonmacnois.[49] They are least common in mid-Ulster. They seem to be derived from primary grave markers, or from the name-stones of Northumbria, and few if any are earlier than the eighth century when the main series began. The earliest which can be dated by inscription have been assigned to 709–12, 783–6 and 787–91, and one early example has the name of a Saxon priest, and a design akin to one found in the Lindisfarne gospels and therefore presumably copied from a Hiberno-Saxon manuscript.[50] The early recumbent cross-slabs are relatively small, becoming increasingly large with time, until they sometimes cover the entire length of the grave. In the early stages of development the designs of the crosses show similarity to those on primary grave markers, but later evolved along their own lines to the very highly ornamented examples that sometimes have inscriptions in Irish minuscules. Inspiration from Northumbria can be detected in many of the later ones, and there seems to have been some

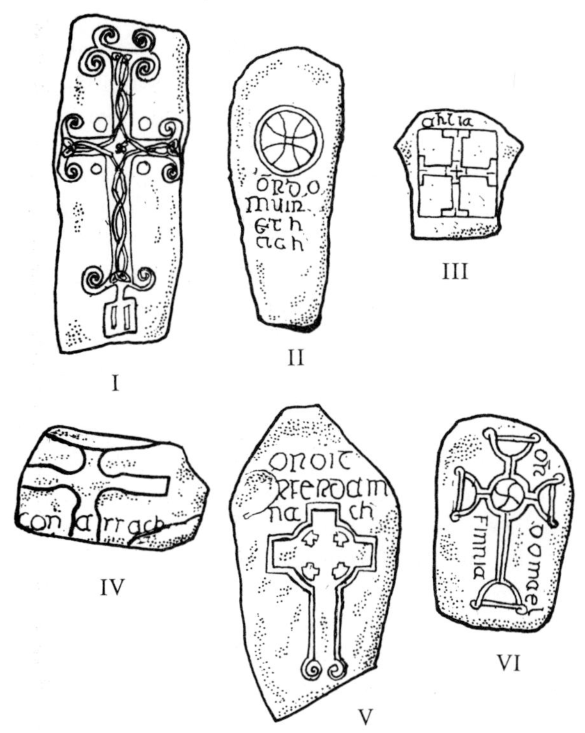

Figure 55 Types of Irish cross slab. Numbered as in text. (I) Inishmurray, Co. Sligo; (II) others, Clonmachois, Co. Offaly (After Lionard)

interplay of designs between monasteries. Fr. Lionard, who has studied these stones, has recognized six main groups based on the type of cross:

- I Plain linear and outline crosses
- II Crosses of arcs
- III Crosses potent without ring
- IV Crosses with hollowed angles without ring
- V Ringed crosses
- VI Expansional crosses, with circular or semicircular expansions at the centre of the terminals.

Many of the types of crosses seem to have been those current outside Ireland – some can be paralleled in the Byzantine world, others in Merovingian Gaul. Crosses of Type I are probably first used in the seventh century, the plain outline not being used till the early eighth. Crosses of arcs were partly evolved from a degenerate Chi-Rho, and first appear on pillars in the sixth century and on recumbent slabs in the eighth century. They appear on upright cross-slabs probably in the seventh century. Types III to V all appear in the early eighth century, and the ninth was dominated by the ringed cross. The expansional cross evolved slowly during the seventh and eighth centuries, and reached its final form in the ninth. In the tenth century it was used almost exclusively, and at Clonmacnois and Glendalough was still being used in the eleventh century to the exclusion of all others.

Irish minuscule seems to have made its appearance at the end of the sixth or beginning of the seventh century. An early example outside an oratory at Kilfountain (Kilfinten), Co. Kerry, bears the saint's name – Finten.

Figural work does not appear on any of the early cross-slabs, but gradually human representations appeared on a number of monuments. Those in the earliest group all have incised outline figures. The *Killeen Cormac* pillar has a remarkable facing bust carrying a cross which must surely be directly, if roughly, copied from a contemporary icon such as the Mount Sinai Saint Peter.[51] The basilica of St Brigid at Kildare was only fifteen miles away, and it is likely that such icons were to be seen there. Icons too seem to be the prototypes for two early Crucifixion slabs from Inishkea North and Duvillaun, Co. Mayo. On the back of the Duvillaun slab is a Maltese cross in a circle and the same motif appears on a slab from Ballyvourney, Co. Cork, where a little figure is depicted carrying a crozier.

Face crosses[52] as a group occur in Ireland, with one outlier at Kiloran, Colonsay, in the Hebrides. The group is distinguished by having a stylized front-view head on the upper arm of the cross. The prototypes, as Thomas has pointed out, are eastern Mediterranean, and crosses of this type can be found in Coptic Egypt, whence other features of cross-slab shape may also have come to Ireland. They first appear in the seventh century, a fine example being known from Kilbroney, Co. Down. In a later development the outline of the stone itself recalls the shape of the head and the arms of the figure. This occurs most notably at Skellig Michael. While it is possible that the inspiration for these crosses is the ornamentation on pilgrim flasks, imported Mediterranean textiles are probably an important factor in the spread of the designs, and indeed in the spread of narrative scenes.

The development of figural art in the seventh century can be well illustrated by a series of relief-decorated cross slabs from Gallen, Glendalough, Drumhallagh and Fahan Mura, as well as the Carndonagh Cross Slab.[53] Appearing here for the first time are the dumpy little ecclesiastics so characteristic of later Irish sculpture – they can be seen on the high crosses (see below). The crosses also display projections at the sides or top which represent an attempt to free the cross from the rigid lines of the slab. An inscription on a slab from Fahan Mura appears to be derived from a Greek manuscript.

Belonging to the same school as the Fahan Cross, but intermediary between the cross-slabs and the high crosses, is the cross at *Carndonagh*. This is cut from a thin slab of sandstone, with sinuous lines, and stands to a height of about 10 feet. One side is covered with broad interlace, the other has an interlaced head. On the shaft, surrounded by four smaller humans, is a frontal full-length figure which presumably represents Christ. Below are three profile figures in a procession. Associated with the Carndonagh Cross are two smaller pillars by the same hand, also with figural work, and a somewhat cruder cross-slab with various decorative elements such as a marigold flabellum (a type of ritual fan of east Christian derivation), which reflect Merovingian Gaulish influence.

Irish high crosses[54] (Plates 28–32)

High crosses date from the eighth to eleventh centuries and are not confined to Ireland, occurring in fewer numbers in both Scotland and England. The origin of the free-standing cross has been debated, and it is uncertain whether they were originally funerary, dedicatory or simply commemorative. Wooden crosses are mentioned in the *Lives of Eastern Saints*, and Adamnan refers to one in Iona existing in the seventh or possibly even the sixth century. Such crosses, with either small straight struts in the four angles of the arms or four arc-struts forming a ring head were probably translated from wood to stone in the seventh century – some cross-slabs seem to depict wooden crosses complete with skeuomorphic wooden features such as the carpenter's nail heads.[55]

Although forerunners may date from the seventh century, no high cross dates from earlier than the eighth. There are between sixty and seventy surviving examples of Irish high crosses, which are characterized by a number of features displayed on nearly all. The cross shaft is rectangular in section and tapers towards the head. It is set on a cubic or slightly pyramidical base, which in turn was probably set in a platform so that the base was at eye level. In the earlier crosses most of the figural compositions appear on the base. Some crosses are made from a single piece of stone, others from blocks tenoned together. The capstone, nearly always a separate block, is shaped either like a house shrine or a cone. The ring of the wheel head is normally openwork. The wheel can be relatively plain, but on some later crosses (ninth-century onwards) stone discs protrude from the arcs or from the hollowed part of the cross. These, frequently carved from fine-grained sandstone, were intended for viewing from various angles, and have corner mouldings, raised bosses and high relief figural carving. The designs are probably inspired in some cases at least by contemporary metalwork and ivories.

There are a number of unfinished crosses which shed light on the method of production. The best example is that known as the *Unfinished Cross of Kells* (Plate 30B). From this it would seem that the cross was hewn out roughly in the quarry before being brought to the site for final work. The panels were first roughed out, then the background deepened, and the interlacing finished. The next stage was the sculpting of the head – the outlines of the figures being put in before the detailed modelling. The crosses were probably painted when completed. The distribution of high crosses lies to the centre and north of Ireland, with only one in the south and a few late examples in the west. On the basis of style they can be divided into seven classes.

Group I (Plate 28A) comprises a small group with a limited amount of figural ornament, very little of which is derived from the usual repertoire of Early Christian iconography. The most typical monuments are the two crosses at Ahenny and one at Kiltieran. These range between 11 and 13 feet high, and have widely spread arms, large rings and conical capstones. High relief rope-mouldings decorate the corners and there is an abundance of non-figural ornament. On the basis of comparison of the decorative details with those found on metalwork the series, which is known as the *Ahenny Group*, can be assigned to the eighth century.

Group II (Plate 28B) is a uniform series with all examples probably the products of one school, and is known as the *Bealin Group* after the best example, from Bealin, Westmeath. Another example is the North Cross at Clonmacnois. They are characterized by low relief ornament with a large expanse of background showing. No scenes are derived from current Christian iconography, though some horsemen characterize the group. The interlace and spiral decoration includes some complex animal interlace. The Bealin Cross is dated by an inscription to the end of the eighth or beginning of the ninth century, and the others are probably contemporaneous.

Group III (Plate 29) comprises a series of crosses carved in granite, not all of the same date. It includes the crosses at Moone, Castledermot, and Old Kilcullen, Co. Kildare. The use of a coarse-grained stone meant that the crosses of this group were heavier and displayed simplified detail. They are in low relief, with flat mouldings at the edges. The Moone Cross is the most impressive of the group, and may date to the ninth century. The base is covered with quaint little figures of almost geometric shape, some with a square body and no arms. The shaft has similar animal ornament. One at least of the Castledermot stones can be ascribed to the ninth century.

Group IV (Plate 30A) consists of the crosses at *Kells*. There are four of these – the Cross of Patrick and Columba (so called because it has an inscription mentioning them), the Unfinished Cross, the Market Cross and the Broken Cross. The shaft survives of the Broken Cross, and the Market Cross is broken in the upper part. The group is distinguished by fine, high relief, figural modelling which may be influenced by ivories and belongs to the ninth century.

Group V is best exemplified by the *Cross of Armagh*, of which only weathered fragments survive, but it is known from engravings. It is characterized by a rigorously logical disposition of the iconographical programme, unlike the more haphazard arrangement found at Kells. The best surviving example of this strict disposition of scenes is the Arboe Cross, Co. Tyrone.

Group VI (Plate 31) consists of a number of exquisitely carved crosses, with originality in the choice of subjects and supreme skill in the carving. They belong to the tenth century and comprise the Cross of Muiredach at Monasterboice, the West Cross at Monasterboice, the Cross of the Scriptures at Clonmacnois and the Cross of Durrow. Of these the Cross of Muiredach is the finest and is regarded as the best surviving example of an Irish high cross. The cross is very substantial, standing to a height of 18 feet, with a thick wide stem nearly twice the usual size.

Group VII (Plate 32A) is distinguished by the carvings of a full-length figure of Christ – in this way the crosses become crucifixes. Usually as well as Christ there is another figure holding a crozier. The best examples of this type are those from Dysert O'Dea and Kilfenora, Co. Clare. They probably date from the eleventh century.

The church as a building in early Ireland

No Irish churches survive from the fifth and sixth centuries, and it may be presumed that they were wooden oratories of the type excavated at Church Island, Co. Kerry. Apart from the timber churches (p. 382) stone churches were also developed in Ireland.

Clochans[56] are beehive cells with corbelled roofs, normally circular, with a single entrance and built without the use of mortar. There can be little doubt that these buildings belong to a long-established native tradition, though there is at present no evidence to date the surviving examples before about AD 700. They are concentrated mainly in the south-west mountainous area of Co. Kerry, where a shortage of timber probably necessitated the use of stone for building at a relatively early date. The clochan is found widely in both ecclesiastical and secular contexts. Mlle Henry has recognized several classes of site that produced such structures: *monasteries*, distinguished by having a rectangular oratory, a cross-slab, a *leacht*, beehive cells and a vallum (though any one site may not have more than one or two of these features); *corbelled stone huts*, of a type also encountered in monasteries but found also in groups of two or three, or singly; *drystone huts*, which do not have corbelled roofs; and *shepherds' structures*, which are rough enclosures usually with small oblong shelters. Such structures are almost impossible to date. Many associated with ecclesiastical sites may date to the eighth century, though most appear to be later. On the evidence provided by secular beehive constructions (as at Leacanabuaile) the domestic sites are also apparently of similar date. Similar structures in France date from the eighteenth century, and it is not unlikely that such buildings were constructed in Ireland as late as the eighteenth or nineteenth centuries by shepherds.

The classic site for the beehive type of cell is the monastery of *Skellig Michael*, Co. Kerry, where there are two oratories. While the date of Skellig is uncertain, it may belong to the eighth century (Fig. 56; Plate 8A).

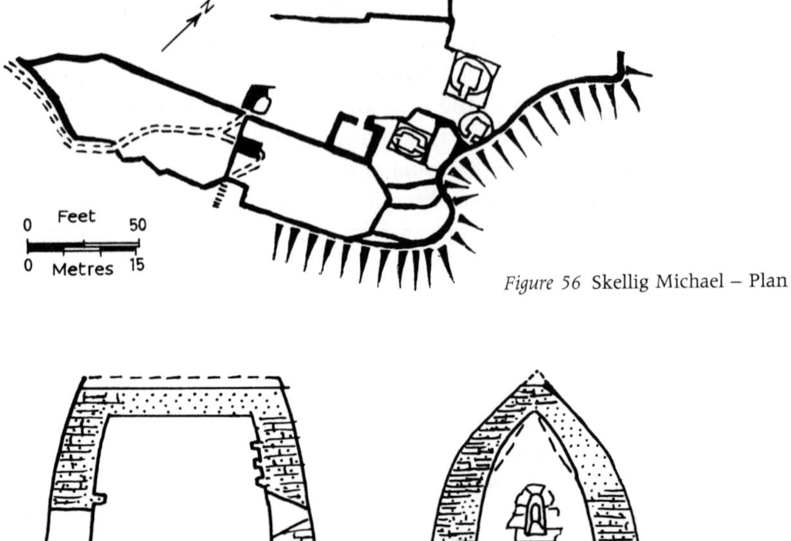

Figure 56 Skellig Michael – Plan

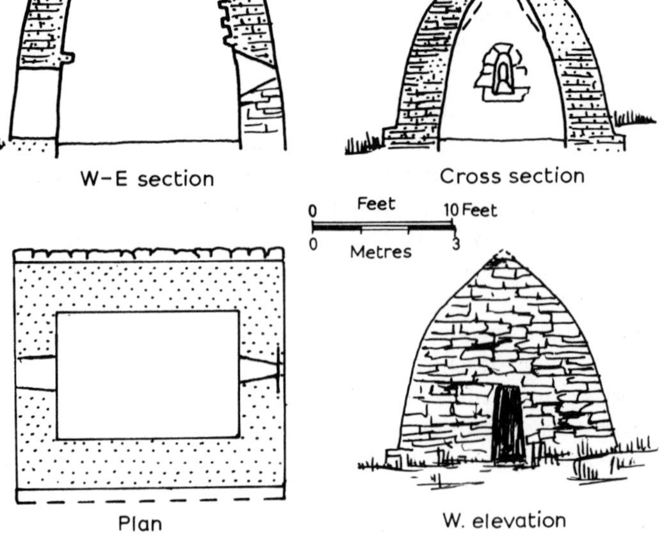

Figure 57 Gallarus oratory, Co. Kerry (After Leask)

The oratories on the Great Skellig compare with the more sophisticated structure known as the *Gallarus oratory* in the Dingle peninsula (Fig. 57). Gallarus has attracted an enormous amount of attention in the past partly because it was the only intact building of its kind, and partly because it was seen to be the 'missing link' between the beehive cells and the later Irish stone churches. A recent examination of the dating evidence for the Gallarus oratory has shown, however, that it is virtually undatable, possibly belonging to as late as the twelfth century.[57] It remains an offshoot from the mainstream of Irish ecclesiastical architecture. In shape it resembles an upturned boat, and is built in the 3 : 2 ratio characteristic of early church plans in western Britain. It has a door at one gable end, and a round-topped window at the other. While it is clear that it is related to the oratories at Skellig, the reason for its shape is not clear. For long it was thought to be a modification of the beehive corbelling of the clochans, but Leask pointed out that its graceful profile might be due to skeuomorphism, the oratory being a stone version of cruck-built timber building.

If Gallarus is accepted as a development peculiar to the west coast of Ireland, the evolution of the Irish stone church from timber antecedents becomes simpler to understand. The evidence for stone skeuomorphism in a number of early churches is seen most clearly in their use of *antae*, butterfly gable finials, and possibly even lintelled doorways (p. 385).[58]

It is possible that the Viking raids hastened the building of stone churches in Ireland, the practice stemming from the Anglo-Saxons. Certainly the earliest stone churches seem to be concentrated in eastern Ireland, nearest to the English shore.

A distinctive feature of the development of Irish ecclesiastical architecture was the development of the stone roof. The incentive behind this was probably the enemy raids, during which timber and shingles would have been vulnerable to fire. The group of churches constructed entirely in stone dates from the ninth to the twelfth centuries. The introduction of mortar enabled corbelled roofs to be constructed with straight sides, triangular in profile both inside and out. St Lua's Church at Killaloe, Co. Clare, and Temple Mac Dara, Co. Galway, are good examples of this. In the case of *Temple Mac Dara* there may have been permanent struts of timber propping the roof – there are signs of props at St Lua's too, though whether they were merely temporary supports while the cement was setting cannot be determined. The date of these two buildings is in dispute, and they may be no earlier than the tenth century. Temple Macdara may date from as late as the twelfth century (Plate 10A).[59]

With the construction of a stone roof with a triangular section, there is an inevitable tendency for it to sag inwards halfway up its length. The timber props were only a partial solution, so a propping arch was devised which also served to roof the vault. This device at the same time provided a space in the vault known as the croft, which could be used if necessary as a room. The earliest example of a roof with a propping arch of this type is *St Columba's House* at Kells. This unicameral building appears too high since the ground level has been lowered by over 5 feet. Internally it measures about 19 feet by 15½ feet. The walls are over 3½ feet thick, have a batter and converge. At the base of the vault was a timber floor, and the croft is divided into three with cross walls, each with a central opening. The building is devoid of architectural detail (except for a triangular-headed and a round-headed window) and, although it could be later, is usually dated to the early ninth century.

Related to St Columba's House is the more complex building known as *St Kevin's Church at Glendalough*, Co. Wicklow, frequently called St Kevin's Kitchen (Plate 9B). Originally a unicameral structure, it had a chancel and sacristy added, both with stone roofs. The chancel was demolished. A round tower was added to the west gable, giving the building a very distinctive appearance.

The final evolution of the Irish stone-roofed church can be seen in *Cormac's Chapel* at Cashel, Co. Tipperary. Architecturally this is a remarkable product of the Irish Romanesque. The roof is very steeply pitched, and changes angle slightly at about half its height. It too has a croft, of which the outer face is made to look like a corbelled structure, but which has very little structural value, the support depending on the inner facing of light calcareous tufa which is neither a true corbelled arch nor a true arch. It has a system of bonding timbers at the base of the vault as an added precaution for the structure.

As well as churches with stone roofs, a series of less pretentious structures flourished which had roofs of a more conventional kind. The earliest are unicameral, and tend to a ratio of 3:2. Later the double square becomes more favoured. Most of the doorways have flat lintels, and many also have the jambs inclining towards one another. These features are found alongside that of battered walls, where the outer long walls of the churches lean inwards slightly. This feature, originally structural in drystone buildings as it gave added strength, was later retained in the mortared churches. As a technique, the battering of walls survived on a peasant level in Ireland until the eighteenth century. A number of doorways are characterized by having a raised border or architrave, and are thus known as architrave lintel doorways. In some cases the lintel is elaborated with a carved or engraved cross. Good examples of architrave lintel doorways can be seen at St Fechin's Church, Fore (Co. Westmeath), and Clonamery (Co. Kilkenny). Frequently the only window was in the east wall above the altar, and most are narrow (sometimes only 6 inches wide). They usually have a single stone at the head which is rounded. The interior may be splayed, sometimes with steps down. Flat and triangular-headed windows as well as triangular windows are sometimes encountered. *Antae* are very typical of Irish churches and continue to the Romanesque. Most churches were small, the early oratories being only large enough for the officiating priest and possibly an acolyte with the congregation remaining outside. Side walls were seldom high (7 feet is common), but gables were often steeply pitched.

Early churches were invariably unicameral, the building of chancels with the churches first taking place, it would seem, in the tenth century. Trinity Church, Glendalough is a tenth-century example of a church with nave and chancel. It also had a round tower rising from a square annexe.

Irish monasteries[60] (Plate 7B)

The introduction of monasticism to Britain in the late fifth century had far-reaching effects on insular Christianity. Nowhere was this more apparent than in Ireland, which from the sixth century became the main stronghold of monasticism in western Europe. Monasteries proliferated, and with them the development of learning and art. Although Irish scholarship of the Early Christian period was less advanced by medieval standards, Irish monks at this time were leading the field in north-west Europe.

Gradually the diocesan organization of the Irish Church was replaced by one in which the main element was the monastic *familia* or *paruchia*, and the bishops ceased to have an administrative function. In the early Irish monasteries there was no adherence to a rule compatible with that of the later medieval monasteries – each monastery followed the rule of its founder. They were not claustral and a characteristic of the Irish monks is that they were frequently driven into exile as a penance, which took them far afield in Europe. By the end of the fifth century Armagh, which may have been the centre of a diocese, had become monastic, and an establishment for both monks and nuns was flourishing at Kildare. Clonard was established by the early sixth century, and during that century monasteries grew up at Clonmacnois, Durrow, Bangor, Nendrum, Glendalough, Inishmurray and many other places.

The sixth century was the golden age of the Irish monasteries. Gradually they became less motivated by religious zeal and more orientated towards the amassing of property and land. By the eighth century there were squabbles between rival monasteries, which brought a reform movement led by the *Céli Dé*, the 'Servants of God', who stressed meditation and the ideal of the monastic state. Many were hermits and their main sphere of operation was the south and east. The movement did not have time to develop as the Viking raids brought about the decrease of the monasteries in Ireland. Many survived, however, and there was something of a spiritual revival in the post-Viking centuries.

Round towers (Plate 32B)[61]

One of the most characteristic of Irish monuments is the round tower built in the Viking Age and after. Although their precise function is uncertain, round towers are usually regarded as bell towers. They are normally about 100 to 120 feet high, and about 16 feet in diameter with walls about 4 feet thick. The tower tapers towards the top, and has a conical stone roof. The doorway is several feet above ground level, and was originally approached by a wooden ladder. Inside was a series of wooden floors (usually five to seven), each storey having a window facing a different way from the others. The top storey had windows facing the four compass points. The windows were narrow, with triangular or lintel heads. There are two examples known of stone floors. The towers were built at a distance from the associated churches, never attached to them.

Certainly it seems likely that they were built first as bell towers, and that they were used as watchtowers in times of emergency. Another probable use was as church treasuries. While their shape and design made them impregnable against normal siege techniques, they would have been vulnerable to fire, acting as chimneys once the ground floor was ignited. This probably explains the accounts of important personages being burned in them. Human bones and charcoal were found in the Kilkenny round tower in 1847.

Round towers span some three centuries, the most elaborate probably being the earliest. They were still being erected in the twelfth century, while the earliest documentary evidence for the building of a round tower is AD 919 (Castledermot). Other references appear in the annals for the years 948, 964, 981 and 994–6. Such references continue through the eleventh and twelfth centuries, so it may be assumed that they were first being constructed in the tenth century. Like the East Anglian series of Anglo-Saxon towers, they are probably imitations of continental prototypes, which first appear in northern Italy in the ninth century. The best preserved examples are those at Kilkenny, Monasterboice, Clondalkin and Kinneigh, where the interiors have been reconstructed.

7 The Norse in Scotland

The period of Scandinavian expansion that began in the late eighth and continued during the ninth and tenth centuries has often been termed the 'Age of Vikings'. It has received much attention both from scholars and the general public, for largely due to the exaggerated contemporary accounts and later saga literature the most memorable picture that has come down to us is of fearless seafarers and adventurers intent on plunder and destruction.

The archaeological evidence for the Age of the Vikings has undoubtedly contributed to popular interest – when Viking archaeology is mentioned one immediately thinks of rich hoards of hacksilver and coins, of ship burials like Gokstad and Oseberg, and some of the magnificent products of Scandinavian art during the period.

To view the Viking adventurer in a cultural vacuum is to obtain a much distorted picture. The term 'Viking' itself is limited, and probably meant to contemporaries only the Scandinavian raider. The culture that the Vikings spread was not peculiar to the raiders, but had been developed in Scandinavia over a period of centuries, in a relatively static society.[1]

The culture of Viking period Scandinavia was essentially the product of a development from the indigenous Iron Age cultures, stimulated by external contact. In Scandinavia natural sources of metal, especially copper and tin, were unusually impoverished. Yet in spite of this, or perhaps because of it, Scandinavia at an early date developed a flourishing trade and indigenous tradition of craftsmanship. The Bronze Age was a period of great prosperity which was paralleled again in the Migration Period. During the Iron Age, contacts with the La Tène Celts, and later with the Romans, brought new influences to the north; during the Roman Iron Age particularly there was contact between Scandinavia and the eastern Mediterranean by way of the east European rivers, and as early as the first century AD a taste for Oriental art was being fostered by such imports as the Gundestrup cauldron.[2] At Havor, in 1961, treasure was found dating from the first century which included Campanian bronzes and a neck ring originating in south Russia. Along such far-flung routes too must have come the concept of writing, for the runic alphabet seems to have been developed around the third century AD possibly from a north Italic stimulus.

The centuries from AD 400 to 800 were years of great wealth in Scandinavia, and more particularly Sweden. During this period Scandinavia increased in political and economic importance, probably due to general social stability, though internal petty squabbles seem to have been common. Jutland and the north European plain were the homeland of many of the groups of barbarians whose migrations were to colour the years from the end of the fourth century until the Age of Charlemagne in Europe. While the migrating peoples did not maintain strong ties with their homeland, the turbulence of the Migration Period was to provide a climate in which cultural and particularly artistic trends were rapidly transmitted and developed. Although now known to have their origins elsewhere, Styles I and II (p. 349) became established in Scandinavia in the fifth to seventh centuries and were the starting point from which the many styles of Viking art developed. This 'golden age' in Scandinavia is marked by a wealth of finds of precious metal. It is characterized by the Vendel culture of Sweden, with its rich burials at Vendel and Valsgarde. It was with the Vendels that the first stage in Scandinavian colonization ventures began, for at Helgö on Malar they established a trading post which is the first of a series that culminated in Viking period sites like Birka. If the northern peoples do not figure much as traders in European history before the Age of Charlemagne, it is probably in part due to domination of north-west Europe by the Frisians from their trading base at Dorestad.

House types of the Migration Period in Scandinavia reflect Iron Age origins, for basically the Scandinavians of the golden age were a late Iron Age society. The same might be said for the Viking Age, which is probably best explained as being the era of the last of the great prehistoric migrations of Europe.

Much attention has been paid to the motivation behind the Viking expansion. It has recently been argued that it was on a much smaller scale than contemporary documentation would suggest,[3] but while true for some regions this cannot apply to an area such as the Northern Isles of Scotland, where even today 99 per cent of placenames are of Scandinavian origin.

A study of the nature of the Viking movements shows they must not be regarded as one entity having the same motivations.[4] Although the Swedes did participate in western raids their main activity was in the east, and more particularly in Russia: they were traders operating on a route through Novgorod and Kiev ultimately to Byzantium, and through Bulgar to Itil on the Caspian. The main sphere of Norwegian activity, outside Britain, was in northern waters – Iceland, Greenland and ultimately America. The Danes travelled less far afield, and were eventually the major menace in England.

What motivated the raids of the Vikings in the west? They began with the development of peaceful trading relationships between Scandinavia and Europe, followed by an ever increasing series of raids (particularly on churches), which eventually terminated in settlement itself. Perhaps the extent of the pillaging has been exaggerated, and some at least of the western European (especially British) goods found in Scandinavian graves may have been obtained in peaceful trade or as gifts. Probably there were four motives at work at various times – pirate raids, political expeditions, colonization ventures and commercial penetration.[5] Of these the second was probably of minimal importance, applying mainly to the Danish expansion occasioned by fear that Charlemagne might annex Danish territory. On the whole, the first and last explanations seem the most likely. Certainly settlement was intended in many cases, particularly in the eighth century, probably because of the increase in population and of Scandinavian rules of primogeniture which left many young men landless. Nevertheless, it would be naïve to suggest that the early 'tip-and-run' raids were motivated by a desire to obtain enough wealth to finance the first settlements. The Vikings became so glutted with precious metal that they were willing to pay for goods and to conduct peaceful trade in Ireland in the tenth century. It is perhaps significant that in Europe the Vikings only settled in the British Isles and Normandy – areas in which their early campaigns seem chiefly designed to exact taxes and not throw open a path for settlement.

The motivations behind the settlements in Scotland were directly influenced by the situation in Norway.[6] Society in west Norway around 800 was essentially pastoral, cultivation being subsidiary and mainly carried out in some of the flatter areas. Economy centred on cattle raising, winter fodder such as birch, alder or willow being collected to keep as many animals alive as possible during the winter months. Hunting and trapping, particularly of deer and seal, were an important adjunct, as probably was fishing. In the century preceding 800 there was a marked increase in the clearance of land, as place-names suggest, following an increase in population. A run of bad seasons may have precipitated the exodus, though recent pollen analyses have shown that there was no overall climatic deterioration. Other factors too may have been instrumental – it has been suggested that the herring shoals migrated towards Scotland – while the social structure in west Norway with its system of odal rights meant the disinheritance of younger sons. The distances across the North Sea were not great – the shortest crossing from Norway to Shetland could have taken between 24 and 36 hours, and the voyagers would only have been out of sight of land for about half this time.

Much of the literary evidence for the period is tendentious, and Scandinavian literature begins in the eleventh century, when the culture which produced the Vikings was already waning. Much of it is not strictly speaking Scandinavian but Icelandic, and consists of the sagas which try to present the Vikings as heroic adventurers. Literature contemporary with the Vikings consists mainly of Christian chronicles, written by clerics who had most to fear from the Vikings. It is not known how the laity reacted to them, though some, at least, even joined them. The climate of the times was such that reports of raids would frequently have been distorted, sometimes for propaganda purposes. The clerics hated the Vikings not only because they raided churches but because they were pagan. It is notable that the conversion of the Vikings made them a part of Europe, and they ceased to be the subject of clerical tirades. Atrocities were a commonplace, but attracted less attention when committed by Christians. It is improbable that Christianity rendered the Norse peaceful or changed their character. Piracy possibly continued in both British waters and the Baltic for some time after the conversion of the Norse, but if so it caused little comment from outside. The *Orkneyinga Saga*, allowing for poetic licence, suggests that the twelfth-century Norse in Orkney were at least as violent as their eighth- or ninth-century ancestors.

The first Norse raids in Scotland (Fig. 58)

The first Viking attacks, excluding a dubious raid entered in the *Anglo-Saxon Chronicle* under the year 787, were concentrated in Northumbria. Lindisfarne was sacked in 793 and an attack in the following year on Jarrow was repulsed. Scottish monasteries probably suffered similar raids a few years later – Iona was raided in the early ninth century. Recent reassessment of the Viking period finds from the Northern Isles suggests a date within the period 790–810 for the first Norse settlements.[7] It is unlikely that settlement took place in the Western Isles any earlier, though a solitary grave at Lamlash in Arran may belong to the eighth century, if indeed it is Viking and the objects were not already old when they were buried.

Documentary sources for early Norse activity in Scotland are either Anglo-Saxon or Irish annals, and events in Scotland are only peripheral to their purpose. The main source is the *Orkneyinga Saga* (p. 183) which is concerned with the Norse earls of Orkney, and which deals with the early history of Scotland in general only by recounting the traditional tale. This version of the Norse colonization is vitiated by an attempt on the part of twelfth- and thirteenth-century Icelandic saga writers to rationalize the colonization of the Atlantic Isles in terms of the exodus from Norway of the opponents of Harald Harfagri after the battle of Hafrsfjord. The date they give for the event is incorrect, and archaeological and placename evidence implies that the settlement took place much earlier than they suggest.[8] In the saga accounts, Harald pursued his enemies, killing those in Shetland and driving out those in Orkney, Caithness and the Hebrides, before going on to Man. Traditionally, he founded the Orkney earldom on his return. Whatever the true story, archaeology shows Orkney to have been settled before the end of the ninth century. It later became a Norse earldom subject to the king of Norway. At first Shetland appears to have been more closely related to Norway than to Orkney, though by the eleventh century the power of Earl Thorfinn the Mighty of Orkney extended to Shetland, the Western Isles and the Scottish earldoms. This supremacy did not go unchallenged, and during the twelfth century the Scottish mainland was reclaimed by the Scotto-Norman kingdom, and in 1263, Norse thassalocracy was destroyed in the west at the battle of Largs. At the height of the Norse period not only were the Northern Isles densely populated, but the adjacent mainland and also probably Lewis had a dominant Norse population. The Hebrides were oriented mainly towards Ireland and Iceland. Many of the most important Icelandic families came via the Hebrides and as Viking saga literature was mostly set down in Iceland, documentation for the Hebrides tends to be fairly detailed in the Icelandic sources. *Eyrbygja Saga* tells how Ketill Flatnose became the first Norse ruler in the Hebrides some time before the mid-ninth century.[9]

Norse placenames, apart from their widespread occurrence in the north mainland and Northern Isles, are to be found throughout the Western Isles (Lewis was probably entirely Norse-speaking in the eleventh century), and the west mainland including Kintyre and Arran.[10] The Norse of the Western Isles seem to have been very rich from the evidence of a number of graves. Ship burials are dated by coins to around the mid-ninth century on Canna and Colonsay and boat rivets suggest another on Arran.[11]

The Norse invaded Galloway and settled round the Solway in the early tenth century, where hybrid Irish-Norse placenames occur.[12] Some at least of these settlers were Christian, though the grave find from Kirkcudbright (p. 202) is pagan in character. In general the Norse settlement of south-west Scotland seems to have been connected with the establishment of the Norse kingdom of Dublin.

Placename studies in general are inconclusive: in Scotland the early forms of placenames do not always survive. A number of detailed studies of particular elements and regions are useful if too wide implications are not read into them, but in general placenames are more useful for demonstrating the extent of Norse settlement than in dating it. They also show, however, that the Norse constituted the chief Scandinavian element in the settlements. Danish names are few – they may be later in date or alternatively may be accounted for by the presence of the occasional Dane among the migrants.

Whether there was any contact between Scotland and Scandinavia before *c.* 800 remains obscure. In spite of attempts to establish evidence for earlier Scandinavian settlement, none that is completely satisfactory has been advanced, though it must remain a possibility.[13] Precise dating for the archaeological material is difficult, though it is possible to assign with confidence most of the pagan graves and a few of the settlements in Scotland to the period 800–50. No recent and authoritative survey has been made of the archaeological material. A study by Sigurd Grieg in 1940 is certainly a useful collection of material, but has many omissions.[14] Another problem is the lack of recent excavation; only a few Norse sites have been explored extensively in the last two decades, and Jarlshof remains the most extensive settlement to

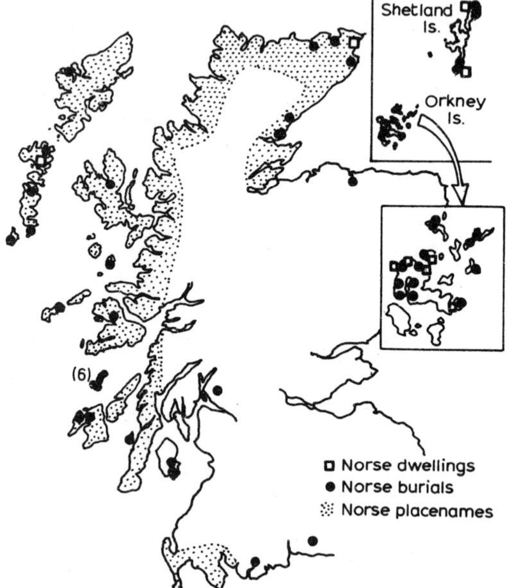

Figure 58 Norse in Scotland

have been both excavated and published. Even though work on the Scottish material has been inadequate, recent advances in Scandinavian archaeology and art history have shed some light on the existing Scottish discoveries.

The Norse in Orkney and Shetland

It has already been suggested that the date and account of the settlements given in the *Orkneyinga Saga* are unreliable. The same story is given in the *Heimskringla*, a collection of royal sagas, where the date for the battle of Hafrsfjord is given as 872. Modern opinion dates the battle nearer to 900, and the *Annals of Ulster* and the *Anglo-Saxon Chronicle* imply that the Scandinavians only began to make serious raids around the last decade of the eighth century in Britain.

Placename evidence adds to the picture provided by the annals.[15] The oldest Scandinavian placenames in the Northern Isles are *byr* names ('bae' in the modern form), which are found in Orkney. Some of these have been claimed as antedating 800 but the majority, if not all, postdate 800. The *byr* element in Orkney means a 'farm' and is related to Danish placenames in England ending in *-by*. Examples in the Northern Isles include Houseby and Trenabie. Names incorporating the elements *land, gardr* and *bolstadr,* which are found in variants of *land, garth* and *bister* and refer to attractive farmland, also antedate 900, and are said to belong to a period of settlement during the ninth century. Most of the other placenames in the Northern Isles postdate 900.

Detailed study of placenames shows that only the elements current in west Norway occur commonly in Scotland, and an overall review of the placename and archaeological evidence points to the homeland of the emigrants as being the coastal regions of Agder, Rogaland, Hordaland, Sogn og Fjordane, Møre og Romsdal and Trondelag, with a few groups of people from Nordland and Troms and possibly South Finnmark.[16] The long-held concept of a peaceful infiltration into largely uninhabited areas cannot now be maintained, though certainly the settlement was successful in completely blanketing out the native population. The settlement can be likened to the Norman Conquest of England – the speech, legal system, building style, political institutions and way of life of the Northern Isles became Norse. That there was a fairly thriving Pictish community in Orkney cannot be doubted and evidence suggests that many of the Pictish ogham inscriptions postdate the Norse colonization. How peaceful it was is difficult to determine. The way in which the St Ninian's Isle treasure was hastily buried might argue a fear of raiders, and camp fires postulated as being those of pirates have been found at Jarlshof, though the evidence is insubstantial. *Olaf's Saga* and other sources hint at a raiding phase, while Irish chronicles indicate that Lewis was used as a winter base for summer raiding parties. Finds of Celtic metalwork from both graves and settlement sites in the north point to raiding as an integral part of Norse life in Scotland till a late date.

In the period up to the advent of Harald Fairhair at the end of the ninth century the main evidence for the Norse occupation of Orkney and Shetland is archaeological. For the period from about 900 to 1200 the main source is the *Orkneyinga Saga,*[17] which was composed in Iceland in the early thirteenth century and gives an account of the history of the Norse earldoms in Caithness, the Orkneys and Shetland. It is therefore important to consider its reliability as a historical narrative. It should be borne in mind that in sagas, even those which purport to be historical narratives, literary effect is more important than factual accuracy. There are different types of sagas: the 'family saga' which deals with a particular family or families and which tends to be literary rather than historical; the 'kings' saga' which is generally historical and deals with the history of Norway and Denmark; the 'sagas of olden time' which are legendary; the 'lying sagas' which are intended as fiction; and some minor works which are translations of saints' *Lives* or deal with other ecclesiastical material. The *Orkneyinga Saga* is unusual in that it incorporates nearly all these elements, the compiler skilfully drawing together information from a wide range of sources. The outcome is an account which is in the main historical though fact may be ornamented in the interests of literary effect, with obviously non-historical material incorporated. While it omits information on certain topics of considerable interest, the *Orkneyinga Saga* remains a remarkable and unique work in the traditions of the best historical writing of thirteenth-century Iceland.

Archaeology has produced spectacular Viking finds from the Northern Isles, particularly from pagan graves and from hoards of hacksilver looted by the Norse. The most important Norse graveyard is that discovered at *Pierowall* on Westray in Orkney.[18] The graves were uncovered gradually by sand blowing away from the site in the nineteenth century. Investigations were first carried out in the period 1839–62, but unfortunately the contemporary accounts are confusing. The minimum number of graves was sixteen, and they belonged to the ninth century, though a sword from one grave may have been made in the eighth century and may have been an heirloom when buried. Most of the burials appear to have been dug into level ground, though a few were possibly inserted into earlier, pre-existing mounds. In several graves horse bones were present, a common feature in Norway. In Grave 7 the skeleton was found headless with the thigh bones crossed. Associated with it was the complete skeleton of a horse, laid on its belly, its head towards the sea and the human skeleton lying in front of its nose. A fragmentary dog's skeleton was also found in the grave. The finds were few, and consisted of a bridle bit, with one of the rings in the horse's mouth, a buckle, a small piece of iron which may have been a weapon, and some indeterminate fragments of iron and bone. Many of the women's graves contained the characteristic 'tortoise' brooches so often found in pagan Norse graves. These large bronze brooches are oval and domical in shape, with bosses and openwork decoration. Other typical finds are bone combs and comb cases, shield bosses, swords, whetstones, beads, ringed pins, an axe, buckles and knives. A magnificent bronze brooch of true penannular shape was found unassociated with any grave group. It was decorated with interlace and with frames for rivet heads, of which only two are still in place. It is almost certainly a product of a native workshop in Scotland and probably was quite old when it found its way into a Viking grave. One of the burials at Pierowall was probably a ship burial, but the account is not adequate to derive any useful information about ship burials in the Northern Isles. There are a number of putative ship burials in the Northern Isles, most notably on Sanday, but none have been excavated.

Another important site which has produced a 'Celtic' object in a Viking context is at Westness on Rousay.[19] There a series of graves was excavated from 1826 onwards, from which a sword still survives. A further grave was discovered in 1963, and was found to be of a young woman buried with a newborn child. In the grave were two iron heckles, a pair of shears, a small knife, a sickle, a long comb, a bronze basin, a whalebone plaque, an iron weaving sword and an iron socket that may have belonged to it, along with some bronze mounts. Round her neck the woman had worn a necklace of different coloured beads, while at her shoulders were a pair of tortoise brooches. She had also worn a gilt-bronze plaque and the magnificent Celtic brooch that has been called the Westness Brooch.

The Westness Brooch was probably at least a century old when it was buried and is similar in type to the famous Tara Brooch from Ireland. It is also a penannular brooch, with the Irish type of 'pseudo-penannular' head, and is made of silver inset with gold panels, amber studs and red glass. On the gold panels is filigree and granular ornament, of which the most notable motifs are two interlacing animals. It dates from around the mid-eighth century, and was probably made on the Scottish mainland.

Following the discovery of the Westness Brooch grave, excavations were begun on the site by Scandinavian archaeologists in 1968. As well as buildings of the Norse period, another grave was excavated which would seem to be evidence of suttee – the custom of killing a woman to accompany her man to the afterlife.[20] This custom is known not only from Scandinavia but also from the Isle of Man.

On the mainland almost opposite Westness another woman's grave was found in 1939. This grave belonged to the Norse settlement on the site of the *Broch of Gurness*, Aikerness.[21] Following the decay of the post-broch settlement, a Norse community was established on the site in the tenth century, a farmstead being built on the levelled remains of the older buildings. A grave at Aikerness contained two tortoise brooches, one of which had the impression of a finely woven wool garment on the reverse, a necklet of sea (or lobster shell?) shells, an iron sickle and a knife with a wooden handle. The woman had been buried in a stone cist, which is an unusual feature, probably to be explained by the nature of the terrain, though a cist burial was also found at Skaill.

In 1970–1 excavations at Buckquoy at Birsay uncovered a male grave with a bronze ring-headed pin, an iron knife, a whetstone, an iron javelin head and half a silver penny of Edmund, the Anglo-Saxon king (940–6 AD). This burial in part overlay the remains of three successive longhouses.[22]

In Shetland there are only two certain Viking graves, both in Unst. The first is a woman's grave at Clibberswick, which produced a pair of tortoise brooches, a trefoil brooch and some objects which have since been lost, and the second is another woman's grave from Unst which produced a tortoise brooch and a circular bronze box. A few stray finds, such as an axehead from

Whiteness or beads from a bog at Hillswick, may represent what were once Viking burials.[23]

At the period when Viking hoards were being buried in Scotland, coins were not being struck by the Scandinavians. Indeed the custom of coining seems to have been taken up by them first in their colony in Dublin, where they began striking a Hiberno-Danish coinage, a comparable Anglo-Danish coinage occurring in the Danelaw in England. Transactions were conducted by weighing out hacksilver. The silver rings were probably a type of ring-money, and possibly served as currency because of their silver weight. Viking graves of the pagan period frequently contain folding balances for weighing metal – one was found in a grave at Gigha in the Hebrides, and another in the excavations at Aikerness.

Prior to the tenth century some Anglo-Saxon coins were coming into Scotland and, in the south-west at least, Northumbrian issues in particular may have enjoyed some circulation. The earliest of the Viking hoards containing Anglo-Saxon and other coins was found in Skye, and comprised coins of Edward and Æthelstan together with plundered Danelaw pieces derived from issues of Alfred. The Skye hoard was buried around 930, and included beside these Anglo-Saxon coins eighteen Arab dirhems struck around 930. During the Viking period Arab or Kufic silver coins were pouring into Scandinavia and were also circulating to a lesser extent elsewhere in Europe. Oriental coins figure in a number of other Viking hoards from Scotland apart from that from Skye. They are mostly of early tenth-century date.

While undoubtedly most of the coins in the earlier hoards were intended as scrap metal, the preference in Scottish, and to some extent in Manx and Irish hoards, for non-portrait issues of Eadgar suggests that these also enjoyed some currency.[24] Stray pennies of Æthelred II have been found at Jarlshof and Galston in Lewis, and such pieces could have been used for trade with England and Ireland, even if they were not in local circulation. A number of Viking period Scottish hoards such as the Tarbat hoard also include Frankish deniers, which may have been for trade with France. The Oriental coins from Scottish hoards are almost invariably cut or pierced, indicating that they were not used as currency. The latest coins to appear in Scottish hoards are those of Cnut, dating from the beginning of the eleventh century; thereafter a gap in the series of Scottish hoards occurs until the mid-twelfth century.

The Viking hoards from the Northern Isles are for the most part late in the period.[25] Five are recorded from Orkney. The two most important hoards are those from Burray and Skaill on Mainland. The *Burray hoard* consisted of thirty silver rings together with a silver armlet, silver rod, intertwined silver necklet, 108 pieces of silver cut off rings, a further decorated ring, a wooden bowl which had contained the hoard, and three silver coins of Edward the Elder, Eadgar and Æthelred II, which would suggest that it was buried at the beginning of the eleventh century.

The *Skaill hoard* was discovered in 1858, and dates from the mid-tenth century. It was found in a rabbit hole at Sandwick, and contained almost 15 lb of silver with nine brooches, fourteen twisted necklets and armlets, twenty-seven armlets of simpler type and an assortment of silver fragments and ingots. Among the whole and fragmentary coins in the hoard were an Anglo-Saxon penny of Æthelstan, a penny of the Anglo-Danish 'St Peter of York' coinage and Samanid and Abbasid dirhems. The Arab coins are among the latest in Britain. The Skaill brooches are penannulars of a type known as 'thistle brooches' because their terminals and pinheads are like thistle heads. A notable feature is the use of Jellinge Style animal ornament on the terminals of one of the brooches. This style of ornament, named after a silver cup found at Jellinge in Denmark, began towards the end of the ninth century, continued in use until *c.* AD 1000 and is associated with Scandinavian settlement in Britain.

Norse settlements in Shetland

The first Norse settlers at Jarlshof (Fig. 59) probably made their *landnamabok* early in the ninth century. They levelled a site on the landward side of the promontory and built a stone farmstead, 70 feet long, with slightly bowed or boat-shaped sides. This was built of stone gathered from the beach, and had two rooms (a kitchen and a living room) with the main entrance leading into the kitchen through the north wall. This type of house is frequently but erroneously called a 'longhouse'. Strictly speaking, a longhouse has animals and humans living under the same roof alignment, byre and dwelling quarters frequently being separated by a cross passage. Although true longhouses are known in Iron Age Scandinavia, the type found in the Northern Isles seems to be a Viking period variant, similar examples being found in Norway and Iceland.

The kitchen was equipped with a long rectangular hearth in the centre of the floor and an oven or cooking pit near it, adjoining the gable end. Stone slabs were set at an angle to enable red-hot stones to be tipped from the hearth into the cooking pit. In the living room there was a stone platform along each side, on which tables and beds would have been set. Another long rectangular hearth stood in the centre of the room. The building was roofed with timber, possibly imported from Norway, and was supported by timber posts in two rows running along the edge of the platforms. From the living room another door in the east wall opened on to the slope behind the house, where there was a midden of burnt stones and peat ash from the central hearth. To the side of the house excavators found a circle of pebbles lying in the sand where a child had obviously been playing with them.

A paved pathway led down from the kitchen door to the outbuildings, which consisted of byre, smithy, barn and a small outhouse which probably served as servants' quarters. These servants were probably the native residents of the now abandoned wheelhouses and passage house, and their possessions included stone pounders and other tools of native type. Near the farmstead was a small building which may have been a temple or a bath-house – it too was equipped with a hearth.

The early Norse settlers were farmers, and there is abundant evidence from the site that they kept sheep, pigs, cattle and ponies. Cultivation is implied by the discovery of burnt grain and sickles. Fishing, later to play an important

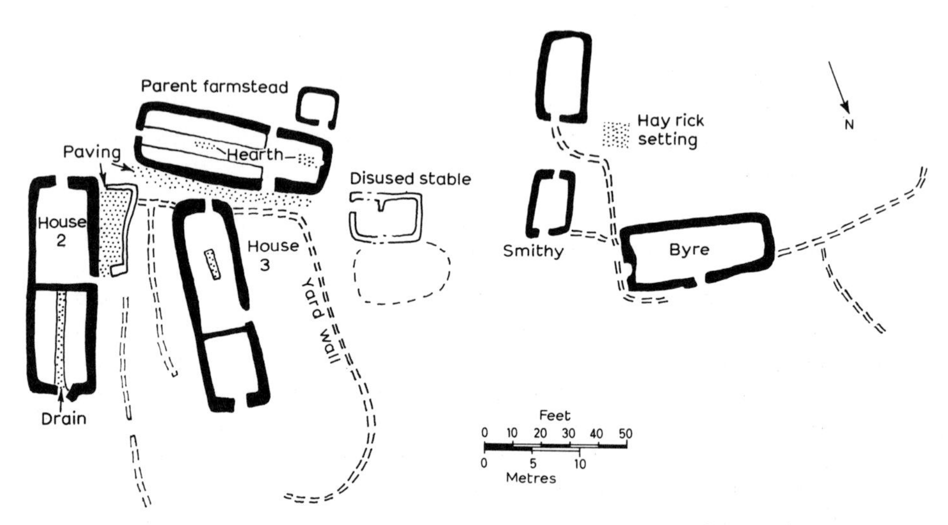

Figure 59 Viking settlement at Jarlshof, Shetland, in the tenth century (After Hamilton).

part in the economy, was apparently of minor importance in the earlier ninth century, though a few line sinkers were found. Bird bones suggest that some were snared.

Iron appears to have been worked in the smithy in a variety of forms. Iron objects from the site include knife blades, hasps, sickles and strike-a-lights, as well as iron clinker nails, used in small boats. Slag was found in considerable quantity at the smithy, where a circular stone setting had probably held a barrel of water for slaking the iron, and where a large, pockmarked stone had been used as an anvil.

Iron was not the only substance worked on the site – bone, including deer antler, was worked into composite combs and pins. Some combs have delicate interlace decoration on them, while the pins have heads fashioned into animal heads or axes.

Soapstone objects are common at Jarlshof. The early Norse did not make pottery, but instead fashioned their vessels out of steatite or soapstone, which is easily carved and is ideal for cooking pots. These were initially imported from Norway, along with soapstone weights used for weighting the warp on looms – they had probably served as ballast in the first ships of the settlers. Later broken fragments of steatite pots were used as loom weights, and later still pebbles of schist or other stone gathered from the beach served the same purpose when perforated. The Norse settlers in Shetland, however, found that there was an indigenous supply of steatite – twelve miles northwards along the coast from Jarlshof at Cunningsburgh the nearest supply was quarried. Here the quarry can still be seen, and the sockets where the early round-bottomed bowls were cut out of the living rock are visible close to the quarry face, while in the less accessible outcrops further up the hill the later square-sided vessels were worked when the other source was exhausted. These square-sided bowls belong to the last phase of the Norse settlement, in the twelfth and thirteenth centuries.

The most impressive finds from the early settlement are a series of incised drawings on slate and sandstone executed by an artist of some skill. Ships, animals and portraits are represented. The finest is a portrait of a young bearded man with a long moustache and curly hair. On the back of the same stone is the portrait of an old man, almost toothless, his beard straggly but his hair still curly. Beside the portrait of the young man is an inept attempt at drawing a hen, presumably by a pupil of the artist who drew the portrait. An interesting series depicts ships. One shows a fine dragon prow, and on the reverse of the same stone is an animal, perhaps a cow, with the prow of a boat beneath. The cow appears to have a knot in its tail. One of the boat drawings shows mast, rigging, steering oar and oarsmen, while another shows a boat with a striped sail. Boat drawings have also been found belonging to the Viking period during the recent excavations at Dublin.

The Jarlshof settlers may not have confined their activities entirely to farming, and a few at least may have joined Viking expeditions. A fine harness mount from the site is of Celtic workmanship with intricate interlace, and was certainly made in Scotland or Ireland. It had been converted into a brooch by the Vikings, who had added a hasp and a catch for the pin. A similar mount was found in a ninth-century grave in Gausel, Norway. Some of the bronze pins from the site may also be loot from elsewhere in Britain, though the ringed pins from the site which are sometimes suggested as being products of Scotland or Ireland were more probably copied by the Norse from Irish prototypes. Apart from such putative raids, the Jarlshof community does not appear to have been very warlike: the only weapons found were an iron spearhead and a spear butt. Down by the shore camp fires of wood ash and fish bones, probably built by returning Vikings, were found. From one came a bronze pin accidentally dropped by a camper.

In the mid-ninth century the original farmstead was extended when a second farm, possibly that of the farmer's sons, was built. It was situated at right angles to the first farm, running down the slope of the mound, and had in addition to the living room a stone-paved byre at the lower end. The area it occupied was demarcated by a yard wall. In this period the temple/bath-house building fell into ruins, and was demolished, and to the north of it a range of outhouses with cobbled floors was built, which probably served as stables.

This extended settlement continued until the end of the ninth century. Around 900 a further farmstead was built, similar in dimensions and style to the second and also with a yard wall. The original farmhouse remained in use, a new outhouse being built in the compound area probably to replace the stable range, and bases were built for haystacks. Due to the shortage of space the second farmhouse was unable to expand easily, and development was confined to an outhouse butted on to the main dwelling.

This particular development of a closely knit community appears unique to Scotland. The same phenomenon can be seen at Birsay, or at Freswick Links in Caithness. It is possible that at Jarlshof and Birsay this type of development was due to the increasing importance of fishing in the economy, agriculture by now playing a lesser role. In the case of Jarlshof, seal fishing seems to have been particularly important.

During the tenth century a huge peat ash midden on the lower slope grew until it covered an area of over 5,000 square feet to a depth of 3 feet. The finds from this midden show the changing character of the material possessions of the occupants of Jarlshof. Loom weights were now made out of water-worn pebbles exclusively, and the hemispherical steatite pots were replaced by trough-shaped vessels. The combs were plainer, without bands of decoration, and the animal-headed pins disappeared, the types current in the tenth century having nail heads with flat expanded tops. Small bone bits were found which appear to have been put in lambs' mouths to prevent them sucking the ewes' milk in late spring. Childrens' toys were found in the midden – tiny querns, line sinkers and little decorated bone pins on which were spun strands of wool.

A very fine gilt-bronze strap end decorated in Ringerike Style of the early eleventh century came from the top of the midden, along with cross-headed pins, which may indicate the conversion of the pagan Norse of Jarlshof.

At the beginning of the eleventh century minor additions were made to the third farmstead, when an outhouse was built.

The site of *Underhoull* on Unst consisted of a boat-shaped dwelling similar to the first house at Jarlshof. In building the house the Vikings made use of stone robbed from an earlier Iron Age settlement, a quern being used as a kerbstone for the pathway from the house. The walls, in keeping with Norse tradition in Scotland, had stone facings on the inside and alternate stone and turf on the outside as windproofing. The rotting turf necessitated periodic rebuilding of the walls, and there was evidence of several such repairs at Underhoull. The roof appears to have been supported on a single line of posts. Due to its position on a slope, the rain-water problem was solved by a system of drains. The house, unlike House 1 at Jarlshof, was a true longhouse, the byre being raised up at the west end.

Finds from Underhoull suggest that occupation was more flourishing in the tenth century than the ninth – finds include a line sinker, a stone vessel for rendering down fish livers, a sandstone sharpening stone that seems to have been used for sharpening fish hooks as well as pins and needles, haunch hones and a series of soapstone bowls both of round and squared shape, one fragment being found along with a slate chisel used in shaping it. Spindle whorls, loom weights, lamps and fragments of a steatite baking board are evidence for some domestic activities, while fragments of gaming boards and counters suggest that board games were played here as at Buckquoy and Jarlshof. As at Jarlshof, toy millstones were found. Black pumice from the floor of the house was probably used as an abrasive, possibly for finishing off wooden articles.

Nearby a boat noost was found, with a curved end some 4 feet deep, suitable for a boat up to 18 feet long. Originally it had been free-standing, and a fragment of a steatite bowl suggests that it was of Viking construction.

Some 263 yards from the house, and probably associated with another house, was a Viking period midden, excavation producing an axehead of iron and bones of cattle, sheep, pigs, rabbit and fish, the axe being similar to one from Iceland.

At a fairly late date in the history of the settlement, an outshot was constructed at the north-east corner of the house, with a central hearth surrounded by a narrow channel with sides of upright slabs, in part covered with flat stones. This was linked to the outside of the house by a further channel, to provide a draught. It would seem that this was used as a drying chamber for grain.

Norse settlements in Orkney (Figs 60–1)

Norse houses of the ninth and tenth centuries have been excavated at several sites, notably Brough of Birsay, Buckquoy and Aikerness.

The occupation at Birsay and Buckquoy can be considered together, since the Brough of Birsay is visible from Buckquoy on the other side of the isthmus. The remains excavated at Buckquoy consisted of three successive longhouses, all incomplete and each being only a part of a more extensive complex.[26] The latest of them, which should probably be assigned to the tenth century since the burial described earlier in the chapter was dug into it, was a house with slightly bowed walls and a paved yard. This overlay a barn with a stone floor. The earliest longhouse was subsequently used as a midden, had a byre at one end and measured about 24 feet. All the houses had turf walls with external stone facings, and were incomplete due to marine erosion. Finds associated with them included small bone pins, composite bone combs, spindle whorls and stone gaming boards. The type of gaming board found here and at Jarlshof was probably used in a battle game akin to chess.

On the tidal island of the *Brough of Birsay*,[27] the remains belong to many periods down to the twelfth century and include the complexes known as 'Earl Sigurd's Hall' and Earl Thorfinn's Palace, and the cathedral (p. 195), as well as the Norse houses.

Two groups have been excavated in particular on the slope to the east of

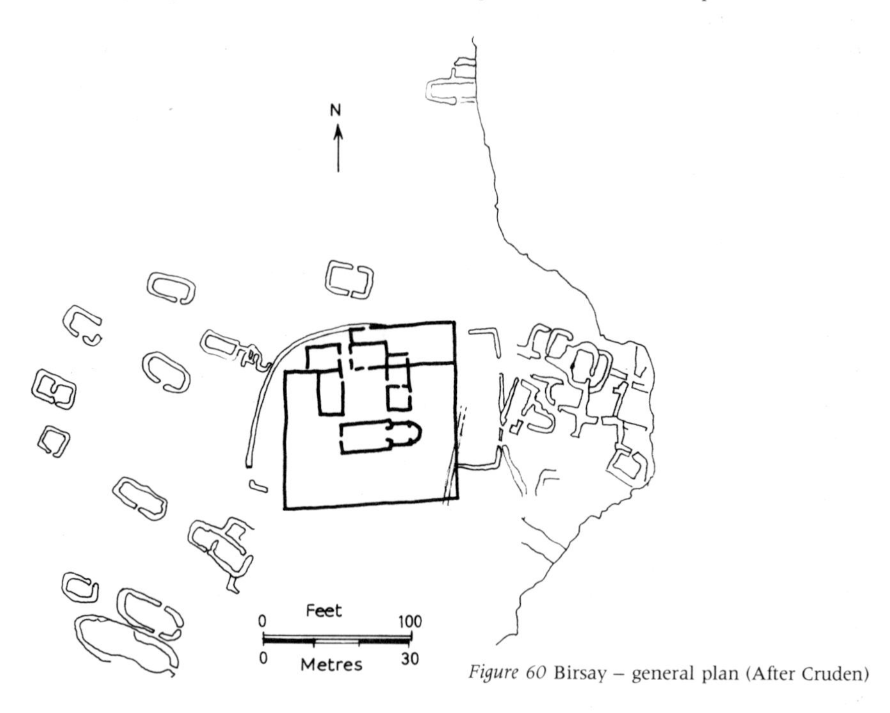

Figure 60 Birsay – general plan (After Cruden)

the cathedral complex. Of these groups (Sites C and D), the earliest consists of two houses side by side separated by a narrow paved passage, probably dating from the ninth century. The older of the two houses was subsequently modified in the tenth or eleventh century. Nearby, Site D has produced three Norse houses of the ninth, tenth and eleventh centuries respectively.

Generally, they are similar in character to the houses at Jarlshof. The earlier houses have walls with stone facings inside and alternating stone and turf outside, while the later have turf cores faced with stone both inside and out. Flagstones were normally used, or sometimes waterworn boulders from the beach. Roofs were supported on double rows of posts, and stone slabs set on end marked the internal visions. The setting of the posts for the roofs was irregular, and the construction seems to have involved continuous purlins on each side to carry rafters, the lower ends of which rested on the inner edge of the turf wall. The roofs were of turf, probably on wickerwork with a thatch covering.

The northern house on Site C was divided by two rectangular stone settings, less than 6 feet square and separated by a passage about 3 feet wide. These were probably the bases of wooden box beds which divided the living room from the byre. The lower corner of the north side of the living room was paved, and was interpreted by the excavators as a smithy. With the exception of the earliest house on Site D, the houses were normally oriented up and

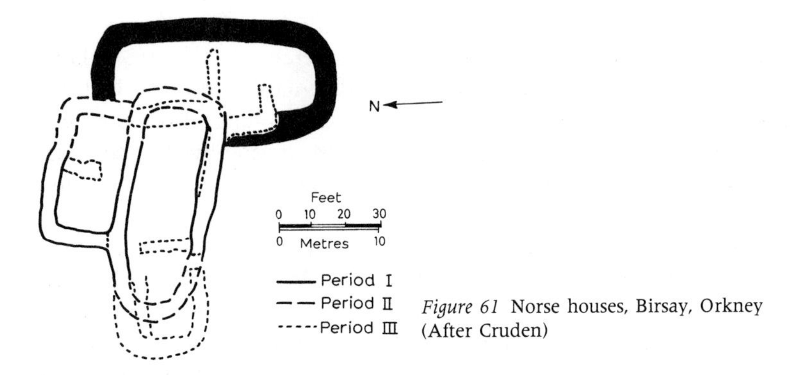

Figure 61 Norse houses, Birsay, Orkney (After Cruden)

down the slope of the hill. Although benches were not encountered in the later houses on Sites C and D, they were a common feature of other houses on the Brough.

The absence of pottery implies that the occupation predates its introduction in the Northern Isles in the twelfth to thirteenth centuries. The latest stage of the occupation is probably contemporary with 'Earl Sigurd's Hall' and Thorfinn's Palace, and they should probably be seen as great establishments like the episcopal palace and farm at Garðar in Greenland. The houses, however, were more probably the accommodation of the earl's officers and guard than farms, the farms belonging to the estate being probably part of the Buckquoy complex.

The Christian Norse in the Northern Isles[28]

The first Norse earl of Orkney was Sigurd the Mighty, who attained the earldom around 880. The early Norse earls were, like the Hebridean Lords of the Isles, virtually independent rulers, owing only nominal allegiance to the kings of Norway or Scotland. From the end of the ninth until the thirteenth century, Orkney was the focal point in a powerful domain extending from Shetland to Caithness, and which from time to time also dominated the Hebrides, and Sutherland. Sigurd himself campaigned in the two northern counties of the Scottish mainland, and was buried in Sutherland on the banks of the Oykell.

His nephew was Einarr, who acquired the epithet Torf because traditionally he introduced the custom of cutting peat for fuel into the islands.

The first great Norse earl after Sigurd the Mighty was Thorfinn, who was born around 999 and made earl of Caithness when five years old, later becoming earl also of Orkney and Shetland. His death is given as *c.* 1065. He was the grandson of Malcolm of Scotland, and following the death of Malcolm in 1033 Thorfinn had to battle with a rival claimant, Rognvald Brusason, who came to claim the earldom in 1037. At the time of Rognvald's arrival, Thorfinn was engaged in campaigns against the Irish, and Duncan of Scotland. Duncan was murdered by Macbeth with whom Thorfinn seems to have formed an alliance. Thorfinn also held considerable estates in Scotland. He finally brought about the death of Rognvald in battle, and travelled first to Norway and then to Rome where he obtained absolution from the Pope for his sins. On his return, he built a cathedral at Birsay and lived on the tidal island till his death. The rule of Thorfinn marks the period when the Norse in the Northern Isles became fully Christian.

He was succeeded by his two sons, who were followed in turn by their sons, Hakon and Magnus. Magnus was murdered by his cousin on Egilsay, and became Saint Magnus, being buried initially on Birsay. His remains were later translated to the new cathedral in Kirkwall which was dedicated in his honour by his nephew Ragnald. Ragnald, who died in Caithness in 1158, was likewise canonized, though he seems not to have been particularly worthy, his chief claim to sanctity resting in his having led a crusade and having a saint for an uncle. With him ended the golden age of the Norse earldom. The Norse earls continued to rule until 1231, but by the mid-twelfth century Scotto-Norman influence was being felt increasingly in the Northern Isles.

Perhaps the most symbolic site of the golden age is *Birsay* (Fig. 62). Here Earl Thorfinn's Palace has been excavated, and represents one phase of the complex of buildings between the cathedral and the sea. The palace incorporates part of Earl Sigurd's Hall, and overlies middens of the tenth to eleventh centuries. Subsequently, in the twelfth century, the palace was burnt, and the site was re-used for a complex of smaller buildings.

The palace, which may not be of one phase of construction, consists of a large building on the north side of an enclosure, facing onto an open court to the south. It centred on a passage, about 5 feet wide, running back from the middle of the south façade. The building was carefully executed, with masonry similar to that used in the cathedral, often squared and set in clay or mortar. The floors had flagstone pavements, and the roof was of turf. To the east of the passage lay two rooms, one a service room containing a firepit for the heating channels of the hall. Behind it lay a small antechamber. The hall itself measured about 21 feet by 45½ feet. The courtyard extended to the cliff, where there was a bath-house. The outer door of the hall is now on the cliff edge, but could originally have been central. The western range consisted of two or three rooms running east and west, with outer walls mostly of turf faced with stone. In front of the main façade was an open, paved courtyard, with a rough boundary wall, through which a passage gave access to a boat slip.

In general, the palace is similar to the episcopal palace at Garðar in Greenland, though somewhat earlier and employing some archaic features such as the turf-cored walls. Possibly the more rational planning and better masonry was inspired by Thorfinn's visit to Rome.

Behind the palace complex lay the cathedral. Dedicated formally as Christchurch, it became known as St Peter's, and quite probably contained some relic of the saint brought back by Thorfinn from Rome. The church consists of a nave, choir and apse, though the builders apparently intended to construct a western tower, which was never completed. The entire church appears to have been built about 1050, and in all is 47 feet 9 inches long internally, the

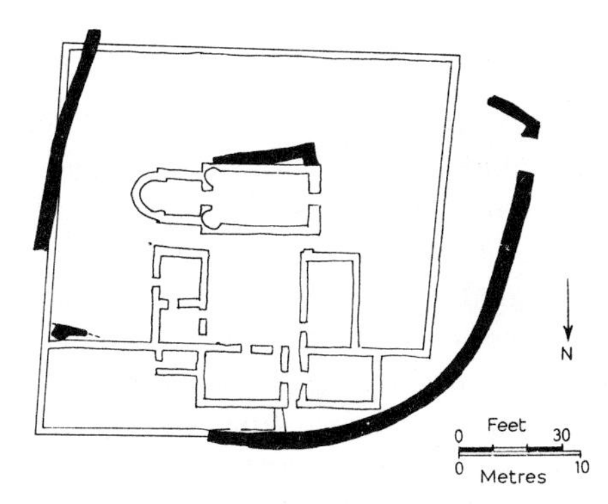

Figure 62 Birsay, Orkney. Ecclesiastical settlement (After Cruden)

nave being 16 feet wide. Excavation in the centre of the nave revealed a grave containing the remains of a skeleton and a wooden coffin. The bones were disarticulated, suggesting that they had been placed in the grave long after death. Possibly this was the original grave of St Magnus. After his remains had been translated to Kirkwall possibly some other notable, perhaps Thorfinn himself, was laid in his place.

The church was enclosed by a rectangular graveyard containing Norse burials. These were laid in stone cists with cover slabs which, in a few cases, were re-used earlier cross-slabs.

To the north of the church three ranges of buildings were grouped about a courtyard, the fourth side being the nave of the church itself. The north range was the most important, and typically domestic, with a hall at the east end and a screen passage in the centre. The west range, which is contemporary or slightly later, was probably a private apartment. The east range was probably storerooms, and was less well built. This complex appears to be contemporary with other modifications in the general plan on the site: at the same time the original entrance to the cemetery was blocked and a new entry made in the south wall of the enclosure. Also about this time two small side altars were set in circular recesses in the east corners of the nave. The closest parallels for them are from Trondheim and the cathedral at Garðar.

These important changes in the church and the construction of the subsidiary buildings are probably to be associated with the establishment of a bishopric at Birsay, some time during the term of office of Bishop William (d. 1168). The ranges of buildings probably constitute a twelfth-century bishop's palace and the additional altars denote an increase in the number of resident clerics.

A group of small houses overlie Earl Thorfinn's Palace: each have two or three small rooms, and are quite unlike the earlier Norse houses, being more similar to medieval farmsteads. They are not farmhouses, however, and are probably the dwellings of the clergy who served the cathedral.

Norse settlement on the Scottish mainland

Norse settlement on the north mainland appears to have been the result of secondary colonization from Orkney in the ninth century.[29] Norse placenames are relatively rare in the west mainland, and tend to be later than those found in the Northern Isles. *Stadr, setr* or *saetr* elements are conspicuously absent and those incorporating *bolstadr* elements are rare, though examples include Ullapool, Eriboll and Arnipol. The *bolstadr* element on linguistic evidence can be shown to be the earliest of the group. The only concentration is around the Kyle of Tongue, probably the result of direct colonization from Orkney. Of the later names, many are connected with hunting, grazing or timbering, and it has been suggested that they are the result of seasonal activities. They occur in the most environmentally suitable areas, such as Gairloch. In Lochaber traditional rights of landowners to use the foreshore may date back to Norse custom.

Norse period finds are rare on the west mainland, though a small hoard was found at Tarbat, Wester Ross, consisting of an armlet, three pieces of 'ring money' and coins of Eadgar, together with some Frankish tenth-century coins. The hoard was found near the church, and was probably deposited some time after 960.

The colonization of the east mainland was on a much greater scale, but still less intensive than in the Northern Isles. Only one *stadr* name is recorded from the area, though there are a number of *setr* or *saetr*, names, particularly in the north-east of Caithness. At the height of the Norse period their control was strongest on the north coast and along the south-east coastland of Sutherland, particularly round the Dornoch Firth. The factors dictating this were both historical and geographical. The Norse depended on suitable sea-ways and open country for penetration. The long inlets of the Dornoch and

1A Dinorben Hillfort, Denbighshire

1B Dinas Powys, Glamorganshire

2A Dinas Emrys, Caernarvonshire. Hillfort. 'The Pool' during excavation

2B Mote of Mark, Kirkcudbright: vitrified rampart during excavation

3A Tynron Doon, Dumfriesshire. Hillfort

3B Broch of Gurness, Aikerness, Orkney, Post-broch settlement

4A South Cadbury, Somerset. Post-Roman hall during excavation

4B Cadbury Congresbury, Somerset. Post-Roman hall during excavation

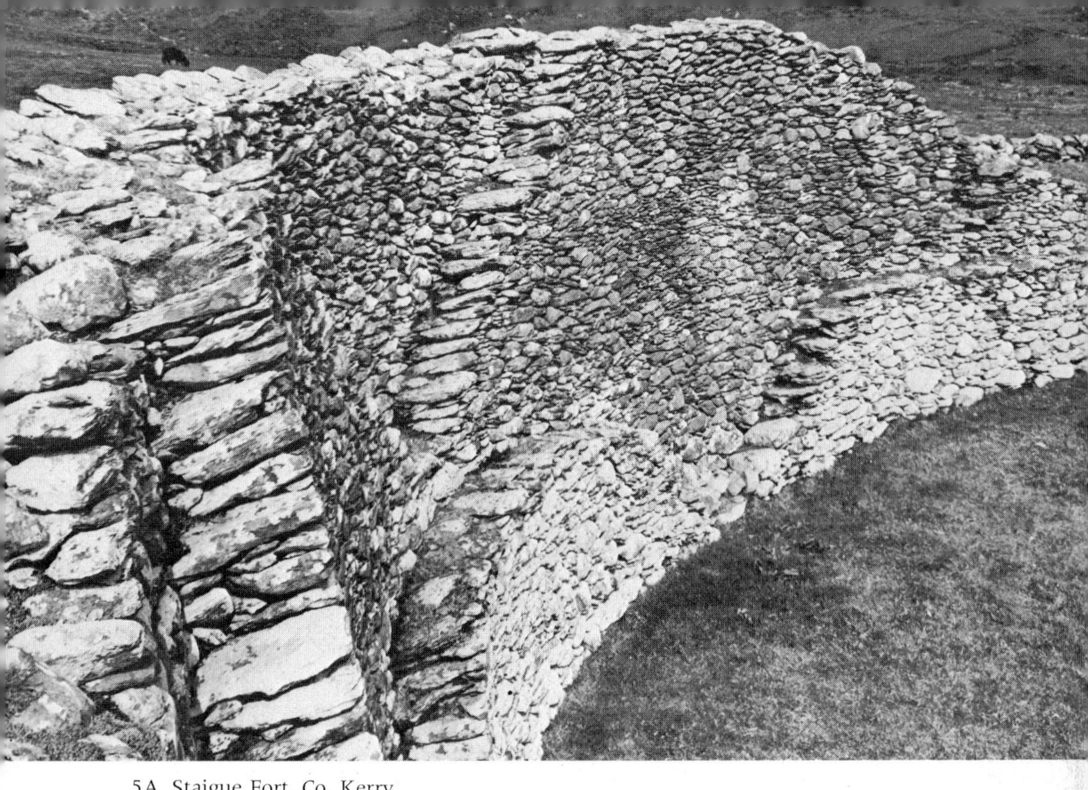

5A Staigue Fort, Co. Kerry

5B Tara, Co. Meath, from the air

6A Raths, near Cork, from the air

6B Dun, Strathtay, Perthshire

7A Tintagel, Cornwall, from the air

7B Inishmurray, Co. Sligo. Monastic site

8A Skellig Michael, Co. Kerry. Monastic cells

8B Eileach-an-Naoimh, Argyll. Monastic site

9A Cashel, Co. Tipperary, from the air

9B St Kevin's Church, Glendalough, Co. Wicklow

10A Temple Macdara Church, Co. Galway

10B Papil, West Burra, Shetland

11A Spooyt Vane Keeill, Michael, Isle of Man

11B The Braaid, Marown, Isle of Man

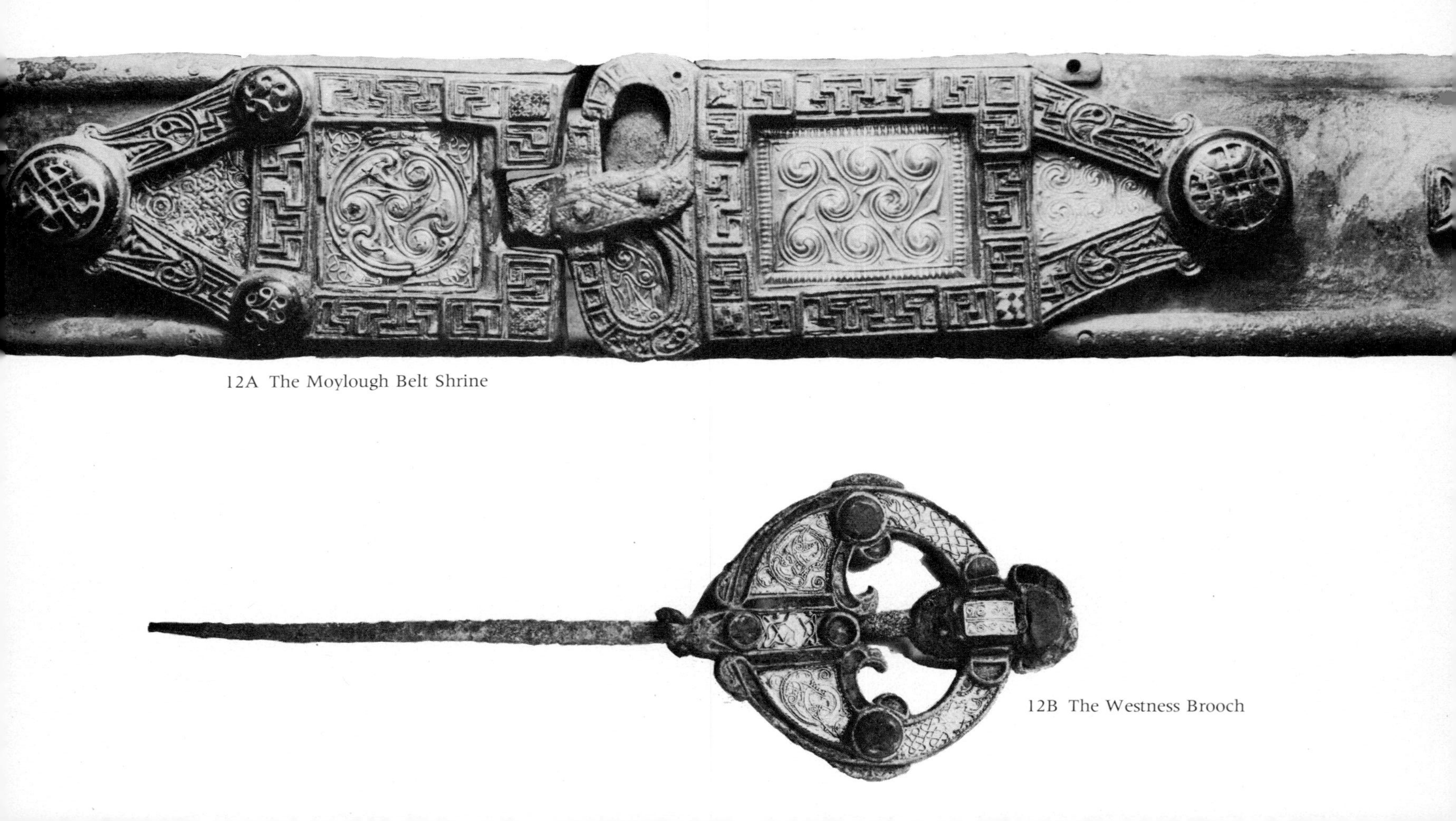

12A The Moylough Belt Shrine

12B The Westness Brooch

13A St Ninian's Isle hanging bowl

13B St Ninian's Isle silver bowl

14A St Ninian's Isle strap end with Pictish inscription

14B St Ninian's Isle, silver mount

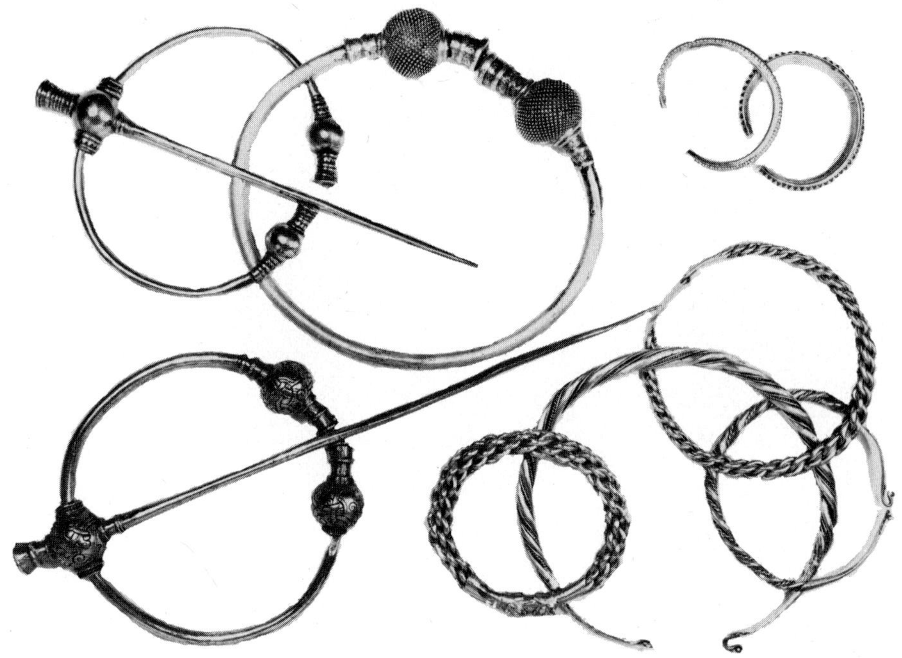

15A Part of Viking silver hoard, Skaill, Orkney

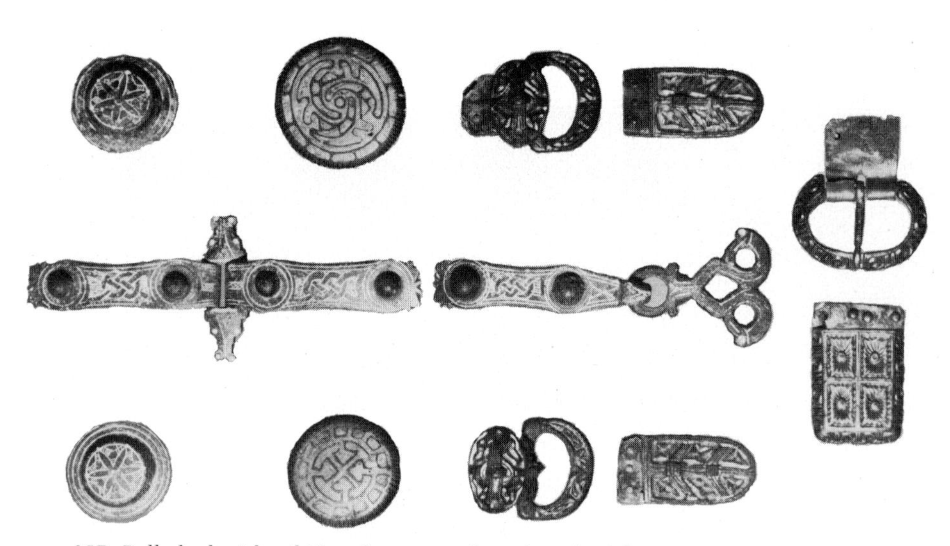

15B Balladoole, Isle of Man, horse gear from boat burial

16A Fragmentary bronze mount, probably Pictish, Stromness, Orkney

16B Pictish wooden box, Birsay, Orkney

17A Pictish cross slab, Papil, West Burra, Shetland

17B 'The Drosten Stone', St Vigeans, Angus

18A Pictish cross slab,
Meigle No. 2, Perthshire

18B Pictish cross slab,
St Vigeans No. 7, Angus

19A Pictish cross slab,
Invergowrie, Angus

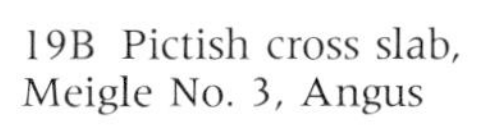

19B Pictish cross slab,
Meigle No. 3, Angus

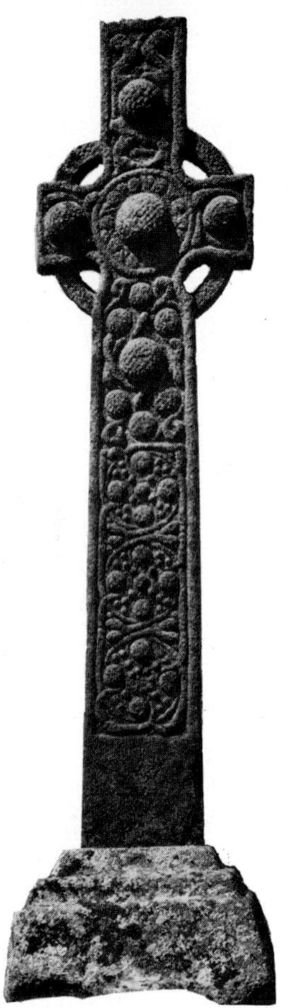

20A Iona – St Martin's Cross

20B Iona – St John's Cross

21A Kildalton, Islay, high cross

21B Cross shaft, Govan, Lanarkshire

21C Kirkinner, Wigtown, cross slab

22A Sueno's Stone, Morayshire

22B Cross slab, Riskbuie, Kiloran, Colonsay

23A Head of Irneit's cross slab, Maughold, Isle of Man

23B 'Crux Guriat' Stone, Maughold, Isle of Man

24A Calf of Man Crucifixion slab

24B Thorwald's cross slab, Andreas, Isle of Man

25A Gaut's Cross,
Michael, Isle of Man

25B Briamail's Cross,
Llandefaelog-Fach, Breconshire

26 Margam, Glamorgan, wheel-headed cross

27A Enniaun's Cross, Margam, Glamorgan

27B Cross shaft fragment, Bardsey, Caernarvonshire

28B Bealin Cross, Co. Westmeath

28A North Cross, Ahenny, Co. Tipperary

29A Moone Cross, Co. Kildare

29B North Cross, Castledermot, Co. Kildare

30A Cross of Patrick and Columba, Kells, Co. Meath

30B East (unfinished) Cross and round tower, Kells, Co. Meath

31 Cross of Muiredach, Monasterboice, Co. Louth

32A Cross, Dysert O'Dea, Co. Clare

32B Round tower, Ardmore, Co. Waterford

Cromarty Firths allowed a reasonable amount of passage, and the flat land of Caithness permitted inland penetration more readily than in the mountainous north mainland of Sutherland and Wester Ross. Historical circumstance too played a part, for the Highlands and coastal plain south of the Moray Firth were in the centre of the Pictish kingdom, and without doubt the habitable regions supported a reasonably large Pictish population. The Picts too may well have had a fleet (though this has been much debated), and if so would have been better able to fend off the Viking menace. The coast of Scotland from Nairnshire round to Kincardine or Angus offers few inlets for a sea-based force, and would be unattractive to raiders or settlers accustomed to fjords. In this context the situation in the lowlands of Easter Ross is particularly interesting, for here, although suitable waterways were present, Pictish control was also strong, with the result that to some extent the dominant element in the population wavered.

The only settlement of the Norse period that has been excavated on the mainland is at *Freswick Links*,[30] Caithness (Fig. 63). The site is mentioned in the *Orkneyinga Saga* as Thraswick from towards the end of the eleventh century. The saga refers to a hall of Freswick, with a farmstead near it in the twelfth century. The site, like Jarlshof, was first discovered owing to sand blowing away. Although the present landscape probably differs greatly from the Norse one, the bay must always have been ideal as a landing place.

Three main phases of settlement can be detected, the first probably dating from the late eleventh century. The settlement was probably abandoned in the thirteenth century, possibly in 1264 when Alexander III of Scotland sent an army to Caithness to exact a fine from the populace for having submitted to Haakon of Norway the previous year.

The earliest structure, of indeterminate date, was an anomalous wattle and daub building with clay floor, which had been destroyed by fire. This was built over by the first main occupation phase: a badly preserved building, one end of which may have been a barn, and which was separated from the (?) dwelling room by a partition wall. In the barn was a corn-drying kiln and a clay-luted basin sunk into the floor, as well as a lined hollow found on excavation to be filled with refuse. The walls were thicker than those of the two successive periods. Finds were few and uninformative, but included pottery which on analogy with that from Jarlshof implies an occupation no earlier than the late eleventh century. Another find was a piece of a metal cauldron with 'paper fastener' rivets, and a rough, fragmentary bone pin.

The next phase on the site was the building of a large dwelling, well preserved and with slightly bow-shaped walls. On the north side the bench was still traceable, though on the south its line was marked only by the post-holes for the roof supports. There was a central hearth, and the floor was covered with kitchen midden refuse, mainly limpet shells. One post-hole, identified by the excavator as possibly coming from the 'high seat', contained remains of willow. The post-holes seem to have been deliberately covered up (one with a quern) and it is possible that reoccupation was intended after its abandonment. Subsidiary buildings adjoined the house. Finds, apart from cooking pots, included a bronze belt chape, a fragmentary comb, broken hones, spindle whorls, pot lids, an iron knife, a fragment of a steatite bowl and a tether.

In the final phase the complex thus comprised two oblong buildings, which may originally have been dwellings, but one of which was converted into a

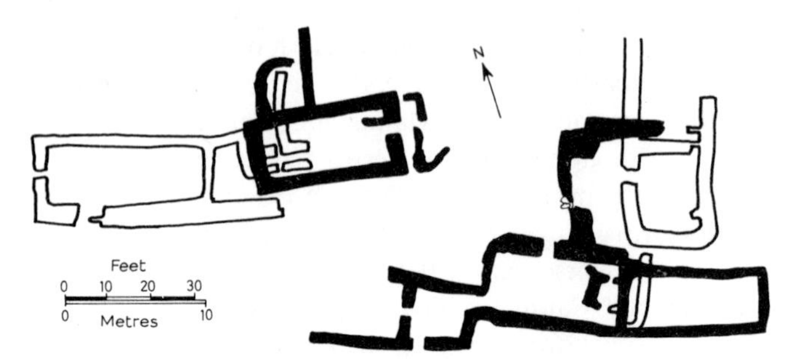

Figure 63 Freswick Links, Caithness. Norse settlement (After Curle)

sauna and the other left derelict, or possibly used as a store, together with the smithy and an annexe, an isolated main dwelling, which may have been a 'woman house', and the boat noost. The complex was roughly grouped about a courtyard.

The finds of the final period were more varied. They included sherds of medieval pottery imported from centres of production further along the east coast, probably in Angus, a penny of Henry III, which provided a rough indication of the date of abandonment, ship rivets, bone door snibs, and a fine eighth-century bronze zoomorphic penannular brooch, probably of Pictish workmanship, although found in a twelfth-century context. Other finds from the site include a bone comb case, and a glass bead.

The overall impression of Freswick, when compared with the equivalent phase at Jarlshof, is that the occupants were more impoverished, though the later finds from Jarlshof were unimpressive.

The north mainland has produced a number of graves and hoards.[31] Burials, most notably around Reay, have been found in Caithness. Women's graves have been recorded from Castletown and Watten, while another male grave is known from Westerseat. In Sutherland most of the finds come from the neighbourhood of Dunrobin Castle, and consist of stray objects which no doubt originally came from graves. Again the earliest datable finds are of the tenth century. Further south, a probable woman's grave is known at Ospisdale near Dornoch.

A few scattered finds from further south on the mainland have also been recorded, though they may not all be burials. One from Ballindalloch in Banff has been tentatively identified as Norse since the burial was accompanied by a horse. A tenth-century sword of Norse type may have come from a grave near Gorten. A possible grave of a woman at Errol, on the Tay east of Perth, may have produced a pair of tortoise brooches. A runic inscription from Knockando churchyard in Banff also amplifies the distribution map of Norse finds on the mainland, as does a tenth-century sword found in Perth itself.

Viking period hoards from the mainland are few, and unimpressive. Apart from the hoard from Tarbat, the only other notable find is from Kirk o'Banks in Caithness, where silver rings were found in a stone cist on the site of a chapel.

The Western Isles (Fig. 64)

It is difficult to assess the Norse occupation of the Western Isles. There is a considerable dearth of excavated sites – the excavated settlement sites at Udal in North Uist and Drimore in South Uist are as yet unpublished except as interim notes. Grave-finds are, however, more numerous (especially in Barra) than elsewhere in Scotland, and are notably rich. The shortage of recorded stone settlement sites may be due in part to the greater availability of wood and turf for building.

When the Norse arrived, a twofold division existed in the Hebrides, the dividing line being somewhere around Ardnamurchan. The northern Hebrides, especially the Long Island, were conservative and backward, retaining a culture which can be demonstrated as a continuation of that of the Iron Age. In contrast, the south Hebrides were flourishing at the time of the Norse. Adamnan, in his *Life of Columba,* describes the north Hebrides as an alien world, though this may partly be due to the rivalry between Iona and the power of the northern monastic foundation at Applecross, in Ross. The population at the arrival of the Norse was if anything smaller than it had been in the Iron Age. During the period from about 400 to 700 the north Hebrides suffered from climatic deterioration, with a resultant increase in the peat bog and reduction in the amount of land for cultivation. Continued reduction of the tree cover by human agency no doubt contributed to the poverty of the land. It is also possible that in the pre-Norse period there was some rise in sea level, as indicated by the number of sites now under water. The *Chronicle of Man* records that King Reginald gave to his brother Olaf the Isle of Lewis which was 'more extensive than the other islands but almost wholly unfit for agriculture'. The same account also states that the inhabitants were almost entirely hunters and fishermen.

It might be expected that colonization would have taken place in a southwards direction from the Orkneys, but this was probably not the case. The Hebrides were used as a base around 900 for raids on Ireland, and it would appear that settlement in the Western Isles followed the establishment of

Norse bases in Ireland.[32] Agricultural colonization was probably initially from Orkney, the temporary winter bases becoming permanent when the terrain proved suitable. Barra is the richest of the islands in Norse period finds. This can no doubt be explained by its good harbourage and its isolation from Dalriada. The relative percentages of Norse placenames in the Western Isles might at first imply that Lewis was the most densely settled (80 per cent of Lewis placenames are Norse in origin), the more southerly islands being progres-

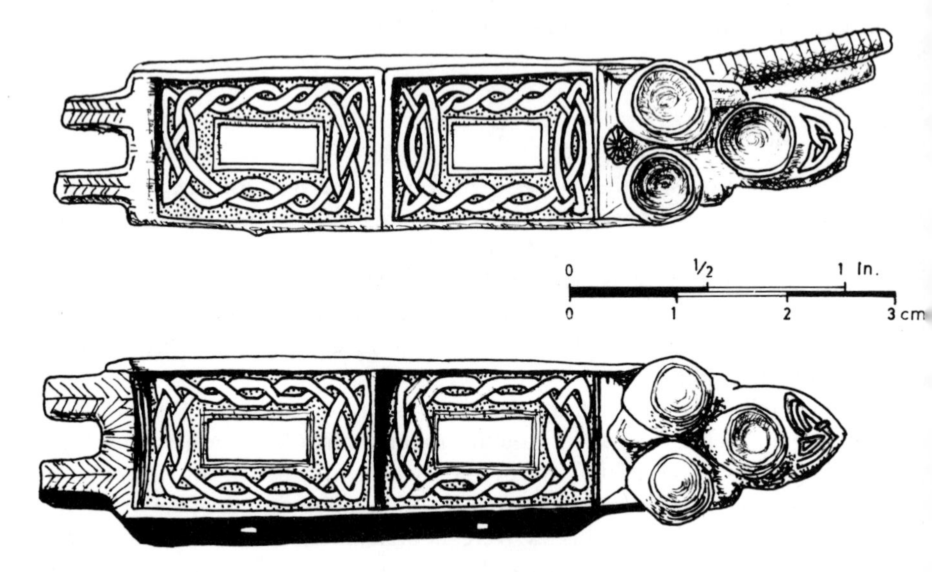

Figure 64 Oblong brooches, probably Irish, from a Viking burial in Oronsay

sively less densely settled. But this phenomenon is probably more apparent than real, for Scots Gaelic was well established in the south isles prior to the Norse settlements, and had even reached Lewis.

The Western Isles remained under Norse domination until the battle of Largs in 1263, but towards the end of the period it is likely that Norse traditions would have been much weakened.

Norse burials in the Western Isles

Not surprisingly, Lewis has produced the fewest Norse burials from the Western Isles. Only one grave has been recorded – a ninth-century woman's at Valtos. It was, however, richly furnished. Two tortoise brooches from St Kilda show that the Vikings reached this isolated outpost. North Uist has produced a spearhead, South Uist a bone comb, presumably associated with a burial since it was found in a stone cist. Eriskay, off South Uist, can boast a fine male grave with a sword with bronze guard and five-lobed pommel, a spearhead and a whetstone. On Barra a double burial of a man and a woman is known from Ardvonrig, in a mound crowned by a standing stone.

On Skye a man's grave was found as a secondary burial in a prehistoric cairn. Eigg has three Norse graves, all male, one with an unusually fine sword. At Ardnamurchan a possible boat grave was excavated at Gorten Bay. Tiree has two sites of Norse burials, one seemingly a small cemetery; Mull has one.

Colonsay, Oronsay and Islay have produced the richest and most noteworthy of the British burials, excepting perhaps two in Man. At Kiloran Bay in Colonsay a very rich boat burial was excavated, dating from the late ninth century. The burial was enclosed in a rectangular area about 15 feet by 10 feet, bounded by schist slabs, two of which were marked with roughly incised crosses. Apart from these, there was no suggestion that the grave might be Christian. The boat probably occupied most of the area of the enclosure, and a man had been laid in it in a crouched position accompanied by a horse. Northumbrian stycas of Eanred and Wigmund of York along with another coin (now lost) provided dating evidence for the burial. The skeleton was accompanied by a sword, shield, iron cauldron and a set of beam scales and weights. The weights were of lead, partly enamelled, two having Arabic designs on them. The scales are probably of Celtic workmanship, and indeed so are some at least of the weights and mounts, though such objects frequently turn up in Norse burials. The other finds included a spear, axe, arrowheads, knife, sickle, series of mounts, whetstone, ringed pin, strap mountings and strap buckle. Other boat graves are known from the island.

On Islay, at Ballinaby, there are three notable burials, besides some lesser finds. One of the Ballinaby burials (of a woman) was set inside a stone enclosure. The associated finds included a fine tortoise brooch, a bronze ladle, a flat silver chain, an ornate silver pin, beads, a glass linen smoother, a bronze needle case, and fragments of repoussé bronze mounts, tin- or silver-plated, of unknown function, which seem to have been joined together in pairs. The male burial was of similar type, but with the appropriate grave goods.

On Gigha a pair of scales was found associated with a set of weights which may have come from a grave, but this is not certain. The scales are of Irish origin, and the terminals of the balance beam are decorated with small birds.

There are two graves from Lamlash on Arran. The one, at King's Cross Point, is noteworthy for being one of the rare instances in Britain of a cremation burial belonging to the Norse period. It appears to have been a woman's burial, but boat rivets suggest that the ashes were laid in a boat. Associated with her was a whalebone plate, decorated with ring-and-dot motifs, and an iron casket hasp. The burial was coin-dated by a Northumbrian styca of Wigmund (837–54). The second Arran grave (male) was at Midhill, and contained a sword, and also a shield of a type obsolete in the homeland by the mid-eighth century.

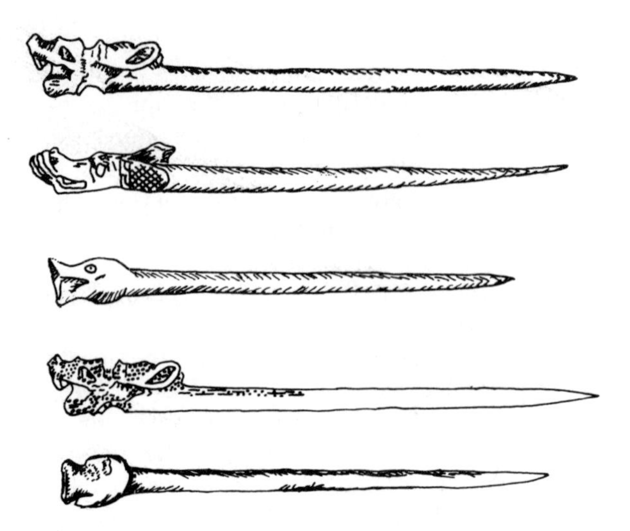

Figure 65 Viking bone pins, Jarlshof (After Hamilton)

Scandinavians in south-west Scotland

There is no evidence for the presence of Scandinavians in the south-west at an early date. During the ninth century the extreme south-west remained predominantly Northumbrian-orientated. Northumbrian stycas continued to circulate well into the ninth century, and the first Scandinavian impact seems to have been around 880 or slightly later, when the bishop of Lindisfarne and Abbot Eadred fled to Whithorn, and Halfdan raided Carlisle, massacring its inhabitants, before penetrating the south-east sector of Dumfriesshire. A few placenames round the Solway may be a relic of this raid and its aftermath, such as Eggerness, Almorness, Heston, Southwick and Satterness.[33] Around 870 the Talnotrie hoard was buried – although the silverwork was Saxon (p. 39), the presence of an Arab dirhem in the hoard and the general character of the hacksilver suggests that it was deposited by a Viking.

The list of Scandinavian finds from south-west Scotland is notably meagre. The only certain burial was in St Cuthbert's churchyard in Kirkcudbright, where a sword, ringed pin and a bead of the tenth century were found together. A handled, dark blue glass linen smoother of tenth-century Viking type was found nearby. Some doubt, however, surrounds the provenance; such linen smoothers were made in the more recent past, and so the find can only be regarded as putatively Norse. An eleventh-century war axe in Dumfries Museum found in a bog in the Borders, though in origin a Scandinavian type, is too late to be associated with the Norse raids, and may well be connected with a Northumbrian Border family's war band.[34] A knobbed bronze macehead from Lilsteads Farm, Canonbie (Dumfries) was probably made in Kiev; the only explanation for its presence here is that it was brought by a

Norseman who had served in the guard of the prince of Kiev. It is probably to be dated to the tenth century. A scatter of such maces is known from northern Europe, but none are published from Britain. From Blackerne comes a silver bracelet.

Two possible tenth-century ship burials are known from Blackshaw and Gretna, and a number of other sites which are probably Norse have been noted. One is a boat-shaped earthwork on a promontory at Milton Loch, Kirkcudbright, known as the Green Island Fort. A structure near Port Mullen in Wigtown has been identified as a Norse signal station, while the ninth-century reoccupation at Castle Haven, Kirkcudbright, may be connected with the Norse, since its local name was 'The Borg', the Norse for 'fort'. The placename Carrickfundle (Carraigfhionngall – the Norseman's rock) may be indicative of Norse occupation of this fort.

During the tenth century and continuing into the eleventh there was considerable settlement in south-east Dumfriesshire by Danes moving out of the Danelaw because of the Norse settlements and the establishment of the Norse kingdom at York. Their presence is attested by placenames which include Torthorwald, Tinwald, Waterbeck and Lockerbie. Their influence is further indicated by Scandinavian elements which were affecting south-west Scottish sculpture around this time (p. 204). Slightly earlier, in 937, the battle of *Brunanburh* (probably fought at Burnswark in Dumfriesshire) had reduced the importance of the Norse in the area. In the battle Olaf Sitricson, the Norse king of Dublin, and Constantine, king of the Dalriadic Scots, were defeated by Æthelstan and his brother, after which Olaf returned with his fleet to Dublin. Belonging to this period of the Hiberno-Norse kingdom is a penny from Whithorn imitating an issue of the 'Crux' type of Æthelred II, and struck in Dublin around 995.[35]

More menacing than the Scandinavian Norse were the *Gallghaideal* – the Norse-Irish – who appear in the Irish annals around 852.[36] They ravaged Bute, Eigg and Kintyre, dominating Argyll and the southern Hebrides. By around 1000 or shortly after, they had acquired most of Strathclyde, Renfrewshire and the Clyde valley, and had extended into Ayrshire, Galloway and Dumfriesshire. Their influence continued to be felt along the west coast into the twelfth century and even later – the last Hiberno-Norse king of Galloway, Alan, was taking part in the war of the Manx succession as late as the 1220s.

It would appear that Galloway was one of the nine Scottish earldoms held by Thorfinn, and he came down to the Solway himself in 1041–2. Magnus Barelegs was likewise an important figure in Galloway. Following his decision to hold the Isle of Man as his main base in 1098, he 'so exerted his power over the men of Galloway that he forced them to fell timber and transport it to the coast for the construction of these [Manx] fortresses'. Norse activity in Galloway effectively came to an end with the battle of Largs in 1263.

The Scandinavian impact on sculpture[37]

The most notable impact of the Scandinavians on south-west Scotland from an archaeological viewpoint lies in the field of sculpture. It has already been seen (p. 40) that there was an offshoot of the Anglian school at work in Whithorn with ramifications elsewhere in Dumfries and Galloway, notably at Hoddam, producing free-standing crosses in the Northumbrian tradition. Dumfriesshire is particularly rich in Northumbrian sculpture, and it is therefore possible to detect increasing Scandinavian influence during the tenth and eleventh centuries in what are basically Northumbrian works. The style of the interlace became looser and less regular, the workmanship less meticulous. A few works are purely Scandinavian in character: a dragon appears on a cross shaft from Glencairn, while at Wamphray there is a stone with a fine interlaced animal design of three dragons, and a hog-backed stone with interlace on one face and tegulae imitating shingles on the other. Such hog-backs are generally regarded as a development of the Danelaw, and are probably skeuomorphs of the roof of a stone house-shaped shrine. They have a long currency in Britain – some are even twelfth century – and in the later stages, when the original meaning of the hipped roof was obscured, the skeuomorphic shingles suggested to the carvers' minds the scales on the back of an animal, so that the stone became zoomorphic, often with animal protomes as terminals. A series of tenth- and eleventh-century Anglian-derived crosses shows the increasing use of Scandinavian imagery – from Closeburn comes a shaft with a spreadeagled boar, a horse, a bird pecking at a fish, a stag with a (?) sun disc on its back, an angel and Gunnar in the snake pit. Other stones in this tradition include one of the late ninth century from Nith Bridge, with twin confronted beasts. Siegfried Fafnirsbane appears on a headstone from Kilmorie in Wigtown, a Viking swastika appears on a stone from Craignaret, and another Scandinavian-influenced stone can be noted at Morton.

There are two purely Anglian crosses from Whithorn. It was, however, in the period of Scandinavian influence that the Whithorn school emerged as a distinct individualistic phenomenon, *c.* 900.[38] The most distinctive product of the school was a type of dumpy, disc-headed cross. The expanded arms of the cross usually follow the form of the disc head. In the centre of the head can usually be found a boss, with others frequently occurring in the spaces between the arms. The head was usually plain – a few ornate examples, such as one from Glasserton, have interlace extending to the head. Some, such as the Kirkinner Cross, have pierced armpits. The main decorative element is ring-chain – the strands frequently have median grooves – and pellets sometimes appear in the plaits. Two stones, one from Whithorn and the other from St Ninian's cave, have runic inscriptions. Taken as a whole, the Whithorn school has much in common with the sculpture of the Isle of Man in the same period, and it seems virtually certain that there was a connection between them.

Further north, in Lanarkshire, the recently discovered stone from Kirkmuirhill may serve to link the Whithorn area with the more northerly Govan school. The Kirkmuirhill stone is a fragment of an unfinished cross shaft of Whithorn type and has Scandinavian-type interlace showing certain similarities to the products of Govan.

The large collection of stones from Govan (p. 41) display an art which is essentially eclectic.[39] Influence from Pictland can be detected in some of the figural work, while the overall character shows much in common with the Whithorn school. The Govan stones date from the tenth to the early twelfth centuries. Originally there were about fifty stones from the site, which must have been an important monastery. The earliest, the so-called sarcophagus of St Constantine, was made to hold the relics of this little-known sixth-century saint who was venerated until the Reformation. The other stones include hogback stones, cross-slabs, cross shafts and two other sarcophagi.

A number of outliers are related to the Govan school. Fragments of a cross shaft and ornamented cross-slab can be noted at Inchinnan in Renfrewshire, along with a very ornamental shrine lid. At Barochan, in Renfrewshire, a free-standing stone cross still stands 11 feet high, decorated with figural compositions. Another fragmentary cross from Kilwinning, Renfrewshire, extends the map of Govan school monuments further, along with a series of Dunbartonshire stones, notably those from Luss, which although mostly later belong to the same tradition.

The style of the Govan school monuments is mixed. The interlace is probably derived from Anglian monuments. The ring-chain and irregular layout is probably Scandinavian. A few motifs, such as snakes' heads projecting from a whorl, can be probably traced to Ireland. Panels with riders have a Pictish ancestry. Taken as a whole, the Govan school is a classic example of how in Early Christian Britain artistic motifs were derived from a common pool of source material, the result of considerable cultural intercourse between regions.

Characteristics of the Scandinavian settlements

There is little evidence for the relationship between Viking and native. In the case of the islands, it is fairly clear that the Norse settlements constituted a blanket over the native population, which continued to live much as before, growing increasingly Scandinavian in character and probably intermarrying with the Norse population. In the Western Isles some intermarriage is recorded. The fact that some placenames and all the ogham inscriptions in Orkney may postdate the coming of the Norse implies some continuation of Pictish culture. The Shetland and North Uist Pictish oghams are likewise probably post-Viking. According to the sagas, some natives went with the Vikings on voyages to Iceland, and others were taken back to Norway. This situation probably holds good for the early centuries following the coming of the Norse. By the eleventh and twelfth centuries a new, more localized nationalism was beginning to take shape – the inhabitants of Orkney and Shetland were beginning to see themselves as Orcadians and Shetlanders, and those of the Hebrides as Hebrideans. They remained oriented towards Scandinavia, but did not regard themselves simply as Scandinavians. On the mainland, the native population was pushed into the poorer land.

The economy of Scandinavian Scotland[40]

The development of nucleated settlements, of which Jarlshof and Freswick are good examples, differs from the pattern in The Faeroes, Iceland or Greenland, where the single farmstead is more typical. The factors behind this are probably geographical, for the amount of arable land in the areas of Scotland settled by the Norse was limited. To some extent the need for good fishing harbourage must have been a factor behind the settlement pattern. Certainly there was a marked preference for coastal settlement in good harbours, and it frequently happened that good land and good harbourage coincided. It is probable that increasing population was the cause behind the growth of fishing. The nature of fishing equipment from excavated sites implies that some deep-water fishing was carried out as well as inshore netting. Small game, birds and eggs no doubt were a valuable supplement to the diet, though bird colonies would have been different in Norse times from the present.

It seems that, unlike the situation in the homeland where autumnal slaughter was a major feature in the farming calendar, in the settlements in Scotland large-scale slaughter did not take place, cattle being stalled in winter. Hay for fodder was important and carefully harvested, the archaeological evidence taking the form of stone bases for ricks, as at Jarlshof. It seems likely that the climate was more clement in the Northern Isles around 1000 AD than it is today (1000 AD was a climatic optimum, when vines were being grown as far north as York), though it is unlikely that conditions were favourable enough for trees to grow, as they would have been stunted by the salt winds.

The Norse farms were probably mainly self-sufficient, but to some extent trade played a part in the economy. One of the main problems lay in obtaining adequate food supplies – Earl Thorfinn had to send to Caithness for supplies – and the buying of cattle, malt and luxury items is frequently mentioned in the sagas. In order to finance such purchases, not only the loot of Viking expeditions but the sale of farm produce was necessary. This probably consisted of skins, hides, whale oil, dried fish and dairy produce as well as woollen cloth. Timber for boat building probably had to be imported, in some instances from Norway. The trade in steatite (soapstone) must have played an important part in Scandinavian economics, as it was used for cooking pots, baking boards, plates, bowls, gaming pieces, fishing weights and weaving equipment. It is not found in Orkney, Iceland or The Faeroes, but was quarried in Shetland and Norway (see p. 188). As yet, however, the nature and extent of the steatite trade is not understood.

Viewed as a whole, the Scandinavian settlement had a profound and far-reaching effect on late Celtic Scotland. It effectively brought to an end the native traditions in the Northern Isles, establishing both a new population and way of life, the effects of which are still felt in the twentieth century. In the Western Isles the effect was only slightly less marked, but here something of the old order survived the Scandinavian occupation to re-emerge in the Middle Ages as an important element in the culture which characterized the area of the Lordship of the Isles. Nevertheless, the emergent society was watered by a Norse strain. On the mainland, the effect was less far-reaching, but in the south-west at least the impact of Scandinavian culture upon the native population, already partly Anglicized by long years of Northumbrian influence, was to be followed too soon by the impact of Scotto-Norman culture and customs. Very little of Celtic Scotland outlived the Age of the Vikings, and what did was merely an echo from a distant past.

8 The Norse outside Scotland

The Vikings in Man

Scandinavian activity in the Isle of Man was similar to that in the Northern Isles. The evidence likewise comprises archaeology, placenames and documentary sources. For Man, the *Orkneyinga saga* and the Irish annals can be used, but more informative is the *Chronicle of Man and the Isles*, compiled at Rushen Abbey in the Middle Ages.

As in the Northern Isles, documentary evidence is uninformative about the first Norse raids and settlements. It seems fairly clear, however, that they were the natural outcome of the extension of the Viking field of raiding from western Scotland. Man was ideally situated as a base for raiding the north coasts of England, Wales and Ireland, and for south-west Scotland. In this the Vikings were following a long tradition, for the island had been the recipient of stimuli from Ireland, Scotland and the English mainland since prehistoric times.

Under the year 798 the Irish annals record a Viking attack on *Innis Patraic*, once thought to be St Patrick's Island off Peel, but now generally believed to be Inispatrick, off the Dublin coast. The first settlers probably reached Man in the decade or so before 900. So far, in marked contrast with Scotland, there is no find from Man earlier than 850. A few grave-finds, which include a sword from St John's with silver on the hilt and others from Ballaugh and Maughold, suggest some settlement prior to 900. The earliest finds from the cemetery at Balladoyne are a sword and a spearhead of *c.* 900.[1] At least some of the graves may be of casual raiders. In all probability Man was first used as a base for raids and expeditions to the adjoining mainlands of Ireland and England, and this picture is borne out by the *Orkneyinga Saga*, which describes Man as a winter base.

A series of four graves, all dating to the first generation of settlement, probably in the very first years of the tenth century, provide a valuable picture of the early Norse in Man.

The first to be investigated was that at *Knock-y-Doonee.*[2] Here in the late 1920s Kermode investigated a boat burial, under a mound. The outline of the boat could only be determined by the rivets, but it was seen to measure about

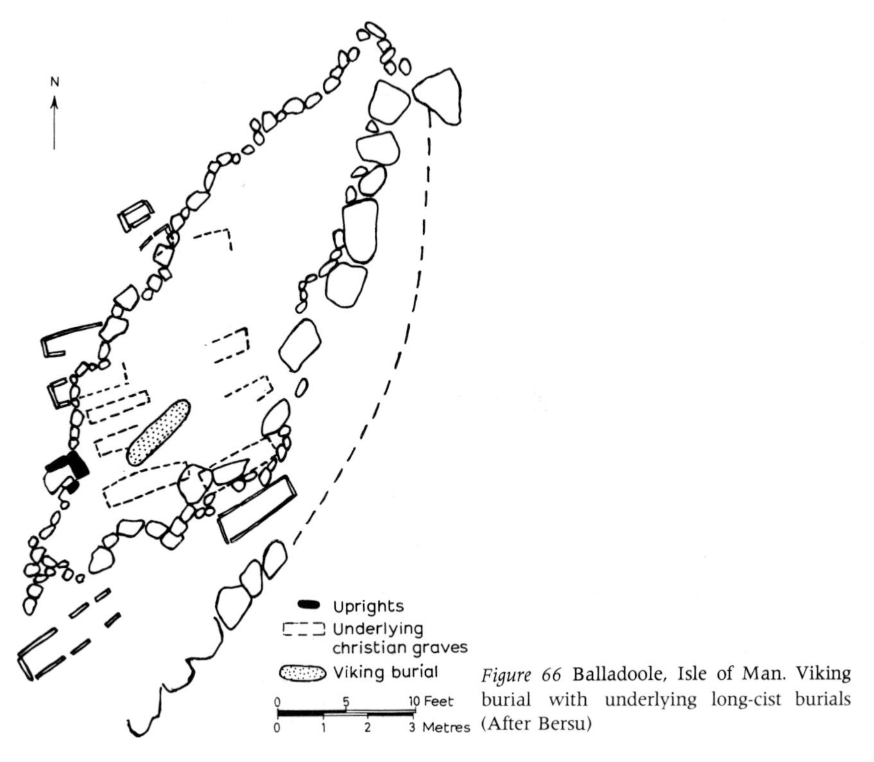

Figure 66 Balladoole, Isle of Man. Viking burial with underlying long-cist burials (After Bersu)

28 feet to 30 feet long. The body had been laid in the boat wrapped in a cloak, and accompanied by sword, shield and spear. Domestic articles, such as fishing gear, a hammer and tongs, were laid in the stern. A horse, and what was identified as a dog, also accompanied the burial. The cloak pin is not the usual type of ringed pin found in Norse burials, but a more peculiarly Irish variety.

While Knock-y-Doonee was the first burial to be scientifically investigated in Man, Bersu subsequently excavated a further series of three burials at Balladoole, Ballateare and Cronk Moar, which have shed more light on Viking burial customs in the British Isles.

Balladoole (Fig. 66; Plate 15B) was a boat burial like Knock-y-Doonee.[3] The dead man was laid in the boat with his belongings and a second body, probably that of a woman killed to accompany him to the afterlife. Due to disturbance, it was not easy to determine the original positions of the objects, but it appears that his cloak had been fastened with a ringed pin, and that he wore a belt with a silver buckle. A hone and a flint strike-a-light were probably contained in a leather bag at his side and he was wearing spurs. At his head was laid a bit and bridle mounts for his horse, the harness gear being spread out over his body. An iron cauldron handle was found near one

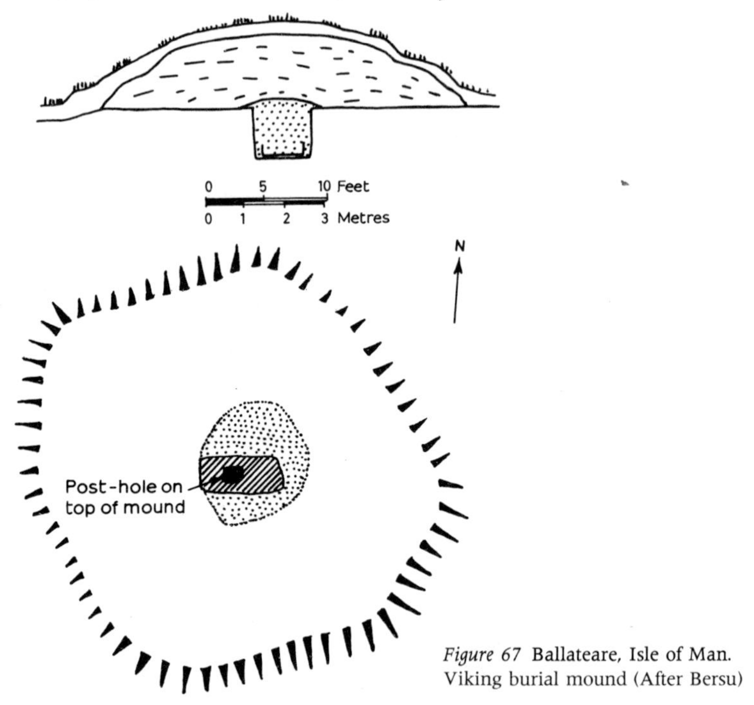

Figure 67 Ballateare, Isle of Man. Viking burial mound (After Bersu)

leg, and a shield was laid above his knees. He was not buried with any weapons. The mound in which the boat was set was capped by a heap of stones, on top of which were burnt bones of horse, ox, pig, sheep, dog and cat – offerings to accompany him to the afterlife. The objects from Balladoole indicate wide contacts – some, such as the cauldron, were of Viking origin. Spurs, buckles and strap ends were continental, probably Carolingian. The stirrups could have been produced under either Carolingian or Anglo-Saxon influence, while the harness mounts and shield were, like the ringed pin, probably Celtic in origin and, as the closest parallels for harness and shield are from Scottish Viking burials, could have come from Scotland.

The burial at *Ballateare* (Fig. 67) was different in character.[4] Here the body was laid in a coffin in a rectangular pit. The man was dressed in a woollen cloak, fastened with a ringed pin, and a knife laid on his chest. His sword was broken into at least two pieces, one spear was laid in the coffin and two on top, and the shield laid to the side of the coffin. The burial pit was then filled in and the mound made up with turves taken from different places not near the mound – possibly symbols of the different parts of the land owned by the dead man, each sod perhaps representing a field. The mound was then built up until it was sufficiently high to be used as a platform on which to lay the body of a sacrificed woman, who had probably been killed elsewhere. In the centre of the platform, above the burial pit, a hole was left for a marker post. Animal ashes were then scattered over the top, and the whole covered over with earth. The objects from the burial were less varied than those from Balladoole, being mostly Viking, though two of the spearheads may have been Celtic. The strap end from the scabbard sling was probably Anglo-Saxon, and can be paralleled by that from Meols in Cheshire.

At *Cronk Moar*[5] the body was laid in a prepared chamber lined with wood, a grave cover being supported by a beam. The associated objects were few in number – a sword, with its ornamented scabbard, a spearhead, a shield, a wooden-handled knife in a leather sheath, a strap distributor and strap end, the latter made from a Celtic (probably Irish) book clasp, and a ringed pin. Most of the finds were Viking, though the book clasp and ringed pin are Celtic, as probably was the scabbard.

The mound at Cronk Moar was situated on top of a ploughed field, though there is no reason to suppose this constituted ritual ploughing. The custom of human sacrifice found at Ballateare and less certainly at Balladoole is known from literature but is rare in archaeology. The twisted body of a female was found on top of another at Birka in Sweden, while there are, nearer home, Anglo-Saxon parallels for the rite. The Cronk Moar man was buried in a shaggy cloak of a type known from a burial on Eigg. Blow-fly pupae from the cloth suggest that the body was left, wrapped in its cloak, for up to three weeks in state before it was buried.

Viking settlements in Man

A number of Viking period settlements have been excavated in Man, a feature of which is the reoccupation of Iron Age promontory forts. *Cronk ny Merriu*[6] is a small promontory fort, in which the main building was a longhouse of fairly standard Norse type, similar to those in Scotland, with slightly bowed walls and benches along the sides. The entrances were opposite one another towards one end of the long sides. It was somewhat shorter than the average longhouse, in order to fit into the area of the promontory, and lacked the kitchen end. It has been interpreted as a lookout rather than a dwelling.

At *Close Ny Chollagh*,[7] Scarlett, the Iron Age fort seems to have been reconstructed in the early first century AD and extensively occupied until about 75, after which it was abandoned until the Viking period. The Viking period farm was butted on to the existing rampart, and the main building measured about 40 feet by 16 feet. There was only one bench, and the character of the plan suggested a late date, possibly after the break with Norway in 1265. There were some outhouses, and finds were nondescript and provided no dating evidence.

The promontory fort at *Cass Ny Hawin*[8] was excavated in 1957. This was distinguished by having a Viking-type house with walls built of turf, not of stone, and benches down the long walls which were created by the unusual method of a hollow being cut in the rock floor of the house to produce a raised area on each side. In the centre of the building was a long characteristic hearth, and there were opposed entrances near one end of the long walls. Typologically it should belong to an early period of the Norse occupation, but medieval pottery implies that it was of thirteenth-century construction. If this is so, and the pottery does not represent a thirteenth-century reoccupation of a tenth-century site (which is unlikely due to the flimsy nature of the walls), then it is possible that the Norse style of house had a long currency in the Isle of Man, and that the Close Ny Chollagh house should be dated possibly as late as the fourteenth century.

A house of Norse type was excavated in 1969 at *Doarlish Cashen*,[9] Kirk Patrick. This was a longhouse with turf walls with some facing stones, benches and a central hearth. Associated with it was a rectangular corn-drying kiln and traces of a boundary wall. Beyond, not explored by excavation, were other structures of unknown date. The only finds were a spindle whorl, a fragment of an iron buckle (unstratified) and a sherd of dark grey unglazed pottery. A medieval date seems likely for it, and it would appear to be the home of a Norse crofter. It was situated on marginal land, but the presence of the corn-drying kiln implies mixed farming. The excavator, Gelling, has very reasonably suggested that the occupation of such land for mixed farming implies fairly dense population on the island in the Norse period.

The first Norse dwelling to be excavated on the island was at *Vowlan*, which is a promontory fort on Ramsey Bay. The site was excavated in 1946 by Bersu who found that the structural remains were very slight, as the buildings were temporary wooden structures, and had probably been lookout posts.[10] The other site is the *Braaid*, excavated initially by Fleure who believed it to be a Bronze Age stone circle and ritual stone alignments.[11] The stone alignments were, however, seen to be the walls of buildings, and Bersu suggested that the site was wrongly interpreted and that it consisted of a round Iron Age hut and Viking longhouses (Plate 11B). This theory was confirmed by excavation in 1962, when two of the alignments were shown to be the bowed-out side walls of a longhouse of exceptional size (68 feet by 41 feet).[12] The short sides are missing – they were probably of timber with a sod backing. The re-excavation produced evidence of a bench along one side at least, but no evidence for the roof supports or any small finds, probably owing to a stream running through the house and removing occupation material. The size of the building and absence of roof supports is remarkable – the dimensions can probably be explained by a native tradition of large hut building in Man. The other alignments were also probably from a Norse house.

Viking period hoards in Man

Viking period hoards have been found in the Isle of Man. For the most part they were found in the nineteenth century and are badly documented.[13] Except for those from Knockaloe and Douglas, they consist mainly of Anglo-Saxon pennies and appear to have been deposited in the tenth century, or in the early part of the eleventh century.

The two Andreas hoards were found in 1867 and consisted of pennies of Eadgar and Eadwig. The Ballaqueeny Cronk hoard was found around 1873 and consisted of coins of Eadwig, Eadmund and Eadred along with a Danish coin of Anlaf and a denier of Charles the Bald of France. The Kirkmaughold hoard was found in a ram's horn in 1834 and consisted of tenth-century Anglo-Saxon and Hiberno-Danish coins, and the similarly composed Kirkmichael hoard was found in the same year. The Rushen hoard, found about 1848, comprised several hundred Anglo-Saxon pennies, of which all except twelve were melted down by a local jeweller. This hoard was probably deposited around 1000.[14]

The only hoards which included ornaments are the Knockaloe find, which is very badly documented, having been found somewhere in the parish prior to 1820 and consisting of Anglo-Saxon pennies of the (?) ninth to tenth centuries along with gold ornaments, and the famous Douglas hoard.[15]

The *Douglas hoard* was found in 1894, and contained at least 180 coins together with gold and silver ornaments. Many coins were thrown away by the finder because he regarded them as too fragile to be of any interest, and many ornaments and coins found their way into private possession without being recovered – the finder retained at least ninety-three coins and nine ornaments. Some ninety-five coins were recovered for the Crown along with eleven ornaments. The hoard constituted mainly Anglo-Saxon pennies although there was at least one Anglo-Danish issue, and was probably deposited around 973 or somewhat later. The ornaments consisted of a twisted gold torc, a series of armlets, half a silver armlet and a finger ring along with a lump of silver from a mould runnel and fragments of two thistle brooches.

Apart from these there have been two finds of Viking silver from Man – a torc and armlet were found in 1868 at Ballacamish, Kirk Andreas, and a silver armlet was found at Nappin, Jurby, as an isolated find.

The coins from the hoards include a large number of pennies of southern English mints – these were probably reaching the Danelaw through peaceful trade, and are a clue to the nature of the Manx hoards. They should probably be seen not as loot from Viking raids but the result of peaceful trading contacts with, probably, the area of Northumbria round York and the Norse kingdom of York itself, though it is also possible that some coins at least came from Chester which around this time appears to have been an important Viking trading port with Dublin, and, probably, Man.

Pagan and Christian in Man

The Vikings in Man were pagan until about the second quarter of the tenth century, as attested by the evidence of grave-finds, which do not postdate *c.* 925. The adoption of Christianity was a slow process, and pagan grave-finds have been found in Christian cemeteries. Churchyards producing Viking finds include Maughold, Michael, Braddan, Malew and Jurby, although in most cases there is no certain evidence for the existence of an early Christian cemetery on the site.

More definitive are the two long-cist cemeteries at Balladoyne and Balladoole. At Balladoyne a long-cist cemetery of thirty-two graves was excavated in 1937, with an associated 'kiln'.[16] A keeill or chapel was known to have once existed nearby. A Viking sword, shield boss and spear were found adjoining one grave, though their context was not properly noted. The grave itself had a cover slab engraved with fairly primitive designs interpreted as a quadruped, a 'grid' or enclosure and a motif that is either a boat or an animal. Another slab with crude engraving was found in a long-cist cemetery, associated with a keeill, at Cronk yn How in 1928.[17]

Some of the grave markers were as early as the eighth century, although one with broken runes was dated to the thirteenth century. The engraved slab had a herd of animals, probably reindeer, on it, and had been built into the foundations of the keeill. There has been much debate about the date of these engraved stones, but since similar crude engravings are known from Jarlshof in the Viking period it is possible that they belong to the same period in the Isle of Man. If so they constitute evidence for Norse burials (not necessarily pagan) in pre-existing Christian cemeteries. The grave at Balladoole (above) was built on top of a long-cist cemetery, and had disturbed one grave when the body was still articulated. While in the case of Balladoole the choice of a cemetery site may have been accidental, the overall picture suggests that the Vikings deliberately used pre-existing Christian cemeteries for burials.

Later, following their conversion, the Vikings seem to have taken over pre-existing keeills. They also took over the native Church organization, but later in the eleventh century in common with the Norse of Orkney and Iceland they became influenced by Roman custom and established a bishopric.

Viking sculpture in Man

The Vikings found an already flourishing school of stone sculpture in Man on their arrival (Plates 23–4), and even after the period of Norse settlement Celtic Christians on the island continued to carve free-standing crosses in accordance with purely Christian taste.[18] Following their conversion, the Norse in Man produced a series of distinctive crosses (which frequently combined with the Christian elements derived from Scandinavian mythology), runic inscriptions and a number of new decorative features. The runic inscriptions are particularly informative, and the Isle of Man has produced more such inscriptions – twenty-nine in number – than the rest of the British Isles, excluding Maes Howe, Orkney.

Only forty-eight – about a third of the stone crosses from Man – belong to the Scandinavian period. Most of them come from the northern parishes, in contrast to the pre-Norse stones. Nine have been found in Andreas, seven in Jurby and two in Rushen for example. Maughold, which has produced most of the pre-Scandinavian stones, has produced seven of the Viking Age. The early Manx crosses are of the wheel-headed Celtic type. During the Viking period, however, the cross-slab was introduced from Scotland, and became the main class of monument. Forty-four names are recorded, of which twenty-two are Norse, and eleven Irish, implying a mixed population. One stone gives a Norse father (Thorleif) with a Celtic son (Fiac), implying a Celtic mother.

Manx sculpture of the Viking period begins with the work of Gaut Bjornson (Plate 25A),[19] whose name is known from two runic inscriptions, the first on a cross-slab from Kirk Michael which reads: 'Melbrigdi son of Adakan the smith erected this cross for his . . . soul, but Gaut made this and all in Man.'

A second stone at Kirk Andreas tells that Gaut was the son of Bjorn, who came from Kuli. This has sometimes been identified as Cooley in the parish of Michael on Man, but is more likely to have been the Hebridean island of Coll. The assertion that he made 'all in Man' was probably correct, if it is taken as meaning all the stones of the Viking Age prior to the date of the inscription. This date has been disputed, but Gaut's work is generally placed in the period 930–50, and it has been suggested that he learned his craft in the north of England and fled from there following the defeat of the Vikings in the north at the battle of Brunanburgh in 937. Certainly the Manx sculpture of the Viking period seems closely related and probably in great part derived from the sculptural traditions of the north. It seems also to have been a fairly short-lived school, for most if not all of the sculptures can probably be assigned to the tenth century; the same motifs appear on typologically early and late stones.

Gaut was a competent craftsman but not an artist of great inspiration. His main concern was with interlace patterns, and he is usually associated with a type of ring-chain motif which also occurs in Cumberland and on an outlying stone from Penmon in Anglesey.[20] The motif is a regularly connecting chain with a midrib, made up of hollow-sided triangles. It is normally confined to sculpture, but there is an example of it on a sword guard from

Hesket, Cumberland, and it can be paralleled in Scandinavia.[21] Although related to the Scandinavian Borre Style, it is a local northern English development. Another of Gaut's motifs, an asymmetrical interlace, is also a northern device, probably developed from vinescroll. One of the motifs, a pattern at the end of the arms of the cross, is without a northern English parallel, but is directly related to Scandinavian Borre work. Animal ornament is absent, though one cross from Treen Church, Nappin in Jurby, which has animal ornament, may be attributable to Gaut.

If the inspiration behind the earliest Manx Viking stones is northern English, Man was the recipient of more direct influences from the mainstream of Scandinavian art. In Scandinavia in the Viking period[22] a number of animal styles evolved. Out of various styles detectable in the Oseberg ship the emergence of the 'gripping beast' can be traced into a fairly uniform tradition known as the Borre Style after a rich burial with characteristic ornaments. It can be detected around the middle of the ninth century, and lasts, in some areas at least, until the end of the tenth. The *Borre Style* is characterized by a lion-like beast, ring-chain akin to Gaut's and a backward-looking animal. Overlapping with the Borre Style from the end of the ninth century is the *Jellinge Style*, named after a site where there is a sculptured memorial stone and a silver cup from a royal grave that are typical of the tradition. Jellinge work is distinguished by its main element being an animal with ribbon-like ornaments, a pigtail and a lip-lappet. The Jellinge Style continued until about 1000, when it gave way to the *Mammen Style*, in which the animal was more substantial and had acanthus-like foliate offshoots. Mammen work was current between about 970 and about 1010, and it in turn developed into *Ringerike Style*, in which the foliation was elongated into exaggerated tendrils which dominate the pattern, and which lasted until the eleventh century.

Manx sculpture was strongly influenced by Jellinge and Mammen Styles, and never progressed much further. On the later Manx stones not only Viking motifs but complete scenes, particularly those derived from the Sigurd story, were depicted with vigour. While some of the animals may be Scandinavian in origin, most seem more closely related to those on northern English or Irish monuments. On a narrative stone from Andreas, Sigurd slays a Jellinge Style dragon, while a slab from Kirk Michael has animals which show many typical Jellinge features and hints of the Ringerike Style that was to follow it. In true Scandinavian style are two stones by the same hand from Kirk Braddan, of which one was erected by Thorleif in memory of his son Fiac, which is in the Mammen tradition in spite of the mixed blood of the man it commemorates.

The House of Keys and treens

Among Manx institutions, the present Manx parliament, the House of Keys, owes its origin to the Scandinavian period.[23] There are still twenty-four representatives – the number determined by Scandinavian historical conditions. The Kingdom of Man and the Isles was regarded as amounting to thirty-two islands (below) and the parliament in the Scandinavian period was fixed at this number. Half of these came from Man, and half from the islands of Scotland. Later, following Somerled's defeat of Godred II in 1156, half the Western Isles were lost, which reduced the number of representatives from the Hebrides to eight, resulting in the present number. Until the First World War, laws enacted by the House of Keys were not regarded as passed until they had been read at the assembly at Tynwald Hill. This was the site of the Norse 'thing' or folk-moot (the 'wald' comes from the Norse word for a meeting place), and it is still used for an annual fair on Tynwald Day, 24 June.

The present parish system is based on the Norse period land divisions, which in turn seem to continue the older land divisions of the Celtic period. These land units, or treens, each had a keeill or chapel, and in this respect Man still preserves a part of the structure of Norse and pre-Norse land divisions.

Man under the Norse[24]

The history of Man under the Norse becomes less nebulous in the eleventh century with the reign of Godred Crovan (1079–95). Godred, whose name is frequently corrupted to Orry, is a figure much like that of Brian Boru in Ireland, a latter-day King Arthur who frequents Manx mythology. He was apparently a Hebridean from Islay, who fought with the Norse under Harold of Norway against Harold of England at Stamford Bridge, and subsequently fled to Man. In 1079, after mustering an army and a fleet, and after two unsuccessful attacks, he at length succeeded in taking the island. Under Godred, the Hebrides and the Isle of Man were united into a kingdom known as the kingdom of Man and the Isles. Although in fact the Isles number several hundred, for administrative purposes they were regarded as thirty-two, and divided up into four units based on the large islands of Lewis, Skye, Mull and Islay. Subsequently the division of the Isles into a north and a south group (Lewis and Skye being known as the Out Isles) came about, and this was to have an effect on administration. For purposes of control, Man was the main island of the confederacy. Little is known of the details of Godred's rule – his power seems to have extended to Dublin, and he died on Islay in 1095.

Following Godred's death there was internal dispute in Man, and to an island weakened with civil war came Magnus Barelegs in 1098, making it his base. His death was followed by further confusion, until the accession of Olaf I in about 1113, who ruled the island well until 1153 and maintained good relations with the neighbouring countries. His successor, Godred II, led an expedition to Ireland and annexed Dublin, but in so doing offended his allies on the venture, the Hebridean chiefs, with the result that on his return he was faced with a war against them. They were led by his brother-in-law, Somerled, ruler of Argyll, and Godred was defeated in a sea battle off Colonsay in 1156. The outcome was a division of the territory of the kingdom of Man and the Isles, Godred retaining Man and the Out Isles. This weakened the power of the king in Man, and Godred sought help first from Henry II of England, then later from Norway, following a further dispute with Somerled and a raid by the latter on Man.

The successor of Godred II was Reginald I (1187–1228); during his reign there was an increasing attempt by England to gain supremacy in the Irish Sea. Henry II had assumed the title of Lord of Ireland in 1171 when he had annexed Dublin and some other ports. King John wished to extend English control in Ireland, and the attempts of Godred II at following his predecessors and interfering in Irish affairs resulted in an English expedition to Man. About the same time there was an attempt by Norway to strengthen its position of authority in Man, and this period marks the beginning of a long struggle for supremacy in Man between the rival factions of England and Norway. By the thirteenth century the North Isles (Lewis and Skye) still belonged to Man, and the others were ruled over by the descendants of Somerled. This situation did not please Alexander III of Scotland, who wished to annex them. An attempt to bargain with Haakon of Norway failed and only led to his coming to Scotland with a fleet and anchoring off Arran. The outcome was a naval battle in which Haakon was defeated off Largs in 1263, and Magnus king of Man (1252–65) submitted to Alexander. Haakon died in Orkney on his return, and by the Treaty of Perth in 1266 the Western Isles and Man were ceded to Scotland in return for a payment of 4,000 merks (£2,666·66) and an annual rent of 100 merks. This brought to an end the period of Scandinavian rule in Man, and the years following 1266 are years of a long struggle between Scotland and England for control of the island.

The Western Isles did not become peacefully absorbed into the Scottish kingdom. Until suppressed by Robert the Bruce the islands were dominated by the chiefs of the Clan Dougall, who claimed descent from Somerled, while subsequently the chiefs of the Clan Donald (who also claimed descent from Somerled) dominated the Isles and held the title of Lord of the Isles. The Lordship of the Isles ended nominally in the reign of James IV, but not until the Statutes and Band of Iona in 1609 did Scottish government have any real effect in the Hebrides.

From the foregoing discussion, it will be apparent that the Scandinavian overlay in Man was considerable and, as in the Northern Isles, was to effectively bring to an end Celtic cultural traditions. Despite this, the linguistic legacy was negligible – the Norse language, which must have been at least as familiar to Manx ears as Celtic, was to leave little trace. Celtic, possibly kept alive due to the peaceful intermarriage between Celt and Viking, was to revive in succeeding centuries. To some extent at least Scots Gaelic may have played a part in this revival, due to the close connection between Man and the Western Isles. Modern Manx is, essentially, phonetically spelled Gaelic.

Norse building customs were to last long, but the longhouse was replaced in the Middle Ages by the sheiling. A Norse origin for the type has been suggested,[25] but as it occurs elsewhere in areas not settled by the Scandinavians, it must be seen as a widespread Highland Zone phenomenon, the adaptation of the medieval peasant house to specialized farming conditions.

North-west England

At the time of the Norse settlements, the old area of Cumbria appears to have remained predominantly British.[26] It seems to have been part of Strathclyde in the years following 900, and a king with the British name of Owen is described as king of the Cumbrians in 927. Owen was probably a son of Donald II of Scotland, and in the early tenth century there is a body of evidence which implies a growing Scottish domination of Cumbria. From this time on the Scottish kings made continuing efforts to dominate what has now become northern England, and this struggle was to be maintained into the eleventh century and later, the boundary between Scotland and England being variable. There is little evidence for Anglo-Saxons in Cumbria – no Anglo-Saxon burials of the pagan period are recorded in Cumberland and Westmorland, and there is very little later evidence for the presence of a strong Anglo-Saxon element in the population. Lancashire likewise seems to have had a hybrid population: only four pagan Saxon burial sites are known from the county, all badly authenticated and two very dubious.[27] There is only one Anglo-Saxon church in the county (at Heysham),[28] and on the eve of the Scandinavian raids Lancashire was probably thinly populated by a mixture of British and Anglo-Saxons. Much of the area was unsuitable for supporting a dense population, but from an early date it had probably provided a thoroughfare linking the men of Wales with the Gwyr Y Gogledd (the Men of the North), easy transit being inhibited by the Chat Moss.[29]

The earliest Norse settlements seem to have affected the area around 900, at a time when Cumbria provided a stepping stone for the Norse of Ireland, Man and Scotland and the Danes of Northumbria. No settlement sites are known, the evidence for the presence of the Scandinavians taking the form of graves, hoards, stray finds and placenames.

The Cumberland and Westmorland graves are fairly numerous: sites include Workington, Eaglesfield, Ormside and Hesket-in-Forest.[30] The last-named burial was a cremation, and although excavated in 1822 is well documented. It contained a sword, spearheads, a shield boss, axehead, buckles, sickle, whetstone and bone comb and also a comb case, which was the only object not showing signs of burning. The weapons had been ritually damaged, as in the Manx find at Ballateare. The burial was covered with a cairn of stones. To this list might be added two burials from Lancashire, at Claughton Hall, near Garstang, and that at Rampside, which is attested by a sword from a churchyard. The list might be extended with the addition of a few stray finds which may have come from burials.

There are a number of Viking period hoards from northern England. A well-known trefoil brooch of silver, with filigree work in spirals and bosses which originally contained garnets (one remains), was found with coins dating between 796 and 854 at *Kirkoswald* in Cumberland.[31] Once held to be Carolingian, it is now generally believed to be the product of an Anglo-Saxon workshop of the late eighth or early ninth century. Halton Moor produced a silver bowl, decorated with medallions containing Sassanian-looking animals and Carolingian-type acanthus. It too has been postulated as Carolingian, but is also more likely to be Anglo-Saxon, influenced by a Sassanian model.[32] It was found with 860 silver pennies, mostly of Cnut, and was deposited probably in the second quarter of the eleventh century. Also in the hoard was a silver torc and six stamped gold pendants.

The hoard from *Cuerdale*[33] was found in 1840 on the banks of the Ribble near Preston, Lancashire. It was composed of over 7,000 coins, together with hacksilver and ornaments. The silver weighed almost 1,000 oz, with the exception of the coins, and included ingots, armlets, rings and fragments of thistle brooches and other penannulars. A strap end was of Anglo-Saxon Trewhiddle Style. Most of the coins were of the type usually ascribed to the Viking mints of the Danelaw, but there were also a number of Anglo-Saxon, continental and Oriental pieces. On the basis of this the date of deposition has usually been taken to be around 903. Considerable debate has surrounded the hoard, which constitutes at least 99 per cent of all the known coins of the Danelaw, though a Danelaw attribution for them has sometimes been contested and recently it has been suggested that they were the product of a Welsh mint. Such a hoard is far too great to have been simply the result of a plundering expedition, and may well have been the contents of a treasure chest lost by the Viking army on its return to Northumbria after the battle of Tettenhall in 911. Another Lancashire hoard, found at the *Hakirke* at Crosby, just north of Liverpool, in 1611, also contained Viking coins of the Danelaw, as well as Anglo-Saxon pennies and continental coins.

Southern Lancashire and Cheshire certainly seem to have been extensively settled in the early tenth century. A series of placenames – Ainsdale, Birkdale, Ormskirk, Formby, Kirkby, Crosby, Skelmersdale, Blundellsands, Meols Cop – all attest intensive Norse settlement. The nature of the settlement seems to have been peaceful, and probably agricultural. The lack of finds can probably be explained by the extensive building operations since the early nineteenth century, the result of Liverpool overspill. Among the finds from Meols in the

Wirral of Cheshire, however, are a number of items which could well be Norse in origin, including two ringed pins of Irish type of the sort so popular among the Norsemen in the British Isles.[34]

Other finds from the north-west include fine thistle brooches which may have once formed parts of hoards and which were found at Penrith and Newbiggin Moor in Cumberland (the sites are near one another and they may constitute a pair),[35] while another thistle brooch has been recorded from Casterton near Kirkby Lonsdale, Westmorland. Another stray penannular silver brooch from the same county was found at Orton Scar.[36]

Chester, which had in all probability remained unoccupied from the end of the Roman period until the ninth century, was still of little consequence when a Danish army wintered there in 894–5, but its strategic position as a port for the Vikings in Ireland was probably soon realized, and Æthelred and Æthelflæda of Mercia 'restored' the city in 907, establishing another burgh at Eddisbury to the south at about the same time.[37] While predominantly Anglo-Saxon, Chester in the tenth and eleventh centuries seems to have owed much of its importance to its being a Viking trading post. There are four late Saxon hoards from the city,[38] all no doubt connected with the unrest caused by the Scandinavians, and the town and its hinterland can boast a fair amount of Viking-influenced sculpture.

Viking period sculpture in northern England

It has already been noted in the discussion of Manx sculpture that there was a notable school of sculpture in north-west England in the Viking period. At first sight the products of the north-west seem degenerate in the extreme when they are compared with the earlier Anglian tradition of Northumbria, yet if studied closely they appear vigorous and preserve elements of the spirit of the Celto-Saxon church of Northumbria.

Several elements can be recognized – the Anglo-Saxon, which reflects the more peaceful days of Northumbrian inhabited vinescroll and careful interlace, the Irish, as exemplified on the high crosses, and the purely Scandinavian.[39] Certainly the overall coarsening of the work is probably to be explained by Viking influence. The Irish influence is explicable since north-west England was mainly affected by Norse from Ireland, and possibly included a Hiberno-Norse element familiar with the monumental style of the ninth and tenth centuries. The main centre of the north-western sculptural tradition appears to have been Cumberland, though related work can be seen in Westmorland, Lancashire, Cheshire and west Yorkshire, and some influence from the school is also apparent in Dumfriesshire and Man (p. 204) with outliers in north Wales.

The most notable feature of the monuments of the period is the figurative decoration. This is both pagan and Christian in inspiration, a phenomenon which can best be explained by the general approach to iconography in the period. The figural compositions were regarded quite simply as ornamental themes, derived from a 'pattern book' of motifs available to the sculptor, and their content was of little importance. Possibly the Church saw some didactic value in the familiar stories from Scandinavian mythology, but more probably it was only concerned that crosses were still being set up and keeping alive traditions, and turned a blind eye to the details of the decoration.[40] Some of the Christian iconography is derived from Ireland – the hart and wolf, for instance, which appear on a cross from Dacre, can be matched on crosses from Ahenny and Castledermot in Ireland.

The classic of the north-west English crosses is the fine example from *Gosforth* chuchyard in Cumberland.[41] This is the highest monument of the pre-Conquest period in England, and still stands 14½ feet. It has a round-sectioned base, partly plain and partly covered with a scale-like pattern, from which stems a square-sectioned tapering rod, formed by slicing away the rounded surface of the shaft. The iconography is extremely detailed, and includes scenes from the life of Christ and the Voluspa, a pagan Norse cycle which tells the story of the world from the creation. The Gosforth Cross is the starting point for a series of round-shaft crosses, though it differs slightly from the majority in Cumberland which are shorter, smaller and more roughly executed. Whether the others are derived from it is unknown – the other Cumberland crosses (of which typical examples can be seen at Beckermet St Bridget and Giant's Grave, Penrith) are more likely to be derived from the products of the Peak District, which belong to the two classes known as 'Peak decorated' and 'Peak plain'.[42] The origin of the type is unknown – it may be a wood skeuomorph or it may be derived from a Carolingian prototype. It is mainly a phenomenon of the Mercian area, and is unlikely to be purely Viking in derivation.

Anglo-Saxon elements can sometimes be detected in sculpture in the north-west. One of the Penrith crosses has degenerate vinescroll. Hybridization is commonplace, however, and sub-Anglian animals are combined with Jellinge interlace at Waberthwaite, Cumberland. At a relatively early date the hog-back spread over the Pennines, and during the second quarter of the tenth century traditions hitherto separate on each site of the Pennines became fused.

The Vikings in Wales

It is significant that in spite of their constant raids on Wales, the Vikings made very little impact. No Viking burial is recorded from the Principality, and no settlement site is known. Stray finds are rare: a lead tablet of the tenth or eleventh century, with an embossed dragonesque design, from Castlemartin, Pembroke; an iron spearhead with a socket decorated with incised chevrons, of the tenth century, from Ty'n Rhosydd, Llantrisant in Anglesey. There are two hoards – one consisting of five silver armlets with stamped geometric ornament from Dinorben Quarries, Anglesey, and a larger hoard from Bangor, which contained fifteen Anglo-Saxon, Danelaw and Kufic coins, along with a fragmentary bracelet and a fragmentary ingot, and which was deposited in 927 or later.[43] A boat, without grave goods or burial, was found at the mouth of the Usk in Pembroke, and is putatively Viking, but this is uncertain.

This sparsity can probably be accounted for in two ways. First, the terrain was unsuited to Scandinavian penetration – inland the north was too mountainous and ill provided with suitable navigable waterways. The south, though more adaptable, was probably fairly densely populated. The second factor appears to have been the efficiency of the Welsh in repelling Scandinavian raids, for Wales had her Alfred in the person of Rhodri Mawr, prince of Gwynedd (844–78). He succeeded in killing Orm (who may have given his name to the two Orme's Heads), the leader of the Hiberno-Danish raid on Anglesey and the north Wales mainland around 855. By the end of his reign Rhodri was king of all north Wales, though his war against the Vikings was not always as successful as his early campaigns. To some extent, too, the Viking failure to colonize Wales may have been due to the subsequent power of the kingdom of Hywel Dda, who succeeded in maintaining internal peace and coherence throughout the country until his death in 950.

The first appearance of the Vikings in Wales was in 795, when they ravaged Glamorgan but were repulsed and went to Ireland.[44] They do not appear in the annals again until the mid-ninth century, when they attacked Anglesey and Gower. The subsequent history of the Viking raids in Wales is mainly an account of hit-and-run attacks, the two main targets being Anglesey and Caernarvonshire in the north and Pembroke in the south.[45] The main attackers were the Irish Vikings from Dublin, though there were also some raids in the early ninth century from the English Danelaw. A few isolated raids were led by more distant chiefs – Eric Bloodaxe, Torf-Einar from Orkney, Olaf Tryggvason and Svein Forkbeard all figured in the later tenth-century attacks, the last being captured by the Welsh.

Probably this period saw some Viking settlement on a small scale in south Wales. There is a scatter of Scandinavian placenames along the coast from Newport to Neath, in Gower and in Pembroke, while documentary sources hint that a few Scandinavians were peacefully settled in this region. A King Sigferth attested a charter of Eadred along with Welsh princes in 955, and his name is surely a corruption of Sigfrid. In 960 a certain Stefni with his foster son Bjorn and daughter Alof are recorded as possessing an estate in south Wales, probably Pembroke. There is also some suggestion that it was Scandinavian-organized trade in the Bristol Channel that led to the early development of Cardiff and Swansea.

Viking attacks continued in Wales in the early eleventh century, but later in the century, as the Scandinavians in Ireland became a part of the Irish community, there was a growing liaison between the Welsh and the mixed communities of the Irish shore against the growing Norman English menace. Gruffydd ap Cynan (1075–1137), king of Gwynedd, was brought up in Dublin, and through marriage was the great-grandson of Sihtric Silkbeard who had fought at Clontarf. Both Norse and Irish fought with Gruffydd in his Welsh battles. The eleventh-century raids were mainly carried out from the Western Isles or elsewhere in the north. Magnus Barelegs took Anglesey, following his raid on Man in 1098, but with little result, although he supposedly returned there for timber to rebuild three of the Manx forts that he had sacked. This more or less marked the end of the Scandinavian raids in Wales, though a few minor raids took place from the Isles and Orkney as late as the twelfth century.

Viking influence in Welsh sculpture (Plates 25–7)

There is some strain of Scandinavian influence in the late Welsh carvings.[46] The influences at work in Welsh art, however, were varied, and the Viking elements were probably not the result of direct influence but rather of the inevitable tendency of Welsh sculptors to draw upon the widespread repertoire of current motifs. The revival of Welsh sculpture in the ninth century was in all probability the outcome of growing contact between Wales and the Anglo-Saxon areas following the settlement of the Easter controversy in 768. Certainly stimulus was given to artistic traditions at the end of the eighth century by the arrival of refugees from Viking-afflicted areas, notably Northumbria and Ireland, and very probably Man, if Manx influence in Welsh carving can be taken to indicate direct contact with Manx sculptural traditions. The period is marked by the early production of fairly accomplished works, followed by a gradual decline which lasted until the Norman Conquest and probably lingered later.

The monuments are concentrated in Anglesey-Caernarvonshire, Pembrokeshire and Glamorganshire, and are grouped in association with major monastic centres such as Penmon (Anglesey), or Bangor (Caernarvonshire). The first two areas coincide with the areas most afflicted by the Viking raids, the third probably marks a gradual expansion of Welsh activity eastwards. The north Welsh crosses seem to be derived for the most part from northern England in their decorative traditions, and are a separate group from those in the south.

Viking influence is mainly felt in the form of individual motifs, though there is a group of ring-headed crosses which are of Anglo-Scandinavian type in Anglesey and Flint, notably at Penmon and Dyserth. In south Wales, the amalgam of influences includes some from the Merovingian and Carolingian world, on stones from Meiford (Montgomery) and Llanynis (Breconshire).

The Vikings in Ireland

The impact of the Vikings in Ireland was considerable, for they provided a much-needed jolt to a nearly stagnant society. Before the first Scandinavian raids, Irish culture had reached a state beyond which it could not develop without fresh impetus. Its art, which had emerged in the seventh century out of the common traditions of the late Celtic world, had reached by 800 a point beyond which it could only decline, its interlace and other decorative schemes degenerating into an over-fussy and badly executed confusion of line and jarring colour. The discipline of the early Church had declined, and the products of the late eighth and early ninth centuries were over-ornate. Society too was static – a world of petty intrigues and local squabbles, based on an essentially pastoral economy. While it is true that the raids resulted in precious works of art being taken to Scandinavia, the overall outcome of the Viking settlements in Ireland was on the positive side for Irish culture. The Vikings made Ireland again aware of its coast and rivers, provided her with towns, and established trade, with all that went with it in a medieval society – systems of weights and measures, and coinage. Viking art styles, which ultimately had a similar origin to the late Celtic, provided a new stimulus for Irish art to develop along fresh lines, while the external menace eventually resulted in greater internal unity.

At the time of the first raids, the Ui Neill (p. 151) were still in control over the north of Ireland, with the ritual centre at Tara, while the south was ruled over from the Rock of Cashel in Tipperary; although probably almost abandoned, the site of Tara still gave its name to the High King of Ireland. The country was still divided into smaller units – Connaught, Munster and Meath were the four largest, Ulster being divided into Ailech, Ulaidh and Oriel.

The first raids were conducted by the Norse, probably from the Hebrides.[47] The first recorded attack was in 795, when the church on Rathlin was burned. Initial attacks were on islands and headlands, and were widespread. By the ninth century the attacks had increased, and attention was concentrated on the west, Norse fleets being stationed on Lough Neagh and Lough Ree. The early campaigns were characterized by the war of the Gaedhill and the Gaill. Of the latter, two elements were distinguished, the 'black foreigners', who appear to have been mainly Danes, and the 'fair foreigners', or Norse.

During the ninth and tenth centuries there were increased attacks and settlement in eastern Ireland, and a number of towns were founded in this period, notably Dublin (which is first mentioned as a Norse town in 841), Wicklow, Waterford, Wexford and Cork. These towns formed the centres of petty Norse kingdoms, and on them Norse activity was based. In due course the east was further affected by Danes, who raided down the east coast and opened up hostilities against the already settled Norse, winning a considerable advantage. The east coastal belt became the main arena of Norse-Danish campaigns, and the native Irish tended to align themselves according to inclination. Dublin was regained for the Norse by Olaf the White in 870, who made it his base for subsequent raids along the Irish Sea province. The later years of the ninth century mark a revival of Danish activities in eastern Ireland. By now established in the Danelaw, the Danes harried the Norse areas. Olaf was, however, an astute commander, whose very mobility gave him additional strength. He is recorded in the annals as raiding Fortrenn and Dumbarton, and it is to this period that much of the Norse activity in Lancashire and in the north of England can be ascribed.

919 marks the recapture of Dublin by the Norse, and in the following period Dublin became joined to the Danish kingdom of York, thus strengthening its position, while Limerick built up its position in Munster. The position of Limerick, however, did not remain unchallenged for long, for north Munster rose against the Norse of Limerick under the leadership of Cenetig and later his son Brian Boru, and became allied to the Irish of Connaught. The rise to power of the Dal Cais, the people of west Munster, was rapid. Brian overthrew the long-established Eóganacht dynasty at Cashel in the year 963 with the help of his brother Mahoun, who had claims of his own to the kingship, and the two brothers continued a policy of aggression towards the Scandinavians of Limerick. Eventually the Norse took up arms against them, only to be defeated at the battle of Sulchoid in 967, when Brian and Mahoun sacked Limerick. Following the murder of Mahoun some years later, Brian became king of Munster, and for the next thirty years built up his position until in 1002 he attained the High Kingship and received the submission of the king of the Ui Neill.

The career of Brian Boru culminated in 1014 in the battle of Clontarf, fought in the suburbs of Dublin.[48] Brian was killed, but the battle effectively marked the end of Scandinavian power in Ireland. A clue to the real importance of this battle can be found in the presence on the battlefield of Earl Sigurd the Stout of Orkney, who would not have gone to Ireland to take part in a battle which had only local significance. Earl Sigurd hoped to annex Ireland and possibly thereafter to gain a foothold on the western mainland of Britain. He died in the battle, his hope unrealized.

Clontarf did not, however, mark the start of a new age of peace in Ireland or the disappearance of Scandinavian influence. Already before the battle there had been considerable intermarriage between Scandinavians and Irish (Brian had married Sihtric of Dublin's mother), and many had been converted to Christianity. In the years following Clontarf, Irish history was once more characterized by petty internal squabbles, mainly over the High Kingship. There was considerable Hiberno-Norse fusion of culture, and probably material culture should be regarded as Hiberno-Norse rather than specifically Irish or Scandinavian – Norse weapons appear on Irish sites, Irish ringed pins and other objects on Norse. In general, however, the Norse concentrated on building up their towns and trade, and remained in occupation until finally ousted by the English in the twelfth century. For the rest of Ireland, the internal dissents had little effect on the cultural progress, and the eleventh and twelfth centuries were a period of general cultural regeneration.

Viking Dublin[49]

In spite of the extensive impact of the Vikings on Ireland, the archaeological evidence is fairly limited. Of the five main Viking cities, Dublin, Limerick, Cork, Waterford and Wexford, only Dublin has produced any substantial evidence of Viking occupation. The majority of Viking grave-finds come from the Dublin cemetery of Kilmainham-Islandbridge, and the remainder consists of a series of stray finds and a considerable number of Viking period hoards.

Recent excavations in Dublin have, however, provided much valuable information about the city. The Viking town seems to have grown up round the confluence of the now subterranean Poddle and the Liffey, where there was a small natural harbour. The area round the meeting of Liffey and Poddle was extremely marshy, hence the name Dublin (*dubh linn*, 'the black pool'). Above the harbour a hill of boulder clay moraines drained easily, and provided a suitable site for settlement, though flooding posed problems and very probably the ground level had to be made up with wattles as in crannogs. Nearby there was a ford which enabled travellers to cross the Liffey on their way to Tara and Armagh, and thus the town acquired its Irish name of Ath Cliath – 'the ford of the hurdles'. There can be no doubt that the Irish settlement of Ath Cliath existed before the Viking raids, for in 836 the annals state that 'Ath Cliath was taken for the first time' and in 840 refer to 'foreigners' building a fort at Dubhlinn. This Viking settlement probably occupied much the same area as the subsequent medieval city, and was in all probability walled.

Excavations carried out on various sites in the city have shown that the town grew up like an Eastern 'tell' above the boulder clay, which being impermeable meant that the levels rapidly became waterlogged. This has provided ideal conditions for excavators, and a clear picture of the timber structures of Viking and early medieval Dublin has been obtained. The evidence shows that from at least the late tenth century the norm in Dublin was wattle construction, with wattle mats on the floors and clay, stone-lined hearths. The wattle sheeting seems to have been re-used frequently, and complete house plans are not readily recoverable due to frequent rebuilding. An interesting technique of construction involved double wattle walls with a space for insulation between. The excavations of 1962–3 at the corner of High Street and Nicholas Street have provided perhaps the best evidence of the Viking period, producing not only information about house types but evidence of industrial activity, such as comb-making, leather working and metal working. Among the small finds was a tenth-century brooch decorated in Borre Style, unique in Ireland, for which the closest parallel must be sought at Birka in Sweden. Other finds included soapstone moulds for casting silver ingots, a bronze needle case, lead weights, bone combs, a wide variety of bronze pins, barrel padlocks and keys, and a Scandinavian spearhead. The 1967 excavations at High Street were mainly of importance for the later levels of the twelfth and thirteenth century, but among the earlier finds were bone trial pieces with both Urnes and Ringerike ornamentation which are of particular value in assessing the Irish-Viking artistic developments of the eleventh and twelfth centuries. In Winetavern Street in 1969 a drawing of a ship similar to that from Jarlshof was found incised on a plank. It is datable to the eleventh century by an associated trial piece in Ringerike Style, and coin evidence. Other finds of the Viking period include wooden vessels, textile fragments, imported pottery, and an Anglo-Saxon pewter brooch of the tenth to eleventh century.

The excavations at the time of writing are still in progress, but so far they have provided a unique picture of the development of the town from its Viking origins through into the medieval city, and have shown clearly that it was an important trading centre with wide contacts in the early Middle Ages. By providing stratigraphical associations, the excavations have also established a detailed chronology for a number of small objects, hitherto ubiquitous but difficult to date precisely, such as certain categories of bronze pin.

The Dublin excavations are mainly of use for constructing a picture of life in the town in the tenth to twelfth centuries. For the earlier period, evidence is afforded by the cemetery at Kilmainham-Islandbridge.[50] Viking Dublin, an elongated city some 600 yards long with crowded streets of timber houses, is separated from the great Viking cemetery a mile upstream at Kilmainham. Here Viking burials were first investigated but badly recorded in the nineteenth century, but further burials came to light around 1933 and three were carefully excavated. A study of the grave-finds, particularly the tortoise brooches and the swords, shows that the cemetery was first in use around 850 – the earliest find is a brooch of the early ninth century which was presumably old when it was buried. The swords include some of the earliest in the Viking series, a number of Frankish weapons and one magnificent example made without doubt in Norway. The finest of the Frankish swords has a silver-inlaid pommel and the name of the maker on the hilt – Hartolfr – and can be compared with another similar example from the site of the crannog of Ballinderry 1. The name Ulfbehrt appears on the sword blade, also on a sword from Kilmainham, on swords from Norway and from the Carolingian world. The majority of burials were inhumations. Cremation in the Viking world was relatively rare.

Apart from weapons the other finds from Kilmainham are generally typical of Viking burials, and include knives, hammers, forge tongs, sickles, spindle whorls, linen smoothers and bronze beam balances. As might be expected quite a number of the objects are of Irish origin, including penannular brooches. One notable object was a gilt-bronze animal which crowned a ship's weather vane.

Apart from Kilmainham, there are very few documented Viking burials in Ireland, and all appear to belong to the early period of the Viking incursions. Outside the Dublin area there are two male graves documented, that from Eyreport, Co. Galway, and another found near Larne, Co. Antrim, about 1840.[51] The Larne burial, with a tenth-century sword, ringed pin and comb as well as a spearhead, came from a grave without distinguishing features, and it appears that the Eyreport burial was similar. Two women's graves are recorded from Ballyholme, Co. Down, and Three-Mile-Water, Co. Wicklow, of the early ninth and early tenth centuries respectively. Apart from a burial under a mound at Donnybrook, Dublin, the only other authenticated burial is that from Navan, where in 1845 two human skeletons, a horse skull, a bronze bridle bit and harness plate, seven gilt-bronze mounts and a series of bronze-plated iron rings were found. The main feature of this burial is that all the finds are Irish in origin, but the presence of the horse skull shows that it is Viking, and an identical series of mounts have been found in an early ninth-century grave at Gausel, Norway, to which date the Navan burial should be assigned.

At the end of the tenth century the Vikings of Dublin began to strike coins on the Anglo-Saxon model and up to that time hoards from Ireland are composed almost entirely of English coins (Fig. 68).[52] That the Dublin mint was in operation by *c.* 995 is shown by the Clondalkin hoard concealed around that year which consisted entirely of Hiberno-Danish copies of coins of Æthelred II, some being fairly faithful imitations while others bear the name of Sihtric III (Silkbeard), a son of Onlaf Quaran who struck coins in the Viking kingdom of York. Some of the coins bear the mint signature of Dublin.

In 997 the English penny types were changed, and a few months later the Hiberno-Norse types emulated them. The ensuing series of coins, also modelled on those of Æthelred II, are of fine style and some even imitate the mint signatures of Lincoln and Winchester. The names of both Æthelred and Sihtric appear on them, while there is a further series mentioning neither but a legend which begins 'Thymn'. For the years following *c.* 1000 the Hiberno-Norse coinage falls into two separate series. First there are imitations of contemporary Anglo-Saxon coins, ending with some copies of coins of Cnut, struck four or five years after the battle of Clontarf. The second series consists of Dublin copies of its own coins, stuck on extremely thin flans. On these coins the name of Sihtric became increasingly blundered. In the 1030s there was a further weight reduction, and some rare coins seem to be imitations of English coins of Harthacnut. With the accession of Edward the Confessor in England a wide variety of portrait types appeared in England, including, towards the end of his reign, a facing portrait type which seems again to have been imitated almost immediately in Dublin, where the coins were by this time of very poor standard.

In the later eleventh century the standard of workmanship was much improved, and there were both copies of the 'Long Cross' coins of Æthelred II, current seventy years previously in England, and some of the types of William I. By the mid-eleventh century, melted down English coins had formed the main source for the metal of the Hiberno-Norse coinage, but this supply seems to have suddenly ceased at the end of the century, depriving Dublin both of her source of metal and of models to copy. The Dubliners again reverted to

Figure 68 Hiberno-Norse coins, Dublin Mint

Æthelred II's Long Cross coins for inspiration, and the standard further declined.

The last stage in the history of the Dublin coinage is reached with the striking of semi-bracteates and bracteates. These coins were struck on wafer-thin metal, and therefore could only have a type on one side, the reverse having the obverse type in incuse. Such coins were a widespread phenomenon in medieval Europe, but were unknown in Britain. The semi-bracteates are the last of the Dublin Norse coins, but a further series of true bracteates (the semi-bracteates were struck by a pair of dies with identical, fitting types, the bracteates with an obverse die only) may have been struck by an Irish king, Toirrdhealbhach O Conchubjair who ruled Connaught between 1106 and 1156 and who traditionally had a mint at Clonmacnois. Whether this attribution is correct or not, no coinage was being struck in Ireland at the time of the Norman invasion, and there is a time gap of about fifty years before the Anglo-Irish began striking a series of rather poor coins under John as Lord of Ireland and John de Courcy.

Viking period hoards in Ireland (Fig. 69)[53]

There are over fifty hoards of the Viking period known from Ireland, and a study of them and their distribution sheds some light on the Viking period as a whole. Half the recorded coin hoards are from five of the thirty-two modern counties, and all five are contiguous and form the eastern half of the old province of Leinster. Leinster has produced two-thirds of the known hoards, Munster and Ulster each providing five hoards and Connaught none. If the distribution by provinces is followed by dividing the hoards into those buried

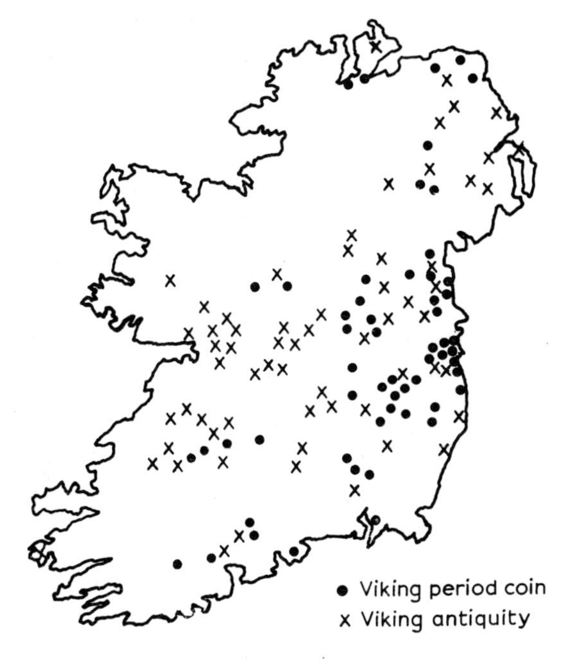

Figure 69 Viking period finds in Ireland (After Dolley)

prior to the setting up of the Dublin mint around 995 and those buried afterwards, the proportion is not significantly different. Three out of seven of all the hoards have been found within ten miles of the sea, and only in Leinster is there a greater proportion of inland hoards than coastal ones. This distribution pattern is in marked contrast to that of stray Viking antiquities, which are scattered all over Ireland. The conclusions that may be drawn from this are obvious. The occurrence of hoards is virtually confined to the main areas of Viking settlement, and therefore it is highly unlikely that the coinage was used by the native Irish but was exclusively Norse. Secondly, the concentration round Dublin shows that the Viking hold over the area was far stronger than over their other towns. Of the seventeen hoards buried after about 1020, only five are from north of Dublin, and two of these are coastal.

9 Celtic survival

The Age of the Vikings, and the hybrid Celto-Scandinavian culture that it produced in Ireland, Scotland and Man, effectively marks the last flourish of late Celtic Britain. Only in Atlantic Scotland, the territory of the Lordship of the Isles, is it possible to trace a Celtic kingdom continuing into the Middle Ages, though even this area was not unaffected by the development of feudal Europe. The greatest single factor in the decline of Celtic culture was the Anglo-Norman advance, which brought the Celtic-speaking areas culturally into line with developments in western Europe.

Medieval Scotland

Nowhere is this more clearly seen than in Scotland. The start of the process of the Anglicization of Scotland can be traced to the foundation of the House of Canmore by Malcolm III.[1] Although first married to the widow of Thorfinn the Mighty of Orkney, somewhere between 1068 and 1070 Malcolm married a Saxon princess, Margaret, who had fled to Scotland after the Norman Conquest with her sister and brother. By Margaret Malcolm had six sons, and under her influence there was a marked increase of English influence in Scotland, the court becoming a refuge for those in opposition to William of England. Under Malcolm's regime a phase of church building in the English manner can be traced. The Benedictine house at Dunfermline, Fife, the foundations of which remain beneath the nave of the Romanesque abbey, was founded by Margaret.

The pro-English policy of the House of Canmore developed into pro-Norman in the reign of Malcolm's youngest son, David I, who succeeded to the throne of Scotland in 1124.[2] He had grown up in the court in England, and his wife was the widow of Simon de Senlis; through her he held the earldom of Northampton and the honour of Huntingdon. The reign of David I marks the beginning of feudal Scotland. David brought many Normans to Scotland, and gave them most of the important offices in the Church and state, as well as extensive territorial holdings. The Scottish aristocracy became French-speaking, and Anglo-Norman feudalism became established as the basis of government. Coinage as a regular means of trade was introduced, copying English models, in 1136,[3] and it was during the reign of David I and to some extent his successor, William the Lion, that many of the important royal burghs were founded by charter; before this time there is little evidence for the existence of towns in Scotland. The twelfth century also marks the beginning of a medieval pottery sequence in Scotland: domestic vessels became fairly widespread at least in the Lowlands.[4] The incentive came from the pottery industry of northern England, particularly Yorkshire, from which the earliest products were directly derived. The extension of trade, particularly with the Continent, that followed the early development of the burghs brought luxury goods to Scotland. The archaeological evidence has not yet been fully studied, but French polychrome and green glazed pottery as well as red painted wares were imported from the twelfth century onwards, while some cooking pots came over from the Rhineland and France. The weight of the trade was first taken by the east coast ports until an extension of the trade operated from France through the Irish Sea brought continental merchandise to south-west Scotland and, probably on a more limited scale, to the Lordship of the Isles.

Scottish architecture, too, developed in the twelfth century. Although there are some possible earlier examples, such as Castle Sween, Argyll, stone castle building in Scotland began around this date.[5] Regular monasticism also flourished as a result of David I's patronage, and his reign is marked by the foundation of a number of major monasteries in Scotland.[6] The process begun by Queen Margaret was continued by her son, Alexander I, who favoured the Augustinian canons regular and introduced them to Scone in about 1120, soon after their arrival in England from France. David I favoured the Tironesians, but was also instrumental in the foundation of Augustinian houses. Some Scottish houses, such as Jedburgh, Selkirk and Kilwinning, appear to have been direct foundations from France. The building of the Scottish monasteries firmly established Romanesque architecture in Scotland, but it was not confined to monastic establishments, and fine examples of the style can be seen in small parish churches such as Dalmeny in Midlothian or Leuchars in Fife.

The spread of Anglo-Norman ideas is most readily represented by the spread of the motte – earthen mounds crowned by and sometimes incorporating a timber tower. These were the strongholds of the Anglo-Normans in Scotland, and they extend as far north as the Beauly Firth. None of the

Scottish mottes appear to predate the twelfth century, but they remained in use even into the fourteenth, when stone castellated architecture had become normal.

The changeover to Norman feudalism was probably a gradual process, however, and there would have been a certain degree of compromise. The essence of the new system was the tenure of land, which seems to have existed side by side with the old 'clan' system, which depended on social grouping based on family and kindred, by acceptance of the chief and admission to a clan. The twelfth and thirteenth centuries witnessed a few Celtic uprisings.[7] Between 1181 and 1187 Donald MacWilliam, grandson of Duncan II, contested William the Lion's throne, being eventually overthrown near Inverness in 1187, while there were further uprisings in 1212–13 led by his son and again in 1230. These, however, were aimed less against the introduction of Norman feudalism than against the right of the later Canmores to hold the throne, and in this connection it is significant that Ferchar Maccintsacairt, a Celtic noble, took up the Canmore cause against Donald Bane, and for his efforts was made a Norman knight.

Politically the end of Celtic rule in Scotland came with the death of Alexander III, the last of the Canmore line, who died by falling off a cliff at Kinghorn, Fife, in 1286, leaving Scotland open to the invasion of Edward I and the events surrounding the competition for the Scottish crown.

Although there were some obvious differences between the feudal Scottish nobility and its English counterpart, there was no essential difference in the material culture available in a Scottish or an English castle between the thirteenth and sixteenth centuries. The concept that the Scottish nobility was impoverished and culturally inferior to the English is not borne out by the archaeological evidence, where it survives. The range of equipment from the moat of Caerlaverock Castle, Dumfries, for example, or Castle Urquhart, Inverness,[8] is closely comparable with that from contemporary English castles, while the surviving inventories show that the range of material which has left no trace in archaeology was equally varied. The picture of the poor Scottish laird is perhaps largely the outcome of the writings of such prejudiced early travellers in Scotland as Aeneas Sylvius, and has little basis on fact, though it is true that the mercantile class was probably less prosperous and Scottish towns compared unfavourably with their English counterparts.

Continuity is naturally apparent on a peasant level. The peasant culture in Scotland south of the Forth was an extension of that in northern England, with the nucleated village widespread. Many of these villages had parochial status as early as the twelfth or thirteenth century, and were often linked with outlying settlements, the group forming a 'shire'. Unity was to be found in the shire centre and the lord, usually the king, bishop, abbot or great layman.[9] Cultivated land extended in a large area round the village, and separate holdings consisted of several rigs scattered round the cultivated land. In addition to this arable land, the adjacent meadow and the common pasture, areas of hill grazing were exploited in the summer from sheilings. Such a pattern was probably due to English influence in the twelfth century, and was a system of farming quite alien to Celtic Scotland. Later in the Middle Ages the infield-outfield system developed and thenceforth the 'fermtoun' (farm township), 'kirtoun' (farm township with parish church) and 'milntoun' (mill township) are recognizable.[10] This pattern survived until the eighteenth-century 'Improvements'. Deserted villages on the English pattern are fairly widespread south of the Forth in the Middle Ages – there are many in Dumfriesshire and Galloway, Berwickshire, Roxburgh and Selkirk, and a few in the Lothians, Ayrshire and Peeblesshire.[11] There has been little study of the medieval villages of Scotland by archaeological techniques, but present evidence indicates that they were similar to the English, with stone 'longhouses' or smaller buildings on one or both sides of a road or street, usually raised in Scotland in contrast to the more common 'sunk way' of English villages. The pattern is, however, essentially English, and is the result of a tradition that must have spread during the twelfth century.

There is some evidence for Early Christian settlement types surviving into the Middle Ages and beyond. In the Lowlands there are hints that scooped settlements of Iron Age type continued into the medieval period – in 1939 Stevenson excavated such a settlement at Manor, Peeblesshire, which consisted of a cluster of quasi-circular huts with roofs supported on more than one post, surrounded by an enclosure wall.[12] Other open settlements of round huts were excavated at Muirkirk, Ayrshire, but are inadequately documented; they appear, however, to be medieval.[13] Crannogs certainly continued in use in the Middle Ages, and several of Iron Age date appear to have been reoccupied, for example Hyndford crannog, Lanark,[14] and Lochspouts crannog, Ayrshire.[15] A few appear to have been built in the Middle Ages or later; one at Eadarloch, Loch Treig, seems to have been constructed not earlier than the sixteenth century,[16] while as late as 1608 an act was passed by the Scottish parliament forbidding the building of 'crannaks'.[17] Similarly duns appear to have been occupied, if not actually built, in medieval Scotland, as for example at Dun Lagaidh (Ross and Cromarty), Dun Fhinn (Kintyre, Argyll), and Kildonan (Argyll), the last being a site with Early Christian occupation. A few sites may have been occupied as late as the eighteenth and nineteenth centuries, as suggested by the finds from Ugadale Point, Kintyre.[18]

The continuing occupation of crannogs and duns in western Scotland raises the question of the nature of the territory of the Lordship of the Isles. Ultimately in the period of its greatest power, the fourteenth and fifteenth centuries, the Lordship of the Isles controlled the whole of the west of Scotland north of Kintyre, and much of the east between Inverness and Kincardine.[19] It was a militant state, constantly at war with the Scotto-Norman feudal kingdom based on Stirling, Fife and the Lothians. It maintained a fleet and had strong Ulster connections, and within its bounds traditions died hard–the bow and arrow still seem to have been used as weapons in the seventeenth century. Local traditions of sculpture, stemming ultimately from Iona, were kept alive until the sixteenth century in the rich and long-lived school of west Highland grave-slabs, which by their iconographic riches provide an interesting side-light on life in the medieval Western Isles. The excavations still in progress at Coileagan an Udail (the Udal) in North Uist are providing a picture of the continuing development of Hebridean culture from the Viking period through to the post-medieval, and have shown that the Hebrides have a distinctive pottery sequence extending down to the craggan ware of the nineteenth century. Building 2 was among the structures excavated belonging to the period of the Lordship of the Isles. It was an ovoid house of massive construction with double infilled walls, which shows a typological relationship to the eighteenth-century thatched houses of North Uist, and indeed to the Hebridean 'black house' as a class.[20]

Medieval Wales

In Wales a situation similar to that in Scotland can be observed. The impact of the Norman penetration was not so great as in Scotland, and the political organization of pre-Norman Wales, with its numerous small lords, required fortifications which were similar in purpose if not in appearance to Norman castles. Ringworks are of considerable importance in studying the divide between Celtic and Norman Wales. The ringwork (i.e. a circular earthen bank broken by an entrance) as a type of field monument has an ancestry going back at least to the Roman Iron Age (Walesland Rath is a good example) and continued in Wales to the time of the Norman advance. There is some evidence to suggest that the ringwork at Dinas Powys was the work of Iestyn ap Gwyrgan, the last native prince of Glamorgan before the Norman invasion, while documentary references to the first castle built in Wales, the 'Castle of King Olaf', built in Gwynedd in the early eleventh century, conceivably refer to a ringwork not a motte.[21] Whatever the case for a pre-Norman origin for ringworks in Wales, the evidence from Castle Tower, Penmaen,[22] and the less direct evidence of surface finds of medieval pottery from a number of other ringworks like Caerau, Ely and Gypsies' Tump, indicate that the ringwork was a feature of the Norman advance, as indeed is the scatter of mottes in Wales, concentrated in the Marches but extending even as far into the mountains of north Wales as Tomen y Mur in Merioneth.[23]

The process of English annexation began as early as the time of William I, who established Norman lords at Chester and Shrewsbury to control the March. The Norman settlement of Wales extended along the coast of south Wales to the mouth of the Teifi and along the north Welsh coast to Rhuddlan. On the lowest-lying part of the coastal belt, especially in south Wales, a pattern of villages of English type grew up, many of them named after Norman founders or owners.[24] To some extent these villages represented a continuity of an already established pattern. The coastal settlement was followed by the gradual penetration of the river valleys of central Wales, with the establishment of lordships and the construction of a rash of mottes, such as that recently excavated at Hen Domen, Montgomery.[25] Attendant on the mottes were vills, established partly as policy, partly as a result of economic necessity. In north Wales the Norman advance was slower, though some castles were established even in the mountainous regions, notably at Dolwyddelan in Merioneth, a stark keep which serves as a reminder that Edward I was not the first Englishman to penetrate Snowdonia.

Benedictine houses were rapidly established following the Norman advance. From the 1130s onwards Cistercian monasteries were being built either in Norman territory or at the request of native Welsh chiefs.[26] Coins were struck by the Normans in south Wales (at Pembroke and St Davids, Cardiff and Rhuddlan), as well as Hereford and Shrewsbury in the English March,[27] though it seems unlikely that coinage as a regular means of trade was early accepted by the Welsh.

The ensuing period until the time of Edward I was one of constant feuds and warfare, the period of the Anarchy of Stephen in particular being marked by Welsh uprisings. The culmination of events was the annexation of the north by Edward I and the defeat of the native Welsh king, Llewelyn Fawr, followed by his execution at English hands in 1283.

Town life was not a feature of medieval Wales, though planned towns, most notably at Caernarvon, were adjuncts of some of Edward I's Welsh castles. Medieval Wales, like its Early Christian predecessor, appears to have been largely aceramic.[28] Kilns may have been established in Norman areas of south Wales in the late eleventh or early twelfth century – there is some pottery from Glamorgan which may have been produced locally around this period. Kilns are known at Newport, Pembroke, and Denbigh, the former of late medieval date. Generally there is very little evidence, however, and the majority of pottery found in south Wales was imported from England to supply English needs. In the north the situation is similar, most of the known pottery coming from the Edwardian castles and proving to be imported, mostly from English centres such as Chester but also from France.

In view of the lack of archaeological evidence in Wales for the later part of the Early Christian period it is difficult to assess the extent of native Celtic survival of settlement types or material culture. Certainly, as in Scotland, the homes of the nobility were as well equipped as those in England with the same types of objects. Documentary evidence indicates that in the later pre-Norman period the basis of Welsh settlement patterns was the *tref*, a township or hamlet, and Welsh society was founded on the bond hamlet with the superimposition of princely and free families, with permanent lowland settlements and temporary summer shelters like the Scottish shielings. From the twelfth century onwards this was replaced by the *gwely*, which was an area of cleared land associated with a single steading occupied by one family, and in its development the bond vill was an important factor. Essentially, the pattern was of gradual change.[29]

A discussion in any detail of the character of medieval peasant settlement sites in Wales is out of place here. As far as the evidence will allow, however, it can be said in general terms that the house types of the Middle Ages constitute a break. The excavations of the Foxes at Gellygaer Common led to the postulation that the medieval 'longhouse' was a characteristic of the Highland Zone, and of Celtic origin,[30] but it is now apparent that the longhouse was widespread in medieval Britain, and is likely to have been an introduction to Wales from outside.[31] On a higher social level, the Welsh medieval hall-house shows English influence.

The Isle of Man and south-west England

In the Isle of Man, as in the Northern Isles of Scotland, Norse occupation was long lived. The Norse character was retained by the Northern Isles into the twelfth century and by the Isle of Man into the thirteenth or fourteenth. By this time the settlement pattern in Man on a peasant level appears to have been changing to one of transhumance from winter lowland to summer highland pastures, and medieval shielings, of a type current throughout the Highland Zone, have been excavated by Gelling at Block Eary and Injebreck.[32] There is little 'Celtic' continuity apparent in Man in the later Middle Ages, and the Manx castles attest feudal influence.

The pattern of medieval settlement in Cornwall and Devon shares many of the characteristics of Wales. The Domesday survey for Cornwall is particularly informative, and on the basis of this and fieldwork it is possible to build up a picture of settlement patterns on the eve of the Norman Conquest. There is some evidence for continuity into the later Middle Ages, but to speak of the south-west in the medieval period as 'Celtic' is impossible from available evidence.

Medieval Ireland

The Normans landed in Co. Wexford in 1169, and by 1200 had captured most of the south and east of the country. The first, military phase resulted in the construction of mottes and subsequently, between 1200 and 1220, stone castles, which were put up in the centre of lordships and at strategic river crossings, as well as round the coast.[33] A number of mottes seem to have been sited on pre-existing raths – at Lismahon, Co. Down, a platform rath seems to have had its low central mound successively heightened till it became a motte with a stilted tower, some time after 1177,[34] and there was a similar conversion of the platform rath at Ballyfounder.[35] At Knocknaholet a motte was added to a rath of ringfort type, and stone buildings appear to have been added to pre-Norman raths at Rahinnane castle, Co. Kerry, and possibly Caher Mortle, Co. Limerick.

Between 1170 and 1300 there were successive settlements in Ireland. The area of Anglo-Norman occupation, approximately two-thirds of the country, was divided up on an English manorial basis.[36] The pre-existing Scandinavian towns of Dublin, Cork and Limerick were developed and inland towns and villages were founded, the former with borough status in many cases. Recent excavations at Dublin[37] show that materially the larger Irish towns were abreast with those in Britain, and the list of imports from Dublin suggests a considerable trade. As in Scotland and Wales ecclesiastical foundations were established in Ireland, and there are many fine examples of both Romanesque and Gothic architecture; the Irish Romanesque, however, had a certain character of its own, and in its sculptural adornment at any rate shows some echoes from a Celtic past.[38] From the twelfth century onwards pottery became commonplace in Ulster, sharing features with that from Chester and Scotland, but was less plentiful elsewhere, where Celtic traditions of wood and leather continued. Coinage, introduced by the Vikings, continued from around 1182 with the issues of John de Courcy.[39]

Artistic continuity

This brief review of the evidence suggests very strongly that the twelfth century marks a convenient divide in the Celtic-speaking areas of Britain. The Norman advance effectively brought late Celtic Britain culturally in line with England and Europe, and though it is unlikely that the Anglo-Norman penetration had any profound effect on basic patterns of settlement or peasant economy, feudalization brought about certain social changes. Archaeology, of course, tells nothing about customs, folk traditions and ideas, but they certainly had a much longer survival than the purely material aspects of Celtic culture.

The problem of the continuity of Celtic art is difficult, for in this at least there are hints of a lingering tradition. In Ireland the Norman invasion marks a more obvious break in artistic traditions than the growth of Norman influence in Scotland and Wales. In the words of Françoise Henry, 'In many ways the Norman invasion marks in Ireland the end of a world, and certainly the death of artistic endeavour. For centuries after that, art in Ireland was almost completely dominated by foreign models, and the old fire of invention was nearly always lacking, though the great sense of proportion and the decorative feeling of the old style survived for a long time.'[40] In Wales there had never been an artistic tradition comparable to that of Ireland, the sole products being the sculptured stones: 'The dying flickers of Welsh Christian art were finally extinguished by the Norman Conquest' (Nash-Williams).[41] In Scotland the west Highland grave-slabs carry the story of Celtic art one stage further, and elsewhere in Scotland a few stones show echoes of an older tradition. Interlace, which sometimes adorns medieval English objects, was occasionally used to decorate metalwork into the sixteenth century – the Barr of Spottes flask is possibly a late example of the tradition. But interlace (p. 349) was never a peculiarly Celtic form of decoration, and the few crude medieval examples are poor indications of continuity.[42] The Fife and Eglinton bone caskets, richly decorated with interlace, have been claimed as late medieval on west Highland evidence, but the case is not strong, and probably they should be regarded as of Early Christian date. A few pieces of metalwork, such as the Guthrie Bell Shrine, carry Scottish ornamental metalworking traditions into the Middle Ages, but not the repertoire of decorative techniques.

The Celtic artistic revival in Scotland appears to be a phenomenon of the sixteenth century. Surprisingly, it took place not in the west Highlands but in the north-east. During the sixteenth to eighteenth centuries, a number of objects, particularly powder horns, were decorated with interlace and other designs. It must be emphasized that this 'Celtic revival' was not connected with Early Christian ornamental traditions, and at present the reason behind it is obscure. Once resumed, this new 'Celtic' art continued, aided by late eighteenth-century romanticism, the writings of Scott and Queen Victoria's enthusiasm for Scotland.

The Celtic Twilight

The Celtic revival is an interesting phenomenon in its own right. The starting point perhaps may be seen in Macpherson's Ossianic poetry and the eighteenth-century Romantics; it came to a head with the 'Celtic Twilight' school of writing in the late nineteenth century, headed by W. B. Yeats. In this century the concept of Celtic nationalism has become confused with political causes, particularly in Ireland.

No serious claim, then, can be made that Celtic Britain outlived the twelfth century. Even in the field of literature, it is scarcely possible to trace continuity. Late Welsh poetry of the Middle Ages may be Welsh in language and in keeping with bardic tradition in its formality, but its fire is spent, and the insidious influence of courtly verse dogs the lines of Dafydd ap Gwilym, while seers like Duncan ban MacIntyre were conscious imitators of a lost art.

In the light of this, the achievement of late Celtic Britain is difficult to assess. In an obvious analysis it lies in its artistic legacy, ranking with Anglo-Saxon art of the Winchester school, the line drawings of Mathew Paris and the work of Constable and Turner as one of the great contributions of the British Isles to the history of art.

From an archaeologist's viewpoint, late Celtic Britain has another importance. Its study brings the last of the great prehistoric cultures of Europe into the dim light of proto-history, and provides a unique glimpse, under the thin disguise of a Christian society, of Europe's undocumented past. The continuity between the culture of the Iron Age Celts and those of the post-Roman period should not be pressed too far. But if the surface appearances were changed, something of the underlying structure remained, and it is this which makes the Early Christian Celts of greater importance to any student of the formation of Europe than their geographical distribution and material achievements might suggest. It is a society with a fundamental structure possibly as early as the spread of Indo-European languages. If the legends surrounding one of the Early Christian Britons deserve the title of the *Matter of Britain*, the history and archaeology of the Early Christian Celts embodies something of the Matter of Europe.

Part 2 The material culture of the Early Christian Celts

10 Technology and trade

Although the Early Christian Celtic peoples were farmers, living a settled life in isolated farmsteads, one element at least in the population was mobile. This element comprised the craftsmen. In the Early Christian period, as in Ireland even in the early twentieth century, crafts such as iron working were carried out by travelling smiths who would have moved from community to community, setting up a forge and repairing old tools as well as making new ones to meet the requirements ofthe residents. In the larger and more prosperous farmsteads the skills and equipment for most everyday crafts were probably available, but it seems unlikely that within every rath there was a skilled blacksmith acquainted with the techniques of smelting or bronze working. On a higher level, ornamental metal working must have been the province of just such itinerant craftsmen, and the lead die for an Irish type of brooch found at Dinas Powys in south Wales shows just how widely such men of art travelled. Monasteries and the homes of the rich, such as the royal crannog at Lagore, would have had their own artisans, but objects such as penannular brooches were used by all sectors of the community except perhaps the poorest, and their production would have been in the hands of itinerant bronze smiths. This fact alone explains the remarkable homogeneity of material culture within the Irish Sea province, and the rapid transmission of new styles and ideas. Regionalism is mainly apparent in the rich objects of the seventh century and later, which were made in monastic workshops. Although little information is available for the earlier centuries of the Early Christian period, evidence shows that in Ireland, from the Viking period onwards, most of the ecclesiastical metalwork was produced by lay craftsmen attached to monasteries, who kept the tradition alive by passing on their skills to their sons, so that their jobs became hereditary.[1]

There is no evidence for the mass production of any merchandise in the Early Christian west, though it had been commonplace in the Roman Empire, and some late Iron Age oppida seem to have produced certain articles in considerable numbers. The La Tène Celts, however, finally possessed both a money economy and a system of markets, developed in Gaul as an extension of the system operating in the Greek colonies in the south; the oppida themselves provided potential markets, and the evidence points to trade being conducted over large areas.[2] In the Early Christian period the situation was different; the two elements essential for extensive trade, markets where the merchandise could be passed on to a sufficiently large number of people, and a money economy to standardize trade procedures, were both lacking. Towns did not exist in the Celtic west until their establishment in Ireland by the Vikings; nor for that matter were there villages or nucleated settlements on the scale of oppida. In this connection it is worth remembering that even in thirteenth-century England the products of pottery kilns do not normally appear to have travelled far from their centre of production[3] – most appear to have been traded within a ten-mile radius of the kilns – while in Anglo-Saxon England a comparable situation can be seen reflected in the products of the Illington-Lackford potter, who seems to be typical of his contemporaries.[4] The distribution of his pots appears to be within a radius of about eight miles – a comfortable day's walk to market and back.

There is surprisingly little evidence for organized overseas trade even in luxury goods or raw materials. All the evidence points to the Celtic craftsman obtaining his raw materials locally as the need arose; in the case of precious metals he seems frequently to have re-used old silver and gold, and probably also scrap bronze and lead. A recent analysis of Pictish silver has shown it to be composed mainly of re-used Roman metal,[5] and some of the scrap bronze at Dinas Powys was probably from Anglo-Saxon buckets.[6] Similarly the fragments of glass vessels from Celtic sites are mostly to be explained as imported raw material for native production of glass beads and inlays. Few if any glass vessels probably actually adorned Celtic tables.

Iron working

Virtually all the sites of the Early Christian period in the Celtic areas of Britain have produced evidence for metal working, particularly iron working, and it may be assumed that the blacksmith's skills were widely known in the population. The same type of furnace was probably used for iron working and bronze working, and the techniques of the bronze smith employed to some extent the same equipment. Furnaces could be simple pits or more elaborate structures with bellows. Steel appears to have been produced only accidentally in the Early Christian era, as there was no way of controlling the carbon content. Low carbon content probably accounts for the worn state of a number of utensils.[7]

The clearest evidence for iron working in the period comes from a ringfort at Garryduff, Co. Cork.[8] Here, as well as shallow hollows used for iron working, a furnace was excavated, consisting of a circular bowl-like structure of clay and small stones, about 4 feet in diameter. When complete it is unlikely to have been more than about 12 inches high. The bottom consisted of a 3-inch layer of clay and the walls were about a foot thick. Some nearby clay was probably used to fasten the tuyère in position.

A number of tuyères, which were used to direct the draught from the bellows into the furnace, were found. When complete, a tuyère measured about 16 inches long and up to 12 inches in diameter, and was cylindrical externally, funnel-shaped internally. The opening as it entered the furnace was only about an inch in diameter, but where the nozzle of the bellows was inserted it was about 8 inches across. Two bellows with wooden nozzles were used, both of which were inserted into the wide end of the tuyère and worked alternately. A heat of 1100° or 1200° C. was required to reduce the ore, which at Garryduff was of poor quality and found locally. Charcoal was mixed with the ore in the furnace. The heat of the smelting caused one end of the tuyère to fuse into pottery, coated with slag, while the other end remained unbaked clay and after the smelt tended to crumble away, so that complete tuyères are very rarely found. So-called 'furnace bottoms' are found in sites where metal working has taken place. These are lumps of slag which take the shape of the bottom of the furnace and are due either to slag collecting higher up in the furnace during the smelt and subsequently sinking, or to a failed smelt, when the whole mass sinks to the bottom. The roughly worked iron was lifted from the furnace by tongs, which are frequent finds on sites of the period, and then hammered into shape with frequent reheating with iron hammers on anvils.

Copper and bronze working

Copper- and bronze-working remains are less frequently found than those of iron smelting, but even so are fairly abundant. A series of sixteen crucibles were examined in the 1920s, and in almost all cases the main trace elements were of copper, with iron second, and tin, lead and other metals thereafter.[9] Examination also showed slag from copper pyrites adhering to the sides of the crucibles, which suggests that they may have been heated in copper-smelting hearths. One crucible from a' Cheardach Mhor in the Hebrides had bronze on its lip, some from Carraig Aille (Co. Cork) had copper and bronze, crucibles from Buston Crannog (Ayrshire), Cadbury Congresbury (Somerset), Garranes (Co. Cork), Clea Lakes Crannog (Co. Antrim), Lagore (Co. Westmeath) and

Glastonbury Tor (Somerset), contained bronze, while one from Lough Faughan had both copper and tin. Precious metals do not seem to have been melted in crucibles, except at Buston and possibly Cadbury Congresbury where scraps of gold were associated with them.

Scrap bronze from Cadbury Congresbury was probably for re-use. From Clea Lakes Crannog comes a sheet of bronze folded up ready for melting down, and similar bronzes come from the Mote of Mark, Kirkcudbright.

Moulds

Ingot moulds are not uncommon, for either straight or curved bars. They occur at Dunadd, Garranes, Kiondroghad and the Mote of Mark. They are usually of stone, with depressions for more than one ingot. At the Mote of Mark two ingots were among the finds. At Lagore, in addition to ingot moulds the excavators found a cake of bronze from a melting pot. Moulds for making small objects are even more common on Early Christian sites. These are normally of clay (though stone moulds also occur) and, to judge by the evidence afforded by the lead model from Dinas Powys for a penannular brooch and the bone pins found with moulds at the Mote of Mark and Birsay, Orkney,[10] the customary procedure was to use a model of lead or some other material, possibly wood, and make the mould round it. At Dunadd, a bone pin was found in the clay mould for which it was the model. From Corraneary came both parts of a bivalve mould for a ring of plano-convex shape, with a funnel cut for the metal to be poured in. The same feature occurs on other moulds indicating that simple objects were cast in such bivalve moulds as well as one-piece moulds. Dunadd produced a mould for a penannular brooch some $\frac{3}{4}$ inch in diameter, along with fragments of a hundred moulds for pins, brooches and rings, one with ornamentation. Garranes produced about thirty moulds for rings, razors, strips, bars, discs and studs. Lagore yielded a mould for a ringed pin, as well as for a large ring, and a bone mould stamp. Lough Faughan has provided a mould for a thistle-headed pin. Moulds from the Mote of Mark include some for penannular brooches, pins and bronze 'combs' (probably rivets) – in one case the 'comb' is preserved in its original matrix – as well as elaborately decorated mounts. Moulds were also found at Kildonan Bay, Argyll, and at Ballinderry 2.

Trial pieces (Figs 70–1)

'Trial' pieces of stone or bone occur on Early Christian period sites. These are usually regarded quite reasonably as artists' sketches, attempts at working out the design before setting it down on the mould or working on the face of the metal. Some may have been simply 'doodles', and a few of these might have been apprentice's work, as they are often technically incompetent. Some

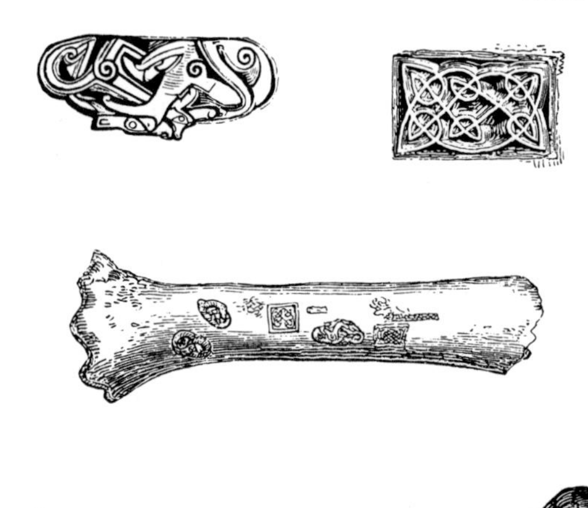

Figure 70 Bone trial pieces, Lagore, Co. Meath

of the bone trial pieces, for example from Lagore, may have had a more immediate use as dies in making the moulds themselves, which would account for the great intricacy and care shown in their execution. Some of the earliest come from Garryduff, and belong to the seventh or eighth century, while there are others from Lissue (Co. Antrim), Dungarvan (Waterford), Killaloe (Clare) and Nendrum (Co. Down).[11] The Nendrum series comes from the ruins of the 'school' and presumably constitutes exercises, which include letters as well as animals and ornaments. One stone trial piece from Dunadd is for a penannular brooch, while another, dating from the last days of the occupation, is purely a decorative scheme. Bone trial pieces are particularly common in the Viking period, and occur outside the Celtic west, for example at York.[12]

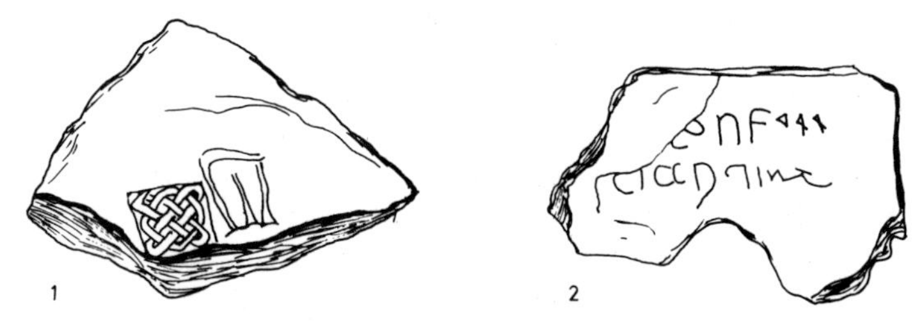

Figure 71 'Trial pieces', Kingarth, Bute. Scale: $\frac{1}{4}$. (1) Piece of slate with incised ornament; (2) Piece of slate with incised letters and scrolls.

Crucibles (Figs 72–3)

Until recently crucibles have been inadequately studied. It was usually thought that the standard crucible of later prehistoric Britain was hemispherical and heated from above, but it seems that this type, which continued into the Early Christian period, is no more common than the triangular. The triangular-shaped crucibles seem to have been heated from above, at least in some examples, such as those from Maiden Castle, Dorset,[13] or Meare, Somerset,[14] and once introduced were to continue. By the Early Christian period a wide variety of new crucible types were in use. Hemispherical crucibles were heated from below, in spite of their thick bases; the other

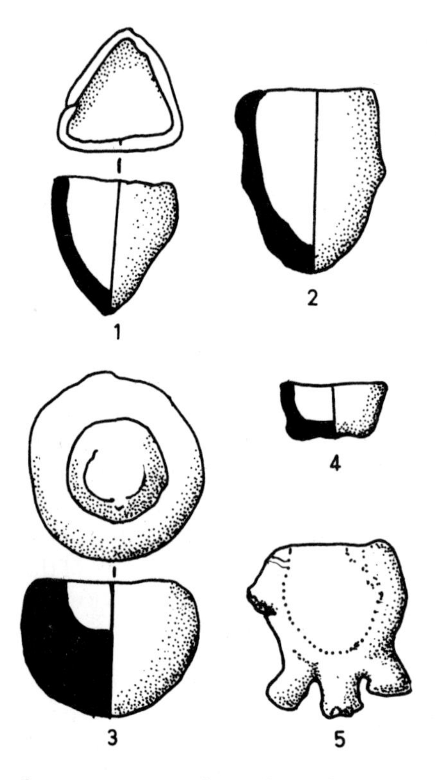

Figure 72 Crucibles, numbered as text. Type (1) Ballinderry 2; (2) Lagore; (3) Garranes; (4) Lagore; (5) Lagore. Scales: (1) $\frac{3}{8}$; (2), (4), (5) $\frac{3}{4}$; (3) $\frac{1}{4}$

forms appear to have been heated from above.[15] They were normally lifted from the fire with tongs, and iron tongs used presumably for this purpose are known from Garranes and Garryduff, and were also used in the Roman period, for example, at Traprain Law, West Lothian.[16] Handles to facilitate lifting were already being added to crucibles in the Iron Age – as in the Meare and Glastonbury examples – and were common in the Early Christian period in a variety of forms.

The lidded crucible seems to have appeared during the Roman period. Lids helped to reduce oxidization in the molten metal, to retain the heat while the metal was being poured, and to prevent ash from contaminating the crucible's contents.[17] There are two putative examples of crucible lids from Roman Britain – one from Llantwit Major and another from Bishopton[18] – but not until the Early Christian period did lidded crucibles become common. They occur at Dunadd, Dinas Powys, Garryduff and less certainly Buston and Iona. Lids appear to have been added to whichever shape of crucible was in use, although at Garryduff the triangular crucibles were adapted slightly to take lids. At Dinas Powys the distinctive pear-shaped crucible with lid has been seen as a form related to the pear-shaped Roman crucibles from Holt, Cheshire.

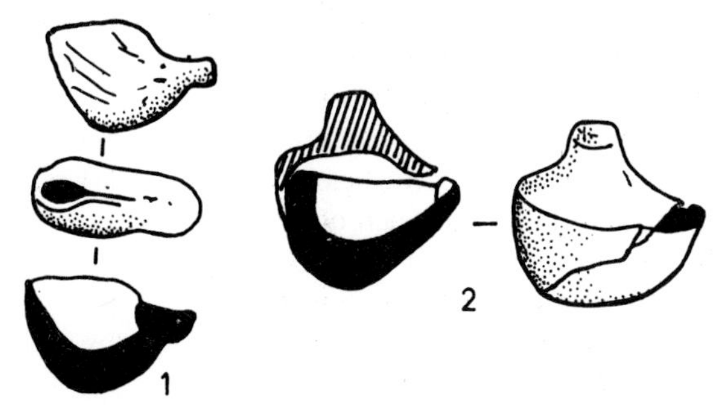

Figure 73 Crucibles. (1) Type 8, Ballinderry 2; (2) Type 9, Dinas Powys. Scale: $\frac{3}{8}$

However, the type is probably just the natural outcome of providing a pouring lip on a more regular form of vessel. The form has a possible predecessor among the Bronze Age crucibles of Dalkey Island, for which, on inadequate evidence, a lid has been claimed.

Crucibles were made of local clay. They sometimes had linings which have been interpreted as serving to prevent contamination from the material previously melted, as in the Bronze Age examples from Dalkey Island, where there were up to three layers of wash. This feature occurs on both lidded and unlidded crucibles. The lining of unlidded crucibles at Dinas Powys and Iona was probably to provide a springing for the lid. Many crucibles show signs of having a partially vitrified 'pumice'-like fabric and heat-crazed exteriors.

The crucibles in use in the Early Christian period can be divided into ten basic types. All except the triangular-mouthed crucibles are rarely found.

(1) *Triangular-mouthed crucible.* This type may be divided into the following classes: 1A, those tapering to a circular horizontal cross-section, with rounded or pointed base; 1B, general type as 1A but with fixed lids; 1C, as 1A but shallower and with a flat base. Types 1B and 1C occur only at Garryduff. These crucibles were current throughout the Early Christian period, though 1B and 1C may have a more restricted chronology which can only be proved by further finds. The type is Iron Age in origin.

(2) *Bag- or cup-shaped crucible.* These have round mouths and profiles similar to 1A, tapering to a pointed or rounded base. The type is Iron Age in origin (an Iron Age example occurs at Long Wittenham, Berks.) and extends throughout the Early Christian period.
(3) *Hemispherical crucible.* The basic type, 3A, is circular at the mouth with a rounded base, and bulges out from the mouth, reaching the greatest diameter lower down the vessel. The clay is thickest towards the base, and the rim is characteristically 'horn-shaped' in section. In type 3B the base is flat. With the exception of some dubious examples from Garryduff, this type is known from two adjacent sites in Argyll – Kildonan and Ugadale Point – and may be a local variant. Type 3C is similar to 3A but made of stone, and is rounded in cross-section. It occurs at Garryduff and is almost indistinguishable from a stone mortar.
(4) *Shallow circular crucible with flat base and straight sides.* This type often has an inturned rim. It does not appear to occur before the Early Christian period but was current probably through much of it.
(5) *Three-legged crucible.* This type is represented at Lagore where it is round-mouthed and somewhat bag-shaped with a lug on one side.
(6) *Rectangular crucible with vertical sides and rectangular flat base.* This type occurs at Glastonbury and the Mote of Mark.
(7) *Cylindrical crucible.* This occurs in the Iron Age at Glastonbury and Maiden Castle and in the post-Roman period at Dunadd.
(8) *Handled crucible, without lid.* This type first appears in the Early Iron Age, but is rare before the Early Christian period. There are a number of different varieties.
(9) *Lidded crucible.* These first appear in Roman Britain, but are extremely rare before the Early Christian period when they are fairly widespread.
(10) *Saucer- or dish-shaped crucible with round mouth, often with a spout.* Certain examples of this type are not known before the Roman period, and they are rare at all times subsequently.

Ornamental metal working

In excavation reports of secular sites, it is usually suggested that the metal-working evidence implies the production of smaller items of ornamental metalwork, such as penannular brooches, studs and pins, the more ornate objects such as reliquaries being produced elsewhere. While it is probable that ecclesiastical metalwork was produced in monastic workshops (for Early Christian monasteries were more like small towns than the small cloistered communities of the Middle Ages), there is no reason to suppose that even the most ornate penannular brooches, hanging bowl escutcheons or mounts were not produced on sites similar to the Mote of Mark or Ballycatteen.

Lagore produced 263 crucibles, implying a considerable scale of metal working, even allowing for the duration of occupation on the site. The trial pieces from Garryduff 1 are closely comparable to designs used in the Lindisfarne gospels and the *Book of Kells*, suggesting that even local craftsmen were accomplished decorators in the seventh to eighth centuries. The objects from both the lead brooch die from Dinas Powys and the pattern stone from Kiondroghad in the Isle of Man would have been finished with champlevé enamel. The head of what is probably a latchet with enamel inlay from Kiondroghad suggests that such objects may have been made on the site, and the evidence was sufficient to suggest that objects as complex as the local bronzes from the Viking grave at Balladoole, Isle of Man, could have been produced there. Elsewhere there is evidence for both glass (millefiori) and enamel production on otherwise primitively equipped metal-working sites. Millefiori has been found on major metal-working sites such as Garranes and Lagore as well as smaller sites such as Dinas Powys.

At one time it was believed that fine ornamental metalwork was essentially an Irish phenomenon, but evidence is accumulating that a high standard of workmanship and artistry was also being attained in other parts of the Celtic-speaking areas, such as south-western Scotland.

Filigree and granular work

Filigree involves the use of finely twisted gold wire soldered on to a metal plate. It is often found in conjunction with granular work, in which tiny beads of gold are applied to a base plate in the same fashion. It is a feature of Anglo-Saxon jewellery, notably Kentish, but in Ireland is developed along separate lines. One of the earliest examples of filigree work is a tiny gold bird from Garryduff, which is possibly an import. The technique of filigree, introduced in the workshops of the later Roman Empire, was developed by Byzantine metal smiths, who may have been influential in its spread among at least some of the barbarians, such as the Lombards.[19] It was widely used among both the Celtic and Germanic peoples of the Migration Period.

Chip carving

Chip carving is derived, as might be imagined, from wood working. In this type of work chips of metal were cut away to leave depressions rather like inverted pyramids to reflect the light. True chip carving is very rare; normally the effect is simulated by *cire perdue* casting, a technique which originated in the Roman Empire. It appears commonly on late Roman military equipment in a broad zone across the northern frontiers of the Empire, and chip-carved belt fittings and other objects turn up in late Roman contexts in Britain.[20] The technique had a long life, and was widely used by the barbarians in Europe down to the eighth century AD. It was probably developed originally in the Black Sea region, but was adopted by the military workshops catering for Germanic taste. It is, however, mainly a Germanic technique, and probably came to the Celtic west by way of Anglo-Saxon England.[21]

Enamel working[22]

Enamelling is a process closely related to glass working – powdered glass is heated until it fuses into an opaque mass. It was developed in La Tène Europe, and is characteristic of the later phases of insular La Tène art in Britain, when red enamel was widely used. Red remained the chief colour used in the Iron Age, but in Romano-British times yellow, blue and other colours were introduced. Enamelwork in Roman Britain seems to have been employed particularly on brooches (notably the dragonesque and plate types) and harness fittings, and is associated with native rather than classical taste. The technique employed was champlevé, in which the areas to be set with enamel were cut away leaving sockets or cavities. A major workshop at Namur produced enamelled trinkets during the third century, but there were no doubt many others, including British workshops.

In cloisonné work thin strips of metal are soldered on to a metal plate to produce cells (cloisons) into which the enamel is set. This is done by melting the vitreous powder when within the cloison, so that it adheres to the base plate as well as to the walls of the cloison. The technique is presumed to be Eastern, but it occurred in Hungary in the fifth century and was not well established in Byzantium until the sixth. Associated with cloisonné enamel work is the use of garnet and other stone inlays, in which the pieces to be set in the cloisons were simply kept in place by the flanges of the walls and were not attached to the base plate. Frequently this type of cloisonné work is associated with an underlay of pierced or faceted gold foil beneath the inlay, to reflect the light, known as a 'paillon'. This polychrome inlay work is presumed to be Eastern, possibly Persian, in origin, but is widespread in Migration Period Europe. Pseudo-cloisonné work was a secondary development, in which the cells are not soldered on to the base plate but cast in one piece with it. It is frequently found with pseudo-filigree, in which the upper edges of the cloisons are indented to imitate the twisted wire or beading of true filigree or granular work.

Evidence of enamelling is rare, though at Garranes it seems to have been produced – a fragment of red enamel and a bronze button with a champlevé pattern on it in red were among the refuse of the industrial activity. Champlevé enamel was fairly common in late Celtic Britain until at least the eighth century. It is probably a survival from the Roman Iron Age, and there is adequate evidence that Romano-British enamelled objects were brought to Ireland during the later days of the Roman Empire. Red enamelwork was also already established in Ireland in the Iron Age on native products, such as the Petrie Crown and one of the Lisnacroghera scabbards. Cloisonné work, on the other hand, is relatively rare in the Celtic west. Where it does occur it is probably due to Anglo-Saxon influence.

There is no conclusive evidence to support the view that enamelling was an important element in the metalworker's repertoire before around 500, the enamel from Garranes being probably the earliest for which there is external dating evidence. The enamelwork of the sixth and seventh centuries consists mainly of red inlays with spiral or whorl patterns, and it is probably to the sixth century, rather than the fifth, that many of the enamelled hanging bowl escutcheons should be assigned. In the eighth century the spiral tended to disappear from champlevé work and was replaced by angular patterns, which were possibly influenced by the shape of millefiori settings or equally probably by the widespread fashion for step pattern cloisonné work in the Anglo-Saxon jewellery of the seventh century. Red and yellow were the predominant colours of the eighth century, occasionally coupled with blue bosses. Area enamel superseded restricted inlay – on eighth-century enamelwork very little of the surface of the bronze is visible.[23]

Millefiori (Fig. 74)

Something of a mystique has grown up in archaeology surrounding the manufacture and use of millefiori in the Early Christian period. Millefiori is a technique which involves fusing together rods of different coloured glass to form a single rod with a coloured pattern running through it. It is still made, and enjoyed a particular vogue in the nineteenth century for paperweights.

In the Early Christian period millefiori was only used in the form of 'slices' taken from the fused rods, for panels of decoration. The technique originated in the East and was developed in the Roman Empire, most notably in Gaul, a third-century workshop being known at Namur. There, as in the Early Christian period in Britain, it was combined with champlevé. There is evidence for the presence of millefiori in Roman Britain in the fourth century – a stud thus decorated was found at Chesterholm, Northumberland. A workshop producing it has been excavated at Garranes, Co. Cork, and there is further evidence for millefiori working at Lagore. Sticks of millefiori have been found in Scotland and Wales, the one a stray find from Luce Sands,[24] the other from the excavations at Dinas Powys, where it may have been part of the stock of an Irish glassworker. Until recently it was believed to be a peculiarly Irish technique, but the last two finds suggest that millefiori was being made elsewhere in the Celtic west. It was not unknown to the Anglo-Saxons. Millefiori was sometimes used to decorate Kentish disc brooches of the early seventh century and it also appears in the Sutton Hoo jewellery. A rod of millefiori was found at the monastery at Jarrow, in what appeared to be a workshop, and more millefiori was found in the sister monastery of Monkwearmouth.[25] The technique of setting millefiori like a jewel rather than fusing glass onto the metal surface is generally regarded as Anglo-Saxon, and the Witham and Scunthorpe hanging bowls have millefiori that closely matches that from Monkwearmouth.

The technique was clearly available to all parts of the Celtic and Anglo-Saxon world, and could easily be a survival from late Roman Britain rather

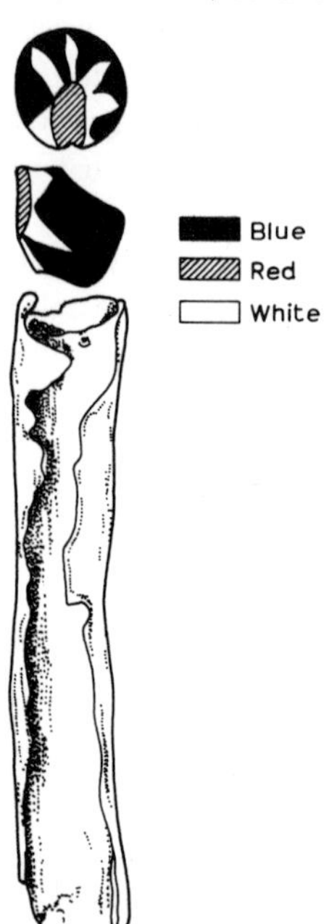

Figure 74 Millefiori glass rod and holder, Garranes, Co. Cork. Scale: $\frac{2}{1}$

than a fresh introduction from the Continent in the Early Christian period. In this connection it is worth noting that the technique used in producing glass bangles of the type discussed in a later chapter (p. 335) is very similar and a fuller understanding of the reason for their reappearance in post-Roman times would probably lead to a fuller understanding of the revival of millefiori. Millefiori appears to have been used in Ireland down to at least the eighth century.

Glass studs (Fig. 75)

One product of the Celtic glass industry apart from bracelets and beads was a category of glass studs for ornamental inlays. A particularly fine stud, decorated with a raised pattern of interlace only 1 centimetre in diameter was found at Garryduff, and at Lagore one was found in the open clay mould in which it had been cast. Other clay stud moulds were also found at Lagore, along with glass rods (Fig. 75) which presumably had supplied the raw material. The Lagore stud had a stepped geometric pattern which can be matched on three objects, a medallion from Killua Castle, Westmeath, an unprovenanced brooch in the British Museum, and a penannular brooch from Westmeath. All belong to the late seventh or eighth century, though as none is exactly similar to the Lagore stud, it cannot be taken as positive evidence for dating.

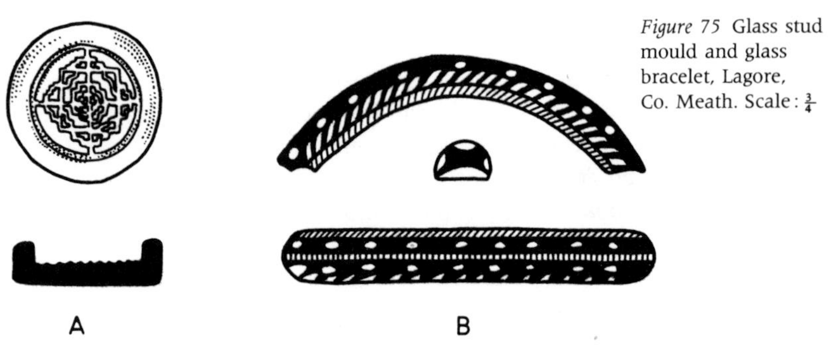

Figure 75 Glass stud mould and glass bracelet, Lagore, Co. Meath. Scale: $\frac{3}{4}$

Industries and crafts

Metal working and glass working are the only crafts that can be classed as true industries of the Early Christian Celtic peoples, though some leather working and wood working may have been the province of highly skilled artisans.

It has recently been shown that a considerable mastery of leather working was required to produce such objects as the budgets or book satchels of the later part of the Early Christian period,[26] and while these were probably the products of monastic workshops a similar degree of skill was involved in the production of some shoes which show, in the words of Dr A. T. Lucas, 'astonishing sophistication'.[27] Some features of Celtic wood working are discussed in connection with the surviving products (p. 262), and here it may simply be noted that manual skill, rather than advanced tools or technology, were involved in both these crafts. The same may be said for spinning, weaving and bone and horn working, all of which were probably domestic rather than specialist crafts.

Stone seems to have been used for a variety of objects, most notably for rotary querns, which in the Early Christian period were sometimes decorated. Stone was also used for rubbers, grinders, whetstones and weights. The objects were probably made as the need arose – there is no evidence at this period for the kind of trade in whetstones that was a feature of late Saxon and medieval England. Querns on the other hand along with millstones may have been produced by specialist quarrymen, though the historical evidence, afforded by a text in Cogitosus's *Life of Bridgit*, suggests that even these were quarried as required by members of the community.[28] No detailed petrological survey is available of Early Christian millstones and quernstones, but where reported the source for quernstones is usually a local outcrop. Worked flints, of the type usually described as 'scrapers', are ubiquitous and occur also on medieval sites. They seem to have served a variety of purposes, from strike-a-lights to engraving tools.

Boats

The only boats to have survived from the Early Christian period are dugout canoes. It is probable, however, that larger boats existed, and a gold model of a boat dating from the early Iron Age known from Broighter, Co. Derry, would imply that even at this date there were boats in Ireland up to 50 feet long.[29] The Broighter boat had eight pairs of oars, a steering oar and a mast. An eighth-century carving of a boat on a pillar at Bantry, Co. Cork, shows what appears to be a rowing boat with four pairs of oars and a steering oar.[30] Although weathered, the overall appearance of the Bantry boat is of a skin-covered vessel similar to the *curraghs* used for inshore fishing in Ireland in recent times. The question as to whether there was a Pictish fleet is debatable, but large skin-covered boats could have been used for the Irish Sea crossing and could have provided a formidable force. The dugouts could only have been used for travel from the water's edge to a crannog or for a limited amount of river travel and fishing.

Canoes are known from both Scotland and Ireland, frequently from crannog sites. One from Buston was 22 feet long.[31] Some seem to have had the stern piece cut out separately and slotted into the open end of the trunk.

Wheeled vehicles

Roads and bridges, with the exception of cobbled paths leading from some raths, are known entirely from literature; such references indicate different classes of roads, some of which may have been modelled on the Roman.[32] Archaeological evidence for wheeled vehicles in the Early Christian period is also largely lacking. There is, however, a wheel from Lough Faughan crannog. Only the fragmentary hub survives, but it is sufficient to indicate that the wheel probably had twelve spokes, the end sections of which were rectangular. Although cruder, it compares with the wheels from Newstead Roman fort or the Iron Age lake village at Glastonbury. It seems too crude to have belonged to a chariot, but could have come from an agricultural waggon.[33]

The Lough Faughan hub raises the question of the origin of the chariot in Ireland.[34] References in Irish saga literature indicate that the chariot was known in Early Christian Ireland, though some references seem almost certainly to be partly derived from classical literary traditions. There are, however, a number of depictions of chariots on high crosses, notably the North Cross at Ahenny, Flann's Cross at Clonmacnois, the tall cross at Monasterboice, the Cross of St Patrick and Columba at Kells and the Kilree Cross. The Ahenny, Kells and Clonmacnois chariots seem to have had eight-spoked wheels, reaching as high as the horse's back. References in Irish literature imply that the Irish chariot of Early Christian times was closely related to modern farm carts, and allude to certain features, such as the use of rere-shafts which do not appear in the sculptures.

Conclusions

From the foregoing review it can be seen that the Early Christian Celtic peoples were largely self-sufficient, producing most of their requirements at home out of materials obtained locally. Although they were considerable craftsmen, they did not engage in large-scale industrial activity, and to a large extent objects that could not be produced at home were manufactured by itinerant smiths and craftsmen. Although boats, vehicles, roads and bridges provided limited facilities for travel, archaeological evidence does not suggest that much long-distance travel or trade was undertaken. While there are a number of exotic objects that have obviously been traded to the Celtic-speaking areas of Britain and Ireland from the Continent and also from Anglo-Saxon England, there is no single category of import, with the exception of pottery, that can be recognized, implying haphazard rather than organized trade with the outside world. In view of this the quantity of imported pottery recognized on Celtic sites requires careful consideration. The various classes of pottery and their date and provenance are discussed in a later chapter (p. 268), but here it should be noted that although it has now been recognized from a number of sites, it is represented by only a few sherds on each and the quantity recovered from Tintagel, Cornwall, is exceptional. In all it need not represent more than a few boatloads. Thomas has stressed the possible liturgical significance of the early imports, and in the light of this it is worth noting that almost all the evidence for direct continental contact with Celtic Britain and Ireland belongs to the fifth to seventh centuries. Until there are more finds it is probably unwise to make many inferences from the pottery about a secular continental trade.

11 Subsistence equipment

The material culture of the Early Christian Celtic peoples was essentially that of a farming society in which trade played a relatively small part. From the highest social ranks to the lowest, the range of equipment was generally similar, and the majority of finds from the royal crannog at Lagore, Co. Meath, differ from those in minor raths and crannogs only in quantity.

Two main problems beset a study of the subsistence equipment of the period. First, much of the material is virtually undatable. Many of the everyday objects in use in Early Christian Celtic Britain and Ireland had reached functional stasis at a much earlier date, and during the period from about 400 to about 1000 underwent very little change. The few categories of objects which were modified seem to have undergone change only slowly, and in the absence of closely datable sites no detailed chronology is possible. Secondly, almost all the evidence comes from a small group of Irish sites. There are a number of reasons for this. In general terms, Irish settlement sites of the period have attracted greater interest than their British counterparts and have been subjected to more recent excavation. They are also more readily recognizable in the field (the majority have a 'defensive' character) and appear to have survived in greater numbers than in Britain (see discussion, p. 155). Furthermore, the most informative sites have been those excavated by the Harvard expedition between the two world wars – Lagore (Co. Meath), the two Ballinderry crannogs (Co. Offaly/Westmeath) and Cahercommaun (Co. Clare), and without the information from these sites much less would be known about the material culture of the Early Christian period generally. A number of the key Irish sites are crannogs, which have preserved organic material in waterlogged conditions. Although there are several crannogs in

Scotland with comparable occupation, notably Buston (Ayrshire) and Loch Glashan (Argyll), all were relatively unimportant compared to Lagore or Ballinderry. There is no comparably ubiquitous class of Early Christian monument in Britain to compare with the Irish rath. Settlement in Wales, south-west England, and less probably Scotland, from the seventh century onwards may have been predominantly open, and most available information comes from the reoccupied hillforts of the earlier centuries. The majority of British sites, and indeed a large percentage of Irish, produce very few finds of the period. A few spindle whorls, perhaps a bead, and an iron knife would make a typical finds list. The few British sites which have provided a significant range of finds – Dinas Powys (Glamorgan), Mote of Mark (Kirkcudbright), Dunadd (Argyll), Buston Crannog (Ayrshire) and perhaps Gwithian (Cornwall), though the latter is not yet fully published, show, however, that the material possessions of the Celtic-speaking occupants of Britain were generally similar and no more impoverished than their Irish counterparts.

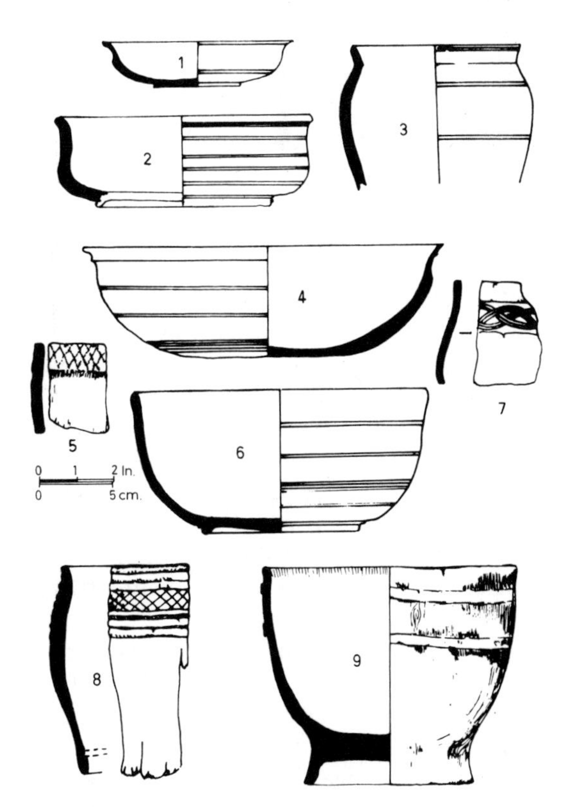

Figure 76 Wheel-turned wooden vessels, Ireland. (1), (2), (4), (6) Lagore; (3) Lissue; (5) Ballinderry 2; (7), (8), (9) Ballinderry 1

Wood working

The main categories of surviving wooden objects are vessels of various types, such as buckets, troughs, bowls and tankards, and utensils such as mallets, paddles, handles, spindles, clubs, pegs, scoops, knobs, lids and spoons, along with more substantial articles such as dugout canoes. From Ballinderry 1 came a fine gaming board and part of what is possibly a pack saddle. Most categories of object are relatively simple, and do not merit detailed discussion, typical examples being shown in the illustrations (Figs 76–80). The bowls, tubs and buckets are worthy of more detailed consideration.

Figure 77 Stave-built wooden vessels, Ireland. (1) Bucket, Ballinderry 1; (2) Churn, Lissue. Height of bucket: 12⅝ins. Height of churn: 20 ins

Carpentry was evidently well developed as early as the Bronze Age in Ireland, and in the Early Christian period wood was worked by a variety of techniques. Adzes were used for rough hewing and dressing, while small objects like bowls or pins were lathe-turned and sometimes decorated either by carving and engraving or by burnishing, after the manner of 'poker work'.

With the exception of the rare imported pottery and some native ware (p. 276), Early Christian Ireland was aceramic and depended on wooden vessels for domestic use. The notable feature of many of these is their similarity to their more recent counterparts, and indeed when such objects turn up as stray finds in peat bogs it is impossible on the grounds of shape alone to attribute them to a particular period.

A series of lathe-turned wooden bowls from Ballinderry and Lagore show the development of the type. Ballinderry 2 has produced parts of fifteen lathe-turned bowls and one platter. Lathe-turned wooden bowls first appear in the Bronze Age in Europe, and there is a series from La Tène.[1] In Britain further examples are known from the lake village of Glastonbury.[2] These Iron Age vessels, however, are markedly different in form from those of the Early Christian period, and it has been postulated that the Irish vessels were

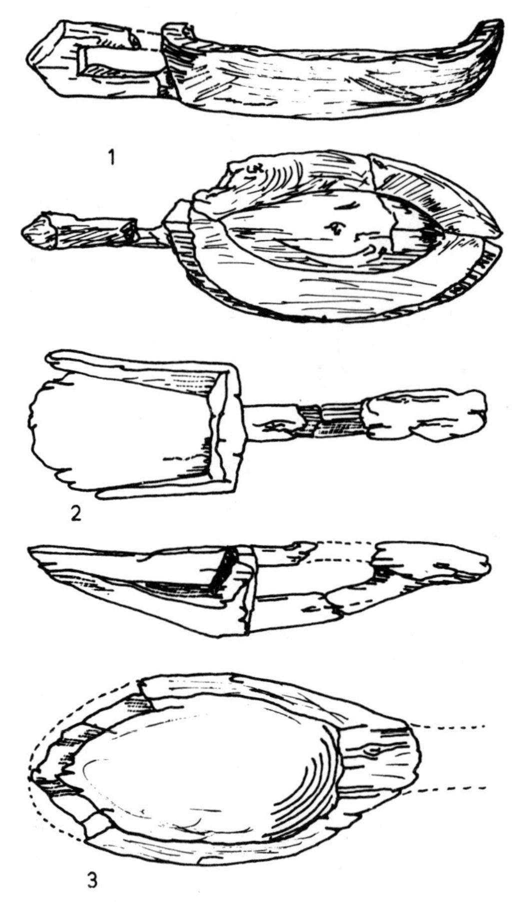

Figure 78 Wooden scoops and shovels, Ireland. (1) Lagore; (2)–(3) Ballinderry 1. Scales: (1) $\frac{3}{16}$; (2) $\frac{3}{32}$; (3) $\frac{3}{8}$

inspired by pottery prototypes. If so, it is difficult to determine the prototype, unless it was a Class E imported bowl. The Ballinderry 2 bowls appear to have lacked foot-rings, and the only decoration encountered was a burned trellis pattern on one. Hazel appears to have been the material most favoured, though wood from fruit trees and elm was also employed. The Lagore vessels are better preserved and more ornate. The earliest are shallow and graceful, the later rather deeper with a more pronounced foot-ring base. Alder and poplar seem to have been the most favoured at Lagore.

The final stage of the development can be seen at Ballinderry 1, where there is a deep, less elegant bowl with a high foot-ring. This sequence from shallow bowls without foot-rings to elegant bowls with foot-rings to deeper bowls with high foot-rings can only be regarded as approximate. A bowl from York, from Anglo-Danish levels, is closer to the early Lagore bowls than the later,[3] while twelfth-century wooden bowls from Oxford show the continuation of the type into the later Middle Ages.[4]

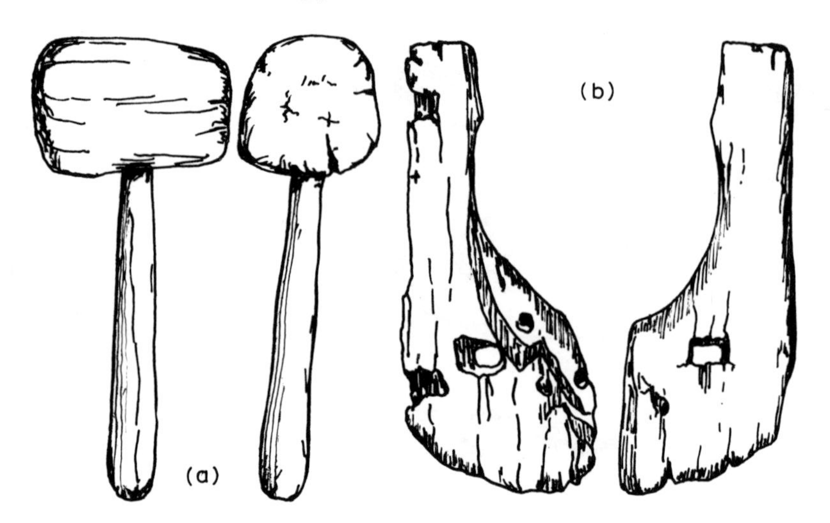

Figure 79 (a) Wooden mallet, Lagore ($\frac{3}{16}$); (b) Wooden pack-saddle, Ballinderry I ($\frac{1}{8}$)

Lissue rath has produced further evidence for lathe-turned vessels. From this site have come a fine deep bowl with small foot-ring, a jar with an everted rim and pairs of burned grooves, and an unfinished bowl, as well as various pieces of waste such as chucks, showing that they were made on the site. They date from around 800. A bowl similar to the first from Lissue came from Inchclough, Co. Kerry.[5]

Ornate decoration other than simple rilling or ribbing is relatively rare on domestic vessels. A wooden tub from Ballinderry 1, decorated with trellis and cordon ornament, was made by hollowing out a piece of trunk, a groove being cut to take a separate bottom plate. This difficult technique of producing wooden vessels is not unknown from post-medieval Ireland at a later date. Ballinderry 1 has also produced a wooden trial piece with interlace on it, and interlace decorated a very elegant bowl from a bog at Cavancarragh, Co. Fermanagh, probably of the ninth or tenth century. Platters and troughs were normally rectangular or oval, and were frequently furnished with a pair of lugs to facilitate lifting.

The other main category of wooden vessel is stave-built, like the Iron Age buckets from Aylesford and Marlborough, or those from Glastonbury lake village. Some staves had projections at the top with a hole to take a metal handle, and such handles, often of twisted iron, are common finds. The hoops were made of a branch split lengthwise and fastened with an iron clamp. The bottom was set in a groove in the staves. Stave-made buckets appear in Roman contexts and were probably widespread in the Germanic world in the post-Roman period. To judge from finds from Dinas Powys, Anglo-Saxon buckets (or at least their bronze mounts) were reaching Wales in the sixth century.

A small complete bucket was recovered from Ballinderry 1, consisting of nineteen staves and two hoops. Two pegs supported each of the hoops after they were hammered into place. From Lissue came a churn of oak, dating from around 800, wider at the base than at the top, with wooden hoops and

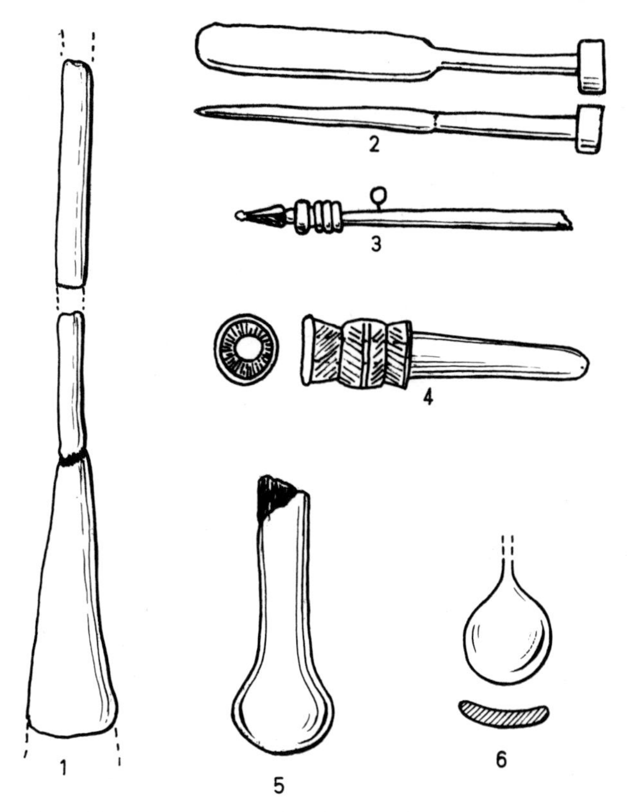

Figure 80 Miscellaneous wooden objects, Ireland. (1) Paddle, Ballinderry 1; (2) Pin, Ballinderry 2; (3) Spindle, Lagore; (4) Knob, Lagore; (5) Handle, Lagore; (6) Spoon, Lagore. Scales: (1) $\frac{1}{8}$; (2)–(5) $\frac{3}{8}$; (6) $\frac{1}{4}$

an iron rim mount, together with two iron hoops. Two iron rings attached to the central iron hoop took cords from which the churn could have been suspended. Such churns which were swung to and fro to make butter were still used in Ireland until the nineteenth century.

Carved wood has not often survived, but there is a carved wooden figure of a nude man from Lagore, and from Ballinderry 1 a gaming board. The latter has a human head and an animal head at opposite sides as handles, and is decorated with ring-chain, key or fret patterns and interlace. The patterns can be most closely paralleled in sculpture in the Isle of Man, and it is likely that the board is a Manx import of the tenth century. The human head is similar to those from the Gosforth or Gainsford crosses. The board was probably used for a version of Fox and Geese, a game played in the early Iron Age, on the evidence of the gaming pieces from a Belgic chieftain's burial at Welwyn Garden City.[6]

Western vessel glass (Fig. 81)

Glass production was established in Roman Britain at Colchester in the second or early third century, though there is no evidence for native glass production in the fourth.[7] Glass working had been familiar to the La Tène Celts, who were not only skilful at making whorled 'eye beads' but produced fine armlets and even figurines. The remains of early Iron Age glass working have been found in the Bavarian oppidum of Manching.[8] During the Roman occupation, natives in northern Britain were producing glass bangles out of melted-down Roman glass.[9] That the Celtic-speaking people of post-Roman

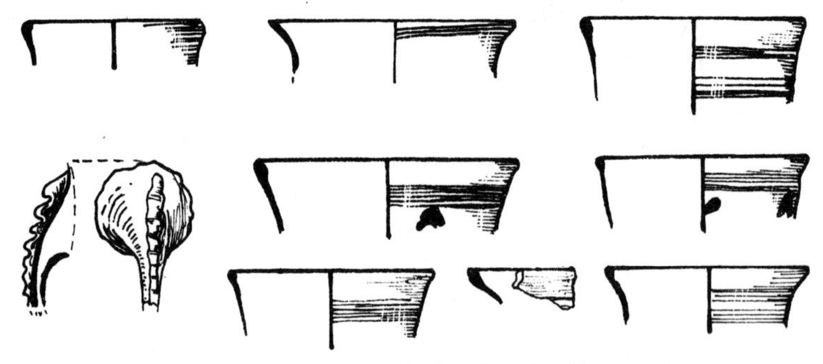

Figure 81 Vessel glass, Dinas Powys. Scale: $\frac{3}{8}$ (After Alcock)

Britain continued the habit of re-using imported glass cannot be doubted, and probably most, if not all, the vessel glass from Early Christian period contexts in western Britain was brought in as scrap. One of the main products of the Celtic glassworkers in the period were bangles not unlike their Romano-British predecessors (p. 335).

Much of the glass in Roman Britain was imported, the main glass-houses being in Syria and the Rhineland. The end of the Roman Empire did not bring an end to Rhineland glass production and the industry continued through the later fourth and fifth centuries. Around the first half of the fifth century there seems to have been a changeover from town to forest glass-houses, and a rapid turnover in glass fashions, so that the products of the fifth century are easily distinguishable from those of the fourth. This continuity of activity from Roman into post-Roman times is characteristic of continental Europe and cannot be paralleled in Britain; it is also reflected in the field of pottery production (pp. 279–80). In the pagan Saxon period products of the forest glass-houses seem to have come to England in considerable numbers and are a regular feature of inhumation cemeteries. Most of this glass came from Belgium, northern France and the Rhine, though there is some evidence that some was being produced at Faversham in Kent.[10]

In the Celtic west vessel glass is relatively rare. The two main sites where it has been found are Dinas Powys (Glamorgan) and the Mote of Mark (Kirkcudbright). The Mote of Mark[11] glass consists of about forty pieces, which range from one late Roman survivor through cone beakers, pouch bottles, stemmed beakers and bowls to a piece of frosted green glass with opaque white and yellow marvered blobs. The types are all the normal forms found in Merovingian and Anglo-Saxon cemeteries of the sixth to early seventh centuries. At Dinas Powys, apart from a few pieces of Roman glass, there were over 300 glass fragments, representing at least thirty-three vessels of fifth- to sixth-century date. As at the Mote of Mark these included a large number of pieces with white trailing. Vessels with trailing are most frequently in the shape of stemmed and bell beakers or cone beakers.

Stray pieces of glass of the period have been found at a few other sites, notably South Cadbury,[12] Gwithian,[13] and Cadbury Congresbury.[14] Tintagel has also produced a single piece of Western glass, along with sherds from four vessels of Eastern origin.[15] Later, in the ninth or tenth century, there was a glass-making industry at Glastonbury.[16] A series of Irish sites – Garranes, Ballycatteen, Garryduff, Dalkey Island, and Ballinderry 2 – have produced fragments of Western glass. All were occupied in the fifth to sixth centuries. Later finds of Western glass are very rare. From Lagore, the folded-over rim of a palm-cup probably belongs to the sixth-century occupation, while a piece of red glass is putatively Carolingian. A vessel of uncertain date was found in a crannog at Mullaroe, Co. Sligo.[17] From Britain the only later glass is from Birsay, Orkney, and belongs to the Viking Age.[18]

Much of the material has come from sites such as Dinas Powys, Garranes, Garryduff and Lagore where there was other evidence for glass working on a minor scale. In the light of this the pieces of glass should be seen as stray imports, possibly from the Anglo-Saxon world, for use as raw material, rather than as evidence of a trade in glass vessels between the Celtic west and the Continent.

Eastern vessel glass[19]

A second category of glass is Eastern in origin. There is very little of this; four vessels from Tintagel are of Romano-Egyptian origin, and datable to the fifth century, while a fragment from Garryduff is dubiously Eastern. Along with these, beads ought to be considered. For example, from Dinas Powys came a clear blue cylindrical bead and a gilded colourless segmented bead of Coptic origin. Both have knocked ends where they were broken off the wire on which they were wound. Of later date is a phial base from St Andrews with an opaque white marvered trail on the body, which is probably eighth- to tenth-century and from the East.

Eastern exotica are by no means unknown from Anglo-Saxon contexts – there are Coptic bowls, cowrie shells and amethyst beads from graves, as well as more imposing objects such as the Anastasius dish from Sutton Hoo. There is also a series of pilgrim flasks deriving from the shrine of St Menas at Alexandria, one at least of which reached the south-west. It is tempting to include these few pieces of Eastern glass in the trade which brought imported pottery from the east Mediterranean. Nevertheless, there is too little glass to draw any conclusions about contacts, and it might well have reached the Celtic west by other channels.

Imported pottery (Figs 82–9)

Following the withdrawal of the Roman legions the Romano-British pottery industry soon declined. It would appear that by about AD 430 the kilns were out of production and the sub-Roman population was relying on old vessels.[20] By the middle of the fifth century even these were no longer available. The Anglo-Saxons introduced into southern and western England new types from the Continent, thus reinforcing an already hybrid tradition of Romano-Saxon and Saxon-Roman pottery that had grown up during the late Empire to meet the requirements of the Germanic element in the Romano-British population. No such impetus, however, was given to the Celtic-speaking areas.

There is evidence that for a while in the fifth century certain types of Roman vessels were still available in the west. In Wales, at Coygan in the south, and Dinorben and Deganwy in the north, there are hints that certain fourth-century types of heavily calcite-gritted jars were in use in the sub-Roman period, though both forms and fabrics were essentially Roman.[21] Elsewhere, there is evidence from Cirencester and a few other Roman towns of a lingering tradition of sub-Roman pottery in the west, though as yet it is poorly understood. At Shakenoak, Oxfordshire, Saxon and apparently Roman pottery appear together in a pit, the latter belonging to the same general class of calcite-gritted ware that is encountered in Wales.[22]

Native pottery is not the only category of ceramic evidence available, for a wide variety of sites in western Britain and Ireland have produced sherds of imported wares. These were first generally recognized following the publication of a group from the monastic site of Tintagel in Cornwall in 1956,[23] and since then intensive research has built up an impressive list of sites with imported pottery. The quantity is as yet insufficient to be used as evidence for regular trade in luxury pottery along the Irish seaboard linking the Celtic areas of Britain with the Continent. The evidence as it stands points to a specialized trade in the fifth century closely connected with the re-establishment of Christianity, which brought amphorae of oil and liturgical vessels from the Mediterranean homeland to the new Christian communities. In the light of this it is important to distinguish between the distribution of Class A and B Wares and of later fabrics. The A and B Wares possibly appear

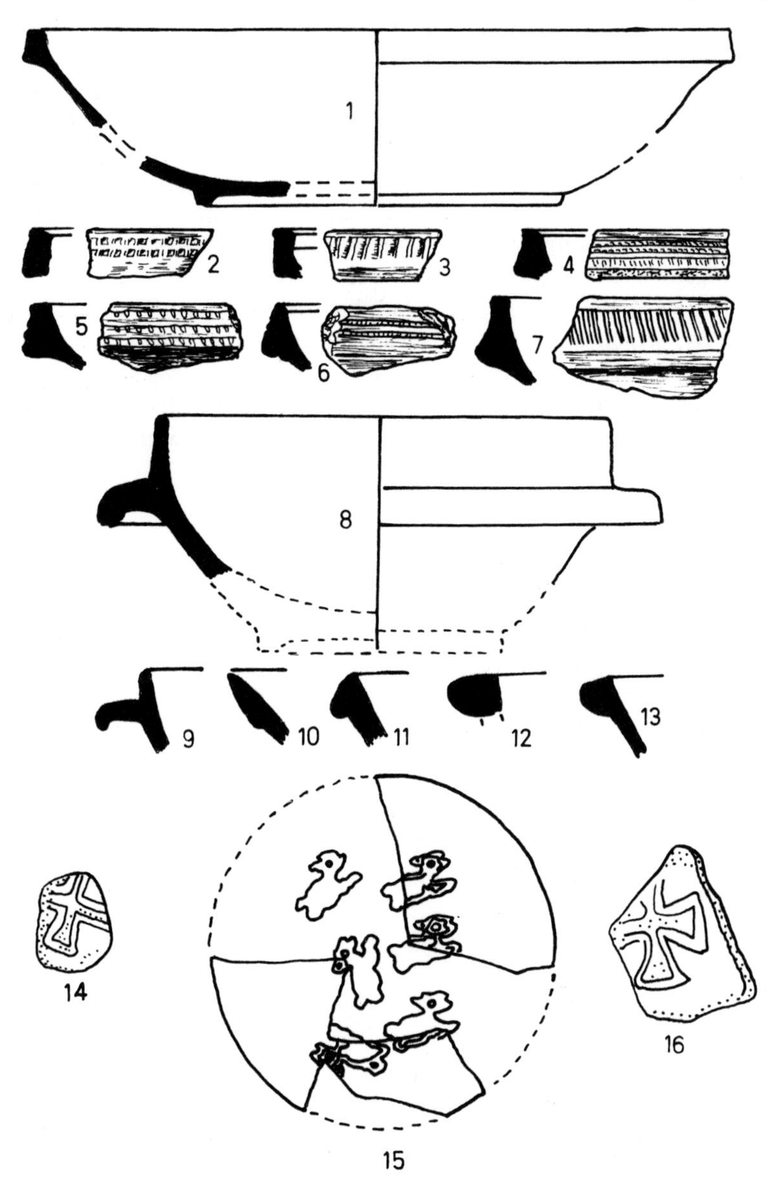

Figure 82 A Ware, all Tintagel except 15, from Dinas Powys. Scale: $\frac{3}{8}$

on secular sites only at second hand, having originally been brought in to supply ecclesiastical requirements. The later classes of imports, particularly Class E Ware, have a wider distribution and were certainly intended from the outset as vessels for domestic use.

Class A[24] Ware consists of a series of bowls and dishes in a brick-red fabric with slightly glossy or red-brown slip. It falls into two main categories: A i, which is soft, with almost no grit and a matt wash, and A ii, which is much harder, has a more lustrous wash the same colour as the body of the vessel (A i is darker) and is found in a shade of buff as well as in the red and pink fabrics found in A i. Class A i vessels are either flanged bowls, similar to Dragendorff 38 bowls of the Roman period, or bowls with upright (or wall-side) rims with rows of rouletting. The bases have small foot-rings. On a few vessels there is a cross stamped on the base, and at Dinas Powys a dish has a random arrangement of stamped animals, probably leopards.

In general, Class A Ware belongs to a family of late Roman and Byzantine stamped pottery, which has a wide distribution in Greece, Asia Minor, the Levant and north Africa. Very close parallels to the British vessels can be found in Athens. The date of Class A Ware has been established by careful research round the Mediterranean and is usually given as extending from about AD 460–70 to about 600.

Figure 83 Distribution of A Ware

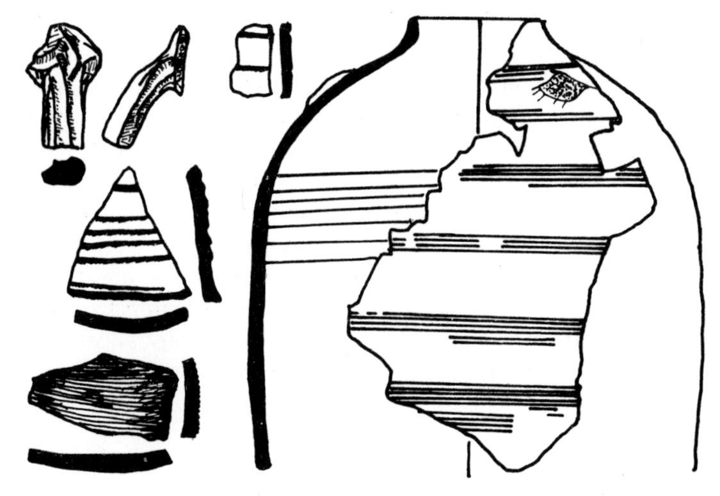

Figure 84 B Ware, Dinas Powys. Scale: $\frac{3}{16}$

Class B[25] Ware consists of a series of amphorae or storage jars with handles. They are in red, pink, buff and creamy coloured fabrics and very frequently have grooves on the body in a continuous spiral to aid handling. They have been divided into four main sub-classes, B iv being the earliest and consisting of small lagenae with a reddish fabric and the inclusion of mica. B iv vessels

Figure 85 Distribution of B Ware

are fairly small with stubby bases, globular bodies and a high constricted bottle neck with two strap handles from neck to shoulder. The grooving on these vessels is confined to broad, shallow fluting. It occurs at Constantinople, and can be dated to the fifth and first half of the sixth centuries. B iii comprises sherds of undecorated amphorae, while B ii consists of jars in a buff ware with very globular profiles and irregularly spaced ridges and fluting. A nearly complete profile of one was eatablished at Gwithian, Cornwall, and in the Mediterranean they may extend from the fourth to the late seventh centuries. B i amphorae are in a pinkish ware with yellow inclusions, and are distinguished by having deep grooves closely set together round the upper part of the vessel. Class B Wares are distributed widely in the east Mediterranean and around the Black Sea, and were used as containers for transporting oil, wine, dried fruit and possibly even nails.

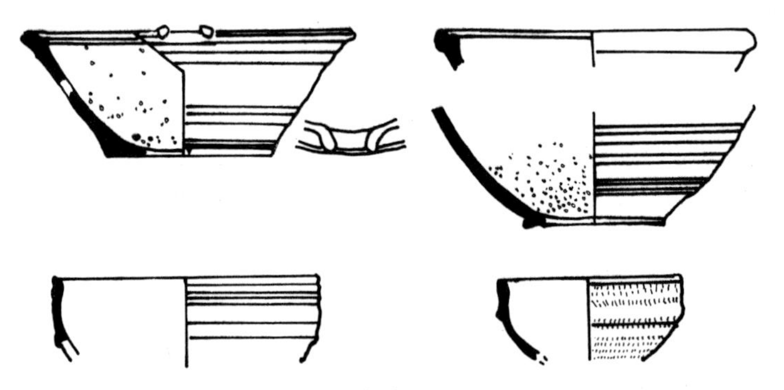

Figure 86 D Ware, Dinas Powys, Scale: $\frac{1}{4}$

Class C[26] Ware is found only at Tintagel, and consists of a series of jugs or pitchers in a coarse grey ware with red-brown surface, occasionally red-brown throughout. They have concave necks, pinched-in spouts and stabbed strap handles. They were once thought to be contemporary with A and B Wares, but current opinion favours the view that they are a local medieval jug form.

Class D[27] consists of mortaria – bowls for mashing fruit and vegetables – descended from the Roman form. Class D vessels are in soft, grey ware with a blue-black wash. They frequently have a small spout for pouring, and like their Roman predecessors have grits to facilitate grinding. Related to the mortaria are smaller bowls and other vessels with external rouletting, and a few larger bowls with stamped decoration. This class as a whole belongs to a family of wares found in France known as *sigillé paléochrétienne grise*, which were once thought to be Visigothic but are now known to be descended from local Roman wares in France. Examples of this ware are widespread in southern and western France in the fifth and sixth centuries, and the closest parallels for the British imports are from the region round Bordeaux. The blue-black wash may have been meant to imitate metal such as silver or pewter.

Class E[28] is the type most frequently found. It consists of cooking pots, bowls, jars, jugs and beakers, and is characteristically hard-fired (almost to stoneware) and pimply to the touch. The colour is usually dirty white on the interior with a grey or yellow exterior shading through to ochre and red or dark grey. The fabric includes quartz and other grits of a white or red colour.

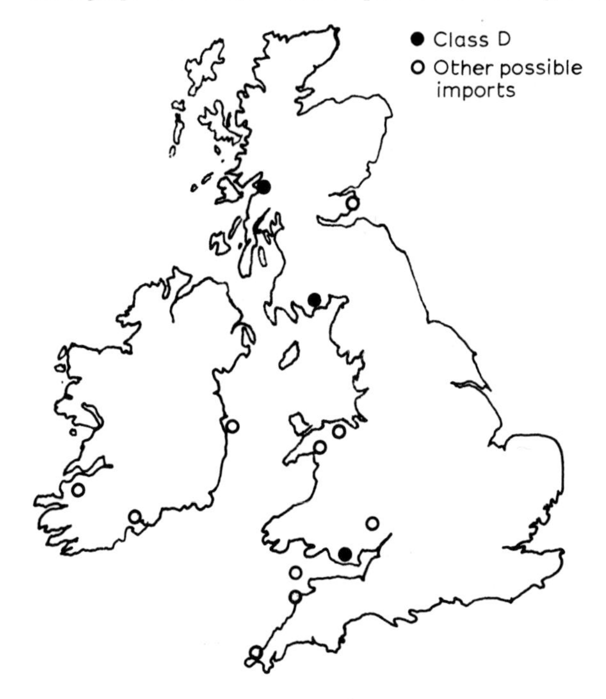

Figure 87 Map of D Ware and other possible imports

On the base there is frequently a raised whirl. The type has turned up on thirty or more sites, and more than 100 vessels are represented. For a long time, because of its general similarity to the products of the Rhineland, E Ware was regarded as a Rhenish export. Problems arose over this attribution, however, since the only area on the Continent where E Ware was known certainly to occur was Britanny, while if the trade was coming from the Rhineland E Ware might be expected to occur in more easterly areas such as Northumbria. Recently the grits in E Ware sherds were examined petrologically and were found to compare most closely with grits from the Paris basin and more particularly Aquitaine. While no E Ware has yet been certainly identified in this area, present opinion places its production around the Charente. It is dated only by association with other imports of datable material in Britain, but does not appear to have been imported prior to 525–50. It continued until about 700 or slightly later.

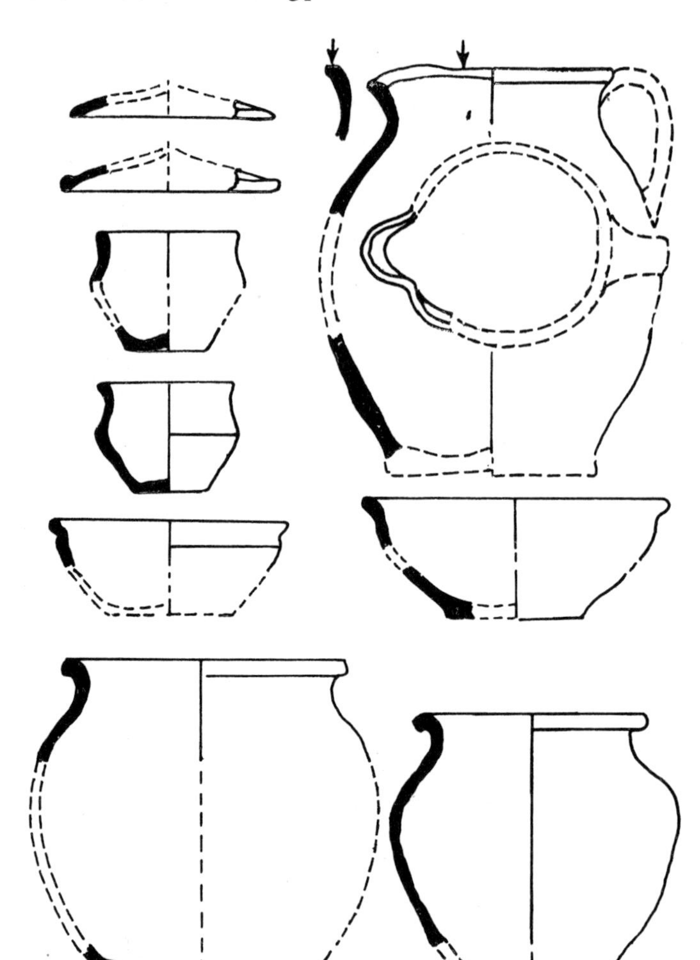

Figure 88 E Ware types. Scale: $\frac{3}{16}$

Class F comprises some thin-walled but large vessels with a laminated fabric and a pearl-grey to pink colour. Its provenance is unknown, and it occurs at only a few sites – Dunadd, Dalkey Island (near Dublin Bay) and Huckhoe, a native site in Northumberland.

Class G comprises small bowls and dishes with a dull red or buff fabric with considerable inclusion of grits. It is widespread in Britain, and is of uncertain origin.[29]

A newly recognized type of flanged bowl of late Roman ancestry in a hard-fired fabric has been found on the Welsh sites of Coygan, Degannwy and Dinorben, and has been considered as possibly imported, but as yet there is insufficient evidence for certainty.[30]

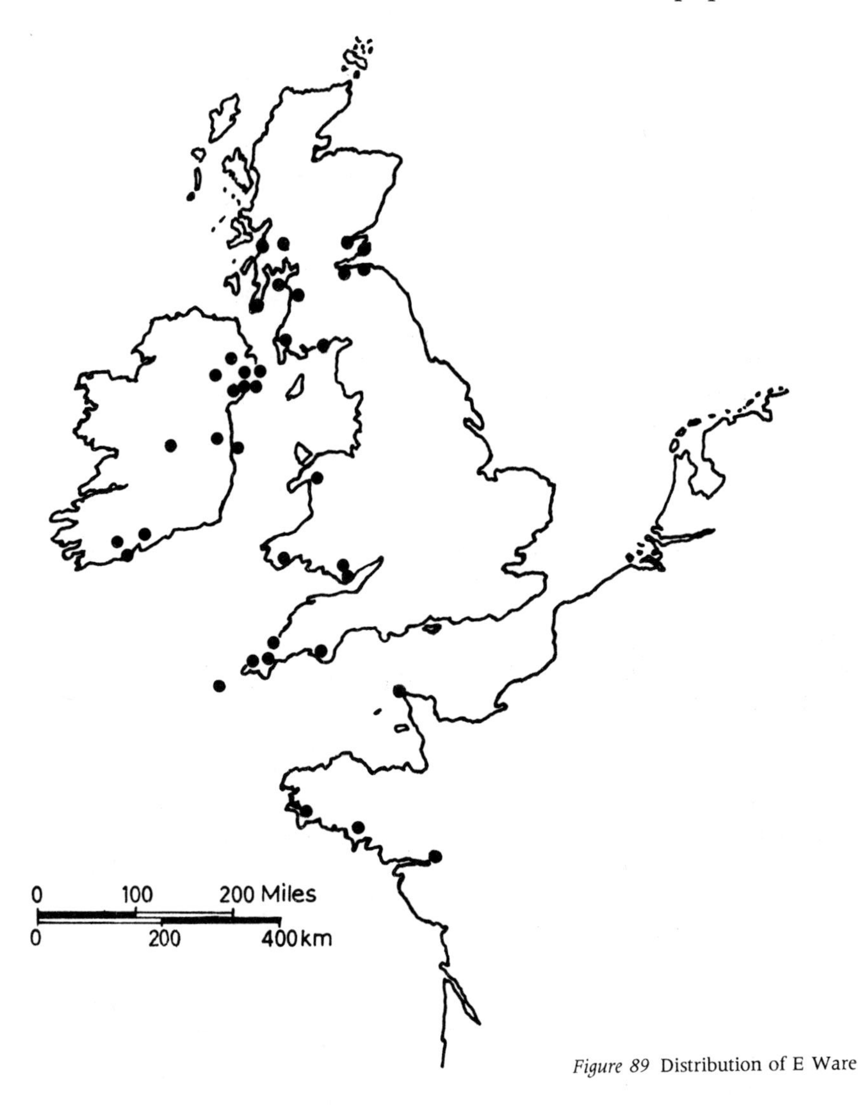

Figure 89 Distribution of E Ware

The distribution pattern of these imports is significant. With the exception of B i amphora sherds, from late fourth- to fifth-century levels in London, all the finds have been from the Celtic west, and all have come from native sites, with the exception of one from the Roman town of Ilchester, Somerset. The overall pattern also differs when A and B Wares are compared with E Ware. The A and B Wares have a southern coastal distribution, being absent from Scotland and northern Ireland. While the southerly distribution of E Ware is similar, it is also found in northern Ireland and Scotland. D and G Wares are absent from northern Ireland, but present in Scotland in a small quantity.

Apart from its value as evidence for a Mediterranean link with western Britain in the Early Christian period (literary evidence and, to a limited extent, epigraphy had previously suggested this connection), the imported pottery is important for establishing a chronology for sites which produce it.

Native pottery

Except in the Atlantic province of Scotland the available native pottery of the Early Christian period is uniformly poor in quality. This raises a problem connected with poor pottery generally, since it cannot normally be used as a viable indicator of culture or date. The German term for poor pottery is *Kummerkeramik*; the British term now most widely used is VCP (Very Coarse Pottery).

It must be recognized that VCP, unless characterized by some distinctive feature, was produced at all times in prehistory subsequent to the Neolithic, and in early historic times, so that it is unattributable. Reports which attribute very poor pottery to the Early Christian period, because of its similarity to poor examples from dated sites elsewhere, are immediately suspect.

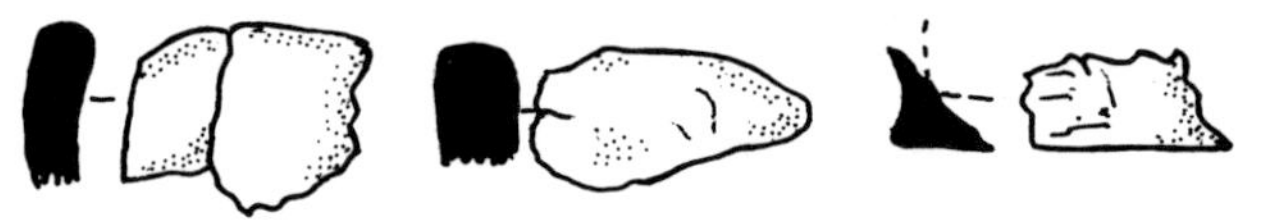

Figure 90 Very Coarse Pottery – Pant-y-Saer, Anglesey. Scale: $\frac{3}{8}$

The pottery found at Castell Odo, Caernarvonshire, was originally regarded as indistinguishable from pottery from Pant-y-Saer in Anglesey (Fig. 90). Subsequently, excavation has shown that the Castell Odo pottery is in fact very coarse Iron Age 'A'.[31] Undecorated pottery from Lyles Hill (Antrim), and similarly 'early' material from Lough Gur (Co. Limerick), once believed to be Neolithic, are suspected in the light of more recent discoveries at Freestone Hill (Co. Kilkenny) of being of Iron Age date.[32]

In Northumberland, Durham and the adjoining Brigantian and Votadinian areas, coarse pottery appears on sites of various periods.[33] It occurs at Traprain Law, West Lothian (Roman Iron Age), Gunnar Peak, Northumberland (second century AD) and Stanwick, Yorkshire (first century AD)[34] as well as on a series of native sites for which close dating is impossible but which generally lie within the Roman Iron Age (Fig. 91). The ultimate origin for this Votadinian VCP (Very Coarse Pottery) has been postulated as being within the ceramic traditions of the local Iron Age 'A', which in the north-east seems to continue very late. VCP is found in the forts of the Welsh Marches, and at Dinorben[35] (where it occurs in the late Roman phase), as well as Garn Boduan, Caernarvonshire,[36] and Pant-y-Saer, Anglesey,[37] in a post-Roman context. A recent study of the Marches pottery, however, has suggested that

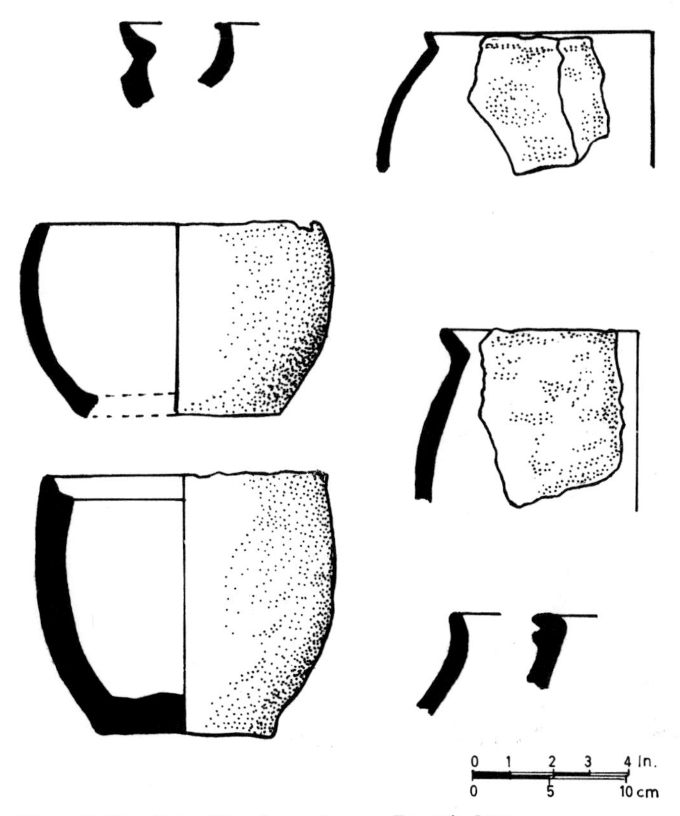

Figure 91 Votadinian Very Coarse Pottery, Traprain Law.

it comes from Iron Age rather than post-Roman contexts, and may not be pottery as such at all, but fired clay from ovens.[38]

Clearly, both fabric and form are related in the case of coarse pottery, the lack of suitable clay necessitating large, straight-walled pots with simple rims and elementary decoration. Whether the choice of very heavily gritted clay was a necessity, or a matter of taste, rims were inevitably either upright or slightly everted, slightly rounded or flattened. Other varieties were a technical impossibility. In this connection it may be added that some post-broch 'wheelhouse' pottery is equally coarse, and its similarity to Bronze Age 'flat-rimmed ware' in some instances must surely be fortuitous. Likewise, similarities between Irish and Scottish flat-rimmed wares, the pottery from two ring-cairns at Mullaghmore, Co. Down, and some of the Votadinian pottery (which is also flat-rimmed) are also probably accidental. Indeed, in the past too much reliance has been put on flat-rimmed ware as a late Bronze Age type fossil.

In addition to these very coarse wares, there are three distinct groups of western native pottery in the Early Christian period: Irish souterrain ware; Cornish grass-marked ware; and wheelhouse and other post-broch pottery of the Atlantic province.

Souterrain ware (Fig. 92) is perhaps a misleading term since this class of pottery is found less often in souterrains than in raths. It is found in east Ulster, Wicklow and Tyrone, and where the grits are identifiable appears to be of local manufacture. Souterrain ware pots are flat-bottomed and 40 per cent are grass-marked. Grass marking should not be confused with grass tempering, where chopped grass is mixed with the clay to strengthen it. In the case

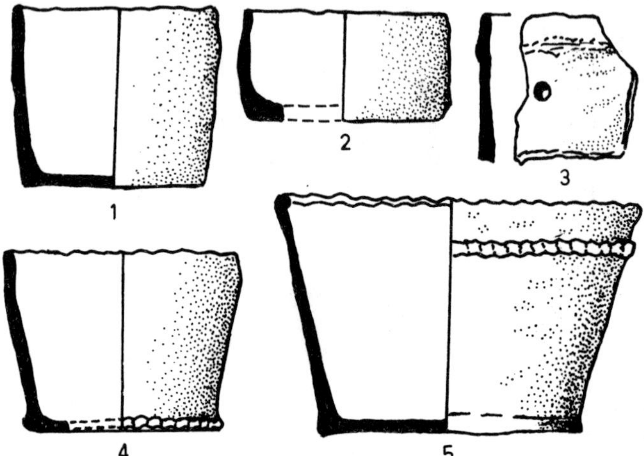

Figure 92 Souterrain ware, Ulster. Scale: $\frac{3}{16}$

of grass-marked pottery the vessel has been set on chopped grass to harden, leaving a grass impression on the base. A typological sequence for it has been worked out on the basis of ornament, but the chronological value of this is doubtful. The decoration is confined to finger-tipping the rim or finger-printing a cordon around the vessel.[39]

Typologically the sequence begins with some pottery from Larrybane, Co. Antrim,[40] which bears incised decoration, chevrons on the rim and fingered rims. One of the Larrybane vessels has a slightly rounded bottom while other sherds show hints of shoulder carination. In the second phase cordons appear. These were present on pottery from Langford Lodge, Co. Antrim,[41] and at Lissue rath, Co. Antrim, where there are also some incurved rims and thumbed bases. The final phase is represented at Shaneen Park, Belfast.[42]

The ancestry of the pottery has been debated. Pottery found by Childe at Larrybane in 1935 prompted him to suggest, on the analogy of the coarse pottery found in Scottish souterrains, that there was a connection between Ulster and Pictland.[43] Later commentators, while seeing the unlikelihood of this suggestion, noted the general similarity between the Larrybane pottery and the undecorated and flat-rimmed ware from Lyles Hill. One deterrent to finding the ancestry of souterrain ware was that almost no Iron Age pottery was recognized in Ireland, the only known examples being from Lugg, Co. Dublin.[44]

The recognition of Iron Age pottery of VCP type stratified with a coin of the fourth century and other late Roman imports at Freestone Hill, Co. Kilkenny, has removed one of the obstacles to finding a likely antecedent to souterrain ware. The Freestone Hill pottery (characterized by perforations below the rim) compares closely not only with the pottery from Lugg, but with coarse pottery from a variety of sites in Ireland. These include Emain Macha, Navan Fort (Armagh), where perforations were absent, and Clogher, Downpatrick and Dunbeg, where the relationship is less close.

It is thus demonstrable that in the Roman Iron Age in Ireland there was at least one tradition of coarse 'jamjar' pots, and that this tradition was current in the fourth century and quite possibly later. Souterrain ware can only be dated in broad terms, though in one case it was clearly associated with E Ware. There is also a radiocarbon date of 480 ± 120 AD for a site producing souterrain ware at Larne, Co. Antrim, suggesting that it was current at least from the end of the fifth to the end of the sixth centuries.[45]

Grass-marked pottery in Cornwall (Figs. 93–4)

The pottery sequence in Cornwall[46] is best demonstrated from Gwithian, Site 1, where in the lowest level (Layer C) stone huts were associated with fine, handmade pottery of local origin. This, produced in the tradition of late Roman pottery and no doubt derived from it, was known as 'Gwithian Style' ware, and was associated with Class A and B imported pottery and a few sherds of grass-marked ware. In the layer above (Layer B) were further sherds of the sub-Roman 'Gwithian Style' pottery, further examples of A and B Wares and some grass-marked pottery. In both Layers B and C there was a limited amount of E Ware. The latest level (Layer A) was dated to around AD 1000 and produced some sherds of grass-marked bar lug pottery. Thus at Gwithian, at least, grass-marked pottery was present in the sixth century, if not the later fifth.

The Cornish grass-marked wares are extremely coarse, and range from browns to grey and black.[47] They appear in two basic forms, the cooking pot and the platter. The platters are probably derived from 'Gwithian Style' dishes; dishes of similar shape, of Roman origin, occur at Porthmeor and Chysauster. They can be up to a foot in diameter. The cooking pots, which are usually carbonized externally, suggesting that they were used in the fire, are normally either flat-rimmed or slightly rounded off with some thickening. There are a few vessels with slightly everted rims. Frequently the pots are slightly narrower at the mouth than at the base, which is flat.

Among the pottery from Layer B at Gwithian were sherds of bar lug wares

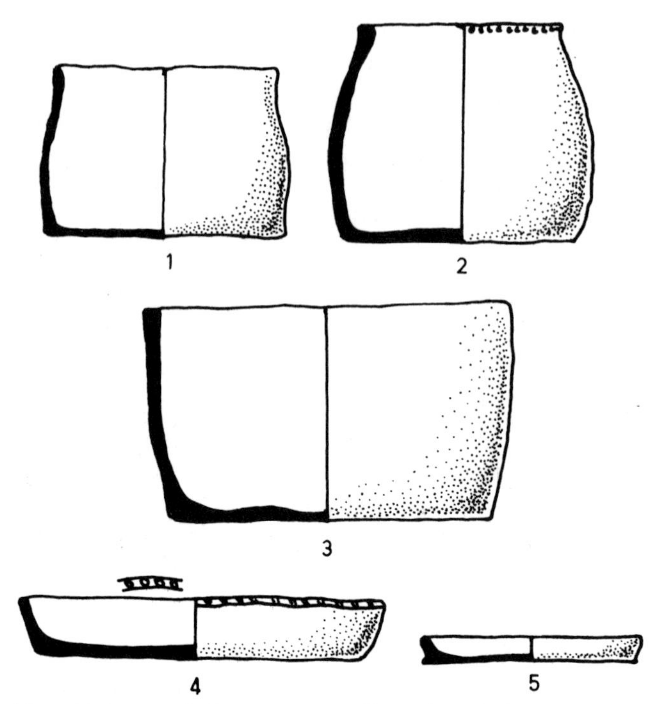

Figure 93 Grass-marked pottery, Cornwall. (1) Chun Castle; (5) Tean, Scilly; Others: Gwithian. Scale: $\frac{3}{16}$

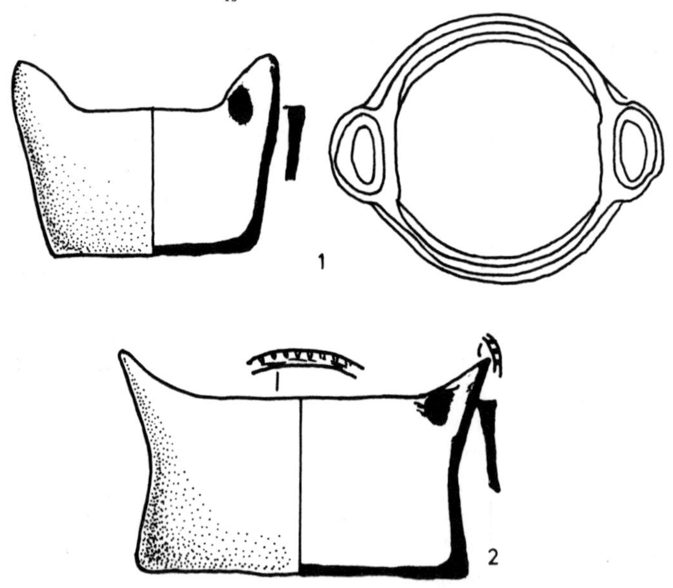

Figure 94 Bar lug pottery, Gwithian, Cornwall. Scale: $\frac{3}{16}$

(Fig. 94). Bar lug pottery appears to have been introduced to Cornwall in the early ninth century from the Low Countries, and also occurs sporadically in eastern England.[48] It would appear to be derived originally from wares produced in Denmark and Schleswig-Holstein in the Roman Iron Age, but its immediate ancestors are not known. On the Continent it was current from the ninth to the eleventh centuries, and is found mainly concentrated in the Netherlands, with extensions into Lower Saxony, Denmark and Sweden. Normally bar lug pottery is globular in shape, with high 'ears' (hence its name), covering bridge spouts, presumably to protect the suspension strings from the fire. Bar lug pottery is coarse and handmade, usually dark in colour.

In Cornwall the bar lug form was taken over by the native potters, who in effect added bar lugs to grass-marked cooking pots. It has been suggested that the presence of grass-marked bar lug pottery in Cornwall was due to the immigration of considerable numbers of Frisians who exploited the Cornish tin streams,[49] but this seems beyond the limits of reasonable inference.

In fabric and general character the grass-marked pottery of the bar lug phase is identical to the earlier pre-bar lug pottery: thus the bases of Cornish bar lug pots are indistinguishable from the bases of earlier vessels, and only when there is a complete assemblage can they be identified.

Evidence from Sandy Lane, Gwithian, suggests that bar lug pottery went out of fashion around 1000, but that grass-marked pottery continued in use in Cornwall for at least a century. Two 'Sandy Lane' styles of pottery have been recognized, Sandy Lane 1 is distinguished by small size, thin walls, and long, oblique finger grooves on the insides of the vessels; Sandy Lane 2 style pots show the rim profiles in common use in the early twelfth century in much of southern England, since their production was begun around 1100–50, when a slow wheel appears to have been used for the first time.[50]

Thomas has suggested that grass-marked pottery was introduced to Cornwall by Irish settlers in the sixth century.[51] Such an introduction would not belong to a primary period of Irish colonization, which has already been postulated from other sources, but to an immigration which is not known from other evidence, with the exception possibly of a few dubious placenames and some saints' *Lives*. There are some problems in this connection. The only feature which the Cornish bar lug has in common with Irish souterrain ware is its use of grass marking on the base. Although there are superficial similarities of form between the Irish and Cornish vessels, these are simply due to the limitations imposed on pot forms by the use of the materials in both instances. Furthermore, grass marking is a technique which might well have been used at any time in the production of handmade vessels, an obvious convenience for preventing the pots sticking to the floor when green-hard. The practice is paralleled by the modern usage of sand. Decoration on the Cornish pots differs from the Irish, though this is arguably because the most developed decoration on souterrain ware (as at Lissue) belongs to a later period than the introduction of grass-marked pottery to Cornwall.

Grass marking has been noted on sherds from Iona and two Hebridean sites, one on the Sound of Harris, the other at the Udal, North Uist. There is a further possible incidence of it in Bute. In the Udal grass marking occurs first in a pre-Norse context and then again after an interval in the late eleventh century. The evidence from Iona points to a similarly recurring native tradition.[52]

Grass tempering has been recently noted on Anglo-Saxon pottery from Porchester.[53] This shows that simple techniques, as distinct from forms and decoration, can appear at any time. Grass tempering also appears in Norse pottery at Jarlshof and Freswick.

Atlantic province pottery (Figs 95–6)

The only other area of late Celtic Britain that had a continuous pottery sequence throughout the Early Christian period was the Atlantic province of Scotland. Here the native Iron Age pottery traditions continued until the time of the Viking settlements. In the Northern Isles the pottery sequence differs from the Hebridean sequence, but represents a parallel series of developments.

In Shetland the pottery at Jarlshof and that at Clickhimin show slight differences. At Jarlshof[54] the earliest wheelhouse period pottery is hard and well fired with flat, roll-top or bead rims and a fine texture, generally red in colour. It is possible to detect in it some continuation from the earliest Iron Age Shetland pottery. At a later stage, however, 'buff ware' made its appearance; it introduced new forms, the most common being a large open bowl with a slightly inverted flat-topped rim. The bases are often slightly splayed. A second class of ware which made its appearance around the same period is grey or grey-black with a smooth, burnished surface. The rims of these pots are sharply everted and the curved shoulders suggest fairly rounded vessels. Finally, in the Passage House phase, the associated pottery is thin-walled and crude, and represents a degenerate form of 'buff ware'. The faces of the pots were pared, and the favourite form was a straight-sided jar with a flat or square-sectioned rim.

At Clickhimin,[55] all the broch period forms survived, the commonest being a large cooking pot with everted rim, plain or fluted, some examples having very pronounced fluting. Neckbands, current in the broch period, were extended to produce bipartite rims. A few smaller barrel-shaped pots continued in use, with slightly flanged flat, everted, or roll-and-bead rims. A few pots are decorated, one having pendent filled triangles, another dimples, while others have shallow curvilinear patterns on the shoulders. Bases were flat, though they often continued the broch period custom of having grooved decoration, frequently spiral, on the underside. Generally the fabric of these wares is the same as the wheelhouse fabrics current at Jarlshof. The late wheelhouse pottery at Clickhimin is identical to the Passage House pottery at Jarlshof. The post-broch pottery from Orkney is not well represented, but generally appears to be similar to that found in Shetland.

In the Hebrides the pottery sequence shows continuity from Neolithic ceramic styles onwards, and the wheelhouse pottery represents a continuation of the traditions of the broch period. There are two main pottery groups in the Early Christian period. The first consists of pots with girth strip decora-

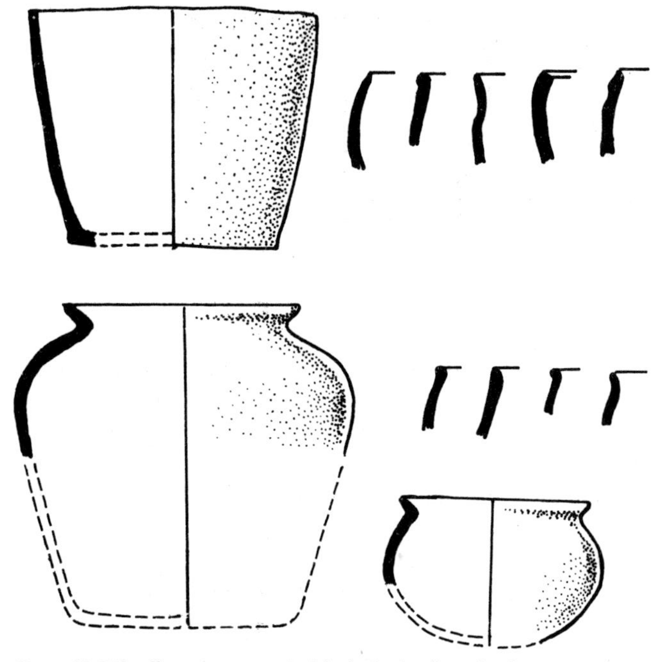

Figure 95 Wheelhouse pottery, Jarlshof, Shetland. Scale: $\frac{3}{16}$

tion and flaring rims, which occur at Dun Cuier, a' Cheardach Mhor and Scurrival.[56] Some vessels of this group continue the Iron Age tradition of employing applied cordons round the neck of the vessel; these were most notably present at Dun Cuier and can also be seen from Clettraval and Unival.

Finally the class of pottery in use prior to the arrival of the Norse was plain, coarse and frequently soot-stained, with a weak profile and occasional finger tipping of the rim. It is particularly common in duns, but also occurs in final phase occupation of wheelhouses and represents a parallel to the Passage House style of pottery current at Jarlshof.

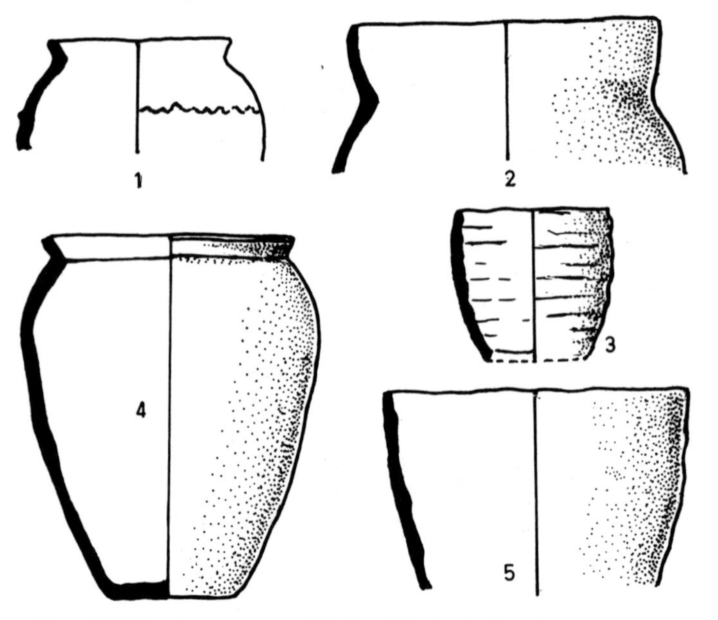

Figure 96 Wheelhouse pottery, Hebrides. (1)–(4), a' Cheardach Mhor. (5), Dun Cuier. Scale: $\frac{3}{16}$

Bone objects

Apart from pins and combs (p. 300) a variety of small objects were made in bone in the Early Christian period, most notably bobbins, toggles, shuttles and mounts for such things as wooden boxes. As a substitute, antler was sometimes used for toggles or handles.

Bone dice were found at La Tène, and are widespread in Europe both in area and time. They occur, for example, in a Migration Period context at Vallhagar in Sweden. In Britain they were first made in the early Iron Age, possibly as early as the first phase, and remained current until the elongated type, hitherto the sole variety, was ousted by the square six-sided die in the Roman period, the latest examples being of the second century AD. Around this date they appeared for the first time in Scotland, and may have spread from there to Ireland.[57] In Scotland they were a feature of the Atlantic province in the post-broch period, and at sites like Bac Mhic Connain, Foshigarry or Dun Cuier are possibly connected with an Early Christian period occupation. In Ireland they were found at Lagore and Ballinderry 2 and occasionally turn up as stray finds. One from Ballinderry 2 is wooden, and another, instead of the normal five dots, has on one face the ogham sign for the Roman numeral V. They were probably used not for scoring throws, but for a game in which four dice are used together and thrown in the air, to fall on a blanket or cloth.[58] All these dice are long (parallelepiped) and are marked on four faces, the ends being open. Bone dice-boxes are also known.

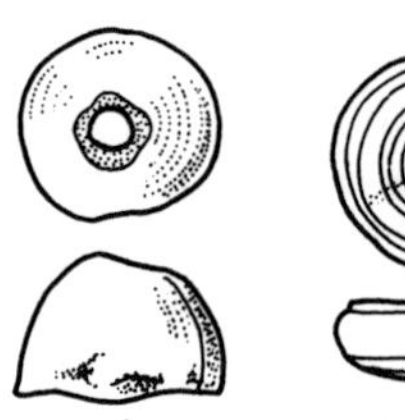

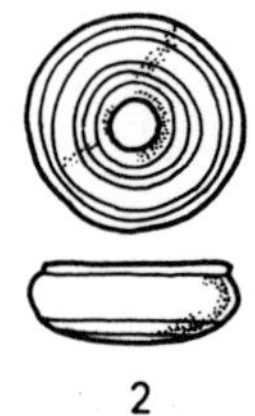

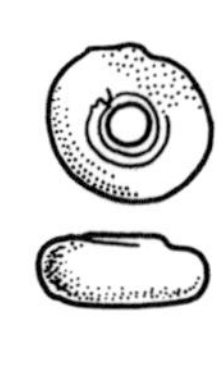

Figure 97 Spindle whorl types, numbered as in text. (1), (2), Cahercommaun, (3), (4), Carraig Aille. Scale: $\frac{1}{4}$

A related gaming piece was found at Dun Cuier, Barra, and simple, round gaming pieces of bone, stone, and occasionally glass, occur in a variety of contexts in the Early Christian period.

Spindle whorls were made of bone in the Early Christian period, and were sometimes decorated, a feature rare at other times.[59] Many were simply made out of a piece cut from the top of a femur and drilled through – such were current at all periods from the Iron Age to the Middle Ages. They belong to four basic types (Fig. 97):

(1) *Plano-convex cut from a femur.* a very common type, current from Iron Age to later medieval times.
(2) *Plano-convex or bowl-shaped.* These were worked to this shape, and were the most common type at Cahercommaun and Lagore.
(3) *Bun-shaped.* This type occurs in the Roman period, for example at Wroxeter and Richborough, and continues into the Early Christian period, for example at Dinas Powys, Ballinderry 2 or Carraig Aille.
(4) *Flat-disc shaped.* This is more often found in other material (e.g. stone), but occurs in bone at Ballinderry 2.

Spindle whorls cannot normally be dated, though decoration is a guide to Early Christian period date.

Ironwork: weapons (Fig. 98)

While weapons are lacking from sites in Britain, with the exception of Dunadd and Buston, which have both produced spearheads, they are common from Irish sites, and the major crannogs have produced a significant range. The weapons were the sword and the spear, the axe being used only occasionally. Many axes claimed as weapons are probably woodmen's tools. The sword was probably confined to the nobility; this would account for the number found at Lagore, which was a royal dwelling.

Irish swords are either double-edged or single-edged.[60] The characteristic features of the *double-edged sword* are square shoulders, a central ridge and a V-shaped point with parallel sides. It appears to be descended from the Roman *spatha* which was itself derived from La Tène types. One of the Lagore swords has sloping shoulders – a feature of La Tène swords. A second type of double-edged sword is generally similar but has a broad, flat tang, with a blade wider near the point than at the hilt, a form which recalls Bronze Age shapes. This type is represented both at Lagore and Ballinderry 2, and there are other examples from Ireland of the same general type. A third variety of double-edged sword has a medial groove or hollow. This feature is normally Viking, but was current in Europe prior to the Viking period and a seventh- or eighth-century example from an Anglo-Saxon context is known from Walthamstow.[61] A unique sword, also from Lagore, is of bronze and has straight sides and a flat straight blade with a similarly straight guard. The blade type is that of the Anglo-Saxon *spatha*; the guard is of a type used on Viking swords.

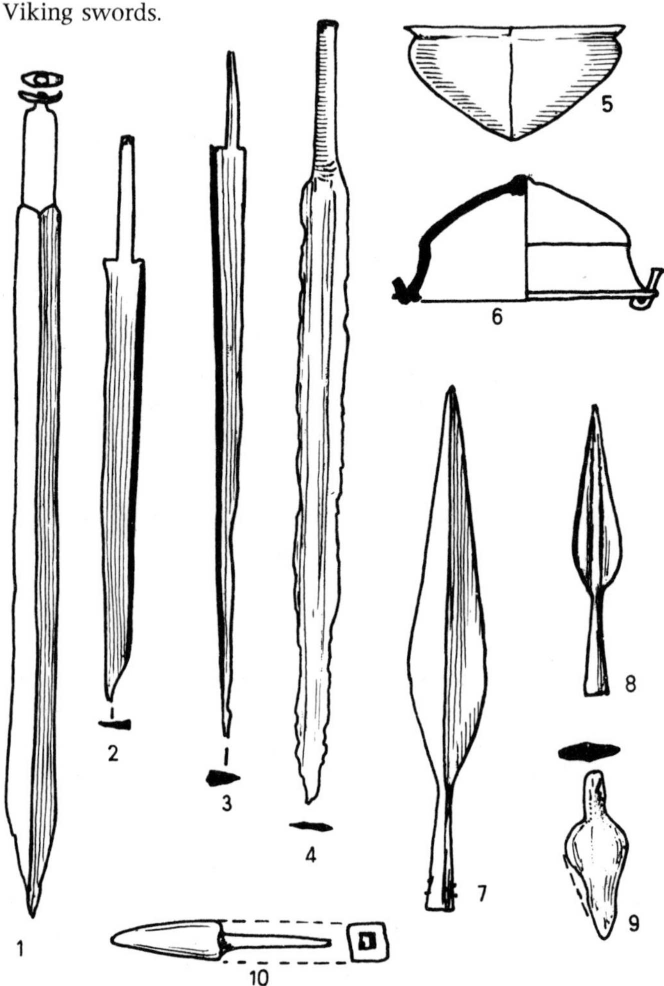

Figure 98 Irish weapons. All from Lagore except 9, from Carraig Aille. Scales: (1)–(3) $\frac{3}{16}$; (4), (7), (8) $\frac{1}{4}$. Others: $\frac{3}{8}$

The *single-edged sword* is the Germanic *scramasax* type. The Irish versions of these weapons are distinctive, and appear to derive from at least two ultimately continental prototypes. All the Irish single-edged swords are smaller and lighter than similar weapons found in the Anglo-Saxon world, but it seems quite likely that they were derived not directly from Europe but from the Anglo-Saxons.

Spears were far more common than swords in the Celtic world. What are normally called spearheads in archaeological literature are in fact javelins (throwing spears), lances (hand-held cavalry weapons) or pikes (infantry hand-held weapons). Spears or their equivalents were used for hunting as well as for war. Two basic types of spearhead occur in Irish contexts. The one is leaf-shaped, the other shouldered. Both types were already present in the European Iron Age and were current in Britain (as shown by finds from Llyn Cerrig Bach), but in later contexts the leaf-shaped spear is more typical of Romano-British weapons and the shouldered spear is more typically Germanic, occurring in Anglo-Saxon graves. The presence of one rivet is a La Tène phenomenon, the presence of two is indicative of Viking influence. One of the many spears from Lagore, of leaf-shaped type, has false damascening on the blade of the type found on Viking examples.

The arrival of the Vikings had considerable impact on the types of Irish weapons.[62] Spears from Ballinderry 1 and Lagore are clearly Irish imitations of Viking weapons with several rivets. Spear ferrules sometimes occur on Irish sites. Those from Lagore have plain tapering covers for the shafts, though a spear butt from the same site has a square section and a long tang for insertion into the shaft. Ferrules of Lagore type again have a La Tène and Roman ancestry. It may be presumed that in Britain the same types of spears were in general use. The spearhead from Buston, however, has the addition of incised grooves on the socket.

The *bow and arrow* were used, though rarely. A bow, 6 feet 1 inch long, and originally slightly longer, was found at Ballinderry 1, and can be presumed to be tenth-century. From Buston came a few arrowheads with heavy, pyramidical heads, rather like Roman *ballista* bolts, and other arrowheads were found at Carraig Aille.

The only armour apparently possessed in the Celtic west was the *shield* – round target-like shields are depicted in the *Book of Kells*[63] – and shield bosses are known from Lagore, Ballinderry 2 and Lough Faughan. The Irish shield bosses are comparatively small, and it is interesting that the Viking examples from the cemetery of Kilmainham-Islandbridge in Dublin were also small, presumably made under the influence of native tradition. The Saxon type of sugar-loaf shield boss is absent, and the Irish examples are more like the Roman.

Knives (Fig. 99). Excavation reports frequently describe knives as typically Early Christian or of 'Dinas Powys' type. In fact, knives of the Early Christian

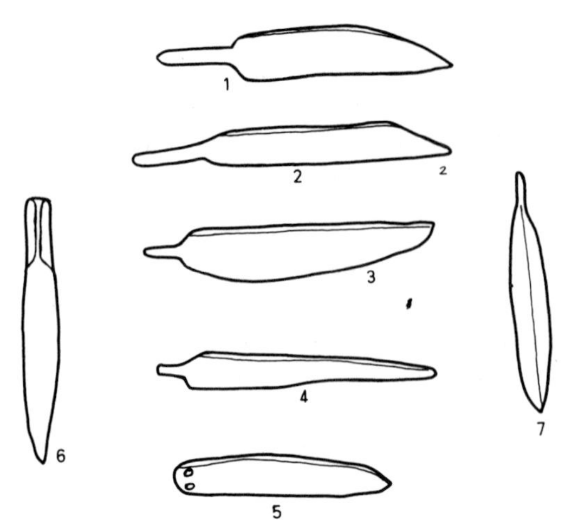

Figure 99 Iron knife types, composite drawing to show shapes. Numbered as in text

period are not particularly distinctive, and are closely related both to Roman antecedents and to medieval forms. The basic types are not peculiar to the west and north, and related forms occur in Anglo-Saxon graves and on Middle Saxon sites such as Maxey, Northamptonshire.[64] It is often difficult to assign knives to particular types as they are usually worn or badly corroded – for this reason the form of the cutting edge should not be accepted as a determinant of form, reliance being placed on the profile of the blunt side for identification. The following are the basic types:

(1) *Knife with curved, backed blade, tang and straight cutting edge.* Worn examples have a shoulder jutting from the cutting side with the rest of the blade offset to the tang. They occur in the early Iron Age, at Traprain Law during the Roman period, and throughout the Early Christian period.

(2) *Knife of scramasax form.* These have a tang, a straight cutting edge, and a back which runs parallel to the cutting edge before running at an angle to the point. The type appears in Iron Age contexts in Scotland and Ireland, later becoming common throughout post-Roman Celtic and Saxon Britain. It survives into the Middle Ages.

(3) *Knife with tang, straight back parallel to the tang, and curved cutting edge.* Some variants of this type have a straight cutting edge running at an angle to the back. This is a common Early Christian type with Roman antecedents and occurs in Anglo-Saxon and Viking contexts. It persists into the Middle Ages.

(4) *Knife with tang, straight back and cutting edge, tapering or pointed at the end.* These knives have Roman antecedents and occur throughout the Early Christian period, continuing into the Middle Ages.

(5) *Knife with flat tang and riveted handle.* The blade takes many forms. This type is current from Roman to medieval times.
(6) *Knife with socketed handle.* This type occurs in Roman Britain and on a few Early Christian sites. It does not appear to have continued into the Middle Ages.
(7) *Flame-shaped bronze knife.* This is a rare form and could be a surgical knife. It has Bronze Age and Iron Age European parallels as well as Roman. It could also have been used as a fleshing knife.

Edge tools. A variety of iron edge tools are encountered in the Early Christian period, most of which have Iron Age and Roman antecedents. The following are the main types:

(1) *Axehead, first type.* This has a small head – the socket is formed by the iron being folded over in a loop and joined to the blade. A good example comes from Buston, and another, slightly 'bearded' blade comes from Lagore.
(2) *Axehead, second type.* This is, strictly speaking, an axe-hammer, since there is a projecting head used as a hammer on the opposite side of the handle from the blade. It occurs at Lagore, Lough Faughan and Cahercommaun.

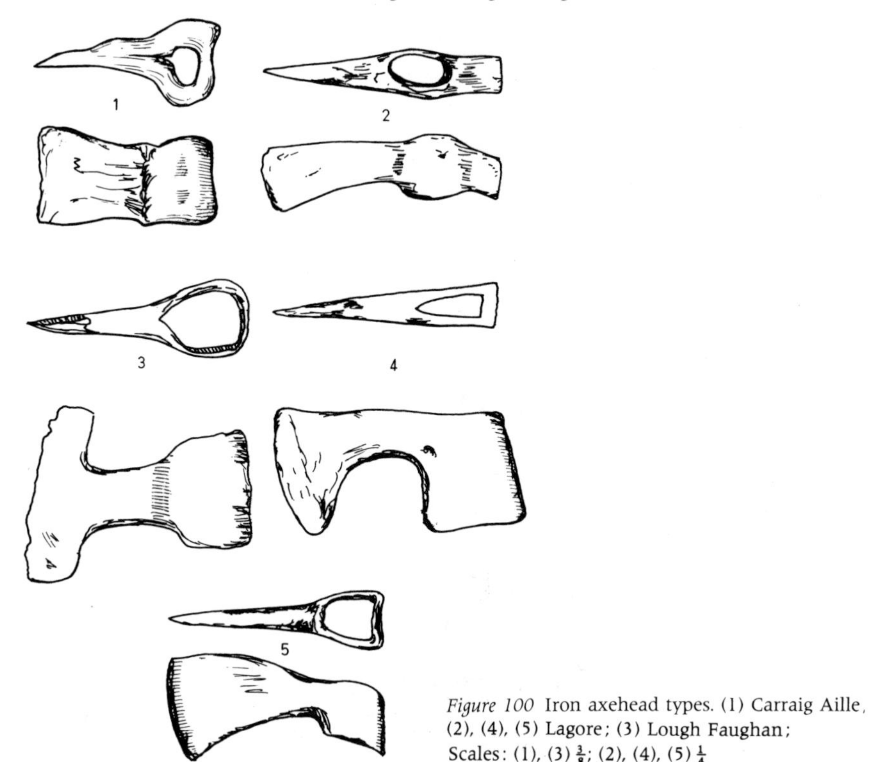

Figure 100 Iron axehead types. (1) Carraig Aille, (2), (4), (5) Lagore; (3) Lough Faughan; Scales: (1), (3) $\frac{3}{8}$; (2), (4), (5) $\frac{1}{4}$

(3) *Axehead, third type.* This is the T-shaped axe, which is ultimately of Frankish origin. It occurs widely in Viking contexts and is illustrated in the Bayeux Tapestry. It is found in England down to the middle of the fourteenth century.[65] It was used for dressing wood. It occurs at Lough Faughan.

(4) *Axehead, fourth type.* This is the 'bearded' axe which was current in Europe from Viking times through the earlier part of the Middle Ages. The socket is formed as in the first type. It is probably derived from a Roman type.

(5) *Axehead, fifth type.* This is similar to the Frankish and Anglo-Saxon *francisca*; it occurs at Lagore and is probably derived from Anglo-Saxon models.

(6) *Shears, first type.* This is a simple type with normal bend and straight-shouldered blades. Shears occur as early as the La Tène period in Europe, and this general type is undatable.

(7) *Shears, second type.* This has a loop at the junction of the arms, a feature which is first noted in pagan Scandinavian graves during the tenth century. It is recorded among the 'old' finds at Lagore, and may be a Viking period type.

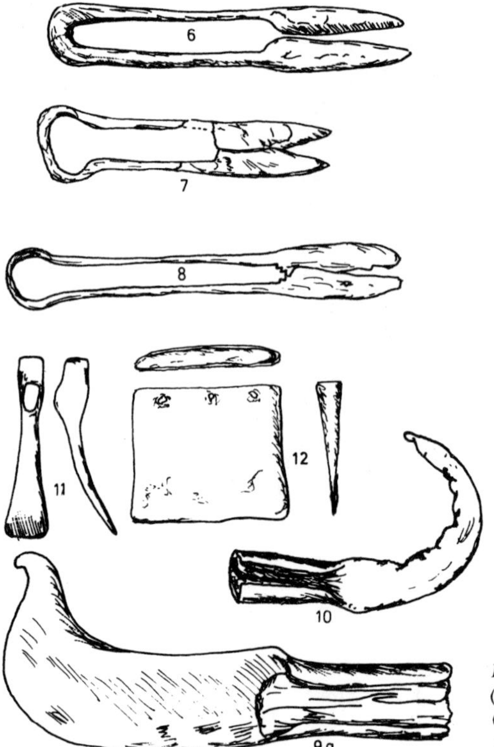

Figure 101 Iron blade tools.
(6) Carraig Aille; (7) Garranes; (8)–(10) Lagore; (11) Ballinderry 2.
Scales: (6)–(9a) $\frac{3}{8}$; (10)–(11) $\frac{1}{4}$

(8) *Shears, third type.* This has semicircular recesses at the top of the blades. It occurs very rarely in Scandinavia in pagan Viking burials of the tenth century; in England it does not occur before the thirteenth century. It is recorded among the 'old' finds at Lagore, and may be a Viking period type.

(9) *Billhook.* This is a fairly common object on Irish sites, and continues later than the Early Christian period. One from Lagore has a curled tip and ash handle.

(10) *Pruning knife or sickle.* This is related to the billhook, and is little different from its modern equivalent.

(11) *Adze.* This common wood-working tool is similar to its modern equivalent.

(12) *Spade.* These are rare, and have the blade riveted to the handle.

Horsegear is relatively rare, and is confined mainly to bits, though a number of harness fittings in bronze are known from Viking graves in the Isle of Man and Scotland.

(1) *Snaffle bit, first type.* This is represented only at Lagore. It is a two-piece bit and has plate cheekpieces with expanded terminals. The general type is represented from the grave at Hintschingen, Baden, dated to the seventh century.[66]

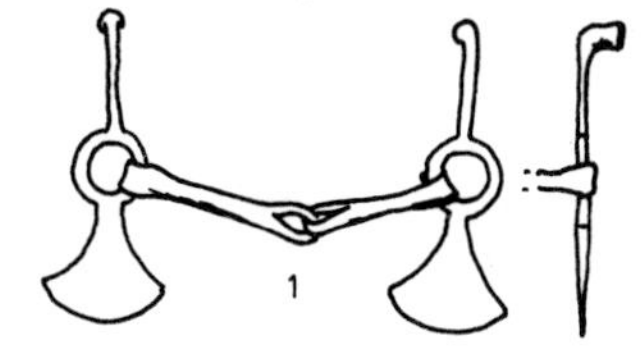

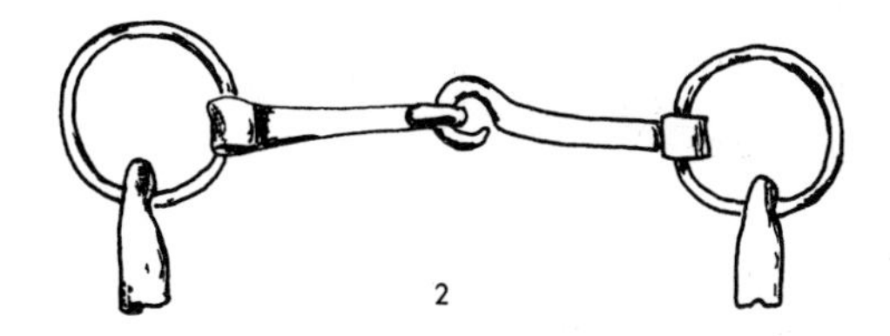

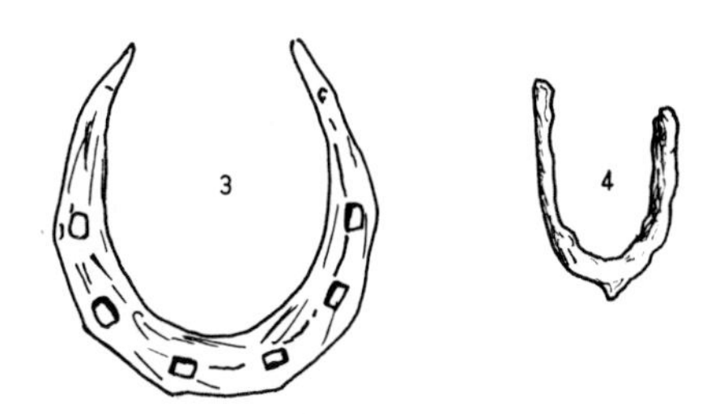

Figure 102 Iron horsegear, Types 1–4. (1)–(3) Lagore; (4) Ballinderry Crannog 1. Scales: (1) $\frac{1}{4}$; (2)–(3) $\frac{3}{8}$; (4) $\frac{1}{4}$

(2) *Snaffle bit, second type.* This occurs at Carraig Aille I and has simple ring cheekpieces. It is a standard type which continued throughout the Middle Ages. It also occurred at Lagore, and at the Mote of Mark.

(3) *Prick spur.* This is represented only by one badly preserved example from Ballinderry 1. The spur, current in Europe among the Carolingians, was probably introduced to Britain by the Vikings, though there are La Tène and Roman examples.

(4) *Horseshoe.* There is some doubt as to the antiquity of the horseshoe from Lagore, and horseshoes do not occur stratified on any other site of the Early Christian period in the Celtic area. The type of shoe represented

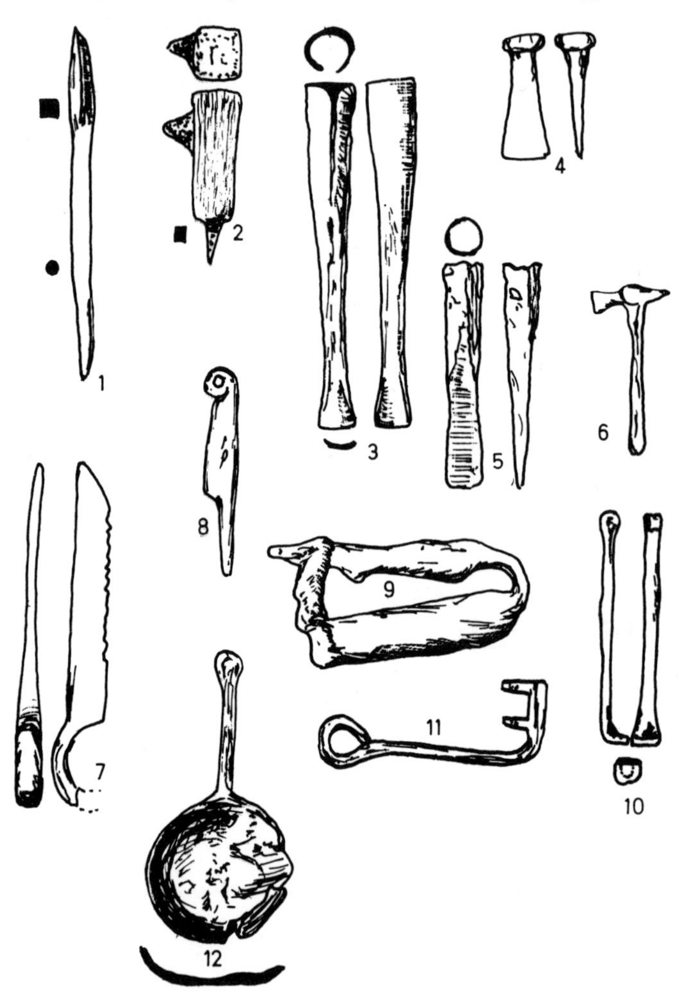

Figure 103 Miscellaneous iron tools. (1), (3)–(7), (11) Lagore; (2), (8)–(10), (12) Garryduff. Scales: (1), (3)–(7) $\frac{1}{4}$; (11) $\frac{3}{8}$. Others about $\frac{3}{8}$

at Lagore, however, is not a medieval type, but has a slightly sinuous outline reminiscent of the type of shoe current in England in the twelfth century, with square nail holes and seemingly without calkins. Horseshoes are known from Roman contexts (e.g. Maiden Castle) and there is documentary evidence for them in Anglo-Saxon England; they may possibly be Early Christian at Lagore.

Metal- and wood-working tools are fairly common types of iron objects. The axes and adzes listed above were also used for wood working. The main types are as follows:

(1) *Awl.* This simple object occurs frequently in a wide variety of forms.
(2) *Anvil.* A small anvil with a spike for setting it in a wooden block and a projection on the side was found at Garryduff. It was probably for ornamental metal working.

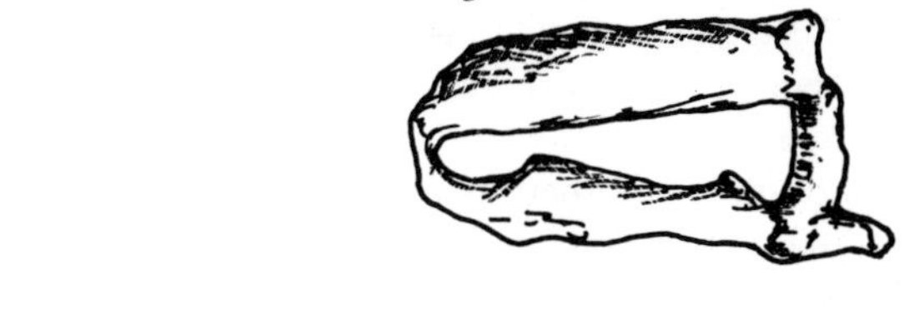

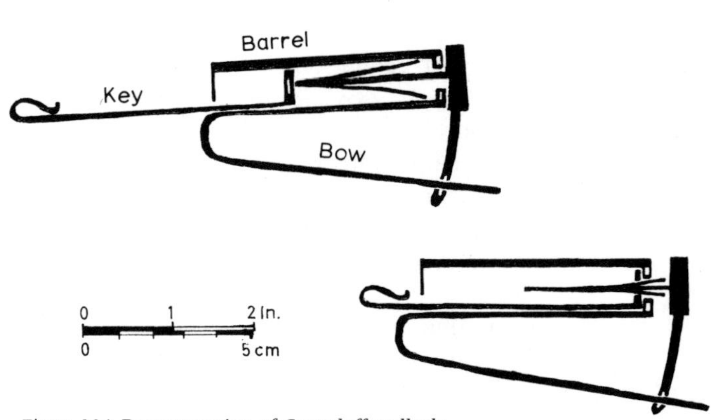

Figure 104 Reconstruction of Garryduff padlock

(3) *Gouge.* There are two basic types, one large and socketed, meant to be used with a hammer, and one smaller, for use by hand. They occur on a number of sites, including Lagore and Cahercommaun.
(4) *Punch or wedge.* These occur at Carraig Aille and Lagore.
(5) *Chisel.* A socketed chisel was found at Lagore.
(6) *Metalsmith's hammer.* Two badly preserved objects from Garryduff have been tentatively identified as such.
(7) *Saw.* The round-handled type is relatively rare: one example is known

from the 'old' finds at Lagore. The smaller, Irish varieties are more common.

(8) *Dividers.* This term has been given to an object of uncertain function which occurs as single legs, and looks like a knife with a hole at one end and a sharp projection at the other. They occur at Garryduff, Cahercommaun and Oldcourt.

Miscellaneous ironwork, mainly domestic. There are a number of objects which do not readily fall into the above classes, mostly connected with the home:

(9) *Barrel padlock* (Fig. 104). These were used in the Roman period and continued until at least the sixteenth century. Examples (or parts of them) have been found at Garryduff, Cahercommaun, Lagore and Buston. Keys for such padlocks are common. The Garryduff padlock was dissected, and it was found that the barrel and bow were all of one piece. The Buston spring, however, seems to have had the bow attached.

(10) *Barrel padlock key.* A number of these have been found, but they seem to have been made more frequently of bronze than iron. Eight iron keys, however, come from Garryduff, and there is another possible example from Cahercommaun. The type is standard, consisting of a flat bar of metal bent over into a right angle with a normally rectangular hole.

(11) *Tumbler lock key.* The only example known is from Lagore. This is a Roman type of padlock.

(12) *Ladle.* Shallow ladles somewhat reminiscent of Roman *paterae* were found at Garryduff and Ballinderry 2, while similar objects have come from Lagore and Strokestown.

(13) *Tether.* These are sometimes found with chains attached. They consist of hinged shackles of various forms and sizes. They are probably animal tethers, though the larger examples may be for prisoners. The general type occurs in the early Iron Age (e.g. at Llyn Cerrig Bach), as well as post 1300.

(14) *Stylus.* This was used for writing on wax tablets and also probably for sketching designs on other materials such as bone. They are common on ecclesiastical sites, but occur also in secular contexts, for example, the Mote of Mark, and usually have an expanded, flat head.

(15) *Trident.* This occurs at Lagore and may have been used in fishing.

(16) *Bucket handle.* Bucket handles, characteristically of a twisted rod of iron, seem to be derived from Roman antecedents. They occur at Lagore and elsewhere.

(17) *Door hinge.* The pivot door hinge seems to have been the type used in the Early Christian period. One was found at Cahercommaun.

(18) *Tongs.* These were used mainly for lifting crucibles from hearths, and accordingly are found on most Irish Early Christian period sites. They may have also been used for a variety of other purposes.

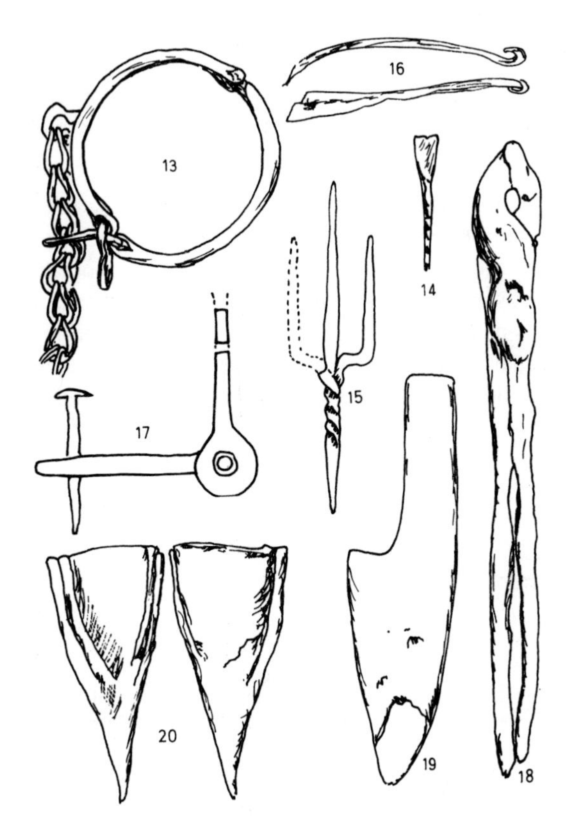

Figure 105 Miscellaneous ironwork. (13), (15), (19), (20) Lagore; (18) Garranes; (14) Carraig Aille; (16), (17) Cahercommaun. Scales: (13) $\frac{1}{4}$; (14), (15), (18) $\frac{3}{8}$; (19), (20) $\frac{3}{16}$; (16) $\frac{3}{8}$

(19) *Plough coulter.* The coulter of the Early Christian period was heavy and sharply angled, and its ancestry is probably to be sought in the Romano-British coulter, which is related to Iron Age types. There is a general similarity between the Irish coulters, which are represented at Lagore and Ballinderry 1, and those of the Germanic Migration Period, which are in turn descended from the Iron Age type current on mainland Europe. Probably the plough coulter reached the west from the Anglo-Saxon world. Medieval coulters are very similar. The Irish coulters seem to have been used in ploughs with a heavy team, possibly on wet ground.[67]

(20) *Ploughshare.* These are found either with or without reinforcements at the sides, and occur at Lagore and Leacanabuaile. The type without reinforcements is known from La Tène contexts.

Objects of types not current in the Middle Ages (Fig. 106)

Most of the iron objects from Early Christian period sites are of types which remained current in later times. A few objects, however, are more distinctive.

(1) *Iron slotted object.* This has a flat expanded head with an elongated slot. It seems to be peculiarly Irish – where it occurs in Britain it is evidence for Irish contact, as for example at Dunadd or Gwithian. Various suggestions have been put forward as to its use: that it was used as a bodkin in weaving some coarse substance such as rush matting;[68] that it was a type of augur;[69] that it was a strike-a-light.[70] None of these explanations seems totally satisfactory. The objects occur at Lagore, Cahercommaun, Lough Faughan, Carraig Aille II, Uisneach and other sites, in contexts down to the tenth century.

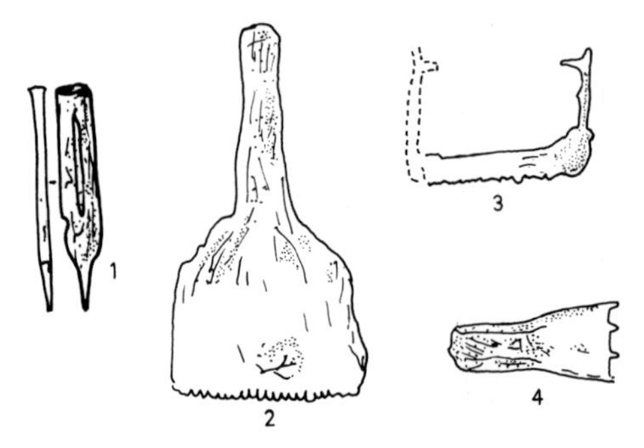

Figure 106 Iron objects of Irish types. (1) Lagore; (2) Dunadd; (3) Garryduff; (4) Cahercommaun. Scale: $\frac{1}{4}$

(2) *Small single-handled saw.* This object occurs at Dunadd and Garryduff, and seems to be peculiar to the Early Christian period. The tang was set in wood and the edge was possibly used for cutting wire.

(3) *Two-handled saw.* Strictly speaking this is a one-handled saw, since the two handles connected a wooden cross-piece, producing an effect rather like a modern fretsaw. The Early Christian saw, however, could not be adjusted for tension. Examples of this type occur at Garryduff and Carraig Aille.

(4) *Socketed pronged object.* This implement has a socketed blade with three or four sharp teeth. These implements tend to be small, and have been found at, for example, Lagore, Garryduff, Dunadd, Cahercommaun and Ballinderry 1. They belong to a general class which occurs in simpler form in the Roman period (for example at Vertault). The Migration Period examples are usually of bronze and more elaborate than the Irish – they also occur in Frisia in the eighth and ninth centuries AD.[71] Their function is unknown though the Roman examples might have been used for scoring tiles.[72]

12 Personal adornment

The Early Christian Celtic peoples, like most barbarian societies, often adorned themselves richly with jewellery and other dress accessories. Most of the adornments worn by the Celts were functional as well as beautiful – penannular brooches, different classes of pins, buckles and studs all served to fasten clothing. Far less common are purely ornamental items of dress, such as necklaces of beads or grass or shale bracelets.

Clothes and weaving

Naturally very little cloth has survived from the period, although spindle whorls from most sites show that spinning and presumably weaving was widespread. Some cloth has been preserved from Ballinderry 2 crannog, showing that tabby weaving was customary in sixth-century Ireland – a type of weaving which had been known in Europe since the Bronze Age. From Lagore the evidence is more abundant and shows that although tabby weaving was predominant other techniques were known. Some diagonal weaving was carried out, and at a very early stage tablet weaving. Tablet weaving was used for producing braid and occurs as early as the Bronze Age in Europe, after which it appears to have died out, to be reintroduced to northern Europe in the Roman Iron Age. Tablet weaving was widespread among the Germanic peoples of the Migration Period, and since evidence for it occurs in Anglo-Saxon graves, it is possible that it came to Ireland by way of Anglo-Saxon England.[1]

Two forms of hand distaffs are known from Ireland, one type represented at Lough Faughan crannog, the other at Lagore and Ballinderry 2 where they were originally described as 'spindles'. It would not be possible, however, to attach spindle whorls to the Lagore and Ballinderry distaffs. Spindle whorls were used on the more normal waist or under-arm distaff. The hand distaff is essentially a Greek or Roman type; outside Ireland it is known from ninth-century Italy, but was not widespread.[2]

Madder appears to have been used for dyeing one piece of cloth from Lagore, while at Inishkea North in Co. Mayo a minor industry seems to have centred round the extraction of dye from the *purpura* shell. Literary references imply that blackberry juice was also used as a dye.

Clothing has to be reconstructed from representations on the high crosses and from literary sources. The garments of the upper classes in Ireland, at least in earlier times, seem to have comprised a linen tunic (*leine*) and a woollen cloak (*brat*) which was worn over it and fastened with a pin or brooch at the breast. While the *brat* was usually wrapped round the body several times, on occasions it was allowed to drag behind. A belt of wool or leather was worn with the *leine*. The *brat* appears to have been coloured; it was usually of one colour but sometimes of several. The *leine* was normally white, but usually had an ornamented border. In the Viking period a tunic and breeches seem to have been worn in Ireland by the lower social orders, and in this period, too, silk seems to have made its appearance.[3]

Leatherwork

Very little leatherwork has survived and most of it is very fragmentary and therefore unidentifiable. Part of a leather jerkin, as yet unpublished, was found at Loch Glashan crannog in Argyll, but most of the other leatherwork is footwear. The finds from Lagore include a wooden last on which the shoes were modelled.

Two classes of shoes were recognized at Ballinderry 2 (Fig. 107). The first has a decorated tongue made in one piece, and round the front of the shoe is a semicircular slit with holes for laces. The tongue is decorated with interlace and a scroll and there is incised ornament on the front. This type does not occur at Lagore and is presumably datable to the sixth century. The second class of Ballinderry shoe has no slit at the sides, but instead a longitudinal join from the toe to the tongue along which were lace holes. This type is also represented at Lagore, and in the *Book of Kells* the Matthew evangelist figure is wearing shoes of this type. It was not possible to relate uppers to soles at Ballinderry 2, but the problem was solved by finds from Lissue where it could be seen that the shoes were made in three pieces, an upper (missing at Lissue), an insole and an outsole. The edges of the insole and outer sole of the Lissue shoe are folded together inwards and sewn with close stitches to the folded-in edge of the upper (Fig. 107). A welt seems to have been used to join upper and sole. A boot of similar type is known from Craigywarren crannog.

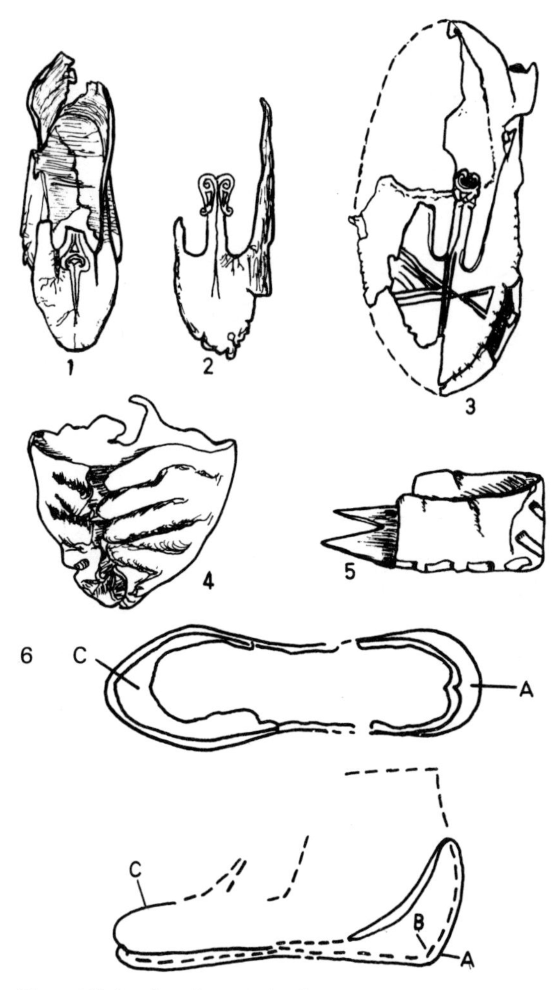

Figure 107 Leather shoes, Ireland. (1)–(2) Craigywarren crannog; (3) Ballinderry crannog No. 2; (4)–(5) Lagore crannog; (6) Reconstruction of Lissue shoe; (a) outer sole; (b) inner sole; (c) upper. Scales: (1)–(2) About $\frac{3}{16}$; (3) $\frac{1}{4}$; (4)–(5) $\frac{3}{8}$; (6) About $\frac{1}{4}$

Hair style

Hair was worn long in the Early Christian period by both men and women. Clerics are depicted in sculpture and manuscripts as cleanshaven, while laymen have drooping moustaches reminiscent of their La Tène predecessors and fork pointed beards, though they could also be cleanshaven. Hairstyles were often elaborate, particularly by the end of the period, as shown by the styles represented on the eleventh-century *Breac Maodhóg*. Dye was sometimes used.[4] *Mirrors* were used, and a mirror handle comes from Inishkea North, Co. Mayo.

Bone combs were one of the chief products of the bone industry, were current throughout the Early Christian period and occur on most sites (Fig. 108). As with many of the other type-fossils of the Celtic west the composite bone comb (which is the commonest type) has an origin in the Romano-British period, ancestral types occurring at the Jewry Wall, Leicester,[5] in the third century and slightly later at Wroxeter,[6] Richborough[7] and Lydney.[8] Several have ring-and-dot decoration, a type of ornament used not only in the

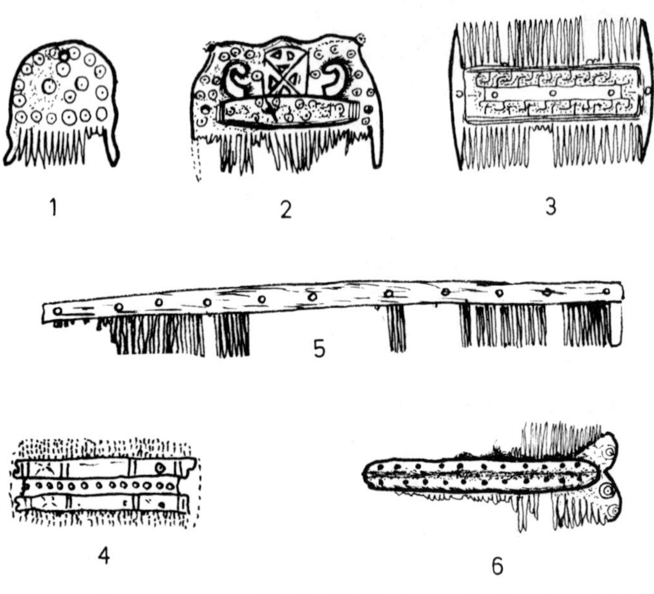

Figure 108 Bone comb types, (1), (3), (4), (5), Lagore, (2) Dun Cuier, (6) Jarlshof. Scale: $\frac{3}{8}$

Celtic west but also on Anglo-Saxon combs of the pagan period, but the general type is somewhat divergent in that the central rib of the Roman combs had longitudinal grooves. The reason why composite bone combs predominate is probably to be found in the nature of the material – most are double-sided and are thus difficult to make out of a single piece of bone. The obvious alternative would be wood, but boxwood, the only variety suitable for cutting fine teeth, does not appear to have been used after the Roman period,[9] possibly because of its scarcity. A wooden comb of unknown but presumably Roman Iron Age date is known from a crannog at Ledaig, Argyll,[10] but otherwise wooden combs are unknown from non-Roman sites. Bone was a cheap substitute for ivory, the most suitable material for combs.

The reason for their abundance in the Early Christian period may be in part explained by the general interest shown by the barbarians in the care of the hair and it is possible that combing and hair cutting were part of some inauguration ritual in the pagan world which was adopted later by Christians. Certainly combs have a liturgical function in the early Church, as shown by that from St Cuthbert's coffin.[11] Miniature combs from pagan Saxon graves show that they had a symbolic significance to the Teutonic peoples,[12] and gifts of combs are not unknown – in the late Middle Ages combs were exchanged as love tokens and a wooden comb used for this purpose is known from Caerlaverock Castle, Dumfriesshire.[13]

It is unlikely that the double-edged combs were worn in the hair, though references in the *Mabinogion* imply that some combs were worn in this way.[14] The double-sided comb was retained, despite the fact that the original reason for having two sides – that one side could have fine teeth and the other coarse – was lost in the Early Christian period when the art of cutting finer teeth was lost and the teeth on both sides were of moderate coarseness.

Combs can be classified into the following main types (Fig. 108):

(1) *Single-edged comb of simple type with high curved back.* This type of comb is common on Anglo-Saxon cemetery sites, miniature versions occurring at Abingdon, Berks.[15] It is found at Lagore, but is absent from later sites, implying a currency up to the seventh century but not much later.

(2) *Single-edged composite comb with ornamental back.* The finest example of this class comes from Dun Cuier, Barra, where the head assumes a zoomorphic form reminiscent of confronted beasts on Germanic buckles. The comb is of openwork design and may be inspired either by a Germanic predecessor or a late Roman model. A characteristic feature of combs of this type is the medial plate which is riveted along each side but does not extend to the ends of the comb. Other examples tend to have backs of tribolate form, and occur at Lagore and Carraig Aille. The first occurrence of the type is not known but it probably continues in the seventh or eighth centuries at least.

(3) *Double-edged composite comb with straight sides.* This is the most common Early Christian period type and appears to have been current until the Viking period.

(4) *Double-sided comb with two braces.* This type of comb is identical to No. 3 except that it has two rather than one medial plate on each side. It appears to be a Viking period type, and occurs at Jarlshof.

(5) *Single-sided long comb with humped back.* This is a common Viking type of comb, current in the twelfth century and later. It appears at Jarlshof.

(6) *Comb with medial plates with double row of rivets.* This is a late Viking type, current at Jarlshof.

(7) *Handled one-sided comb.* This is a Viking period type.

Toilet articles

Another class of bone toilet article is a type of pin with an expanded, curved point similar to nail cleaners or Roman ear scoops. Examples from Lagore are very ornate, with animal or human heads in two cases. They seem to be derived from Roman antecedents.

Dress fasteners

A study of the different forms of dress fastener current in the Early Christian period is of particular archaeological value. The great diversity of brooch and pin types, and their relative abundance compared with other classes of material culture, make them useful as chronological indicators. They are difficult, however, to date precisely, some particular pin types being very long lived. Brooches were more subject to fashion, and while basic forms may have had a long currency, decorative schemes were short lived. It should not be forgotten that many of the brooches are important works of art in their own right. The Tara, Kilmainham, or Hunterston Brooches, for example, are very well known, and because of their superb artistry have tended in the past to be viewed in isolation. Yet, remarkable though they are, they belong to a long tradition of penannular brooches which stretches back to the early Iron Age, and which also embraces many less well-known but fine artistic achievements.

Perhaps the most notable feature of the dress fasteners is the extent to which they are modelled on late Roman forms. While the penannular brooches and various classes of ringed and ring-headed pins originated in the Iron Age, the immediate inspiration was the prototypes of Romano-British date, just as the artistic motifs that decorate other classes of fifth- and sixth-century metalwork were greatly inspired by designs current in the late Roman Empire, particularly among the native population.[16] To some extent a conscious revival of native craftsmanship and art can be seen in the dress fasteners: a revival not of the old traditions of the pre-Roman Iron Age but of schools of minor craftsmanship within Roman Britain itself. It was in northern Britain that this revival took place in the fourth and fifth centuries, whence it was transmitted to Ireland, though there Roman imports may have contributed to its early development. Anglo-Saxon metalwork played an important part in its subsequent growth, contributing both new forms and decorative techniques and language: the Moylough Belt Shrine belongs to a world far removed from native Celtic tradition.

Penannular brooches

The most common type of dress ornament in the Early Christian period was the penannular brooch. Basically this is a hoop of metal with two confronted terminals and a pin which runs along the hoop. Some confusion exists over the nomenclature for different types of dress fastener which are related to the penannular tradition, and for this reason some definition of the terms used in this book is necessary. A *pseudo-penannular brooch* is one in which the terminals of the hoop are joined together, either by a septum, or by septa, or simply by casting plate terminals in one expansion of the ring, the former penannular shape being preserved through skeuomorphism in the decorative scheme. A *ring brooch* is a penannular or pseudo-penannular brooch in which the hoop's diameter is less than a third of the length of the pin – normally the hoop has a diameter not greater than 1½ inches. A *loose ringed pin* is one in which the hoop is a simple ring without terminals or terminal skeuomorphs, and in which the length of the pin is at least three times the diameter of the ring. An *annular brooch* (which is not a type current in the Early Christian Celtic areas) is a simple hoop or ring with a pin which is not more than twice the diameter of the ring in length. A *ring-headed pin* is one which has a fixed ring, cast in one with the shank. In any classification of the brooches the important element is the terminals, though the form of the pin attachment is also significant.

The simplest forms of penannular brooches developed in Britain about the third century BC out of the older Hallstatt-derived series of ring-headed pins.[17] Elsewhere in Iron Age Europe the penannular brooch in variant forms can be found in Iberia and the north. During the Roman occupation of Britain it continued to survive alongside other, more ornate, forms of fibula, a characteristic product of native craftsmanship and wear. They appear to have had some appeal to the Roman army and are notably frequent on Roman military sites, particularly those associated with auxiliaries.[18]

In the Early Christian period there was a marked revival of the popularity of the type. This revival is particularly noteworthy in the Highland Zone, though penannular brooches also occur in some numbers in pagan Saxon contexts, hinting at a British substratum in the population. One characteristic type of Anglo-Saxon brooch, the Quoit Brooch, produced in Kent, is more or less an elaboration of the traditional type of penannular.[19] The forms current in the fifth and sixth centuries were derived from Roman and pre-Roman ancestors and generally were of 'zoomorphic' type, that is, with zoomorphic terminals, often stylized beyond recognition. Ornament on the terminals was limited, but during the sixth century some more elaborately decorated types began to appear, and these brooches, together with related types with millefiori inlay, continued into the seventh. The period from the end of the sixth century is also characterized by the increasing tendency to flatten the terminals into expanded flanges, and the majority of the ornate eighth-century brooches are derived from this type. While the true penannular remained current in Britain, the pseudo-penannular evolved in Ireland. First the terminals were bridged, and later they became solid, though the ornamentation continued to reflect the penannular origin.

Both simple and more ornate forms remained current until the time of the Viking invasions. New types enjoyed a currency in the Viking period, when

Viking women regarded 'foreign' (frequently penannular) brooches as status symbols. The more ornate forms of penannular and pseudo-penannular brooches do not seem to have outlived the Viking period, the circular brooch being preferred in the Middle Ages.[20]

The chronology of penannular brooches can only be established in relative terms. Almost all the more ornate examples are stray finds or come from Viking period burials and are frequently much earlier than the date of burial. Most of the earlier, simpler types are either without association, or not associated with closely datable material. While typology is a useful clue to sequence it can be taken only as a rough guide to date, usually within a horizon of about a century. Except in the case of the very ornate examples, such as the Tara Brooch, art historical considerations are of limited value since the extent of the ornamentation is too restricted to permit close comparison. Nevertheless, attempts have been made to date brooches within very limited brackets.

Representations in Irish sculpture suggest that the brooches were worn with the pin pointing upwards, and this would seem to be confirmed by the decorative schemes on some of the more ornate brooches.[21] Some of the later ornate examples were almost certainly ecclesiastical and were used for fastening chasubles, but the simpler brooches and probably many of the ornate examples were worn by laity. The *Senchas Mhor*, a collection of Irish law tracts, related the wearing of brooches to rank:

> (When they are in fosterage) there must be brooches of gold having crystal inserted in them, with the sons of the king of Erin and of the king of a province, and brooches of silver with the sons of the king of a territory; or the sons of each king is to have a similar brooch as to material, but that the ornamentation of all these should appear in that brooch.
>
> (*Ancient Laws of Ireland*, II, 146–7)[22]

The typology of penannular brooches (Figs 109–13)

The scheme normally followed in classifying penannular brooches down to the end of the sixth century is that set out by Fowler in two papers.[23] This scheme uses an alphabetical system of classification, Classes A and B being Iron Age types, Class I being the latest of the Early Christian. Within the broad classes, various sub-classes are indicated by arabic numerals. This scheme has been followed below, with certain modifications where the larger classes have seemed capable of further subdivision, and slight rearrangement of the sequence has thus been necessary. As the Fowler scheme was devised to cover essentially the fifth and sixth centuries, it has been extended to include some later types of brooches.[24]

(1) *Fowler A5*. This type has thistle-like knob terminals and it is related to Romano-British brooches. It has a long survival but is relatively rare. It was probably still current in the Viking period.

(2) *Fowler B3*. The terminals on this type are bent outwards into the form of birds' heads. The type originates in the Romano-British brooches of Fowler's Type B. In Ireland the type may have evolved independently from 'omega' brooches, but is more likely to be derived from Welsh models and was subject to Anglo-Saxon influence. It does not appear to outlive the fifth to sixth centuries.

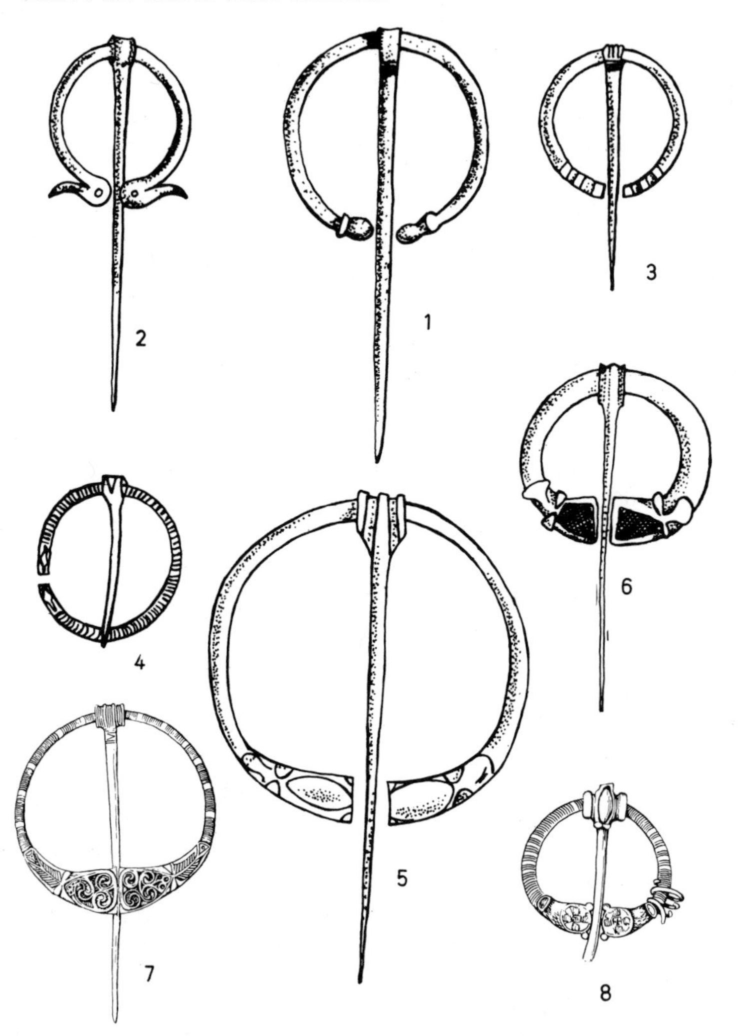

Figure 109 Penannular brooches types 1–8. (1) Lagore; (2) Ballyfallon; (3) Ballycatteen; (4) Birdoswald; (5) Ardagh; (6), (7), (8) Ireland, unprovenanced. Scale: $\frac{3}{4}$

(3) *Fowler D7.* The terminals on this type consist of three ribs separated by deep, squared grooves. The type is related to the Romano-British D6 and probably developed at the end of the fourth century in England, later spreading to the west. It probably had a long life, current at least until the seventh century. From Castlehaven Fort in Kirkcudbrightshire there is an example which is possibly as late as the Viking period.

(4) *Fowler E.* A small brooch with zoomorphic terminals on which the features of the animal's head are all discernible. This type is probably derived from Fowler D4 and D5 brooches which were current in the first to second centuries. The type became popular in the mid fourth century, and occurs on Roman military sites. The type may have been acquired by Irish raiders in the area of Hadrian's Wall. True E brooches appear to be confined to the fourth to fifth centuries; the more devolved type (Fowler E1), in which the delimiting features are less distinct, were current in the sixth century and possibly later.

(5) *Fowler F.*[25] This is a large zoomorphic brooch which is particularly common in the fifth to sixth centuries. The zoomorphism on the early examples is already stylized, and later the animal heads are virtually unrecognizable. The type probably evolved out of Type E in the late fourth century and spread to Ireland from Britain, where the Irish Type F has larger terminals of flatter shape with a more projecting ovoid tail. The basic Type F is probably mainly fifth-century.

(6) *Fowler F1.* This evolved early out of Type F, and is distinguished by having the terminals inlaid with a blob of enamel, usually red. It is probably fifth-century in date.

(7) *Fowler F2.* This is related to Type F and has the entire terminal richly ornamented with champlevé enamel and sometimes millefiori. It is basically an Irish type, though a lead die found at Dinas Powys in Glamorgan suggests that some were made thereabouts. There is also one from Mull. The earliest are probably mid- to late fifth-century, but they continue into the sixth.

(8) *Fowler F3.* In these brooches the general tradition of F brooches is elaborated into a more specialist form in which the terminals are rounded, acquire rounded, projecting 'eyes' and are inlaid with enamel or millefiori. There is a tendency on these brooches for the pin to become longer, and the type is almost exclusively Irish. It is probably a sixth- to seventh-century form.

(9) *Fowler F3* (variant). This type is similar in form to (8) above but lacks the inlay and is more zoomorphic. In a few cases the eyes alone may have inlay.

(10) *Fowler G.*[26] In these brooches the terminal is squared or faceted, with a central dot or diamond containing four dots. The type is probably of Roman origin, stemming from Fowler's Class D series, and may have

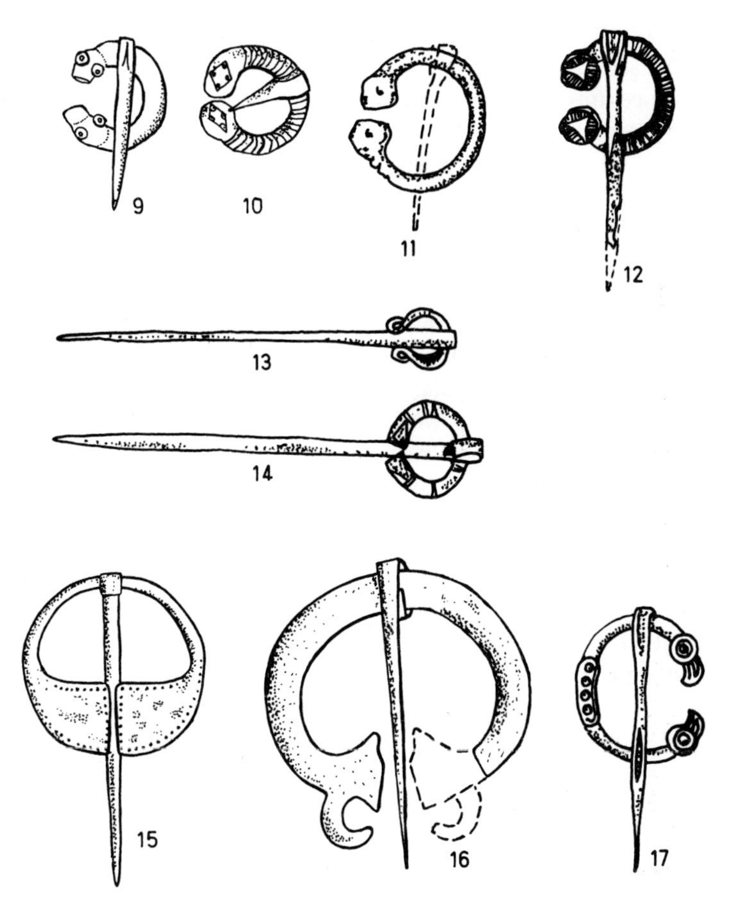

Figure 110 Penannular brooches, Types 9–17. (9) Glenluce; (10) Sleaford; (11), (12) Luce Sands; (13), (14), (15) Lagore; (16) Richborough; (17) Antrim, unprovenanced. Scale: $\frac{3}{4}$

developed in the Midlands. A feature of many of the brooches is the silvering or tinning that they show. Dating is uncertain: the earliest are Romano-British, the latest are probably of the eighth to ninth century. An early series (fourth- to sixth-century), and a late series (eighth- to ninth-century), have been suggested, but there is no reason to suppose that the type was totally obsolete for upwards of two centuries. An unusual silver example is that from the ninth-century Anglo-Saxon hoard from Trewhiddle, Cornwall. A characteristic of many is grooving on the hoop.

(11) *Fowler H2.* This has round, flattened terminals, and a Romano-British origin. Probably because of its simplicity it had a long life, extending into the seventh century and possibly later.

(12) *Fowler H3.* In this type the round terminal is decorated, sometimes with enamel, sometimes with incised linear patterns. It is basically a sixth- to seventh-century type. In many cases the brooch is small with a long pin, making it more a ring brooch than the usual penannular.

(13) *Fowler B.* This is a simple type of brooch with curled-over terminals. It is the Iron Age 'Belgic' type, and is often found in Saxon contexts. It is represented at Lagore.

(14) *Fowler H/F.* This type marks the transition from F to Type H following. It has flattened expanded terminals together with some features of true zoomorphic brooches, notably the flaring tail and sometimes the snout of Type F. It is so far only known from Ireland and is probably contemporary with the more regular Type F brooches in Britain.

(15) *Fowler H.* On brooches of this type the terminal is extended and flat, and is in the form of a curved triangle. There is often an internal groove or line following the edge. This type is important, due to its obvious relationship to the later elaborate brooches including those of 'Tara' type. Fowler has suggested that it developed out of the Scots Aa brooch in the Roman period and was current from the fifth to the eighth centuries.[27] In origin it certainly appears to be a British, rather than an Irish type, but this does not necessarily preclude the possibility of its development out of Type H/F or the common prototype, Type F. In this connection a true penannular from Ballinderry 1, Co. Westmeath, which Fowler has placed in her Class H/F, might be seen as the transitional stage between Types F and H, though the Ballinderry brooch is exceptionally late and remains an anomaly. The only example that is almost certainly late fifth- or early sixth-century is that from Garranes, Co. Cork, which differs from the others known in that the terminals are joined to form a plate, making it a pseudo-penannular brooch.[28] In this respect it belongs rather to a separate series of brooches and is of little value for dating. Most Type H brooches come from sites producing E Ware (i.e. occupied *c.* 525/550–700 or slightly later), and the evidence from Norrie's Law, Fife, would almost certainly suggest that it was current in the seventh century. While not excluding the possibility that it was in use in the fifth century, a sixth- to seventh-century date is here preferred.

(16) *Fowler H4.* A miscellaneous class of brooches related to Class H, with terminals flattened inwards or outwards and frequently with hooks or crescentic projections.

(17) *Fowler B3.* The type was distinguished by Fowler as belonging to her B3 class, because of the birds' head terminals. The birds' heads are confronted and show some affinities to Type H3 brooches with rounded terminals. The type is relatively rare: there is one from Lagore and another from Co. Antrim. The Antrim brooch shows some 'Pictish' features, and it may in fact be a Pictish product – it links the Lagore

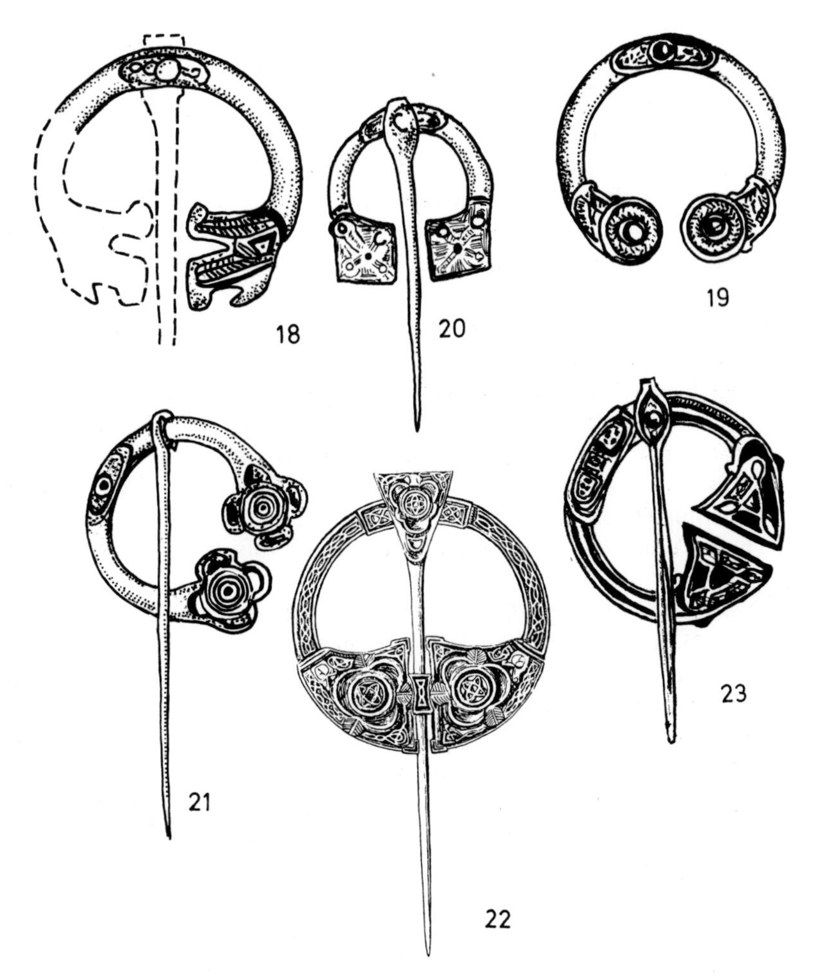

Figure 111 Penannular brooches, Types 18–23. (18) Freswick; (19) Croy, Inverness; (20) St Ninian's Isle; (21) Machrin's, Colonsay; (22) Lagore. Scale $\frac{3}{4}$

brooch with a more developed brooch known only from a mould from Birsay, which has parrot-like birds and is undoubtedly Pictish work of the late seventh or eighth century.[29] As a group, the brooches like (17) link B3 with the brooches like (18) and provide a possible ancestry for dragon brooches. The inspiration was probably Anglo-Saxon.

(18) *Fowler H5.* In this class of brooch the terminals are elaborated into facing dragon heads. The most famous example is the St Ninian's Isle brooch No. 28, but a slightly different example was found in a twelfth-century context at Freswick, Caithness. They date from the eighth or ninth century.

(19) *Fowler H3*. This is an elaboration of (12) above. It is distinguished by having a round terminal, frequently with a central inlay or concentric decoration. An example from Kildonan, Argyll, is probably of seventh-century workmanship, and there is another from the Croy hoard, Inverness.[30] Another fragment is known from a Viking grave in the Hebrides. The type is Pictish and dates from the eighth to ninth centuries.

(20) *Fowler H5*. This is represented only in the St Ninian's Isle hoard.[31] It is characterized by a flattened terminal of square shape and is otherwise similar to (19).

(21) *Fowler H3*. Brooches of this type have round terminals related to (19), with the addition of lateral projections or cusps. The most usual type has three cusps with a pseudo-cusp formed by a curved line separating the terminal from the ring. The ring is frequently decorated with an ornamental panel with curved ends, and the pin is of lentoid head type. This type of brooch is Pictish and is best exemplified by finds from St Ninian's Isle, Rogart and Kilmainham.[32] It dates from the eighth to ninth centuries. Moulds for brooches of this type are known from Birsay.[33]

(22) *Fowler H5*. This type of brooch employs the cusped form of the terminal of (21) as the main decorative element on expanded, flattened terminals of Type H derivative brooches. Brooches of this type may be true penannulars (like the North Gate (Canterbury) Brooch)[34] or pseudo-penannulars (such as the Lagore brooch). The true penannulars are probably Pictish, the pseudo-penannulars Irish derivative types. The finest example is the Breadalbane Brooch. They date from the eighth to ninth centuries.

(23) *Fowler H5*. This is a large group and includes all brooches with flattened flaring terminals of Type H derivative form. The examples with very pronounced flaring, exemplified by St Ninian's Isle Nos 17 and 18, are Pictish. The shape of the central decorative element on the terminal frequently follows the shape of the terminal itself, as on the examples from Pierowall (Orkney) or Bonsall (Derbyshire). The Tara and Hunterston Brooches are elaborate versions of the same type.[35] The expansion and elaboration of the terminals led to the use of a septum or septa to join the terminals to give greater strength. Where this occurred the pin-head was fitted with a bolt or rivet so that it could be detached from the hoop. The type dates mainly from the eighth to ninth centuries.

(24) This type is a derivative of Type G and preserves the square or faceted terminal with central incuse diamond. Brooches of this type can be divided into two groups. (24A) consists of slight elaborations of the Type G form, the terminals being joined by a septum. Sometimes the pin-head matches the terminals. (24B) has the terminals built up with openwork as in the Killucan (Co. Westmeath) Brooch, or built into a solid plate, the latter type being ancestral to (25). Late eighth to ninth century.

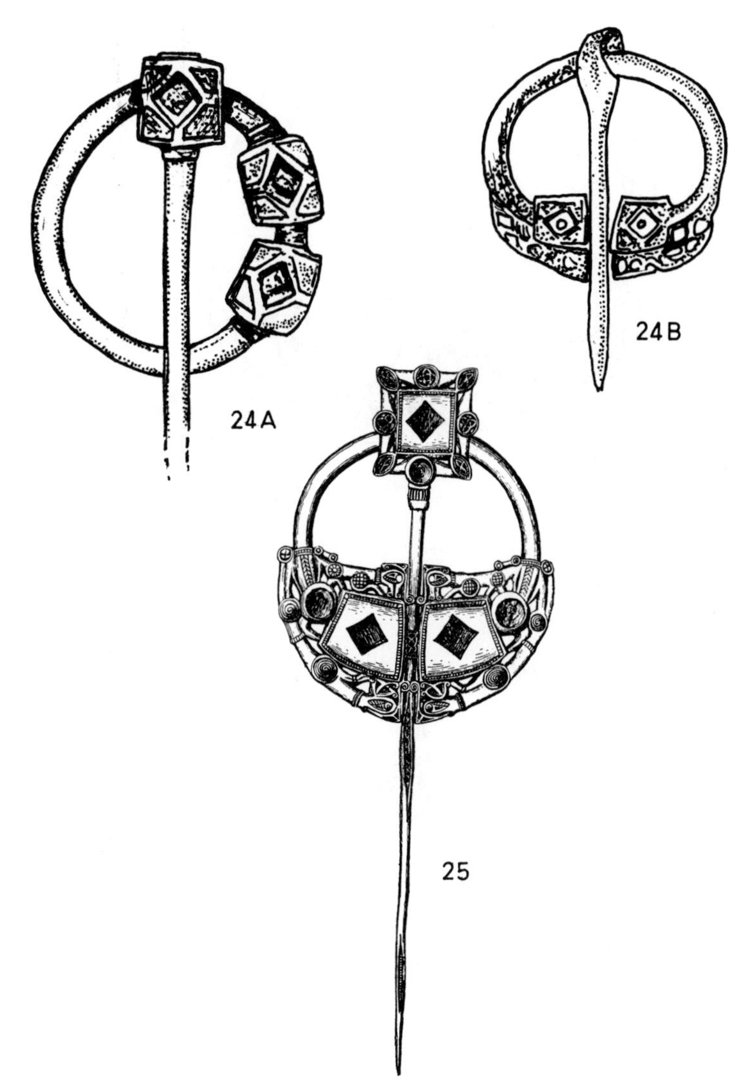

Figure 112 Penannular brooches, Types 24–5. (24A) Tralee, Co. Kerry; (24B) Killucan, Co. Westmeath; (25) Co. Limerick, found with Ardagh Chalice. Scale: (24) $\frac{3}{4}$, (25) $\frac{1}{3}$

(25) *Fowler H5.* On these brooches the terminal form of the Class G brooch has been developed into a decorative panel on what is otherwise a brooch of Type H5. It is best exemplified by the two brooches found with the Ardagh Chalice and by the Killamery Brooch.[36]

(26) *Fowler H3.* This is related to (24) and is distinguished by openwork building up the terminal. Frequently the terminal is round and similar to those like (19), with a central circular inlay – a brooch of this type

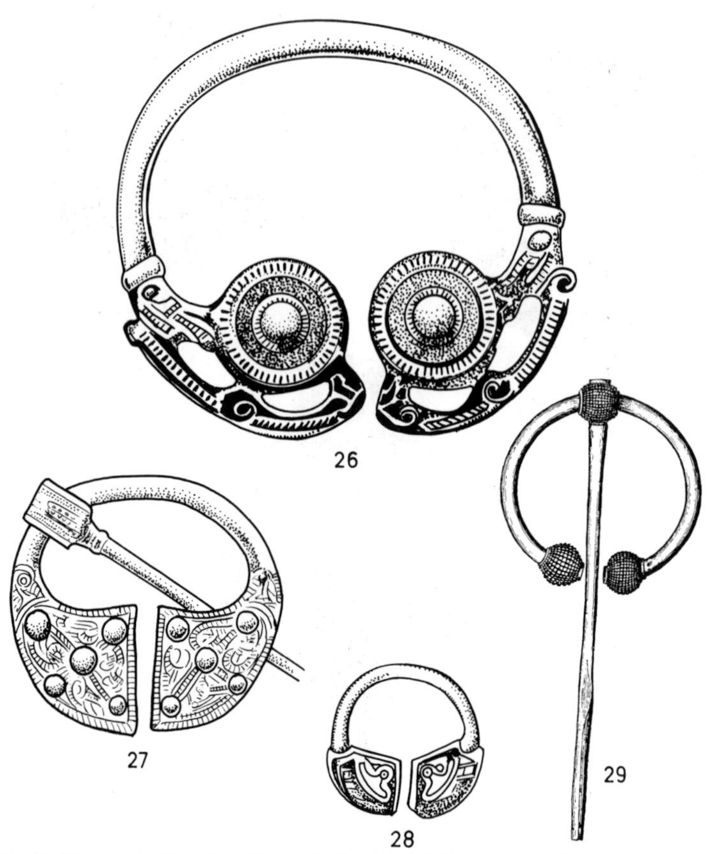

Figure 113 Penannular brooches, Types 26–9. (26) Goldsborough, Yorks, (27), (28) Ireland, unprovenanced, (29) Co. Limerick, found with the Ardagh Chalice. Scale (all): $\frac{3}{4}$

occurs in a Viking hoard from Goldsborough, Yorks.[37] In a number of examples the openwork is replaced by solid metal. Ninth-century.

(27) *Fowler H5.* This is a Viking period variant of (23). Brooches of this class have flat, engraved plate terminals decorated with very large bosses. These were probably produced in England and occur in northern England, Ireland and Norway, and may possibly be assigned to the kingdoms of Dublin and York. They date from the tenth century.[38]

(28) *Fowler H5.* This is possibly related to (27), but has the hoop as a separate element from the plate terminals, which are frequently engraved.

(29) *Fowler I.* Brooches of this type are usually termed 'thistle brooches' and have thistle-shaped terminals and head to the pin. They can be either brambled, or plain, with engraved decoration. They are a product of Viking culture, were produced in the late ninth and tenth centuries, and show Oriental as well as Celtic influence.

Of the above brooches, (24) should possibly be regarded as a development of Fowler's Class G, in which case (24A) should be G1 and (24B) G2. (26) might be regarded in terms of Fowler's scheme as an H3 variant.

It should be noted that while in the fifth and sixth centuries all the Celtic-speaking areas produced or at least wore penannular brooches, from the seventh century onwards the brooches were confined to Ireland and Scotland. This may be due to the accident of survival, but it should be remembered that apart from a few brooches of Class G, penannulars are absent from much of south-west England also. Where penannular brooches do occur in Britain it may be due to direct Irish or Pictish contacts.

Decorative motifs from penannular brooches

There is considerable hybridization of the various types of penannular brooch, and there can be considerable variation within each type. Within the series as a whole regional characteristics can be noted. While true penannulars of the seventh century onwards do occur, the pseudo-penannular is the more

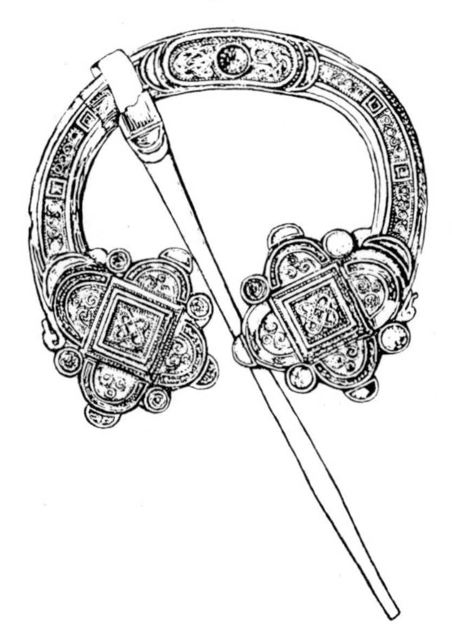

Figure 114 The Kilmainham Brooch. Actual size.

common type in Ireland. In Scotland true penannulars were the normal type, and in at least two cases imported Irish brooches had the junction between the terminals removed to convert them to the penannular form, the most notable example being the Breadalbane Brooch. A stylistic crosscurrent can be seen in the close similarity between the Pictish brooches of the type illustrated as (21), and examples from Ireland, which are distinguishable by a septum joining the terminals – as for instance on a brooch from Skryne,

Co. Meath.[39] The Irish brooches are rare, in contrast to the Pictish, and there can be little doubt that they are derivative. Once established in Ireland, however, the type eventually inspired the essentially Irish brooches of the type of (22). The absence of a septum suggests that the Kilmainham brooch is a Pictish import to Ireland rather than an Irish copy (Fig. 114).

In the sixth and seventh centuries the pin-heads were predominantly of barrel shape, or simply looped over the ring as they had been in the Roman period. In Pictland the pin had a lentoid head and this simple type seems to have continued even later, in the more elaborate brooches. In Ireland a trapezoidal panel (sometimes square or triangular), usually richly decorated, obscured the hook of the pin on the later, more ornate brooches. On some Irish brooches the square pin-head is ornamented with a hollow diamond with sockets for inlay at the angles. This may be an echo of a type of Irish stick pin current in the same period, which has an open diamond-shaped head with bosses at the angles (such as Fig. 125 (No. 37)) or the cushion-headed pin (Fig. 124 (No. 22)).

Throughout the period of production of penannular brooches, they reflected current developments in the ornamental repertoire of the metalworker. The ornamentation of fifth- and sixth-century brooches draws upon the repertoire employed in other contemporary arts – the range of motifs which belongs partly to the late Roman world. The basic elements were the palmette, the spherical triangle and the spiral. Single spirals under the influence of the triskele were elaborated into the double spiral. This can be seen most clearly on the brooches of Fowler Class F3. The spiral, double spiral and running scroll – the only elements to be found on the most accomplished brooches – are stylistically similar to motifs on some latchets and hanging bowl escutcheons. These pieces are probably contemporaneous, and represent a small artistic subgroup which Kilbride-Jones termed 'School B'.[40] While some may be the products of a single workshop, they are few in number and do not constitute a 'school' in the usual sense. Almost all are unprovenanced. Another group appears to be mainly confined to southern and eastern Ireland – in these the main motif is a pelta which in the later brooches becomes degenerate. The latest brooches employ millefiori inlay, and a cross (a result of Christian influence) was sometimes used as a terminal motif.[41]

The ornate brooches

Fine granular work as exemplified by the Dunbeath or Hunterston Brooches (Fig. 115) is quite possibly a Scottish feature.[42] Of the highly decorated brooches of Class H5 (22–3) the earliest employ filigree-outlined animals, pseudo-filigree and the device of making an openwork hollow platform on the top of gold panels to emphasize the relief of the filigree and granular decoration. This technique, which occurs in fifth- and sixth-century Sweden, seems to be Germanic in origin, and was probably transmitted to the Celtic world

Figure 115 The Hunterston Brooch, Ayrshire. Actual size.

by the Anglo-Saxons. The earliest brooches of the series include the finest. The Tara, Westness and Hunterston Brooches (Figs 115–17; Plate 12B), along with the Dunbeath Brooch, belong stylistically to the period of the Lindisfarne gospels and a little later, perhaps the first quarter of the eighth century. The brooches similar to (22) include the Breadalbane, 'County Cavan', Snaasen (Norway) and Lagore Brooches, and cover a period from the eighth to the beginning of the ninth centuries. Apart from the Pictish brooches, those akin to (25) seem to come from south of Dublin and include the Ballyspellan, Killamery and Cahercommaun Brooches and the brooches found with the Tara Brooch, all of which are eighth-century. Brooches such as the Londesborough Brooch, in the British Museum, are difficult to assign to any one group, though this example probably belongs to the same category as (23).

Of the Pictish brooches, the Rogart Brooches are probably the earliest, and that with lobed terminals has cast birds' heads riveted to the lobes, which

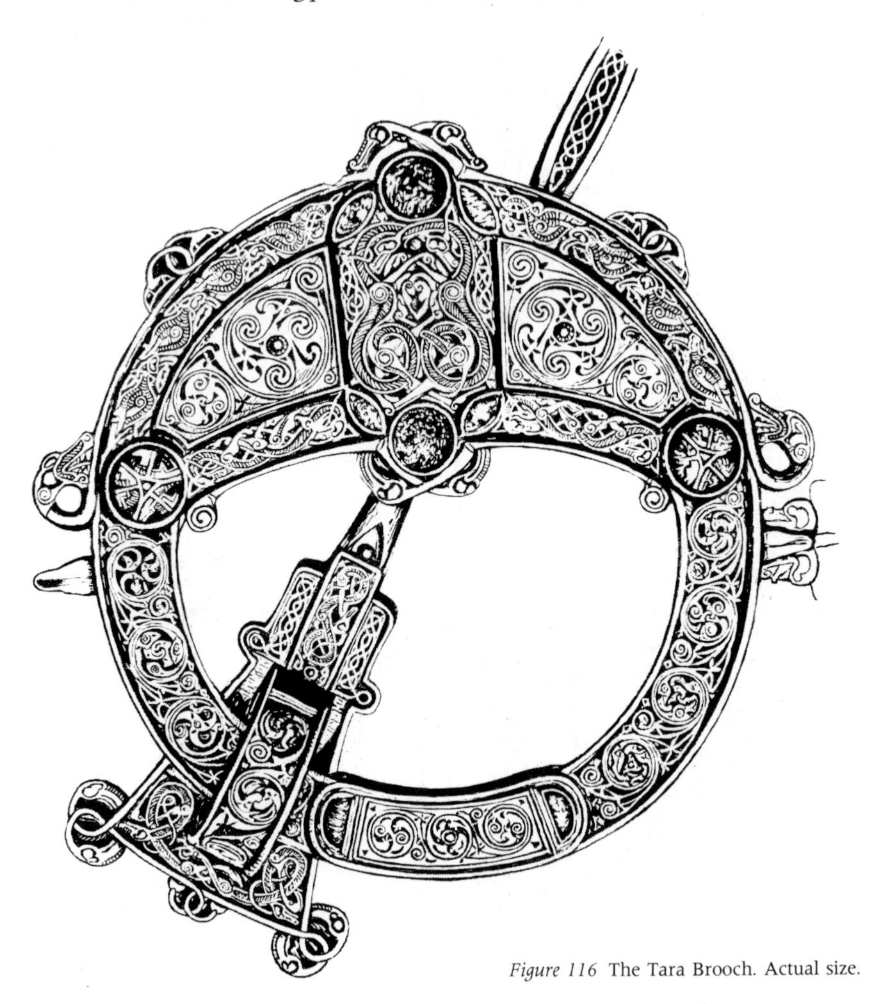

Figure 116 The Tara Brooch. Actual size.

may be ancestral to the vestigial birds' heads on later brooches.[43] The Croy Brooches are coin-dated to the mid-ninth century.

The Westness Brooch has a hoop to carry a chain or wire on the ring. This was probably to wind round the pin, like the fastening for a true ringed pin, or that of the Tara Brooch.

Ring brooches (Fig. 118)

The dividing line which separates penannular brooches from a series of pins with heads copying brooches is slight. In the ring brooch series, the pin tends to be very long and the head (i.e. the penannular ring) small.

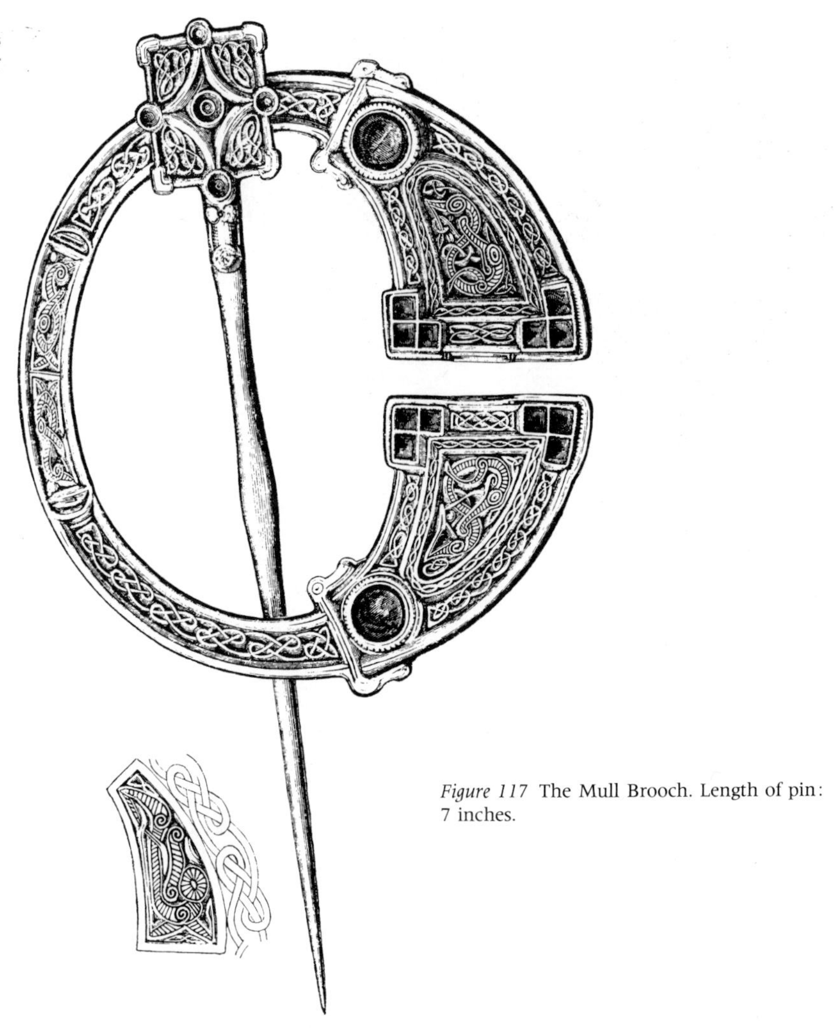

Figure 117 The Mull Brooch. Length of pin: 7 inches.

There are two series of ring brooches; those which are simply small penannular brooches with elongated pins, and which fall into the same types as the larger penannulars; and those which have a fixed pin which swivels in a notch in the hoop, which seem to be almost exclusively Irish (there are two examples from Scotland) and are relatively rare. The heads have terminals like (23) but because of their size are normally less intricately decorated. For the most part they belong to the eighth to ninth centuries.

A further series of ring brooches, 'disc pins', have a flat round plate-head which is hinged to the pin, and are thus closely related to the penannular ring brooches. They are characterized by the absence of decoration. E. C. R. Armstrong regarded them as being derived from the ring brooches,[44] but in view

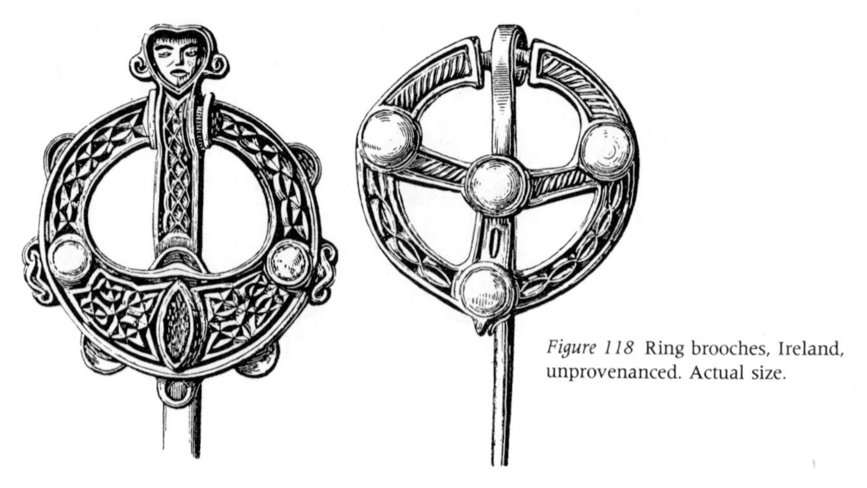

Figure 118 Ring brooches, Ireland, unprovenanced. Actual size.

of their early occurrence at Garryduff 1, Co. Cork, this does not seem likely, though it is possible that they developed from simpler penannular brooches like (15).

Kyte brooches (Fig. 119)

A rare category of Irish dress fastener is the kyte brooch, which is characterized by a hinged head attached to a large pin. The hinged head or pendant hangs down from the pin due to the thickness of the hinge, which suggests that they were used for very thick material such as fur or leather.[45] From the pendant a metal chain is usually suspended, to be wound round the pin to secure it. The pendants are richly decorated and vary slightly in shape, the classic example being that from Clonmacnois, Co. Offaly, now lost, which had a head resembling the shape of the Alfred Jewel. The similarity is probably fortuitous, since the Alfred Jewel was almost certainly the head of a pointer

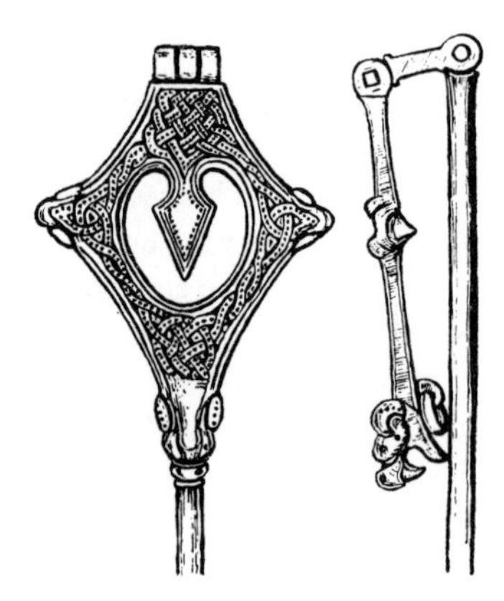

Figure 119 Kyte brooch, Co. Kilkenny

used in reading. The Clonmacnois Brooch, along with another surviving example from the same place, belongs to the ninth to tenth centuries. A silver kyte brooch from Ballinderry 1 was dated by Hencken to around 1000 AD. The head, of animal form, was extremely stylized. It probably represents the latest stage in the development of the type.

Loose ringed pins (Figs 120–1)

The loose ringed pin was the most common form of dress fastener in the Early Christian period, and survived for almost a millennium. There are about 500 examples known, of which at least 400 have come from Ireland. The spread of the ringed pin in Britain was probably due in great part to Viking adoption of the type – they seem to have been used as shroud pins – though evidence from various finds in Scotland, and from Meols in Cheshire, show that some at least were in use on the mainland prior to the arrival of the Vikings.

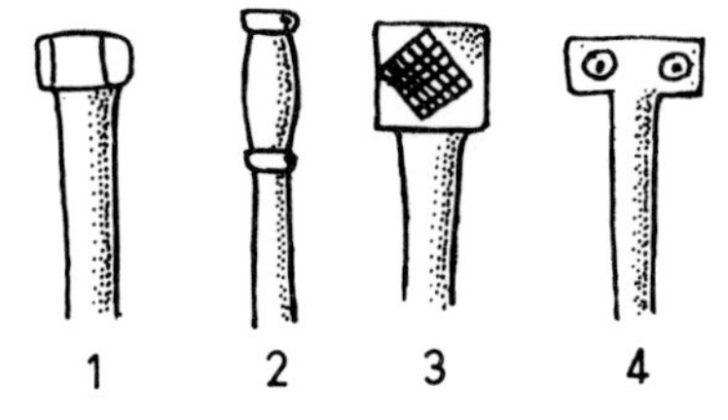

Figure 120 Types of heads of ringed pins. (1) Loop; (2) Baluster; (3) Polyhedral; (4) Crutch

Loose ringed pins have recently been studied by Fanning.[46] The essence of the loose ringed pin is a swivel ring held in a looped or perforated head. As in the case of some of the more elaborate penannular brooches, the pin was probably kept in place by a cord or wire, a theory which seems to be corroborated by the discovery of a loose ringed pin with a cord still attached to the ring from a Viking burial in The Faroes.

The origin of the type is difficult to determine. Loose ringed pins occur in Bronze Age and early Iron Age Europe, but are absent from the early Iron Age in Britain and Ireland. During the Roman and early post-Roman period the basic pin type was the stick pin (p. 324), though a few instances of loose ringed pins are known from late Roman and Anglo-Saxon contexts in England. The origin of the series should probably be sought in a sub-Roman context, though Anglo-Saxon influence is possible – the earliest ringed pins from Ireland occur, however, in contexts too early to be directly influenced by the Anglo-Saxons.

Classification of loose ringed pins is based on the two basic elements, the ring and the pin-head. There are six main types of ring – *spiral, plain, kidney, stirrup, rib* and *knob*. The pin-heads have fewer varieties, comprising the *baluster, loop, polyhedral* and *crutch*. The rings are more useful than the pins for

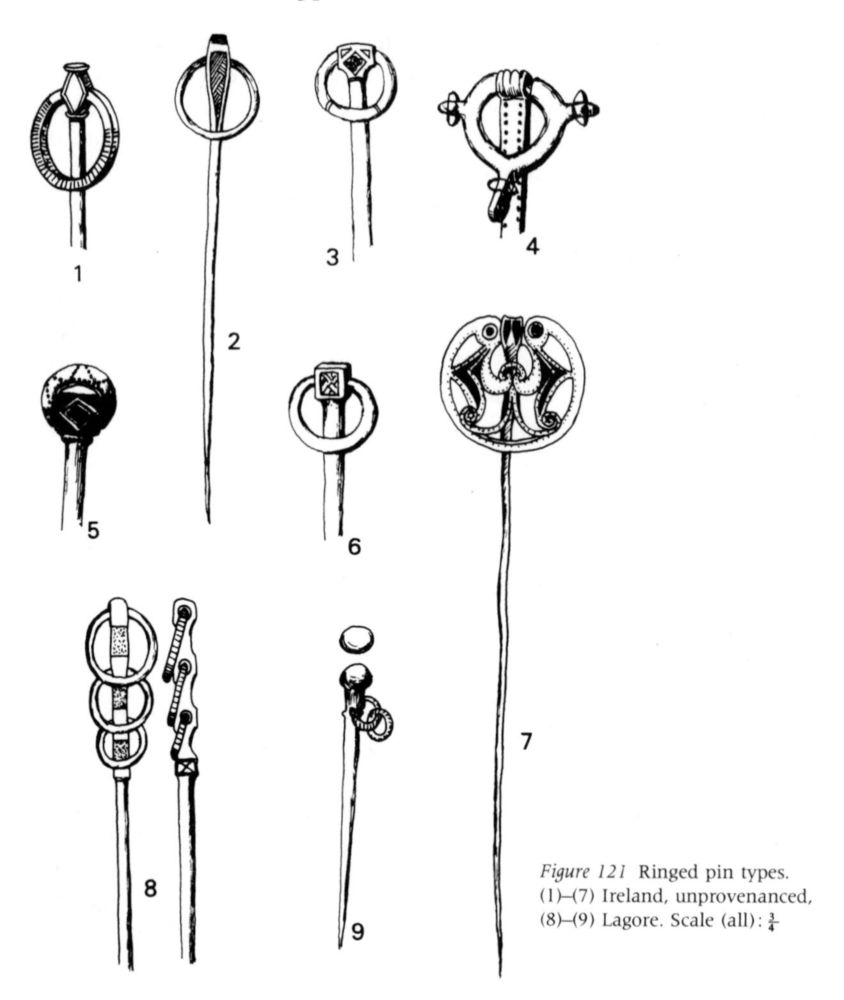

Figure 121 Ringed pin types.
(1)–(7) Ireland, unprovenanced,
(8)–(9) Lagore. Scale (all): $\frac{3}{4}$

the classification of the types. The two primary types were the *spiral-ringed* and the *plain-ringed*. From the plain-ringed variety evolved types with increasingly smaller rings, fitting closer to the pin-head. The pin-head also became larger, probably to facilitate a variety of decorative schemes. Pins with larger heads and pins with close-fitting rings were in vogue at the time of the Vikings. From these the *kidney-ringed* pin evolved: in the first stages of evolution of the kidney rings the ring was cast separately and fitted on to the pin-head; later it was soldered on to the pin; and finally it was cast as one with the pin, resulting in a skeuomorph. This late form was current in medieval Ireland, probably lasting until the thirteenth century. The *stirrup-ringed* pin is a related form also current until at least the twelfth century. Later the ringed pin was replaced, notably by the annular brooch.

Loose ringed pins were normally made of bronze, though iron examples are not uncommon and are of identical types. Silver ringed pins also occur, the most notable example being the Adare Pin. Decoration is usually confined to the pin-head and in the period prior to the Vikings was relatively simple. In the Viking period more elaborate designs appeared.

(1) *Spiral-ringed pin.* The ring consists of a spiral strip of bronze threaded through the baluster or looped pin-head. It is early and occurs on sites of the fifth and sixth centuries, but probably continued in use in Ireland until the Viking period. Examples have been found associated with E Ware. The terminal date for use of the type is probably late eighth or early ninth century. They do not appear to have been made in Scotland.
(2) *Loop-headed plain-ringed pin.* This type, because of its simplicity, was very long-lived. It occurs in early contexts along with (1) but also occurs in Viking graves. It may have continued into the early medieval period.
(3) *Polyhedral-headed ringed pin.* The heads are faceted and bear simple decoration in many cases. The pins themselves are related to a series of stick pins which enjoyed wide currency in the Viking period and later (p. 329, (21)). Pins of this type occur in contexts from the ninth to the eleventh centuries, as at Ballinderry 1 or Dublin High Street.
(4) *Knobbed-ring pin.* These pins are closely related to (2) but are distinguished by having up to three projections on the ring. It is a relatively rare type, current during the Viking period.
(5) *Kidney-ringed pin.* This invariably has a large polyhedral-headed pin often ornamented with brambling, a type of decoration which occurs on thistle brooches and on stick pins and which can be ascribed to the Viking period. The kidney-ringed pin seems derived from (3) and where examples have been found stratified they range from the late tenth to the thirteenth centuries.
(6) *Stirrup-ringed pin.* Pins of this type have crutch heads into which the stirrup ring is socketed by means of small tenons. The type is related to the preceding one and appears to have been current in the eleventh to twelfth centuries. Dot-and-circle ornamentation is characteristic of both rings and pin-heads. They have occurred stratified at Ballinderry 1 and Dublin High Street.
(7) *Rib-ringed pin.* A rare type in which the ring is segmented like a wheel with ribs or spokes radiating from a central boss, usually placed off centre. The circumference of the ring may also carry knobs, or more frequently sockets for inlay. Early examples are related to ring brooches and carry decoration on the ring – these probably date from the ninth century. Most, however, should probably be assigned to the tenth.
(8) *Double-ringed pin.* A relatively rare type, in which there are two rings, one of more regular style, the other passing through the shank lower

down. In the case of a pin from Lagore, Co. Westmeath, there are three tiers of rings. Such pins are probably contemporary with more common forms.

(9) *Ringed pin with secondary ring.* These have a second ring, or a bead looped on to the first, as on the Lagore example. This appears to be an elaboration of the basic ringed pin type, examples usually being similar to (1).

In addition to the above forms a number of variants can be noted. Normally the rings themselves are plain, but (1) and a hybrid of (3) and (5) can be decorated with grooving or more bulbous ribbing.

Hand-pins and their predecessors (Fig. 122)

The hand-pins are a class of dress fastener which has received much attention in the past, though the type is relatively rare. Formerly believed to be an Irish development,[47] it now can be seen to have evolved out of prototypes current in northern Britain.[48] Typologically the development of the hand-pin

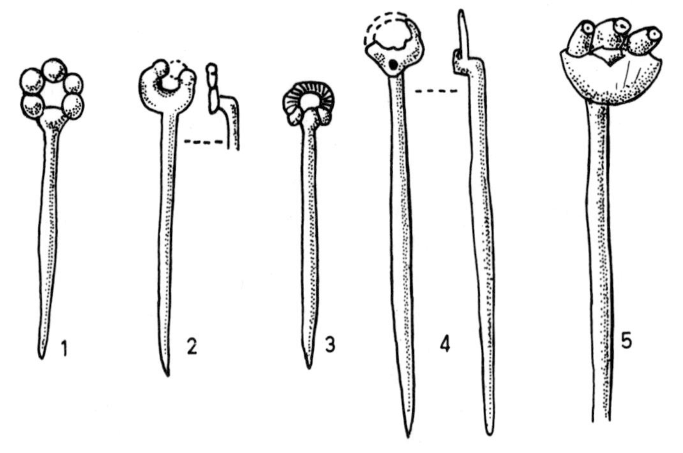

Figure 122 Development of the hand-pin. (1) Rosette pin, Covesea; (2) Proto-hand-pin, Covesea; (3) Beaded end corrugated Pin, Covesea; (4) Ibex-pin, Dundrum Sandhills; (5) Hand-pin, Hallum Terp. Scale: All $\frac{3}{4}$ except (5), $\frac{1}{1}$

appears fairly clear.[49] The starting point was a series of ring-headed pins, current in the early Iron Age, in which the head projects from the shank of the pin. The ultimate ancestry of these pins may either be in the sunflower pins of the late Bronze Age, or, more probably, a rare type of pin with a double curve and projecting head current in England and related to the convoluted brooches of the second century BC. Whatever the origin, the projecting ring-headed pin appears to have been current in Scotland in the early centuries AD. In much of Scotland it does not appear to have greatly outlived the third century, but in the wheelhouse cultures of the Hebrides these pins seem to have been used for making impressed decoration on pottery as late as the seventh or eighth century.[50] Related to it are a number of later types:

(1) *Rosette pin.* This type has a ring head decorated with either small or large beads on the circumference, those with the large beads constituting the 'rosette pin' proper. Typologically the small beaded ring pins are earlier than the larger, but both types were probably current in the second century AD, continuing into the fourth.
(2) *Proto-hand-pin.* The proto-hand-pin is distinguished from (1) in that it has from three to six beads round the upper part of the ring only. It probably evolved out of (1) in the third or fourth century AD and is primarily a northern British form.
(3) *Beaded and corrugated pin.* This type, well represented at Covesea, Moray, is characterized by having a corrugated upper portion to the ring and a beaded lower portion. It is related to (4).
(4) *Ibex-headed pin.* This is similar in general form to (3) but is distinguished by having concave-sided projecting side heads, like ears. In more evolved examples the lower beading may be replaced by a plate, but they also have side projections giving the overall impression of an ibex head. Ibex pins are probably fourth-century in origin, though a case has been advanced for an earlier date within the Roman period in Britain. They seem, however, to have had the widest currency in the sub-Roman period.
(5) *Early hand-pin.* The early type of hand-pin evolved out of the proto-hand-pin in the fourth century AD. It evolved when the lower part of the ring had developed into a crescentic plate and the upper part, which consisted of beading, had straightened out into a row of projections or 'fingers'. The hand-pin appeared in Ireland when fully developed, and evidence suggests that the early stages of its development took place in northern Britain where the essential elements of hand-pins were already present. These elements comprise the basic form and the use of enamelling to decorate the plate or 'palm' of the hand. This was demonstrably already existing in the fourth century in north Britain; Halton Chesters (Northumberland) produced a ring-headed pin with a plain upper part and lower part expanded slightly into a plate with enamelled double scrolls. Silver pins from Ireland provide more of the basic decorative elements used on the early hand-pins.

    Dating for the earliest hand-pins is probably provided by the find of a worn example from Hallum Terp, Friesland, which would suggest that they were in use in the late fifth and sixth centuries.[51]
(6) *Developed hand-pin.* As the hand-pin developed, its form was regularized. The 'fingers' were increased from three to five, became more elongated,

and gave the appearance of a row of tubes filled with enamel. The open space between the plate and the fingers diminished to a pinpoint and then disappeared, while the plate itself became a true semicircle of larger size and was more intricately decorated, though the decorative schemes were always fairly simple. The loose scroll or linked spiral design of the early pins were replaced by a pelta and 'eyed-peak' motif. Developed hand-pins continued into the seventh century at least. An example from Ballycateen, Co. Cork, has been ascribed to the late sixth to early seventh centuries. A relatively simple hand-pin from Carraig Aille II suggests that they may have continued in use until the beginning of the eighth century.

Stick pins (Figs 123–5)

With the exception of a few rarer types and those listed above, the remainder of the pin types current in the Early Christian period are of the 'stick' variety with solid heads.[52] Stick pins were made in metal (normally bronze) or bone – usually the bone pins are of identical type to the bronze. Bone and wooden pins, of which a few examples survive, probably served as models for moulds for the metal types. Bone pins have been found associated with the moulds made from them at Birsay (Orkney) and Mote of Mark (Kirkcudbright). Ball-, bead- and nail-headed pins are almost certainly of Roman ancestry, the Early Christian examples being, however, considerably shorter for the most part than the Romano-British and frequently having a hip on the shank to prevent the pin slipping out. Stick pins are common in Ireland at all periods, but in Britain are relatively rare except in the Western and Northern Isles of Scotland. Very few types from Scotland have exact counterparts in Ireland, and it must be assumed that they are the product of a continuing native tradition, though Dalriadic connections with Ireland might have kept it flourishing. A large percentage of the Scottish pins were of types current at the time of the Viking raids. It is possible that the Scandinavian movements were instrumental in the spread of different types of personal adornment, including stick pins, leading to a period of increased popularity.

It is difficult to construct a 'type series' for stick pins, for although certain types occur with some frequency, a great many are known only from single examples. The following list therefore is not intended as exhaustive, but includes a sufficient range to illustrate the diversity of types.

(1) *Pin with zoomorphic head.*[53] This is closely related to Fowler Class D4 and D5 Romano-British penannular brooches, but may have evolved out of the swan's-necked pin. The distribution is concentrated in the Military Zone of Roman Britain and it is possible that this type developed there in the late third or fourth century when the D4 and D5 penannular

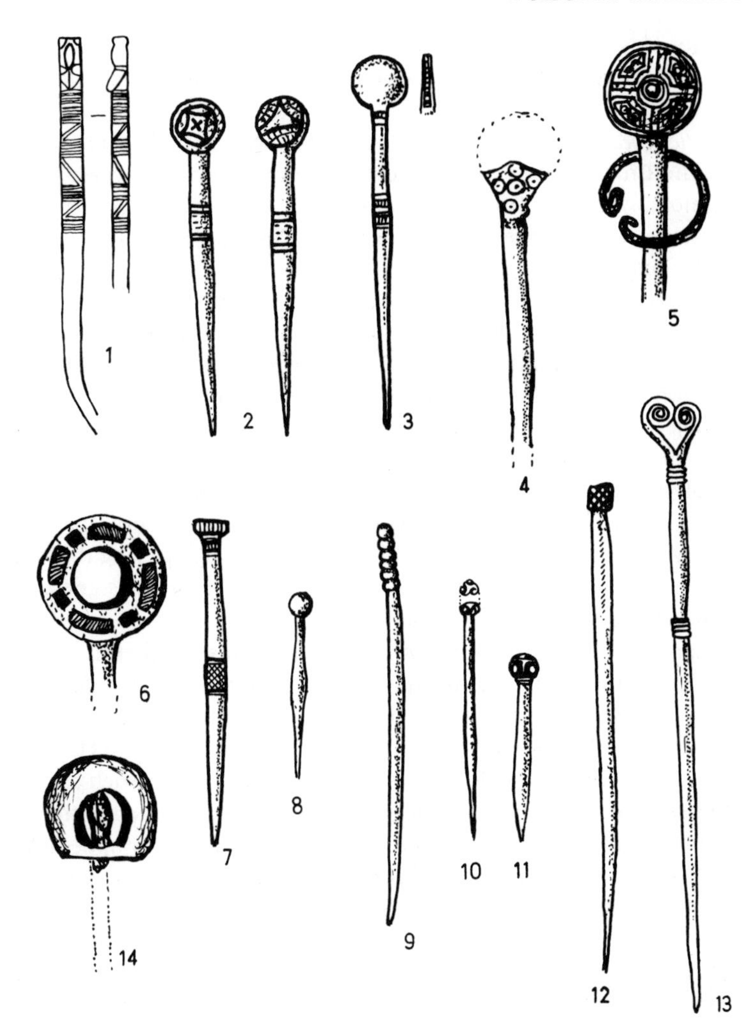

Figure 123 Stick pins, Types 1–14. Scale: $\frac{3}{4}$. (1) Traprain Law; (2) Orkney; (3) Broch of Burray, Orkney; (4) Blackhall House, Strathtay, Perthshire; (5), (7), (13) Ireland, unprovenanced; (6), (9) Birsay, Orkney; (8) Broch of Burrian, Orkney; (10) Borreray Sands; (11) Rosemarkie; (12) Vallay, Uist; (14) Brough of Birsay, Orkney

brooches were evolving. The type continues into the fifth and sixth centuries.

(2) *Pin with round head, sometimes enamelled.* This is seen by Fowler as related to the zoomorphic-headed pins, and examples are characterized by simple, rounded heads, sometimes with a dimple or hollow, probably for enamel; they are probably related to H2 and H3 penannular brooches and may have evolved in the late second or third century AD. The red

enamel dot was sometimes replaced later by geometric designs. The type was current in the fourth to fifth centuries, some surviving into the sixth.

(3) *Pin with flattened, round head.* Pins of this type are related to (2). They occur at the Broch of Burrian (Orkney) and on Scottish west coast sites, but are notably absent from the major Early Christian period sites in Ireland that postdate the seventh century. They presumably did not outlive the sixth century.

(4) *Racquet-headed pin.* This is probably related to (3) but the head is more expanded and frequently decorated, sometimes with ring-and-dot, sometimes with more elaborate designs. The type is fairly common in later Anglo-Saxon contexts, for example at Whitby[54] or York,[55] and a related type of object with a similar head may have been used as a stylus. There is a fairly ornate example from Meols, Cheshire.[56] Anglo-Saxon influence is probably responsible for the development of the type.

(5) *Ringed racquet pin.* This is an Irish type with a round head, usually more elaborately decorated than on pins like (4) and with a wire ring through the shank not far below the head. The ring was used for the same type of attachment as the ring of a loose ringed pin.

(6) *Wheel-headed pin.* These have flat, open wheel heads, frequently inlaid with enamel panels. The shank may carry a perforation just below the head for a wire ring, as in (5). There is one example from Birsay (Orkney),[57] the others are all Irish. Probably seventh- to eighth-century.

(7) *Nail-headed pin.* This type is Romano-British in origin. Some, such as one from Buston crannog, have glass insets which can be compared with late Roman pins from Lydney, Gloucestershire. The type certainly appears as early as the sixth century (at Ballinderry 2) and was presumably also current in the fifth. It does not appear to have outlived the Viking period although it occurs in an early Norse context at Jarlshof, Shetland.

(8) *Ball-headed pin.* Such pins are so simple that they are of little chronological value. They were not current before the Roman period but gained widespread popularity within the Empire. They are found on early sites of the Early Christian period and are very common in the seventh and eighth centuries. They are absent from Period III at Lagore (i.e. the mid-tenth century) and presumably did not outlast the Viking invasions.

(9) *Multiple ball-headed pin.* These pins are similar to ball-headed pins (8) but have two, sometimes three, beads or balls, instead of one, and are probably of later date. They may be Scottish in origin.

(10) *Triskele pin.*[58] This is a specialized variant of (8). They are normally hipped and have a simple triskele on the head. Some have incised decoration on the stem, such as a cross. They are probably a sixth-century type, though some examples with very devolved hatching on the head may be later.

(11) *Ball-headed pin with settings.* Pins of this type are probably degenerate versions of the triskele pin, in which the triskele has broken down and the curved terminals have become the sockets for insets. On some, the original triskele form is still more or less distinguishable. They occur in Ireland at Lagore, and at Rosemarkie, Ross, in Scotland. The earliest are probably seventh-century, the latest probably contemporary with and influenced by the bramble-headed pins (12).

(12) *Bramble-headed pin.* These have round heads with projections similar to those on thistle brooches, for which reason they are usually regarded as being tenth-century. A pre-Viking example, however, occurs in the final wheelhouse phase at Jarlshof, Shetland.

(13) *Double spiral-headed pin.* These occur in Ireland and Wales and are probably derived from a type current in Anglo-Saxon cemeteries in the sixth century.[59] The Irish type is distinguished by having a knop on the shank, a feature derived from another type of Anglo-Saxon pin with a knobbed head. In Ireland the type is seventh-century. A related type, represented at Culbin Sands, Moray, has a double crook head rather than a true spiral.

(14) *Iron pin with bone head.* This type may be a Scottish development, related to the jet-headed iron pins of the Roman Iron Age at Traprain, in West Lothian. The pins occur in post-broch contexts and on Irish sites, notably Ballinderry and Lagore. They seem to have been current not later than the seventh century.

(15) *Single spiral-headed pin.* This type occurs at Carraig Aille I, in the earliest levels of Lagore (IA) and at Dunadd. It is normally of iron and is probably sixth- to ninth-century.

(16) *Vase- or thistle-headed pin.* This is a very long-lived type and belongs to the family of Roman-derived pins. It occurs at Buston crannog, Ayrshire, the Broch of Burrian, Orkney, a number of Scottish west coast sites, and in Ireland. It was also an important type at Jarlshof in the Viking period.

(17) *Mushroom-headed pin with radial grooves.* This type of pin is characterized by a small, slightly globular head usually rising to a point in the middle and decorated with grooves from the centre. In origin the type may be related to Romano-British penannular brooches of Type A2 and there are a few Romano-British examples. They are particularly common on the west coast of Scotland, and may be regarded as a native type. There are a few Irish examples, and one from Whitby, Yorkshire. The range of date is wide; most seem to be sixth- to seventh-century, but one from Ballinderry 1 implies continuity until the tenth century. Plain mushroom-headed pins are probably contemporary.

(18) *Projecting disc-headed pin.* This rare type has a round, solid projecting head and is probably derived from the open projecting ring-headed pins of the Iron Age. It occurs in Ireland, a plain example occurring at

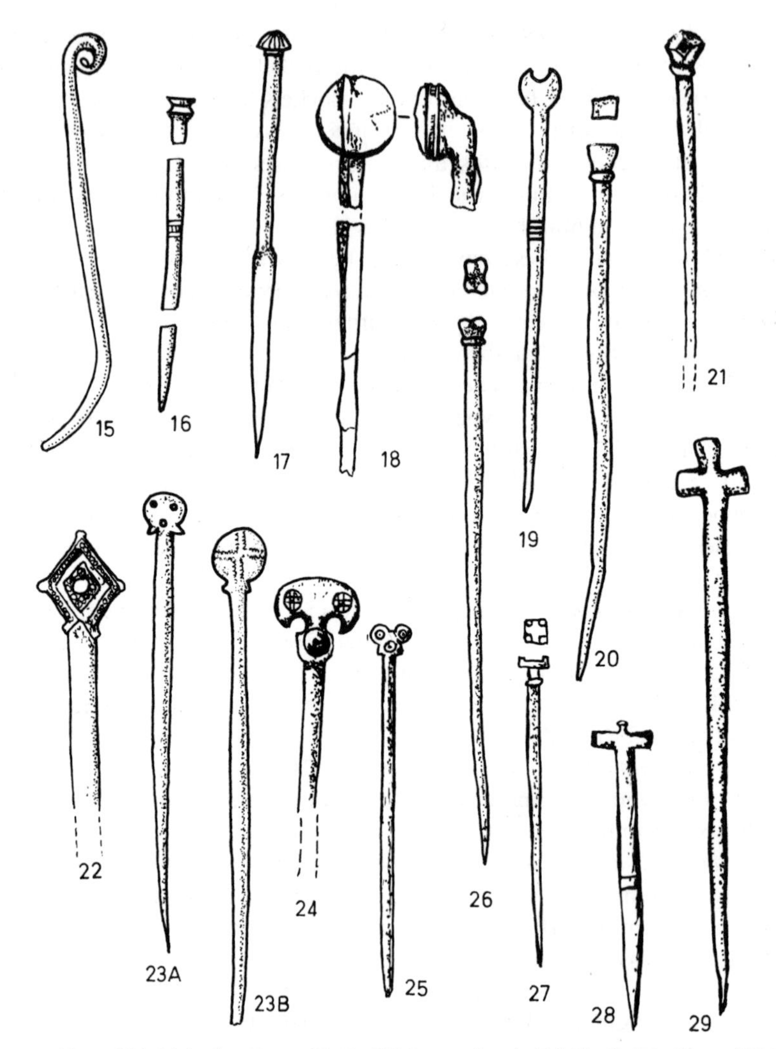

Figure 124 Stick pins, Types 15–29. (15) Lagore (iron); (16) North Ronaldsay; (17) Ross; (18) Garranes; (19) Boreray, Harris; (20) Lismore, Argylle; (21) Culbin Sands, Moray; (22) Birsay, Orkney; (23) A. Freswick; B. Harris; (24) Lagore; (25) Dublin; (26) Uig, Lewis; (27) Galston, Lewis; (28) Birsay (bone); (29) Jarlshof. Scale: $\frac{3}{4}$

Garranes, Co. Cork. Some occur decorated with C-scrolls or interlace, implying continuity of the type into the seventh or eighth century.

(19) *Pin with crescentic plate-head.* This appears to be a variant of (3) and is rare. It appears to be a Scottish type, and in the absence of associations cannot be dated precisely.

(20) *Frustum-headed pin.* These pins have heads shaped like a trapeze in face with a rectangular section, usually rising above an abacus, and are

found in Scotland. Dating is uncertain – they do not appear to have been current later than the early Viking period and do not occur in contexts that suggest a date earlier than the eighth century.

(21) *Faceted diamond-headed pin.* This seems to be related to the cushion-headed pin (22) and is probably contemporary, belonging to the Viking period. The facing plane may be decorated with a link knot of the type that occurs on some Viking period ringed pins.

(22) *Cushion-headed pin.* This type of pin has a flat, diamond-shaped head, sometimes with projections at the corners. It is a late type, probably descended from some pins like (12). The earliest examples may be tenth-century, the type probably continuing into the eleventh. One from Birsay, Orkney, has silver inlay.

(23) *Pin surmounted by a round or oval head above a fillet.* Pins of this type fall into two groups: those which have solid wheel heads, often inlaid or otherwise decorated, with the fillet integrated with the head; and those which have flatter heads, in which the fillet becomes a projection on either side of the shank below the head, and in which the decoration where present is confined to engraving of 'rocked tracer' type. The earliest are probably of the eighth to ninth centuries; the developed examples may be later.

(24) *Butterfly-headed pin.* (These pins have flattened, bifoliate heads.) It has been postulated that these are derived from double spiral-headed pins. A split-headed bone pin from the Broch of Burrian, Orkney, may, however, also be an ancestral type, as may some early pins similar to (3) where the terminal is not a complete disc but somewhat fan-shaped. The classic example is one inlaid with millefiori from Lagore. Possibly seventh-century.

(25) *Lobed-headed pin.* This type is closely related to (24), the lobes being decorated with ring-and-dot. Viking period. It occurs at Jarlshof and Dublin.

(26) *Astragaloid-headed pin.* This is an extremely rare type, possibly related to (20). Both are Scottish variants.

(27) *Pin with rectangular head with projections.* This type of pin has a flat rectangular plate-head at right angles to the stem, with projecting knobs at the corners. One example is known, from Scotland. It may be derived from (26).

(28) *Axe-headed pin.* Also a Viking type, found at Jarlshof. Later ninth- to tenth-century.

(29) *Cross-headed pin.* A Viking type, found at Jarlshof and also at Beginish in Ireland. Later ninth- to tenth-century.

(30) *Animal-headed pin.* This is a predominantly Viking type and again was current at Jarlshof in the ninth century. A variant form is recorded from the Norse cemetery at Islandbridge, Dublin. The Jarlshof examples are

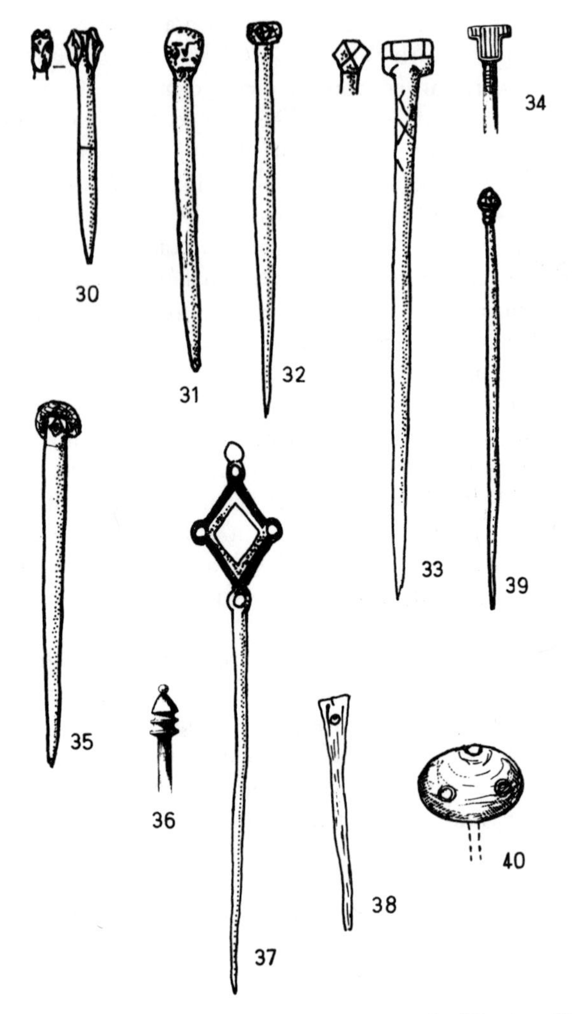

Figure 125 Stick pins. Types 30–40. (30) Broch of Burrian; (31) Lagore; (32) Kildonan, S. Uist; (33) Birsay, Orkney; (34), (36) Ireland, unprovenanced; (35) Valtos, Lewis; (37) Tiree (Length: 14·5 cms); (38) Jarlshof, Shetland; (39) Boreray, Harris; (40) Mote of Mark, Kirkendbright. Scale: $\frac{3}{4}$

bone, the Dublin one is bronze. A second category of animal-headed pin has a curved head, usually in the form of a facing head of a horse. A bone pin of this type is known from the Broch of Burrian and there are several Irish examples. It is probably an earlier type than the Viking 'dragon' series and may be related to a class of Roman pins.

(31) *Human-headed pin.* This very rare type, represented at Lagore, is probably derived from a Roman type of pin. The Lagore pin was unstratified but stylistically is in accordance with a seventh- or eighth-century date.

(32) *Faceted-headed pin.* This has a square head with facets and is related to the faceted heads of some Viking period ringed pins, sharing the same decorative schemes. A variant, related to brambled pins, has a square head with cross-hatching.

(33) *Crutch-headed pin.* Closely related to the crutch-headed pins of the stirrup- and kidney-ringed pins. Some are decorated with ring-and-dot, some with incised lines, others are left plain. They are a Viking period type, of the tenth century or later.

(34) *T-headed pin.* This Irish type has a T-shaped plate-head. It is probably related to crutch-headed pins and is presumably late.

(35) *Kidney-ring skeuomorph pin.* This very late type is a solid-cast skeuomorph of a ringed pin with a kidney ring. They occur at Dublin as late as the twelfth century. A few examples are known from Scotland, mainly from Viking or later Norse period sites.

(36) *Lantern-headed pin.* This has a domed head, sometimes crowned by a bead, with corrugations below. It is an Irish type, and is probably eighth-century.

(37) *Pin with open diamond head.* This type is closely related to the cushion-headed pins, and has an open head of diamond shape. It is a Viking period type.

(38) *Bone pin with triangular head.* Pins of this type are probably the commonest of the Early Christian period, and have expanded heads which may or may not be perforated. They are common in Viking contexts, and continue into the Middle Ages; they also occur in the pre-Viking period, for example in wheelhouses.

(39) *Domical headed pin.* This is related to the mushroom pin with grooves. It may have the head decorated with lattice, surmounted by a bead, and may have two or more lobes.

(40) *Bone-headed pin with inlay.* This type has a bead-shaped head, metal pin shank and inlays of metal on the head. It is best exemplified by one from the Mote of Mark, Kirkcudbright, and presumably is a late fifth- to sixth-century type.

Latchets (Fig. 126)

The type of dress fastener known as the 'latchet' possibly evolved out of the ring-headed pin, or, more probably, out of one of its predecessors, the 'shepherd's crook' pin or 'swan's-necked' pin.[60] The characteristic features of the latchet are the bend in the shank and the plate-head. There are no examples in Ireland which illustrate the early development of the type, though in England examples are known with a twist in the middle of the shank.

At some unknown point in time the latchet acquired a solid plate-head

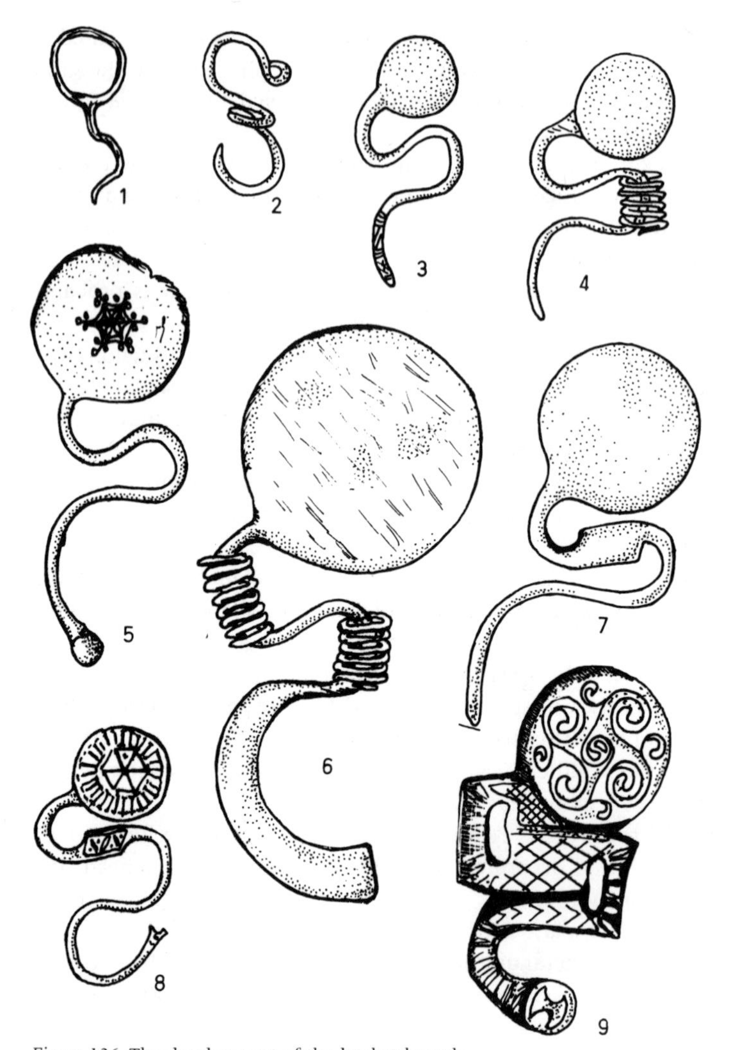

Figure 126 The development of the latchet brooch

instead of a ring. Originally latchets had spirals of wire wound round the stem and the bends in the shank – this coil of wire could be turned like a corkscrew in the cloth to grip it securely. In a few cases the spirals still survive.

The first stage in latchet typology was the flattening out of the tip of the shank to prevent it from sliding through the wire coil. At a later stage the coils were kept apart by flattening out the middle, and in the final stage the two loops of the S-curve were turned into a plate, with two slots in it for the wire coil. In spite of the latchet's similarity to a Roman belt plate, the most evolved type is probably not earlier than the seventh or eighth century AD.

Due to the absence of finds from excavations (the latchet is in any case a fairly rare type of dress fastener) a chronological scheme cannot be established, but it is probable that examples at various stages of the typological sequence existed contemporaneously. Some have undecorated heads, others have heads decorated with marigolds and other designs, some of which are reminiscent of hanging bowl escutcheons. The series probably belongs to the period from the fifth to the seventh or early eighth centuries AD, and on stylistic grounds most of those with decorated heads belong to the period after 600. The latest examples are enamelled. A fragment of what appears to be a latchet from Kiondroghad, Isle of Man, possibly suggests that they were being made as late as the Viking raids.

Buckles (Fig. 127)

Buckles were rare in the Early Christian period. Principal evidence for their use comes from Lagore, Co. Meath, where three examples were found. The buckle probably came to Ireland in the sixth century as a result of contact with the Anglo-Saxon world, or less probably the Germanic Continent. The Irish examples are closely comparable with the Anglo-Saxon. The earliest, which may date from the early seventh century or possibly the sixth, comes

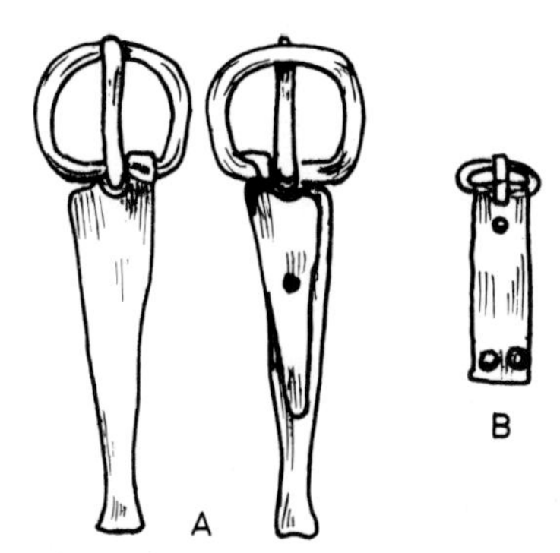

Figure 127 Buckles, Lagore. Scale: $\frac{3}{8}$

from Uisneach, Co. Westmeath, and there is another from Cahercommaun, Co. Clare. The Uisneach example has a simple rectangular plate, and one of the Lagore buckles has a similar plate, rather more elongated than the majority of Anglo-Saxon examples. A second buckle from Lagore has a triangular plate, a form current in Anglo-Saxon graves of the early seventh century, an exceptional example of which is the Taplow buckle. Two buckles of similar shape come from Rathtinaun, Lough Gara (Co. Sligo) and Garryduff (Co. Cork), the former richly decorated with enamel. The third Lagore buckle, while inspired by triangular Germanic types, is without doubt a native development, having a slightly triangular plate from which extends a stem for the strap attachment. The plate is richly decorated with three scrolls, and probably should be assigned to the eighth century. There are other iron and bronze buckles from Dooey, Donegal.

An unsual buckle decorated with millefiori was among the finds from Derry, Co. Down. This lacks a plate, and presumably the belt was looped round it in the manner of later buckles rather than being riveted or sewn on to it. It is probably of the seventh or eighth century. An enamelled object, usually regarded as a buckle, is among the old finds from Lagore. It may, however, be a strap attachment rather than a buckle, and dates probably from the seventh century. The buckle on the Moylough belt shrine was never used as such and the fastening was riveted. It dates from the end of the seventh or beginning of the eighth century, and is modelled on a Frankish prototype (p. 359).[61]

In the Viking period, buckles probably became more common in the Celtic west. There is an example from Ballinderry 1, and examples are known from Viking graves, notably Balladoole in the Isle of Man.

Tanged studs (Fig. 128)

Domed studs with tangs are fairly common finds, a less common form having a flat head like a button. They appear at Garranes, Cahercommaun, Creevykeel, Cush and Lagore in Ireland, and at Dinas Powys in Wales. The type

Figure 128 Tanged studs, Lagore. Scale $\frac{3}{8}$

first appears in the Roman Empire, and they are fairly common in Migration Period graves in Switzerland. In Ireland and Wales the prototypes are probably Anglo-Saxon and one such stud is among the finds from Sutton Hoo. In Ireland they seem to span a period from the sixth century to the ninth. The heads are frequently decorated.

Finger rings and bracelets (Fig. 129)

Finger rings are rare from the Early Christian period. One example in the collection of the Royal Irish Academy is decorated with a design closely related to that used on some F2 penannular brooch terminals, and is probably contemporary.[62] A bronze finger ring from Garryduff 1 has an oval flattened bezel, decorated with incised lines and chip-carved triangles. At Lagore a similar ring has a cross incised on the bezel. Another ring is penannular, with overlapping ends, made of sheet bronze decorated with dots. Instead of having a bezel it is expanded at the front. A spiral bronze finger ring was among the finds from Garranes.

Bracelets are not common before the Viking period, with the exception of a series of glass armlets and a rarer series made of shale or lignite. There are a few of bronze, with limited decoration.

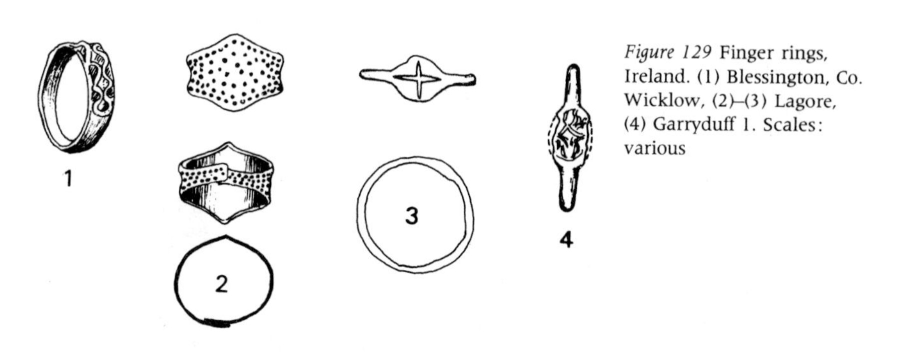

Figure 129 Finger rings, Ireland. (1) Blessington, Co. Wicklow, (2)–(3) Lagore, (4) Garryduff 1. Scales: various

Glass armlets[63] (Fig. 75)

Armlets were being produced in north Britain in the second century AD from re-used Roman glass. Elsewhere in Britain they are rarely found, though one was found on an Iron Age site in Cornwall, and there are others from Welwyn, Herts.[64] Certainly their production was a fairly widespread La Tène craft, and they were made among other glass products at Manching, Bavaria.[65] In Ireland they occur at Lagore (Co. Meath), Larriban (Co. Antrim), Cahercommaun (Co. Clare) and Ballinderry 1 (Co. Westmeath) among other places. A feature of the bracelets is their similarity to the type current in north Britain in the Roman Iron Age, from which they were probably descended. They are plano-convex in section and decorated with cable-patterned bands, akin to some of the beads. Threads of white glass were twisted round a blue rod, which was drawn thin, the cable thus formed being applied to the body of the bracelet. The cables were pressed into the wall of the bracelet, and do not project above the surface. White spots were also used for ornamentation. There are some instances of similarly worked glass objects from the Anglo-Saxon areas. From the seventh century there are a couple of pendants with raised cable ornament from the Sibbertswold cemetery, Kent, while the Gravesend Cross also has a glass border produced in this fashion. Fused cables are also in evidence on beads from Whitby, Yorkshire.[66]

Beads[67] (Fig. 130)

Necklaces were as common in the Early Christian period as at other periods, and beads are among the most common finds from settlement sites. These were made of amber, bone, stone and glass, which was the most popular substance. Some of these glass beads, notably plain dark blue and possibly spotted types, were probably produced in the Celtic west. The majority, however, were almost certainly imported from the Teutonic world. Beads of materials other than glass are normally round and undecorated, though some bone beads may be cordoned or ribbed, being lathe-turned. The main glass bead types are:

(1) *Plain blue bead.* Mainly dark blue and small. They are round or, less frequently, drum-shaped and occur at all periods from the Bronze Age in Europe.

(2) *Plain yellow bead.* Similar in size and shape to (1) and very ubiquitous.

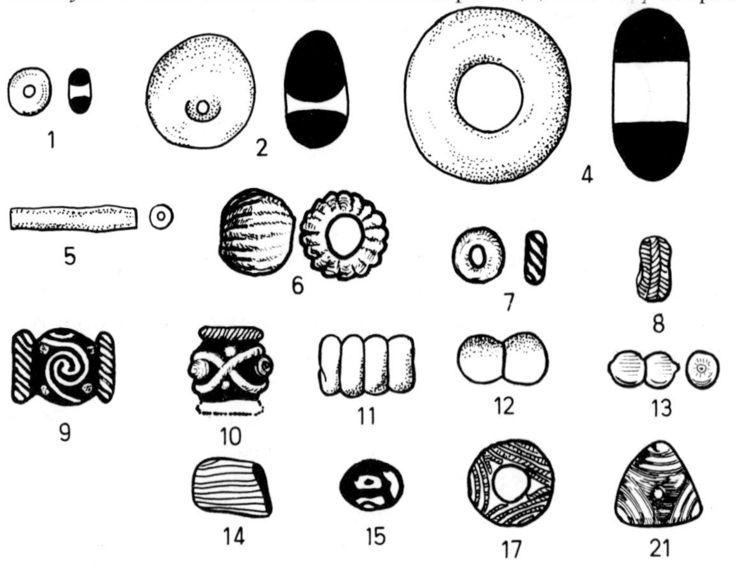

Figure 130 Glass beads. All Lagore except (10) Carraig Aille, (15) Kirkconnel, Dumfries, and (21) Culbin Sands, Moray. Scale (all): $\frac{3}{4}$

(3) *Plain white bead.* Some show slight traces of blue colouring. Similar to (1) and (2).

(4) *Plain khaki-coloured bead.* These are very rare in Britain but fairly common on the Continent down to the Viking period, first appearing in Roman times. They occur in Frankish graves of the fifth to sixth centuries.

(5) *Large green bead.* These occur in Iron Age Britain at Glastonbury, and also in Roman Britain. They appear in Scandinavia from the third to fifth centuries, and thereafter, being particularly common in the Viking period. They are found in Anglo-Saxon graves.

(6) *Opaque red bead.* Plain round beads of this type, sometimes with a marvered spot, are common Germanic types and occur in Anglo-Saxon graves. They are rare in the west – one was found at Dinas Powys.

(7) *Green tubular bead.* A common Anglo-Saxon type which continued in northern Europe to the Viking period.

(8) *Melon bead.* This is a standard pre-Roman and Roman type which is rare in the post-Roman period. It is distinguished by corrugations or grooves.

(9) *Cable bead.* This is made with one or more cables of different coloured glass threads twisted together. In western Europe it is a pre-Roman technique and occurs at Meare in an Iron Age context. This type is rarer among the Germanic peoples than other types, and some in Scandinavia have been regarded as Irish imports. Hencken recognized three types at Lagore: (1) annular beads made with one cable; (2) zig-zag beads: these have herringbone cables and are rare in the Germanic area but occur at Dunadd, Mote of Mark, Lagore and Ballinderry 2, as well as at Cush; (3) beads with cables not covering the whole surface. These are an Iron Age type current also in the Roman period; in the Early Christian period they are usually regarded as Irish. Examples come from Lagore.

(10) *Horned eye bead.* This category covers all beads with knobs on which are spirals of different coloured glass. They are predominantly an Iron Age type and are rare in western Europe in the Early Christian period, though they occur in the Viking period.

(11) *Blue segmented bead.* A recurring type from the Roman Iron Age to the Viking period. One was found at Lagore, another at Dunadd. They are frequently found in Frankish cemeteries.

(12) *Unperforated dumbbell bead.* This is strictly speaking a toggle. It is a peculiarly Irish type. Examples come from Lagore.

(13) *Double yellow striated bead.* Beads of this common type are dumbbell-shaped and have a longitudinal perforation. They have fine striations lengthwise along the surfaces. It occurs in Anglo-Saxon cemeteries and Frankish graves. In northern Europe examples exist from the Roman Iron Age to the Viking period and in Hungary the type continues until the twelfth century. They were found at Lagore and elsewhere.

(14) *Bead with stripes parallel to the piercing.* These can be of a number of varieties, either annular or elongated in shape. On the whole they do not occur much before the sixth century and they lasted until the Viking period.

(15) *Eye bead.* This is distinguished by having trailed white opaque glass with central dark-coloured glass spots (usually dark blue) against a dark blue or other dark-coloured background. They appear to be mainly sixth- to seventh-century in date, and occur at Trier in this period, as well as in Anglo-Saxon cemeteries. British finds include one from Kirkconnel (Dumfriesshire), and there are many from Ireland.

(16) *Millefiori bead.* Beads of this type are very rare and are cylindrical with millefiori insets and sometimes stripes. They are found in Anglo-Saxon graves and are otherwise widely distributed in the Migration Period. One came from Lagore.
(17) *Clear glass bead with yellow spirals.* This is an Iron Age type, which is found at Maiden Castle and Meare. They are fairly common in Ireland, but not elsewhere, and may be a survival.
(18) *Annular bead with haphazard spots.* These are frequently black with spots of various colours. They are a particularly Germanic type, and were current until the Viking period in northern Europe. They occur at Ballinderry 2 and Lagore, and are very common – they may have been made in Ireland as well as being imported.
(19) *Plain bead with 'icing'.* A few beads have a trailed raised pattern 'iced' onto the surface in a haphazard fashion. They are not closely datable. One comes from Garranes.
(20) *Swirled bead.* This is a very rare type in which the colours are swirled together. One comes from Lagore, where it had been made in two pieces which were joined together. A few are known from Anglo-Saxon contexts.
(21) *Triangular yellow and black bead.* Triangular beads with stripes of yellow and white are apparently a Pictish product, being confined to the north-east Scottish mainland.

Buttons and badges

Buttons were used as dress fasteners as early as the late Neolithic in Europe, but thereafter various classes of pins and brooches seem to have been favoured. Buttons of the Early Christian period are rare, but possible examples have been found at Garryduff 1 (Co. Cork) and Lagore (Co. Meath).[68]

A few finds from Early Christian period sites appear to be dress adornments, but the precise method of wearing them is not always clear. Into this category falls the miniature gold bird in filigree from Garryduff 1, which may have been sewn on clothing in a similar fashion to the gold and garnet cicadas sewn on to the robes of the Merovingian king, Childeric.[69] Into the same category comes a roundel with interlace from Dunadd, Argyll, which is comparable in style to the bracteates found in pagan cemeteries in Kent. The bracteates were probably worn as necklace pendants, and the Dunadd disc may have been used in similar fashion.[70]

13 Art and craftsmanship

The art of Britain and Ireland in the Early Christian period has received more attention in the past than any other aspect of the archaeology of the period, because of its finest achievements. This art has been widely regarded as an Irish phenomenon, representing the survival in Ireland of La Tène artistic traditions, the disappearance of which from Britain is accounted for by the overlay of other, classical traditions during nearly four centuries of Roman rule. This interpretation appears to oversimplify the issues, and the position adopted in the following pages is that Early Christian 'Celtic' art is a complex amalgam of artistic traditions which became blended together in the fifth to seventh centuries. In this formative period works cannot be recognized which are specifically 'Irish', 'Scottish' or 'Welsh' since the Irish Sea province seems to have shared common artistic traditions. Only in the seventh century, or possibly the late sixth, can regional 'schools' be discerned.

Early Christian 'Celtic' art can be recognized in the three main media of medieval art – manuscripts, sculpture and metalwork. In most discussions of Christian Celtic art attention is focused on manuscripts, and comparisons are drawn between the ornament displayed in works such as the *Book of Durrow*, the *Lindisfarne Gospels* or the *Book of Kells* and the products of La Tène art. Such comparisons are at once rendered suspect since they overlook one important fact. Manuscripts by their nature belong to Antique tradition, and their inspiration stems directly from the world of Christian Rome. The fundamental iconography of evangelist figures and canon tables, was taken directly from late Antique prototypes, and while the interpretation was Celtic, it was the interpretation of Celtic clerics schooled in classical thought. The art of the La Tène Celts was essentially that of the metalworker, and any attempt therefore to argue a continuity in Celtic art should begin with a study of the metalwork. It is for this reason that this chapter is confined almost exclusively to metalwork. While manuscripts are surviving material culture, and therefore of concern in archaeology, they are invariably without original archaeological association: manuscripts are not found in excavation, nor are they found associated in any other way with other classes of material culture. Study of them is based entirely on the internal evidence of the manuscripts themselves, and while comparisons can be made between ornamental details in manuscripts and those in metalwork or sculpture, they are of limited value. Although sculpture is discussed on a regional basis in the appropriate chapters, many of the points made about manuscripts likewise apply to this medium. Although the La Tène Celts produced some sculpture, it was never of major importance, and it, too, is usually without archaeological association.

The problem of Early Christian art in the British Isles

Study has tended, for obvious reasons, to be concentrated on the major works of Early Christian art. This has led to such works receiving a prominence which has eclipsed the study of the less imposing products of the milieu in which they were produced, and, indeed, of that milieu itself.

The majority of the great works of Early Christian art in the British Isles, with the exception of certain categories of sculpture, are without precise provenance and association. Chronology for them is based to a great extent on general art historical considerations.

Because two objects or motifs are the same it does not necessarily imply that they are the products of the same centre or of the same date, but only that both are drawing upon the same tradition. One of the characteristics of barbarian art is that it does not necessarily follow a direct evolutionary line. Comparisons between works in different media for chronological or regional attribution are particularly futile. The producers of metalwork or sculpture tend to be conservative. This applies both to secular works and to works produced under clerical patronage. Manuscripts were executed in monastic scriptoria; metalwork and stone carving were the products mainly of lay workshops, and it is probable that there was usually a time lag before a new motif in one medium was widely adopted in another. It is impossible to establish dates from associations in Scandinavian sites, since the objects could be of considerable antiquity before they were taken to Scandinavia, and could have remained there for some time before they were buried. Grave-finds in particular cannot be dated to the time of burial. It must be stressed that particularly before the ninth century the chronology of metalwork is a relative matter, and experts differ on dates by as much as a century.

Provenance too is complicated to establish, since manuscripts and other objects were taken from one monastery to another, the most ornate and valuable being the most likely to move from the place of production.

In the case of the isolated great works of art, detailed comparative study with regard to provenance tends to obscure the picture. As Clapham so rightly observed in 1934, one should concentrate on the general development of Early Christian ornament, as far as it can be ascertained, and then, and only then, will the masterpieces fit into their proper place in the general scheme.[1]

Barbarian art in Europe

Throughout European prehistory an artistic tradition is apparent which was concerned less with naturalism and the accurate representation of human, animal or plant life than with design.

The evolution of this barbarian art, if indeed the term 'evolution' can be used at all, was far from simple, as shown so clearly by Sandars[2] and Powell.[3] There was no clear line of development: naturalism and impressionism, realism and abstraction could exist side by side at any point in time or could be combined in a variety of ways. The sources of the La Tène Celtic style or the Early Christian Celtic styles can be recognized, but, like all art, ultimately defy analysis.

Just as Celtic art of the pre-Roman Iron Age belonged to the larger family of barbarian art in prehistoric Europe, so was the Celtic art of the Early Christian period part of the larger family of barbarian art of post-classical Europe. Developed Viking art, such as the products of the Ringerike or Urnes Styles, was the linear descendant of Styles I and II in Scandinavia, which in turn owed much to earlier, prehistoric traditions.[4] It has been argued that the art of the Pictish symbol stones was an Early Christian period survivor of a long tradition of animal art the origins of which can be sought among the nomads of the Steppes.[5] Because of the basic relationship between the various traditions, the same motifs, the same ornamental elements, even the same preferences for forms and compositions constantly recurred. While there were complex and ultimately indistinguishable borrowings between the different groups of peoples at different times, resulting in new, distinct styles, in essence all were part of the same perception.

It must be stressed that the barbarian tradition displayed an eclecticism which was not confined to borrowings purely from other barbarian styles. Just as classical motifs and schemata borrowed from the repertoire of Eastern iconography contributed to the development of La Tène art, so too in the Early Christian period artists drew upon the classical art of late Antique Rome and the art of Coptic Egypt to form new and exciting expressions.

In the light of this, the endeavour to explain the apparent hiatus between La Tène art and the art of Early Christian Britain and Ireland seems irrelevant. The basic tradition survived in various forms beyond the Roman *limes* and there was ample opportunity in the period of barbarian movements in the later days of the Roman Empire for its transmission and promulgation.

Continental La Tène art

Sandars has compared the essence of Celtic (La Tène) art with a triskele of tension, ambiguity and the ideal. The tension is 'an artistic tension in which symmetry and asymmetry balance and imbalance, and are continually being played off against each other in a kind of visual counterpoint'.[6] The ambiguity is one in which the motifs are capable of more than one interpretation, and the ideal is the 'close adherence to the schemata or readily definable basic artistic vocabulary of the La Tène craftsman'.[7] To some considerable extent this quality is also shared by the art of the Early Christian period.

The elements that were to come together in what Jacobsthal classified as his 'Early' Style of La Tène art were varied. Contrary to what is sometimes thought, behind the full flowering of Celtic art lay a period of innovation and experimentation. This phase, lasting from the early fifth into the mid-fourth century BC, was largely dominated by the influence of plant ornamentation from the classical world.[8] These motifs, mainly flowers and palmettes, were combined with more exotic elements ultimately derived from the 'Orientalizing' art of the east Mediterranean. A major contributor in the transmission of this Eastern art was the 'situla' art from the head of the Adriatic.[9] Situla art, which takes its name from the bronze buckets of the sixth to fourth centuries BC, introduced to the Celtic world formalized scenes of feasting, wrestling and processions, combined with fantastic animals of the type that are found on Greek proto-Geometric pottery. Through situla art passed an eclectic mixture of Greek, Cypriot and Etruscan styles into those of Early La Tène. Here these two exotic elements, the Orientalizing and the classical, were combined with the indigenous traditions of the preceding Hallstatt culture. From this stage onwards through the succeeding Waldalgesheim, Plastic and Sword Styles the development of Celtic art, which was to terminate with the conquests of Caesar in the mid-first century BC, can be traced.

La Tène art in Britain

It is increasingly apparent that La Tène art came to Britain as late as the late second century BC and that the few early pieces were exceptional and did not give rise immediately to insular schools.[10]

British La Tène art retained its individuality, though motifs current in mainland Europe were used extensively. Regional groups were more apparent than on the Continent. The essence of insular art was swirling designs, often in groups of three, with stylized birds' heads, curved-sided triangles or trumpet spirals used as linking or terminal elements. It was much less representational than the continental – anthropomorphic features were as rare as animals, though the latter became more common nearer the Roman conquest.[11]

The final phase of La Tène insular art began at the end of the first century BC and is the one with which this study is most concerned. On the whole the work in mainland Britain was degenerate and increasingly influenced by the Roman. The Waterloo Bridge helmet has a stalk pattern with enamel studs, and there are a series of collars with spiral ornament which show signs of Roman formalism. Cross-hatching is replaced by stipple for the infill of voids. The berried rosette appeared as a new motif in the workshops of north-east England.

It is not easy to determine how late native works can be recognized in La Tène or La Tène derivative style in Britain and Ireland. The art found among the Romano-Britons in the Civil Zone of the province owed little to Celtic models. It is impossible to distinguish much of Celtic art in the rough-and-ready plastic ornament or painted scrolls of Castor and New Forest pottery. There are, however, a few late examples of metalwork. The Elmswell Mount from Yorkshire had good La Tène lyre scroll combined with vinescroll borrowed from the Roman but enriched with trumpet spirals. Combined with champlevé red and blue-green enamel it bears certain affinities to a decorated fragment from London and to the Balmacellan mirror handle from Kirkcudbrightshire. With it can be classed a few other works, notably brooches, such as those from Greatchesters (Aesica) on Hadrian's Wall, and Tr'er Ceiri in north Wales, which belong to the end of the first century AD and constitute native copies of imported fantailed brooches. Although usually thought of as a northern product, the Aesica Brooch along with the Wraxhall Collar may have been made in the south-east. From such works as these can be recognized a late style, aptly termed by Megaw 'art nouveau' of the first and early second century AD in England.[12] A faint hint of the old Celtic birds' heads can also be seen in other brooches of the Roman period, notably those of Birdlip type.

Of greater interest, however, must be some brooches and mounts from the northern part of the province, notably the garishly enamelled animal brooches that enjoyed a currency in the second century, and the equally brash but attractive dragonesque brooches. The latter, though probably inspired by Roman hippocamps, nonetheless bear a curious similarity to the 'swimming elephant' of Pictish art in the treatment of their terminals.[13]

A pair of large mounts from South Shields with an openwork design of a triquetra of trumpets, along with one from Icklingham, Suffolk, represent the first of a series of openwork horse fittings produced from the second century onwards throughout the Empire and which are particularly common in northern Gaul and the Rhineland.[14] The same openwork trumpet motifs appear on brooches. The provenance of these pieces is unknown, but they are crucial in determining the true origins of Early Christian art motifs.

In Scotland, the end of the development comes probably around the time of Severus, in the decades around 200. The last products were the massive bronze armlets of the 'Caledonian' school, which as well as the bracelet from Culbin Sands, Moray, are decorated in rather crude plastic ornament and enamel, and probably represent the extension of a general Brigantian Style to be found also in northern England.[15]

The chronology of the last products of the late La Tène world in Ireland has been violently disputed. It has been argued that if something of the old style could linger on in Britain, in spite of Roman domination, until the second century, products could still have been made in Ireland in the third and fourth centuries to form a continuous sequence with the metalwork of the Early Christian period. Various dates are arguable for the Bann Disc, Petrie Crown and the Cork Horns, but because they are in harmony with the last phase of La Tène art in Britain and compare favourably with for instance the dragonesque fibulae and Aesica type of brooches, they should probably be dated no later than the first or second century AD.[16] The basic element in them is a broken-backed scroll with birds' head terminals, a device also employed in later Early Christian art in Ireland.

A series of products do seem to link the Iron Age with the post-Roman period in Britain. These are the animal heads, normally those of oxen, which appear as handle attachments for bronze-mounted buckets in the Iron Age and in Roman Britain. Hawkes has shown that the buckets they adorn belong to an Iron Age, even Bronze Age tradition, which seems to have been kept alive by native craftsmen in the Romano-British period.[17] The oxen themselves belong to the tradition of symbolic animals that were so popular with the La Tène Celts, and the ancestors of the Romano-British ox heads can be seen in a series of similar bronzes such as that from Ham Hill, Somerset, or the Lexden Tumulus, Colchester, while ox heads also adorn the iron fire dogs of Iron Age Britain.[18] The bucket-handle ox heads occur in the Belgic hoard from near Felmersham, Bedfordshire, and there are a series leading to the unique Mount Sorrel bucket from Leicestershire, probably of the late third century AD. From an Anglian cemetery at Twyford, Leicestershire, comes a fragmentary bucket with an ox head attachment, which was made presumably by a British craftsman. A further bucket, of bronze-bound yew wood from Ty'r Dewin (Brynkir, Caernarvonshire) is of uncertain date, but probably belongs to the Early Christian period. These few late examples of bucket animals cannot be regarded as the last survivors of a dead tradition, they belong rather to a continuing industry which must have enjoyed a new lease of life as pottery gradually went out of use in the fifth century.

Roman metal openwork (Fig. 131)

It may be argued, then, that the last threads of insular La Tène art can be traced into the second century AD, though there were lingering traditions of native craftsmanship that may have kept alive something of the repertoire of motifs, if not the art itself, on a fairly humble level.

Most of the ornamental motifs to be found in metalwork of the fifth and sixth centuries can also be found in Roman Britain on metal openwork, of the type represented at South Shields and Icklingham. The taste for openwork seems to have been deep-rooted among the barbarians, both Celt and German, and there are numerous examples of it in La Tène contexts.[19] Probably as early as the first century AD some Roman openwork bronzes were being produced, as can be seen for example at Newstead.[20] By the later second to mid-third century a type of openwork brooch developed, characterized by a divided foot, which is found in contexts as far apart as Dura-Europos and Richborough.[21] That they reached Ireland as well as Britain can be demonstrated by the development of the Navan type of brooch, ultimately inspired

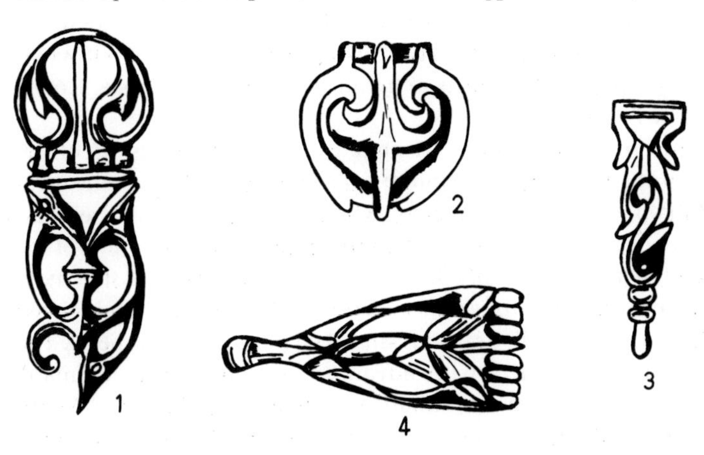

Figure 131 Roman metal openwork and (4) The Navan type of brooch (After Jope)

by these divided brooches. In other contexts it has been demonstrated by Jope and Wilson that by the second century the influence of Roman provincial workshops was being felt in Ireland, as can be seen for example in the connection between the bowls from a mirror burial at Colchester[22] and that from Keshcarrigan, Co. Leitrim.[23]

A special category of Roman openwork may also have contributed to the basic repertoire of motifs current in late Roman Britain. This is the series of buckles, plates and other miscellaneous bronzes particularly popular among the barbarian federates in the late Roman Empire, which were imported to Britain and copied extensively mainly in the fifth century.[24] These 'Vermand' Style bronzes were produced in accordance with Germanic taste but following Roman prototypes, and occur in a broad belt across the northern *limes*.

Some embryonic elements of Early Christian art can also be distinguished in a series of late Romano-British objects ranging from the hoard of late

Roman silverwork from Traprain Law to an engraved bone from Lydney. Late Roman silver hoards, such as that from Coleraine, are considered to have been loot from Britain carried over to Ireland, and could easily have provided inspiration for Irish craftsmen. It is now known that Roman mosaics were being laid in the late fourth century at, for example, Great Casterton villa (Rutland), Hinton St Mary's (Dorset) and Frocester Court (Gloucester). In view of this it is possible that mosaics could have contributed some motifs, notably guilloche and chequer patterns, to Celtic Christian art.[25]

The Eurasiatic animal style (Figs 132–3)

The Eurasiatic animal style of the Steppes was perhaps the most extensive, pervasive and long-lived art tradition in history.[26] Basically, this tradition employed, in a decorative fashion, animals of a lively character. Scythian art marked the greatest flowering of the style. Its influence was to be felt wherever the Steppe peoples had contacts – it can be detected in Persia, Korea, Japan and central Europe.

Hints of a preference for animal art among the remote ancestors of the Steppe people, in the late third millennium BC, come especially from the great tumulus at Maikop in the Kuban region, where gold and silver vessels and appliqués for hangings show a variety of animal representation.[27] Most of the characteristics of what is generally known as Eurasiatic animal style now appear to have been the result of contacts between the Scythians and related peoples on the one hand and Urartians and Assyrians on the other.[28] The latter were settled city dwellers with advanced art, which included many animal motifs. A result of extended military activity in the eighth and seventh centuries BC among all these peoples was a great enrichment of Scythian equipment and art, and, in due course, bridging the turn of the sixth and fifth centuries BC, the expansion of the Achaemenid Empire across Asia Minor to European Thrace further reinforced the supply of Oriental motifs.

From the sixth century BC examples of animal style ornament, which may have contributed to La Tène art can be recognized in the Carpathians and Lower Danubian regions. From the third to the first century BC there appears to have been trade or other contact from Celtic groups settled near the Middle Danube and in the Carpathians, reaching as far north as Denmark. The bronze cauldron with ox head protomes from Brå is an outstanding example probably of the third century BC. The silver cauldron from Gundestrup, and the silver cups from Mollerup, show stronger Thracian, or Dacian inspiration, and may be dated to the late second or early first century BC. Finally, some examples of a powerful animal style in the shape of silver *phalerae* for horse gear found their way as far west as the Rhone and the Channel Islands. These objects in the style of Pontic workshops of the first century BC were probably carried west by Thracian mounted auxiliaries in the Roman army.[29]

Figure 132 Animal art in Europe. I Backward looking animals. (1) Silver mount, Carinthia; (2) Ordos bronze; (3) Howletts quoit brooch; (4) Alfriston buckle plate; (5) From a brooch, Nordheim, Vestfold, Norway; (6) Killamery Brooch, Ireland; (7) Detail from beaker, Lilla Jøred; (8) From a pole top, Kurgan near Ul', Kuban; (9) From Aberlemno Cross, Angus; (10) Pictish stone, Rossie, Perthshire; (11) Beltclasp, Koban well grave; (12) Bone plate, Zharotin, Lower Dniepr; (13) Aylesford bucket, Kent

The animal style art of the Steppes had some representation, then, in Iron Age Europe. There is at present no reason to suppose that it was a part of insular La Tène tradition, and the animal art of the Scottish Iron Age that Thomas has seen as the precursor of the Pictish is on the whole a far cry from the traditions of the Scythians.[30] Certainly in England there is nothing comparable, and the suggestion that it was a peasant art, transmitted from Europe through textiles, pottery and even tattoos, seems unlikely. To argue in favour of such an Iron Age transmission would require more positive evidence than a rough similarity between some animal representations from Scotland and some from continental Europe.

Figure 133 Animal art in Europe. II Shoulder spirals. (1) Basse-Yutz flagon, France; (2) Lullingstone hanging bowl; (3) Papil stone, Shetland; (4) Ordos bronze; (5) Grantown, Elgin; (6) *Book of Durrow*. Scales: various

While it is possible that Scottish Iron Age animal art may have contributed to the art of the Pictish symbol stones, it is more likely that the motifs were the outcome of influences from a new source. At present it is only possible to recognize in various contexts hints of the animal style in post-Roman Britain and Ireland. Shoulder spirals, a distinctive feature of Eurasiatic animal art, appear in Pictish sculpture, in Hiberno-Saxon manuscripts, on the Lullingstone hanging bowl and on Viking period stones from the Isle of Man (Fig. 133). Perhaps the common source for the re-emergence of Eurasiatic elements is to be found in Scandinavia; they may have passed thence to Anglo-Saxon England. The Eurasiatic style is certainly an element in Germanic art, and has been regarded as a contributory element in the formation of the art of the Goths, who seem to have adopted it in the Ukraine from the Sarmatians.

The problem is complicated, for Germanic art of the Migration Period owes much to the products of late Antique workshops, in which a hybrid repertoire of Antique and barbarian styles was current.

Germanic art

Another contributor to Early Christian 'Celtic' design is the Germanic tradition, most notably the Styles I and II of northern Europe, first recognized by Salin in 1904.[31]

Style I was not the first Germanic style in Britain – the Quoit Brooch Style preceded it, but was more restricted in its distribution.[32] Although mainly centring on Canterbury, the Quoit Brooch Style represents, in all probability, the work of Germanic craftsmen operating in a native late Romano-British tradition. One of the interesting features of the group of metalwork in this style is the form of the Quoit Brooch itself – it is quite simply a penannular brooch round which a circular plate (the 'quoit') has been added, and as such belongs to the tradition of penannular brooches.

Salin's Style I embraced all animal ornament of the fifth century in northern Europe, continuing into the sixth. The style, which probably stems from late Roman metalwork, is characterized by semi-naturalistic animals, in which the elements are broken down into individual shapes. It can best be explained by illustration (Fig. 134).

Style II shows a new element, ribbon ornament, composed of ribbon-like animals distorted into twining serpents or lacertines. The bodies are flat, and the intertwining not necessarily symmetrical. Salin was inclined to believe that this ribbon interlace had a north European origin, but it soon became apparent that its appearance in north Europe was prompted by external stimulus – southern or Byzantine ribbon interlace – which, it was suggested, became disseminated in Europe following the Lombard invasion of Italy in 568.[33] Some recent discoveries have modified this picture further. The finds from a princess's grave from Cologne and of the grave of Queen Arnegunde of the Franks at St Denis have shown that ribbon interlace and a type of Style II ornament were known in the Frankish world at least as early as 575, while Hawkes has recently pointed out that northern contact with Italy began as early as the time of Theudibert I, who died in 548.[34] On the basis of this evidence it would be reasonable to suppose that ribbon interlace became disseminated in Europe in the late sixth century.

An important feature, however, of Style II interlace is its regionalism – Kentish and East Anglian Style II (the latter represented by the Sutton Hoo treasure) is in the final assessment an individualistic art, which owes something at least to underlying native traditions. So too should the Scandinavian variants of the style be regarded. The finds from the great cemetery site at Valsgarde, Uppland, Sweden, have led to the recognition of five different

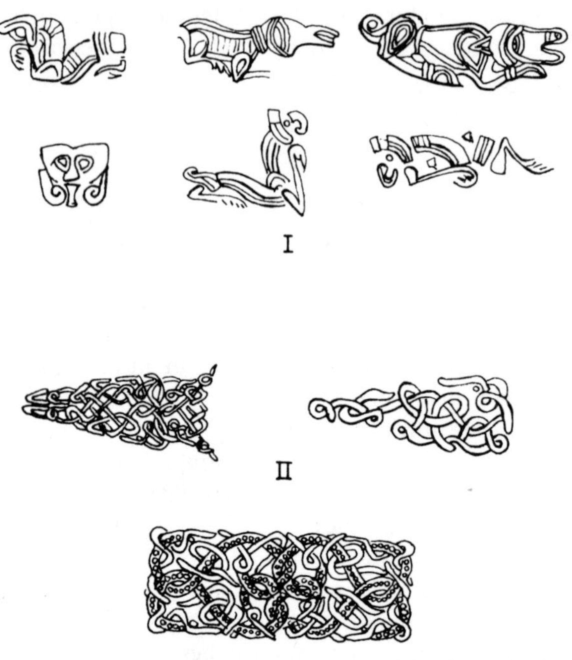

Figure 134 Styles I and II – typical ornamental details, England and Europe (After Aberg 1928)

types of animal art, of which three are variants of the basic Style II. Behind the full flowering of Scandinavian Style II can be seen an earlier tradition that is certainly native and owes nothing to Mediterranean models.[35] This style can be traced in a series of bracteates – thin gold plates originally made to imitate Roman coins – of which Class D in particular can be seen in the Jutish phase in Kent (*c.* 490–525 AD).[36] On these bracteates a loose type of interlace can be recognized, which developed into a type of ribbon ornament, well exemplified on a late native bracteate from Kent, a roundel from a cemetery at Rhenen in the Netherlands and a disc from Dunadd in Argyll, recently illustrated in another context by Fowler (Fig. 135).[37]

Ribbon interlace appeared first in Celtic metalwork around 600, when it occurred on moulds from the Mote of Mark, Kirkcudbright.[38] Among the moulds dated on site evidence is one for a mount, similar to one from Caenby, Lincs, of approximately the same date, while interlace also occurs on other moulds for mounts and for penannular brooches of Fowler Class H. It next appeared later in the seventh century, when it was used in manuscripts and on several pieces of metalwork, including the Moylough belt shrine.

The Mote of Mark interlace, which includes double-strand ribbons, is not animal interlace and, though similar in many respects to Style II lacertine ornament, should be regarded as a separate tradition. Its contemporaneity with Anglo-Saxon interlace suggests that it is not derived from Anglo-Saxon England, especially in view of the restricted nature of contact between Celts and Saxons around 600, and more probably a direct continental origin should be sought. The most likely explanation is not that it came from northern Europe but rather from the Mediterranean, where interlace of similar type (including double strand) was current from the fifth century onwards. Coptic textiles, as shown by an example now in Manchester,[39] were frequently decorated with interlace, and Coptic influence from Egypt is probably the most likely explanation. Later Hiberno-Saxon manuscripts show evidence for

Figure 135 Three roundels showing widespread occurrence of ribbon ornament. (1) Rhenen; (2) Kent; (3) Dunadd. (After Fowler)

Coptic influence (see appendix, p. 390), and Coptic imports are quite probable if the nature of the Mediterranean trade in pottery in the Irish Sea region is considered.

Later seventh-century interlace could represent a development of that used at the Mote of Mark, but equally probably could be due to fresh ideas reaching the Celtic world from Anglo-Saxon England or the Continent.

The melting pot of traditions

Fowler has drawn up a list of the elements to be found in 'Celtic' art of the fifth and sixth centuries, and from this it can be seen that all the components could be found in some form or other in Roman Britain (Fig. 136).[40] Even if the range is extended to include works of the early seventh century, there is nothing in the basic range of ornament that was not available from the common pool of designs. It may be argued that this or that design has no apparent prototype in the region in which it was found, but this is irrelevant. It is increasingly apparent that in the fifth and sixth centuries there was an amalgam of basic motifs derived from a wide range of sources available to artists working in different parts of Britain and Ireland. In the troubled times of the fifth century, raids and folk movements could have spread motifs and articles. By the end of the century the seeds of regionalism were sown, the hand-pin 'eye peak' in Ireland, for example, that was to develop fully in the seventh century.

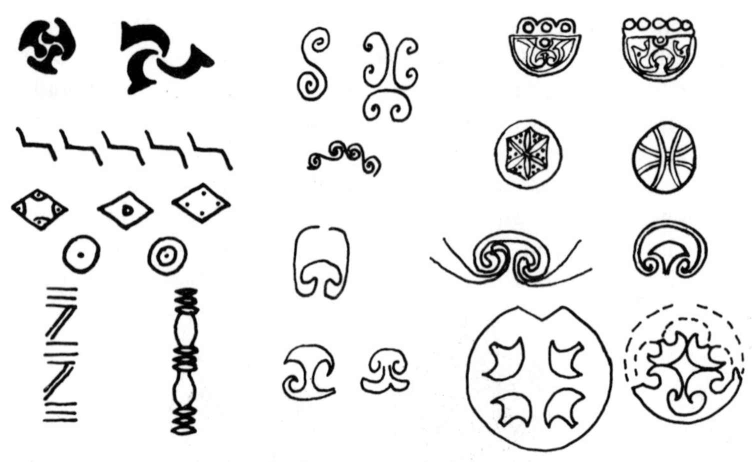

Figure 136 'Grammar' of Dark Age art (After Fowler 1963)

Roman Britain in the late fourth or early fifth century was a different world from that of the first or second: it was already barbarous, with a strong admixture of Germanic peoples, as metalwork and a recent study of the pottery shows. By the fifth century the Romano-Britons were distinct from their barbarian neighbours in political organization and religion rather than in material culture. A mixed population in lowland Britain would explain the eclectic character of art exemplified in the hanging bowl escutcheons of the later fifth to seventh centuries.

Celtic ornamental metalwork

The formative period for Celtic ornamental metalwork seems to have been the late seventh century AD. By around 700 the techniques were mastered and the most superb products of the tradition, such as the Ardagh Chalice or the Tara Brooch, were being produced. Certainly the impetus behind this great period of creativity was Anglo-Saxon work, although the flowering of Irish metal working was much later than the period of its inspiration: most of the Kentish jewellery was produced in the first half of the seventh century, and the East Anglian workshops that made the jewels for Sutton Hoo were in operation in the first three decades of the century. This hiatus, which is just one of many at present afflicting the study of Early Christian art in the Celtic west, may be more apparent than real. It is possible that some of the well-known objects should be down-dated – there is, for example, no conclusive argument why the Tara Brooch should not be dated earlier in the seventh century than the date usually ascribed to it.

Hanging bowls[41] (Fig. 137)

Hanging bowls have probably prompted more studies than any other subject in the field of post-Roman archaeology. Because they were believed to be Irish, and most were known from Anglo-Saxon graves, mystery surrounded their place of manufacture and a similar confusion grew up surrounding their purpose.

Hanging bowls can now be seen to be derived from a series of late Roman metal bowls and are part of the general tradition of sub-Roman metalwork in Celtic Britain. They seem to have served several purposes: in some cases the term 'hanging bowl' is clearly a misnomer. They appear to have been in general use among both Celtic and Anglo-Saxon elements in the population. They were made mainly during the fifth to seventh centuries and the few related objects of later date, such as the Ballinderry 1 hanging lamp, are not

Figure 137 Triskele motifs from hanging bowl escutcheons. (1) Barlaston; (2) Winchester; (3) Barrington. (After Leeds)

true hanging bowls. There are almost as many different designs as there are hanging bowl escutcheons, and their diversity defies classification or detailed chronology. On present evidence the development seems to have followed several parallel courses – typologically 'early' and 'late' features may be seen on the same bowl. In general terms bowls with undecorated escutcheons can be distinguished from those with openwork decoration, or those with enamelled decoration. Some, if not all, of the undecorated examples seem to be Romano-British, while if comparison with late Roman open metalwork is valid, a small group of openwork escutcheons should probably be placed in the fifth (to later sixth?) century. Those with enamelling belong to the sixth and seventh centuries in all probability. Further discovery, however, may question even so simple a scheme.

The first outstanding problem that should be considered is the question of Irish provenance. Now that it is recognized that enamelwork and millefiori were being produced on both sides of the Irish Sea, the claim that all hanging bowls are Irish because most of them are thus decorated is open to doubt. Until recently there were no recognized hanging bowls from Ireland, but a distinctive group is now becoming apparent in Ireland and Scandinavia. This group (Group C of Mlle Henry's classification) is distinguished by having the rim of the bowl rolled over an iron wire to strengthen it.[42] It is best represented by the famous Miklebostad vessel from Norway, with its fine enamelled human-shaped escutcheons, or in Ireland by the escutcheons from Ferns and Clonmacnois. The notable feature of this Irish group is the way in which it draws upon a variety of elements from other vessels. It seems likely that the hanging bowl was not a common Irish product until the late seventh to eighth centuries.[43] Roman ancestral types are necessarily lacking in Ireland; there is one openwork escutcheon from the Bann, but the general absence of openwork motifs from the Irish bowls might imply that the technique was used in Britain prior to the adoption of hanging bowls in Ireland.

Recently attention has been drawn to a group of three triangular hanging bowls, from Cuillard (Co. Roscommon), Kilgulbin East (Co. Kerry) and Ballynacourty (Co. Waterford), of wood, bronze and stone respectively. Their similarity to a silver dish from the Traprain treasure has suggested an earlier date for them than their British counterparts, although the bronze example has an ogham inscription which could not be earlier than the mid-seventh century and which cannot be proved to be a later addition to the bowl.[44] As a group they are diagnostic, and their shape sets them aside from the main tradition of round hanging bowls, relating them more to the tradition of the Ballinderry lamp.

The second problem of the hanging bowls is that of function. Various suggestions have been put forward – that they were decorative hanging vases,[45] lamps,[46] hand basins[47] or votive chalices.[48] It is probable that hanging bowls served different functions according to particular requirements. That all served as lamps seems very unlikely – the fish at the bottom of the Sutton Hoo bowl, for example, was clearly intended to be seen, and would be most explicable if it were intended to be seen swimming in clear water rather than oil. A text from Bede suggests that the bowls were most often intended as secular vessels for washing hands.[49] It has recently been suggested that the bowls were not suspended from a height, which would have put too much strain on the relatively weak escutcheon loops, but were supported from a tripod.[50]

The immediate antecedents of the hanging bowls can be found in a series of late Roman vessels, such as those from Finningley and Irchester, which have slightly thickened inward-inclined rims, and hooks cast either in the form of birds or animals, usually with triangular escutcheons. Usually there were three or four escutcheons, and decoration was confined to the animal attachments. This type of bowl is fourth-century in origin, and occurs in fifth-century Anglo-Saxon graves. A further development seems to have taken place in the fifth century, when the rim was folded over and hammered down, from which the escutcheons were outbent. The earliest example is on a vessel from a grave at Sleaford, Lincolnshire. About the same time there seems to have been a progression from the plain escutcheon of oval type, which was a relatively rare Roman form, to a round openwork one, the openwork idea being taken over from some of the late Roman metal openwork which enjoyed a wide currency in the late fourth to early fifth centuries. Plain triangular (heater) and bird-shaped escutcheons continued to be made alongside the new openwork type, sometimes engraved ornament being added – a few examples come from datable contexts, such as from Ballinderry 2 or Ford Down (sixth-century).

On present evidence there are forty-five isolated escutcheons, twenty-five bowls, and seven bowl fragments surviving. Of these, nine are openwork and ten plain. Two bowls at least (Wilton and Keythorpe) and a great number of escutcheons were lost from excavated Anglo-Saxon graves. In all, the total number of escutcheons recorded is in the neighbourhood of seventy to eighty, of which fifty to sixty are from Anglo-Saxon contexts. While some of the isolated escutcheons may be from bowls that have perished, quite possibly many were preserved as objects of intrinsic value, long after the bowls to which they were attached had corroded, and were placed in the graves simply as ornaments. With the exception of two silver vessels (one lost, from the Witham, Lincolnshire, the other from St Ninian's Isle) which are probably late Northumbrian variants, the bowls were made of very thin beaten or spun bronze and were very fragile. The Sutton Hoo bowl was repaired with an elaborate silver patch, while the Lullingstone bowl's elaborate ornament may have been for strengthening purposes. The Baginton bowl was also patched.

It has been suggested that escutcheons with red enamel only date from the fifth century, possibly continuing into the sixth, while those with both millefiori and enamel date from the sixth.[51] Those with yellow enamel are the latest, since there is no evidence for its introduction prior to the seventh century. Most of the motifs employed in escutcheon ornament are variants of the standard repertoire of fifth- to seventh-century art. The most frequent are developed pelta or trumpet patterns, frequently in a triquetra arrangement. Interlace is rare, and does not appear to have been used before the mid-seventh century. Christian motifs appear on what seem to be late escutcheons. One from Faversham, Kent, shows a cross between two serpents. Such motifs would be compatible with a liturgical use of some bowls, and Irish monastic finds, coupled with evidence from Whitby (Yorkshire) and Glastonbury (Somerset) might imply that some were produced in monastic workshops.

The recent discovery of a hanging bowl escutcheon mould from Craig Phadrig, Inverness, in Pictland (discussed on p. 64),[52] shows that some hanging bowls at least were being made in Pictland, and that the openwork type of escutcheon, hitherto believed by many to be exclusively of the fifth century, continued in production well into the sixth.

Ornamental metalwork 650–800

The hanging bowls represent the greatest known achievements of Celtic art of the fifth to seventh centuries, and are the only large pieces of ornamental metalwork to have survived. Along with the penannular brooches, latchets, pins, studs and other small articles used as dress attachments (discussed in Chapter 12), they constitute the evidence for the art of the metalworker in those centuries. That is not to suppose that larger objects were not produced, and the sophisticated character of the surviving examples of late seventh-century ornamental ecclesiastical metalwork suggests that some predecessors existed, none of which has survived. Nevertheless, the Church in the Celtic-speaking areas in the early centuries of the post-Roman period appears to have been assiduous in its adherence to the ideal of simplicity and poverty, and not until the Irish monasteries began to grow during the later seventh century did highly ornate and complex ornamental metalwork develop.

Until the seventh century there was a general tradition of 'Irish Sea province' metalwork, with regional distinctions of minimal importance. Already, however, by the late sixth and early seventh centuries there were signs in the development of penannular brooches, and other types of dress fastener, that regionalization of styles was beginning; by the later seventh century a distinctive Irish art was developed which was connected with the development of the monastic Church in Ireland. All the surviving ornamental metalwork, with the exception of brooches and pins, is ecclesiastical. Much of it was probably produced in monastic workshops, and most that has survived takes the form of reliquaries or parts of reliquaries, other categories of Church furniture being conspicuously rare or absent.

The pre-eminence of Ireland in this connection should not obscure the fact that metalwork was being produced elsewhere. There is ample evidence that Pictish metal smiths were producing fine works in many ways comparable to the Irish, from shrines such as the Monymusk reliquary to richly ornamented penannular brooches.[53] Other workshops, too, seem to have been in operation in Scotland: some of the moulds from the Mote of Mark, Kirkcudbright, are for complex objects produced in the late sixth and early seventh centuries, while other objects found in Scotland, such as the Hoddom crozier shrine, may also have been produced in local schools.[54]

The importance of Northumbrian metal-working and manuscript and sculptural art must be appreciated to understand fully the nature of the Irish tradition of ornamental metal working. The variety of sources contributory to Northumbrian art can best be demonstrated from the sources for some of the early manuscripts. The sources of the *Book of Durrow*, for instance, which can be classified under six headings: (a) decorative elements derived from the general tradition of British art of the Early Christian period which in turn owes much to late Roman metalwork; (b) elements derived from the mainstream of Anglo-Saxon metalwork, and which are in turn related to European barbarian art traditions; (c) elements which are derived possibly from Romano-British art; (d) elements derived directly from late Antique art transmitted to Northumbria through manuscripts imported from Italy; (e) elements derived from Pictish art or the tradition of animal art it represents; (f) elements derived from Coptic and other Eastern artistic traditions. These varying traditions were to come together in Northumbria as a result of the great cultural revival which centred round the monasteries of Monkwearmouth and Jarrow. To some extent the same sources were available in seventh-century Ireland, with the exception of (b), (c) and (e), and where there are features in Irish art that seem to be derived from any of these three sources a Northumbrian model is likely, though it is possible that the model was introduced to Ireland from a more direct source. Considerable attention has been paid to Northumbrian manuscript and sculptural art in the past, and very little to Northumbrian metalwork. To some extent this has been due to its relative scarcity and fragmentary character, but it should not be overlooked in a study of Early Christian metalwork. The series of book mounts and other decorated objects from the monastery of Whitby are particularly informative for comparative purposes.[55]

In the late seventh century a general artistic blossoming was generated in the Columban monasteries stemming from the foundation of Iona and Lindisfarne. In this context Iona has probably been greatly underestimated in the past as a centre of artistic production. There is good reason to suppose that the *Book of Kells* was begun if not completed there. At a slightly later date a vigorous and important school of sculpture grew up on the island, characterized by high crosses which are clearly linked to the Irish series. Recent excavation, too, has shown that metal working was carried out there.

The metalwork of the late seventh century is characterized by its continuing use of enamel, usually set in T-, L- or S-shaped patterns or in the form of a cross.[56] In the late seventh century red was used as a background for yellow and green enamel and insets of blue and white or black and yellow millefiori. The geometric arrangement is almost certainly due to the influence of Anglo-Saxon metal-working techniques. The other feature of metalwork of this period is the use of engraving on the surface of the metal, usually deeply cut but still with the character of a freehand sketch. This technique of engraving appears to be generally alien to Anglo-Saxon England or even northern Gaul, though to judge by its appearance on the Monymusk reliquary it was a feature also of Pictish work. The basic techniques were cross-hatching or dots for background and openwork, with a sheet of metal of a different colour showing through. Early in the eighth century this type of relatively shallow engraving was replaced by a type of relief, and about the same time 'pseudo chip carving' was acquired from the Anglo-Saxons, one of the earliest examples being on a crozier head from Copenhagen.

In the second half of the eighth century high relief casting became popular, the main elements being trumpet and spiral patterns. The Ekerö crozier and the St Germain shrine finials belong to this category. At the end of the eighth century high relief work was abandoned in favour of rectilinear interlace done in chip-carved technique, which continued into the ninth century.

Ornamentation on the metalwork consists of two elements: geometric designs based on spirals, trumpet patterns and trilobate designs, of the type current in the sixth and seventh centuries; and animal interlace derived probably from Style II products in Anglo-Saxon England. A few animals closely resembling Style II creatures appear early – they are present for example on the terminals of a brooch found at Bergøy – but in general the Irish lacertine and its Scottish counterpart is a different animal. It is more realistic than the Anglo-Saxon, with a fairly naturalistic head, eye with pupils, teeth and claws, and normally has the distinctive feature of joint and crest spirals and hatching on the body. The spirals show its affinity to the Pictish animals as does its naturalism, which is removed from the abstraction of Style II beasts. Whether it is influenced by Pictish art, or whether it has the same ultimate origin, is impossible to tell. Earlier in the eighth century the engraved work shows influence from the Hiberno-Saxon Lindisfarne Style, and the 'Lindisfarne bird' makes an occasional appearance on Irish metalwork. The human figure is very rare, and when it does occur is both stylized and distinctive. Human figures adorn the escutcheons of the Myklebostad hanging bowl. They have enamelled rectangles for bodies and slightly almond-shaped heads with distinctively amygdaloid eyes without pupils, which recur in Irish art down to the full Romanesque period. The Athlone Crucifixion plaque, which once adorned a book cover, shows the Irish lack of interest in naturalism, the heads of the figures being tilted at impossible angles and the mouths being simply down-turned crescents.

The surviving reliquaries are often fragmentary due to their composite construction, panels of ornament being made separately and riveted. The most common category is the house-shaped shrine with hipped gable roof – a little box in the stylized form of a chapel into which any type of relic could be inserted. A second class, also fairly common, is the crozier shrine, made to encapsulate the staff of an early saint. These were shaped like walking sticks, with a straight drop and usually a crest with knops on the stem. Shrines were also made for such things as the bells, books or belts of early saints. Specific corporeal reliquaries are rarer, but include an arm-shaped shrine and another for a foot. These are, however, later in date than the house-shaped shrines. Reliquaries of these general types continued to be made throughout the Early Christian period and even later in the Middle Ages in Ireland.

Major examples of metalwork, c. 650–800 AD

The principal surviving pieces of metalwork of the period are briefly listed below in the approximate order of production.

(1) *The Moylough belt shrine* (Plate 12A)[57] was found in peat-cutting in 1943 at Tubbercurry, Moylough Townland (Co. Sligo), and at the time of its discovery was believed to be simply an ornamental belt. Careful examination has shown, however, that the metal casing covers a leather original. It shows strong Anglo-Saxon influence and dates probably from the very end of the seventh century. It consists of four hinged segments, each incorporating a section of belt between bronze plates, and is decorated with medallions, rectangular panels and a skeuomorphic buckle, of a form clearly derived from Germanic prototypes. The segments of the belt and buckle are decorated with champlevé enamels, millefiori, coloured glass, studs with metal inlay, embossed plates of silver, plates of openwork silvered bronze with mica backing, and other devices. The motifs employed are those in current use in the late seventh century for hanging bowls and other works – simple interlace, trumpet patterns, hairspring spirals, triskeles, long-beaked birds' heads, curled-snout open-jawed animal heads and yellow enamel in L-, T- and S-shaped frames. Animal interlace and chip carving are both absent, and the fact that they are used on the Ardagh Chalice implies that the Moylough belt shrine is earlier.

(2) *The Ekerö crozier*[58] was found at the Scandinavian trading site of Ekerö near Stockholm in 1955, and is a crozier head comprising a volute on a socket. It is difficult to date, but most probably was made around 700. The volute ends in an animal head with gaping jaws, in which a human head is gripped, representing Jonah and the whale. The socket and one side of the volute has extensive inlay with enamel and millefiori, while the other side is adorned with sharp relief hatched modelling, of chip-carved type.

(3) *The Ardagh Chalice.*[59] Found in 1868 in a rath at Ardagh, Co. Limerick, by a boy digging for potatoes, the Ardagh Chalice was concealed under a stone slab with four brooches and a small bronze chalice. It was probably made around 700 AD, although the brooches show that it was not buried until at least Viking times. It is liturgical, and is usually regarded as one of the finest achievements of late Celtic art. It is made of two hemispheres of sheet silver joined together by a rivet which is hidden by a gilt-bronze band with chased decoration. The handles and plaques which attach them to the bowl together with two medallions on each side of the bowl are decorated with filigree and red and blue enamels. A decorated band runs round the bowl, just below the rim, while another runs round the foot. The bowl is lightly engraved with the names of the twelve apostles and some animal interlace. The enamels were produced from a clay mould fitted with a metal grill. The cup also has blue glass beads encrusted with gold spirals produced by the same method and set on the foot and the handles. Other glass studs were

simply moulded. The filigree is particularly fine, and was produced by using several gold wires of varying thicknesses soldered one above the other to form interlace or animals in outline. The use of such studs is probably in imitation of continental ecclesiastical metalwork, but the result is essentially Celtic.

(4) *The Tara Brooch* (Fig. 116).[60] The provenance of this brooch is unknown, and its name was given it by a firm of Dublin jewellers in the 1870s who were producing replicas of it to sell as souvenirs. It is a large penannular brooch, and is discussed in its context (p. 315). It is probably nearly contemporary with the Ardagh Chalice (i.e. datable to *c.* 700) and employs similar decorative techniques, but is far less restrained and therefore less successful to modern eyes.

(5) *Athlone Crucifixion plaque.*[61] This was found at St John's, near Athlone, Co. Westmeath, and is an openwork depiction of the Crucifixion with two angels above and Stephanus and Longinus below. It is of iron, originally copper gilt. It is the earliest of a series of openwork Crucifixion plaques, and dates from the mid-eighth century. The figures, which are very stylized, are decorated with ornamental spirals, fret patterns and interlace. It may have served as a book mount, or, less probably, the mount for a pax panel.

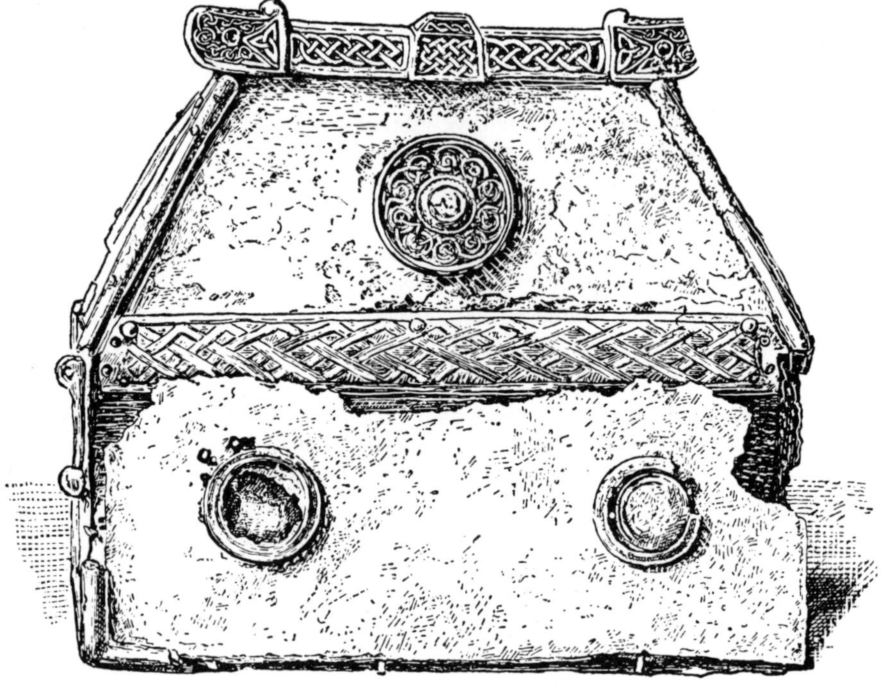

Figure 138 The Lough Erne shrine

(6) *The Lough Erne shrine* (Fig. 138)[62] was found between Belleek and Enniskillen, on Lough Erne, Co. Fermanagh. It is a house-shaped shrine consisting of a yew wood box covered with bronze plates with ornamental bronze attachments. Inside was a smaller undecorated shrine of similar type. It dates from the early eighth century. The surviving decoration consists mainly of geometric interlace, confined to ridge, roundels and binders.

(7) *Monymusk reliquary* (Fig. 139).[63] This object appears never to have been lost. It is sometimes termed the Brecbennoch of St Columba, is said to have been carried at Bannockburn and is mentioned in landgrants of the early fourteenth century. It is a house-shaped shrine, and dates from around 700. It is 4 inches long, carved out of solid wood, cased with bronze plates fastened with hollow-moulded angle strips. The front is faced with engraved silver. It has hinged strap terminals for a carrying strap, and like the Lough Erne shrine is decorated with ornamental roundels. It is probably of Pictish workmanship.

(8) *The Shannon shrine*[64] was found in the Shannon and is now in the National Museum of Antiquities in Edinburgh. It is a house-shaped

Figure 139 The Monymusk reliquary

shrine of bronze. Binding strips, hinges and all but one of the rectangular ornamental mounts are missing. It is of eighth-century date.

(9) *The Emly shrine.*[65] Of uncertain provenance, this shrine was for long in the possession of the Monsell family of Tervoe, Co. Limerick, hence its other name 'The Monsell of Tervoe' shrine. It is now in the Museum of Fine Arts, Boston. It is of yew wood covered with bronze decorated with ornamental roundels, set against a step pattern background. Late seventh-century.

(10) *The Copenhagen shrine.*[66] This was found in Norway, but the provenance is unknown. It presumably was taken as loot by the Vikings. It is a house-shaped shrine, and dates from the early eighth century. The face is decorated with engraved interlace, and it carries the usual three roundels. These have trilobate patterns reminiscent of hanging bowl escutcheons. The interlace is reminiscent of the *Book of Durrow.* It has a runic inscription 'Ranvaig owns this casket', which has been suggested as Manx Viking rather than Scandinavian. A Manx origin for the object has been suggested, but it is more probably Irish.

(11) *The Saint-Germain reliquary terminals.*[67] These two objects of uncertain provenance are now in the Museum of Saint-Germain-en-Laye, France. They have recently been identified as the butterfly wings of the finials of an unusually large house-shaped shrine. They are bronze, and D-shaped. They date probably from the early eighth century. On one side of each are six raised bosses with spiral ornament, from each of which two or three snake-like animals extend, with wolf, bird, dragon or human heads. Their bodies mostly have herringbone markings and in general appearance and character are similar to the figures on the Ekerö crozier. The face masks correspond almost exactly to those of Ekerö.

(12) *The Melhus shrine.*[68] Found in a Viking ship burial of *c.* 800 AD at Melhus, Norway, this house-shaped shrine is made of yew wood covered with bronze plates. The decoration is confined to the attached roundels and the hinges. Only one roundel survives, of silver, decorated with spiral and trumpet patterns. The one surviving hinge has millefiori inlay of blue and white set in red enamel. On account of the millefiori, the style of decoration on the surviving roundel and its overall character, a late seventh-century date is more probable than the eighth-century date usually ascribed to it.

(13) *The Oseberg bucket.*[69] This was found in the famous Viking ship burial at Oseberg, in south Norway. It is a stave-built bucket with bronze mounts, and although not buried until the ninth century it dates from the eighth. It has escutcheons for the handles in the form of squatting human figures, their legs crossed and their bodies decorated with enamel inlay in a cruciform pattern, as well as millefiori. Stylistically they are very similar to the figures on the Myklebostad bowl.

(14) *The Romfohjellen mount.*[70] Found at Romfohjellen in More, Norway, this rectangular gilt-bronze mount has animal figures modelled in high relief, springing from raised bosses. The bodies of the animals are decorated with herringbone ornament and they have red glass studs for eyes. The surface between the animals is decorated with animal interlace of Tara Brooch type, and the mount should presumably be assigned to the early eighth century.

(15) *The Birka bucket.*[71] This was found during excavations at the Swedish trading post of Birka, in Grave 507. It is made of birchwood staves, covered with a thin sheet of bronze. It dates probably from the early eighth century. It is decorated with engraved bird interlace in zones and has triangular handle escutcheons ornamented with bosses and openwork. The cross-hatching of the scrolls which run round the lower register is very reminiscent of the infill of similar designs on 'Mirror Style' mirrors of the pre-Roman Iron Age in south-east England, but the similarity is probably fortuitous. The handle escutcheons are very reminiscent of Anglo-Saxon buckles. Precise Irish parallels for it are difficult to find, and it should probably be regarded as Pictish or Northumbrian – the engraving shows certain affinities to that on the Monymusk reliquary.

(16) *The Bergen censer.*[72] This was found in a Viking woman's grave in Norway, and is now in Bergen Museum. It has been identified, with some probability, as a censer, and consists of a bronze box of almost circular form. It has lightly engraved decoration in zones, which though not as accomplished has close affinities to that on the Birka bucket. It dates from the eighth century.

Ornamental metalwork, c. 800–1050 AD

There is relatively little metalwork from the period of the Viking raids, and most of it is fragmentary. To some extent the lack may be due to a number of ninth-century pieces being ascribed to the late eighth century, and to the fairly extensive looting of metalwork by the Vikings. This alone is not enough to explain the dearth which is better explained in terms of a general decline and limited production, partly due to Viking disturbance. Certain features of the period can, however, be established from the pieces that survive.[73] Enamelwork became very rare, and filigree became coarser. Niello, the black paste which had been used in Romano-British metalwork and had later fallen out of favour, was revived in the ninth century. It is characteristic of the Trewhiddle Style of Anglo-Saxon metalwork,[74] and its appearance in Ireland was probably due to contacts with Anglo-Saxon England. Interlace in this period was geometric and monotonous, while other types of ornament that had been current in the preceding centuries, such as spirals and peltas, fell out of popularity. Instead there was an increase in the use of foliage, which reflects the widespread revival of acanthus and other leaf decoration that was one of the characteristics of Carolingian art. Such foliage was the result of a conscious classical revival, and the ultimate ancestry is to be found in late Antique manuscripts. Once established, it gained great popularity on the Continent and in Anglo-Saxon England, where it is well represented in the Winchester school.

The known metalwork of this period is entirely Irish, with the possible exception of a crozier head from Hoddom, Dumfriesshire, and certain pieces of Pictish origin, and the works so ornamented were almost invariably ecclesiastical, with shrines as the main category.

The main works are briefly listed below:

(1) *The Ballinderry lamp* (Fig. 140).[75] This bronze hanging lamp was found in Ballinderry 1 crannog, and has usually been ascribed to the period around 1000 AD, though it now seems likely that it is an early ninth-century

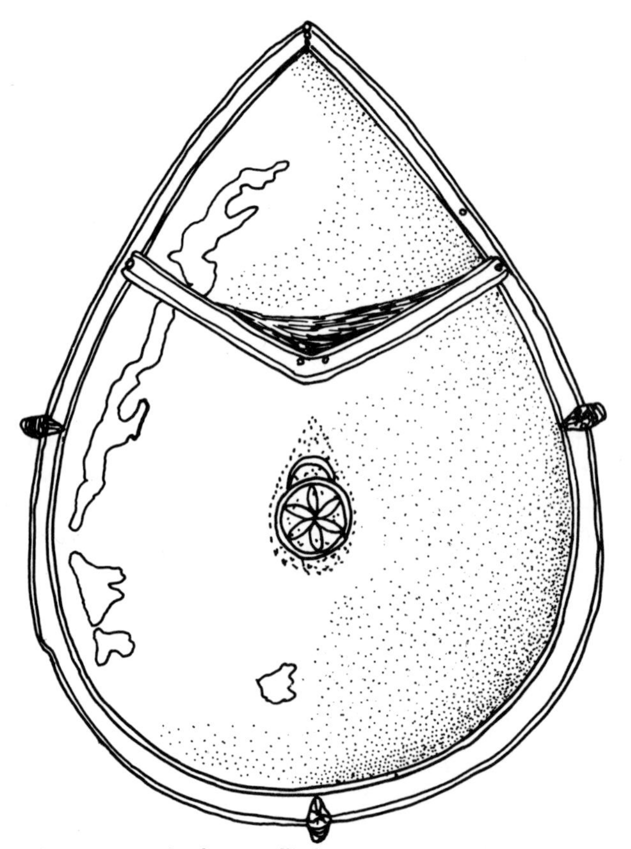

Figure 140 Hanging lamp, Ballinderry I crannog. Scale ½

work and should be seen as the last stage of the hanging bowl tradition. It is ovoid and has a pointed spout, which is separated from the rest of the lamp by a filter. The lamp has three zoomorphic escutcheon hooks, decorated with enamel, now dark green but once possibly red. The rest of the decoration is engraved, including a band of foliage below the rim and a marigold on the inside of the base.

(2) *The Prosperous crozier.*[76] This unaccomplished work was found in 1840 in a turf bog in Kildare, near Prosperous. It consists of a yew wood staff enclosed in bronze sheets. It dates from around 1000 AD, and differs from the other croziers of the period because it has enamel decoration on the knops, the foot and the drop of the crozier head. The crest, which may be a later addition, has a series of bird silhouettes produced by cutout and silver inlays. There are two rows of eight human heads on the ferrule.

(3, 4 and 5) *The British Museum crozier and the croziers of St Dympna and St Mel.*[77] These three croziers can be considered together since they are of similar type. The British Museum crozier, sometimes called the 'Kells crozier' although it has no association with Kells, was found behind a solicitor's cupboard in London in the nineteenth century. St Mel's crozier was found in the nineteenth century at Ardagh, while the crozier of St Dympna was bought from the hereditary keepers by George Petrie in 1835 and was passed on to the National Museum in Dublin. All lack the enamelling of the Prosperous crozier, and are decorated with small lozenge-shaped or triangular panels, each panel with a separate motif – interlace, animal interlace or foliage. They date from the late ninth or tenth century. Two have inscriptions; that on St Dympna's is almost illegible, but the translation of that on the British Museum crozier reads 'Pray for Cuduilig and Maelfinnen'. Attempts have been made to identify these personages, without success.

(6) *The Soiscél Molaise.*[78] Soiscél means 'book satchel'. This object is a *cumdach* or book shrine for the Gospel of St Molaise, and was converted in the eleventh century from a house-shaped shrine of the seventh or eighth century which was originally decorated with enamelled escutcheons for strap attachments. In its present form it is generally assumed to date from the early eleventh century. The cover is decorated with the four evangelists' symbols and inscriptions naming them. An inscription also states that it was done by Gill Biathin who was abbot of St Molaise's monastery on Devenish Island, Lough Erne. The symbols are in low relief in the four compartments of a cross of filigree in a rectangular frame. One of the sides of the box has a figure of an evangelist – the others, if they existed, are missing. The evangelist is surrounded by small intertwined animals, which belong to the general tradition of Irish animals with curling lappets.

(7) *The Corp Naomh.*[79] The name means 'Holy Body' though why it should be so called is not known. It was found at Temple Cross, Westmeath, and is a bell shrine dating from the tenth century with medieval additions. The crest was cast in one piece, with a figure holding a book on one side, flanked by a horseman and a bird. The work is in low relief with an openwork crest, and the background is an overall guilloche.

(8) *The British Museum stemmed disc.*[80] This round bronze two-faced disc with a short stem may have come from a processional, or free-standing, cross. Its surface is divided into panels with a border of lozenges with transverse lines, which may be copied from a Carolingian imitation of a classical ivory. The motif is rare, but occurs on a few other ninth-century objects. The disc is probably of ninth-century date.

(9) *Clonmacnois Crucifixion plaque.*[81] Found at Clonmacnois, Co. Offaly, this bronze openwork plaque is the finest of a series of Crucifixion plaques probably used as mounts for book covers. The earliest of the series is the Athlone plaque; the majority, including the Clonmacnois, date from the late ninth to tenth centuries. Another from Dublin is a plate of bronze with relief decoration, while a third from Dungannon (Tyrone) is now in Edinburgh. All show affinities to contemporary sculpture and also to the evangelist figure on the Soiscél Molaise.

Ornamental metalwork, after 1025 AD

There was a considerable revival in the art of the metalworker in the early eleventh century, and a number of complete, or nearly complete, reliquaries have survived. The main factor in the development of this renaissance was the impact of the art of the Vikings. By its very nature Viking art was close to the spirit of the Irish, being a flamboyant animal art in which pattern was more important than realism. First the Ringerike, then the Urnes Styles were to have a considerable impact on metalwork. A rich style was thus achieved in the twelfth century.[82] Intricacy, and detail in design, were then regarded as of less importance than a flamboyant overall effect; nevertheless, some very fine designs were displayed on individual works. Chronology is simplified for the period by a number of dated works. These objects are:

(a) The *cumdach* of the Stowe Missal: 1045–52
(b) The *cumdach* of the Cathach of St Columba: last years of the eleventh century.
(c) The shrine of St Patrick's bell: 1094–1105
(d) The Lismore crozier: 1090–1113
(e) The shrine of St Lachtin's arm: 1118–21
(f) The Cross of Cong: 1123–7

The dating is provided by inscriptions, which also give information about the metalworkers: it seems that they were frequently laymen attached to major monasteries, as in the case of Armagh or Kells.

The number of fine objects that have survived attest the wealth of the Irish monasteries of the period, which rivalled continental houses, and indeed they represent only a few survivors out of what must have been an impressive catalogue, since they were regarded with great cupidity by later generations and a considerable number were probably looted by Anglo-Normans. While it is likely that some metalwork was being produced in Scotland, and less probably in Wales during this period, it is unlikely that this was ever as abundant and impressive as that from Ireland. Two examples of later Scottish ecclesiastical metalwork that have survived, the Kilmichael Glassary and Guthrie bell shrines, of the thirteenth and fourteenth centuries respectively, show that similar but less accomplished work was being done in Scotland.

The general techniques of ornamentation were similar in the eleventh and twelfth centuries to those that had gone before. Filigree work tended to be coarse, and chip carving continued. The gilding employed was not fused on to the metal surface but was plated, a piece of gold foil being used to cover the surface of the worked metal. Enamel continued, but instead of yellow on red, red on yellow was favoured. Niello became increasingly popular, possibly because of the Anglo-Saxon, Viking and Byzantine use of it for inlay.

Two new techniques appeared in the eleventh and twelfth centuries. The first consisted of making borders with plaits of red copper and silver wire hammered into grooves, which were then polished to give a two-coloured rope pattern. The technique was used in Merovingian Gaul and Scandinavia, and by this date was becoming obsolete on the Continent. The second technique involved the insetting of silver ribbons into shallow grooves cut on a bronze ground, usually accompanied by bands of niello on either side. It appears on the Clonmacnois crozier and the shrine of St Lachtin's arm, and originally would have appeared as a silver tracery with black borders against a gold ground, as the bronze would probably have been gilded. The technique may be Byzantine in origin.

The centre for this new Viking-inspired art was probably Kells. The style probably evolved there around the mid-eleventh century, and can be seen in the repaired knop of the British Museum crozier where a pure Ringerike Viking design was used employing acanthus in silver and niello. The foliage of the pure Ringerike, however, was not long popular, and an Irish version in which the foliage became zoomorphic replaced it. This Irish version can be seen in the shrine for the Cathach of St Columba. The Urnes Style, which replaced the Ringerike, was more popular in Ireland, and indeed was developed there to a degree of excellence surpassing any example in its homeland.

The main examples of the metalwork of the period are listed below:

(1) *The Stowe missal shrine.*[83] This bronze box was altered at various periods;

the upper part is entirely medieval, but the lower part is eleventh-century. The work is a curious mixture of the vigorous and the stereotyped, and the iconography is difficult to interpret. The decoration consists of openwork bronze plaques wrapped in silver foil and backed by gold on a red copper plaque which covers the wooden box. One panel shows two ecclesiastics, one with a bell, the other with a crozier, on either side of a harpist and an angel, in a style recalling tenth-century sculpture. The other panels are less archaic. Enamel, glass and chip carving envigorate the composition.

(2) *The Innisfallen crozier.*[84] This was found in the river Laune in Co. Kerry, near Innisfallen. It is built up of silver plates round a wooden staff and has four knops, the lowest merging with the ferrule. It dates from the mid-eleventh century. The middle knops are archaic in style, reflecting the more general tradition of the croziers of St Mel and Dympna, and are divided into compartments with animal motifs originally gold-plated and set in silver frames. The upper and lower knops have foliage decoration. It is the earliest of the Viking-inspired works.

(3) *The cumdach of the Cathach of Columba.*[85] This is the shrine made for Columba's Cathach, a psalter. It is a rectangular wooden box covered with metal sheets. The upper plate is fourteenth-century, the others, except for some additions, are eleventh-century. The animal ornament is in Ringerike or Irish Style, similar to that on the Innisfallen crozier, and is set in panels along with corded interlace, palmettes and foliage scrolls. The top is obscured by later work, the bottom is openwork. The side panels have as a principal motif two animals in a figure-of-eight pattern with bands of silver and niello.

(4) *The Misach of St Columba.*[86] This is the shrine of a relic of unknown nature, and consists of a yew box covered with bronze plates. The upper part was remade in the sixteenth century, but the rest is eleventh-century, and similar in style to the *cumdach* of the Cathach, except that the decoration is more extravagant and flamboyant.

(5) *The shrine of St Patrick's bell* (Fig. 141).[87] This late eleventh-century shrine was made to contain the iron bell traditionally used by St Patrick. The reliquary was probably made in Armagh, and is a box made of thick bronze plates held in place by rounded joint covers. On the plates are openwork decorations in high relief. The general character of the decoration is similar to that on Urnes Style works, and the principal motifs are Urnes Style animals. The filigree is particularly elaborate, reminiscent of the Ardagh Chalice but coarser.

(6) *The crozier of the abbots of Clonmacnois.*[88] This crozier is closely related in style to the *cumdach* of the Cathach, and has on the crook double-looped bands, linked at the centre with free ends at the terminals. It is inlaid in silver and niello. The animals' heads are closely comparable

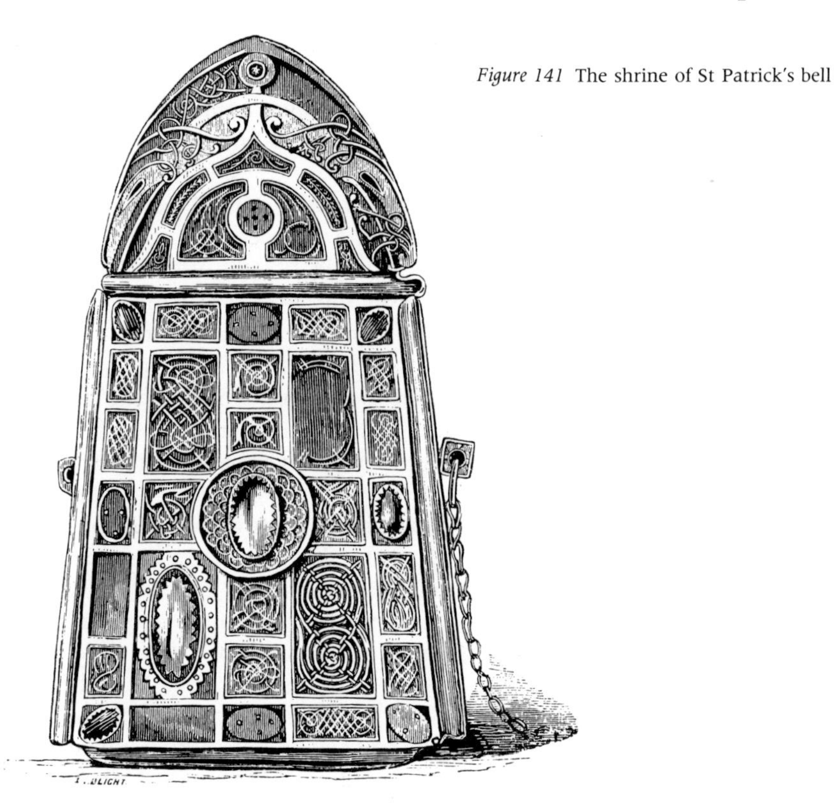

Figure 141 The shrine of St Patrick's bell

with the carvings in the stave church at Urnes itself, but the animals themselves are more transitional in style from Ringerike. It dates from the eleventh century.

(7) *The Lismore crozier.*[89] This crozier, which was found walled up in Lismore castle, consists of heavy bronze plates riveted together, with an openwork crest ornamented with three-dimensional terminal animal heads with lappets and moustaches in degenerate Ringerike Style. The shaft of the crozier is smooth, and the decoration is confined to the crest, knops and binding strip. The knops have lattice-like bronze openwork, with circular settings for enamels at the crossings. In the interstices are panels with patterns in gilt-bronze, including human interlace and Urnes Style animals. The studs are enamelled in red, blue and white.

(8) *The shrine of St Lachtin's arm.*[90] This early twelfth-century shrine comes from Freshford, Co. Kilkenny. Arm shrines were not uncommon, but only this and the shrine of St Patrick's arm have survived. The shrine consists of a wooden cylinder covered with metal plaques, terminating in a clenched fist. It is well preserved, and the decoration in general is similar to that on the Lismore croziers, the eight plaques that make up

the arm being inlaid with damascened motifs and every portion of the surface except the finger nails covered with ornament. The ornament consists mainly of tightly woven intertwining animal bodies, in Urnes Style, with some foliage. There is also some fine filigree work on the surface.

(9) *The Cross of Cong.*[91] This is a large processional cross (2 feet 6 inches high) which also served as a reliquary for a fragment of the True Cross. It comes from Cong in Co. Mayo. It is made, like the other reliquaries, out of bronze plates riveted together in the form of a Latin cross, below which is a handle of which the upper part is cast in the form of an animal head that grips the bottom of the shaft in its jaws. The reliquary proper is a silver truncated cone set in the centre of the arms and holding a hemisphere of rock crystal which magnified a small splinter of the Cross set below it. The type, which can be paralleled in Spain, was common in the twelfth century. It was probably made at Clonmacnois. Along the edges of the shaft and transom there are settings for red and yellow enamel. Along the back of the shaft, above the crossing and on the arms are openwork cast bronze mounts with zoomorphic interlace in Urnes Style. Similar interlace adorns the front of the cross. In all, it is a superb example of twelfth-century craftsmanship.

(10) *The shrine of St Manchan.*[92] This is a gabled shrine some 19 inches high, now in Boher Church, Co. Offaly. It covers a floor space 2 feet by 16 inches. It is made of yew with bronze and enamel fittings, and contains bones, one being part of a femur, traditionally that of St Manchan who

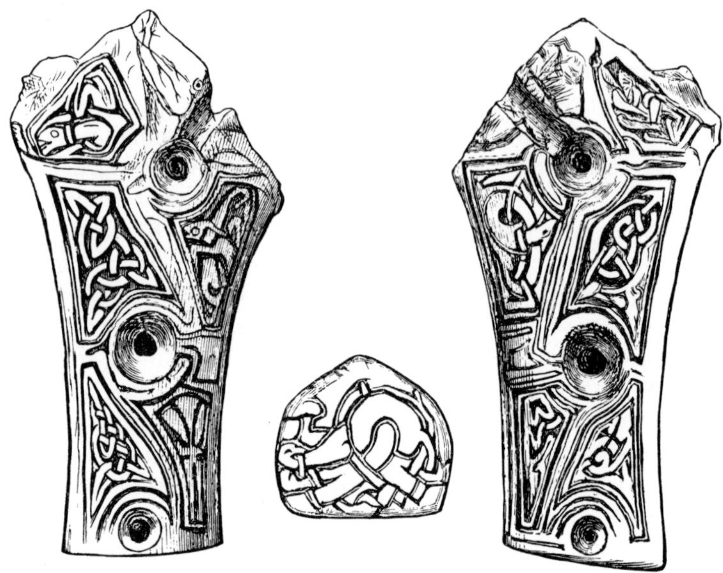

Figure 142 The Hoddom crozier shrine

died in 664. It is possibly a copy of a much earlier slab shrine. The ornament is in Urnes Style and almost identical to that on the Cross of Cong, but probably very slightly later. In addition a series of human figures was added not long after it was made, cast in high relief, and imitating continental Romanesque crucifix figures.

The shrine of St Manchan marks the end of the major Irish works of ornamental metalwork. Of the twelfth century there are a great number of other, slightly lesser, pieces, which are none the less of some note in their own right: the *Bearnan Cuilean* (the bell of St Cuilean), a fine Tau crozier (the surviving example of what was a more common type, to judge by literary references and sculptural representations), the *cumdach* of the *Book of Dimna,* are all worthy of mention. This review may be concluded, however, by considering one important object which carries the account forward into the thirteenth century. This is the *Breac Maodhóg,* a shrine of house-shaped type reminiscent of seventh- or eighth-century predecessors. The shrine in its present form, however, dates from the mid-eleventh century or possibly even later (Françoise Henry suggests a date in the thirteenth century)[93] and is decorated with plaques with rich figural decoration, reminiscent of St Molaise's shrine. There are only a few panels surviving, and the original scheme is now lost.

Bells

A series of objects which span the Early Christian period are the 'Celtic' bells, some of which are decorated. The type is probably related to the cow bell, an example of which is illustrated on a Pictish stone from Fowlis Wester, Angus. No fixed bells of the Early Christian period are known, possibly because the technology for casting large bells for suspension in towers was not known in the Celtic regions of Britain or Ireland. Certainly it seems that hand bells were the type rung even in the round towers of Viking period Ireland. They were not provided with clappers, and were rung by striking.

The usual material for Celtic bells was iron coated with bronze, though later in the period bronze bells are also known. They were hammered and riveted, and the bronze was applied to the iron by a process akin to tinning. Invariably they were four-sided, tall and tapering. The ends were flattened and the sides bulged. They were provided with a handle so that they could be swung by hand. The type seems to have been developed in Ireland, but they also occur in Scotland and Wales. The rectangular shape was necessitated by the use of iron – the later bronze bells are skeuomorphs (Fig. 143).

Romilly Allen recognized four basic classes of bronze bell, and one class of iron, the iron examples always being simple and undecorated.[94] The four classes of cast bronze bell are as follows:

(1) cast bronze without ornament
(2) cast bronze without ornament, but inscribed
(3) cast bronze with ornamented handles
(4) cast bronze with ornamented bodies

Class 1 is widespread in Scotland and Ireland and one example is known from Wales. Class 2 is known from Ireland and Brittany, and appears to be fairly late, of the ninth to tenth centuries. Class 3 falls into two subgroups,

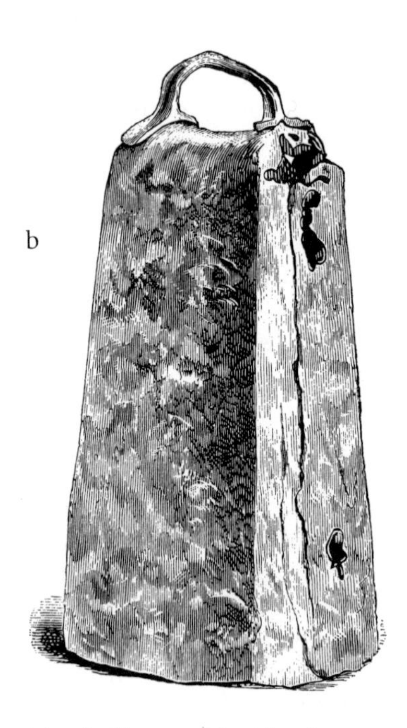

Figure 143 Celtic bells. (a) the Armagh bell, bronze, (b) the Birnie bell, iron.

those with zoomorphic handles and those with phyllomorphic. The former has animal heads joining the handle with the body of the bell, as on an example from Llangwynodl, Caernarvonshire, the latter has a leaf in the same postition, exemplified by a bell from Saint-Pol-de-Leon. Cast bronze bells seem to belong to the period from the end of the eighth century, though the two most notable, the Bangor bell and the Lough Lene bell, probably belong to the early ninth. Both have a key pattern border round the lip and a cross and circle in the case of the Lough Lene. These two, along with a third similar example from Cashel, Co. Tipperary, belong to Class 4 of the series.

The largest bell known is the Birnie bell from Nairnshire, which is 1 foot 2 inches high. The smallest are about 4 inches in height, the average is about 9 inches. They give a good tone, but are not loud.

Leather budgets[95]

Indirectly related to some of the metalwork discussed above are a group of three leather book satchels or budgets, one for the *Breac Maodhóg* (p. 371), one for the *Book of Armagh* and one for a manuscript at Corpus Christi College, Cambridge. These are important examples of leather working, and two, the *Breac Maodhóg* and the Armagh budget, are richly decorated. An early date has recently been suggested for them, but none need be earlier than the tenth century.

14 The Church

Although perhaps the role of the Church in the everyday life of the post-Roman Celts has been overestimated, it cannot be denied that Christianity was of major importance in their world; it was the inspiration behind their art, and apart from language was the main factor that united the scattered groups in all parts of the Celtic west.

There is a growing body of evidence to support the theory that there was some survival of Christianity, and with it the structure of the diocesan church in Britain, into the post-Roman period. Bishops and priests are mentioned on memorial stones of the fifth and sixth centuries, and bishops are mentioned in documentary sources. Gildas implies that in his day the Church was diocesan, and both Ninian and Patrick are described by their biographers as bishops.[1]

While Christianity perished in the areas that became England, overwhelmed by the Anglo-Saxon invasions and their aftermath, it probably survived elsewhere. In the south-west and Wales there is very little conclusive evidence for Roman Christianity. Certainly, however, there appears to have been a flourishing Christian community in the area of Hadrian's Wall, particularly round Carlisle. The evidence here mainly consists of a series of late Roman Christian tombstones from the western end of the Wall.[2]

In the fifth and sixth centuries there was a new wave of Christian activity in the Irish Sea province, stemming directly from the Continent, particularly from Gaul but to a lesser extent possibly from the eastern Mediterranean. The evidence for this comprises memorial stones with continental formulae and imported pottery, which initially may have been brought to Britain to meet liturgical requirements.[3]

The fifth and sixth centuries are often termed the 'Age of the Saints' and are traditionally represented as a period when wandering evangelical saints set out to convert the heathen in a wide area of hinterland. Such a picture is a distortion of the truth, for the fathers of the early Church were probably more concerned with preaching and ministering to an already existing Christian community than with missionary work.

This diocesan structure appears to have lasted in Britain until the seventh century, when it was shaken by a new element, monasticism, also introduced from the Continent. Monasticism was introduced from the Mediterranean and north Africa to south-west Britain in the late fifth century, and there can be little doubt that the movement in Britain was reinforced by influences from southern Gaul, Aquitaine and northern Spain during the sixth century.[4] The distribution of early monasteries in mainland Britain coincides with that of imported pottery (they are notably coastal), implying continuing influences along the same lines of contact. The earliest in Britain is almost certainly Tintagel in Cornwall (p. 141) and the extension of monasticism can be traced from Cornwall round the south Welsh coast in the years prior to 500, to Ireland in the sixth century and, by extension of the original Irish foundations, to the north-west of mainland Britain in the late sixth century. From the British areas monasticism spread to Northumbria in the seventh century.

The spread of monasticism meant a break in the development of the Church in Britain, since as has been implied, the fifth- and sixth-century Church was essentially connected with the world of the late Roman Empire, and bore few traces of the distinguishing features associated with the later so-called 'Celtic' Church. Once established in Britain the monasteries grew in importance and an administrative structure based on the monastery began to replace the old diocesan framework.

The nature of the evidence

The most valuable categories of evidence for Christianity in the Celtic areas of Britain are the sites themselves and the contemporary documentary sources. Information can also be gleaned from memorial and other stones, references in later documentary sources, placenames, dedications and portable objects. Of these categories, the last two are of very limited value. While it is true that a number of relics and reliquaries such as bells, croziers or house-shaped shrines became associated with particular churches, or in some cases families of hereditary keepers, the associations can frequently be traced back only to the Reformation or at best the Middle Ages. Such objects moved around in antiquity, and there is seldom any reason to suppose that the church now associated with a particular object is that in which it originally reposed. Church dedications are equally problematic, for one cannot often be certain at what date down to the sixteenth century a church was dedicated to a particular saint. In some cases dedications to sixth- or seventh-century saints are due to a medieval revival of interest in the particular cult, or to deliberate antiquarianism. Nevertheless, it does seem likely that dedications to early and fairly obscure local saints owe their origins to the Early Christian period rather than later. It has been suggested that many dedications to Irish saints in Scotland were derived from commemorative lists used in the liturgies of the mother houses of the monastic *paruchiae*. If this is the case, much information can be gleaned concerning the allocation of particular churches to particular *paruchiae*. The large number of Irish saints with churches dedicated to them in Scotland, who also appear in the martyrologies compiled in Ireland, implies that dedications were frequently drawn from official lists. Another problem concerning dedications is that many saints shared the same name, and without adequate documentation it is not always possible to distinguish the saint involved.

Placename evidence is also difficult to assess. Much depends on establishing the original form of the placename which has often changed because it was corrupted through usage. Antiquarianism is sometimes responsible for the revival of early placename forms. Charters, though seldom earlier than the twelfth century, are usually the most informative sources for early placenames. Used with caution, placenames can provide information about the existence of sites of which no trace now survives, and can sometimes provide clues to the status of a site. There are a substantial number of ecclesiastical placename elements, some of which seem to be exclusively Early Christian in origin, while others continued to be applied in later medieval times. Names such as *dysert* or *diseart* are derived from Latin *desertum* (a desert place) and refer to anchorite's cells, sometimes attached at some distance to a monastery. The term *abthaine* in Scotland, meaning literally 'abbacy' or 'abbey lands', occurs in medieval charters, sometimes in its Latin form *abthania*, but apparently always refers to Early Christian monastic sites. Other Scottish placenames – *annat*, found by itself or in compounds; and *teampull* (from Latin *templum*) – are known to refer to specific kinds of church, though their precise meanings remain in some doubt. In wider usage *kil, cille, llan, keeill, merthyr, land*, can all provide clues to the presence of small chapel sites.

The main pieces of documentary evidence are the various annals and, all to be used with great caution, saints' *Lives*. Medieval charters and other documents can refer to sites now vanished, while later antiquaries' accounts can often be useful for providing information about lost sites and stones.

Memorial stones provide evidence from their find-spots and their inscriptions or carvings. It is often supposed that Early Christian stones are located today where they have always been, or that if they are inside a church they originally stood in the churchyard. This however is erroneous: in the eighteenth century and more particularly in the nineteenth century there was a tendency to move stones to churchyards or churches partly to protect them and partly because it was felt more appropriate that they should stand there than in perhaps some farmyard or wood. In nineteenth-century Scotland, too, there was a tendency to wish to hallow Scottish presbyterianism with an ancestry going back to Ninian and Columba, and to enhance a church site with greater antiquity by setting up an Early Christian stone in it.

The classification of Early Christian sites

Early Christian sites can be generally classified into *monastic sites* and *cemetery* and *chapel* sites. One category tends to merge into another, and to some extent the classification is dependent on literary sources, for archaeological evidence alone is not sufficient to provide a distinction between various classes. In particular, major monasteries are almost impossible to define archaeologically.

Monasteries generally speaking were enclosed by a *vallum monasterii*, normally an earth bank with an outer quarry ditch. This served as a spiritual and legal boundary line, and must seldom have been regarded as defensive. In contrast to cemetery enclosures it has been suggested that monastic enclosures were often initially of roughly rectangular plan. The concept was derived from the East, where by the fifth or sixth centuries monasteries were enclosed by a substantial wall following a rectilinear plan.[5] The type is well represented in St Catherine's monastery, Mount Sinai, and can also be seen at R'safah. Such plans are fairly widespread in the east Mediterranean, in Egypt, Syria, Greece, north Africa, the Balkans and the Caucasus. It is possible that they initially served a defensive purpose and that the early monasteries were indeed fortresses for the soldiers of God, for in remote desert situations raids from hostile tribesmen could not have been infrequent.

Two sites on which rectilinear valla can be particularly well studied are Clonmacnois and Iona (Fig. 144). Each enclosed an area of 10 acres or more. At Iona the plan is complicated by subsidiary earthworks of various dates, and where it has been sectioned shows differing construction at various points. The west side has a bank, ditch and a little outer bank, but the south side consists of a stone-faced bank with a ditch, of more regular construction. The monastic enclosure at Glendalough appears to have been of generally similar shape.

In contrast to these early monasteries there is another group in which the enclosure appears to have been circular in plan. Examples of circular or near circular valla are widespread.[6] They occur for instance at Inchcleraun in Ireland, at Kirk Maughold on the Isle of Man, Kingarth in Bute, Applecross in Wester Ross, and there are outliers in Northumbria and Mercia implying that the shape was transmitted from the Celtic to the Anglo-Saxon areas with the spread of monasticism. The vallum was in some cases stone-built as at Nendrum (Co. Down) or Kingarth (Bute). It is likely that in a number of cases existing circular fortifications were reoccupied. There is some documentary evidence for earlier fortified sites being handed over for such a purpose: the Roman fort at Caer Gybi on Holyhead was a gift to St Gybi, the ruined Saxon shore fort of Burgh Castle, Suffolk, was given to St Fursa, and that at Reculver, Kent, was a donation to the priest Bassa.

Sometimes the site chosen was ideally suited to an enclosed community. River bends were particularly suitable, as at Old Melrose on the Tweed (Roxburghshire) or Old Deer (Aberdeenshire). The larger monasteries, unlike the smaller, were selected not for their remote positions but for their convenience. Island monasteries – both major and minor – are not uncommon. The classic example is the remote site of Skellig Michael, Co. Kerry, but there are others, such as Inishmurray or Iniscealtra in Ireland or Iona, Lismore, Birsay and Papil in Scotland, or Priestholm off Anglesey in Wales. Similarly

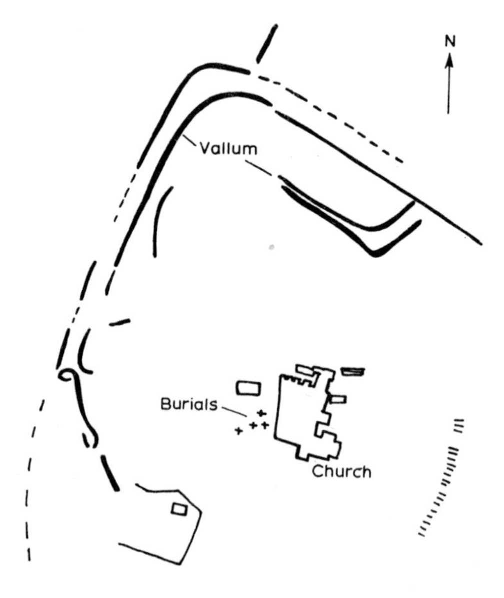

Figure 144 Iona – Plan of vallum

promontories were sometimes utilized, as at St Abb's Head, Berwickshire, or the Brough of Deerness, Orkney, both probably making use of earlier promontory forts.

The smaller monasteries probably differed little in character from the larger foundations, but many fall into the category of the classic small island eremitic sites, such as Skellig Michael or the Brough of Deerness. The earliest of these eremitic monasteries probably dates to the seventh rather than to the sixth century.

Into the category of *hermitages* should probably be assigned a number of the chapel sites in remote situations, such as that on North Rona, to the north of the Butt of Lewis, the scattered remains on Eilean Mor, off Argyll, or the chapel site on Pygmies' Isle off the coast of Lewis. A related category are the cave sites which are associated with hermits, such as Ellory (Argyll) or Weem, near Aberfeldy (Perthshire). St Ninian's cave, Physgyll (Wigtown), is a classic example of the type.

The larger monasteries were in effect enclosed villages, comprising haphazard agglomerations of small buildings surrounded by their valla. The buildings varied according to their function, from the cells of the monks (two monks often occupied one cell) to the scriptorium, guest house and refectory. Within the enclosure were plots of land and buildings associated with farming, workshops and possibly a 'school'. Living cells and public buildings were probably distributed at random inside the enclosure. Instead of the single church found in the Middle Ages there were several chapels, all relatively small. Larger buildings would usually have been rectilinear in plan, smaller ones rectilinear or circular. Up to the eighth century at least, building would normally have been in wood. At the opposite end of the scale, a hermitage

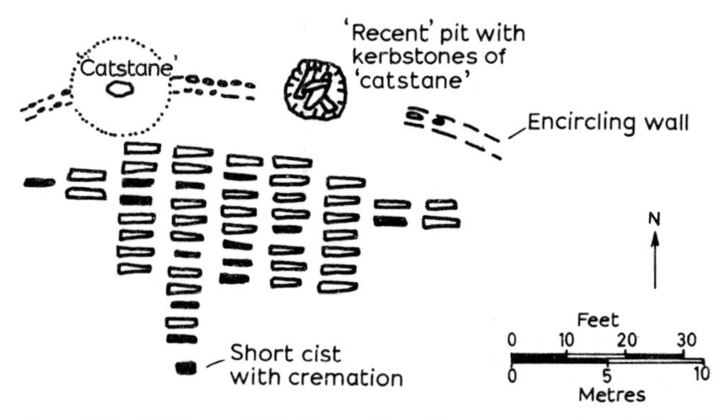

Figure 145 Kirkliston, Midlothian – Plan of catstane cemetery. (After Thomas)

might comprise simply an oratory and one or two living cells. The pattern is best observed on the Irish sites of Nendrum, Co. Down, and Inishmurray, Co. Sligo (Plate 7B). At Nendrum, though the monastic buildings themselves were destroyed, probably in the Viking raids, the monastery was found to have been built within a fort similar to that at Cahercommaun, and between the inner and outer stone walls were excavated artisans' huts and a building known as the 'school', since it produced thirty slates with trial designs on them, a compass arm and several iron styli.

Cemetery[7] sites can be either simple burial grounds without such associated features as chapels or founder's tombs, or sites in which the burials are subordinate to the associated structures. While some cemetery sites may have developed from simple graveyards with the construction of chapels, living huts, shrines and other above-ground features within pre-existing cemeteries, many cemeteries were undoubtedly intended as places of religious observance from the outset, and indeed the oratory or chapel may have been the key element, the graveyard being of secondary importance.

By the fourth century the standard burial practice in Roman Britain was inhumation. In Early Christian cemeteries bodies were normally simply laid in the ground or in a hollow worked out of bedrock (known as *dug graves*), in stone-lined cists (*cist graves*) or in stone cists with a capping of stones (*lintel graves*). Stone sarcophagi are relatively rare.

Many of the earliest known Christian cemeteries comprise unenclosed groups of burials, as at Cannington in Somerset and the long-cist cemetery at Parkburn in Midlothian. More important are the series of enclosed cemeteries, which are normally surrounded by a curvilinear vallum which symbolically separated the holy from the profane and the dead from the living. There is some evidence of continuity of burial site from pagan to Christian times, Christian burials sometimes being associated with Iron Age funerary

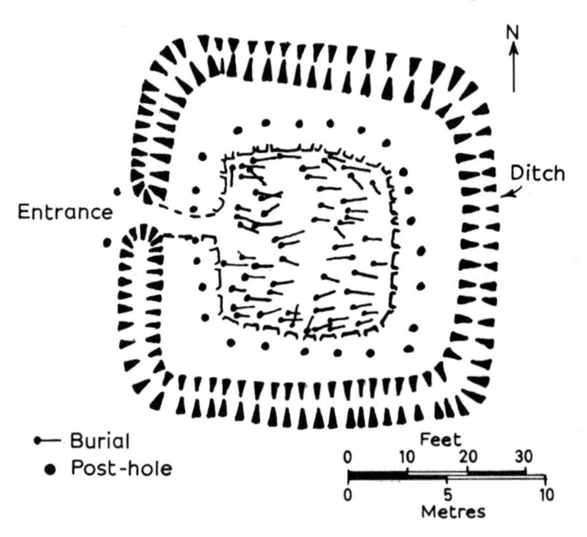

Figure 146 Hill of Knockea, Co. Limerick – plan (After O'Kelly)

sites or, more frequently, Roman. The custom of demarcating special burials with a circular surround also appears to be of prehistoric and Roman ancestry, as indeed do the few Early Christian burials with rectangular surrounds, such as that from Llandegai, Caernarvonshire. The excavated site at the Hill of Knockea, Co. Limerick, comprised a regular ditch, 6 feet wide and 2 feet deep, enclosing a rectangular area about 45 feet square (Fig. 146). Within the ditch was a low bank with an internal stone revetment, along the crest of which were the sockets for twenty-six posts. In the central area, about 25 feet across, were at least sixty-six inhumations, mostly oriented and therefore Christian.

The spread of the custom of venerating relics seems to have reached Britain in the fifth century from the Mediterranean, and from this time onwards various structures are recognizable in Early Christian cemeteries that were designed to hold the relics of saints.[8] A group of such structures, probably dating from the early seventh century, occur in south-west Ireland, where they are found associated with surrounds of rectilinear plan. These structures have been designated *slab shrines*, and consist of a hollow dug into the ground roofed with two sloping stones and two triangular end gables, the overall appearance being that of a ridge tent. One of the finest examples is at Killabuonia, Co. Kerry, where the gable stone is furnished with a porthole to enable the relics to be touched.

Another early series of outdoor shrines is derived from a particular type of wooden superstructure above a grave known as a *totenmemoria*. These had hipped roofs like miniature chapels, which in turn were wooden copies of ridge-lidded sarcophagi representing chapels. No timber *totenmemoria* are as yet known from Britain, but there are stone counterparts, the earliest of which probably do not antedate 700. The first transitional stage from wooden to stone shrines can be seen in the Jedburgh shrine, which dates from about 700 and is associated with St Boisil of Old Melrose. The long sides are set

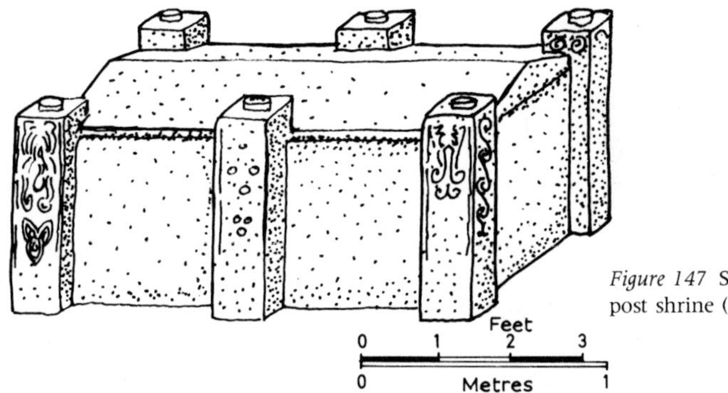

Figure 147 St Ninian's Isle corner-post shrine (After Thomas)

in grooves in the slightly overlapping end panels in a technique common in wood working. The Jedburgh shrine only involved the use of six pieces, the two sides and the end panels, together with two roof panels. The later composite stone shrines have either eight or thirteen pieces, excluding the roof slabs. The earliest are the *corner-post shrines*, which have four stone pillars with grooves on two faces, into which end slabs are slotted. The lid is either flat or the two end slabs rise into gables, to support two roof slabs. Frequently one slab could be removed to allow the relics within to be touched. The distribution of corner-post shrines appears to be north British, the only known Irish examples being very late and developed. The norm is the single shrine, but there are a few double shrines, probably of Northumbrian origin, such as one from St Ninian's Isle, Shetland (Fig. 147). A slightly more sophisticated variant of the corner-post shrine is the *corner-block shrine*, which has neatly made large rectangular blocks at the corners. Good examples are that from Monifeith, Angus, and the famous *St Andrews Shrine*.

The final stage in the development of stone shrines is the solid shrine, consisting of a solid house-shaped piece of stone, that was put over a grave. An example from Clones, Co. Monaghan, is an exact copy of a timber prototype, including imitation locks and hasps.

In Mediterranean Christianity, as early as the fourth century, open-air altars are sometimes associated with tombs, either erected above the grave or constituting the lid of the tomb itself. The idea of this superstructure above a saint's tomb appears to have been transmitted to Britain along with other facets of Mediterranean Christianity, its outcome being the structure known commonly in Irish as a *leacht*. Essentially, a *leacht* is a small rectangular construction of stones or slabs, or sometimes a single block, with a flat top to which stones may be attached. It is unknown whether *leachta* covered burials in Britain – no excavation has ever tested this – but they show such features as surrounds which are comparable to those round important graves, and the

Figure 148 'Altoir Beag' *leacht,* Innishmurray

name itself (which is derived from Latin *lectus,* a bed) implies funerary connections. However, the other features of *leachta* are not in keeping with graves but have more in common with altars: they stand to the average altar height (about 3 or 4 feet) and the stones set in them are unlike the usual funerary cross slabs but have a central cross flanked by four smaller ones, as on an altar mensa. The most famous collection is on Innishmurray, Co. Sligo, where they are spaced out round the perimeter of the island and were used until recently as processional stations. Nine of the eleven *leachta* have specific names. The best-known is *Altoir Beag* ('little altar') which has pebbles on top of it of a type found elsewhere, for instance on Islay, associated with votive custom and prayer, the pebbles sometimes being turned as prayers were said (Fig. 148).

The church as a building

Until the seventh century the tradition of building in the Celtic-speaking areas was in wood, not stone. Until recently the evidence for this was entirely literary, but excavations have now provided archaeological evidence for timber oratories or chapels. Bede provides a reliable account of the transition from wooden- to stone-church building in Northumbria and there are references in saints' *Vitae* and early Irish sources of various types. In Ireland, a wooden chapel is distinguished from a stone one by a special term – *dairtech*, or 'house of oak'.[9] It should be noted that this building tradition is in direct variance with that encountered from the earliest days of the Augustinian mission in Kent, where stone churches were built along conventional Roman lines, sometimes employing re-used Roman brick. In the Celtic-speaking areas, however, the timber church was essentially a product of native tradition, and the small timber oratories should not be attributed either to a Romano-British survival or to an introduction from continental Europe.

Archaeological evidence for chapels comes mainly from one site in Ireland and one in Scotland. The Irish site is *Church Island*, near Valencia, Co. Kerry, where three phases were recognized (Fig. 149). The first phase consisted of

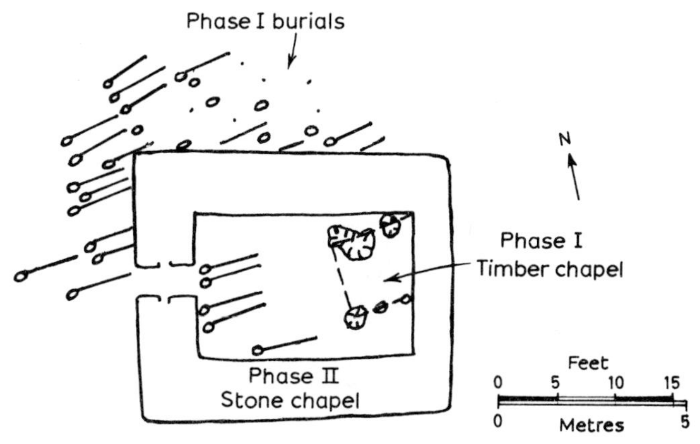

Figure 149 Church Island, Co. Kerry – Plan (After O'Kelly)

an unenclosed cemetery in which was erected a timber oratory, about 6 feet by 9 feet, outlined in excavation by six post-holes. Nearby was a circular living cell, about 18 feet in diameter. Some burials on either side of the oratory were aligned along its axis, and a cross slab was set up to mark what may be presumed to have been the grave of the founder. This phase should probably be dated to the seventh century. In Phase II the timber oratory was replaced by a stone chapel, $18\frac{1}{2}$ feet by $12\frac{1}{2}$ feet, which was partly built over the timber oratory and its associated graves. The wooden hut was likewise replaced by a stone one, and further burials were aligned with the new chapel. This phase possibly belongs to the early eighth century.

The second site is *Ardwall Island*, off the coast of Kirkcudbright (Fig. 150). Here, usage of the site begàn with a cemetery, probably initially unenclosed, of dug graves, possibly first used in the late fifth or sixth century. A group of badly disturbed graves was associated with a hollow dug out of the rock, which may have been the below-ground element of a slab shrine. The next phase is represented by the construction of a small timber oratory, 11 feet by 7 feet 6 inches, partly overlying the hollow of the shrine. In this phase some burials were orientated along the axis of the chapel, and a group of associated post-holes have been identified as those of a corner-post shrine. In a third phase a stone-walled chapel was built, partly overlying the timber oratory and on a slightly different axis.

Apart from the archaeological traces of the chapels themselves, the presence of an earlier timber oratory can sometimes be detected from previous burials. In such cases oriented graves lie underneath a stone chapel of later date, as for example at St Ninian's Point, Bute.

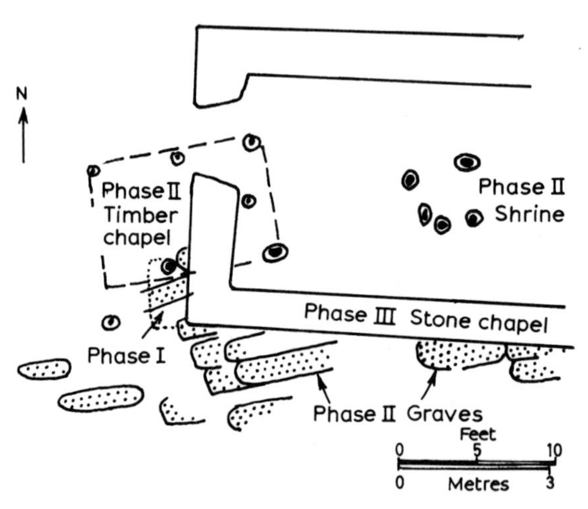

Figure 150 Ardwall Isle, Kirkcudbright – Plan (After Thomas)

Wood skeuomorphism in early stone churches

The earliest stone churches in the west probably do not antedate AD 700 though it is possible that in some areas where timber was in short supply and stone was readily available such oratories were being erected in the seventh century. Among the earliest are the stone 'whalebone' corbelled churches, represented by the Gallarus Oratory, Co. Kerry, and the buildings on Skellig Michael (p. 172).[10] The Skellig buildings are typologically the earliest, with high, corbelled elevations, oval in form, but with a rectangular ground plan. The Gallarus Oratory had interior dimensions of 15 feet 3 inches by 10 feet 2 inches. This 2:3 ratio can be observed in timber oratories at Church Island and Ardwall, and in the majority of early stone chapels. It has been suggested as the accepted ratio for the church proportions in the Early Christian period in Ireland and parts at least of Britain. By the Romanesque period the classical ratio of 1:2 was increasingly favoured, and the nearer the internal proportions are to the classic 2:3 the earlier the chapel is likely to be.

The shape of the Gallarus Oratory led Leask to suggest that it is a stone version of a timber prototype, the form being the result of copying a timber cruck building.[11] This is difficult to prove, but other features of early Irish stone chapels suggest that the stone buildings were timber skeuomorphs. Elbow crucks have been seen to be the precursors of the *antae* that adorn the front and back elevations of a number of Irish churches down to the Romanesque period. These *antae* are continued up the gable to the roof ridge, and may represent the slotting of planks into elbow crucks in a timber building. The feature can be observed at Temple Macdara, Co. Galway (Plate 10A).

Even more convincing are the butterfly finials associated with a number of stone chapels. In cruck building it was not uncommon to decorate the point where the crucks crossed, and projected above the line of the roof, by

Figure 151 Butterfly gable finials. (1) Freshford, Kilkenny; (2) Iniscealtra, Clare (After Leask)

adding a butterfly-shaped ornamental finial.[12] Such finials of stone are known from a number of Irish sites: Iniscealtra, Temple Macdara, Freshford and Church Island, for example, and a fragment of one from Ardwall (Fig. 151).

Most of the surviving early chapels are small and unicameral (Plate 11A). The presence of a chancel can generally be taken to indicate a late date. Columba's biographer, Adamnan, describes an *exedra* or porch to the timber church at Iona, but this was probably exceptional. Apart from the buildings with stone roofs in Ireland, roofs have not generally survived, but representations on later hog-backed tombstones imply that they were roofed for the most part with lapped semicircular shingles, slates or stones.

All the early chapels are of drystone construction, without the use of mortar, which probably came to the Celtic areas by way of Northumbria, where it was in use in the seventh century. It probably reached Ireland in the eighth century. Many early chapel walls, however, are bonded with clay, cob or mud. In west and north Scotland it is fairly common to find stones laid in yellow clay. Plastering was rarely carried out, though it seems to have been traditional in Cornwall.

Appendices

Appendix A Celtic manuscript art

Celtic manuscript art is a specialist study which is more the province of the art historian than the archaeologist. Its general development should be familiar to any student of the period, however, because of its importance in any assessment of Celtic culture and art.

Before the Book of Durrow

Although very few manuscripts survive that predate the late seventh century, a few fragmentary examples are of fundamental importance in any consideration of the origins of Celtic manuscript art. From these it is apparent that the *Book of Durrow*, the earliest of the great Celtic manuscripts, was not suddenly created as a new Celtic art form but marks the culmination of nearly a century of ornamental development. As in other fields of Celtic art, discussion of provenance only serves to confuse the account of development; whether produced in Ireland, Northumbria, Scotland or even south Wales manuscripts were the product of a particular artistic milieu essentially eclectic in character and owing little to La Tène antecedents. Manuscript art is a medium alien to pagan Celtic traditions; it is something which is both Christian and classical in inspiration, and though the ornamental techniques may owe much to barbarian artistic traditions the overall conception is classical and the iconographical models for evangelist figures and symbols, canon pages and even spacial relationships between ornament and text come clearly from late Antique models.

Three types of ornamental device employed in the classic Celtic manuscripts are to be found in the pre-*Durrow* works: interlace, spirals and zoomorphic ornament. Of these, spiral ornament was derived from native Celtic traditions, and was probably taken over from metalwork. Interlace was of Mediterranean origin, being current in Coptic Egypt as early as the fifth century. It also occurred in the Byzantine world and in Italy, whence it may have been disseminated by the Lombards in the later sixth century. Interlace probably came to Celtic Britain directly from the Mediterranean, along with other facets of Mediterranean Christian art and creed. It is apparent in Scottish metalwork as early as the first quarter of the seventh century, but does not appear in manuscripts until the middle of the century or later. It may have come to Celtic Britain and Ireland along with another decorative device of early manuscripts, the use of red dots to accentuate letter outlines, an essentially Coptic device. Although zoomorphic ornament was a feature of La Tène Celtic art, it was not a distinctive feature of Celtic Christian art in the fifth and sixth centuries, except in a moderate degree, and the sudden appearance of animal ornament on a lavish scale in the manuscripts of the late seventh century onwards is almost certainly due to Anglo-Saxon influence from Northumbria. The influence of Anglo-Saxon polychrome jewellery has probably been overestimated though it undoubtedly played some part in the development of the 'carpet pages'. The influence of Romano-British art (particularly mosaic pavements) on carpet pages has been suggested, but this seems increasingly improbable, and if indeed mosaic floors played any part in their development the prototypes should be sought on the Continent, not in Britain.

It is convenient to divide manuscript art into three phases: early, classical and degenerate. The pre-*Durrow* manuscripts may be termed 'early', those from *Durrow* to the *Book of Kells* 'classical' and those later than the *Book of Kells* 'degenerate'. Of the early manuscripts the most important are:

(1) *The Cathach of St Columba.* This fragment of a psalter is in very poor condition, and may genuinely have belonged to the saint or, if not, cannot be much later than his death (*s.a.* 597). The decoration is sparse, and confined to large capitals, which were surrounded with red dots. The interiors of some letters were filled in, probably with yellow.

(2) *Codex Usserianus Primus.* This manuscript was probably produced at Bobbio by Irish monks in the first half of the seventh century. In many respects similar to the *Cathach*, it has some features borrowed directly from Italian manuscripts. It is a gospel book, and is in poor condition.

(3) *The Durham Cathedral A II 10.* A fragment of a large-sized gospel book, consisting of only twelve pages, the *A II 10* is of considerable importance since it employs all the main decorative elements. The end of St Matthew's Gospel has three loops of interlace, while the text of the Gospel of St Mark has a large decorated opening capital. The colours are very bright, and in addition to interlace it employs groups of spirals

in trumpet patterns and animal ornament. It dates from the mid-seventh century or slightly earlier.

The classical Celtic manuscripts

The main period of Celtic manuscript illumination extends from the *Book of Durrow* (end of seventh century) to the *Book of Kells* (*c.* 800). By the end of this period ornament was over-ornate and, in the *Book of Kells*, almost baroque in its exuberance. Technically, however, the *Book of Kells* is a work of supreme calligraphic skill, and the works that postdate it are far less careful in their execution. The most important and famous manuscripts of this period are *Durrow, Lindisfarne, Kells, Echternach* and *Lichfield*, the latter being in some ways more extravagant than the *Book of Kells*. There are in addition a number of lesser known but none the less important works.

(1) *The Book of Durrow*. This work is a copy of the gospels preceded and followed by canons of concordance and summaries of the text. Each gospel begins with an evangelist symbol in a plain expanse bordered by interlace. This is followed by a carpet page, the inspiration for which is probably Coptic, and facing this, the first page of the text with an ornamented capital. The decorated pages for each gospel are all present, with the exception of the carpet page for St Matthew. The canon pages are framed in borders of interlace, and there are some other decorations. The only colours employed are orange-red, green, yellow and brown (which appears only on a few pages). New to the *Book of Durrow* is the use of a mass of intertwining animals on the carpet page preceding the Gospel of St John. The style of these is considerably influenced by Anglo-Saxon work, particularly metalwork. It is difficult to date, but probably belongs to the second half of the seventh century.

(2) *The Durham Cathedral A II 17*. Slightly later than the *Book of Durrow*, the *A II 17* represents a development of the style. At the beginning of the Gospel of St Mark there is a Crucifixion instead of an evangelist symbol, and only one decorated initial survives. It dates from 700 or slightly earlier.

(3) *The Echternach gospels*. There are several manuscripts ascribed to Echternach in Luxembourg, a foundation of Saxon (and probably Irish) monks established at the end of the seventh century. The manuscript of the Echternach gospels in Paris is the earliest and the most important, the ornament of which is Celtic in style and represents a development from *Durrow*. It is characterized by its lack of animal ornament (except for the evangelist symbols) and its use of fine interlace and spirals.

(4) *The Lindisfarne gospels*. Produced at Lindisfarne, a colophon states that this manuscript was the work of a Saxon abbot called Eadfrith. It dates

from around 700. Although essentially it follows the layout of *Durrow*, it employs evangelist portraits with their symbols above them, instead of symbols alone, and in this iconography it is copying Antique models. The animal ornament is much more developed in this work, and the initials have become so elaborate that they occupy much of the first page of each gospel. The colours are much more varied in tone than those in *Durrow*.

The canon tables in the Lindisfarne gospels differ from those in *Durrow* in their use of arches, reminiscent of Eastern manuscript design. They are, however, decorated with interlace.

(5) *The Lichfield gospels (Gospels of St Chad).* Closely related in its ornament to the Lindisfarne gospels, the manuscript of the Lichfield gospels is probably nearly contemporaneous. It is incomplete, but the two surviving evangelist pictures are in a different style from Lindisfarne, and may have Coptic models behind them. The figure of Luke is composed almost entirely of curves, and is symmetrical. The ornament includes Lindisfarne birds, particularly well deployed on a cruciform carpet page. In some respects the evangelist figures recall the style of the earlier Echternach gospels.

(6) *Durham Cathedral B II 30.* This manuscript, dating from around 725, is notable for its two full-page illustrations of David, one as harpist and one as warrior. It is a copy of Cassiodorus' *Commentary on the Psalms*. The importance of the work lies in the new attempted realism in figural representation, done in a linear technique. The ground and border for the figure is made up of good interlace and animal heads.

(7) *St Gall gospels.* Executed probably in the monastery at St Gall, Switzerland, an Irish foundation, this purely Celtic-style manuscript was made around 750. The figures in this work represent a transitional stage between the style of the Lichfield gospels and that of the *Book of Kells*. It has only one carpet page, but apart from the usual evangelist portraits has at the end of St John's Gospel two pages depicting the Crucifixion and the Last Judgement. The colours used (blue, red, yellow and green) are unusually bright, even garish. Realism is of negligible importance, and representations are expressed in terms of abstract design.

(8) *Book of MacRegol.* Named after the monk who probably produced it, this book dates from the late eighth century, and is now in the Bodleian Library in Oxford. Its treatment tends to be careless and disorderly. Of related style and date are the smaller *Book of Dimna* and *Book of Mulling*.

(9) *Book of Armagh.* This is the best of a group of early ninth-century manuscripts. It was made by Ferdomnagh for the abbot of Armagh, 807–8. The decoration is elegant and linear, and is a foretaste of the style represented in the *Book of Kells*.

(10) *The Book of Kells.* Along with *Lindisfarne* and *Durrow* this ranks as one of the greatest Celtic manuscripts. Begun probably at Iona around 800, it was taken to Kells by monks fleeing from Viking raiders, and may have been further decorated there.

The ornament of the *Book of Kells* shows that the artists had some familiarity with current Carolingian work, which is particularly reflected in the canon tables, while Coptic influence can be seen in the portrait of the Virgin and Child. The last page of St Mark's Gospel reflects the design of an Essen manuscript, while the type of capital employed frequently echoes Merovingian models, as indeed does the wealth of amusing detail. The style of the work is, however, distinctive, and always represents a Celtic interpretation of the models. The ornament is frequently used to illustrate the text. There are six types of decoration in the book: (1) canon tables, (2) evangelist symbols, (3) portraits of Christ and the evangelists, on separate pages, (4) miniatures of the Temptation of Christ (the so-called 'Temple Page'), the Virgin and Child and the Betrayal of Christ, (5) cruciform pages, preceding each gospel (i.e. carpet pages) and (6) decorative text pages, of which the XPI monogram page is perhaps the most ornate.

After the Book of Kells

The *Book of Kells* effectively marks the end of vigorous Celtic manuscript art; very few works survive that postdate it and all are of a lesser quality. A few are listed below.

(1) *Turin Gospel Book.* This badly mutilated work was destroyed in a fire in 1904, with the exception of a few pages. It is important for showing that other books of comparable richness to the *Book of Kells* were being produced in the early ninth century. Although the layout is similar to that employed in the *Book of Kells,* it shows some affinities with the St Gall tradition of manuscripts. The picture pages show Byzantine inspiration, and depict the Ascension and the Last Judgement.

(2) *The Book of Mac Durnan.* This work is in many ways closely related to the *Book of Armagh,* and it has been suggested it was also executed by Ferdomnach, though this is unlikely and it should probably be assigned to the later ninth century. The colours used are very vivid, and the arrangement of the decoration careful and orderly. Interlace predominates as the decorative element.

(3) *Cotton Psalter.* Dating from the early tenth century, this manuscript was badly damaged by the Cotton fire. Its importance lies in its obvious relationship to contemporary sculpture. The style is vigorous, and shows a mixture of realism and stylization. Two surviving picture pages show David the Musician and David and Goliath.

(4) *Southampton Psalter* (St John's College, Cambridge, Psalter). Possibly early eleventh-century, this work was modelled on the Cotton Psalter. It is perfectly preserved, with very bright colours, and appears to copy, without fully understanding its model.

Appendix B The chronology of some historical personages mentioned in the book

Northumbria

Æthelfrith 593–617
Edwin 616–633
Oswald 634–642
Oswy 642–670
Ecgfrith 670–685
Aldfrith 685–705
Osred 705–716
Coenred 716–718
Osric 718–729
Ceolwulf 729–737
Eadberht 737–757/8
Alhred 765–774
Æthelred I 774–778/9
Ælfwald 778/9–789
Æthelred I 790–796
Eanred 806/8–840/1
Æthelred II 840/1–849
Redwulf 844
Osberht 848/50–867

Kings in Wales

Maelgwyn (see below)
Merfyn Vrych 800–844
Rhodri Mawr 844–877
Hywel Dda *c.* 927–*c.* 949

British Chiefs of the fifth to sixth century
(dates mainly approximate)

Vortigern *c.* 425–*c.* 459
Ambrosius *c.* 460–*c.* 475
Arthur *c.* 475–*c.* 515
Aurelianus
Maelgwn *c.* 520–551
Vortepor *c.* 515–*c.* 540
Urien *c.* 570–*c.* 590
Owain *c.* 590–*c.* 595
Rydderch *c.* 560–*c.* 600

Kings of Dalriada

Gabran 541–560
Conall 560–574
Aedan mac Gabran 574–609
Domnall Brecc *c.* 630–*c.* 643
Ferchar 680–696

Kings of Pictland

Bridei mac Maelcon 554–584
Drest 663–672
Bridei mac Bili 672–693
Taran 693–697
Bridei mac Derelei 697–706
Nechtan mac Derelei 706–724
Oengus mac Fergus 724–761
Kenneth mac Alpin 830–860
(united Picts and Scots)

Abbreviations of Journals

Act. Arch.	*Acta Archaeologica*
Arch. Camb.	*Archaeologia Cambrensis*
Ant.	*Antiquity*
Ant. J.	*Antiquaries Journal*
Arch.	*Archaeologia*
Arch. Ael.	*Archaeologia Aeliana*
Arch. J.	*Archaeological Journal*
Arch. Scot.	*Archaeologia Scotica*
B.B.C.S.	*Bulletin of the Board of Celtic Studies*
B.M.Q.	*British Museum Quarterly*
C.A.	*Cornish Archaeology*
Current Arch.	*Current Archaeology*
Co. Louth A.J.	*County Louth Archaeological Journal*
G.A.J.	*Glasgow Archaeological Journal*, New Series
J.B.A.A.	*Journal of the British Archaeological Association*
J.C.H.A.S.	*Journal of the Cork Historical and Archaeological Society*
J. Galway H.A.S.	*Journal of the Galway Historical and Archaeological Society*
J.R.S.	*Journal of Roman Studies*
J. Manx Mus.	*Journal of the Manx Museum*
J.R.I.C.	*Journal of the Royal Institute of Cornwall*
J.R.S.A.I.	*Journal of the Royal Society of Antiquaries of Ireland*
Med. Arch.	*Medieval Archaeology*

N.C.	*Numismatic Chronicle*
Oxon.	*Oxoniensia*
Prehist.	*Préhistoire*
P.P.S.	*Proceedings of the Prehistoric Society*
P.R.I.A.	*Proceedings of the Royal Irish Academy*
P.S.A.S.	*Proceedings of the Society of Antiquaries of Scotland*
Proc. Brit. Acad.	*Proceedings of the British Academy*
Proc. D.A.E.S.	*Proceedings of the Devon Archaeological Exploration Society*
Proc. Devon A.S.	*Proceedings of the Devon Archaeological Society*
P.D.N.H.A.S.	*Proceedings of the Dorset Natural History and Archaeological Society*
P.O.A.S.	*Proceedings of the Orkney Antiquarian Society*
Proc. Soc. Ant. Lond.	*Proceedings of the Society of Antiquaries of London*
P. U. Bristol Spel. Soc.	*Proceedings of the University of Bristol Speleological Society*
Proc. Somerset A. & N.H.S.	*Proceedings of the Somerset Archaeological and Natural History Society*
P.W.C.F.C.	*Proceedings of the West Cornwall Field Club*
R.C.H.A.M.	*Royal Commission for Historical and Ancient Monuments, Inventories (by counties)*
S.A.C.	*Sussex Archaeological Collections*
S.A.F.	*Scottish Archaeological Forum*
S.C.M.B.	*Seaby's Coin and Medal Bulletin*
S.H.R.	*Scottish Historical Review*
Trans. Birmingham A.S.	*Transactions of the Birmingham Archaeological Society*
Trans. Cymm.	*Transactions of the Honourable Cymmrodorion Society*
Trans. C.H.S.	*Transactions of the Caernarvonshire Historical Society*
Trans. B. & G.A.S.	*Transactions of the Bristol and Gloucester Archaeological Society*
Trans. C. & W.A.A.S.	*Transactions of the Cumberland and Westmorland Antiquarian and Archaeological Society*
T.D.A.	*Transactions of the Devonshire Association*
Trans. D. & G.N.H.A.S.	*Transactions of the Dumfries and Galloway Natural History and Antiquarian Society*
T.H.S.L.C.	*Transactions of the Historical Society of Lancashire and Cheshire*
W.H.R.	*Welsh Historical Review*

Select Bibliography

Section A gives a short list of general works of a non-specialist nature which cover the history and archaeology of late Celtic Britain. Section B provides a basic bibliography for the regions covered in Part I of the book, arranged according to chapter. Section C is a selective list of publications relating to the material culture of the Early Christian Celts, again on a chapter basis. Most of the material relating to this subject is to be found in the main excavation reports listed in Section B.

Section A

ALCOCK, L. *Arthur's Britain,* London (1971)

ASHE, G. *The Quest for Arthur's Britain,* London (1968)

CHADWICK, H. M. *Early Scotland,* Cambridge (1949)

CHADWICK, N. K. (ed.) *Studies in Early British History,* Cambridge (1954)

CHADWICK, N. K. *The Age of the Saints in the Early Celtic Church,* London (1961)

CHADWICK, N. K. *Celtic Britain,* London (1963)

CHADWICK, N. K. *The Celts,* Harmondsworth (1970)

DE PAOR, M. & L. *Early Christian Ireland,* London (1958)

DILLON, M. (ed.) *Early Irish Society,* Dublin (1954)

DILLON, M. & CHADWICK, N. K. *The Celtic Realms,* London (1967)

HARDEN, D. (ed.) *Dark Age Britain,* London (1956)

HENDERSON, I. *The Picts,* London (1967)

HENRY, F. *Irish Art,* London, 3 vols (1965–70)

HUGHES, K. *The Church in Early Irish Society,* London (1966)

JACKSON, K. H. *Language and History in Early Britain*, Edinburgh (1953)

NORMAN, E. R. & ST JOSEPH, J. K. *The Early Development of Irish Society*, Cambridge (1969)

THOMAS, A. C. *The Early Christian Archaeology of North Britain*, Oxford (1971)

THOMAS, A. C. *Britain and Ireland in Early Christian Times, A.D. 400–800*, London (1971)

WAINWRIGHT, F. T. *The Problem of the Picts*, London (1955)

Section B

Southern Scotland

BALDWIN-BROWN, G. 'Notes on a necklace of glass beads found in a cist in Dalmeny Park, South Queensferry', *P.S.A.S.* XLIX (1914–15), 332–8.

BARBOUR, J. 'Notice of a stone fort near Kirkandrews', *P.S.A.S.* XLI (1906–7), 68–80.

BURLEY, E. 'A survey and catalogue of the metalwork from Traprain Law', *P.S.A.S.* LXXXIX (1955–6), 118–226.

CALLANDER, J. G. 'A collection of prehistoric relics from Stevenston Sands, Ayrshire', *P.S.A.S.* LXVII (1932–3), 26–34.

COCHRAN-PATRICK, R. 'Notes on some explorations in a tumulus called the Court Hill, Dalry', *P.S.A.S.* X (1874), 281–5.

CORMACK, W. 'Northumbrian coins from Luce Sands', *Trans. D. & G.N.H.A.S.* XLII (1965), 149–50.

CRAMP, R. 'The Anglian sculptured crosses of Dumfriesshire', *Trans. D. & G.N.H.A.S.* XXXVIII (1961), 9–20.

CURLE, A. O. 'Report on the excavation of a vitrified fort at Rockcliffe, known as the Mote of Mark', *P.S.A.S.* XLVIII (1913–14), 125–68.

CURLE, A. O. 'Excavations on Traprain Law', *P.S.A.S.* XLIX (1914–15), 139–202.

FEACHEM, R. 'The fortifications of Traprain Law', *P.S.A.S.* LXXXIX (1955–6), 284–9.

FEACHEM, R. 'The hillforts of northern Britain', in Rivet, A. (ed.), *The Iron Age in Northern Britain* (1966), Edinburgh, 59–87.

GRESHAM, C. '*The Book of Aneuirin*', *Ant.* XVI (1942), 237–57.

HENSHALL, A. S. 'The long cist cemetery at Parkburn, Midlothian', *P.S.A.S.* LXXXIX (1955–6), 252–83.

HOGG, A. H. A. 'The Votadini', in Grimes, W. (ed.), *Aspects of Archaeology in Britain and Beyond* (1951), London, 214–19.

HOGG, A. H. A. 'Garn Boduan and Tre'r Ceiri', *Arch. J.* CXVII (1960), 1–39.

HUNTER-BLAIR, P. 'The origins of Northumbria', *Arch. Ael.* XXV (1947), 1–51.

HUNTER-BLAIR, P. 'The Bernicians and their northern frontier' in Chadwick, N. (ed.) *Studies in Early British History* (1958), Cambridge, 137–72.

JACKSON, K. H. 'The Gododdin of Aneurin', *Ant.* XIII (1939), 25–34.

JACKSON, K. H. 'The Britons in southern Scotland', *Ant.* XXIX (1955), 77–88.

JACKSON, K. H. *The Gododdin Poem* (1969).

JOBEY, G. 'Excavation at the native settlement at Huckhoe, Northumberland', *Arch. Ael.* XXXVII (1959), 217–78.

JOBEY, G. 'Homesteads and settlements of the frontier area', in Thomas, C. (ed.), *Rural Settlement in Roman Britain* (1966), London, 1–14.

KENT, J. P. C. 'Coins and the evacuation of Hadrian's Wall', *Trans. C. & W.A.A.S.* LI (1952), 4–16.

LAING, L. R. & CLOUGH, T. 'Excavations at Kirkconnel, Waterbeck, Dumfriesshire, 1968', *Trans. D. & G.N.H.A.S.* XLVI (1969), 128–39.

MACIVOR, I. *Dumbarton Castle* (1958).

MACKIE, E. 'The Scottish Iron Age', *S.H.R.* XLIX (1970), 1–32.

MAXWELL, H. 'Notes on a hoard of personal ornaments from Talnotrie, Kirkcudbright', *P.S.A.S.* XLVII (1912–13), 12–16.

MORRIS, J. 'Dark Age dates', in Dobson, B. & Jarrett, M., *Britain and Rome* (1965), 145–85.

MUNRO, R. *Ancient Scottish Lake Dwellings* (1882), Edinburgh.

NEWALL, F. *Excavations at Walls Hill, Renfrewshire* (1960), Paisley.

PIGGOTT, S. 'Native economies and the Roman occupation of north Britain', in Richmond, I. (ed.), *Roman and Native in North Britain* (1958), 1–27.

RADFORD, C. A. R. 'Excavations at Whithorn, 1949', *Trans D. & G.N.H.A.S.* XXVII (1950), 85–126.

RADFORD, C. A. R. 'St Ninian's cave', *Trans. D. & G.N.H.A.S.* XXVIII (1950–1), 96–8.

RADFORD, C. A. R. 'Excavations at Chapel Finnian, Mochrum', *Trans. D. & G.N.H.A.S.* XXVIII (1951), 28–40.

RADFORD, C. A. R. 'Hoddom', *Trans. D. & G.N.H.A.S.* XXXI (1954), 174–97.

RADFORD, C. A. R. 'Two reliquaries connected with south-west Scotland', *Trans. D. & G.N.H.A.S.* (1955), 115–23.

RADFORD, C. A. R. & DONALDSON, G. *Whithorn and Kirkmadrine* (1957).

REID, R. C. 'Physgill', *Trans. D. & G.N.H.A.S.* XXVIII (1951), 99–103.

SCOTT, J. *South-West Scotland* (1966), London.

SIMPSON, D. & SCOTT-ELLIOT, J. 'An excavation at Camp Hill, Troughouton', *Trans. D. & G.N.H.A.S.* XLI (1964), 125–34.

STEVENSON, R. B. K. 'The nuclear fort of Dalmahoy and other Dark Age capitals', *P.S.A.S.* LXXXIII (1948–9), 186–97.

THOMAS, A. C. 'Excavations at Trusty's Hill, Anwoth, 1960', *Trans. D. & G.N.H.A.S.* XXXVIII (1961), 58–70.

THOMAS, A. C. 'An Early Christian cemetery and chapel at Ardwall Isle, Kirkcudbright', *Med. Arch.* XI (1967), 127–88.

THOMAS, A. C. 'The evidence from north Britain', in Barley, M. & Hanson, R. (eds.), *Christianity in Britain, 300–700* (1968), Leicester, 93–122.

THOMAS, A. C. *The Early Christian Archaeology of North Britain* (1971), Oxford.

TRUCKELL, A. E. 'An excavation at Blacketlees, Annan', *Trans. D. & G.N.H.A.S.* XXXV (1958), 138–9.

TRUCKELL, A. E. 'Dumfries and Galloway in the Dark Ages: some problems', *Trans. D. & G.N.H.A.S.* XL (1963), 89–97.

TRUCKELL, A. E. 'Tynron Doon 1964–5', *Trans. D. & G.N.H.A.S.* XLIII (1966), 147–9.

WAINWRIGHT, F. T. *The Souterrains of Southern Pictland* (1963).

WILLIAMS, J. 'Tynron Doon, Dumfriesshire: a history of the site with notes on the finds, 1924–67', *Trans. D. &. G.N.H.A.S.* XLVIII (1971), 106–20.

WILSON, D. M. & BLUNT, C. E. 'The Trewhiddle hoard', *Arch.* XCVIII (1961), 75–122.

Northern Scotland

ALLEN, J. ROMILLY & ANDERSON, J. *The Early Christian Monuments of Scotland* (1903), Edinburgh.

ANDERSON, A. O. *Early Sources for Scottish History, 500–1286*, I, Edinburgh (1922).

ANDERSON, J. *Scotland in Early Christian Times* (1880), Edinburgh.

ANDERSON, M. O. 'The lists of the kings', *S.H.R.* XXVIII (1949), 108–18.

ANDERSON, M. O. 'The lists of the kings', *S.H.R.* XXIX (1950), 13–22.

BAKKA, E. 'Some English decorated metal objects from Norwegian graves', *Årbok fur Universitet i Bergen, humanistik serie I* (1963), 1–66.

BEVERIDGE, E. 'Excavation of an earth-house at Foshigarry and a fort at Dun Thomaidh, in North Uist', *P.S.A.S.* LV (1930–1), 299–356.

BEVERIDGE, E. & CALLANDER, J. G. 'Earth houses at Garry lochdrach and Bac Mhic Connain, in North Uist', *P.S.A.S,* LXVI (1931–2), 32–66.

BLUNT, C. E. 'The date of the Croy hoard', *P.S.A.S.* LXXXIV (1949–50), 217.

CHADWICK, H. M. *Early Scotland* (1949), Cambridge.

CHADWICK, N. K. *Celtic Britain* (1963), London.

CHRISTISON, D. & ANDERSON, J. 'Excavation of forts on the Poltalloch estates, Argyll, 1904–5', *P.S.A.S.* XXXIX (1904–5), 259–322.

CRAW, J. H. 'Excavations at Dunadd and other sites in the Poltalloch estates, Argyll', *P.S.A.S,* LXIV (1929–30), 111–47.

CRUDEN, S. H. *The Early Christian Monuments of Scotland* (1964), Edinburgh.

CURLE, C. L. 'The chronology of the Early Christian monuments of Scotland', *P.S.A.S.* LXXIV (1939–40), 60–116.

EDWARDS, A. J. H. 'A massive double-linked silver chain', *P.S.A.S.* LXXIII (1938–9), 326–7.

EELES, F. 'The Monymusk reliquary or Brecbennoch of St Columba', *P.S.A.S.* LXVIII (1933–4), 433–8.

FAIRHURST, H. 'The galleried dun at Kildonan Bay, Kintyre', *P.S.A.S.* LXXXIII (1938–9), 185–228.

FAIRHURST, H. 'The stack fort on Ugadale Point, Kintyre', *P.S.A.S.* LXXXVIII (1954–6), 15–22.

FEACHEM, R. 'Fortifications', in Wainwright, F. T. (ed.), *Problem of the Picts* (1955), 66–86.

FOWLER, E. 'Celtic metalwork of the fifth and sixth centuries', *Arch. J.* CXX (1963), 98–160.

GRIEG, C. 'Cullykhan', *Current Arch.* III (1972), 227–31.

GRIEG, C. 'Excavations at Cullykhan Castle Point, Banff', *S.A.F.* 3 (1971), 15–21.

GRIEG, S. 'Scotland', being Part II of Shetelig, H. (ed.), *Viking Antiquities of Great Britain and Ireland* (1940–54), Oslo.

HAMILTON, J. R. C. *Excavations at Jarlshof, Shetland* (1956), Edinburgh.

HAMILTON, J. R. C. *Excavations at Clickhimin, Shetland* (1968), Edinburgh.

HENDERSON, I. *The Picts* (1967), London.

HENDERSON, I. 'The origin centre of the Pictish symbol stones', *P.S.A.S.* XCI. (1957–8), 44–60.

HENDERSON, I. 'The meaning of the Pictish symbol stones', in Meldrum, P. (ed.), *The Dark Ages in the Highlands* (1971), 53–68.

JACKSON, K. H. 'Notes on the ogham inscriptions of southern Britain', in Bruce-Dickins (ed.), *Early Cultures of North-West Europe* (1950), Cambridge, 197–213.

JACKSON, K. H. *Language and History in Early Britain* (1953), Edinburgh.

JACKSON, K. H. 'The Pictish language', in Wainwright, F. (ed.), *The Problem of the Picts* (1955), 129–66.

JACKSON, K. H. 'The St Ninian's Isle inscription', *Ant.* XXXIV (1960), 38–42.

JACKSON, K. H. 'The ogham inscription at Dunadd', *Ant.* XXXIX (1965), 300–2.

KILBRIDE-JONES, H. E. 'A bronze hanging bowl from Castle Tioram and a suggested absolute chronology for British hanging bowls', *P.S.A.S.* LXXI (1936–7), 206–47.

LETHBRIDGE, T. C. *The Painted Men* (1956).

MACALISTER, R. A. S. *Corpus Inscriptionum Insularum Celticarum*, I (1945), Dublin.

MACDONALD, J. 'Historical notices of the "Broch" of Burghead in Moray', *P.S.A.S.* IV (1860–2), 2–51.

MACKIE, E. 'Radiocarbon dates and the Scottish Iron Age', *Ant.* XLIII (1969), 15–26.

MACKIE, E. 'The Scottish Iron Age: a review', *S.H.R.* XLIX (1970), 1–32.

MARSHALL, D. N. 'Report on excavations at Little Dunagoil', *Trans. Bute N.H.S.* XVI (1964).

RADFORD, C. A. R. 'From prehistory to history', in Piggott, S. (ed.), *Prehistoric Peoples of Scotland* (1962), London, 125–54.

RADFORD, C. A. R. 'The early Church in Strathclyde and Galloway', *Med. Arch.* XI (1967), 105–26.

RICHARDSON, J. *The Broch of Gurness, Aikerness, Orkney* (1948), Edinburgh.

RICHMOND, I. A. 'Ancient geographical sources for Britain north of the Cheviot', in Richmond, I. A. (ed.), *Roman and Native in North Britain* (1958), London, 131–49.

SCOTT, L. 'Gallo-British colonies; the aisled round-house culture in the north', *P.P.S.* XIV (1948), 46–125.

SIMPSON, W. D. 'The early Romanesque tower at Restenneth Priory, Angus', *Ant. J.* XLIII (1963), 269–83.

SKENE, W. F. *Chronicles of the Picts, Chronicles of the Scots and other Memorials of Scottish History* (1867).

SMALL, A. 'Burghead', *S.A.F.* 1 (1969), 61–8.

SMALL, A. *Craig Phadrig* (1972), Dundee.

SMALL, A., THOMAS, C. & WILSON, D. M. *St Ninian's Isle and its Treasure*, 2 vols (1973), Aberdeen.

STEVENSON, R. B. K. 'Dalmahoy and other Dark Age capitals', *P.S.A.S.* LXXXIII (1948–9), 186–97.

STEVENSON, R. B. K. 'Celtic carved box from Orkney', *P.S.A.S.* LXXXVI (1951–2), 187–90.

STEVENSON, R. B. K. 'Pictish art', in Wainwright, F. T. (ed.), *Problem of the Picts* (1955), London, 97–128.

STEVENSON, R. B. K. 'The Inchyra stone and other unpublished Early Christian monuments', *P.S.A.S.* XCII (1958–9), 33–55.

STEVENSON, R. B. K. 'Pictish chain, Roman silver and bauxite beads', *P.S.A.S.* LXXXVIII (1954–6), 228–30.

STEVENSON, R. B. K. 'The Gaulcross hoard of Pictish silver', *P.S.A.S.* XCVII (1963–4), 206–11.

STEVENSON, R. B. K. 'Sculpture in Scotland in the sixth to ninth centuries AD', *Kolloquium Uber Spatantike Und Fruhmittelalteriche Skulptur* (1970), Mainz, 65–74.

TAYLOR, H. M. & TAYLOR, J. *Anglo-Saxon Architecture* (1965), Cambridge.

TAYLOR, D. B. 'Excavations at Hurly Hawkin, Angus', *S.A.F.* 3 (1971), 11–14.

THOMAS, A. C. 'Excavations at Trusty's Hill, Anwoth, 1960', *Trans. D. & G.N.H.A.S.* XXXVIII (1961), 58–70.

THOMAS, A. C. 'Animal art of the Scottish Iron Age', *Arch. J.* CXVIII (1961), 14–64.

THOMAS, A. C. 'The interpretation of the Pictish symbols', *Arch. J.* CXX (1963), 31–97.

WAINWRIGHT, F. T. 'The Picts and the problem', in Wainwright, F. T. (ed.), *The Problem of the Picts* (1955).

WAINWRIGHT, F. T. 'Picts and Scots', in Wainwright, F. T. (ed.), *The Northern Isles* (1962), 91–116.

WAINWRIGHT, F. T. *Souterrains of Southern Pictland* (1963), London.

WILSON, D. M. *Reflections on the St Ninian's Isle Treasure* (Jarrow Lecture, 1969).

YOUNG, A. 'An aisled farmhouse at the Allasdale, Isle of Barra', *P.S.A.S.* LXXXVII (1952–3), 80–105.

YOUNG, A. 'Excavations at Dun Cuier, Isle of Barra', *P.S.A.S.* LXXXIX (1955–6), 290–328.

YOUNG, A. 'The sequence of Hebridean pottery', in Rivet, A. (ed.), *The Iron Age in North Britain* (1966), 45–58.

YOUNG, A. & RICHARDSON, K. M. 'a' Cheardach Mhor, Drimore, S. Uist', *P.S.A.S.* XCIII (1959–60), 135–73.

YOUNG, H. 'Notes on the ramparts of Burghead as revealed by recent excavations', *P.S.A.S.* XXV (1890–91), 435–47.

Wales and Man

ALCOCK, L. 'Dark Age objects from Lesser Garth Cave, Glamorgan', *B.B.C.S.* XVIII (1958–60), 221–7.

ALCOCK, L. 'Post-Roman sherds from Longbury Bank Cave Penally', *B.B.C.S.* XVIII (1958–60), 77–8.

ALCOCK, L. *Dinas Powys, an Iron Age, Dark Age and Medieval Settlement in Glamorgan* (1963), Cardiff.

ALCOCK, L. 'Excavations at Degannwy Castle, Caernarvonshire, 1961–6', *Arch. J.* CXXIV (1967), 190–201.

ALCOCK, L. 'Was there an Irish Sea culture-province in the Dark Ages?', in Moore D. (ed.), *The Irish Sea Province in Archaeology and History* (1970), London, 55–65.

ALCOCK, L. *Arthur's Britain* (1971), Harmondsworth.

BERSU, G. 'Celtic homesteads in the Isle of Man', *J. Manx Mus.* V (1941–6), 177–82.

BOWEN, E. G. 'Clawdd Mawr, Carmarthenshire', *B.B.C.S.* VIII (1937), 383–5.

BOWEN, E. G. *The Settlements of the Celtic Saints in Wales* (1956), Cardiff.

BU'LOCK, J. D. 'Early Christian memorial formulae', *Arch. Camb.* CV (1956), 133–41.

BU'LOCK, J. D. 'Vortigern and the Pillar of Eliseg', *Ant.* XXXIV (1960), 49–53.

CHADWICK, N. K. (ed.) *Studies in Early British History* (1959), Cambridge.

CHADWICK, N. K. (ed.) *Celtic Britain* (1963), London.

CHADWICK, N. K. (ed.) *Celt and Saxon: Studies in the Early British Border* (1963), Cambridge.

CHADWICK, N. K. *The Celts* (1970), Harmondsworth.

CHADWICK, O. 'The evidence of dedications in the early history of the Welsh Church', in Chadwick, N. (ed.), *Studies in the Early British Church* (1954), Cambridge, 173–88.

DAVIES, W. H. 'The Church in Wales', in Barley, M. & Hanson, R. P. C. (eds.), *Christianity in Britain, 300–700* (1968), Leicester, 131–50.

FOSTER, I. 'The emergence of Wales', in Foster, I. & Daniel, G. (eds.), *Prehistoric and Early Wales* (1965), London, 213–35.

FOWLER, P. 'Hillforts 400–700', in Jesson, M. & Hill, D., *The Iron Age and Its Hillforts* (1971), Southampton, 203–13.

FOX, A. 'Early Christian period I: settlement sites and other remains', in Nash-Williams, V. (ed.), *A Hundred Years of Welsh Archaeology* (1946), 105–22.

FOX, C. 'Wat's Dyke, a field survey', *Arch. Camb.* LXXXIX (1934), 205–78

FOX, C. *A Find of the Early Iron Age from Llyn Cerrig Bach, Anglesey* (1946), Cardiff.

FOX, C. *Offa's Dyke* (1955), London.

GARDNER, W. & SAVORY, H. N. *Dinorben* (1964), Cardiff.

GELLING, P. S. & STANFORD, S. 'Dark Age pottery or Iron Age ovens?', *Trans. & Proc. Birmingham A.S.* LXXXII (1967), 77–91.

GRESHAM, C. 'Interpretation of settlement patterns in N.W. Wales', in Alcock & Foster, *Culture & Environment*, (1963), London, 263–79.

GRIFFITHS, W. E. 'The excavation of an enclosed hut group at Caer Mynydd, Caernarvonshire', *Ant. J.* XXXIX (1959), 33–60.

GRIMES, W. F. *The Prehistory of Wales* (1951), Cardiff.

HAGUE, D. B. 'A medieval church on the Island of St Tudwal', *T.C.H.S.* XXI (1960), 6–13.

HAGUE, D. B. 'Burryholms', *Med. Arch.* X (1966), 184.

HOGG, A. H. A. 'The date of Cunedda', *Ant.* XXII (1948), 201–5.

HOGG, A. H. A. 'Garn Boduan and Tr'er Ceiri', *Arch. J.* CXVII (1960), 1–39.

HOGG, A. H. A. 'Early Iron Age Wales', in Foster, I. & Daniel, G. (eds), *Prehistoric and Early Wales* (1965), 109–50.

HOGG, A. H. A. 'Native settlements in Wales', in Thomas, C. (ed.), *Rural Settlement in Roman Britain* (1966), 28–38.

HOGG, A. H. A. 'Hillforts in the coastal areas of Wales', in Thomas, C. (ed.), *The Iron Age in the Irish Sea Province* (1972), London, 11–23.

HOULDER, C. & MANNING, W. H. *South Wales* (1966), London.

HUGHES, H. 'Ynys Seiriol', *Arch. Camb.* I (1901).

HUGHES, H. 'An ancient burial ground at Bangor', *Arch. Camb.* LXXX (1925), 432–6.

JACKSON, K. H. 'Notes on the ogham inscriptions of southern Britain', in Fox, C. & Bruce-Dickins (eds), *Early Cultures of North-West Europe* (1950), 199–213.

JARRETT, M. Revised ed. of Nash-Williams, V. E., *The Roman Frontier in Wales* (1969), Cardiff.

JOHNS, C. N. 'The Celtic monasteries of north Wales', *T.C.H.S.* XXI (1960), 14–43.

LETHBRIDGE, T. & DAVID, H. 'Excavation of a house site on Gateholm, Pembroke', *Arch. Camb.* LXXXV (1930), 366–74.

MEGAW, B. R. S. 'The ancient village of Ronaldsway', *J. Manx Mus.* IV (1938–40), 181–2.

MEYER, K. 'Early relations between Gael and Brython', *Trans. Cymm.* (1895–6), 55–86.

MEYER, K. 'The expulsion of the Dessi', *Y Cymmrodor*, XIV (1900), 101–35.

NASH-WILLIAMS, V. E. *The Early Christian Monuments of Wales* (1950), Cardiff.

NASH-WILLIAMS, V. E. *The Roman Frontier in Wales* (1954), Cardiff.

NEELY, C. J. H. 'Excavations at Ronaldsway, Isle of Man', *Ant. J.* XX (1940), 72–86.

NICHOLSON, E. W. 'The dynasty of Cunedag', *Y Cymmrodor*, XXL (1908), 61–104.

PALMER, A. N. 'Notes on the early history of Bangor-is-Coed', *Y Cymmrodor*, X (1890), 12–28.

PHILIPS, C. W. 'The excavation of a hut group at Pant-y-Saer', *Arch. Camb.* LXXXIX (1934), 1–36.

RICHARDS, M. 'The Irish settlements in south-west Wales', *J.R.S.A.I.* LXXX (1960), 133–62.

RICHMOND, I. A. 'Roman Wales', in Foster, I. and Daniel, G. (eds), *Prehistoric and Early Wales* (1965), 151–76.

SAVORY, H. N. 'Some sub-Romano-British brooches from south Wales', in Harden, D. (ed.), *Dark Age Britain* (1956), London, 40–58.

SAVORY, H. N. 'Excavations at Dinas Emrys, Beddgelert, Caerns.' *Arch. Camb.* CIX (1960), 13–77.

SKINNER, F. G. & BRUCE-MITFORD, R. 'A Celtic balance beam of the Early Christian period', *Ant. J.* XX (1940), 87–102.

WAINWRIGHT, G. *Coygan Camp* (1967), Cardiff.

WHEELER, R. E. M. & WHEELER, T. V. *Report on Excavations at Lydney Park, Gloucestershire* (1932).

WRIGHT, R. P. & JACKSON, K. H. 'A late inscription from Wroxeter', *Ant. J.* XLVIII (1968), 296–300.

South-west England

ALCOCK, L. 'Excavations at South Cadbury Castle, 1968', *Ant. J.* XLIX (1969), 30–40.

ALCOCK, L. *Arthur's Britain* (1971), Harmondsworth.

ALCOCK, L. *By South Cadbury is that Camelot* (1972), London.

APSIMON, A. 'The Roman temple on Brean Down, Somerset', *Proc. Univ. Bristol Spel. Soc.* X (1965), 195–258.

BRUCE-MITFORD, R. 'A Dark Age settlement at Mawgan Porth, Cornwall', in Bruce-Mitford (ed.), *Recent Archaeological Excavations in the British Isles* (1956), London, 167–96.

CLIFFORD, E. M. 'The Roman villa of Witcombe, Glos.', *Trans. B. & G.N.H.A.S.* LXXIII (1954), 5–69.

CUNLIFFE, B. *Roman Bath* (1969), London, Soc. Ant. Res. Rep.

DEXTER, T. H. *Old Cornish crosses* (1938), London.

FOWLER, P. & RAHTZ, P. 'Cadcong 1970', *Current Arch.* II (1970), 337–42.

FOWLER, P. 'Hillforts, AD 400–700', in Jesson, M. & Hill, D. (eds.), *The Iron Age and Its Hillforts* (1971), Southampton, 203–13.

FOX, A. 'A Dark Age trading site at Bantham, S. Devon', *Ant. J.* XXXV (1955), 55–67.

FOX, A. *South-West England* (1964), London.

FRERE, S. S. 'The end of towns in Roman Britain', in Wacher, J. (ed.), *Civitas Capitals of Roman Britain* (1966), Leicester, 87–100.

GREEN, J. C. S. 'Excavations in the Roman cemetery at Poundbury, Dorchester, 1969', *P.D.N.H.A.F.C.* XCI (1969), 183–6.

HENCKEN, H. O'N. *The Archaeology of Cornwall and Scilly* (1932), London.

HURST, H. R. *Excavations in Gloucester, 1970* (1970), Gloucester.

LAING, L. R. 'Dark Age timber halls in Britain – some problems', *Trans. D. & G.N.H.A.S.* XLVI (1969), 110–27.

LANGDON, A. G. *Old Cornish Crosses* (1896).

LEEDS, E. T. *Early Anglo-Saxon Art and Archaeology* (1936), Oxford.

MACALISTER, R. A. S. *Corpus Inscriptionum Insularum Celticarum*, II (1949), Dublin.

MEANEY, A. & HAWKES, S. C. *Two Anglo-Saxon Cemeteries at Winnall, Hampshire* (1970), London.

MYRES, J. N. L. 'Wansdyke and the origins of Wessex', in Trevor-Roper, H. (ed.), *Essays in British History* (1964), 1–28.

MYRES, J. N. L. *Anglo-Saxon Pottery and the Settlement of England* (1969), Oxford.

O'NEIL, H. 'Excavation of a Celtic hermitage on St Helens, Isles of Scilly', *Arch. J.* CXXI (1964), 40–69.

POLLARD, S. M. 'Neolithic and Dark Age settlements on High Peak, Sidmouth, Devon', *Proc. Devon A.S.* XXIII (1966), 35–59.

RADFORD, C. A. R. 'Tintagel, the castle and Celtic monastery', *Ant. J.* XV (1935), 401–19.

RADFORD, C. A. R. 'Report on the excavations at Castle Dore', *J.R.I.C.*, I, Appendix (1951).

RAHTZ, P. 'The Roman temple at Pagan's Hill', *P.S.A.N.H.S.* XCVI (1951), 112–42.

RAHTZ, P. 'Cannington hillfort', *P.S.A.N.H.S.* CXIII (1969), 56–68.

RAHTZ, P. 'Excavations at Glastonbury Tor, Somerset', *Arch. J.* CXXVII (1970), 1–81.

RAHTZ, P. 'Sub-Roman cemeteries in Somerset', in Barley, M. & Hanson, R. (eds.), *Christianity in Britain, 300–700* (1968), 193–6.

RAHTZ, P. & FOWLER, P. 'Somerset AD 400–700', in Fowler, P. (ed.) *Archaeology and the Landscape* (1972), London, 187–221.

THOMAS, A. C. 'Evidence for the post-Roman occupation of Chun Castle', *Ant. J.* XXXVI (1956), 75–8.

THOMAS, A. C. 'Dark Age imported pottery in western Britain', *Med. Arch.* III (1959), 89–111.

THOMAS, A. C. *People and Pottery in Dark Age Cornwall* (1960) (West Cornwall Field Club publ.).

THOMAS, A. C. 'Post-Roman rectangular house plans in the south-west', *Proc. W.C.F.C.* II (1960), 156–61.

THOMAS, A. C. 'Cornwall in the Dark Ages', *Proc. W.C.F.C.* II (1960), 62–5.

THOMAS, A. C. *Gwithian, Ten Years' Work, 1949–58* (West Cornwall Field Club, 1958).

THOMAS, A. C. & FOWLER, P. 'Arable fields of the pre-Norman period at Gwithian', *Cornish Arch.* I (1962), 61–84.

THOMAS, A. C. 'The character and origin of Roman Dumnonia', in Thomas (ed.), *Rural Settlement in Roman Britain* (1966), London, 74–98.

THOMAS, A. C. *Christian Antiquities of Camborne* (1967), St Austell.

THOMAS, A. C. 'Lundy 1969', *Current Arch.* II (1969), 138–42.

WHEELER, R. E. M. & T. *Report on the Excavation of the Prehistoric, Roman and Post-Roman Site in Lydney Park, Gloucestershire,* (London, Soc. Ant. Res. Rep. 1932).

Ireland

ANON 'Navan fort', *Current Arch.* II (1970), 304–8.

ANON 'Dun Ailinne', *Current Arch.* II (1970), 308–11.

BERSU, G. 'The rath at Towland, Lissue', *U.J.A.* (1947), 30–58.

BIELER, L. *The Life and Legend of St Patrick* (1949), Dublin.

BINCHY, D. 'Patrick and his biographers: ancient and modern', *Studia Hibernica,* II (1962), 7–173.

COLLINS, A. E. P. 'Excavations at the Dressogagh rath, Co. Armagh', *U.J.A.* XXIX (1966), 117–29.

COLLINS, A. E. P. 'Excavations at Lough Faughan crannog, Co. Down', *U.J.A.* XVIII (1955), 45–80.

COLLINS, A. E. P. 'Settlement in Ulster, 0–1100', *U.J.A.* XXXI (1968), 53–8.

DE PAOR, L. & M. *Early Christian Ireland* (1958), London.

DICKINSON, C. W. & WATERMAN, D. M. 'Excavation of a rath with motte at Castleskreen, Co. Down', *U.J.A.* XXII (1959), 67–82.

DICKINSON, C. W. & WATERMAN, D. M. 'Excavations at Castleskreen, Co. Down', *U.J.A.* XXIII (1960), 63–77.

DUIGNAN, M. 'Irish agriculture in early historic times', *J.R.S.A.I.* LXXIV (1944), 124–45.

EVANS, E. E. *Prehistoric and Early Christian Ireland* (1966), London.

HARBISON, P. 'How old is Gallarus Oratory?', *Med. Arch.* XIV (1970), 34–59.

HENCKEN, H. O'N. 'Ballinderry 1 crannog', *P.R.I.A.* XLIII (1936), 103–226.

HENCKEN, H. O'N. *Cahercommaun, a Stone Fort in Co. Clare, J.R.S.A.I.* special volume (1938).

HENCKEN, H. O'N. 'Ballinderry 2 crannog', *P.R.I.A.* XLVII (1942), 1–75.

HENCKEN, H. O'N. 'Lagore, a royal residence of the seventh to tenth centuries AD', *P.R.I.A.* LIII (1950), 1–247.

HENRY, F. 'A wooden hut at Inishkea North, Co. Mayo', *J.R.S.A.I.* LXXXII (1952), 163–78.

HENRY, F. *Irish Art in the Early Christian Period* (1965), London.

HENRY, F. *Irish Art During the Viking Invasions, 1020–1170 A.D.* (1967), London.

HENRY, F. 'Early monasteries, beehive huts and dry-stone houses in the neighbourhood of Caherciveen and Waterville, Co. Kerry', *P.R.I.A.* LVIII (1956–7), 45–166.

HENRY, F. *Irish High Crosses* (1964), Dublin.

HUGHES, K. *The Church in Early Irish Society* (1966).

JOPE, E. M. 'Iron Age brooches in Ireland: a summary', *U.J.A.* XXV (1962), 25–38.

LEASK, H. G. *Early Irish Churches and Monastic Buildings*, I: The Early Period and the Romanesque (1955), Dundalk.

LIONARD, P. 'Early Irish grave slabs', *P.R.I.A.* LXI (1961), 95–169.

MACALISTER, R. A. S. *The Memorial Slabs at Clonmacnois, King's County* (1909), Dublin.

MACALISTER, R. A. S. & PRAEGER, R. L. 'Report on excavations at Uisneach', *P.R.I.A.* XXXVIII (1928), 69–127.

MACALISTER, R. A. S. *Corpus Inscriptionum Insularum Celticarum*, 2 vols (1943 and 1949), Dublin.

O'KELLY, M. J. 'St Gobnet's House, Ballyvourney', *J.C.H.A.S.* LVII (1952), 18–40.

O'KELLY, M. J. 'Excavations and experiments in ancient Irish cooking places', *J.R.S.A.I.* LXXXIV (1954), 105–56.

O'KELLY, M. J. 'An island settlement at Beginish, Co. Kerry', *P.R.I.A.* LVII (1956), 159–94.

O'KELLY, M. J. 'The excavation of two earthen ringforts at Garryduff, Co. Cork', *P.R.I.A.* LXIII (1962), 17–124.

O'KELLY, M. J. 'Beal Boru, Co. Clare', *J. Cork H.A.S.* LXVII (1962), 1–27.

O'RIORDAN, S. P. 'The excavation of a large earthen ring-fort at Garranes, Co. Cork', *P.R.I.A.* XLVII (1942), 77–150.

O'RIORDAIN, S. P. & FOY, J. B. 'The excavation of Leacanabuaile fort, Co. Kerry', *J.C.H.A.S.* XLVI (1943), 85–98.

O'RIORDAIN, S. P. & HARTNETT, P. J. 'The excavation of Ballycatteen fort, Co. Cork', *P.R.I.A.* XLIX (1943), 1–43.

O'RIORDAIN, S. P. 'The genesis of the Celtic cross', in Pender, S. (ed.), *Feilscribhinn Torna* (1947), Cork, 108–14.

O'RIORDAIN, S. P. 'Roman material in Ireland', *P.R.I.A.* LI (1947), 35–82.

O'RIORDAIN, S. P. 'Lough Gur excavations: Carraig Aille and the "Spectacles"', *P.R.I.A.* LII (1949), 39–111.

O'RIORDAIN, S. P. 'Lough Gur excavations: the great stone circle at Grange Townland', *P.R.I.A.* LIV (1951–2), 37–74.

O'RIORDAIN, S. P. & MACDERMOTT, M. 'Excavation of a ringfort at Letterkeen', *P.R.I.A.* LIV (1952), 89–119.

PROUDFOOT, V. B. 'The economy of the Irish rath', *Med. Arch.* V (1961), 94–122.

PROUDFOOT, V. B. 'A rath at Boho, Co. Fermanagh', *U.J.A.* XVI (1953), 41–57.

PROUDFOOT, V. B. 'Excavations at Cathedral Hill, Downpatrick', *U.J.A.* XIX (1956), 57–72.

PROUDFOOT, V. B. 'Ancient Irish field systems', *Adv. of Science* XIV (1958), 369–71.

PROUDFOOT, V. B. 'Irish raths and cashels: some notes on origins, chronology and survivals', *U.J.A.* XXXIII (1970), 37–48.

RAFTERY, B. 'Freestone Hill, Co. Kilkenny: an Iron Age hillfort and Bronze Age cairn', *P.R.I.A.* LXVIII (1969), 1–108.

RAFTERY, B. 'Irish hillforts', in Thomas, A. C. (ed.), *The Iron Age in the Irish Sea Province* (1972), London, 37–58.

RAFTERY, J. 'The Turoe stone and the rath of Feerwore', *J.R.S.A.I.* LXXIV (1944), 23–52.

RAFTERY, J. 'Iron Age and Irish Sea: problems for research', in Thomas, C. (ed.), *Iron Age in the Irish Sea Province* (1972), 1–10.

RYNNE, E. 'The introduction of La Tène into Ireland', *Bericht. V. Internat. Kong. Var-und Frügesch., Hamburg* (1958), Berlin, 705–9.

THOMAS, A. C. *The Early Christian Archaeology of North Britain* (1971), London.

WAILES, B. 'Excavation at Dun Ailinne, Co. Clare', *J.R.S.A.I.* C (1970), 79–90.

WATERMAN, D. M. 'The excavation of a house and souterrain at White Fort, Drumaroad', *U.J.A.* XIX (1956), 73–86.

WATERMAN, D. M. 'Excavations at Lismahon, Co. Down', *Med. Arch.* III (1959), 139–76.

WATERMAN, D. M. & COLLINS, A. E. P. *An Archaeological Survey of Co. Down* (1966), Belfast.

WATERMAN, D. M. 'Excavations at Langford Lodge', *U.J.A.* XXVI (1963), 43–54.

WESTROPP, T. J. 'The ancient forts of Ireland', *P.R.I.A.* XXXI (1896–1901), 579–730.

The Norse in Scotland

ANDERSON, J. *Scotland in Pagan Times* (1883), Edinburgh.

ANDERSON, J. 'Notes on the contents of two Viking graves in Islay', *P.S.A.S.* XIV (1879–80), 51–62.

ANDERSON, J. 'Notice of bronze brooches, personal ornaments, from a ship burial in Oronsay . . . a ship burial of the Viking time at Kiloran Bay, Colonsay', *P.S.A.S.* XLI (1906–7), 437–50.

ARBMAN, H. *The Vikings* (1961), London.

BALFOUR, J. A. 'Notes on a Viking mound at Millhill, Lamlash, Arran', *P.S.A.S.* XLIV (1909–10), 221–4.

BARBOUR, J. 'Notice of a stone fort near Kirkandrews', *P.S.A.S.* XLI (1906–7), 68–80.

BRØGGER, A. *Ancient Emigrants* (1929), Oxford.

BRØGGER, A. *Den norske bosetnigen pa Shetland-Orknoyene* (1930), Oslo.

BRONSTED, O. *The Vikings* (1965), Harmondsworth.

BRYCE, T. H. 'Note on a balance and weights of the Viking period found in Gigha', *P.S.A.S.* XLVII (1912–13), 436–43.

CHILDE, V. G. 'Another late Viking house from Freswick', *P.S.A.S.* LXXVII (1942–3), 5–17.

CLOUSTON, J. S. *History of Orkney* (1932), Kirkwall.

CRUDEN, S. H. 'Excavations at Birsay, Orkney', in Small, A. (ed.), *Transactions of the Fourth Viking Congress* (1965), Aberdeen, 22–31.

CURLE, A. O. 'A Viking settlement at Freswick, Caithness', *P.S.A.S.* LXXIII (1938–9), 71–110.

CURLE, J. 'On recent Scandinavian finds from the Island of Oronsay, and from Reay, Caithness', *P.S.A.S.* XLVIII (1913–14), 292–315.

GRIEG, S. 'Scotland', being Part II of Shetelig, H. (ed.), *Viking Antiquities of Britain and Ireland* (1940–54).

HAMILTON, J. R. C. *Excavations at Jarlshof, Shetland* (1956), London.

HAMILTON, J. R. C. 'Jarlshof, a prehistoric and Viking settlement in Shetland', in Bruce-Mitford, R. (ed.), *Recent Archaeological Excavations in Britain* (1956), London, 197–222.

JACOBSEN, J. *The Place-names of Shetland* (1936), London.

MACDONALD, A. & LAING, L. R. 'Early ecclesiastical sites in Scotland: a field survey, Part I', *P.S.A.S.* C (1967–8), 123–34.

MACLEOD, D. J. & CURLE, J. 'An account of a find of ornaments of the Viking time from Valtos, Uig, Isle of Lewis', *P.S.A.S.* L (1915–16), 181–90.

MACPHERSON, N. 'Notes on antiquities from the Island of Eigg', *P.S.A.S.* XII (1878–9).

MARWICK, H. 'The place-names of North Ronaldsay', *P.O.A.S.* 1 (1922–3), 53–64.

MARWICK, H. 'Orkney farm name studies', *P.O.A.S.* IX (1930–1), 25–34.

MARWICK, H. *The Place-names of Rousay* (1947), Kirkwall.

MAXWELL, H. 'Notes on a hoard of personal ornaments, implements and Anglo-Saxon and Northumbrian coins from Talnotrie', *P.S.A.S.* XLVII (1913–14), 12–16.

NICHOLAISEN, W. 'Norse settlements in the Northern and Western Isles', *S.H.R.* XLVIII (1969), 6–17.

RADFORD, C. A. R. 'Excavations at Whithorn', *Trans. D. & G.N.H.A.S.* XXVII (1950), 85–136.

RADFORD, C. A. R. 'From prehistory to history', in Piggott, S. (ed.), *Prehistoric Peoples of Scotland* (1962), London, 125–54.

RADFORD, C. A. R. *The Early Christian and Norse Site at Birsay* (1959).

RADFORD, C. A. R. 'Hoddom', *Trans. D. & G.N.H.A.S.* XXXI (1954), 174–97.

RADFORD, C. A. R. 'The early Church in Strathclyde and Galloway', *Med. Arch.* XI (1967), 105–26.

SCOTT, J. G. 'A glass linen smoother of Viking type from Kirkcudbright', *P.S.A.S.* LXXXVIII (1954–6), 226.

SCOTT, J. G. 'An eleventh-century war axe in Dumfries Museum', *Trans. D. & G.N.H.A.S.* XLIII (1966), 117–20.

SMALL, A. 'Excavations at Underhoull, Shetland', *P.S.A.S.* XCVIII (1964–6), 225–48.

SMALL, A. 'The Viking Highlands – a geographical view', in Meldrum (ed.), *The Dark Ages in the Highlands* (1971), Inverness, 69–90.

STEVENSON, R. B. K. *Sylloge of the Anglo-Saxon Coins in the National Museum of Antiquities, Edinburgh* (1966).

TAYLOR, A. B. *Orkneyinga Saga* (1932), Edinburgh.

THOMPSON, J. D. A. *Inventory of British Coin Hoards, 600–1500* (1956).

THORSTEINNSON, A. 'The Viking burial place at Pierowall, Westray', in Niclasen, B. (ed.), *Transactions of the Fifth Viking Congress* (1965), Torshavn, 150–73.

TURVILLE-PETRE, G. *The Heroic Age of Scandinavia* (1951), London.

WAINWRIGHT, F. T. 'The Scandinavian settlement' in Wainwright, F. (ed.), *The Northern Isles* (1962), Edinburgh, 117–62.

The Vikings outside Scotland

BANKS, M. *The Problem of Cuerdale* (1967), Newcastle.

BERSU, G. 'A promontory fort on the shore of Ramsey Bay', *Ant. J.* XXIX (1949), 62–79.

BERSU, G. 'Three Viking graves in the Isle of Man', *J. Manx Mus.* VI (1957–65), 15–18.

BERSU, G. & WILSON, D. M. *Three Viking Graves in the Isle of Man* (London, Soc. Med. Arch., 1966).

BRUCE, R. & CUBBON, W. 'Cronk yn How', *Arch. Camb.* LXXXV (1930), 267–308.

COFFEY, G. & ARMSTRONG, E. C. 'Scandinavian objects found at Islandbridge and Kilmainham', *P.R.I.A.* XXVIII (1910), 107–48.

COWEN, J. D. 'Viking burials in Cumbria', *Trans. C. & W.A.A.S.* XLVIII (1948), 73–7.

COWEN, J. D. 'Viking burials in Cumbria: a supplement', *Trans. C. & W.A.A.S.* LXVII (1967), 31–4.

CUBBON, M. *The Art of the Manx Crosses* (1971), Douglas.

CUBBON, M. & MEGAW, B. R. S. 'The Western Isles and the growth of the Manx parliament', *J. Manx Mus.* V (1941–6), 57–62.

DAVIDSON, H. R. & MEGAW, B. R. S. 'Gaut the sculptor', *J. Manx Mus.* V (1941–6), 136–9.

DOLLEY, M. 'The mint of Chester', *J. Chester & N. Wales A. & A.H.S.* XLII (1955), 1–21.

DOLLEY, M. 'Viking Age coin hoards from Ireland and their relevance for Anglo-Saxon studies', in Dolley, M. (ed.), *Anglo-Saxon Coins* (1961), London, 241–65.

ELLIS, H. E. 'The story of Sigurd in Viking art', *J. Manx Mus.* V (1941–6), 87–90.

FANNING, T. 'Viking grave goods near Larne', *J.R.S.A.I.* C (1970), 71–8.

FLEURE, H. J. & DUNLOP, M. 'Glendarragh circle and alignments, The Braaid, I.O.M.', *Ant. J.* XXII (1942), 39–53.

FOSTER, I. 'Wales and North Britain', *Arch. Camb.* CXVIII (1969), 1–16.

FOX, A. 'Early Christian period I – settlement sites and other remains', in Nash-Williams, V. (ed.), *A Hundred Years of Welsh Archaeology* (1946), Cardiff, 105–22.

GELLING, P. S. 'Close ny Chollagh; an Iron Age fort at Scarlett, Isle of Man', *P.P.S.* XXIV (1958), 85–100.

GELLING, P. S. 'Recent excavations of Norse houses in the Isle of Man', *J. Manx Mus.* VI (1957–65), 54–6.

GELLING, P. S. 'The Braaid site', *J. Manx Mus.* VI (1957–65), 201–5.

GELLING, P. S. 'Medieval shielings in the Isle of Man', *Med. Arch.* VI–VII (1962–3), 156–72.

GELLING, P. S. 'A Norse homestead near Doarlish Cashen, Kirk Patrick, Isle of Man', *Med. Arch.* XIV (1970), 74–82.

HENRY, F. *Irish Art during the Viking Invasions 1070–1120* (1967), London.

KENDRICK, T. D. *A History of the Vikings* (1930), London.

KENDRICK, T. D. *Late Saxon and Viking Art* (1948), London.

KERMODE, P. C. M. *Manx Crosses* (1907).

KERMODE, P. C. M. 'An engraved stone pillar from the Isle of Man', *Ant. J.* IX (1929), 372–5.

KERMODE, P. C. M. 'Ship burial in the Isle of Man', *Ant. J.* X (1930), 126–33.

KERMODE, P. C. M. *List of Manx Antiquities* (1932), Douglas.

KINVIG, J. *A History of Man* (1944; 2nd ed. 1951), Liverpool.

KIRBY, D. P. 'Strathclyde and Cumbria, a survey of historical development to 1092', *Trans. C. & W.A.A.S.* LXII (1962), 77–94.

KLINDT-JENSEN, O. & WILSON, D. M. *Viking Art* (London, 1966).

LITTLE, G. *Dublin Before the Vikings* (1957).

LYON, C. S. S. 'The Northumbrian Viking coins in the Cuerdale hoard', in Dolley, M. (ed.), *Anglo-Saxon Coins* (1961), London, 96–121.

MEANEY, A. *Gazetteer of Early Anglo-Saxon Burial Sites* (1964), London.

MEGAW, B. R. S. 'Weapons of the Viking Age found in Man', *J. Manx Mus.* III (1935–7), 234–6.

MEGAW, B. R. S. 'The Douglas treasure trove', *J. Manx Mus.* IV (1938–40), 77–80.

MEGAW, B. R. S. 'An ancient cemetery at Balladoyne, St John's', *J. Manx Mus.* IV (1938–40), 11–14.

MEGAW, B. R. S. 'The monastery of St Maughold', *Proc. I.O.M.N.H.A.S.* V (1950), 169–80.

NASH-WILLIAMS, V. E. *Early Christian Monuments of Wales* (1950), Cardiff.

O'RIORDAIN, B. 'Excavations at High Street and Winetavern Street, Dublin', *Med. Arch.* XV (1971), 73–86.

O'SULLIVAN, W. *The Earliest Irish Coinage* (1961), Dublin.

RAFTERY, J. 'A Viking burial in County Galway', *J. Galway H.S.* XXIX (1960–1), 1–6.

SEABY, P. 'Some Cuerdale queries', *S.C.M.B.* June–September (1967).

SHETELIG, H. 'Manx crosses relating to Great Britain and Ireland', *Saga Book of the Viking Club,* IX (1925), 253–74.

SHETELIG, H. (ed.) *Viking Antiquities of Great Britain and Ireland,* 5 parts (1940–54), Oslo.

SHETELIG, H. 'The Norse style of ornamentation in the Viking settlements', *Acta Arch.* XIX (1948), 69–118.

TALBOT-RICE, D. *English Art 871–1100* (1952), Oxford.

TAYLOR, H. M. & TAYLOR, J. *Anglo-Saxon Architecture* (1965), Cambridge.

THOMPSON, J. D. A. *Inventory of British Coin Hoards, 600–1500* (1956), London.

VARLEY, W. J. 'Excavation of Castle Ditch, Eddisbury, 1935–8', *H.S.L.C.* CII (1950), 1–69.

WILSON, D. M. *A Catalogue of Anglo-Saxon Metalwork in the British Museum, 700–1100* (1964) London.

WILSON, D. M. *The Vikings and their Origins* (1970), London.

Section C

Technology and trade

HARBISON, P. 'The old Irish chariot', *Ant.* XLV (1971), 171–7.

HENRY, F. 'Emailleurs d'Occident', *Préhistoire* II, fas. 1 (1933), 65–146.

HENRY, F. 'Irish enamels of the Dark Ages and their relation to the cloisonné techniques', in Harden, D. (ed.), *Dark Age Britain* (1956), London, 71–90.

JOHNSTONE, P. 'The Bantry boat', *Ant.* XXXVIII (1964), 277–84.

LUCAS, A. T. 'Footwear in Ireland', *Co. Louth Arch. J.* XIII (1956), 367–82.

MOSS, R. J. 'A chemical examination of the crucibles in the collection of the Royal Irish Academy', *P.R.I.A.* XXXVII (1927), 175–93.

STEVENSON, R. B. K. 'Pictish chain, Roman silver and bauxite beads', *P.S.A.S.* LXXXVIII (1954–6), 228–30.

Subsistence equipment

DUIGNAN, M. 'Irish agriculture in early historic times', *J.R.S.A.I.* LXXIV (1944), 124–45.

GELLING, P. S. & STANFORD, S. C. 'Dark Age pottery or Iron Age ovens?', *Trans. Birmingham A.S.* LXXXII (1967), 77–91.

HARDEN, D. B. 'Glass vessels in Britain, AD 400–1000', in Harden, D. (ed.) *Dark Age Britain* (1956), London, 132–57.

PIGGOTT. S. 'An iron object from Dunadd', *P.S.A.S.* LXXXVI (1952–3), 194.

RADFORD, C. A. R. 'Imported pottery found at Tintagel, Cornwall', in Harden, D. (ed.) *Dark Age Britain* (1956), 59–70.

RIGOIR, J. 'Les sigillées paléochrétiennes grises et oranges', *Gallia*, XXVI (1968), 177–244.

THOMAS, A. C. 'Imported pottery in Dark Age western Britain', *Med. Arch.* III (1959), 89–111.

THOMAS, A. C. *People and Pottery in Dark Age Cornwall* (1960), Truro.

THOMAS, A. C. & PEACOCK, D. 'Class E imported pottery: a suggested origin', *Cornish Arch.* VI (1967), 35–46.

THOMAS, A. C. 'Grass-marked pottery in Cornwall', in Coles, J. & Simpson, D. (eds), *Studies in Ancient Europe* (1968), Leicester, 311–32.

Personal adornment

ARMSTRONG, E. C. R. 'Irish bronze pins of the Christian period', *Arch.* LXXII (1921–2), 71–86.

FANNING, T. 'The ringed pins in Limerick Museum', *North Munster Antiquarian Journal* XII (1969), 6–11.

FOWLER, E. 'The origin and development of the penannular brooch in Europe', *P.P.S.* XXVI (1960), 149–77.

FOWLER, E. 'Celtic metalwork of the fifth and sixth centuries AD', *Arch. J.* CXX (1963), 98–160.

JOPE, E. M. 'The ibex-headed pin from Dunfanaghy Sandhills', *U.J.A.* 13 (1950), 52–4.

KILBRIDE-JONES, H. 'Scots zoomorphic penannular brooches', *P.S.A.S.* LXX (1935–6), 124–38.

KILBRIDE-JONES, H. 'The evolution of penannular brooches with zoomorphic terminals in Great Britain and Ireland', *P.R.I.A.* XLIII C (1935–7), 379–455.

LASKO, P. 'The comb', in Battiscombe, C. F. (ed.), *The Relics of St Cuthbert* (1956), Durham, 336–55.

RAFTERY, J. 'A bronze zoomorphic brooch from Toomullin, Co. Clare', *J.R.S.A.I.* LXXI (1941), 56–60.

RYNNE, E. 'Excavations at Ardcloon, Co. Mayo', *J.R.S.A.I.* LXXVI (1956), 203–14.

SAVORY, H. N. 'Some sub-Romano-British brooches from south Wales', in Harden, D. B. (ed.), *Dark Age Britain,* Essays to E. T. Leeds (1956), London, 40–53.

SMITH, R. A. 'The evolution of the handpin in Great Britain and Ireland', in *Opuscula Archaeologica Oscari Montelio Septuagenaria Dicata* (1913), 36–289.

SMITH, R. A. 'Irish serpentine lachets', *Proc. Soc. Ant. Lond.* XXX (1917–18), 120–31.

SMITH, R. A. 'Irish brooches through five centuries', *Arch.* LXV (1913–14), 223–50.

STEVENSON, R. B. K. 'Native bangles and Roman glass', *P.S.A.S.* LXXXVIII (1954–6), 208–21.

STEVENSON, R. B. K. 'Pins and the chronology of brochs', *P.P.S.* XXI (1955), 282–94.

STEVENSON, R. B. K. 'The brooch from Westness, Orkney', in Niclasen, B. (ed.), *The Fifth Viking Congress* (1965), Torshavn 25–31.

WILSON, D. M. 'A group of penannular brooches of the Viking period', in Eldjarn, K. (ed.), *The Third Viking Congress* (1958), 95–100.

Art and craftsmanship

ANDERSON, J. *Scotland in Early Christian Times* (1881), Edinburgh.

BOE, J. 'An ornamental bronze object found in a Norwegian grave', *Bergens Mus. Årbok* (1924–5), 1–34.

CLAPHAM, A. 'Notes on Hiberno-Saxon art', *Ant.* VII (1934), 43–57.

DUIGNAN, M. 'The Moylough and other Irish belt shrines', *J. Galway A. & H.S.* XXIV (1951), 83–94.

FOWLER, E. 'Celtic metalwork of the fifth and sixth centuries AD', *Arch. J.* CXX (1963), 98–160.

FOWLER, E. 'Hanging bowls', in Coles, J. & Simpson, D., *Studies in Ancient Europe* (1968), Leicester, 287–310.

GOGAN, L. S. *The Ardagh Chalice* (1932), Dublin.

HASELOFF, G. 'Fragments of a hanging bowl from Bekesbourne, Kent, and some ornamental problems', *Med. Arch.*, II (1958), 72–103.

HAWKES, C. F. C. 'Bronze workers, cauldrons and bucket animals in Iron Age and Roman Britain', in Grimes, W. (ed.), *Aspects of Archaeology in Britain and Beyond* (1951), London, 172–99.

HENRY, F. 'Hanging bowls', *J.R.S.A.I.* LXVI (1936), 209–310.

HENRY, F. 'Deux objets de bronze irlandais au Musée des Antiquités nationales', *Préhistoire*, VII (1938), 65.

HENRY, F. *Irish Art during the Early Christian Period, to A.D. 800* (1965), London.

HENRY, F. *Irish Art during the Viking Invasions, 800–1020* (1967), London.

HENRY, F. *Irish Art during the Romanesque Period, 1020–1170* (1970), London.

HOLMQVIST, W. 'An Irish crozier found near Stockholm', *Ant. J.* XXXV (1955), 46–51.

HUNT, J. 'On two D-shaped objects in the Saint-Germain Museum', *P.R.I.A.* LVII (1956), 153–7.

KENDRICK, T. D. 'British hanging bowls', *Ant.* VI (1932), 161–84.

KENDRICK, T. D. & SENIOR, E. 'St Manchan's shrine', *Arch.* LXXXVI (1937), 105–18.

LIESTOL, A. 'The hanging bowl, a liturgical and domestic vessel', *Act. Arch.* XXIV (1953), 163–70.

MAHR, A. & RAFTERY, J. *Christian Art in Ancient Ireland*, Dublin, 2 vols (I, ed. Mahr, 1932; II, ed. Raftery, 1941).

O'KELLY, M. J. 'The Cork Horns, the Petrie Crown and the Bann Disc', *J. Cork H. & A.S.* LXVI (1961), 1–12.

O'KELLY, M. J. 'The belt shrine from Moylough, Sligo', *J.R.S.A.I.* XCV (1965), 149–88.

RADFORD, C. A. R. 'Two reliquaries connected with S.W. Scotland', *Trans. D. & G.N.H.A.S.* XXXII (1955), 115–23.

RAFTERY, J. 'The Cuillard and other unpublished hanging bowls', *J.R.S.A.I.* XCVI (1966), 29–38.

STOKES, M. 'Observations on two ancient Irish works of art . . . the Breac Moedog . . . and the Soicel Molaise', *Arch.* XLIII (1871), 131–50.

STOKES, M. *Early Christian Art in Ireland* (1928), London.

WATERER, J. W. 'Irish book satchels or budgets', *Med. Arch.* XII (1968), 70–82.

WILSON, D. M. *Reflections on the St Ninian's Isle Treasure* (Jarrow Lecture) (1969).

The Church

AITKEN, W. G. 'Excavation of a chapel at St Ninian's Point, Bute', *Trans. Bute N.H.S.* XIV (1955), 62–76.

BRUCE, J. R. & CUBBON, W. 'Cronk yn How, an Early Christian and Viking site', *Arch. Camb.* LXXXV (1930), 267–99.

BRYCE, T. H. & KNIGHT, G. A. F. 'Report on a survey of the antiquities on Eileach an Naoimh', *Trans. Glasgow Arch. Soc.* N.S. 8, pt. 2 (1930), 62–102.

BU'LOCK, J. D. 'Early Christian memorial formulae', *Arch. Camb.* CV (1956), 133–41.

BURN, A. R. 'Holy men on islands in pre-Christian Britain', *Glasgow A.J.I.* (1969), 2–6.

CHADWICK, N. K. *The Age of the Saints in the Early Celtic Church* (1961), Oxford.

CRAWFORD, G. S. 'Iona', *Ant.* VII (1934), 202–4.

DE PAOR, L. 'A survey of Sceilg Mhichil', *J.R.S.A.I.* LXXXV (1955), 174–87.

HENRY, F. 'Early monasteries, beehive huts, and dry-stone houses in the neighbourhood of Caherciveen and Waterville (Kerry)', *P.R.I.A.* LVII (1957), 45–166.

HENSHALL, A. S. 'The long cist cemetery at Parkburn, Midlothian', *P.S.A.S.* LXXXIX (1955–6), 252–83.

KENDRICK, T. D. 'Gallen Priory excavations, 1934–5', *J.R.S.A.I.* LXIX (1939), 1–20.

LAWLOR, H. C. *The Monastery of St Mochaoi at Nendrum* (1925), Belfast.

LEASK, H. G. *Irish Churches and Monastic Buildings*, I The Early Phases and the Romanesque (1955), Dundalk.

MACALISTER, R. A. S. 'The history and antiquities of Inis Cealtra', *P.R.I.A.* XXXIII (1916), 93–174.

MACALISTER, R. A. S. *Monasterboice, Co. Louth* (1946), Dundalk.

NISBET, H. C. & GAILEY, R. A. 'A survey of the antiquities of North Rona', *Arch. J.* CXVII (1962), 88–115.

O'KELLY, M. 'Church Island, near Valencia, Co. Kerry', *P.R.I.A.* LIX (1958), 57–136.

O'KELLY, M. 'Knockea, Co. Limerick', in Rynne, E. (ed.), *North Munster Studies* (1967), Limerick, 72–101.

O'NEIL, H. E. 'Excavation of a Celtic hermitage on St Helen's, Isles of Scilly', *Arch. J.* CXXI (1964), 40–69.

RADFORD, C. A. R. 'Tintagel; the castle and Celtic monastery – interim report', *Ant. J.* XV (1935), 401–19.

RADFORD, C. A. R. 'Excavations at Whithorn, 1949', *Trans. D. & G.N.H.A.S.* XXVII (1950), 85–126.

RADFORD, C. A. R. 'St Ninian's cave', *Trans. D. & G.N.H.A.S.* XXVIII (1951), 96–8.

RADFORD, C. A. R. 'Two Scottish shrines, Jedburgh and St Andrews', *Arch. J.* CXII (1955), 43–60.

RADFORD, C. A. R. 'Excavations at Whithorn (final report)', *Trans. D. & G.N.H.A.S.* XXXIV (1957), 131–94.

RADFORD, C. A. R. 'The Celtic monastery in Britain', *Arch. Camb.* CXI (1962), 1–24.

RADFORD, C. A. R. 'The early Church in Strathclyde and Galloway', *Med. Arch.* XI (1967), 105–26.

RAHTZ, P. A. 'Sub-Roman cemeteries in Somerset', in Barley, M. & Hanson, R. *Christianity in Britain, 300–700* (1968), Leicester, 193–6.

THOMAS, A. C. *Christian Antiquities of Camborne* (1967), St Austell.

THOMAS, A. C. 'An Early Christian cemetery and chapel on Ardwall Isle, Kirkcudbright', *Med. Arch.* XI (1967), 127–88.

THOMAS, A. C. 'The evidence from north Britain', in Barley, M. & Hanson, R. P. C. *Christianity in Britain, 300–700* (1968), 93–122.

THOMAS, A. C. 'Lundy, 1969', *Current Arch.* II (1969), 138–42.

THOMAS, A. C. *The Early Christian Archaeology of North Britain* (1971), Oxford.

WAKEMAN, W. F. *A Survey of the Antiquarian Remains on the Island of Inismurray (Inis Muireadhaigh)* (1893), Dublin.

Addenda

Since this was written a number of important studies relating to the period have appeared in print. The most important of these is a collection of papers on early Celtic monasteries which appears as *Scottish Archaeological Forum*, V, Edinburgh (1973). The following should also be noted:

HUGHES, K. *Early Christian Ireland; an Introduction to the Sources*, London (1972).

GRAHAM-CAMPBELL, J. 'Two groups of ninth century Irish brooches', *J.R.S.A.I.* CII (1972), 113–28.

MORRIS, J. R. *The Age of Arthur*, London (1973).

LAING, L. R. 'The Mote of Mark', *Current Arch.* IV (1973), 121–5.

A few papers now in press ought to have appeared in print by the time this book is published, and which expand on subjects dealt with briefly here. Of these three are by the author; 'People and pins in Dark Age Scotland' and 'The Angles in Scotland and the Mote of Mark' are due to appear in *Trans. D. & G.N.H.A.S.L*, and 'The Mote of Mark and the origins of Celtic interlace' is due to appear in *Antiquity*. A study of the Hunterston Brooch by R. B. K. Stevenson ought to have appeared in *Med. Arch.*

The iron age background is now admirably discussed in Cunliffe, B. *Iron Age Communities in Britain*, London (1974).

Notes

Chapter 1

1 A. H. M. Jones, *The Later Roman Empire* (1964).
2 H. O'N. Hencken, 'Indo-European languages and archaeology', *Amer. Anthrop. Assoc. Memoir*, 84 (1955).
3 Cultural continuity in Bronze Age Europe argued in M. Gimbutas, *Bronze Age Cultures in Central and Eastern Europe* (1965).
4 T. F. O'Rahilly, *Early Irish History and Mythology* (1946), 205–8.
5 K. H. Jackson, *Language and History in Early Britain* (1933), 5.
6 Convenient summary in S. Piggott, *Ancient Europe* (1965), 145–60.
7 Convenient accounts in T. G. E. Powell, *The Celts* (1958) and J. Filip, *Celtic Civilization and its Heritage* (1961).
8 General reviews in C. F. C. Hawkes, 'The ABC of the British Iron Age' in S. S. Frere (ed.) *Problems of the Iron Age in Southern Britain* (1961), 1–16; F. R. Hodson, 'Cultural grouping within the British pre-Roman Iron Age', *P.P.S.* XXX (1964), 99–110.
9 Current position summarized in C. F. C. Hawkes, 'New thoughts on the Belgae', *Ant.* XLII (1968), 6–16.
10 Ammianus Marcellinus xxi, 1, 1.
11 M. & L. de Paor, *Early Christian Ireland* (1958), 25.
12 Discussion of Niall in O'Rahilly, *Early Irish History* . . . (1946), 209–34.
13 S. P. O'Riordain, 'Roman material in Ireland', *P.R.I.A.* LI (1947), 35–82.
14 Convenient summary in A. C. Thomas, *Britain and Ireland in Early Christian Times* (1971), 63–7.
15 Ibid., 67–9.
16 C. Fox, *The Personality of Britain* (1932).
17 L. Alcock, 'The Irish Sea Zone in the pre-Roman Iron Age', in A. C. Thomas (ed.) *The Iron Age in the Irish Sea Province* (1972), 106.
18 H. J. Mackinder, *Britain and the British Seas* (1902), discussed in E. G. Bowen, 'Britain and the British seas', in D. Moore (ed.) *The Irish Sea Province in Archaeology and History* (1970), 13–28.
19 V. B. Proudfoot, 'The economy of the Irish rath', *Med. Arch.* V (1961), 94–122.
20 Ibid., 119.
21 M. Duignan, 'Irish agriculture in early historic times', *J.R.S.A.I.* LXXIV (1944), 124–45.
22 L. Alcock, *Dinas Powys* (1963), 40–2; L. Alcock, 'Wales in the fifth to seventh centuries AD' in I. Foster & G. Daniel, *Prehistoric and Early Wales* (1965), 208.
23 Social structure summarized in M. Dillon, *Early Irish Society* (1954).
24 Useful discussion in L. Alcock, *Arthur's Britain* (1971), 310–13; see also historical discussions *passim* in *Angles and Britons* (O'Donnell Lectures, 1963).
25 J. N. L. Myres, *Anglo-Saxon Pottery and the Settlement of England* (1969), 136.
26 N. K. Chadwick, *The Age of the Saints in the Early Celtic Church* (1961).
27 Discussions of Celtic literature in N. K. Chadwick, *The Celts* (1970), 255–91; N. K. Chadwick, *Celtic Britain* (1963), 99–116.
28 Convenient discussion in L. Alcock, *Arthur's Britain* (1971), 1–20.

Chapter 2

1 E. MacKie, 'The Scottish Iron Age', *S.H.R.* XLIX (1970), 1–32.
2 C. M. Piggott, 'The excavations at Hownam Rings, Roxburghshire', *P.S.A.S.* LXXXII (1947–8), 193–225.
3 S. Piggott, 'A scheme for the Scottish Iron Age', in A. L. F. Rivet (ed.), *The Iron Age in North Britain* (1966), 1–16.
4 R. B. K. Stevenson, 'Metalwork and some other objects in Scotland and their cultural affinities', in Rivet (ed.), *The Iron Age in North Britain* (1966), 17–44.
5 I. A. Richmond, 'Ancient geographical sources for Britain north of the Cheviot', in I. Richmond (ed.), *Roman and Native in North Britain* (1958), 131–9.
6 R. W. Feachem, 'The fortifications of Traprain Law', *P.S.A.S.* LXXXIX (1955–6), 284–9.
7 R. W. Feachem, 'The hill-forts of northern Britain', in Rivet (ed.), *The Iron Age in North Britain* (1966), 79.
8 S. S. Frere, *Britannia* (1967), 110–11.
9 Ibid., 122–3.
10 C. Daniels, 'Problems of the Roman northern frontier', *S.A.F.* 2 (1970), 97–8.
11 Ibid., 99.
12 R. E. Birley, 'Excavation of a Roman fortress at Carpow, Perthshire', *P.S.A.S.* XCVI (1962–3), 184–207.
13 S. Piggott, 'Native economies and the Roman occupation of north Britain', in I. Richmond (ed.), *Roman and Native in North Britain* (1958), 25.
14 G. Jobey, 'Homesteads and settlements of the frontier area', in A. C. Thomas (ed.), *Rural Settlement in Roman Britain* (1966), 13.
15 A. Robertson, 'Roman coin finds in Scotland', *P.S.A.S.* XLIV (1960), 137–69; J. Curle, 'Objects of Roman and provincial Roman origin found on sites in Scotland', *P.S.A.S.* LXVI (1931–2), 277–397.
16 I. A. Richmond, 'Roman and native in the fourth century and after', in I. Richmond (ed.), *Roman and Native in North Britain* (1958), 114.
17 J. P. C. Kent, 'Coins and the evacuation of Hadrian's Wall', *T.C. & W.A.A.S.* LI (1952), 4–16.
18 Richmond, 1958, 130.
19 E. Burley, 'A catalogue and survey of the metalwork from Traprain Law', *P.S.A.S.* LXXXIX (1955–6), 118–226.
20 A. C. Thomas 'The evidence from north Britain' in M. Barley & R. P. C. Hanson, *Christianity in Britain, 300–700* (1968), 105.
21 Background in P. Hunter-Blair, 'The Bernicians and their northern frontier', in N. Chadwick (ed.), *Studies in Early British History* (1959), 137–72 – list of burials 149. See also P. Hunter-Blair, 'The origins of Northumbria', *Arch. Ael.* XXV (1947), 1–51. Burials listed in A. Meaney, *A Gazetteer of Anglo-Saxon Burial Sites* (1964), 198–9 (Northumberland), 83–4 (Durham).
22 G. Baldwin Brown, 'Notes on a necklace of glass beads found in a cist in Dalmeny Park, South Queensferry', *P.S.A.S.* XLIX (1914–15), 332–8.
23 Unpublished, in N.M.A.S.
24 J. G. Callender, 'A collection of prehistoric relics . . . and other objects in the National Museum', *P.S.A.S.* LXVII (1932–3), 33–4.
25 D. M. Wilson, 'The Trewhiddle hoard', *Arch.* XCVIII (1961), 86–7.
26 Unpublished, in N.M.A.S.
27 Note in *Med. Arch.* X (1966), 176–7.
28 G. Baldwin Brown, *The Arts in Early England* V (1921), *passim*; L. Stone, *Sculpture in Britain: The Middle Ages* (1955), 16–17.
29 A. E. Truckell, 'An excavation at Blacketlees, Annan', *Trans. D. & G.N.H.A.S.* XXXV (1958), 138–9.
30 D. Simpson & J. Scott-Elliot, 'An excavation at Camp Hill, Troughouton', *Trans. D. & G.N.H.A.S.* XLI (1964), 125–44.
31 D. P. Kirkby, 'Strathclyde and Cumbria: a survey of historical development to 1092', *Trans. C. & W.A.A.S.* LXII (1962), 77.
32 Ibid., 79–80.
33 Ibid., 82–4.
34 J. Williams, 'Tynron Doon, Dumfriesshire: a history of the site with notes on the finds, 1924–67', *Trans. D. & G.N.H.A.S.* XLVIII (1971), 106–20.
35 L. de Paor, 'Some vine scrolls and other patterns in embossed metal from Dumfriesshire', *P.S.A.S.* XCIV (1960–1), 184–95.
36 1973 excavations as yet unpublished. The 1913 excavations in A. O. Curle, 'Report on the excavation of a vitrified fort at Rockcliffe', *P.S.A.S.* XLVIII (1913–14), 125–68.
37 R. Munro, *Ancient Scottish Lake Dwellings* (1881), 202.
38 Ibid., 190–239.
39 I. MacIvor, *Dumbarton Castle* (1958).

40 W. F. Cormack, 'Northumbrian coins from Luce Sands', *Trans. D. & G.N.H.A.S.* XLII (1965), 149–50.
41 J. G. Callendar, 'A collection of prehistoric relics from Stevenson Sands, Ayrshire', *P.S.A.S.* LXVII (1932–3), 26–32.
42 H. Maxwell, 'Notes on a hoard of personal ornaments from Talnotrie, Kirkcudbright', *P.S.A.S.* XLVII (1912–13), 12–16.
43 Wilson, 'The Trewhiddle hoard' (1961), 121.
44 Unpublished, in Dumfries Burgh Museum.
45 R. Cramp, 'The Anglian sculptured crosses of Dumfriesshire', *Trans. D. & G.N.H.A.S.* XXXVIII (1961), 9–20.
46 C. A. R. Radford, 'Hoddom', *Trans. D. & G.N.H.A.S.* XXXI (1954), 174–97.
47 W. F. Nicholaisen, 'Scottish placenames; 24, *slew-* and *Sliabh*', *Scottish Studies* IX (1965), 91–106.
48 This, and another possibly early Irish element, *kil-*, discussed with refs in A. C. Thomas, 'An Early Christian chapel and cemetery on Ardwall Usle, Kirkcudbright', *Med. Arch.* XI (1967), 179–80.
49 E. Rynne, 'A bronze ring-brooch from Luce Sands, Wigtownshire', *Trans. D. & G.N.H.A.S.* XLII (1965), 99–113.
50 C. Thomas, 'Ardwall Isle: the excavation of an Early Christian site of Irish type, 1964–5', *Trans. D. & G.N.H.A.S.* XLIII (1966), 112.
51 Thomas, 'The evidence from north Britain' (1968), 111–16.
52 C. A. R. Radford & G. Donaldson, *Whithorn & Kirkmadrine* (1957), 38–9.
53 Thomas, 'The evidence from north Britain' (1968), 103.
54 Ibid., 105.
55 A. S. Henshall, 'The long cist cemetery at Parkburn. Midlothian', *P.S.A.S.* LXXXIX (1955–6), 252–83.
56 Thomas, 'The evidence from north Britain' (1968), 113.
57 The Anglian pottery is unpublished in N.M.A.S. The strap end listed by Wilson, 'The Trewhiddle hoard' (1961), 121.
58 Note in *Med. Arch.* IX (1965), 177–8.
59 C. A. R. Radford, 'Two reliquaries connected with S. W. Scotland', *Trans. D. & G.N.H.A.S.* XXXII (1955), 115–23.
60 Not fully published – description from personal examination.
61 Discusses briefly with reference in A. E. Truckell, 'Dumfries and Galloway in the Dark Ages: some problems', *Trans. D. & G.N.H.A.S.* XL (1963), 91.

Chapter 3

1 I. Henderson, *The Picts* (1967), 161–2.
2 E. MacKie, 'The Scottish Iron Age', *S.H.R.* XLIX (1970), 17–19; E. MacKie, 'Radiocarbon dates and the Scottish Iron Age', *Ant.* XLIII (1969), 15–26.
3 E. MacKie, 'Brochs and the Hebridean Iron Age', *Ant.* XXXIX (1965), 266–78; E. MacKie, 'The origin and development of the broch and wheelhouse building cultures of the Scottish Iron Age', *P.P.S.* XXXI (1965), 124–8, represent one school of thought. Another represented by J. R. C. Hamilton, *Clickhimin* (1968), 101–9.
4 Mackie, 'Brochs and the Hebridean Iron Age' (1965), 266–78.
5 MacKie, 'Origin and development . . .' (1965), 126–7; E. MacKie, 'English migrants and Scottish brochs', *Glasgow A.J.* 2 (1971), 39–71.
6 I. A. Richmond, 'Ancient geographical sources for Britain north of the Cheviot', in I. Richmond (ed.), *Roman and Native in North Britain* (1958), 131–49.
7 M. Simpson, 'Massive armlets in the north British Iron Age', in J. Coles & D. Simpson (eds), *Studies in Ancient Europe* (1968), 233–254; R. B. K. Stevenson, 'Metalwork and other objects and their cultural affinities', in A. L. F. Rivet (ed.), *The Iron Age in North Britain* (1966), 31–2.
8 M. MacGregor, 'The early Iron Age metalwork hoard from Stanwick, N.R. Yorks', *P.P.S.* XXVIII (1962), 17–57.
9 Main sources for this section are M. O. Anderson, 'The lists of the kings', *S.H.R.* XXVIII (1949), 108–18 and XXXIX (1950), 13–22; W. F. Skene (ed.), *Chronicles of the Picts, Chronicles of the Scots and other Early Memorials of Scottish History* (1867); F. T. Wainwright, 'The Picts and the problem', in F. Wainwright (ed.), *Problem of the Picts* (1955), 1–53; I. Henderson, *The Picts* (1967), 42–66.
10 K. H. Jackson, 'The Pictish language', in F. T. Wainwright (ed.), *Problem of the Picts* (1955), 129–66.
11 C. A. Gordon, 'Carving technique on the symbol stones of north-east Scotland', *P.S.A.S.* LXXXVIII (1954–6), 40–6.
12 K. H. Jackson, 'The St Ninian's Isle inscription', *Ant.* XXXIV (1960), 38–42.
13 Originally defined by J. Romilly Allen & J. Anderson, *The Early Christian Monuments of Scotland* (1903).

14 R. B. K. Stevenson, 'Sculpture in Scotland in the sixth to ninth centuries AD', *Kolloquium Uber Spatantike Und Fruhmittelalteriche Skulptur* (1970), 65–74.
15 Jackson, 'The Pictish language' (1955), 153.
16 Most recent discussion of date: A. C. Thomas, 'Animal art of the Scottish Iron Age', *Arch. J.* CXVIII (1961), 44–5; *contra* Stevenson (1970), and Stevenson, 'Pictish chain, Roman silver and bauxite beads', *P.S.A.S.* LXXXVIII (1954–6), 228.
17 A. C. Thomas, 'The interpretation of the Pictish symbols', *Arch. J.* CXX (1963), 65.
18 Ibid., 93.
19 Ibid., 88–9.
20 I. Henderson, 'The meaning of the Pictish symbol stones', in P. Meldrum (ed.), *The Dark Ages in the Highlands* (1971), 53–68.
21 I. Henderson, 'The origin centre of the Pictish symbol stones', *P.S.A.S.* XCI (1957–8), 44–60.
22 R. B. K. Stevenson, 'Pictish art', in F. Wainwright (ed.), *Problem of the Picts* (1955), 102.
23 A. J. H. Edwards, 'A massive double-linked silver chain', *P.S.A.S.* LXXIII (1938–9), 326–7, gives list.
24 A. C. Thomas, 'Excavations at Trusty's Hill, Anwoth, 1960', *Trans. D. & G.N.H.A.S.* XXXVIII (1961), 58–70, discusses context.
25 R. B. K. Stevenson, 'The Gaulcross hoard of Pictish silver', *P.S.A.S.* XCVII (1963–4), 206–11.
26 Main discussion in Stevenson, 'Pictish art' (1955); Stevenson, 'Sculpture in Scotland . . .' (1970); see also C. L. Curle, 'The chronology of the Early Christian monuments of Scotland', *P.S.A.S.* LXXIV (1939–40), 60–116; I. Henderson, *The Picts* (1967), 104–60; S. H. Cruden, *The Early Christian and Pictish Monuments of Scotland* (1964); R. B. K. Stevenson, 'The Inchyra stone and other unpublished Early Christian monuments', *P.S.A.S.* XCII (1958–9), 33–55.
27 Cruden, *Early Christian and Pictish Monuments* (1964).
28 Stevenson, 'Pictish art', 151–6.
29 Ibid., loc. cit.
30 Stevenson, 'Pictish art' and Stevenson 'Sculpture in Scotland . . .' (1970), 74.
31 Henderson, *The Picts* (1967), 134–57.
32 Ibid., 144.
33 Ibid., 149–50.
34 H. E. Kilbride-Jones, 'A bronze hanging bowl from Castle Tioram', *P.S.A.S.* LXXI (1936–7), Figs 2, 3.
35 R. B. K. Stevenson, 'Note on a mould from Craig Phadrig', in A. Small (ed.), *Craig Phadrig* (1972), 49–51.
36 E. Fowler, 'Celtic metalwork of the fifth and sixth centuries', *Arch. J.* CXX (1963), 110.
37 Kilbride-Jones, 'A bronze hanging bowl . . .' (1936–7).
38 Unpublished, now with D.o.E.
39 J. Anderson, *Scotland in Early Christian Times* (1880), 241.
40 Discussed in D. M. Wilson, *Reflection on the St Ninian's Isle Treasure* (Jarrow Lecture, 1969), 8–9; E. Bakka, 'Some English decorated metal objects found in Norwegian graves', *Årbok for Universitet i Bergen, humanistik serie I* (1963).
41 S. Grieg, 'Scotland', in H. Shetelig (ed.), *Viking Antiquities of G.B. and Ireland* (1940), II, 200–1.
42 Unpublished, information from Mrs C. Curle.
43 Grieg, 'Scotland', 201.
44 Literature extensive. Full report in press, meanwhile see D. M. Wilson, *Reflections . . .* (1969); R. L. S. Bruce-Mitford, 'The St Ninian's Isle hoard', *Ant.* XXXIII (1959), 241–68; A. C. O'Dell, *The St Ninian's Isle Treasure* (1960).
45 D. MacRoberts, 'The ecclesiastical significance of the St Ninian's Isle treasure', *P.S.A.S.* XCIV (1960–1), 301–3.
46 R. B. K. Stevenson, 'Celtic carved box from Scotland', *P.S.A.S.* LXXXVI (1951–2), 187–90; W. Kirkness, 'A further note on the Celtic carved box from Orkney', *P.S.A.S.* LXXXVII (1952–3), 195.
47 R. W. Feachem, 'Fortifications', in F. Wainwright (ed.), *Problem of the Picts* (1955), 66–86; R. B. K. Stevenson, 'The nuclear fort of Dalmahoy and other Dark Age capitals', *P.S.A.S.* LXXXIII (1948–9), 186–97.
48 F. T. Wainwright, *Souterrains of Southern Pictland* (1963).
49 W. D. Simpson, 'The early Romanesque tower at Restenneth Priory, Angus', *Ant. J.* XLIII (1963), 269–83.
50 H. M. Taylor & J. Taylor, *Anglo-Saxon Architecture*, II (1965), Appendix A, 710–13.
51 Quoted by C. A. R. Radford, 'From prehistory to history', in S. Piggott (ed.), *Prehistoric Peoples of Scotland* (1962), 136.
52 W. F. Skene, *Chronicle of the Picts* (1867), 130.
53 N. Chadwick, *Celtic Britain* (1964), 59.
54 Skene, *Chronicle* . . . (1867), 308.

55 K. H. Jackson, 'The ogham inscription at Dunadd', *Ant.* XXXIX (1965), 300–2.
56 W. F. Nicholaisen, 'Scottish placenames; 24, *slew* and *sliabh*', *Scottish Studies* IX (1965), 91–106.
57 *Med. Arch.* V (1961), 310.
58 Useful general survey in O. G. S. Crawford, 'Iona', *Ant.* VII (1933), 453–67.
59 Best survey in C. A. R. Radford, 'The early Church in Strathclyde and Galloway', *Med. Arch.* XI (1967), 114–16.
60 *Med. Arch.* I (1957), 150.
61 *Med. Arch.* III (1959), 300.
62 A. C. Thomas, *Britain and Ireland in Early Christian Times* (1971), Fig. 37.
63 R. B. K. Stevenson, 'The chronology and relationship of some Irish and Scottish crosses', *J.R.S.A.I.* LXXXVI (1956), 84–96.
64 J. R. C. Hamilton, *Jarlshof* (1956), 58.
65 MacKie, 'Origin and development . . .' (1965), 129.
66 Ibid., 138.
67 *Med. Arch.* XV (1971), 137.
68 F. T. Wainwright, 'Picts and Scots', in F. Wainwright (ed.), *The Northern Isles* (1962), 93.
69 I. A. Crawford, *Excavations at Coileagean an Udail (The Udal) N. Uist, 9th Report* (1972), 5–6.
70 A. Young, 'The sequence of Hebridean pottery', in A. L. F. Rivet (ed.), *The Iron Age in North Britain* (1966), 54.
71 A. C. Thomas, 'The evidence from north Britain', in M. Barley & R. P. C. Hanson, *Christianity in Britain, 300–700* (1968), 105.
72 Ibid., 106.
73 Wainwright, 'Picts and Scots' (1962), 92.
74 Henderson, *The Picts* (1967), 82.
75 A. C. Thomas, *The Early Christian Archaeology of North Britain* (1971), 41.
76 Ibid., *passim.*

Chapter 4

1 S. C. Stanford, 'Invention, adoption and imposition – the evidence of the hill-forts', in M. Jesson & D. Hill (eds), *The Iron Age and its Hillforts* (1971), 44.
2 H. N. Savory, *Early Iron Age Art in Wales* (1968); H. N. Savory, 'The Tal y Llyn hoard', *Ant.* XXXVIII (1964), 18–31.
3 A. H. A. Hogg, 'Hillforts in the coastal areas of Wales', in A. C. Thomas (ed.), *The Iron Age in the Irish Sea Province* (1972), 11–24; H. N. Savory, 'Later prehistoric migrations across the Irish Sea', in D. Moore (ed.), *The Irish Sea Province in Archaeology and History* (1970), 48.
4 P. Harbison, 'Wooden and stone *chevaux-de-frise* in central and western Europe', *P.P.S.* XXXVII (1971), 201–3.
5 The literature is extensive. Basic material to be found in M. Jarrett (ed.), revision of V. E. Nash-Williams, *The Roman Frontier in Wales* (1969); G. Simpson, *Britons and the Roman Army* (1964); I. A. Richmond, 'Roman Wales' in I. Foster and G. Daniel (eds), *Prehistoric and Early Wales* (1965), 151–75.
6 A. H. A. Hogg, 'Native settlement in Wales', in A. C. Thomas (ed.), *Rural Settlement in Roman Britain* (1966), 28.
7 R.C.H.A.M., *Inventory of Caernarvonshire*, I (1956), 96.
8 A. H. A. Hogg, 'Garn Boduan and Tr'er Ceiri', *Arch. J.* CXVII (1960), 1–39.
9 P. S. Gelling, 'The hillfort of South Barrule', *J. Manx Mus.* VI (1957–65), 146–8.
10 P. S. Gelling, 'Close ny Chollagh: an Iron Age fort at Scarlett, Isle of Man', *P.P.S.* XXIV (1958), 85–100.
11 G. Bersu, 'Celtic homesteads in the Isle of Man', *J. Manx Mus.* V (1945–6), 177–82.
12 B. R. S. Megaw, 'The ancient village of Ronaldsway', *J. Manx Mus.* IV (1938–40), 181–2; G. J. H. Neely, 'Excavations at Ronaldsway, Isle of Man', *Ant. J.* XX (1940), 72–86; F. G. Skinner & R. L. S. Bruce-Mitford, 'A Celtic balance-beam of the Early Christian period', *Ant. J.* XX (1940), 87–102.
13 S. S. Frere, *Britannia* (1967), 339.
14 L. R. Laing, *Coins and Archaeology* (1969), 233–4.
15 K. Meyer, 'Expulsion of the Dessi', *Y. Cymmrodor*, XIV (1900), 113.
16 K. Meyer, 'Early relations between Gael and Brython', *Trans. Cymm.* (1895–6), 58.
17 See discussion in L. Alcock, *Dinas Powys* (1963), 58.
18. Frere, *Britannia* (1967), 378.
19 Meyer, 'Early relations . . .' (1895–6), 59–61.
20. Ibid.
21. M. Richards, 'The Irish settlements in south-west Wales', *J.R.S.A.I.* XC (1960), 139.
22 Ibid.
23 L. Alcock, 'Was there an Irish Sea culture-province in the Dark Ages?', in D. Moore (ed.), *The Irish Sea Province in Archaeology and History* (1970), 65.
24 General discussions in V. E. Nash-Williams, *Early Christian Monuments of Wales* (1950), 3–8; see also Richards, 'The Irish settlements . . .' (1960), 141–8.
25 Richards, 'Irish settlements . . .' (1960), 139.

26 Ibid., 145.
27 Ibid., 147.
28 Ibid.
29 E. G. Bowen, 'Clawdd Mawr, Carmarthenshire', *B.B.C.S.* VIII (1937), 383–5.
30 L. Alcock, 'Dark Age objects from Lesser Garth Cave, Glamorgan', *B.B.C.S.* XVIII (1958–60), 221–7.
31 H. N. Savory, 'Some sub-Romano-British brooches from south Wales', in D. Harden (ed.), *Dark Age Britain* (1956), 40–53.
32 Ibid., 45.
33 A. Fox, 'Early Christian period I: settlement sites and other remains', in V. E. Nash-Williams (ed.), *A Hundred Years of Welsh Archaeology* (1946), 105–22.
34 T. Lethbridge & H. David, 'Excavation of a house site on Gateholm, Pembroke', *Arch. Camb.* LXXXV (1930), 366–74.
35 Alcock, *Dinas Powys* (1963), 121–2.
36 G. Wainwright, 'Excavation of a fortified settlement at Walesland rath, Pembroke', *Britannia*, II (1971), 48–108.
37 J. Ward, 'Roman remains at Cwmbrwyn, Carmarthenshire', *Arch. Camb.* 6th Ser. VII (1907), 175–209.
38 W. G. Thomas & R. F. Walker, 'Excavations at Trelissey', *B.B.C.S.* XVIII (1959), 295.
39 A. C. Thomas, *Britain and Ireland in the Early Christian Period* (1971), 58–60.
40 C. Guest (trs.) *The Mabinogion* (Everyman Ed., 1906), 81.
41 J. D. Bu'lock, 'Vortigern and the Pillar of Eliseg', *Ant.* XXXIV (1960), 49–53.
42 E. W. Nicholson, 'The dynasty of Cunedag', *Y Cymmrodor*, XXI (1908), 63–105; L. Alcock, *Arthur's Britain* (1971), *passim* but esp. 125–9; P. H. Blair, 'The origins of Northumbria', *Arch. Ael.*[4] XXV (1947), 28–37.
43 A. H. A. Hogg, 'The date of Cunedda', *Ant.* XXII (1948), 201–5; Alcock, *Dinas Powys* (1963), 70–2.
44 Lethbridge & David, 'Excavation ... on Gateholm' (1930), 366–74.
45 A. O. Curle, 'Excavations at Traprain Law', *P.S.A.S.* XLIX (1914–15), 139–202.
46 C. W. Philips, 'The excavation of a hut group at Pant-y-Saer', *Arch. Camb.* LXXXIX (1934), 1–36.
47 Hogg, 'Garn Boduan' (1960), 1–39.
48 Bowen, 'Clawdd Mawr' (1937), 383–5.
49 Discussed in Alcock, 'Was there an Irish Sea culture-province ...' (1970), 58.
50 Nash-Williams, *Early Christian Monuments of Wales* (1950), No. 138.
51 L. Alcock, *Arthur's Britain* (1971), 122.
52 Convenient summary of Welsh history in N. Chadwick, *Celtic Britain* (1963), 65–76 and also I. Foster, 'The emergence of Wales', in I. Foster & G. Daniel, *Prehistoric and Early Wales* (1965), 213–35.
53 For summaries, see n. 52 above, and also J. E. Lloyd, *A History of Wales* (3rd ed., 1939); W. Rees, *An Historical Atlas of Wales*, I (1951); A. H. Williams, *An Introduction to the History of Wales*, I (1941); N. Chadwick (ed.), *Studies in Early British History* (1959), esp. chapters III and V.
54 C. Fox, 'Wat's Dyke: a field survey', *Arch. Camb.* LXXXIX (1934), 205–78.
55 C. Fox, *Offa's Dyke* (1955).
56 J. J. North, *English Hammered Coinage*, I (1963), 20.
57 General discussion in P. Fowler, 'Hillforts 400–700', in M. Jesson & D. Hill (eds), *The Iron Age and its Hillforts* (1970), 203–13; this discusses the context of reoccupied forts, concentrating on England.
58 W. J. Varley, 'Excavations at the Castle Ditch, Eddisbury', *Trans. Hist. Soc. Lancs. and Chesh.* CII (1950), 53–6.
59 W. J. Varley, 'Hillforts of the Welsh Marches', *Arch. J.* CV (1948), 41–60.
60 Most of the above listed in Fox, 'Early Christian period I ...' (1946), 105–22.
61 General background in W. H. Davies, 'The Church in Wales', in M. Barley & R. P. C. Hanson (eds), *Christianity in Britain, 300–700* (1968), 131–50; P. A. Wilson, 'Romano-British and Welsh Christianity, continuity or discontinuity?', *W.H.R.* III (1966), 5–21; E. G. Bowen, *The Settlements of the Celtic Saints in Wales* (1956).
62 H. Hughes, 'Ynys Seiriol', *Arch. Camb.* I (1901), 85–108.
63 R.C.H.A.M., *Inventory of Anglesey* (1937), 123.
64 R.C.H.A.M., *Inventory of Caernarvonshire* (1960), 201–6.
65 Ibid., 39–41.
66 C. N. Johns, 'The Celtic monasteries of north Wales', *T.C.H.S.* XXI (1960), 14–43.
67 D. B. Hague, 'A medieval church on the island of St Tudwal', *T.C.H.S.* XXI (1960), 6–13.
68 A. N. Palmer, 'Notes on the early history of Bangor Is Coed', *Y Cymmrodor* X (1889), 12–28.
69 R. B. White, 'Rescue excavations on the New Theatre site, University College Park, Bangor', *T.C.H.S.* XXXIII (1972), 246–7; H. H. Hughes, 'An ancient burial ground

at Bangor', *Arch. Camb.* LXXX (1925), 432–6.

70 R. E. M. Wheeler, *Segontium and the Roman Occupation of Wales* (1923), 95–101.

71 D. B. Hague, 'Burryholms', *Med. Arch.* X (1966), 184.

72 Davies, 'The Church in Wales' (1968), 142 n. 2.

73 Wheeler, *Segontium* (1923), 129–30; G. C. Boon, 'A temple of Mithras at Caernarvon-Segontium', *Arch. Camb.* LXV (1960), 136–71.

74 R. P. Wright & K. H. Jackson, 'A late inscription from Wroxeter', *Ant. J.* XLVIII (1968), 296–300.

75 H. M. & J. Taylor, *Anglo-Saxon Architecture*, II (1965), 694.

76 Nash-Williams, *The Roman Villa at Llantwit Major Arch. Camb.* CII (1953) 103.

77 Nash-Williams, *Early Christian Monuments of Wales* (1950); J. D. Bu'lock, 'Early Christian memorial formulae', *Arch. Camb.* CV (1956), 133–41.

78 A. C. Thomas, *The Early Christian Archaeology of North Britain* (1971), 124–6.

79 Bowen, *Settlements of the Celtic Saints* (1956); O. Chadwick, 'The evidence of dedications in the early history of the Welsh Church', in N. K. Chadwick (ed.), *Studies in the Early British Church* (1954), 173–88.

Chapter 5

1 B. Cunliffe & D. W. Philipson, 'Excavations at Eldon's Seat, Encombe, Dorset', *P.P.S.* XXXIV (1968), 230–7, sets the beginnings of the Dorset Iron Age in perspective.

2 A. Fox, 'South-western hillforts', in S. Frere (ed.), *Problems of the Iron Age in Southern Britain* (1961), 35–60.

3 C. S. Bate, 'A British cemetery near Plymouth', *Arch.* XL (1866), 500–9.

4 A. C. Thomas, 'Character and origins of Roman Dumnonia', in Thomas (ed.), *Rural Settlement in Roman Britain* (1966), 78–80.

5 Ibid., 81.

6 D. Peacock, 'A contribution to the study of Glastonbury ware from south-west England', *Ant. J.* XLIX (1969), 41–61.

7 Thomas, 'Character and origins . . .' (1966), 76.

8 J. Brailsford, 'Early Iron Age "C" in Wessex', *P.P.S.* XXIV (1958), 101–19; S. S. Frere, 'Some problems of the later Iron Age' in S. Frere (ed.), *Problems of the Iron Age in S. Britain* (1961), 84–92.

9 G. Wainwright, 'The excavation of a Durotrigian farmstead near Tollard Royal in Cranborne Chase, southern England', *P.P.S.* XXXIV (1968), 102–47.

10 A. Fox, *South-west England* (1964), 136–40.

11 B. Cunliffe, 'The Somerset Levels in the Roman period', in A. C. Thomas (ed.), *Rural Settlement in Roman Britain* (1966), 71.

12 S. S. Frere, *Britannia* (1967), 74.

13 B. St J. O'Neill, 'The Roman villa at Magor Farm, near Camborne, Cornwall', *J.B.A.A.* XXXIX (1933), 116.

14 Thomas, 'Character and origins . . .' (1966), 85.

15 Unpublished.

16 H. R. Hurst, *Excavations in Gloucester, 1970* (1970), 7–9.

17 S. S. Frere, 'The end of towns in Roman Britain', in J. Wacher (ed.), *Civitas Capitals of Roman Britain* (1966), 94; J. Wacher, 'Cirencester 1962', *Ant. J.* XLIII (1963), 16. Other finds unpublished.

18 B. Cunliffe, *Roman Bath* (1969), 162–3.

19 J. C. S. Green, 'Excavations in the Roman cemetery at Poundbury, Dorchester, 1969', *P.D.N.H.A.F.C.* XCI (1969), 183–6.

20 'Wroxeter', *Current Arch.* III (1971), 45–9.

21 A. Fox, 'Roman Exeter' in J. Wacher (ed.), *Civitas Capitals of Roman Britain* (1966), 45–51; A. Fox, *Roman Exeter* (1962), 21.

22 Frere, 'The end of towns . . .' (1966), 95.

23 E. M. Clifford, 'The Roman villa of Witcombe, Glos.', *Trans. B. & G.N.H.A.S.* LXXIII (1954), 26–7.

24 P. A. Rahtz, 'The Roman temple at Pagan's Hill', *P.S.A.N.H.S.* XCVI (1951), 112–42.

25 R. E. M. Wheeler, *The Excavations at Lydney Park, Glos.* (1932), 23–39.

26 *Archaeological Excavations, 1968* (1969), 18–19.

27 A. C. Thomas, *People and Pottery in Dark Age Cornwall* (1960), 1.

28 F. C. Hirst, 'Excavations at Porthmeor, 1933–5', *J.R.I.C.* XXIV (1936).

29 R. A. S. Macalister, *Corpus Inscriptionum Insularum Celticarum*, I (1945), 479–85.

30 A. C. Thomas, *Christian Antiquities of Camborne* (1967), 42–3.

31 H. Hencken, *The Archaeology of Cornwall and Scilly* (1932), 215–18; Thomas, *People and Pottery in Dark Age Cornwall (1960), 3–5.*

32 A. C. Thomas, *Gwithian, Ten Years' Work* (1958), 18–24.

33 Thomas, *Britain and Ireland in Early Christian Times* (1971), 62–7.

34 G. C. Boon, 'The latest objects from Silchester, Hants', *Med. Arch.* III (1959), 87.

35 R. P. Wright & K. H. Jackson, 'A late inscription from Wroxeter', *Ant. J.* XLVIII (1968), 296–300.
36 General discussion in P. Fowler, 'Hillforts AD 400–700' in M. Jesson & D. Hill, *The Iron Age and its Hillforts* (1972), 203–13.
37 Ibid., 209.
38 L. Alcock, *Arthur's Britain* (1971), 222.
39 J. G. D. Clark & C. Fell, 'The early Iron Age site at Micklemoor Hill, West Harling', *P.P.S.* XIX (1953), 13; W. F. Grimes, 'Some smaller settlements', in S. Frere (ed.), *Problems of the I.A. in S. Britain* (1961), 25–8.
40 B. Cunliffe, 'Danebury', *Current Archaeology*, III (1972), 180.
41 S. C. Stanford, 'Credenhill Camp, Hereford; an Iron Age hillfort capital', *Arch. J.* CXXVII (1970), 82–129.
42 Discussion of the problem in L. R. Laing, 'Timber halls in Dark Age Britain – some problems', *Trans. D. & G.N.H.A.S.* XLVI (1969), 118–21 with refs.
43 Discussed in I. A. Richmond, 'Irish analogies for the Romano-British barn dwelling', *J.R.S.* XXII (1932), 96–106.
44 P. Fowler & A. C. Thomas, 'Arable fields of the pre-Norman period at Gwithian', *Cornish Arch.* I (1962), 61–84.
45 Discussed in length in Thomas, *Christian Antiquities of Camborne* (1967); Hencken, *Archaeology of Cornwall & Scilly* (1932); R. A. S. Macalister, *Corpus Inscriptionum Insularum Celticarum*, I (1945), 435–78 and II (1949), 177–88, lists the E. C. stones from the south-west. Sub-Roman cemeteries in P. Rahtz, 'Sub-Roman cemeteries in Somerset', in M. Barley & R. P. C. Hanson, *Christianity in Britain, 300–700* (1968), 193–6.
46 C. Thomas, *Christian Antiquities of Camborne* (1967), 41–50.
47 Ibid., 48–50.
48 A. G. Langdon, *Old Cornish Crosses* (1896); H. Hencken, *Archaeology of Cornwall & Scilly* (1932), 203–86; T. & H. Dexter, *Cornish Crosses* (1938).
49 J. N. L. Myres, *Anglo-Saxon Pottery and the Settlement of England* (1969), 78–80.
50 Ibid., 44–5.
51 Ibid., 100–2.
52 A. Meaney & S. C. Hawkes, *Two Anglo-Saxon Cemeteries at Winnall, Hampshire* (1970).
53 Myres, *Anglo-Saxon Pottery ...* (1969), 113.
54 E. T. Leeds, *Early Anglo-Saxon Art and Archaeology* (1936), 38.
55 Myres, *Anglo-Saxon Pottery* (1969), 115.
56 Ibid., 116–17.
57 J. N. L. Myres, 'Wansdyke and the origins of Wessex', in H. Trevor-Roper (ed.), *Essays in British History* (1964), 1–28.
58 A. Meaney, *Gazetteer of Anglo-Saxon Burial Sites* (1964), 219.
59 H. Hencken, *Archaeology of Cornwall & Scilly* (1932), 246–56.

Chapter 6

1 J. Raftery, 'Iron Age and the Irish Sea: problems for research', in A. C. Thomas (ed.), *The Iron Age in the Irish Sea Province* (1972), 2.
2 'Navan fort', *Current Arch.* II (1970), 305–6.
3 E. Rynne, 'The introduction of La Tène into Ireland', *Bericht. V. Internat. Kong. Vor-und Frügesch. Hamburg* (1958), 705–9.
4 R. B. K. Stevenson, 'Metalwork and other objects found in Scotland', in A. L. F. Rivet (ed.), *The Iron Age in North Britain* (1966), 24.
5 C. Fox, *A Find of the Early Iron Age from Anglesey* (1946), 44.
6 J. Raftery, 'The Turoe stone and the rath of Feerwore', *J.R.S.A.I.* LXXIV (1944), 23–52.
7 Raftery, 'Iron Age and Irish Sea...' (1972),2.
8 B. Raftery, 'Irish hill-forts', in A. C. Thomas (ed.), *The Iron Age in the Irish Sea Province* (1972), 51.
9 H. Hencken, 'Lagore crannog: an Irish royal residence of the seventh to tenth centuries AD', *P.R.I.A.* LIII (1950), 14–17.
10 The original publication is in H. Hencken, *Cahercommaun, A Stone Fort in Co. Clare* (1938). Dating disputed by Raftery in 'Irish hill-forts' (1972), 51.
11 S. P. O'Riordain, 'Lough Gur excavations: Carraig Aille and the "Spectacles"', *P.R.I.A.* LII (1949), 62–3.
12 S. P. O'Riordain, 'Roman material in Ireland', *P.R.I.A.* LI (1947), 35.
13 M. & L. de Paor, *Early Christian Ireland* (1958), 26.
14 R. A. S. Macalister, 'On some antiquities discovered upon Lambay', *P.R.I.A.* XXXVIII (1929), 240–6.
15 E. M. Jope, 'Iron Age brooches in Ireland, a summary', *U.J.A.* XXV (1962), 25–38.
16 J. Raftery, 'A hoard of the Early Iron Age', *J.R.S.A.I.* XC (1960), 2–5.
17 Raftery, 'Irish hill-forts' (1972).
18 V. B. Proudfoot, 'Excavations at the Cathedral Hill, Downpatrick', *U.J.A.* 19 (1956), 57–72.

19 P. Harbison, 'Wooden and stone *chevaux-de-frise* in central and western Europe', *P.P.S.* XXXVII (1971), 195–225.
20 Raftery, 'Irish hill-forts' (1972), 54.
21 E. E. Evans, *Prehistoric and Early Christian Ireland* (1966), 24.
22 M. O'Kelly, 'An early Bronze Age ringfort at Carrigillihy, Co. Cork', *J.C.H.A.S.* LVI (1951), 69–86.
23 S. P. O'Riordain, 'The excavation of conjoined ringforts at Cush', *P.R.I.A.* C (1940), 83–181.
24 Raftery, 'Turoe stone . . .' (1944).
25 V. B. Proudfoot, 'Irish raths and cashels: some notes on chronology, origins and survivals', *U.J.A.* 33 (1970), 37–48; V. B. Proudfoot, 'The economy of the Irish rath', *Med. Arch.* V (1961), 94–122; A. E. P. Collins, 'Settlement in Ulster, 0–1100 AD', *U.J.A.* 31 (1968), 53–8; T. J. Westropp, 'The ancient forts of Ireland', *P.R.I.A.* XXXI (1896–1901), 579–730.
26 R. A. S. Macalister, 'Kiltera', *P.R.I.A.* XLIII (1935), 1–16.
27 Proudfoot, 'Irish raths and cashels . . .' (1970), 42.
28 D. M. Waterman, 'Excavations at Langford Lodge', *U.J.A.* 26 (1963), 43–54.
29 Proudfoot, 'Irish raths and cashels . . .' (1970), 42.
30 C. W. Dickinson & D. M. Waterman, 'Excavation of a rath with motte at Castleskreen, Co. Down', *U.J.A.* 22 (1959), 69; D. M. Waterman & C. W. Dickinson, 'Excavations at Castle Skreen, Co. Down', *U.J.A.* 23 (1960), 73.
31 For Dressogagh, A. E. P. Collins, 'Excavations at the Dressogagh Rath, Co. Armagh', *U.J.A.* 29 (1966), 117–29; others in Proudfoot, 'Irish raths and cashels . . .' (1970), 42.
32 D. M. Waterman, 'Excavations at Lismahon, Down', *Med. Arch. III (1959), 139–76.*
33 S. P. O'Riordain, 'Lough Gur excavations; the great stone circle (B) in Grange Townland', *P.R.I.A.* LIV (1951–2), 37–74.
34 Proudfoot, 'Irish raths and cashels . . .' (1970), 39.
35 Dickinson & Waterman, 'Excavation of a rath . . . at Castleskreen', (1959), 71–2.
37 D. M. Waterman, 'The excavation of a house and souterrain and White Fort, Co. Down', *U.J.A.* 19 (1956), 73–86.
38 Unpublished: discussed briefly in Proudfoot, 'Economy of the Irish rath' (1961), 103.
39 D. M. Waterman & A. E. P. Collins, *An Archaeological Survey of Co. Down* (1966), 115.
40 Useful discussion in E. E. Evans, *Prehistoric & E. C. Ireland* (1966), 28–30.
41 Ibid., 31.
42 Ibid., 30.
43 Patrician literature extensive. But see particularly L. Bieler, *The Life and Legend of St Patrick* (1949); D. Binchy, 'Patrick and his biographers: ancient and modern', *Studia Hibernica*, II (1962), 7–173.
44 K. Hughes, *The Church in Early Irish Society* (1966), 50–1.
45 R. A. S. Macalister, *Corpus Inscriptionum Insularum Celticarum* (1945), I.
46 A. C. Thomas, *The Early Christian Archaeology of North Britain* (1971), 116.
47 H. N. Savory, 'Excavations at Dinas Emrys, Caernarvonshire', *Arch. Camb.* CIX (1960), 61.
48 Thomas, *Early Christian Archaeology . . .* (1971), 125.
49 R. A. S. Macalister, *The Memorial Slabs from Clonmacnois, King's County* (1909).
50 P. Lionard, 'Early Irish grave slabs', *P.R.I.A.* LXI (1961), 98.
51 F. Henry, *Irish Art in the Early Christian Period* (1965), 122.
52 Thomas, *Early Christian Archaeology . . .* (1971), 128–30.
53 Henry, *Irish Art . . .* (1965), 128.
54 Extensive literature. Main discussions, on which the ensuing section is based, in F. Henry, *Irish High Crosses* (1964); F. Henry, *Irish Art during the Viking Invasions* (1967), 133–94; Henry, *Irish Art . . .* (1965), 131–57.
55 S. P. O'Riordain, 'The genesis of the Celtic cross', in S. Pender (ed.), *Féilscríbhinn Torna* (1947), 108–14.
56 F. Henry, 'Early monasteries, beehive huts and dry-stone houses in the neighbourhood of Caherciveen and Waterville, Co. Kerry', *P.R.I.A.* LVIII (1956–7), 45–166.
57 P. Harbison, 'How old is Gallarus Oratory?', *Med. Arch.* XIV (1970), 34–59.
58 H. G. Leask, *Irish Churches and Monastic Buildings*, I (1955), 55–6.
59 Ibid., 27–41.
60 Useful summary in de Paor, *Early Christian Ireland* (1958), 49–72.
61 Henry, *Irish Art during the Viking Invasions* (1967), 49–57.

Chapter 7

1 D. M. Wilson, *The Vikings and their Origins* (1970), 46.

2 T. G. E. Powell, 'From Urartu to Gundestrup: the agency of Thracian metalwork', in J. Boardman, M. Brown & T. Powell, *The European Community in Later Prehistory* (1971), 183–210.
3 P. H. Sawyer, *The Age of the Vikings* (2nd ed., 1971), 9, 121.
4 Ibid., 5–6.
5 J. Brondsted, *The Vikings* (2nd Penguin ed., 1965), 31.
6 A. Small, 'The Viking Highlands – a geographical view', in E. Meldrum (ed.), *The Dark Ages in the Highlands* (1971), 69–70.
7 F. T. Wainwright, 'The Scandinavian settlement', in F. T. Wainwright (ed.), *The Northern Isles* (1962), 117–62; A. W. Brogger, *Ancient Emigrants* (1929), 5.
8 G. Turville-Petre, *The Heroic Age of Scandinavia* (1951), 115–17.
9 H. Arbman, *The Vikings* (1961), 53.
10 W. Nicholaisen, 'Norse settlements in the Northern and Western Isles', *S.H.R.* XLVIII (1969), 6–17.
11 H. Shetelig (ed.), *Viking Antiquities in Great Britain & Ireland*, VI (1954).
12 J. MacQueen, '"Kirk-" and "kil-" in Galloway placenames', *Archivum Linguisticum* VIII (1956), 135–49.
13 The case largely depends on the date of a spearhead from Skaill, Orkney; W. G. Watt, 'Notice of the discovery of a stone cist, with an Iron Age interment, at Skaill Bay', *P.S.A.S.* XXII (1887–8), 283–5; eighth-century date for it advanced in A. Brogger, *Den norske bosetningen pa Shetland-Orknoyene* (1930), 182–4; see also A. Brogger, *Ancient Emigrants* (1929), 122. Shetelig disagreed: H. Shetelig, *Viking Antiquities* (1954), 101–2.
14 S. Grieg, 'Scotland' (part II of H. Shetelig (ed.), *Viking Antiquities* . . . (1940)).
15 Literature extensive, but useful summary in Wainwright, 'The Scandinavian settlement', (1962), 134–40. See also Nicholaisen, 'Norse settlements . . .' (1969), 6–17.
16 Wainwright, op. cit., 146.
17 A. B. Taylor (ed.), *The Orkneyinga Saga* (1938), Introduction, *passim*.
18 A. Thorsteinnson, 'The Viking burial place at Pierowall, Westray, Orkney', in B. Niclasen (ed.), *Fifth Viking Congress* (1965), 150–73.
19 R. B. K. Stevenson, 'The brooch from Westness, Orkney', in A. Niclaisen (ed.), *Fifth Viking Congress* (1968), 25–31.
20 Med. Arch. XII (1968), 164.
21 N. Robertson: 'A Viking grave found at the Broch of Gurness, Aikerness, Orkney', *P.S.A.S.* CI (1968–9), 289–90.
22 *Med. Arch.* XV (1971), 137 and information from excavator.
23 Wainwright, 'The Scandinavian settlement' (1962), 148; R.C.H.A.M., *Inventory of Orkney and Shetland* I, Introduction (1948), *passim*.
24 Stevenson, *Sylloge of Coins of the British Isles, National Museum of Antiquities of Scotland*, I (1966), xix.
25 Hoards listed in J. D. A. Thompson, *Inventory of British Coin Hoards, c. 650–1500* (1956), *passim* with refs. Also discussed in R. B. K. Stevenson, *Sylloge of the Coins of the British Isles, National Museum of Antiquities of Scotland, Edinburgh*: I *Anglo-Saxon Coins* (1966), xvi. Also listed in Grieg, *Viking Antiquities*, II (1940), 119–42.
26 Information from the excavator, Dr Anna Ritchie.
27 S. H. Cruden, 'Excavations at Birsay, Orkney', in A. Small (ed.), *Transactions of the Fourth Viking Congress* (1965), 22–31; C. A. R. Radford, 'Art and architecture, Celtic and Norse', in F. Wainwright (ed.), *The Northern Isles* (1962), 163–80; C. A. R. Radford, *The Early Christian and Norse Site at Birsay* (1959), 18–23.
28 J. S. Clouston, *History of Orkney* (1932).
29 Convenient summary in Small, 'The Viking Highlands . . .' (1971).
30 A. O. Curle, 'A Viking settlement at Freswick, Caithness', *P.S.A.S.* LXXIII (1938–9), 71–110; V. G. Childe, 'Another late Viking house at Freswick, Caithness', *P.S.A.S.* LXXVII (1942–3), 5–17.
31 Grieg, *Viking Antiquities* (1940), 17–18 with refs.
32 Small, 'The Viking Highlands . . .', (1971).
33 General discussion in A. E. Truckell, *The Scandinavians in South-West Scotland* (n.d.), Dumfries Burgh Museum leaflet.
34 J. G. Scott, 'An eleventh-century war axe in Dumfries Museum', *Trans. D. & G.N.H.A.S.* XLIII (1966), 117–20.
35 R. H. M. Dolley & W. F. Cormack, 'A Hiberno-Norse penny of Dublin found in Wigtownshire', *Trans. D. & G.N.H.A.S.* XLIV (1967), 122–5.
36 C. A. Radford, 'Excavations at Whithorn', *Trans. D. & G.N.H.A.S.* XXVII (1950), 97.
37 C. A. R. Radford, 'The early Church in Strathclyde and Galloway', *Med. Arch.* XI (1967), 124–6.
38 C. A. R. Radford & G. Donaldson, *Whithorn and Kirkmadrine* (1953), 12–14.

39 Radford, 'The early Church in Strathclyde and Galloway' (1971), loc. cit.
40 Convenient summary in Small, 'The Viking Highlands . . .' (1971).

Chapter 8

1 Summary of evidence in G. Bersu and D. M. Wilson, *Three Viking Graves in the Isle of Man* (1966), xiii. See also B. R. S. Megaw, 'Weapons of the Viking Age found in Man', *J. Manx Mus.* III (1935–7), 234–6.
2 P. C. M. Kermode, 'Ship burial in the Isle of Man', *Ant. J.* X (1930), 126–33.
3 Bersu & Wilson, *Three Graves . . .* (1966).
4 Ibid.; G. Bersu, 'Three Viking graves in the Isle of Man', *J. Manx Mus.* VI (1957–65), 15–18.
5 Bersu & Wilson, ibid.
6 P. S. Gelling, 'Recent excavations of Norse houses in the Isle of Man', *J. Manx Mus.* VI (1958), 85–100.
7 P. S. Gelling, 'Close ny Chollagh: an Iron Age fort at Scarlett, Isle of Man', *P.P.S.* XXIV (1958), 85–100.
8 Gelling, 'Recent excavations . . .' (1957–65), 55.
9 P. S. Gelling, 'A Norse homestead near Doarlish Cashen, Kirk Patrick, Isle of Man', *Med. Arch.* XIV (1970), 74–83.
10 G. Bersu, 'A promontory fort on the shore of Ramsey Bay', *Ant. J.* XXIX (1949), 62–79.
11 P. S. Gelling, 'The Braaid site', *J. Manx Mus.* VI (1957–65), 201–5; H. J. Fleure, & M. Dunlop, 'Glendarragh Circle and alignments, The Braaid, I.O.M.' *Ant. J.* XXII (1942), 39–53.
12 Gelling, 'The Braaid site' (1957–65), 205.
13 Listed with refs in H. Shetelig (ed.), *Viking Antiquities of Great Britain and Ireland,* V (1954),
14 Ibid.; also listed with refs in J. D. A. Thompson, *Inventory of British Coin Hoards* (1956), *passim* and in P. C. M. Kermode, *List of Manx Antiquities* (1932).
15 B. R. S. Megaw, 'The Douglas treasure trove', *J. Manx Mus.* IV (1938–40), 77–80.
16 B. R. S. Megaw, 'An ancient cemetery at Balladoyne, St Johns', *J. Manx Mus.* IV (1938–40), 11–14.
17 R. Bruce & W. Cubbon, 'Cronk yn How', *Arch. Camb.* LXXXV (1930), 267–99; P. M. C. Kermode, 'An engraved stone pillar from the Isle of Man', *Ant. J.* IX (1929), 372–5.
18 The literature is extensive. Main sources: P. M. C. Kermode, *Manx Crosses* (1907); A. M. Cubbon, *The Art of the Manx Crosses* (1971); H. Shetelig, 'Manx crosses relating to Great Britain and Ireland', *Saga Book of the Viking Club* IX (1925), 253–74; B. R. S. Megaw, 'The monastery of St Maughold', *Proc. I.O.M.N.H.A.S.* V (1950), 169–80; H. R. Davidson & B. R. S. Megaw, 'Gaut the sculptor', *J. Manx Mus.* V (1941–6), 136–9; O. Klindt-Jensen & D. Wilson, *Viking Art* (1966).
19 Klindt-Jensen & Wilson, *Viking Art* (1966), 114–15, most recent survey.
20 Ibid., 108.
21 H. Shetelig, 'The Norse style of ornamentation in the Viking settlements', *Acta Arch.* XIX (1948), 69–113.
22 Useful summary in D. M. Wilson, *The Vikings and Their Origins* (1970), 122–9.
23 J. Kinvig, *A History of Man* (1944), 92–5.
24 W. Cubbon & B. R. S. Megaw, 'The Western Isles and the growth of the Manx parliament', *J. Manx Mus.* V (1941–6), 57–62; Kinvig, *History of Man.*
25 P. S. Gelling, 'Medieval shielings in the Isle of Man', *Med. Arch.* VI–VII (1962–3), 156–172.
26 D. P. Kirby, 'Strathclyde and Cumbria, a survey of historical development to 1092', *Trans. C. & W.A.A.S.* LXII (1962), 77–94.
27 A. S. Meaney, *Gazetteer of Anglo-Saxon Burial Sites* (1964), 143.
28 H. M. Taylor and J. Taylor, *Anglo-Saxon Architecture* (1965), I, 312–16.
29 I. Foster, 'Wales and north Britain', *Arch. Camb.* CXVIII (1969), 1–16.
30 J. D. Cowen, 'Viking burials in Cumbria', *Trans. C. & W.A.A.S.* XLVIII (1948), 73–6. J. D. Cowen, 'Viking burials in Cumbria: a supplement', *Trans. C. & W.A.A.S.* LXVII (1967), 31–4.
31 D. M. Wilson, *Anglo-Saxon Metalwork in the British Museum, 700–1000* (1964).
32 D. Talbot Rice, *English Art 871–1100* (1952), 231.
33 Cuerdale has an extensive literature: see especially M. Banks, *The Problem of Cuerdale* (1967); P. J. Seaby, 'Some Cuerdale queries', *S.C.M.B.* June–September 1967; C. S. S. Lyon, 'The Northumbrian Viking coins in the Cuerdale hoard', in M. Dolley (ed.), *Anglo-Saxon Coins* (1961), 96–121.
34 J. D. Bu'lock, 'Celtic, Saxon and Scandinavian settlement at Meols, Wirral', *H.S.L.C.* CXII (1960), 1–28, Fig. 3.
35 Shetelig, *Viking Antiquities,* V. (1954).

36 Ibid.
37 M. Dolley, 'The mint of Chester', *J. Chester & N. Wales A. & A.H.S.* XLII (1955), 1–21.
38 J. D. A. Thompson, *Inventory of British Coin Hoards, c. 650–1500* (1956), *passim*.
39 Klindt-Jensen & Wilson, *Viking Art* (1966), *passim*.
40 T. D. Kendrick, *Late Saxon and Viking Art* (1948), 68–9.
41 Ibid., 72–3.
42 Ibid., 70–1.
43 Viking finds in Wales listed with refs in A. Fox, 'Early Christian period I: settlement sites and other remains', in V. E. Nash-Williams (ed.), *A Hundred Years of Welsh Archaeology* (1946), 105–22. Hoards in Thompson, *Inventory . . .* (1956), *passim*.
44 T. D. Kendrick, *A History of the Vikings* (1930), 323–7.
45 Ibid., loc. cit.
46 V. E. Nash-Williams, *The Early Christian Monuments of Wales* (1951), 27–32.
47 Kendrick, *History of the Vikings* (1930), 274–99.
48 S. J. Ryan, 'The battle of Clontarf', *J.R.S.A.I.* LXVIII (1938).
49 G. Little, *Dublin Before the Vikings* (1957), gives background; B. O'Riordain 'Excavations at High Street and Winetavern Street, Dublin', *Med. Arch.* XV (1971), 73–86.
50 Finds conveniently gathered in H. Shetelig, *Viking Antiquities . . .* III (1940), Ireland. Earlier finds in G. Coffey & E. C. Armstrong, 'Scandinavian objects found at Islandbridge and Kilmainham', *P.R.I.A.* XXVIII, C (1910), 107–48.
51 T. Fanning, 'Viking grave goods discovered near Larne', *J.R.S.A.I.* C (1970), 71–8.
52 W. O'Sullivan, *The Earliest Irish Coinage* (1961).
53 R. H. M. Dolley, 'Viking coin hoards from Ireland and their relevance for Anglo-Saxon studies', in M. Dolley (ed.) *Anglo-Saxon Coins* (1961), 241–65.

Chapter 9

1 W. C. Dickinson, *Scotland from the Earliest Times to 1603* (1961), 70.
2 Ibid., 83.
3 I. H. Stewart, *The Scottish Coinage*, 2nd ed. (1968), 190.
4 Bibliography extensive; summary in L. R. Laing, 'Cooking pots and the origins of the Scottish medieval pottery industry', *Arch. J.* CXXX (1974), 183–216.
5 S. H. Cruden, *The Scottish Castle* (1960), 22–3.
6 S. H. Cruden, *Scottish Abbeys* (1960), 48–9.
7 Dickinson, op. cit. (1961), 57–8.
8 Publication of the finds from these sites by the author forthcoming.
9 G. W. S. Barrow, 'Rural settlement in central and eastern Scotland', *Scottish Studies*, VI (1962), 125.
10 L. R. Laing, 'Medieval settlement archaeology in Scotland', *S.A.F.* 1 (1969), 71.
11 Ibid., 71–2.
12 R. B. K. Stevenson, 'Medieval dwelling sites and a primitive village in the parish of Manor, Peeblesshire', *P.S.A.S.* LXXV (1941), 92–115.
13 A. Fairbairn, 'Notes on excavations of prehistoric and later sites at Muirkirk, 1913–27', *P.S.A.S.* LXI (1927), 269–89.
14 The medieval finds from this site are in N.M.A.S., unpublished.
15 R. Munro, *Ancient Scottish Lake Dwellings* (1882).
16 J. Ritchie, 'The lake dwelling or crannog in Eadarloch, Loch Treig', *P.S.A.S.* LXXVI (1941–2), 8–78.
17 I. A. Crawford, 'The divide between medieval and post-medieval in Scotland', *Post-Medieval Archaeology*, I (1967), 88.
18 H. Fairhurst, 'The stack fort on Ugadale Point, Kintyre', *P.S.A.S.* LXXXVIII(1954–6), 20–1.
19 Crawford, 'The divide between medieval and post-medieval in Scotland' (1967), 85.
20 I. A. Crawford, *A Preliminary Report of Excavations at Udal, North Uist* (1964), 6.
21 L. Alcock, *Dinas Powys* (1963), 87.
22 L. Alcock, 'Castle Tower, Penmaen; a Norman ringwork in Glamorgan', *Ant. J.* XLVI (1966), 178–210.
23 L. Alcock, *Dinas Powys* (1963), 87.
24 L. A. S. Butler, 'The study of deserted medieval settlements in Wales (to 1968)', in M. Beresford & J. Hurst, *Deserted Medieval Villages* (1971), 252.
25 P. A. Barker, 'Hen Domen Montgomery', *Arch. J.* CXXV (1968), 303.
26 J. E. Lloyd, *Outlines of the History of Wales* (1906), 177.
27 J. J. North, *English Hammered Coinage*, I (1963), 164–5 and *passim*.
28 E. J. Talbot, 'Welsh Ceramics: a documentary and archaeological survey', *Post-Medieval Archaeology*, 2 (1968), 119–39.
29 Butler, 'Deserted medieval settlements in Wales' (1971), 250, with refs.
30 A. Fox, 'Early Welsh homesteads on

Gelligaer Common, Glamorgan, excavations in 1938', *Arch. Camb.* XCIV (1939), 163–200.

31 J. G. Hurst, 'A review of archaeological research (to 1968)' in M. Beresford & J. Hurst, *Deserted Medieval Villages* (1971), 107.

32 P. S. Gelling, 'Medieval shielings in the Isle of Man', *Med. Arch.* VI–VII (1962–3), 156–172.

33 R. E. Glasscock, 'Ireland: deserted medieval settlements (to 1968)', in Hurst and Beresford, *Deserted Medieval Villages* (1971), 287.

34 D. M. Waterman, 'Excavations at Lismahon, Co. Down', *Med. Arch.* III (1959), 139–76.

35 D. M. Waterman, 'Excavations at Ballyfounder rath, Co. Down', *U.J.A.* 21 (1958), 39–61.

36 Glasscock, op. cit. (1971), 287.

37 B. O'Riordain, 'Excavations at High St and Winetavern St, Dublin', *Med. Arch.* XV (1971), 73–85.

38 H. G. Leask, *Irish Churches and Monastic Buildings*, I (1955), 81.

39 W. O'Sullivan, *The Earliest Anglo-Irish Coinage* (1964), v.

40 F. Henry, *Irish Art in the Romanesque Period* (1970), 25.

41 V. E. Nash-Williams, *Early Christian Monuments of Wales* (1950), 31.

42 Drummond, *Sculptured Monuments of Iona and the West Highlands* (1881).

Chapter 10

1 This evidence comes mainly from inscriptions on the metalwork – see *passim* R. A. S. Macalister, *Corpus Inscriptionum Insularum Celticarum*, II (1949); F. Henry, *Irish Art During the Romanesque Period* (1970), 77.

2 J. R. Collis, 'Functional and theoretical interpretations of British coinage', *World Archaeology* (1971), 3–71; J. R. Collis, 'Markets and money', in M. Jesson & D. Hill, *The Iron Age and its Hillforts* (1971), 97–103.

3 H. E. Jean le Patourel, 'Documentary evidence and the medieval pottery industry', *Med. Arch.* XII (1968), 101–26.

4 J. N. L. Myres, *Anglo-Saxon Pottery and the Settlement of England* (1969), 132–6.

5 R. B. K. Stevenson, 'Pictish chain, Roman silver and bauxite beads', *P.S.A.S.* LXXXVIII (1954–6), 228–30.

6 L. Alcock, *Dinas Powys* (1963), 105–6.

7 Ibid., 219. See also discussion on iron working in the Iron Age in E. M. Clifford, *Bagendon, A Belgic Oppidum* (1961), 189.

8 M. J. O'Kelly, 'Two ringforts at Garryduff, Co. Cork', *P.R.I.A.* LXIII (1962), 99–103.

9 R. J. Moss, 'A chemical examination of the crucibles in the collection of the Royal Irish Academy', *P.R.I.A.* XXXVII (1927), 175.

10 Unpublished, information from the excavator Mrs C. Curle.

11 H. C. Lawlor, *The Monastery of St Mochaoi at Nendrum* (1925), 144.

12 D. M. Waterman, 'Late Saxon, Viking and medieval finds from York', *Arch.* XCVII (1959), Pl. XX, 1.

13 R. E. M. Wheeler, *Maiden Castle, Dorset* (1943), 378.

14 A. Bulleid & H. St G. Gray, *Glastonbury Lake Village*, I (1917), 300.

15 For example at Meare – L. Alcock, *Dinas Powys* (1963), 141.

16 E. Burley, 'A survey of the metalwork from Traprain Law, West Lothian', *P.S.A.S.* LXXXIX (1955–6), 213.

17 L. Alcock, *Dinas Powys* (1963), 143.

18 Ibid., 144.

19 P. Verzone, *From Theoderic to Charlemagne* (1967), 135.

20 S. C. Hawkes & G. C. Dunning, 'Soldiers and settlers in Britain, the fourth and fifth centuries', *Med. Arch.* V (1961), 1–70.

21 F. Henry, *Irish Art during the Early Christian Period* (1965), 96–7.

22 F. Henry, 'Emailleurs d'Occident', *Préhistoire* II fas. 1 (1933), 65–146; F. Henry, 'Irish enamels and their relation to the cloisonné techniques', in D. B. Harden (ed.), *Dark Age Britain* (1956), 71–88.

23 F. Henry, *Irish Art* (1965), 96.

24 R. Cramp, 'Decorated window glass and millefiori from Monkwearmouth', *Ant. J.* L (1970), 333.

25 Ibid., 331–2.

26 J. Waterer, 'Irish book satchels or budgets', *Med. Arch.* XII (1968), 70–82.

27 A. T. Lucas, 'Footwear in Ireland', *Co. Louth Arch. J.* XIII (1956), 367.

28 *Vita Secunda*, cap. 8, quoted in A. C. Thomas, *The Early Christian Archaeology of North Britain* (1971), 210–11.

29 A. Evans, 'On a votive deposit of gold objects from the north-west coast of Ireland', *Arch.* LV (1894–7), 391–408.

30 P. Johnstone, 'The Bantry boat', *Ant.* XXXVIII (1964), 277–84.

31 R. Munro, *Ancient Scottish Lake Dwellings or Crannogs* (1882), 237.
32 M. & L. de Paor, *Early Christian Ireland* (1958), 98–9.
33 Some block wheels are also known, see A. T. Lucas, 'A block wheel car from Co. Tipperary', *J.R.S.A.I.* LXXXII (1952), 135–144.
34 Extensive literature on this topic. Main discussions in P. Harbison, 'The chariot of Celtic funerary tradition', in O.-H. Frey, *Marburger Beitrage zur Archäologie der Kelten, Festschrift Dehn* (1969), 34–58; P. Harbison, 'The old Irish chariot', *Ant.* XLV (1971), 171–7; D. Green, 'The chariot as described in Irish literature', in A. C. Thomas (ed.), *The Iron Age in the Irish Sea Province* (1972), 59–74.

Chapter 11

1 P. Vouga, *La Tène* (1923), Pl. xxix.
2 A. Bulleid & St G. Gray, *Glastonbury Lake Village*, I (1910), 310–27.
3 K. M. Richardson, 'Excavations in Hungate, York', *Arch. J.* CXVI (1960), 86.
4 E. M. Jope, H. M. Jope & S. Rigold, 'Pottery from a late twelfth century well-filling and other medieval finds from St John's College, Oxford', *Oxon*, XV (1950), 55.
5 Wood-Martin, *Ancient Irish Lake Dwellings* (1889), 101.
6 I. M. Stead, 'A La Tène III burial at Welwyn Garden City', *Arch.* CI (1967), 19.
7 D. B. Harden, 'Ancient glass II – Roman', *Arch. J.* CXXVI (1969), 51.
8 W. Kramer, 'The oppidum of Manching', *Ant.* XXIV (1960), 197.
9 R. B. K. Stevenson, 'Native bangles and Roman glass', *P.S.A.S.* LXXXVIII (1953–5), 208–21.
10 D. B. Harden, 'Glass vessels in Britain, 400–1000', in D. B. Harden (ed.), *Dark Age Britain* (1956), 132–57, esp. 146–8.
11 Ibid., 149–51. The 1973 finds are not yet published.
12 C. A. R. Radford & J. S. Cox, 'Cadbury Castle, South Cadbury', *Proc. Somerset A. & N.H.S.* 99–100 (1954–5), 106–13.
13 Harden, 'Glass vessels in Britain, 400–1000', in *Dark Age Britain* (1956), 149.
14 P. Fowler & P. Rahtz, 'Cadcong 1970', *Current Arch.* II (1970), 342.
15 Harden, 'Glass vessels in Britain' (1956), 149.
16 C. A. R. Radford, 'Glastonbury Abbey', in G. Ashe, *The Quest for Arthur's Britain* (1968), 105 (of paperback edition).
17 Harden, 'Glass vessels in Britain . . . (1956), 154.
18 Ibid., 154.
19 Ibid., 155.
20 S. S. Frere, *Britannia* (1967), 372.
21 G. Wainwright, *Coygan Camp* (1967), 157.
22 A. C. Broadribb, A. R. Hands & D. R. Walker, *Excavations at Shakenoak Farm near Wilcote*, Oxford, III (1972), 54–9.
23 C. A. R. Radford, 'Imported pottery found at Tintagel, Cornwall', in Harden (ed.), *Dark Age Britain* (1956), 59–70.
24 Original definition in Radford, ibid., developed by A. C. Thomas, 'Imported pottery in Dark Age western Britain', *Med. Arch.* III (1959), 90–1; recent reassessment in J. W. Hayes, *Late Roman Pottery* (1972), 13–322.
25 Radford (1956), ibid; Thomas (1959), ibid., 91–4; Eastern occurrences in M. Irimia, 'Cuptoraeale Romano-Bizantine de ars ceramica de la Oltina (Jud. Constanta)' in *Pontice, studii si materiali de istorie, arheologie si muzeographie* (1968), 408 (French summary).
26 Thomas, 'Dark Age imported pottery . . .' (1959), 94.
27 Ibid., 94–5; J. Rigoir, 'Les sigillées paléochrétiennes grises et oranges', *Gallia*, 26 (1968), 177–244.
28 Thomas, ibid., 96–8; D. Peacock & A. C. Thomas, 'Class E imported post-Roman pottery: a suggested origin', *Cornish Arch.* 6 (1967), 35–46.
29 Thomas, 'Dark Age imported pottery . . .' (1959), 95.
30 L. Alcock, *Arthur's Britain* (1971), 206.
31 L. Alcock, 'Wales in the fifth to seventh centuries', in I. Foster & G. Daniel (eds), *Prehistoric and Early Wales* (1965), 196. For the problem of Welsh pottery ascribed to this period, see also L. Alcock, 'Pottery and settlements in Wales and the March', in I. Foster & L. Alcock (eds), *Culture and Environment* (1963), 281–302.
32 B. Raftery, 'Freestone Hill, Co. Kilkenny: an Iron Age hillfort and Bronze Age cairn', *P.R.I.A.* LXVIII (1969), 86–96.
33 A. H. A. Hogg, 'The Votadini', in W. Grimes (ed.), *Aspects of Archaeology* (1951), 214–19.
34 R. E. M. Wheeler, *The Stanwick Fortifications* (1954), 38–41.
35 W. Gardner & H. Savory, *Dinorben* (1964), 192.

36 A. H. A. Hogg, 'Garn Boduan and Tre'r Ceiri', *Arch. J.* CXVII (1960), 38.
37 C. W. Phillips, 'The excavation of a hut group at Pant-y-Saer', *Arch. Camb.* LXXXIX (1934), 6.
38 P. S. Gelling & S. C. Stanford, 'Dark Age pottery or Iron Age ovens?', *Trans. Birmingham A.S.* LXXXII (1967), 77–91.
39 Characteristics and distribution in D. M. Waterman & A. E. P. Collins, *Archaeological Survey of County Down* (1966), 133–5.
40 V. B. Proudfoot & B. C. S. Wilson, 'Further excavations at Larrybane promontory fort, Co. Antrim', *U.J.A.* 24–5 (1961–2), 97–103.
41 D. M. Waterman, 'Neolithic and Dark Age site at Langford Lodge, Co. Antrim', *U.J.A.* 26 (1963), 51–2.
42 V. B. Proudfoot, 'Further excavations at Shaneen Park, Belfast', *U.J.A.* 21 (1958), 23–8; E. Evans, 'Rath and souterrain at Shaneen Park', *U.J.A.* 13 (1950), 6–27.
43 V. G. Childe, 'A promontory fort on the Antrim coast', *Ant. J.* XVI (1936), 197; stated in greater detail in V. G. Childe, *Prehistoric Communities of the British Isles* (1940), 210–11.
44 H. E. Kilbride-Jones, 'Excavation of a composite E.I.A. monument with henge features at Lugg, Co. Dublin', *P.R.I.A.* LIII (1951), 311–12.
45 *Archaeological Survey of County Down* (1966), 133; *Radiocarbon*, III (1961), 36.
46 A. C. Thomas, *People and Pottery in Dark Age Cornwall* (1956), 2–4.
47 A. C. Thomas, 'Grass-marked pottery in Cornwall', in J. Coles & D. Simpson, *Studies in Ancient Europe* (1968), 322–3.
48 G. C. Dunning, J. G. Hurst, J. N. L. Myres and F. Tischler, 'Anglo-Saxon pottery, a symposium', *Med. Arch.* III (1959), 48–9.
49 Ibid., 49.
50 Ibid., *passim*.
51 Thomas, 'Grass-marked pottery in Cornwall' (1968), 328–9.
52 I. A. Crawford, *Excavations at Coileaghan an Udail, (The Udal) N. Uist – 9th Interim Report* (1972), 9.
53 B. Cunliffe, 'The Saxon culture-sequence at Portchester Castle', *Ant. J.* L (1970), 68–72.
54 J. R. C. Hamilton, *Excavations at Jarlshof* (1956), 88.
55 J. R. C. Hamilton, *Excavations at Clickhimin* (1968), 144.
56 A. Young, 'The sequence of Hebridean pottery', in A. L. F. Rivet (ed.), *The Iron Age in North Britain* (1966), 48–56.
57 D. Clarke, 'Bone dice and the Scottish Iron Age', *P.P.S.* XXXVI (1970), 217–18.
58 Ibid., 226.
59 L. Alcock, *Dinas Powys* (1963), 153–4.
60 H. Hencken, 'Lagore, a royal residence of the seventh to tenth centuries AD', *P.R.I.A.* LIII (1950), 88–94.
61 R. E. M. Wheeler, *London and the Saxons* (1935), 175.
62 E. Rynne, 'The impact of the Vikings on Irish weapons', *Atti del VI Congresso Internazionale delle Scienze Preistorische e Protohistorische Sezioni V–VIII* (1966), 181–6.
63 L. Alcock, *Arthur's Britain* (1971), 332.
64 P. V. Addyman, 'A dark-age settlement at Maxey, Northants', *Med. Arch.* VIII (1964), Fig. 16, 1–6.
65 *London Museum Medieval Catalogue* (1954), 114.
66 J. Werner, *Munzdatierte Austrasische Grafunde* (1935), 101.
67 M. Duignan, 'Irish agriculture in early historic times', *J.R.S.A.I.* LXXIV (1944), 136–40.
68 H. Hencken, *Cahercommaun* (1938), 53.
69 S. P. O'Riordain, 'Carraig Aille', *P.R.I.A.* LII (1949), 79.
70 H. Hencken, *Cahercommaun* (1938), 53.
71 A. Roes, *Bericht Rijkd. Oudheidk. Bodemond. in Nederland*, IV, 2 (1953), 31.
72 S. Piggott, 'An iron object from Dunadd', *P.S.A.S.* LXXXVI (1952–3), 194.

Chapter 12

1 E. Crowfoot & S. C. Hawkes, 'Early Anglo-Saxon gold braids', *Med. Arch.* XI (1967), 42–86, with refs.
2 H. L. Roth, *Studies in Primitive Looms* (1918), Fig. 91c.
3 General discussion of clothing in M. & L. de Paor, *Early Christian Ireland* (1958), 101–5.
4 Ibid., 104.
5 K. Kenyon, *The Jewry Wall Site, Leicester* (1947), Fig. 92, 3.
6 J. P. Bushe-Fox, *Wroxeter, 1913* (1913), Pl. IX, 4.
7 J. P. Bushe-Fox, *Excavations at Richborough*, III (1932), Pl. XIII, 42.
8 R. E. M. Wheeler, *Excavations at Lydney Park, Gloucestershire* (1932), Pl. XXXII, 181.
9 P. Reynolds, *Excavations at Caerhun* (1938), Fig. 63, 7.
10 R. Munro, *Ancient Scottish Lake Dwellings* (1882), Fig. 27.

11 P. Lasko, 'The comb', in C. F. Battiscombe (ed.), *The Relics of St Cuthbert* (1956), 336–355.
12 Useful discussion in L. Alcock, *Dinas Powys* (1963), 156–8.
13 Publication by the author pending.
14 L. Alcock, *Dinas Powys* (1963), 156.
15 E. T. Leeds, *Early Anglo-Saxon Art and Archaeology* (1936), Pl. X; discussed in A. Meaney, *A Gazetteer of Early Anglo-Saxon Burial Sites* (1964), 16.
16 E. Fowler, 'Celtic metalwork of the fifth and sixth centuries', *Arch. J.* CXX (1963), 134–5.
17 E. Fowler, 'The origins and development of the penannular brooch in Europe', *P.P.S.* XXVI (1960), 155–8; 160.
18 Ibid., 171.
19 S. C. Hawkes, 'The Jutish Style A, a study of the Germanic animal art in southern England', *Arch.* XCVIII (1961), 52.
20 *London Museum Medieval Catalogue* (1954), 273.
21 F. Henry, *Irish Art during the Viking Invasions* (1967), Pl. 79, shows this on Muiredach's Cross, Monasterboice.
22 F. Henry, *Irish Art in the Early Christian Period* (1965), 102, n. 2.
23 Fowler, 'Origins and development of the penannular brooch . . .' (1960); Fowler, 'Celtic metalwork of the fifth and sixth centuries' (1963).
24 Alternative schemes to Fowler's in H. E. Kilbride-Jones, 'The evolution of penannular brooches with zoomorphic terminals in Great Britain and Ireland', *P.R.I.A.* XLIII, C (1935–7), 379–455; H. E. Kilbride-Jones, 'Scots zoomorphic penannular brooches', *P.S.A.S.* LXX (1935–6), 124–38; H. N. Savory, 'Some sub-Romano-British brooches from south Wales' in D. B. Harden (ed.), *Dark Age Britain* (1956), 40–53; J. Raftery, 'A bronze zoomorphic brooch from Toomullin, Co. Clare', *J.R.S.A.I.* LXXI (1941), 56–60.
25 This class discussed in Kilbride-Jones, 'The evolution of penannular brooches . . .' (1935–7) and in Kilbride-Jones, 'Scots zoomorphic penannular brooches . . .' (1935–1936).
26 This class discussed in particular in Savory, 'Some sub-Romano-British brooches . . .' (1956).
27 Fowler, 'Celtic metalwork of the fifth and sixth centuries' (1963), 110.
28 S. P. O'Riordain, 'The excavation of a large earthen ringfort at Garranes, Co. Cork', *P.R.I.A.* XLVII, C (1942), 93–4 and Fig. 3, 265.
29 Unpublished, information from Mrs C. Curle.
30 Dating discussed in R. A. Smith, 'Irish brooches through five centuries', *Arch.* LXV (1913–14), 234 and C. E. Blunt, 'The date of the Croy hoard', *P.S.A.S.* LXXXIV (1949–50), 217.
31 Conveniently figured in A. C. O'Dell *et al.*, 'The St Ninian's silver hoard', *Ant.* XXXIII (1959), Pl. XXXIIIb; discussion 255–7.
32 D. M. Wilson, 'Reflections on the St Ninian's Isle treasure' (Jarrow Lecture, 1969), 3–4. Other brooches in Smith, 'Irish brooches . . .' (1913–14), 235–7.
33 Unpublished; information from Mrs C. Curle.
34 Smith, 'Irish brooches . . .' (1913–14), 231 and Fig. 6.
35 Most convenient discussion of Tara in Henry, *Irish Art in the E.C. Period* (1965), 108–10; Hunterston in J. Anderson, *Scotland in Early Christian Times* (1881), Ser. 2, 1 and G. Stephens, 'Note on the Hunterston Brooch, Ayrshire', *P.S.A.S.* XXII (1886–7), 462.
36 Smith, 'Irish brooches . . .' (1913–14), Pl. XXVII, No. 3.
37 Ibid., Pl. XXVIII, No. 2.
38 D. M. Wilson, 'A group of penannular brooches of the Viking period', in K. Eldjarn, *Third Viking Congress* (1958), 95–100.
39 Smith, 'Irish brooches . . .' (1913–14), Pl. XXVI, No. 3.
40 Kilbride-Jones, 'The evolution of penannular brooches . . .' (1936), 412–18.
41 Cf. Kilbride-Jones, ibid., Fig. 17/52.
42 R. B. K. Stevenson, 'The brooch from Westness, Orkney' in Niclasen, B. (ed.), *The Fifth Viking Congress* (1965), 27.
43 Anderson, *Scotland in E.C. Times* (1881), II, 7; *P.S.A.S.* XXII (1886–7), 271–3; *P.S.A.S.* VIII (1869–70), 305.
44 E. C. R. Armstrong, 'Irish bronze pins of the Christian Period', *Arch.* LXXII (1921–2), 77.
45 This class of brooch in F. Henry, *Irish Art during the Viking Invasions* (1967), 128–31; the Alfred Jewel in J. Kirk, *The Alfred and Minster Lovell Jewels* (1948).
46 T. Fanning, 'The ringed pins in Limerick Museum', *North Munster A.J.* XII (1969), 6–11; detailed study by Fanning forthcoming in *P.R.I.A.*

47 R. Smith, 'The evolution of the hand-pin in Great Britain and Ireland', in *Opuscula Archaeologica Oscari Montelio Septuagenaria Dicata* (1913), 36–289.

48 Fowler, 'Celtic metalwork of the fifth and sixth centuries' (1963), 120–9; R. B. K. Stevenson, 'Pins and the chronology of the brochs', *P.P.S.* XXI (1955), 282–9.

49 Iron Age antecedents in G. C. Dunning, 'Swan's-neck and ring-headed pins of the early Iron Age in Britain', *Arch. J.* XCI (1934), 269–95; later development in Stevenson, 'Pins . . .' (1955), 282–94.

50 A. Young, 'An aisled farmhouse at the Allasdale, Isle of Barra', *P.S.A.S.* LXXXVII (1952–3), 84, Pl. IX, 4.

51 Fowler, 'Celtic metalwork of the fifth and sixth centuries' (1963), 126.

52 Main discussions to date in Armstrong, 'Irish bronze pins . . .' (1921–2), 71–86, and Stevenson, 'Pins and the chronology of brochs' (1955), 282–94.

53 This and the next type in Fowler, 'Celtic metalwork of the fifth and sixth centuries' (1963), 120–2.

54 C. A. R. Radford & C. Peers, 'The Saxon monastery of Whitby', *Arch.* LXXXIX (1943), Fig. 13, 1 and 7.

55 Waterman, D. M. 'Late Saxon, Viking and early medieval finds from York', *Arch.* XCVIII (1959), Fig. 11, 1–3.

56 J. D. Bu'lock, 'Celtic, Saxon, and Scandinavian settlement at Meols, Wirral', *T.H.S.L.C.* CXII (1960), Fig. 3c.

57 Unpublished, in N.M.A.S.

58 Armstrong, 'Irish bronze pins . . .' (1921–2), 72–3.

59 E. Rynne, 'Excavations at Ardcloon, Co. Mayo', *J.R.S.A.I.* LXXVI (1956), 212–13.

60 R. A. Smith, 'Irish serpentine latchets', *Proc. Soc. Ant. Lond.* XXX (1917–18), 120.

61 V. Evison, 'Quoit Brooch Style buckles', *Ant. J.* XLVIII (1968), 234.

62 G. Coffey, *Guide to the Celtic Antiquities of the Christian Period in the National Museum, Dublin* (1910), 23.

63 R. B. K. Stevenson, 'Native bangles and Roman glass', *P.S.A.S.* LXXXVIII (1953–1955), 208–21.

64 I. A. Stead, 'A La Tène III burial at Welwyn Garden City', *Arch.* CI (1967), 17.

65 W. Kramer, 'The oppidum of Manching', *Ant.* XXXIV (1960), 197.

66 Radford & Peers, 'Whitby' (1943), 72–3.

67 Hencken, 'Lagore . . .' (1950), 132–45, best list of beads.

68 O'Kelly, 'Garryduff' (1962), 38, discussion.

69 Ibid., 27–30.

70 See comparative roundels, Fig. 135.

Chapter 13

1 A. Clapham, 'Notes on the origins of Hiberno-Saxon art', *Ant.* VIII (1934), 43–57.

2 N. K. Sandars, *Prehistoric Art in Europe* (1968).

3 T. G. E. Powell, *Prehistoric Art* (1966).

4 Convenient summary in D. M. Wilson, *The Vikings and Their Origins* (1970), 122–9.

5 A. C. Thomas, 'The animal art of the Scottish Iron Age', *Arch. J.* CXVIII (1961), 14–63

6 J. V. S. Megaw, *Art of the European Iron Age* (1970), 38.

7 Ibid., 38.

8 Sandars, op. cit., 234–9; Megaw, op. cit. 17.

9 W. Lucke & O.-H. Frey, *Die Situla in Providence* (Rhode Island) (1962); see also Sandars, op. cit. 223–5.

10 Sandars, op. cit., 258–9; First phase of Celtic insular art also in E. M. Jope, 'The beginnings of the La Tène ornament style in the British Isles', in S. Frere (ed.), *Problems of the Iron Age in Southern Britain* (1961), 69–83.

11 Sandars, op. cit., 273; Megaw, op. cit., 37.

12 Megaw, op. cit., 37.

13 W. Bulmer, 'Dragonesque brooches and their development', *Ant. J.* XVIII (1938), 146–53; R. W. Feachem, 'Dragonesque fibulae', *Ant. J.* XLVIII (1968), 100–2.

14 See discussion in N. P. Toll, *Dura Europos*, Final Report, IV, 1 (1949), 58.

15 M. Simpson, 'Massive armlets in the north British Iron Age', in J. Coles & D. Simpson (eds), *Studies in Ancient Europe* (1968), 233–254; Caledonian metalwork also in R. B. K. Stevenson, 'Metalwork and some other objects in Scotland and their cultural affinities', in A. L. F. Rivet (ed.), *The Iron Age in North Britain* (1966), 31–2; Brigantian metalwork in M. MacGregor, 'The Iron Age metalwork hoard from Stanwick, N.R. Yorks', *P.P.S.* XXVIII (1962), 17–57.

16 Main discussions of late La Tène art in Ireland in M. O'Kelly, 'The Cork Horns, the Petrie Crown and the Bann Disc', *J. Cork H. & A.S.* LXVI (1961), 1–12; Raftery, J. 'Bronze mount from Feltrim Hill, Co. Dublin', *J.R.S.A.I.* C (1970), 175–9. The Feltrim Hill mount is of openwork type.

17 C. F. C. Hawkes, 'Bronze workers, cauldrons and bucket animals in Iron Age and

Roman Britain', in W. Grimes (ed.), *Aspects of Archaeology* (1951), 172–200.
18 S. Piggott, 'Firedogs in Britain and beyond', in J. Boardman, M. Brown & T. G. E. Powell, *The European Community in Later Prehistory* (1971), 245.
19 Cf. P. Jacobsthal, *Early Celtic Art* (1944), No. 293, etc.
20 J. Curle, *Newstead, a Roman Frontier Post and its People* (1911), Pl. LXXVI, Nos. 1–3.
21 E. M. Jope, 'Iron Age brooches in Ireland, a summary', *U.J.A.* XXV (1962), 25–38.
22 C. Fox, *Pattern and Purpose* (1958), 93–4.
23 E. M. Jope, 'The Keshcarrigan bowl and a bronze mirror handle from Ballymoney, Co. Antrim', *U.J.A.* 17 (1954), 92–6.
24 S. C. Hawkes & G. C. Dunning, 'Soldiers and settlers in Britain, fourth to fifth century', *Med. Arch.* V (1961), 10–21 useful summary.
25 First suggested by T. D. Kendrick, *Anglo-Saxon Art to A.D. 900* (1938), 32–6.
26 Best general discussion in K. Jettmar, *Art of the Steppes* (1964) and M. Rostovtzeff, *The Animal Style in South Russia and China* (1929). Useful series of comparative illustrations in E. Minns, 'The art of the northern nomads', *Proc. Brit. Acad.* XXVIII (1942), 47–99.
27 Conveniently illustrated in S. Piggott, *Ancient Europe* (1965), Fig. 37.
28 T. G. E. Powell, 'From Urartu to Gundestrup, then agency of Thracian metalwork', in J. Boardman, M. Brown and T. G. E. Powell, *The European Community in Later Prehistory* (1971), 183–210.
29 D. F. Allen, 'The Sark hoard', *Arch.* CIII (1971), 1–31.
30 A. C. Thomas, 'Animal art of the Scottish Iron Age', *Arch. J.* CXVIII (1961), 14–64.
31 B. Salin, *Altgermanische Thierornamentik* (1904).
32 Main discussions in S. C. Hawkes, 'The Jutish Style A. A study of Germanic animal art in southern England', *Arch.* XCVIII (1961), 29–74; V. Evison, *The Fifth Century Invasions South of the Thames* (1965); E. Bakka, 'On the beginnings of Salin's Style I in England', *Universitet i Bergen Årbok* (1958), 1–83.
33 Discussed in C. F. C. Hawkes, 'Sutton Hoo, twenty-five years after', *Ant.* XXXVIII (1964), 253.
34 Ibid.
35 Discussion in P. Lasko, *The Kingdom of the Franks* (1971), 59.
36 E. T. Leeds, 'Denmark and early England', *Ant. J.* XXVI (1946), 22–37; C. F. C. Hawkes, 'The Jutes of Kent', in D. B. Harden (ed.), *Dark Age Britain* (1956), 104.
37 E. Fowler, 'Hanging bowls' in J. Coles & D. Simpson (eds), *Studies in Ancient Europe* (1968), 300, Fig. 71.
38 Unpublished excavation by the author 1973.
39 P. Lasko, op. cit. (1971), Fig. 62.
40 E. Fowler, 'Celtic metalwork of the fifth and sixth centuries', *Arch. J.* CXX (1963), 134.
41 The literature is extensive. The main studies, however, are E. Fowler, 'Hanging bowls' in *Studies in Ancient Europe* (1968), 287–310; F. Henry, 'Hanging bowls', *J.R.S.A.I.* LXVI (1936), 209–46; T. D. Kendrick, 'British hanging bowls', *Ant.* VI (1932), 161–84; G. Haselohf, 'Fragments of a hanging bowl from Bekesbourne, Kent, and some ornamental problems', *Med. Arch.* II (1958), 72–103; A. Liestol, 'The hanging bowl, a liturgical and domestic vessel', *Acta Arch.* XXIV (1953), 163–70.
42 Henry, 'Hanging bowls' (1936), 239–44.
43 Henry, ibid., 244.
44 J. Raftery, 'The Cuillard and other unpublished hanging bowls', *J.R.S.A.I.* XCVI (1966), 29–38.
45 C. A. R. Radford & C. Peers, 'The Saxon monastery of Whitby', *Arch.* LXXXIX (1943), 47.
46 Henry, 'Hanging bowls' (1936), 211–13.
47 Suggested by Liestol, 'Hanging bowls' (1953), 163.
48 D. MacRoberts, 'The ecclesiastical significance of the St Ninian's Isle treasure', *P.S.A.S.* XCIV (1960–1), 304–5.
49 Bede, *H.E.* II, 16.
50 Fowler, 'Hanging bowls' (1968), 290.
51 F. Henry, *Irish Art in the Early Christian Period* (1965), 96.
52 R. B. K. Stevenson, 'Note on the mould from Craig Phadrig', in A. Small (ed.), *Craig Phadrig* (1972), 49–51.
53 See general discussion in D. M. Wilson, *Reflections on the St Ninian's Isle Treasure* (Jarrow Lecture, 1969).
54 C. A. R. Radford, 'Two reliquaries connected with south-west Scotland', *Trans. D. & G.N.H.A.S.* XXXII (1955), 115–23.
55 Radford & Peers, 'Saxon monastery of Whitby' (1943), Pl. XXVI.
56 F. Henry, *Irish Art in the Early Christian Period* (1965), 96–8.
57 M. Duignan, 'The Moylough (Co. Sligo) and other Irish belt shrines', *J. Galway A. & H.S.* XXIV (1951), 83–94; M. O'Kelly,

'The belt shrine from Moylough, Sligo', *J.R.S.A.I.* XCV (1965), 149–88.

58 W. Holmqvist, 'An Irish crozier found near Stockholm', *Ant. J.* XXXV (1955), 46–51.

59 L. S. Gogan, *The Ardagh Chalice* (1932); Henry, *Irish Art* (1965), 106–8.

60 J. Raftery, *Christian Art in Ancient Ireland*, II (1941), 25–6 with refs.

61 Henry, *Irish Art* (1965), 114.

62 G. Coffey, *R.I.A. Guide to Celtic Antiquities of the Christian Period in the National Museum, Dublin* (1909), 42–3.

63 J. Anderson, *Scotland in Early Christian Times* (1881), 241; F. Eeles, 'The Monymusk reliquary or Brecbennoch of St Columba', *P.S.A.S.* LXVIII (1933–4), 433–8.

64 Anderson, ibid., 246.

65 Raftery, *Christian Art in Ancient Ireland*, II (1941), 109–10.

66 Anderson, *Scotland in Early Christian Times* (1881), 248.

67 J. Hunt, 'On two D-shaped objects in the Saint-Germain Museum', *P.R.I.A.* LVII (1956), 153–7.

68 Raftery, *Christian Art* ... II (1941), 107.

69 H. Shetelig, *Osebergfunnet*, II (1920), Figs 32–3.

70 Henry, *Irish Art* (1965), 106.

71 H. Arbman, *Birka, I, Die Graber* (1940–3), I, Pls 203–4; II, 147–8.

72 J. Boe, 'An ornamented bronze object found in a Norwegian grave', *Bergens Mus. Arbok* (1924–5), 1–34.

73 F. Henry, *Irish Art During the Viking Invasions* (1967), 131.

74 D. M. Wilson, 'The Trewhiddle hoard', *Arch.* XCVIII (1961), 75–122.

75 H. Hencken, 'Ballinderry 1' (1936), 191.

76 Raftery, *Christian Art* ... II (1941), 145–6.

77 B. M. Crozier in M. MacDermott, 'The Kells crozier', *Arch.* XCVI (1955), 59–113; the others in M. MacDermott, 'The croziers of St Dympna and St Mel and tenth-century Irish metalwork', *P.R.I.A.* LVIII (1957), 167–95.

78 M. Stokes, 'Observations on two ancient Irish works of art known as the Breac Moedog, or shrine of St Moedoc of Ferns, and the Soicel Molaise', *Arch.* XLIII (1871), 131–50. Henry, *Irish Art During the Viking Invasions* (1967), 120.

79 Ibid. (1967), 125.

80 Ibid. (1967), 123.

81 M. MacDermott, 'An openwork Crucifixion plaque from Clonmacnois', *J.R.S.A.I.* LXXXIV (1954), 36–40.

82 Henry, *Irish Art During the Romanesque Period* (1970), 74–122.

83 G. F. Werner, *The Stowe Missal* (1906).

84 Henry, *Irish Art in the Romanesque Period* (1970), 85.

85 Ibid., 91.

86 E. C. R. Armstrong & H. S. Crawford, 'The reliquary known as the Misach', *J.R.S.A.I.* LII (1922), 105–11.

87 Coffey, *R.I.A. Guide to Celtic Antiquities* ... (1909), 47–8.

88 Raftery, *Christian Art* ... II (1941), 159–60.

89 M. Stokes, *Early Christian Art* (1928), 85 and 87; Raftery, *Christian Art* ... II (1941), 159.

90 Ibid. (1928), 85–6.

91 Extensive literature, summarized with refs in Henry, *Irish Art in the Romanesque Period* (1970), 106–7.

92 T. D. Kendrick & E. Senior, 'St Manchan's shrine', *Arch.* LXXXVI (1937), 105–18.

93 Henry, *Irish Art in the Romanesque Period* (1970).

94 J. Anderson, *Scotland in Early Christian Times* (1881).

95 J. W. Waterer, 'Irish book satchels or budgets', *Med. Arch.* XII (1968), 70–82.

Chapter 14

1 A. C. Thomas, *The Early Christian Archaeology of North Britain* (1971), 13. This is the main source used for this chapter.

2 A. C. Thomas, 'The evidence from north Britain', in M. Barley & R. P. C. Hanson, *Christianity in Britain, 300–700* (1968), 99–100.

3 Summarized in Thomas, *The E.C. Archaeology of North Britain* (1971), 22–6.

4 Ibid., 27.

5 Ibid., 32.

6 Ibid., 41.

7 Ibid., 48–68.

8 Ibid., 132–66.

9 H. G. Leask, *Irish Churches and Monastic Buildings*, I (1955), 6.

10 L. de Paor, 'A survey of Sceilg Mhichil', *J.R.S.A.I.* LXXXV (1955), 174–87.

11 Leask, *Early Irish Churches* (1955), 44.

12 Ibid., 46–7.

Index

All types of settlement listed under settlement

Aed Finn, 50
Aeneas Sylvius, 234
Aeron, 31, Fig. 8
Aeternus, 25
Aethelbald (k. of Mercia), 104
Aethelflaeda (q. of Mercia), 221
Aethelfrith (k. of Bernicia), 30, 50
Aethelred (k. of Mercia), 221
Aethelstan (k. of England), 105, 205
Aethelwulf (k. of Northumbria), 104
Abercorn, Midlothian, 29, 45, Fig. 9
Aberdaron, Caerns., 115, 118
Aberlady, E. Lothian, 29
Aberlemno, Angus, 60–3
Abernethy, Perths., 71, Fig. 9
a'Cheardach Mhor, S. Uist, 84–5, 87, Fig. 26
Adamnan, 30, 49, 169, 199
Agricola, 22, 33, 90
Aidan mac Gabran (k. of Dalriada), 30, 50
Aikerness, Orkney, 186, 191
Alan (k. of Galloway), 203
Alclud (Dumbarton Rock), Dunbarton, 30, 31
Aldbar, Angus, 62
Alexander III (k. of Scotland), 197, 218, 233, 234
Allasdale, Barra, 84
Allectus, 93
Almorness, Wigtown, 36
Ambrosius Aurelianus, 106
Ammianus Marcellinus, 8
Andreas, I.O.M., 99, 213, 215, Pl. 24B
Aneurin, 17, 27
Anglo-Saxons, 20, 27, 30, 36, 38
Anglo-Saxon Chronicle, 30, 143, 180, 182
Annait, Skye, 88
Annales Cambriae, see *Annals of Wales*
Annals of the Four Masters, 18, 93, 156
Annals of Innisfallen, 151
Annals of Wales, 18, 31
Annals of Tigernach, 18, 31, 72, 75
antae, 174
Antonine Wall, 23, 51
Applecross, Ross & Cromarty, 78, 88, 199
Ardagh Chalice, 359–60
Ardderydd, battle of, 38
Ardestie, Angus, 70
Ardwall Island, Kirkcudbright, 42, 112
areani, 24, 25
Arran, 181
Athflotla, 49
Athlone crucifixion plaque, 360
Attacotti, 24, 25
Aurelius Caninius, 102

Bac Mhic Connain, Vallay, N. Uist, 85
Bacon Hole, Glam., 98
Baginton, Warwicks., 143
Ballacaggan, I.O.M., 92
Ballacamish, I.O.M., 213
Balladoole, I.O.M., 209–10, 214, Fig. 66, Pl. 15B

Balladoyne, I.O.M., 208, 214
Ballanorris, I.O.M., 92
Ballaugh, I.O.M., 208
Ballateare, I.O.M., 210–11, 220, Fig. 67
Balliehill Island, 36
Ballindalloch, Banff, 198
Ballinderry, Co. Offaly/Westmeath, crannogs, 12, 14, 149–50, 161–2, Fig. 52
lamp, 364, Fig. 140
Ballintoy, Co. Antrim, 125
Ballycatteen, Co. Cork, 149, 155, 156
Ballygalley Head, Co. Antrim, 154
Ballykinler, Co. Down, 161
Ballymacash, Co. Antrim, 13
Ballyvourney, Co. Cork, 168
Bamburgh, Northumberland, 27
Bangor, Caerns. (Bangor Fawr), 113, 118, 224
Bangor-Is-Coed, Flint, 113
Bantham, Devon, 133
Bardsey, Caerns., 113, 118
Barochan, Renfrew, 205
Barr of Spottes, Dumfries, 45
Barrasford, Northumberland, 27
Bath, Somerset, 123
Beaker people, 4
Beal Boru, Co. Clare, 156
Beddgelert, Caerns., 118
Bede, 16, 30, 38, 49, 79, 83
Beginish, Co. Kerry, 160
Belgae, 21, 48, 122
Bells, 371–2, Fig. 143
Bergen censer, 363
Bernicia (Berneich, Bryneich), 27, 28, 30, 42, Fig. 6
Bewcastle, Cumberland, 24, 29
Bidford-on-Avon, Warwicks., 143
Birka, Sweden, 178
bucket, 65, 363
Birrens, Dumfries, 29
Birrenswark, Dumfries, 23
Birrier, Yell, Shetland, 88
Birsay, Orkney, 56, 61, 65, 190, 191–6, Figs 60, 61, 62
box, 68, Pl. 16B.
Blackerne, Dumfries, 203
Blacketlees, Dumfries, 29
Blackshaw, Dumfries, 203
boats, 14, 258
Bodafon, Caerns., 118
Boho, Co. Fermanagh, 12
bone objects, 284–5
combs, 300–1
Book of Armagh, 392, 393
Book of Durrow, 18, 55, 67, 391
Book of Echternach (Echternach Gospels), 55
Book of Kells, 63, 67, 393
Book of Mac Durnan, 393
Braaid, I.O.M., 212, Pl. 11B
Braddan, I.O.M., 214
Braich y Dinas, Caerns., 92
Brandsbutt Stone, Aberdeens., 58
Brean Down, Somerset, 131, 132
Brechin, Angus, 71, Figs 19, 20
Brecon Gaer, Brecks., 93
Breedon, Leics., 40
Breiddin, Mont., 106
Brian Boru, 151, 226
Bridei mac Maelcon (k. of Picts), 49, 68, 83
British, 20, 26
settlements, 126–37, Fig. 38
British Museum crozier, 365
British Museum stemmed disc, 366
Broch of Burrian, Orkney, 59
Broch of Gurness, Orkney, 48, 80, 81, 185, Fig. 25, Pl. 3B. *See also* Aikerness
Brunanburgh, battle of, 215
Brycheiniog, 102
Brynkir, Caerns., 95
Buckquoy, Birsay, Orkney, 83, 185, 191–2
Builth, 102
Burghead, Moray, 68–9
Burgred (k. of Mercia), 105
Burray, Orkney, hoard, 186
Burry Holms, Glam., 112–14
Buston crannog, Ayrs., 37, Fig. 8

Cadbury Congresbury, Somerset, 127–8, 132, 143, Fig. 39, Pl. 4A
Cadfan, 104
Cadwallon, 104
Caer Gybi, Anglesey, 9, 93, 113
Caerhun, Caerns., 114
Caerlaverock, Dumfries, 234
Caerlon, Mon., 90, 111
Caer Mynydd, Caerns., 111
Caernarvon, 90, 93

Caerwent, Mon., 111, 114
Cahercommaun, Co. Clare, 12, 147–9, 154, 155, Fig. 47
Caherguillamore, Co. Limerick, 13
Cairngryffe, Lanarks., 32
Caledonians, 56
Caledonii, 48, 49
Calleva, *see* Silchester
Cambuslang, Lanarks., 44
Camps Hill, Trohoughton, Dumfries, 30
Canna, Inverness, 181
Cannington, Somerset, 126–7, 131
Caracalla, 23
Caractacus, 102
Caradog, 113
Carausius, 93
Cardiff, Glam., 9, 93
Cardinham, Cornwall, 140, Fig. 45
Carlisle, Cumb., 30, 42, 43, Fig. 9
Carlungie, Angus, 70, Fig. 18
Carndonagh, Co. Donegal, 168–9
Carn Fadrun, Caerns., 92
Carpow, Perths., 23
Carraig Aille, Co. Limerick, 14, 149
Cashel, Co. Tipperary, 141, Pl. 9A
Cass ny Hawin, I.O.M., 212
Castell Dwyran, Carmarth., 93, 101
Casterton, Westmorland, 221
Castle Dore, Cornwall, 11, 34, 121, 126, 130–1, 132, 133, Fig. 42
Castle Haven, Kircudbright, 36, 203
Castlehill, Dalry, Ayrs., 38
Castlemartin, Pembroke, 98
Castle Point, Kircudbright, 22
Castle Skreen, Co. Down, 154, 156
Castle Sween, Argyll, 233
Castle Tioram, Inverness, 64
Castletown, Caithness, 198
Castle Urquhart, Inverness, 234
Cathach of St Columba, 390
Catstane, Midlothian, 44
  cemetery, Fig. 145
Catterick, Yorks., 27
Catuvellauni, 21
Celts, La Tène, 172, 246
Celtic language, 4, 218–19
  Brythonic, 10, 51, 73, 99, 103
  Gaulish, 11
  Goidelic, 10, 51, 73, 74, 96, 99, 125
  Manx, 219
  Primitive Welsh, 103
  Scots Gaelic, 74
cemeteries, 30, 44, 377, 379
Ceretic (Coroticus), 30
chapels, 138–9, 377
Chapel Finnian, Wigtowns., 44
Charlemagne, 178, 179
Charles the Bald (k. of France), 99, 105
Chatto Craig, Rox., 27, 38
Chester, 9, 90, 103, 104, 221
Chesterholm, Northumberland, 25
Christianity, 42–5, 112–19, 137–9, 164–76, 181, 193–6, 214–16
Chronicle of Dalriada (C. of the Scots), 72
Chronicle of Man and the Isles, 199, 208
Chun Castle, Cornwall, 30, 121, Fig. 41
Church, The, 17, 60–7, 87–8, 97, 117–19
  building, 112–15, 171–6, 382–5
Church Island, Co. Kerry, 42, 112
Cinhil, 30
Circinn, 49
Cissbury, Sussex, 131
Clatchard's Craig, Fife, 46, 64, 69, Fig. 8
Claughton Hall, Lancs., 226
Clawdd Mawr, 97, 101
Clettraval, S. Uist, 84
Clibberswick, Shetland, 185
Clochans, 171
Clondalkin, Co. Dublin, 176
Clonmacnois, Co. Offaly, 79, 166
  crucifixion plaque, 366
Closeburn, Dumfries, 41, 204
Close ny Chollagh, I.O.M., 92, 211–12
clothes, 297–8
Cluim, 30
Clumland, Shetland, 81
Clynnog Fawr, Caerns, 118
Codex Usserianus Primus, 390
Coel Hen, 31
Coileagan an Udal *see* Udal
coins, 6, 29, 39, 106, 186, 198, 201, 202, 223, 229–30, 233, 237, 239, Fig. 68. *See also* hoards
Coldingham, Berwicks., 39
Collin, Dumfries, 39, Fig. 7
Colonsay, 181, 201
Columba, S., 49, 50, 83, 78–9, 87–8
Colwyn Bay, Caerns., 112
Concenn (k. of Powys), 105
Conspiratio Barbarica, 24
Constans, 24
Constantine (k. of Dalriada), 203

Constantine (k. of Dumnonia), 102
Constantius Chlorus, 29
Copenhagen shrine, 362
Corbridge, Northumberland, 27
Cormac's Chapel, Cashel, Co. Tipperary, 174
Cormac's Glossary, 93, 125
Cornovii, 102
Corpus Christi 197 MS, 55
Corp Naomh, 366
Cotton Psalter, 393
Coygan Camp, Carmarthen, 11, 92, 106
Coylton, Ayrs., 31
crafts, 257–9, chapter 13
Craig Phadrig, Inverness, 64, 68
crannogs, *see* settlements
Cranstock, Cornwall, 137
Crickley, Glos., 126
Crith Gabhlach, 13, 157
Crock Cleugh, Rox., 26
Cronk Sumark, I.O.M., 92
Cronk yn How, I.O.M., 214
Cross of Cong, 370
Croy hoard, Inverness, 65
crozier of the Abbots of Clonmacnois, 368–9
crucibles, 250–2, Figs 72, 73
Cuerdale hoard, Lancs., 220
Cruithne (legendary k. of Picts), 49
Cruithni, 49
Culbin (Sands), Moray, 28, 49
Cullykhan, Banff, 68
Culter, Lanarks., 32
Culver Hole, Glam., 98
Cumdach of Cathach of Columba, 368
Cunedda, 15, 25, 26, 43, 96, 100, 101, 102
Cuneglasus, 102
Cunningsburgh, Shetland, 189
Cush, Co. Limerick, 13, 154
Cuthred (k. of Wessex), 50
Cwmbrwyn, Carmarthen, 90, 98

Dalmahoy, Midlothian, 22, 26, Fig. 3
Dalmeny, Midlothian, 28, Fig. 3
Dalriada, 9, 50–1, 61, 71–9
Dalry, Ayrs., 24, 132, Fig. 8
Damnonii, 22, 23, 25
Danebury, Hants., 132
Danuting, 31
David I (k. of Scotland), 232–3
Deerness, Orkney, 88
Degannwy castle, Caerns., 107–8
de Maximis Pretiis, edict, 24
Desi, 9, 93, 99
Deskford, Banff, 49
Deywr, 27
Dinas Emrys, Caerns., 11, 106–7, 117, Fig. 33, Pl. 2A
Dinas Powys, Glam., 11, 15, 18, 98, 109–10, 132, 133, 148, 149, 245–6, Figs 35, 36, Pl. 1B
Dinllaen, Caerns., 96
Din Lligwy, Caerns., 91, Fig. 28
Dinorben, Caerns., 91, 92, 110, 132, Pl. 1A
Din Silwy, Caerns., 92
Dio Cassius, 49
Doarlish Cashen, I.O.M., 212
Domnnall Brecc (k. of Dalriada), 50
Doon Hill, E. Lothian, 27, 28, 38, 132, Fig. 8
Dorestad, 178
Douglas, I.O.M., 213
Downpatrick, Co. Down, 11, 156
Dream of Maxen Wledig, 100
dress fasteners, 302. *See also* jewellery
- buckles, 333–4, Fig. 127
- handpins, 322–4, Fig. 122
- kyte brooches, 318–19, Fig. 119
- latchets, 331–3, Fig. 126
- loose ringed pins, 319–22, Figs 120, 121
- penannular brooches, 302–18, Figs 109–13
- stick pins, 324–31, Figs 123–5
- tanged studs, 334, Fig. 128

Drimore, S. Uist, 199
Dromiskin, Co. Louth, 68
Drosten, 52
Duan Albanach, 71
Dublin, 203, 225, 227–30
Dumbarton Rock, 31, 38, Figs 8, 9
Dumngual Hen, 31
Dumnogenus, 44
Dumyat, Stirling, 69
Dunadd, Argyll, 11, 18, 51, 73, 75, 77, 83, 97, 98, Fig. 22
Dun Aengus, Aran Isles, 154
Dun Ailinne, Co. Kildare, 151, 154, 157
Dun Beag, Co. Down, 154
Dunbeath, Caithness, 65

Dun Bhuirg, Iona, 78, 79
Duncan II (k. of Scotland), 234
Duncarnock, Renfrews., 23, 37
Dun Cuier, Barra, 86–7, Fig. 27
Dundonald, Ayrs., 37
Dundrum, Co. Down, 13
Dundurn, Perths., 19, 69, 75, Fig. 22
Dunearn, Fife, 70
Dunfallandy, Perths., 61
Dunfermline, Fife, 232
Dunkeld, Perths., 48
Dun Mhor Vaul, Tiree, 82
Dunollie, Argyll, 72
Dunragit, Wigtowns., 30
Dunseverick, Co. Antrim, 73
Duplin, Perths., 62
Durham cathedral,
MS AII 17, 390–2;
MS AII 30, 390–2;
MS AII 10, 390–2
Durotriges, 122
Dutigirn, 27
Duvillarn, Co. Mayo, 168
Dyserth, Flints., 224
Dyfed, 97, 101, 102, 103, 105

Eadberht (k. of Northumbria), 39, 50
Eadred, Abbot, 39, 202
Eardulf, b. of Lindisfarne, 39
Ecgfrith (k. of Northumbria), 31
Echternach Gospels, 391
Economy, 12–15, 23, 179, 206–7, 235
Eddisbury, Chesh., 106, 221
edge tools, 289–91, Figs 100, 101
Edinburgh, Midlothian, 26, 27
Edwin (k. of Northumbria), 30, 103
Eigg, 78
Eildon Hill, North, Rox., 22, 23
Eileach an Naoimh, Garvellochs, Argyll, 88, Pl. 8B
Einarr, 194
Ekerö crozier, 357, 359
Elmet, 103, 104
Emly shrine, 362
Erickstanebrae, Dumfries, 29
Errol, 199
Exeter, 123
Eyrbygja Saga, 181

Fahan Mura, Co. Donegal, 168
Fardel, 125
Fareham, Hants., 143
Feerwore, Co. Galway, 146, 154, 156
Fergus mac Erc (k. of Dalriada), 72
Ffestiniog, Merioneth, 116
Fib, 49
Florentius, 43
foederati, 214
Fórden Gaer, Mont., 93
Forthriu, 49
Fortrenn, 69
Foshigarry, N. Uist, 85
Fowlis Wester, Angus, 61
Franks Casket, 60, 63
Freswick Links, Caithness, 190, 197–8, Fig. 63
Frontinus, 90

Gabran (k. of Dalriada), 49
Gallarus Oratory, Co. Kerry, 172, Fig. 57
Gallehus, 63
Gallen, Co. Offaly, 168
Gardar, Greenland, 193, 196
Garn Boduan, Caerns., 32, 100, 108, Fig. 34
Garranes, Co. Cork, 12, 13, 14, 149, 155, 156
Garryduff, Co. Cork, 149, 156, 157, 158
Garry Iochdrach, N. Uist, 85
Garrynamona, Co. Clare, 156
Gateholm, Pembroke, 98, 100, 111
Gaulcross, Banff, 59
Gaut Bjornson, 215
Geography of Ptolemy, 22
Gigha, 75, 186
Gildas, 18, 83, 93, 100, 102, 118, 142
Glamis, Angus, 66
Glasserton, Wigtown, 204
glass studs, 256–7, Fig. 75
vessels, 266–8, Fig. 81
Glastonbury, Somerset, 121, 267
Glencairn, Dumfries, 41
Gododdin, 26, 27, 42, 100, Figs 8, 9
poem, 18, 27, 31
Godred II (k. of I.O.M.), 217–18
Godred Crovan, 217
Gokstad, ship, 177
Gorten, 199
Gosforth, Cumberland, 222
Govan, Lanarks, 62, 205, Pl. 218
Grange, Co. Limerick, 156
graves, 27, 28. *See also* cemeteries

Green Island fort, Kirkcudbright, 203
Gretna, Dumfries, 203
Grianan of Aileach, Co. Derry, 153, 154
Gruffyd ap Cynan (k. of Gwynedd), 224
Gulval, Cornwall, 125
Gundestrup, 63, 178
Gwerthyrion, 102
Gwithian, Cornwall, 97, 98, 124, 125, 133–5, Figs 37, 43
Gwynedd, 96, 99, 102, 104, 105

Haakon (k. of Norway), 197
Haddington, E. Lothian, 58
Hadrian, 22
H's Wall, 23, 24, 25, 27
hairstyles, 299
Hakirke, Lancs., 220
Halfdan, 202
hanging bowls, 353–55, Fig. 137
Harald Fairhair, 183
Harald Harfagri, 181
Hardown Hill, 143
Harelaw, E. Lothian, 27
Hatfield Chase, battle of, Yorks., 104
Havor, 178
Heathrow, Middlesex, 132
Hebrides, 84–7
Helgo, Sweden, 178
Helmskringla, 182
Hen Domen, Mont., 237
Henley Wood, Somerset, 131, 132
hermitages, 378–9
  hermitage chapels, 139
Herodotus, 5
Hesket in Forest, Cumberland, 219
Heysham, Lancs., 219
High Peak, Devon, 126
High Rochester, Northumberland, 24
hillforts, *see* settlements
Hillswick, Shetland, 186
Hilton of Cadboll, Ross & Cromarty, 61, 63
hoards, 93, 186, 187, 213–14, 220, 223, 231. *See also* coins
Hoddom, Dumfries, 38, 40, 44, 45, Fig. 9
  crozier shrine, Fig. 142
Hod Hill, Dorset, 122
horsegear, 291–3, Fig. 102
Hough on the Hill, Lincs., 39
House of Keys, 216, 217
Howick, Northumberland, 27
Hownam Law, Rox., 26
Hownam Rings, Rox., 21, 25
Hurly Hawkin, Angus, 69
Hyndford, Lanarks., 37
Hywel Dda (k. of Wales), 15, 25, 99, 105–6, 223

Ida (k. of Bernicia), 27
Ilchester, Somerset, 123
Inchinnan, Renfrews., 205
industries, 257–8
Inishkea North, Co. Mayo, 160, 168
Inispatrick, 20
Innisfallen crozier, 368
Iona, 61, 74, 78–9, 199, Fig. 144, Pls 20A, 20B
Ireland, 145–77
Irish Annals, 78, 208
Irish people, *see* Scots
Irish Sea Province, 10
Irish settlements, 8, 9, 10, 41–2, 92–9, 115–16, 124–6
Iron Age, 5–7, 11, 20, 21–4, 26, 29, 31, 42, 47–8, 55, 89–90, 120–1, 178
ironwork, *see* metalwork
Island MacHugh, Co. Tyrone, 160

Jarlshof, Shetland, 81, 82, 84, 182, 183, 187–91, 192, 197, 206, Fig. 59
Jedburgh, Rox., 28
jewellery, buttons and badges, 338
  finger rings, 334–5, Fig. 129
  beads, 336–338
  bracelets, 334–5
  glass armlets, 335
  See also dress fasteners
Jocelyn of Furness, 38
Jurby, I.O.M., 214, 215

Kaimes Law, Midlothian, 22, 25
Kells, unfinished cross, Pl. 30B
  monastery, 169–70
Kelvingrove Museum, Glasgow, 41
Kenfig Burrows, Glam., 98, 100
Kenneth mac Alpin (k. of Scots), 51, 61
Ketill Flatnose, 181
Kiev, 179, 203
Kilbroney, Co. Down, 168
Kildalton, Islay, 61, 79
Kildonan Bay, Argyll, 11, 76–7, Fig. 24
Kildreenagh, Co. Kerry, 166

Kilfountain, Co. Kerry, 168
Kilkenny, 176
Killeen Cormac pillar, 168
Kiloran, Colonsay, 168
Kiltera, Co. Waterford, 155
Kilwinning, Renfrews., 205
Kingarth, Bute, 78
King's Weston, Bristol, 131
Kirkconnel, Dumfries, 38, 41, Fig. 8, 132
Kirkinner, Wigtown, 204, Pl. 21C
Kirk Michael, I.O.M., 215
Kirkmuirhill, Lanarks., 205
knives, 287–9, Fig. 99
Knock-y-Doonee, I.O.M., 43, 209
Knockando, Banff, 199
Kyle, Ayrs., 39

Lagore, Co. Meath, 9, 12, 98, 147, 150, 161, 162–3
lake dwellings, *see* settlements
Lamlash, Arran, 201
Lancaster, 93
Langford Lodge, 155
Largs, Ayrs., 181
Lanherne, Cornwall, 140
Latinus stone, 43, Fig. 10
Leacanabuaile, Co. Kerry, 14, 171, Fig. 49
leacht, 171
leatherwork, 298, 373, Fig. 107
Leinster, 150
Lesser Garth Cave, Glamorgan, 97, 98
Letterkeen, Co. Mayo, 13
Lichfield Gospels (Gospels of St Chad), 392
Life of St Carannog, 94, 96
St Columba, 199
St Kentigern, 38
St Samson of Dol, 117, 118
Lillsteads farm, Dumfries, 202
limes, 24
Lindisfarne, 45, 180, 202
Gospels, 18, 56, 65, 67, 202
Linford, Essex, 38
Lismahon, Co. Down, 155, 238
Lismore, Argyll, 78
Lismore crozier, 369
Lisnacroghera, Co. Antrim, 146
Lisnagade, Co. Down, 155
Lissue, Co. Antrim, 13, 156, 157, Fig. 50
Lives of Eastern saints, 169

Llanaelhaern, Caerns., 103
Llanbeblig, Caerns., 114
Llandegai, Caerns., 114
Llanfaelog, Anglesey, 96
Langadwaladr, Anglesey, 104
Llangybi, Caerns., 112, 114
Lantrisant, Anglesey, 115, 118
Llanynis, Brecon, 224
Llefelys, 17
Llewellyn Fawr, 118
Llewellyn ap Gruffydd, 107
Lleyn, 96
Lludd, 17
Llyn Cerrig Bach, Anglesey, 146
Loch Glashan, Argyll, 76
Lochlee, Ayrs., 36, 37
Lochspouts, Ayrs., 36, 37
Longbury Bank, Pemb., 111
Lough Erne shrine, 361, Fig. 138
Lough Faughan, Co. Down, 161, 162
Lough Gur, Co. Limerick, 13, Fig. 51
Lough na Shade, Co. Armagh, 146
Luce Sands, Wigtown., 39
Lullingstone hanging bowl, Kent, 57
Lundy Island., 138
Luss, Dumbarton, 205
Lydney Park, Glos., 131

Mabinogion, the, 17
Macbeth (k. of Scotland), 194
Maeatae, 23, 49
Maelcon (k. of Pictland), 49
Maelgwn (k. of Gwynedd), 49, 100, 102, 107
Maes Howe, Orkney, 215
Maglocunun, 102
Magnus Barelegs, 203, 217, 224
Magnus Maximus, 100, 101
Maiden Castle, Dorset, 122
Mailros, *see* Old Melrose
Malcolm III (k. of Scotland), 72, 232
Malew, I.O.M., 214
Man, Isle of, 43, 92, 99, 208–19
Manau, 25, 26, 50, 100, Fig. 8
Manorwater, Peebles, 44
manuscripts, 59–60, 369–94
Marcus Aurelius, 22
Marshal Moor, Renfrews., 38
Maughold, I.O.M., 208, 214, 215, Pls 23A, 23B
Mavorius, 43

Mawgan Porth, Cornwall, 135–7, Fig. 44
Maxey, Northants., 148
Meare, Somerset, 121
Meifort, Mon., 224
Meigle, Perths, 61, 66
Melhus shrine, 362
memorial stones, 42–3, 113–17, 125
  164, 165
Mercia, 104, 105
Merfyn Vrych, 103
metalworking, 146, 246–54, 285–96,
  339–73, Figs 132–7
  Anglo-Saxon, 57
  bronze, 247–8
  Caledonian, 49
  chip carved, 253–4
  enamelled, 254–5
  filigree, 253
  granular, 253
  iron, 246–7, 294–6
  moulds, 248
  ornamental, 35, 47, 352–71
  Pictish, 63–8
  Roman openwork, 344–6, Fig. 131
  Trewhiddle Style, 28
Michael, I.O.M., 214, Pl. 25A
Midhowe, Orkney, 80, 81
millefiori, 98, 255–6, Fig. 74
Milton Loch, Kirkcudbright, 36
Minchin Hole, Glam., 98
Misach of St Columba, 368
Monasterboice, Co. Louth, 176
monasteries, 137–9, 171, 175, 233, 237,
  Pl. 7B. *See also* hermitages
Moncrieffe Hill, Perths., 69
Monifeith, Angus, 59
Monker Green, Orkney, 65
Mons Badonicus, battle of, 142
Monybuie, Dumfries, 45
Monymusk reliquary, 64–5, 361, Fig. 139
Morcant, 31
Mote of Mark, Kirkcudbright, 33–6,
  Fig. 5, Pl. 2B
Mount Batten, Devon, 121
Mousa, Shetland, 81
Moylough belt shrine, 359, Pl. 12A

Nantstallon, Devon, 122
Nappin, I.O.M., 213, 216
Navan, Co. Armagh, 154, 157
  brooches, 150
Nechtan mac Derelei (k. of Picts), 50, 88
Nechtan's Mere, battle of, 31, 50
Nendrum, Co. Down, 13
Nennius, 18, 27, 83, 96, 100, 102
Nevern, Pemb., 95
Newbiggin Moor, Cumberland, 221
Newgrange, Co. Meath, 150
Newton Stone, Aberdeens., 51
Niall of the Nine Hostages, 9, 150
Nigg, Perths., 63, 67
Ninian, *see* St Ninian
Nith Bridge, Dumfries, 204
Norrie's Law, Fife, 55, 58, 64–5
Norse, 177–231. *See also* Vikings
Northmavine, Shetland, 88
Northumbria, 20, 26, 30, 39, 50, 55, 59,
  60, 67
Notitia Dignitatum, 25
Novantae, 22, 23, 29
Novgorod, 179
Nudus, 26

Oengus mac Fergus (k. of Dalriada), 50,
  61, 75
Offa's Dyke, 97, 104
ogham, 115, 125, 139, 164–5, 205, Figs
  29, 30
  bilingual, 95–6, 116
  Irish, 95–6, Fig. 30
  Pictish, 51, 55, 74, 83
Olaf I (k. of Norway), 217
Olaf's Saga, 183
Olaf Sitricson (k. of Dublin), 203
Olaf the White, 226
Oldbury Camp, Wilts., 131
Old Melrose, Rox., 44, 45
Old Oswestry, Salop, 106
oratories, timber, 138
  stone, 172–3
Ordovices, 90
Orkneyinga Saga, 180, 182, 183, 184, 197,
  208
Orton Scar, Westmorland, 221
Oseberg, ship burial, 362
  bucket, 362
Oswiu (k. of Northumbria), 30
Over Kirkhope, Peebles, 44
Owain ap Hywel Dda (k. of Dyfed), 31

Padstow, Cornwall, 137
Pagan's Hill, Somerset, 124

Paisley, Lanarks., 44
Pant y Saer, Anglesey, 100, 111
Papil, Shetland, 61, 83, 88, Pls 10B, 17A
Parkburn, Midlothian, 44
Parkhill, Aberdeens., 58
Paternus, 25
Pelagian heresy, 115
Pencaernisiog, Anglesey, 96
Penda (k. of Mercia), 104, 123, 143
Peniel Heugh, Rox., 26
Penmachno, Caerns., 115
Penmon, Anglesey, 112, 118, 215, 224
Pennershaughs, Dumfries, 38
Penpont, Dumfries, 41
Penrith, Cumberland, 221
Pentrefoelas, Denbigh, 116
Perran, Cornwall, 137
Picts, 9, 10, 11, 24, 26, 33, 44, 46–7, 48, 49, 50, 51, 55–6, 57, 59, 66–71, 72–6, 183, 205
  language, 47, 51–2
  symbol stones, 26, 33, 53–63, 64, 66, 74, 75, 83, Figs 12–17
Pierowall, Orkney, 184
Pillar of Eliseg, 18, 100, 104
Pilsdon Pen, Dorset, 129, 132
placenames, 41
  Irish, 96–7, 75, Figs 21, 29
  Manx, 99
  Norse, 181, 183, 196, 202, 220, 223
  Danish, 203
  Pictish, Fig. 11
ploughs, 15
  Belgic, 23
  coultered, 13
Porth Dafarch, Anglesey, 112
Porthmeor, Cornwall, 124
pottery, Atlantic province, 282–3
  bar lug, 135, 281, Fig. 94
  buckelurnen, 142, 143
  Glastonbury Ware, 121
  grassmarked, 279–82, Fig. 93
  Gwithian Style, 124, 134, 279
  imported, 123, 129, 133, 268–76, Figs 82–9
  Iron Age, 89
  native, 276–9, Figs 90, 91
  Roman, 24, arretine, 150, samian, 150
  stehende bogen, 142
Poundbury, Dorset, 123
Powys, 22, 102, 104, 105, Fig. 32
Prosperous crozier, 365
Ptolemy, 22, 94, 122

Quethiock, Cornwall, 141

Ragnald, 194
Rampside, Lancs., 220
Rathcrogan, Co. Roscommon, 154
Rathlin Island, 225
Rath of the Synods, *see* Tara
Rathtinaun, Co. Sligo, 146
Ravenna Cosmography, 22
Reginald I (k. of I.O.M.), 218
Restenneth, Angus, 70, 71
Rheged, 27, 28, 30, 31, 42, Figs 8, 9
Rhodri Mawr (k. of Gwynedd), 99, 105, 223
Rhydderch Hael (k. of Strathclyde), 30
Ribchester, Lancs., 103
Ripon, Yorks., 31
Risingham, Yorks., 24
Robert I, the Bruce (k. of Scotland), 218
Rock of Cashel, Co. Tipperary, 225
Rognvald, 194
Romans, 7–9, 11, 21, 23, 24, 90–2, 177
Romfohjellen mount, 363
Ronaldsway, I.O.M., 92
Rossie, Angus, 61
runes, 28, 36
  runic inscriptions, 199
Rushen, I.O.M., 215
  hoard, 213
Ruthwell Cross, Dumfries, 28, 40

St Abb's Head, Berwicks., 45
St Andrew, 61
St Andrew's Shrine, 61, 63
St Augustine, 137
St Bueno, 119
St Bueno's chapel, Caerns., 113
St Columba's House, Kells, Co. Meath, 173
St Constantine's sarcophagus, 203–5
St Cuthbert's churchyard, Kirkcudbright, 202
St Gall Gospels, 392
St Germain reliquary terminals, 362
St Gobnet's House, Ballyvourney, Co. Cork, 159, 160
St Jerome, 25
St Kentigern (St Mungo), 119

St Kew, 137
St Kevin's Church, Glendalough, Co. Wicklow, 174, Pl. 9B
St Lachtin's arm shrine, 369–70
St Manchan's shrine, 370
St Martin of Tours, 119
St Ninian, 43, 88, 99
St Ninian's Cave, Wigtown, 40, 44
St Ninian's Isle Treasure, 18, 44, 65–8, Pls 13A, 13B, 14A, 14B
St Ninian's Point, Bute, 44
St Patrick, 150, 164
St Patrick's Bell shrine, 368, Fig. 141
St Peter, 119
St Peter's Stone, Whithorn, Wigtowns., Fig. 10
St Regulus (St Rule), 71
St Tysilo, 119
St Vigeans, Angus, 61, Pls 17B, 18B
Sallagh, Co. Antrim, 155
Sancreed, Cornwall, 140
Santon stone, Cornwall, 43
Saxons, 16–17, 24–7. *See also* Anglo-Saxons
Scandinavians, 202–7
  settlements, 205–6
  see also Vikings and Norse
Scotland, 20–87
Scots, 11, 24, 50, 51, 71–9, 88
sculptures, 28, 29, 32, 40–1, 45, 79, 139–41, 165–9, 169–71, 204–5, 214–16, 221–2, 224, Figs. 4, 7, 10, 16, 17, 45, 55, 71, Pls 17A–32A
Segontium (Caernarvon), 114
Selgovae, 22, 23, 29
Septimius Severus, 23, 49
settlements, 235–9
  brochs, 48
  cashels, 12
  caves, 24
  Celtic, 16
  ceremonial sites, 151
  cliff castles, 121
  courtyard houses, 121, 124
  crannogs, 11, 12, 13, 21, 22, 24, 36, 76, 160–1, 235, Fig. 52
  duns, 11, 21, 36, 39, 69, 86, 154, 235, Fig. 24, Pl. 6B
  ecclesiastical dwellings, 171
  enclosed hut groups, 21, 24, 26, Fig. 28
  figure of eight houses, 83, 86
  fogous, 121, 163
  hillforts, 11, 30, 31, 32, 37, 89–90, 106, 121–2, 126–33, 151–3, Fig. 48
  homesteads, 21, 38
  Irish, 151–64
  lake villages, 121
  native British, 90–2
  nuclear forts, 153–5
  Pictish, 19, 68–71
  promontory forts, 153–5
  raths, 12, 13, 76, 78, 98, 99, 151, 154, Fig. 50, Pl. 6A
  rounds, 121–2
  Saxon, 16
  scooped, 11
  souterrains, 12, 21, 24, 70, 163–4, Fig. 18
  stack forts, 78
  stonewalled forts, 153
  vici, 25
  Viking, 211–13
  villas, 122
  wheelhouses, 11, 47, 81–2, 84–5
Sgor Nam Ban Naomha, Canna, 88
Shannon shrine, 361–2
Shaw Craig, Peebles, 26
Shetland, 79–84
Shiehallion (mountain), Perths., 48
shrines, 380–2, Fig. 147
Sigurd the Mighty (E. of Orkney), 193–4
Sigurd the Stout, 226
Earl Sigurd's Hall, Birsay, Orkney, 192, 193
Silchester (Calleva), Hants., 125
Silures, 90, 102
Skaill, Orkney, 187, Pl. 15A
Skellig Michael, Co. Kerry, 88, 168, 172, Fig. 56, Pl. 8A
Slamannan, Stirling, 41
Soiscel Molaise, 365
Somerled, 217, 218
Somerset, Co. Galway, 150
Southampton Psalter, 393
South Barrule, I.O.M., 92
South Cadbury, Somerset, 11, 15, 121, 128–9, 132, 133, 143, Fig. 40, Pl. 4B
Staigue Fort, Co. Kerry, 153, Pl. 5A
Stevenston Sands, Ayrs., 39
Stilicho, 3
Stobshiel, E. Lothian, 27

Stowe Missal Shrine, 367–8
Stratford, Warwicks., 143
Strathclyde, 44, 50, 62
Sueno's Stone, Moray, 62, Pl. 22A
Suie Hill, 36
Sutton Hoo, 28, 40
Syagrii, 25

Tacitus, 9
Taezali, 48, 49
Taliesin, 17, 30
Talnotrie, Kirkcudbright, 39, 202
Tal-y-Llyn, Merioneth, 146
Tamshiel Rig, Rox., 23
Tamworth, Staffs., 104
Tara, Co. Meath, 133, 150, 151, 225, Pl. 5B
  Rath of the Synods, 9
  Tara Brooch, 60, 185, 360, Fig. 116
Tarbat, Ross & Cromarty, 196, 199
Tasciovanus, 21
technology, 245–59
Thady's Fort, Co. Clare, 156
Theodosius, 25
Thorfinn the Mighty (E. of Orkney), 181, 194, 195, 203, 206, 232
Earl Thorfinn's Palace, Birsay, Orkney, 192, 193, 194–6
Tintagel, Cornwall, 137, 141, Fig. 46, Pl. 7A
toilet articles, 301–2
tools, 293–4, Fig. 103
Torr Abb, Iona, 79
Torrs pony cap, 146
trade, 14, 259
Traprain Law, W. Lothian, 22, 24, 25, 27, 56, 58, 100, Fig. 2
Trebarveth-in-Lizard, Cornwall, 124
Tre'er Ceiri, Caerns., 92, 109
Trelissey, Pemb., 90, 98
Tremadoc, Caerns., 114
Trevor Rocks, Mont., 112
Trewhiddle hoard, Cornwall, 135
Trinian, 99
Trusty's Hill, Kirkcudbright, 11, 32, 59, Fig. 6
Tummel Bridge, Perths., 64
Turin Gospels, 393
Turin Hill, Angus, 70
Two Mile Stone, 13
Tynron Doon, Dumfries, 32, 33, Fig. 8, Pl. 3A
Tynwald Hill, I.O.M., 217
Typiaun, 26

Udal, S. Uist, 199, 236
Ugadale Point, Argyll, 78
Ui Neill, 151, 225
Uisneach, Co. Westmeath, 13
Underhoull, Unst, 190–1
Unst, 185
Urien (k. of Rheged), 27, 30, 31, 36, 105
Urnfield people, 5

Vacomagi, 4, 8, 49
vehicles, wheeled, 14, 258–9
Vendel culture, Sweden, 178
Venicones, 48, 49
Vikings, 42, 81, 105, 113, 205. *See also* Norse
Vinjum, Norway, 65
Viventius, 43
Viventius' stone, Kirkmadrine, Wigtown, Fig. 10
Vix, France, 6
Vortepor, 101, 102
Vortigern, 15, 100, 101
Votadini, 22, 23, 24, 25, 30, 100
Vowlan, I.O.M., 212

Walesland Rath, Pembroke, 98
Walls Hill, Renfrews., 23, 38
Wamphray, Dumfries, 204
Wansdyke, 143
Wareham, Dorset, 137
Wat's Dyke, 97, 104
Watten, Caithness, 198
weapons, 285–91
weaving, 297–8
Wessex, 105
Westerseat, 198
West Harling, Norfolk, 132
Westness, Rousay, Orkney, 185
  Westness Brooch, 185
Whitecleugh, Lanarks., 58, 59
White Fort, Drumaroad, Co. Down, 157
Whiteside Rig, Peebles, 26
Whithorn, Wigtown, 30, 39, 42, 43, 44, 202, 204, 205, Fig. 9
William the Lion (k. of Scotland), 233, 234

Witcombe, Glos., 123
Witham, Lincs., bowl, 67
Woden Law, Rox., 26
woodworking, 262–6, Figs 76–80
wool industry, 24
  woollen cloaks, 24
Worthy Park, Hants, 142–3
Worlebury, Somerset, 132
Yardhouses, Lanarks., 21
Yarrow, Selkirk, 26
  Yarrow stone, 44
Yeavering, Northumberland, 27, 28, Fig. 8
Yetholm, Rox., 28
Ynys Seiriol, Anglesey, 112, 118